Advanced MVS JCL Examples

Using MVS/ESA on the Job

James G. Janossy
DePaul University

John Wiley & Sons, Inc.
New York • Chichester • Brisbane • Toronto • Singapore

This book is dedicated to the memory of Joe Baker (1954–1994), a colleague whose help with DePaul's lab facilities was much appreciated.

Publisher: Katherine Schowalter
Editor: Theresa Hudson
Managing Editor: Elizabeth Austin
Composition: Impressions, a division of Edwards Brothers

This text is printed on acid-free paper.

Published by John Wiley & Sons, Inc.

Library of Congress Cataloging-in-Publication Data:

Janossy, James G.
Advanced MVS JCL examples: using MVS/ESA on the job / James G. Janossy.
p. cm.
Includes index.
ISBN 0-471-30990-7 (paper)

Printed in the United States of America
10 9 8 7 6 5 4 3 2 1

About the Author

James Janossy is a full-time faculty member of the Department of Computer Science and Information Systems at DePaul University, Chicago. He teaches COBOL, MVS/ESA JCL, systems analysis and design, software testing, project management, relational database, and on-line programming on IBM, VAX, and Unix systems. Prior to joining DePaul he worked in the industry for 17 years as programmer, project leader, and manager. From 1979 to 1987 he held positions of project leader, assistant manager, and most recently Manager of System and Programming for the city of Chicago Datacenter. He joined the faculty of DePaul University in 1987. Jim earned his B.A. at Northwestern University and his M.S. at California State University, Los Angeles, and is completing a Ph.D. in computer science.

Jim has written several books including *Practical MVS JCL Examples, VS COBOL II: Highlights and Techniques, VAX COBOL On-Line, Practical VSAM* (with Richard Guzik), and *Practical TSO/ISPF For Programmers and the Information Center,* published by John Wiley and Sons. He has authored columns and numerous articles for *Data Training* magazine and *Enterprise Systems Journal* and has given presentations on course development at the annual Data Training conference. Jim also conducts professional seminars and provides custom course development through Caliber Data Training, Chicago.

Contents

Preface		xi
1	The Evolution of MVS and JCL	1
2	Improving Job Stream Control with IF/ELSE Operators	11
3	IF/THEN/ELSE Tests for Systems and User Abends	41
4	JCLLIB: Private Proc and JCL Libraries	85
5	Nested Procs as Building Blocks	133
6	Tuning Up Old Procs	157
7	Handling Failed MVS/ESA Jobs	173
8	Building Rerunnable MVS/ESA Jobstreams	227
9	JCL for C, COBOL, and Assembler PARMs and Intercommunication	247
10	Introducing SMS: Storage Management Subsystem	309
11	System-Determined Block Sizes and AVGREC	337
12	Miscellaneous MVS/ESA New Techniques	349
	Appendixes	359
A	The DFDSS Utility	359
B	VSAM Key Sequenced Data Set (IDCAMS) Examples	402
C	Diagnosing File Status Errors in VS COBOL II	432
D	IBM Utility Program Return Code Reference	438
E	System Completion Code Reference	445
F	Obtaining JCL and Programs for Local Use	463
Index		464

Preface

In 1993, I wrote *Practical MVS JCL Examples* to help newcomers to the IBM mainframe environment quickly become comfortable with the MVS/ESA operating system and its job control language. In this sequel I show both seasoned JCL users and newcomers how to master the facilities of MVS/ESA Version 4 to create easily maintained production job streams.

IBM's newest version of its MVS/ESA operating system, Version 4, brings you modern conveniences such as IF/ELSE logic, private proc (procedure) libraries, nested procs, and system management of disk data set creation and management. If you're an experienced JCL user or a relative newcomer to the mainframe environment, you'll find the full-length examples and explanations in this book ideal for your direct use. The way JCL has been coded from 1964 through 1993 (that's 29 years!) has not changed very much. But with Version 4 of the MVS/ESA operating system, new features have been introduced that let you create JCL that is more understandable and modifiable.

In the first part of this book I cover MVS/ESA Version 4 features for newly developed job streams. In Chapters 6 through 8, I show you how to adapt new MVS/ESA features to existing job streams to make them more readable and let them process more efficiently. In Chapter 9, I illustrate JCL supporting subprogramming and the C language in the modern MVS environment, since C is emerging as a viable alternative to assembler coding for access to low-level functions. You use JCL to compile, link edit, and run C programs, and I demonstrate how to do this.

Data Facility Storage Management Subsystem (DFSMS) is beginning to affect the work of most programmers in large IBM mainframe installations. This major new addition to the MVS environment fits the significant part of its acronym "DFSMS" in an entirely suitable way. The storage management subsystem is intended to achieve *system managed storage*. I explain its effect on your JCL in the latter parts of this book, in Chapters 10, 11, and 12, and show you examples and system reporting related to it.

The appendixes to this book were also carefully designed for your convenience. Appendix A provides an overview of the DFDSS utility, new to the mainframe scene and becoming a part of everyday life in this environment. Appendix B provides some pithy coverage of VSAM file creation using IDCAMS and JCL. Appendixes C, D, and E consolidate error code reference information concerning input/output processes, utility programs, and MVS/ESA system reporting. In combination with examples in the main part of the book, the appendixes are intended to make this book an on-the-job manual for today's busy programmers.

How is this book different from a JCL manual and many other JCL books? A major difference is that, unlike almost all other books, I provide full-length examples here, not hypothetical code fragments. All of the examples here have actually been run on modern ES/9000 mainframes. You see MVS/ESA JCL in context, and you see the output it produces when it is run. You can copy the examples and run them yourself to quickly learn new features and adapt them to your own work. A second difference is that, unlike the case with most manuals and books, the figures here have been produced directly from executable JCL on computer screens using desktop publishing techniques. This eliminates almost all potential for typographical errors, which can cause you hours of frustration.

A third major difference—perhaps the biggest difference of all between this and most other technical mainframe books—is that I have designed the figures and illustrations to tell a story with concise annotations rather than lengthy legends or text. My goal in creating these examples is to get important points across with pictures rather than words, and to separate figure placement from typeset narrative as much as possible. You'll find here what goes into the MVS/ESA system, and what it produces as output, concisely and accurately depicted. Important things are pointed out as if I was sitting at a computer terminal with you, explaining things while looking over your shoulder at what you had on the screen.

I couldn't have created this book alone. I'd especially like to thank Hal Breitenberg, Jim Turk, and Michael Haupt for their significant contributions. Hal Breitenberg developed and composed the introduction to Storage Management Subsystem that you'll find in Chapter 10, while Jim Turk edited and fleshed out Appendix A, dealing with DFDSS. Michael Haupt provided considerable insight in shaping the introductory chapters, refining my chronology of MVS. Both Hal and Michael provided assistance in achieving unambiguous wording throughout the book with their detailed technical reviews.

I'd also like to thank Reverend John Minogue, C.M., president of DePaul University; Dr. Susy Chan, vice president for University Planning and Information Technology; Dr. Helmut Epp, chair of the Department of Computer Science and Information Systems; and Dr. Edward Allemand, director of the Division of Information Systems, for providing and maintaining our new IBM ES/9000 mainframe, which I used to develop most of the examples in this book. The ES/9000 has joined our Unix, VAX, Hewlett-Packard, and 3Bx computer systems and is dedicated to student use in support of TSO/ISPF, MVS JCL, VS COBOL II, C, CICS/ESA, DB2, and assembler language instruction.

Finally, I'd like to thank Wiley author Gary Brown for the service he did the computer industry with his original System/360 JCL book of the 1970s. My earlier *Practical MVS JCL Examples* (1993) and *Advanced MVS JCL Examples* are both designed as companions that complement Gary's third edition, *System/390 JCL*. Gary and I cover much of the same ground but with different intent; by design, there is no functional overlap between our books. Gary's book provides extensive references, while my books provide full-length examples of typical on-the-job situations and explain how to diagnose and surmount common problems. Combined, our three books form a set that provides the coverage of the modern MVS/ESA environment which today's busy programmers and end users need to address their mainframe work.

Jim Janossy

1

The Evolution of MVS and JCL

1.1 System/360 Ancestry and JCL
1.2 Why MVS/ESA?
1.3 Differences Between MVS/ESA Versions 3 and 4
1.4 The Role of Storage Management Subsystem (DFSMS)
1.5 How Your JCL Will Change with MVS/ESA Version 4
1.6 "Promoted" Parameters Can Simplify Your JCL

1.1 System/360 Ancestry and JCL

Newcomers to the mainframe environment, and even many experienced personnel, are often surprised to learn that the architecture and personality of mainframe IBM computers was set in place in 1963-64. During that period, John F. Kennedy was president, the Beatles were a new phenomenon, no human had yet set foot on the moon, and there were no small computers—mini, personal, or otherwise. All computers were mainframes, and very nearly all business computers were dedicated to supporting batch applications such as payroll and accounting. Into this environment, IBM launched what was then a revolutionary family of computers named the System/360.

The System/360 represented one of the first civilian uses for integrated circuits where at least hundreds of transistors were manufactured already wired into logic circuits as "chips." This meant that the assembly of electronic components could begin on circuit boards at a higher level than individual transistors. The System/360 was intended to replace the unique and varied vacuum tube and transistor computers that IBM's competitors and IBM itself had offered prior to 1964. The System/360 was the product of shrewd marketing as much as it was the product of innovative engineering (a strategy of how it would be marketed played a major role in its design).

The System/360 became an enormous success, and its influence has dominated business data processing to the present day. It did so because it was not one machine but rather a "scalable" family of machines that could meet the computing power requirements of a broad range of moderately small to very large computer installations. Unlike the case with many competing machines, an installation using the System/360 could gradually acquire more and more computing horsepower as its needs grew, without losing its investment in existing programs, by upgrading from one model of System/360 to another. The machine language of all System/360s was the same. Even programs written in assembler, the lowest-level language short of machine language itself, remained the same across System/360 models. And the machine language remains the same now, across three decades of hardware progress.

A typical System/360 of the 1960s used magnetic core memory, a technology that was eclipsed in the 1970s by semiconductor memory. We are now accustomed to inexpensive memory chips that house 4 million or more transistors (bits) in an area about the size of a postage stamp. Magnetic core memory, however, 1964 style, could fit only a few hundred bits in this space, and was, by comparison, very expensive and power-hungry. It should come as no surprise that a mainframe of the 1960 era might have had as little as 8 kilobytes of real memory, although a more typical memory size was 64 to 256 kilobytes. This is far less than contained in a rather ordinary PC or Apple microcomputer of today, far less even than found in today's common laser printer or used by an action video game.

Memory size constrains the sophistication and complexity of the software a computer can execute. It is to IBM's considerable credit that its teams of software engineers developed an operating system for the System/360 that so well suited its purpose within the confines of the resources then available. That operating system continues to live, to this day, in the form of MVS/ESA.

The patriarch of today's MVS/ESA was OS, the original high-end operating system developed for the System/360 and immodestly christened "Operating System" as a trademarked name. OS was endowed with machine memory addresses of 24-bit size, which meant that it could address 2^{24} memory locations, which is 16,777,217 bytes (16 megabytes). The designers of OS, just like the designers of MS-DOS 17 years later, underestimated how fast and how far memory circuit technology would progress, and the 24-bit address eventually proved insufficient. The disk devices of the era included the Model 2311 and Model 2314, the largest of which stored only 29 megabytes on a single disk volume. The Model 3330, with 100 megabytes of storage (later 200 megabytes) was introduced in 1970.

The human interface to the original OS operating system was Job Control Language, JCL. As OS progressed from its original form through MVS (Multiple Virtual Storages) in the 1970s, and MVS metamorphosed into MVS/XA (Extended Architecture) in the 1980s, JCL did not change. The System/370 of 1970 replaced magnetic core memory with semiconductors, and its MVS was an adaptation of OS enhanced with the ability to manage memory using virtual storage (swap-memory-to-disk) techniques. It eventually offered larger capacity disk devices (the Model 3350 of 1975, with 317 megabytes per volume). Tape data storage density increased to 6,250 bytes per inch. But, aside from a few new parameter values, *JCL did not change.*

Extremely high density circuits replaced less dense circuits in the 1980s. Mainframe models such as the System/370 Models 3081 and 3090 supplied liquid cooling to chips compacted in sealed aluminum "thermal conduction modules" with coolant plumbing that made mainframe computer internals look like a diesel engine. In its MVS/XA version, MVS began supporting 31-bit addresses (2^{31} memory addresses) to expand the potential memory range to 2,147,482,048 bytes (over 2 billion bytes). Fiber optic con-

Figure 1.1 An IBM ES/9000 Mainframe
Huge mainframes such as this 512-megabyte ES/9000 Model 900 are cost effective in support of large enterprisewide business applications because of their operational stability and economies of scale. MVS/ESA Version 4 is the primary operating system of these mammoth machines, and MVS job control language is the command language of this operating system. (Photo courtesy of International Business Machines Corporation)

nections were designed to replace slower wire connections for disk devices with the Model ES/3090 of the late 1980s, and disk data storage expanded to 630, 1,200, and 2,400 megabytes (2.4 gigabytes) per disk unit. Tape storage leaped to a storage density of 38,800 bytes per inch on tape cartridges. Figure 1.1 shows you such a machine. *Yet JCL did not change.*

A remarkable consistency pervades the world of JCL. Depending on your point of view, JCL continues to be as good, or as bad, as it originally was, right on through to the present. A programmer knowledgeable of JCL in 1965, who, like Rip van Winkle, fell asleep for 20 years, then awoke, would find a world vastly different from the one she last saw. But she could could count on one thing. She could go right back to work and use the JCL she had been working with in 1965. The same JCL that would work in 1965 would work in 1985. In fact, pretty much the same JCL would work on your mainframe even in the 1990s, until your installation upgraded to MVS/ESA Version 4 and Storage Management Subsystem. With Version 4 and DFSMS, things have finally changed.

1.2 Why MVS/ESA?

IBM introduced MVS/ESA as the most recent evolution of its most popular mainframe operating system with the current family of mainframes, named the ES/9000. The "ES" in this name means "enterprise system." The name arises from a marketing attempt to distinguish large computers from smaller ones by their intended use. An "enterprise" is a business, and mainframes are business machines, as opposed to personal systems ("PS"), IBM's marketing name for its current crop of personal computers. While its heart is now composed of even higher density integrated circuits, the soul of ES/9000 computers is still an OS-derived operating system. MVS/ESA stands for *Multiple Virtual Storages/Enterprise System Architecture.*

MVS/ESA ushers in the Storage Management Subsystem (DFSMS), a major advance for working with disk space. The use of DFSMS is optional with MVS/ESA, but it looks as if IBM's intention is to eventually have most or all mainframe installations enthusiastically use it. MVS/ESA itself adds certain capabilities and features to JCL. DFSMS adds additional JCL parameters and modifies the way that some existing parameters, such as SPACE, operate. In this book, I show you advanced JCL coding techniques and practices suited to the production mainframe environment. Though many of the techniques shown here work under MVS/ESA Version 3, this book is really intended to help you make the transition to MVS/ESA Version 4.

1.3 Differences Between MVS/ESA Versions 3 and 4

The most current version of MVS/ESA is Version 4, which has been marketed since 1991. Storage Management Subsystem is supported by the MVS/ESA Version 3. But Version 4 provides these major feature enhancements over earlier versions:

- IF/ELSE statement coding, which allows you to replace COND CODE testing
- Private proc libraries, which make instream proc testing (and the PEND statement, and certain third-party products) irrelevant and unneccesary
- Nested procedures (procs), which allow you greater flexibility in customizing and packaging your production JCL to "hide" details and make job stream coding easier

With DFSMS installed, Version 4 also gives you more features, such as:

- System-determined block sizes for new data sets
- A new parameter named AVGREC that changes the way the SPACE parameter works
- The ability to eliminate coding UNIT when you create a disk data set
- Newer, simpler ways to specify standardized new data set attributes, performance, and availability criteria using DATACLAS, STORCLAS, and MGMTCLAS parameters
- Greater flexibility with generation data group data sets, which are now called *generation data sets* (GDS)

MVS/ESA Version 4 provides the most significant upgrade in JCL features in almost 30 years. I wrote this book to help you, either as an experienced JCL user or a relative newcomer to mainframes, get the most out of MVS/ESA Version 4 JCL with the least frustration and bother.

1.4 The Role of Storage Management Subsystem (DFSMS)

Storage Management Subsystem (DFSMS) is one of the newest major features offered by MVS/ESA. In this introductory chapter, I give you the "big picture" of DFSMS, so that you can see how it fits into the MVS/ESA Version 4 environment. As you read through this introduction, you'll see that DFSMS has the potential to change the way you code JCL. But a wide variety of circumstances affects the way changes to your JCL occur as DFSMS is implemented at your company. I cover general JCL changes of MVS/ESA Version 4—those not related to DFSMS—first in this book. I put details about DFSMS operation into Chapter 10.

Storage Management Subsystem provides tools to mainframe installations to automate the management of disk space resources. "Management" means the specification of data set characteristics such as data set organization, the determination of what disk device a data set will be housed on, when the data set should be backed up, and when it should be removed from disk and "archived" to less expensive (and slower to access) storage mediums. As a by-product, DFSMS has the potential to make JCL coding easier, once you understand how DFSMS becomes responsible for disk data set management.

To use the Storage Management Subsystem, your installation has to evaluate the types of disk data sets already in place and categorize them in terms of their attributes (such as record format, record length, and data set organization) and disk space requirements (DATACLAS), performance and availability (STORCLAS), and criteria related to their backup, migration, and expiration specifications (MGMTCLAS). Names (DATACLAS, STORCLAS, and MGMTCLAS) must be agreed upon and established for each category of disk data set. These are not decisions that can be made by individual programmers. Rather, disk space administration personnel usually handle the implementation of DFSMS, in coordination with systems programmers, and in collaboration with end users who must ultimately agree to pay for specified levels of data set performance. Your JCL is simplified if the new data sets that you create can be assigned the characteristics of an already-defined category.

Storage Management Subsystem is for the modern mainframe environment shorn of obsolete vestiges of the original System/360, such as uncataloged data sets and the obsolete Indexed Sequential Access Method (ISAM). All DFSMS-managed data sets are cataloged, and indexed files are supported by Virtual Storage Access Method (VSAM) key sequenced data sets. In addition, although they are not obsolete, DFSMS does not (at least at this time) deal with tape data sets, the SYSOUT print spool, or instream data.

DFSMS is not available with earlier versions of MVS, such as MVS/XA. DFSMS is, however, available with versions of MVS/ESA prior to Version 4. Regardless of MVS/ESA version, DFSMS may be installed but "shut off" in an inactive state. Storage Management Subsystem adds 10 new JCL parameters, most of which deal only with new cataloged disk data sets. Some of these new JCL features become available to you as soon as DFSMS software is present on your system, even if it is not active. You gain access to other features—even for disk data sets not managed by DFSMS—only if DFSMS is active.

In Chapters 2, 3, 4, and 5, I show you practical examples of MVS/ESA Version 4 features of entirely general applicability. The features in these chapters, such as IF/ELSE job stream control, private proc libraries, nested procs, and enhanced proc add/override treatment, are available to you even if your installation has not yet installed the Storage Management Subsystem. Chapters 10 and 11 focus on DFSMS itself and new JCL features for which DFSMS is required. I cover miscellaneous other new MVS/ESA capabilities and JCL coding in Chapter 12, including an additional format of the partitioned data set called the Partitioned Data Set Extended (PDSE).

1.5 How Your JCL Will Change with MVS/ESA Version 4

From its origin in 1964, JCL has fostered a variety of reactions and some nasty opinions. To some extent, negative opinions arise because JCL represents a second grammar programmers have to learn in order to process programs on mainframes. To a larger degree, some people resent JCL because it reflects the terse abbreviations and acronyms chosen by early day assembler-oriented personnel, and it is often written in a compacted form suited to minimizing the number of punched cards (lines) used to house it. Although JCL does represent a rather commonsense approach to communication to the operating system, JCL became, and continues to be, fashionable for everyone to knock, from programmer trainees to Unix gurus.

Negative opinions about job control language may certainly continue. JCL still exhibits a remarkable consistency with the past in format and appearance. MVS/ESA Version 4 JCL is still oriented to punched card images, it still starts with slashes //, it still uses the same three basic statement types of JOB, EXEC, and DD, and it still uses old abbreviations such as RECFM (record format) and LRECL (logical record length). JCL still ends in column 72 on what could actually be a punched card, even though you use TSO/ISPF to electronically prepare and store it. And all of your old JCL coding practices will continue to work, subject to dictates from your data administration group about specific code eliminations made necessary by local use of the Storage Management Subsystem.

But in MVS/ESA Version 4 JCL, you now optionally eliminate the DCB parameter as a group and code separate RECFM, LRECL, and other data set attributes, as I demonstrate below. You can use the new JCLLIB statement immediately after your JOB statement to specify the libraries where MVS should look for any cataloged procedures (procs) to be executed. You can code an IF . . . THEN statement on a line of JCL preceding an EXEC statement, an ELSE after one or more EXECs, and an END/IF statement after one or more subsequent EXECs to control step execution. You can omit the block size from your JCL for a new data set and have MVS compute the best block size for you. You can (with DFSMS installed) code the new AVGREC parameter to specify SPACE by records rather than blocks. You can use LIKE and REFDD in DD statements as special purpose references to data set labels and other DD statements to specify data set attributes. How, exactly, do you use these things? *See my examples throughout this book!*

The many MVS/ESA Version 4 improvements make it possible for you to create new job streams that are easier to build and modify. You can now also tune up older procs for efficiency, enjoy a greater flexibility in concatenating data sets, and incur fewer problems in overriding parameters in production procs via execution JCL. You can also use the DFDSS utility to move data from one disk volume to another and bring data into the Storage Management Subsystem environment or take it out of it.

In short, in the MVS Version 4 environment, you can continue to do many of the things you have always done with JCL. But you can also increase your productivity, gain a greater reliability of your job streams, ease the maintenance burden associated with your JCL, and make it easier and faster for newcomers to become familiar with the mainframe processes you have orchestrated with JCL. Mainframes are no longer the only game in town. Some folks even call the software on them "legacy" systems, as if someone or something had died and left them behind.

But mainframes are still at the heart of vital business processes and will continue to be for several years. Many personnel who learn programming on Unix systems, Windows NT systems, AS/400s, or microcomputers will still ultimately find themselves assuming responsibility for the support of mainframe applications. As we move from mainframe dominance to cooperative computing involving mainframes communicating with other computer systems, we will all have to understand several different operating systems, not fewer, and simplifications will become especially productive. Start making your MVS JCL easier for everyone to deal with in the ways that MVS/ESA Version 4 supports!

1.6 "Promoted" Parameters Can Simplify Your JCL

For the first time in almost 30 years, JCL gives you several new statement types, several new parameters, and the ability to simplify your JCL coding format through "promoted" parameters. As an introduction to advanced MVS/ESA techniques and Version 4, let me show you two examples that will also let you see the unique style of this book.

Promoted parameters are one of the simpler improvements MVS/ESA allows you to make in your JCL. Parameter promotion involves the elimination of "DCB=(. . .)" coding. In Figure 1.2, I have coded a simple data set housekeeping deletion step involving the IEFBR14 program, followed by an execution of the IEBGENER utility to allocate a new data set of the same name and populate it with records. I purposely coded this in the cramped format that was standard with punched cards. As you can see in Figure 1.2, you can continue to code the DCB parameter with MVS/ESA as you have always done, enclosing RECFM, LRECL, BLKSIZE within parentheses.

In Figure 1.3, I have coded a second version of the same job stream shown in Figure 1.2. In this case, I coded the JCL in the more modern format that is productive with the use of TSO/ISPF for JCL formation rather than punched cards. Same-line comments make the JCL easier to read. You can see how the separate subparameters that were formerly a part of DCB have become parameters of their own. You can use promoted parameters with any version of MVS/ESA, just as you can use the modern JCL format shown

```
EDIT ---- CSCJGJ.ADV.CNTL(A1OLD) - 01.03 -------------------- COLUMNS 001 072
COMMAND ===>                                                  SCROLL ===> PAGE
****** ***************************** TOP OF DATA ******************************
000001 //CSCJGJA    JOB 1,'BIN 7--JANOSSY',CLASS=A,MSGLEVEL=(1,1),
000002 //   MSGCLASS=X,TIME=(0,6),REGION=2048K,NOTIFY=CSCJGJ
000003 //* TYPRUN=SCAN
000004 //*
000005 //* ILLUSTRATE A JCL FORMAT COMMONLY USED BEFORE MVS/ESA VERSION 4
000006 //* THIS JCL IS STORED AT CSCJGJ.ADV.CNTL(A1OLD)
000007 //*
000008 //*-----------------------------------------------------------------
000009 //* DELETE DATA SET BEFORE CREATING A NEW COPY OF IT
000010 //*-----------------------------------------------------------------
000011 //STEP010  EXEC  PGM=IEFBR14
000012 //DELETE1    DD   DSN=CSCJGJ.ADV.TESTDATA,DISP=(MOD,DELETE),
000013 //              UNIT=SYSDA,SPACE=(TRK,0)
000014 //*-----------------------------------------------------------------
000015 //* CREATE A NEW COPY OF DATA SET
000016 //*-----------------------------------------------------------------
000017 //STEP020  EXEC  PGM=IEBGENER
000018 //SYSPRINT   DD   SYSOUT=*
000019 //SYSIN      DD   DUMMY
000020 //SYSUT1     DD   DSN=CSCJGJ.CSC.WORKERS,DISP=SHR
000021 //SYSUT2     DD   DSN=*.STEP010.DELETE1,DISP=(,CATLG),
000022 //              DCB=(RECFM=FB,LRECL=80,BLKSIZE=3840),UNIT=SYSDA,
000023 //              SPACE=(3840,(50,10),RLSE)
000024 //
```

This is old-style job control language. The DD statement at SYSUT2 includes several parameters on the same line, typical of punched card coding, and the DCB parameter is coded with multiple subparameters RECFM, LRECL, and BLKSIZE. This JCL will still work with MVS/ESA Version 4, but you can now make major improvements in it to make it more readable and more maintainable.

Figure 1.2 A Common Older Punched Card Format of JCL

in Figure 1.3. Decide for yourself which format of JCL you find easier to read, understand, explain to others, and maintain.

All of the MVS/ESA examples I show you in this book are in the more modern JCL coding format, which I describe with examples in Chapter 6. All of the illustrations you'll see here carry self-explanatory annotations

```
EDIT ---- CSCJGJ.ADV.CNTL(A1NEW) - 01.03 -------------------- COLUMNS 001 072
COMMAND ===>                                                  SCROLL ===> PAGE
****** ****************************** TOP OF DATA ******************************
000001 //CSCJGJA   JOB 1,                   ACCOUNTING INFORMATION
000002 //  'BIN 7--JANOSSY',                 PROGRAMMER NAME AND DELIVERY BIN
000003 //  CLASS=A,                         INPUT QUEUE CLASS
000004 //  MSGLEVEL=(1,1),                  HOW MUCH MVS SYSTEM PRINT DESIRED
000005 //  MSGCLASS=X,                      PRINT DESTINATION X A L N OR O
000006 //  TIME=(0,6),                      SAFETY LIMIT: RUN TIME UP TO 6 SECS
000007 //  REGION=2M,                       ALLOW UP TO 2 MEGS VIRTUAL MEMORY
000008 //* TYPRUN=SCAN,                     UNCOMMENT THIS LINE TO DO SCAN ONLY
000009 //  NOTIFY=CSCJGJ                    WHO TO TELL WHEN JOB IS DONE
000010 //*
000011 //* AN EXAMPLE OF MODERN JCL IN THE MVS/ESA VERSION 4 ENVIRONMENT
000012 //* THIS JCL IS STORED AT CSCJGJ.ADV.CNTL(A1NEW)
000013 //*
000014 //*-----------------------------------------------------------------
000015 //* DELETE DATA SET BEFORE CREATING A NEW COPY OF IT
000016 //*-----------------------------------------------------------------
000017 //STEP010  EXEC  PGM=IEFBR14
000018 //DELETE1    DD  DSN=CSCJGJ.ADV.TESTDATA,          DATA SET TO BE
000019 //  DISP=(MOD,DELETE),                              RE-CREATED
000020 //  UNIT=SYSDA,
000021 //  SPACE=(TRK,0)
000022 //*-----------------------------------------------------------------
000023 //* CREATE A NEW COPY OF DATA SET
000024 //*-----------------------------------------------------------------
000025 //STEP020  EXEC  PGM=IEBGENER
000026 //SYSPRINT   DD  SYSOUT=*                          STATUS REPORT
000027 //SYSIN      DD  DUMMY                             OPTIONAL COMMANDS
000028 //SYSUT1     DD  DSN=CSCJGJ.CSC.WORKERS,           INPUT
000029 //  DISP=SHR
000030 //SYSUT2     DD  DSN=*.STEP010.DELETE1,            OUTPUT (SAME NAME
000031 //  DISP=(NEW,CATLG,DELETE),                        AS DELETED ABOVE)
000032 //  UNIT=SYSDA,
000033 //  RECFM=FB,
000034 //  LRECL=80,
000035 //  BLKSIZE=3840,
000036 //  DSORG=PS,
000037 //  SPACE=(3840,(50,10),RLSE)
000038 //
```

MVS/ESA now promotes what used to be subparameters of DCB to be full parameters of their own. This and the modern self-documenting coding style described in Chapter 6 lets you quickly develop job control language that is clear and easy to maintain.

Figure 1.3 TSO/ISPF Format for JCL with "Promoted" DCB Parameters

with arrows such as in Figure 1.3, for easy, quick reading. And all of the illustrations you'll see are taken from TSO/ISPF screens and show you error-free JCL as it actually appears when you work with it, rather than typeset for publication or as if JCL were still coded on punched cards. MVS/ESA Version 4 is for the modern environment. So is this book.

2

Improving Job Stream Control with IF/ELSE Operators

2.1 IF/ELSE Logic Improves JCL
2.2 What the EXEC Statement Does
2.3 How MVS Tells You What EXEC Did
2.4 Confusing Synonyms Exist for COND CODE!
2.5 Completion Code Is Abend Reporting!
2.6 Job Stream Control
2.7 Quick Review of COND Coding
2.8 A Basic COND Example
2.9 A Basic IF . . . THEN Example
2.10 IF Test for a Step That Did Not Execute
2.11 Applying IF/ELSE Logic in Your JCL
2.12 IF/ELSE Coding Rules
2.13 IF/ELSE "Blanket" Coding Analogous to COND=(4,LT)
2.14 Coding an IF/ELSE Against a Step in a Proc
2.15 Trying Out IF/ELSE and RC Testing Against a Proc Step

2.1 IF/ELSE Logic Improves JCL

MVS/ESA Version 4 makes a major improvement in your ability to control the execution of steps in job streams. In earlier versions of MVS you had only the COND parameter of the EXEC statement to dictate whether or not a step was executed. In MVS, Version 4, you can now use IF/ELSE statements to accomplish job stream control. This is one of the biggest improvements provided by MVS/ESA over earlier versions of MVS. Although MVS/ESA Version 4 continues to support coding the COND parameter on EXEC statements, you will want to explore how IF/ELSE makes JCL easier to develop, test, and understand.

In this chapter, I'll show you the basics of the new IF/ELSE job control feature. Then, in Chapter 3, I'll illustrate more advanced IF/ELSE features such as testing the run status of a prior step for generic or specific abend.

2.2 What the EXEC Statement Does

Every EXEC statement cites either a program to be executed, or "canned JCL" to be executed as a procedure. Each EXEC that cites a program causes MVS to accomplish three actions for the program to be executed.

1. Before program execution, EXEC calls upon MVS to examine the DD statements associated with the step and "allocate" devices needed for the program, such as disk and tape drives, and memory for the program itself.
2. When devices are ready, EXEC causes MVS to load the program into memory and give it control (execute the program).
3. After program execution, EXEC causes MVS to reclaim devices and memory used by the program ("deallocate" them).

When the second of these actions is under way, the program is being

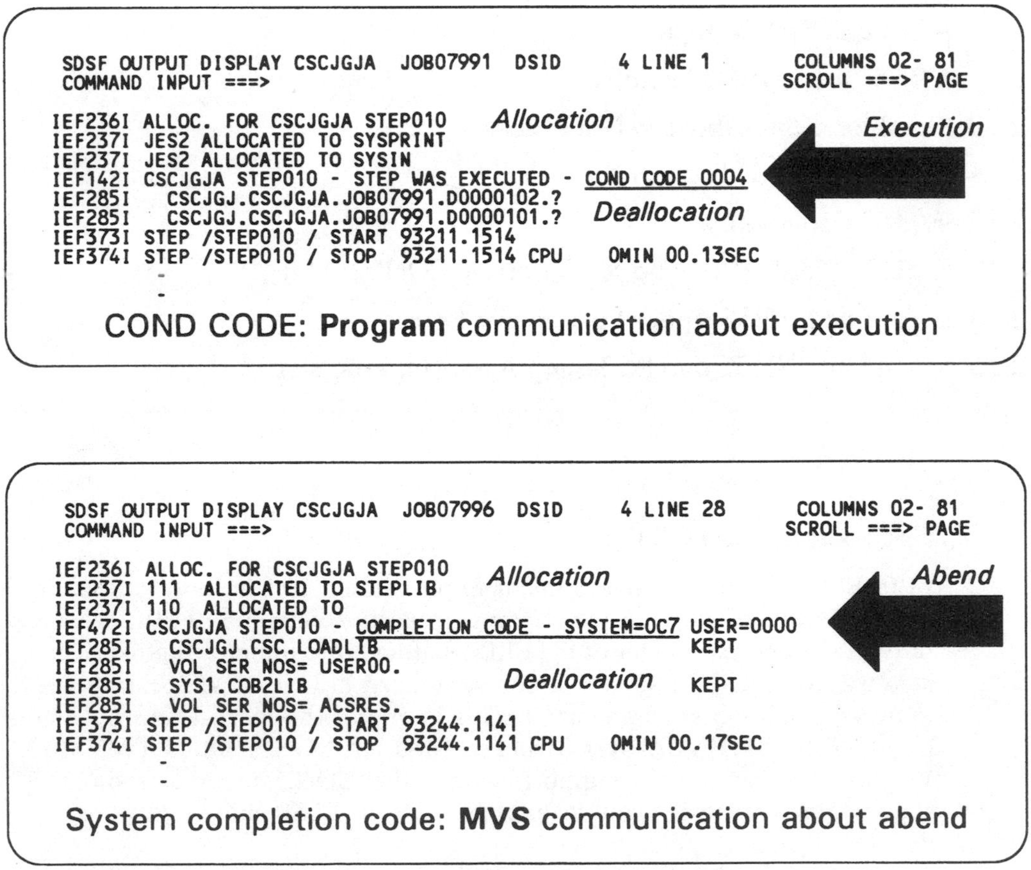

```
SDSF OUTPUT DISPLAY CSCJGJA  JOB07991  DSID     4 LINE 1        COLUMNS 02- 81
COMMAND INPUT ===>                                              SCROLL ===> PAGE

IEF236I ALLOC. FOR CSCJGJA STEP010     Allocation               Execution
IEF237I JES2 ALLOCATED TO SYSPRINT
IEF237I JES2 ALLOCATED TO SYSIN
IEF142I CSCJGJA STEP010 - STEP WAS EXECUTED - COND CODE 0004
IEF285I   CSCJGJ.CSCJGJA.JOB07991.D0000102.?
IEF285I   CSCJGJ.CSCJGJA.JOB07991.D0000101.?  Deallocation
IEF373I STEP /STEP010 / START 93211.1514
IEF374I STEP /STEP010 / STOP  93211.1514 CPU    0MIN 00.13SEC
        -
        -
```

COND CODE: **Program** communication about execution

```
SDSF OUTPUT DISPLAY CSCJGJA  JOB07996  DSID     4 LINE 28       COLUMNS 02- 81
COMMAND INPUT ===>                                              SCROLL ===> PAGE

IEF236I ALLOC. FOR CSCJGJA STEP010     Allocation                Abend
IEF237I 111  ALLOCATED TO STEPLIB
IEF237I 110  ALLOCATED TO
IEF472I CSCJGJA STEP010 - COMPLETION CODE - SYSTEM=0C7 USER=0000
IEF285I   CSCJGJ.CSC.LOADLIB                           KEPT
IEF285I   VOL SER NOS= USER00.
IEF285I   SYS1.COB2LIB                 Deallocation    KEPT
IEF285I   VOL SER NOS= ACSRES.
IEF373I STEP /STEP010 / START 93244.1141
IEF374I STEP /STEP010 / STOP  93244.1141 CPU    0MIN 00.17SEC
        -
        -
```

System completion code: **MVS** communication about abend

Figure 2.1 How COND CODE and System Completion Code Appear in MVS System Output

executed. The second action concludes when the program stops executing, reaching either a normal end or an abnormal end ("abend"). If the program ends execution normally, MVS conveys a four-digit "condition code," which it makes visible in its reporting as the COND CODE, such as 0000 or 0004, or any other value up to 4095 as set by the program. The top part of Figure 2.1 shows a typical COND CODE. If the program being executed by the JCL ends by abending ("blowing up"), MVS retains and makes visible a "completion code" for the step as shown in the bottom part of Figure 2.1. *COND CODE and completion code are not the same thing.* COND CODE is communication from a program that executed successfully. A completion code is communication from either the program or MVS itself, issued when a program failure has occurred.

2.3 How MVS Tells You What EXEC Did

Whenever you submit JCL to MVS to execute one or more programs, MVS reports back to you what happened, with several lines of output. You use the TSO/ISPF SDSF ("=s.h") function to view this output as shown in Figure 2.1. The type of messages shown in Figure 2.1 are repeated for each program you execute.

The messages produced by MVS before the line carrying the COND CODE or completion code are generated during the device allocation processes (see point 1 in the preceding section). The COND CODE or completion code line is printed when program execution has ended. The messages following the COND CODE or completion code line are printed after program execution has ended and describe the device deallocation actions MVS has performed.

If anything has gone wrong during device allocation or program execution, it will be reflected in the form of MVS system reporting shown in Figure 2.1, and reading it is part of the joy of dealing with MVS. But the task of interpreting MVS system output is complicated by the fact that the same things are referred to by various different names in IBM software and publications.

2.4 Confusing Synonyms Exist for COND CODE!

COND CODE is printed as a four-digit decimal value in the range 0000 through 4095. Several synonyms exist for the COND CODE in various IBM manuals and documentation. It isn't good technical writing to use many different names for the same thing. But this arises with MVS because so many people—literally thousands of people—have had a hand in designing, coding, enhancing, and documenting MVS since 1964. The COND CODE is also referred to as:

- the condition code
- the return code
- RC

To make matters even more confusing, "return code" is a term that is also used differently in various software products and may mean something other than COND CODE.

COND CODE is communication from the *program* being executed, not MVS. Most programming languages give you the capability to put a value into the MVS system reporting COND CODE field. In COBOL, for example, you put a value in the range 0 through 4095 into a register named RETURN-CODE to convey it to the COND CODE field. IBM-supplied utility programs follow a convention of using COND CODE 0000 to indicate successful execution, 0004 to indicate a slight problem causing warning messages to be generated, 0008 for serious problems, and higher values in increments of 4 for even more significant problems.

Note that the term "completion code" does not appear in the list of synonyms for COND CODE. COND CODE is printed by MVS only for programs that execute and end normally. Completion code is printed when a program abends.

2.5 Completion Code Is Abend Reporting!

Completion code is the MVS term for communication about a program failure. Two forms of completion codes exit: system completion codes and user completion codes.

System completion code is set by MVS itself when a program fails by overstepping its memory or other resource allocation, violates a processing requirement such as attempting arithmetic on nonnumeric data, or when some form of system software input/output error occurs. System completion code is a three-character code expressed in hexadecimal and is printed with the letter S or the word SYSTEM in front of it, such as S0C7 or SYSTEM=0C7. When a program abends, MVS preempts communication to you, and the system completion code will be printed in system reporting, not a COND CODE. That is, you will see *either* a COND CODE for a step or a completion code, but not both.

User completion code is a code set by a program when it has triggered an abend under its own control. Why would a program do this? Most often, a program triggers an abend to call attention to a significant failure, to force the abandonment of further processing in the job stream, and to communicate information about the problem to the outside world via the MVS system reporting.

User completion codes can be confusing, because they are printed as four-digit numbers, just like COND CODE values. To make matters worse, some IBM compilers, such as VS COBOL II, automatically generate user completion codes in the range 1000 to 1999 for conditions that older compilers allowed MVS to intercept. I will show you the effect of user completion codes on your JCL and MVS system reporting in Chapter 3.

As you can see in the lower part of Figure 2.1, the MVS system output message that carries the completion code has places for both system completion code and user completion code. Only one of these fields will ever carry a value. When this message line is used for system completion code, USER=0000 is printed for the user completion code.

When the completion code line is used to carry a user completion code, SYSTEM=000 is printed on the line.

2.6 Job Stream Control

A *job* consists of a JOB statement and one or more EXEC statements. Each EXEC statement marks the beginning of a "step" of the job. A *job stream* is just a job that contains two or more steps.

COND CODE and completion code both provide the basis for control over whether the programs named at steps in a job stream execute or do not execute. If a program executes successfully but its logic is arranged to identify and detect some condition that should prevent a subsequent job step (program) from executing, it can "tell" (via the COND CODE it sets) the program(s) at subsequent steps not to execute. If a program abends, MVS usually dictates whether or not subsequent steps are given attention for execution, but you can override its actions and still make subsequent steps execute, as I describe in Chapter 3.

The subject of job stream control deals with controlling the execution of steps based on COND CODEs or completion codes. Prior to MVS/ESA Version 4, exercising job stream control required you to code the COND parameter on the EXEC statements of most steps. With Version 4, you can now use IF . . . THEN/ELSE coding.

2.7 Quick Review of COND Coding

Since its invention in 1964, MVS JCL has suffered from the lack of a full and complete mechanism for controlling the execution of steps based on COND CODEs and completion codes. The designers of JCL seem to have been concerned only with giving you a means to shut off steps based on the COND CODE of earlier steps. If you have used JCL to any practical extent, you have no doubt been exposed to the COND parameter of the EXEC statement. You can code COND on any EXEC statement to define up to eight conditions under which the step will be shut off:

```
//STEP010  EXEC PGM=A111
   -
   -
//STEP020  EXEC PGM=B222,COND=(0,EQ,STEP010)
   -
   -
//STEP030  EXEC PGM=C333,COND=(0,LT,STEP010)
   -
   -
```

In this example, STEP020—program B222—will be shut off (will not execute) if the program at STEP010 leaves behind a return code of 0000. This is so because COND=(0,EQ,STEP010) means "if 0 is equal to the condition code of STEP010, shut off the execution of program B222."

Similarly, STEP030 will be shut off if 0 is less than the condition code of STEP010. For example, STEP030—program C333—will not execute if the program at STEP010 leaves behind a condition code of 0004, because "0 is less than 4." (Compound condition coding such as COND=((0,EQ,STEP010),(4,LT,STEP020)) at a single step always implies an "OR" condition, but I have not illustrated that here.)

2.8 A Basic COND Example

You can confirm how COND works by looking at Figures 2.2 and 2.3. STEP010 of the JCL in Figure 2.2 executes the IDCAMS utility to set a condition code of 0004. Steps STEP020 and STEP030 execute the "nothing" program IEFBR14 purely for demonstration purposes. Since IEFBR14 contains no logic at all except the assembler instruction BR14 (assembler's "stop" instruction), a step at which it is executed will always receive COND CODE 0000. COND=(0,EQ,STEP010) at STEP020 will shut it off if STEP010 leaves behind COND CODE 0000. COND=(0,LT,STEP010) at STEP030 will shut off that step if STEP010 leaves behind a COND CODE such as 0004, 0008, or any other nonzero value.

The JCL in Figure 2.2 works, as you can see from the output it produces, which is shown in Figure 2.3. IDCAMS returned a COND CODE of 0004. The arrows point to the result of STEP020, which has executed, and the indication that STEP030 was not executed.

```
EDIT ---- CSCJGJ.ADV.CNTL(B1COND) - 01.01 ------------------- COLUMNS 001 072
COMMAND ===>                                                   SCROLL ===> PAGE
****** ****************************** TOP OF DATA ******************************
000001 //CSCJGJA   JOB 1,              ACCOUNTING INFORMATION
000002 //   'BIN 7--JANOSSY',          PROGRAMMER NAME AND DELIVERY BIN
000003 //   CLASS=A,                   INPUT QUEUE CLASS
000004 //   MSGLEVEL=(1,1),            HOW MUCH MVS SYSTEM PRINT DESIRED
000005 //   MSGCLASS=X,                PRINT DESTINATION X A L N OR O
000006 //   TIME=(0,6),                SAFETY LIMIT: RUN TIME UP TO 6 SECS
000007 //   REGION=2M,                 ALLOW UP TO 2 MEGS VIRTUAL MEMORY
000008 //*  TYPRUN=SCAN,               UNCOMMENT THIS LINE TO DO SCAN ONLY
000009 //   NOTIFY=CSCJGJ              WHO TO TELL WHEN JOB IS DONE
000010 //*
000011 //* DEMONSTRATE HOW TRADITIONAL COND CODING WORKS
000012 //* THIS JCL IS STORED AT CSCJGJ.ADV.CNTL(B1COND)
000013 //*-----------------------
000014 //STEP010  EXEC  PGM=IDCAMS
000015 //SYSPRINT   DD  SYSOUT=*
000016 //SYSIN      DD  *
000017      SET LASTCC = 4
000018 //*-----------------------
000019 //STEP020  EXEC  PGM=IEFBR14,COND=(0,EQ,STEP010)      SHUT OFF IF RC=0
000020 //*----------------------------------------------------------------
000021 //STEP030  EXEC  PGM=IEFBR14,COND=(0,LT,STEP010)      SHUT OFF IF RC>0
000022 //
```

Old COND parameter coding

Figure 2.2 Typical Pre-MVS/ESA Version 4 COND Coding

```
                   J E S 2  J O B  L O G  --  S Y S T E M  I B M 1  --  N O D E  N 1

16.45.09 JOB03556  IRR010I  USERID CSCJGJ   IS ASSIGNED TO THIS JOB.
16.45.10 JOB03556  ICH70001I CSCJGJ   LAST ACCESS AT 16:30:49 ON SATURDAY, JUNE 26, 1993
16.45.10 JOB03556  $HASP373 CSCJGJA  STARTED - INIT  1 - CLASS A - SYS IBM1
16.45.10 JOB03556  $HASP395 CSCJGJA  ENDED

------ JES2 JOB STATISTICS ------
    26 JUN 93 JOB EXECUTION DATE
           21 CARDS READ
           56 SYSOUT PRINT RECORDS
            0 SYSOUT PUNCH RECORDS
            4 SYSOUT SPOOL KBYTES
         0.01 MINUTES EXECUTION TIME

        1 //CSCJGJA   JOB 1,                ACCOUNTING INFORMATION               JOB03556
          //  'BIN 7--JANOSSY',             PROGRAMMER NAME AND DELIVERY BIN
          //  CLASS=A,                      INPUT QUEUE CLASS
          //  MSGLEVEL=(1,1),               HOW MUCH MVS SYSTEM PRINT DESIRED
          //  MSGCLASS=X,                   PRINT DESTINATION X A L N OR O
          //  TIME=(0,6),                   SAFETY LIMIT: RUN TIME UP TO 6 SECS
          //  REGION=2M,                    ALLOW UP TO 2 MEGS VIRTUAL MEMORY
          //* TYPRUN=SCAN,                  UNCOMMENT THIS LINE TO DO SCAN ONLY
          //  NOTIFY=CSCJGJ                 WHO TO TELL WHEN JOB IS DONE
          //*
          //* DEMONSTRATE SIMPLE, TRADITIONAL IF/ELSE
          //* THIS JCL IS STORED AT CSCJGJ.ADV.CNTL(B1COND)
          //*-------------------------------------------------------------------
        2 //STEP010  EXEC  PGM=IDCAMS
        3 //SYSPRINT   DD  SYSOUT=*
        4 //SYSIN      DD  *
          //*-------------------------------------------------------------------
        5 //STEP020  EXEC  PGM=IEFBR14,COND=(0,EQ,STEP010)      SHUT OFF IF RC=0
          //*-------------------------------------------------------------------
        6 //STEP030  EXEC  PGM=IEFBR14,COND=(0,LT,STEP010)      SHUT OFF IF RC>0

ICH70001I CSCJGJ   LAST ACCESS AT 16:30:49 ON SATURDAY, JUNE 26, 1993

IEF236I ALLOC. FOR CSCJGJA STEP010
IEF237I JES2 ALLOCATED TO SYSPRINT
IEF237I JES2 ALLOCATED TO SYSIN
IEF142I CSCJGJA STEP010 - STEP WAS EXECUTED - COND CODE 0004
IEF285I   CSCJGJ.CSCJGJA.JOB03556.D0000102.?              SYSOUT
```

IDCAMS executed and left behind a condition code of 0004

Figure 2.3 MVS System Reporting for Executed and Shut-Off Steps

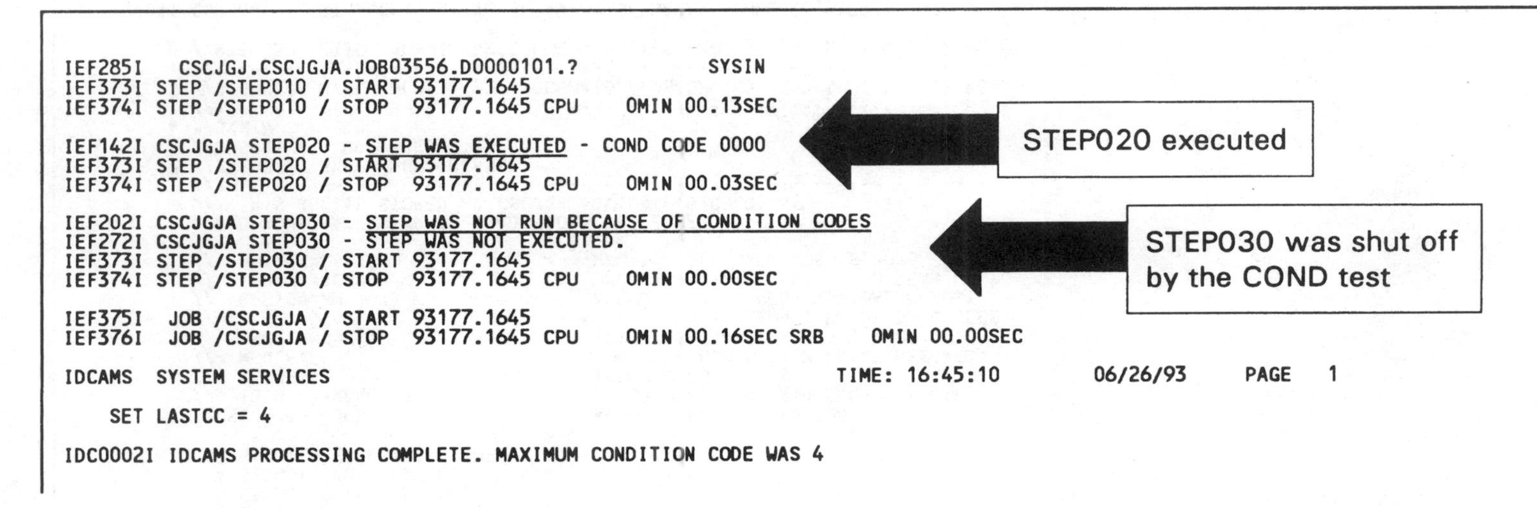

```
IEF285I   CSCJGJ.CSCJGJA.JOB03556.D0000101.?          SYSIN
IEF373I STEP /STEP010 / START 93177.1645
IEF374I STEP /STEP010 / STOP  93177.1645 CPU    OMIN 00.13SEC

IEF142I CSCJGJA STEP020 - STEP WAS EXECUTED - COND CODE 0000
IEF373I STEP /STEP020 / START 93177.1645
IEF374I STEP /STEP020 / STOP  93177.1645 CPU    OMIN 00.03SEC

IEF202I CSCJGJA STEP030 - STEP WAS NOT RUN BECAUSE OF CONDITION CODES
IEF272I CSCJGJA STEP030 - STEP WAS NOT EXECUTED.
IEF373I STEP /STEP030 / START 93177.1645
IEF374I STEP /STEP030 / STOP  93177.1645 CPU    OMIN 00.00SEC

IEF375I  JOB /CSCJGJA / START 93177.1645
IEF376I  JOB /CSCJGJA / STOP  93177.1645 CPU    OMIN 00.16SEC SRB    OMIN 00.00SEC

IDCAMS  SYSTEM SERVICES                               TIME: 16:45:10       06/26/93     PAGE    1

    SET LASTCC = 4

IDC0002I IDCAMS PROCESSING COMPLETE. MAXIMUM CONDITION CODE WAS 4
```

STEP020 executed
STEP030 was shut off by the COND test

Figure 2.3 (continued)

2.9 A Basic IF . . . THEN Example

COND coding is workable for job stream control. Those of us who develop job streams have "made do" with COND for about 30 years. But COND forces you to think in reverse (it always shuts off steps, rather than expresses when a step will execute), and each COND only works for one step (EXEC). A more straightforward way to express what I am trying to do in the JCL in Figure 2.2 is to say: "If STEP010 leaves behind a condition code greater than 0, execute STEP020, otherwise execute STEP030."

This is in the form of a relational ("conditional") expression. It is the way you probably would think about your program execution requirements. MVS/ESA Version 4 finally makes it possible for you to code your JCL the way you think about program execution requirements, without having to translate your thinking into COND's limited and convoluted "shut off" capabilities.

In Figure 2.4, I have coded an IF at line 19 for STEP020, and an ENDIF at line 21. The coding for the IF states:

```
//   IF ( STEP010.RC > 0 ) THEN
```

and is followed by an EXEC statement. The program at the EXEC following this IF will be executed if this condition is met (the COND CODE from STEP010 is greater than 0), otherwise this EXEC will be shut off. This is "positive" logic, not the "negative" shut off logic of the COND parameter.

```
EDIT ---- CSCJGJ.ADV.CNTL(B2IFEL) - 01.01 ------------------- COLUMNS 001 072
COMMAND ===>                                                  SCROLL ===> PAGE
****** ***************************** TOP OF DATA ******************************
000001 //CSCJGJA   JOB 1,                  ACCOUNTING INFORMATION
000002 //   'BIN 7--JANOSSY',              PROGRAMMER NAME AND DELIVERY BIN
000003 //   CLASS=A,                       INPUT QUEUE CLASS
000004 //   MSGLEVEL=(1,1),                HOW MUCH MVS SYSTEM PRINT DESIRED
000005 //   MSGCLASS=X,                    PRINT DESTINATION X A L N OR O
000006 //   TIME=(0,6),                    SAFETY LIMIT: RUN TIME UP TO 6 SECS
000007 //   REGION=2M,                     ALLOW UP TO 2 MEGS VIRTUAL MEMORY
000008 //*  TYPRUN=SCAN,                   UNCOMMENT THIS LINE TO DO SCAN ONLY
000009 //   NOTIFY=CSCJGJ                  WHO TO TELL WHEN JOB IS DONE
000010 //*
000011 //* DEMONSTRATE HOW THE NEW IF/ELSE CODING WORKS
000012 //* THIS JCL IS STORED AT CSCJGJ.ADV.CNTL(B2IFEL)
000013 //*-------------------------------------------------------------------
000014 //STEP010   EXEC  PGM=IDCAMS
000015 //SYSPRINT    DD  SYSOUT=*                  Relational expression
000016 //SYSIN       DD  *
000017     SET LASTCC = 4
000018 //*---------------------------------
000019 //     IF ( STEP010.RC > 0 ) THEN                      RUN IF RC>0
000020 //STEP020   EXEC  PGM=IEFBR14                         MEANS SAME AS
000021 //     ENDIF                                          SHUT OFF IF RC=0
000022 //*-------------------------------------------------------------------
000023 //     IF ( STEP010.RC = 0 ) THEN                      RUN IF RC=0
000024 //STEP030   EXEC  PGM=IEFBR14                         MEANS SAME AS
000025 //     ENDIF                                          SHUT OFF IF RC>0
000026 //
```

Figure 2.4 Simple Use of MVS/ESA Version 4 IF/THEN Coding

The ENDIF at line 21 ends the scope of this IF statement. Similarly, the IF at line 23 says in a positive way,

```
//  IF ( STEP010.RC = 0 ) THEN
```

which means the program at the EXEC for STEP030 will be executed if STEP010 leaves behind a return code of 0000. The ENDIF at line 25 ends the scope of this IF statement.

IF statements are evaluated by MVS/ESA Version 4 to determine a logical true or false value. If the value determined is true, the EXEC after the IF is allowed to execute. As you can see in the system output shown in Figure 2.5, the final effect of this newer "IF" form of coding on step execution is the same as the older COND coding. And as you can see, MVS/ESA provides some new message text when you use IF coding, stating where (in the MVS-applied numbering of your JCL statements) the IF that controls each EXEC is coded.

2.10 IF Test for a Step That Did Not Execute

When you test the COND CODE of a step that didn't execute, a value of false is assumed for an IF relational test. That is, if you make the following test at STEP030 but STEP020 did not execute, the IF before STEP030 will provide a logical value of false, and program C333 will not execute:

```
//----------------------------------------
//   IF ( STEP010.RC = 0 ) THEN
//STEP020   EXEC  PGM=B222
     -
     -
     ENDIF
//----------------------------------------
//   IF ( STEP020.RC = 0 ) THEN
//STEP030   EXEC  PGM=C333
     -
     -
     ENDIF
//----------------------------------------
```

Does not execute if STEP020 did not execute

2.11 Applying IF/ELSE Logic in Your JCL

The JCL in Figure 2.4 simply uses the new IF operator to implement positive step-by-step job stream control, more or less as an "opposite" to COND's negative "shut off" coding. Yet MVS/ESA Version 4 gives you more capability than that. You can now structure job streams with full IF/ELSE capabilities, as I demonstrate in Figure 2.6.

In Figure 2.6, STEP010 executes IDCAMS to set a COND CODE for example purposes. But lines 20, 21, and 22 show three EXEC statements, all within the scope of one IF:

```
                  J E S 2  J O B  L O G  --  S Y S T E M  I B M 1  --  N O D E  N 1

16.58.11 JOB03574  IRR010I  USERID CSCJGJ   IS ASSIGNED TO THIS JOB.
16.58.12 JOB03574  ICH70001I CSCJGJ   LAST ACCESS AT 16:57:34 ON SATURDAY, JUNE 26, 1993
16.58.12 JOB03574  $HASP373 CSCJGJA  STARTED - INIT  1 - CLASS A - SYS IBM1
16.58.12 JOB03574  $HASP395 CSCJGJA  ENDED

------ JES2 JOB STATISTICS ------
   26 JUN 93 JOB EXECUTION DATE
          25 CARDS READ
          60 SYSOUT PRINT RECORDS
           0 SYSOUT PUNCH RECORDS
           4 SYSOUT SPOOL KBYTES
        0.01 MINUTES EXECUTION TIME

        1 //CSCJGJA   JOB 1,                    ACCOUNTING INFORMATION
          //  'BIN 7--JANOSSY',                 PROGRAMMER NAME AND DELIVERY BIN
          //  CLASS=A,                          INPUT QUEUE CLASS
          //  MSGLEVEL=(1,1),                   HOW MUCH MVS SYSTEM PRINT DESIRED
          //  MSGCLASS=X,                       PRINT DESTINATION X A L N OR O
          //  TIME=(0,6),                       SAFETY LIMIT: RUN TIME UP TO 6 SECS
          //  REGION=2M,                        ALLOW UP TO 2 MEGS VIRTUAL MEMORY
          //* TYPRUN=SCAN,                      UNCOMMENT THIS LINE TO DO SCAN ONLY
          //  NOTIFY=CSCJGJ                     WHO TO TELL WHEN JOB IS DONE
          //*
          //* DEMONSTRATE HOW THE NEW IF/ELSE CODING WORKS
          //* THIS JCL IS STORED AT CSCJGJ.ADV.CNTL(B2IFEL)
          //*-------------------------------------------------------------------
        2 //STEP010   EXEC  PGM=IDCAMS
        3 //SYSPRINT   DD  SYSOUT=*
        4 //SYSIN      DD  *
          //*-------------------------------------------------------------------
        5 //     IF ( STEP010.RC > 0 ) THEN                      RUN IF RC>0
        6 //STEP020  EXEC  PGM=IEFBR14                           MEANS SAME AS
        7 //     ENDIF                                           SHUT OFF IF RC=0
          //*-------------------------------------------------------------------
        8 //     IF ( STEP010.RC = 0 ) THEN                      RUN IF RC=0
        9 //STEP030  EXEC  PGM=IEFBR14                           MEANS SAME AS
       10 //     ENDIF                                           SHUT OFF IF RC>0

ICH70001I CSCJGJ   LAST ACCESS AT 16:57:34 ON SATURDAY, JUNE 26, 1993
```

Expressions involving IF are "relational" in that they compare two values. In this case the "return code" (RC) from STEP010 is compared to the literal value 0. The outcome of this expression is determined as true or false. This truth outcome determines whether or not the EXEC (or EXECs) coded after the IF are processed.

Figure 2.5 MVS System Reporting of an IF/THEN Logic Test

```
IEF236I ALLOC. FOR CSCJGJA STEP010
IEF237I JES2 ALLOCATED TO SYSPRINT
IEF237I JES2 ALLOCATED TO SYSIN
IEF142I CSCJGJA STEP010 - STEP WAS EXECUTED - COND CODE 0004
IEF285I   CSCJGJ.CSCJGJA.JOB03574.D0000102.?           SYSOUT
IEF285I   CSCJGJ.CSCJGJA.JOB03574.D0000101.?           SYSIN
IEF373I STEP /STEP010 / START 93177.1658
IEF374I STEP /STEP010 / STOP  93177.1658 CPU    0MIN 00.13SEC

IEF142I CSCJGJA STEP020 - STEP WAS EXECUTED - COND CODE 0000
IEF373I STEP /STEP020 / START 93177.1658
IEF374I STEP /STEP020 / STOP  93177.1658 CPU    0MIN 00.03SEC

IEF206I CSCJGJA STEP030 - STEP WAS NOT RUN BECAUSE OF CONDITIONAL EXPRESSION ON STATEMENT 8
IEF272I CSCJGJA STEP030 - STEP WAS NOT EXECUTED.
IEF373I STEP /STEP030 / START 93177.1658
IEF374I STEP /STEP030 / STOP  93177.1658 CPU    0MIN 00.00SEC

IEF375I  JOB /CSCJGJA / START 93177.1658
IEF376I  JOB /CSCJGJA / STOP  93177.1658 CPU    0MIN 00.16SEC SRB    0MIN 00.00SEC

IDCAMS  SYSTEM SERVICES                                      TIME: 16:58:12

    SET LASTCC = 4

IDC0002I IDCAMS PROCESSING COMPLETE. MAXIMUM CONDITION CODE WAS 4
```

Relational expressions are also called **"conditional" expressions** in MVS/ESA system reporting. System reporting uses these new terms and tells you the statement number on which each condition was coded.

Figure 2.5 (continued)

```
EDIT ---- CSCJGJ.ADV.CNTL(B3IFEL) - 01.01 -------------------- COLUMNS 001 072
COMMAND ===>                                                  SCROLL ===> PAGE
****** ******************************* TOP OF DATA *******************************
000001 //CSCJGJA    JOB 1,                  ACCOUNTING INFORMATION
000002 //   'BIN 7--JANOSSY',               PROGRAMMER NAME AND DELIVERY BIN
000003 //   CLASS=A,                        INPUT QUEUE CLASS
000004 //   MSGLEVEL=(1,1),                 HOW MUCH MVS SYSTEM PRINT DESIRED
000005 //   MSGCLASS=X,                     PRINT DESTINATION X A L N OR O
000006 //   TIME=(0,6),                     SAFETY LIMIT: RUN TIME UP TO 6 SECS
000007 //   REGION=2M,                      ALLOW UP TO 2 MEGS VIRTUAL MEMORY
000008 //*  TYPRUN=SCAN,                    UNCOMMENT THIS LINE TO DO SCAN ONLY
000009 //   NOTIFY=CSCJGJ                   WHO TO TELL WHEN JOB IS DONE
000010 //*
000011 //* DEMONSTRATE IF/ELSE WITH MULTIPLE STEPS WITHIN SCOPE
000012 //* THIS JCL IS STORED AT CSCJGJ.ADV.CNTL(B3IFEL)
000013 //*-------------------------------------------------------------------
000014 //STEP010   EXEC  PGM=IDCAMS
000015 //SYSPRINT    DD  SYSOUT=*
000016 //SYSIN       DD  *
000017      SET LASTCC = 4
000018 //*-------------------------------
000019 //     IF ( STEP010.RC > 0 ) THEN
000020 //STEP020   EXEC  PGM=IEFBR14
000021 //STEP030   EXEC  PGM=IEFBR14
000022 //STEP040   EXEC  PGM=IEFBR14
000023 //     ELSE
000024 //STEP050   EXEC  PGM=IEFBR14
000025 //STEP060   EXEC  PGM=IEFBR14
000026 //     ENDIF
000027 //
```

You can code multiple EXEC statements within the scope of an IF or ELSE. All of the EXECs within the scope are either given control or not given control.

Figure 2.6 How to Group Multiple EXECS Within an IF/THEN/ELSE

```
//     IF ( STEP010.RC > 0 ) THEN
//STEP020   EXEC   PGM=IEFBR14
//STEP030   EXEC   PGM=IEFBR14
//STEP040   EXEC   PGM=IEFBR14
//     ELSE
    -
    -
```

Steps 020, 030, and 040 will all execute if STEP010 leaves behind a COND CODE greater than 0. If STEP010 leaves behind a COND CODE of 0, the EXECs following the ELSE at line 23—namely, STEP050 and STEP060—will execute. The MVS system output shown in Figure 2.7 confirms this operation and demonstrates how you will see the results of such coding.

The examples you have seen thus far, in Figures 2.2 through 2.7, will help you become familiar with the use of IF/ELSE coding in your MVS JCL. Now let's consider some formal MVS/ESA Version 4 rules for IF/ELSE use.

2.12 IF/ELSE Coding Rules

IF/ELSE coding in JCL is not difficult, but there are several ways you can go astray with this new coding form. Here are several rules you will have to know and follow:

1. IF has to be coded indented at least one space from the slashes that start a

```
                         J E S 2  J O B  L O G  --  S Y S T E M  I B M 1  --  N O D E  N 1

17.04.55 JOB03582  IRR010I  USERID CSCJGJ   IS ASSIGNED TO THIS JOB.
17.04.56 JOB03582  ICH70001I CSCJGJ   LAST ACCESS AT 16:58:12 ON SATURDAY, JUNE 26, 1993
17.04.56 JOB03582  $HASP373 CSCJGJA  STARTED - INIT  1 - CLASS A - SYS IBM1
17.04.57 JOB03582  $HASP395 CSCJGJA  ENDED

------ JES2 JOB STATISTICS ------
   26 JUN 93 JOB EXECUTION DATE
          26 CARDS READ
          71 SYSOUT PRINT RECORDS
           0 SYSOUT PUNCH RECORDS
           4 SYSOUT SPOOL KBYTES
        0.01 MINUTES EXECUTION TIME

        1 //CSCJGJA   JOB 1,                    ACCOUNTING INFORMATION                JOB03582
          //   'BIN 7--JANOSSY',                PROGRAMMER NAME AND DELIVERY BIN
          //   CLASS=A,                         INPUT QUEUE CLASS
          //   MSGLEVEL=(1,1),                  HOW MUCH MVS SYSTEM PRINT DESIRED
          //   MSGCLASS=X,                      PRINT DESTINATION X A L N OR O
          //   TIME=(0,6),                      SAFETY LIMIT: RUN TIME UP TO 6 SECS
          //   REGION=2M,                       ALLOW UP TO 2 MEGS VIRTUAL MEMORY
          //*  TYPRUN=SCAN,                     UNCOMMENT THIS LINE TO DO SCAN ONLY
          //   NOTIFY=CSCJGJ                    WHO TO TELL WHEN JOB IS DONE
          //*
          //* DEMONSTRATE IF/ELSE WITH MULTIPLE STEPS WITHIN SCOPE
          //* THIS JCL IS STORED AT CSCJGJ.ADV.CNTL(C3IFEL)
          //*-----------------------------------------------------------------
        2 //STEP010  EXEC  PGM=IDCAMS
        3 //SYSPRINT   DD  SYSOUT=*
        4 //SYSIN      DD  *
          //*-----------------------------------------------------------------
        5 //     IF ( STEP010.RC > 0 ) THEN
        6 //STEP020  EXEC  PGM=IEFBR14
        7 //STEP030  EXEC  PGM=IEFBR14
        8 //STEP040  EXEC  PGM=IEFBR14
        9 //     ELSE
       10 //STEP050  EXEC  PGM=IEFBR14
       11 //STEP060  EXEC  PGM=IEFBR14
       12 //     ENDIF

ICH70001I CSCJGJ   LAST ACCESS AT 16:58:12 ON SATURDAY, JUNE 26, 1993
```

You can code multiple steps within the scope of an IF or ELSE

Figure 2.7 Statement Number Reporting by MVS for Steps That Are Not Executed

```
IEF236I ALLOC. FOR CSCJGJA STEP010
IEF237I JES2 ALLOCATED TO SYSPRINT
IEF237I JES2 ALLOCATED TO SYSIN
IEF142I CSCJGJA STEP010 - STEP WAS EXECUTED - COND CODE 0004
IEF285I   CSCJGJ.CSCJGJA.JOB03582.D0000102.?             SYSOUT
IEF285I   CSCJGJ.CSCJGJA.JOB03582.D0000101.?             SYSIN
IEF373I STEP /STEP010 / START 93177.1704
IEF374I STEP /STEP010 / STOP  93177.1704 CPU    0MIN 00.13SEC

IEF142I CSCJGJA STEP020 - STEP WAS EXECUTED - COND CODE 0000
IEF373I STEP /STEP020 / START 93177.1704
IEF374I STEP /STEP020 / STOP  93177.1704 CPU    0MIN 00.03SEC

IEF142I CSCJGJA STEP030 - STEP WAS EXECUTED - COND CODE 0000
IEF373I STEP /STEP030 / START 93177.1704
IEF374I STEP /STEP030 / STOP  93177.1704 CPU    0MIN 00.03SEC

IEF142I CSCJGJA STEP040 - STEP WAS EXECUTED - COND CODE 0000
IEF373I STEP /STEP040 / START 93177.1704
IEF374I STEP /STEP040 / STOP  93177.1704 CPU    0MIN 00.03SEC

IEF206I CSCJGJA STEP050 - STEP WAS NOT RUN BECAUSE OF CONDITIONAL EXPRESSION ON STATEMENT 5
IEF272I CSCJGJA STEP050 - STEP WAS NOT EXECUTED.
IEF373I STEP /STEP050 / START 93177.1704
IEF374I STEP /STEP050 / STOP  93177.1704 CPU    0MIN 00.00SEC

IEF206I CSCJGJA STEP060 - STEP WAS NOT RUN BECAUSE OF CONDITIONAL EXPRESSION ON STATEMENT 5
IEF272I CSCJGJA STEP060 - STEP WAS NOT EXECUTED.
IEF373I STEP /STEP060 / START 93177.1704
IEF374I STEP /STEP060 / STOP  93177.1704 CPU    0MIN 00.00SEC

IEF375I  JOB /CSCJGJA / START 93177.1704
IEF376I  JOB /CSCJGJA / STOP  93177.1704 CPU    0MIN 00.22SEC

IDCAMS  SYSTEM SERVICES                         TIME: 17:04:56      06/26/93     PAGE   1

   SET LASTCC = 4

IDC0002I IDCAMS PROCESSING COMPLETE. MAXIMUM CONDITION CODE WAS 4
```

Statement number is where IF is coded, not the affected EXECs!

Figure 2.7 (continued)

JCL statement, or it will be interpreted as a statement label (stepname). You can code a label ("name") on the IF statement immediately after the slashes and before the word IF, but unlike the stepname on an EXEC, such a name will not appear in any MVS system reporting (it's not a program-executing step and doesn't cause allocation/deallocation messages).

2. You will notice from the JCL in Figures 2.4 and 2.6 that I have coded the word THEN after the IF condition code test. Unlike the case with programming languages, you always have to code the word THEN. It is not a "noise" word in JCL as it is in some languages such as VS COBOL II.

3. ENDIF is not optional. You must code the word ENDIF after any IF or IF/ELSE. Like IF, ENDIF has to be indented at least one space from the // that start the JCL statement or it will be mistaken for the name of a new statement.

4. You always have to have at least one EXEC after an IF or ELSE.

5. You can't put JOB, JCLLIB, JOBCAT, JOBLIB, SYSCHK, or XMIT JCL statements within an IF or IF/ELSE.

6. You can code relational expressions using symbols such as = and > and >=, or you can use operators similar to COND operators such as EQ, GT, and GE as shown in Figure 2.8. Although you can code a test such as STEP010.RC=0 without spaces delimiting the "=" operator, you have to put a space before and after the mnemonic forms such as EQ:

```
//     IF ( STEP010.RC=0 ) THEN
```

This is valid; no spaces needed in RC=0

or

```
//     IF ( STEP010.RC EQ 0 ) THEN
```

This is valid; must uses spaces around EQ, GT, and others

7. You can code a NOT in front a relational expression to negate it:

```
//     IF NOT ( STEP010.RC=0 ) THEN
```

But if you are interested in IF/ELSE coding to improve job stream clarity over the negative logic of COND coding, using NOT hardly seems like

---

Figure 2.8 MVS/ESA Version 4 IF/THEN/ELSE Symbol Operators and Their Character Equivalents (see facing page)

<table>
<tr><th>Operator</th><th>Meaning</th><th>Character Form</th></tr>
<tr><td>=</td><td>Equal</td><td>EQ</td></tr>
<tr><td>></td><td>Greater than</td><td>GT</td></tr>
<tr><td><</td><td>Less than</td><td>LT</td></tr>
<tr><td>>=</td><td>Greater than or equal to</td><td>GE</td></tr>
<tr><td><=</td><td>Less than or equal to</td><td>LE</td></tr>
<tr><td>&</td><td>And</td><td>AND</td></tr>
<tr><td>|</td><td>Or</td><td>OR</td></tr>
<tr><td>¬</td><td>Not</td><td>NOT</td></tr>
<tr><td>¬=</td><td>Not equal</td><td>NE</td></tr>
<tr><td>¬></td><td>Not greater than</td><td>NG</td></tr>
<tr><td>¬<</td><td>Not less than</td><td>NL</td></tr>
</table>

`STEPyyy.RC <= 4`	Did STEPyyy have a COND CODE less than or equal to 4?
`STEPyyy.PS010.RC ¬= 0`	Did STEPyyy have a COND CODE not equal to zero?
`ABEND` `ABEND=TRUE`	Did any prior step abend with any system or user completion code?
`STEPyyy.ABEND` `STEPyyy.ABEND=TRUE`	Did prior step STEPyyy abend with any system or user completion code?

`NOT ABEND`
`ABEND=FALSE`
`STEPyyy.ABEND=FALSE`
	True if no prior step incurred a system or user abend

`STEPyyy.PS010.ABEND` `STEPyyy.PS010.ABEND=TRUE`	Did step PS010 in a proc executed at prior step STEPyyy abend?
`ABENDCC=Sxxx`	Did any prior step abend with system completion code Sxxx?
`ABENDCC=Unnnn`	Did any prior step abend with user completion code Unnnn?
`STEPyyy.RUN` `STEPyyy.RUN=TRUE`	Did prior step STEPyyy execute and end normally (not abend)?
`NOT STEPyyy.RUN` `NOT STEPyyy.RUN=TRUE`	Was prior step STEPyyy not given control?

Notes:

1. If you code the combination operators such as >= or ¬= the > or ¬ must always come first. For example, it is incorrect to code => or =< as an operator.
2. You must always code a space before and after & and | but this is optional for words such as ABEND=TRUE.

progress. NOT is a throwback to the type of negative logic that COND forces. You can also use the logical symbol ┌ (available on IBM 3270-type terminals but not on PC keyboards) instead of the word NOT:

```
//      IF ┌  ( STEP010.RC=0 ) THEN
```

8. You can code compound conditions using the words AND and OR. The symbols & and | also stand for these compound joining words as shown in Figure 2.8. This is a big departure from older forms of JCL coding. While COND also allows you to express compound conditions, COND provides only an implicit OR, since any condition being true causes a step to be shut off. For the first time, IF/ELSE allows the compound AND:

```
//      IF ( STEP010.RC <= 8 AND STEP020.RC <=4 ) THEN
```

   Figure 2.9 shows you how I used a compound AND at the "GO" step (line 67) of our "tuned up" VS COBOL II compile, link, and go proc at DePaul University. In Figure 2.9, the "GO" step at line 68 executes only if both the COB2 and LKED steps produced return codes of less than 4. Although you could accomplish the same intent with COND, you could not code COND in the positive way I have shown here.

9. If you code compound relational expressions and NOTs (I don't recommend this), you have to understand that MVS will first process NOT keywords, then comparisons, and only afterwards will process AND and OR. A string of clauses may not be interpreted as you intend unless you code parentheses to clearly indicate your intended processing grouping of terms.

10. As with programming languages, you can use parentheses to specify the relational hierarchy you want:

```
//     IF (STEP010.RC  >= 4 AND STEP020.RC = 0) OR STEP030.RC > 8 THEN
```

   In this case the next EXEC executes if STEP010 had a COND CODE of 0004 or greater *and* STEP020 had a COND CODE of 0000. The next EXEC will also execute if STEP030 had a COND CODE greater than 8.

11. To continue a lengthy relational expression, just break it at any point where you would ordinarily code a space, and continue it indented on the next line, beginning anywhere from column 4 through column 16. For example, I could have coded the IF statement shown above as:

```
//      IF (STEP010.RC >= 4 AND STEP020.RC = 0)
//         OR STEP030.RC  > 8 THEN
```

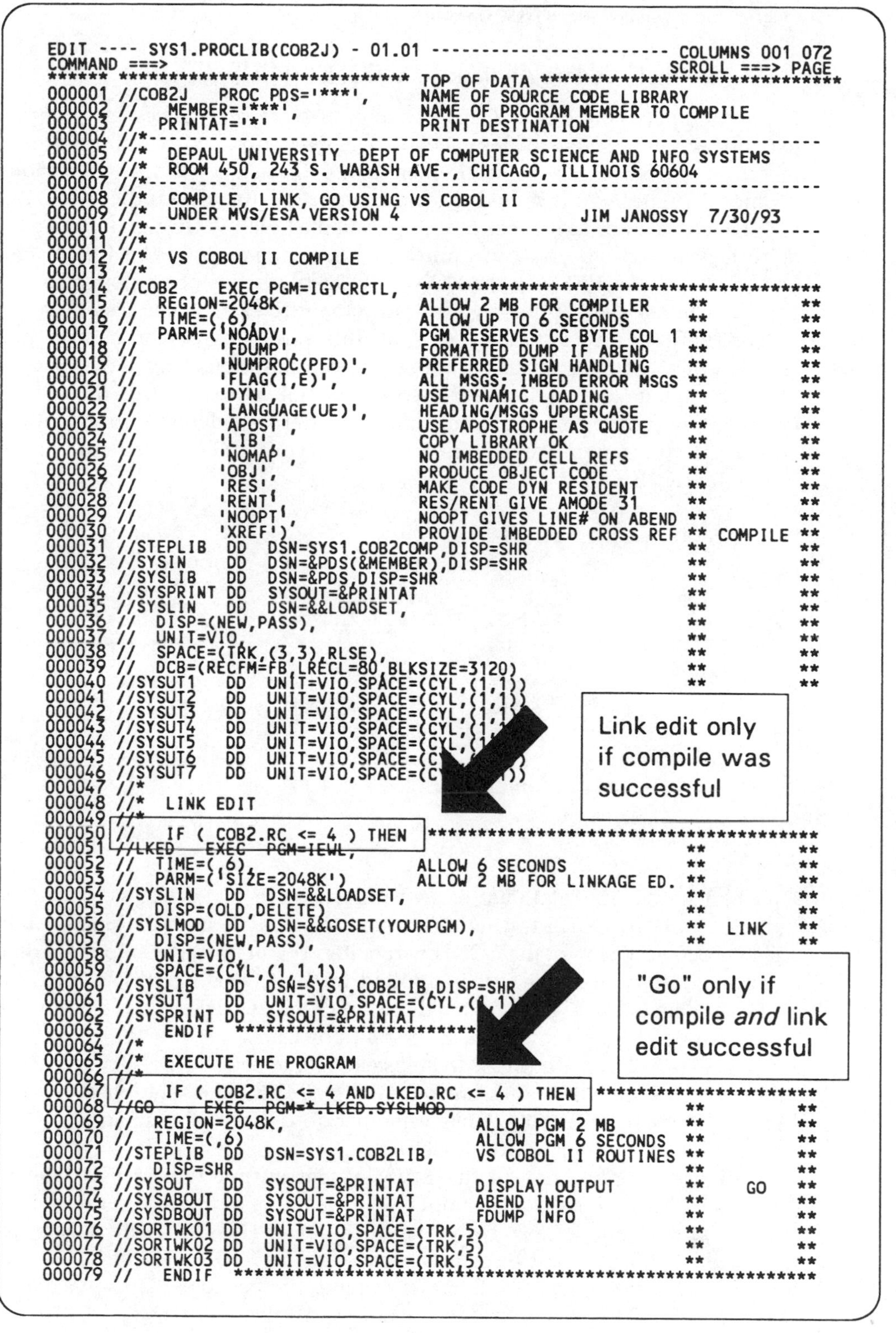

```
EDIT ---- SYS1.PROCLIB(COB2J) - 01.01 ---------------------- COLUMNS 001 072
COMMAND ===>                                                  SCROLL ===> PAGE
****** ***************************** TOP OF DATA ******************************
000001 //COB2J    PROC PDS='***',       NAME OF SOURCE CODE LIBRARY
000002 //   MEMBER='***',               NAME OF PROGRAM MEMBER TO COMPILE
000003 //   PRINTAT='*'                 PRINT DESTINATION
000004 //*---------------------------------------------------------------------
000005 //*  DEPAUL UNIVERSITY  DEPT OF COMPUTER SCIENCE AND INFO SYSTEMS
000006 //*  ROOM 450, 243 S. WABASH AVE., CHICAGO, ILLINOIS 60604
000007 //*---------------------------------------------------------------------
000008 //*  COMPILE, LINK, GO USING VS COBOL II
000009 //*  UNDER MVS/ESA VERSION 4                       JIM JANOSSY  7/30/93
000010 //*---------------------------------------------------------------------
000011 //*
000012 //*  VS COBOL II COMPILE
000013 //*
000014 //COB2    EXEC PGM=IGYCRCTL,     ***************************************
000015 //   REGION=2048K,               ALLOW 2 MB FOR COMPILER      **          **
000016 //   TIME=(,6),                  ALLOW UP TO 6 SECONDS        **          **
000017 //   PARM=('NOADV',              PGM RESERVES CC BYTE COL 1 **          **
000018 //         'FDUMP',              FORMATTED DUMP IF ABEND      **          **
000019 //         'NUMPROC(PFD)',       PREFERRED SIGN HANDLING      **          **
000020 //         'FLAG(I,E)',          ALL MSGS; IMBED ERROR MSGS **          **
000021 //         'DYN',                USE DYNAMIC LOADING          **          **
000022 //         'LANGUAGE(UE)',       HEADING/MSGS UPPERCASE       **          **
000023 //         'APOST',              USE APOSTROPHE AS QUOTE      **          **
000024 //         'LIB',                COPY LIBRARY OK              **          **
000025 //         'NOMAP',              NO IMBEDDED CELL REFS        **          **
000026 //         'OBJ',                PRODUCE OBJECT CODE          **          **
000027 //         'RES',                MAKE CODE DYN RESIDENT       **          **
000028 //         'RENT',               RES/RENT GIVE AMODE 31       **          **
000029 //         'NOOPT',              NOOPT GIVES LINE# ON ABEND **          **
000030 //         'XREF')               PROVIDE IMBEDDED CROSS REF ** COMPILE **
000031 //STEPLIB  DD  DSN=SYS1.COB2COMP,DISP=SHR                  **          **
000032 //SYSIN    DD  DSN=&PDS(&MEMBER),DISP=SHR                  **          **
000033 //SYSLIB   DD  DSN=&PDS,DISP=SHR                           **          **
000034 //SYSPRINT DD  SYSOUT=&PRINTAT                             **          **
000035 //SYSLIN   DD  DSN=&&LOADSET,                              **          **
000036 //   DISP=(NEW,PASS),                                       **          **
000037 //   UNIT=VIO,                                              **          **
000038 //   SPACE=(TRK,(3,3),RLSE),                                **          **
000039 //   DCB=(RECFM=FB,LRECL=80,BLKSIZE=3120)                   **          **
000040 //SYSUT1   DD  UNIT=VIO,SPACE=(CYL,(1,1))                  **          **
000041 //SYSUT2   DD  UNIT=VIO,SPACE=(CYL,(1,1))
000042 //SYSUT3   DD  UNIT=VIO,SPACE=(CYL,(1,1
000043 //SYSUT4   DD  UNIT=VIO,SPACE=(CYL,(1
000044 //SYSUT5   DD  UNIT=VIO,SPACE=(CYL,(1
000045 //SYSUT6   DD  UNIT=VIO,SPACE=(C
000046 //SYSUT7   DD  UNIT=VIO,SPACE=(C      1))
000047 //*
000048 //*  LINK EDIT
000049 //*
000050 //     IF ( COB2.RC <= 4 ) THEN  ***************************************
000051 //LKED    EXEC  PGM=IEWL,                                    **          **
000052 //   TIME=(,6),                  ALLOW 6 SECONDS              **          **
000053 //   PARM=('SIZE=2048K')         ALLOW 2 MB FOR LINKAGE ED.  **          **
000054 //SYSLIN   DD  DSN=&&LOADSET,                              **          **
000055 //   DISP=(OLD,DELETE)                                      **          **
000056 //SYSLMOD  DD  DSN=&&GOSET(YOURPGM),                        **   LINK   **
000057 //   DISP=(NEW,PASS),                                       **          **
000058 //   UNIT=VIO,
000059 //   SPACE=(CYL,(1,1,1))
000060 //SYSLIB   DD  DSN=SYS1.COB2LIB,DISP=SHR
000061 //SYSUT1   DD  UNIT=VIO,SPACE=(CYL,(1,1
000062 //SYSPRINT DD  SYSOUT=&PRINTAT
000063 //     ENDIF  ***********************
000064 //*
000065 //*  EXECUTE THE PROGRAM
000066 //*
000067 //     IF ( COB2.RC <= 4 AND LKED.RC <= 4 ) THEN  **********************
000068 //GO      EXEC  PGM=*.LKED.SYSLMOD,                         **          **
000069 //   REGION=2048K,                      ALLOW PGM 2 MB        **          **
000070 //   TIME=(,6)                          ALLOW PGM 6 SECONDS   **          **
000071 //STEPLIB  DD  DSN=SYS1.COB2LIB,     VS COBOL II ROUTINES     **          **
000072 //   DISP=SHR                                                **          **
000073 //SYSOUT   DD  SYSOUT=&PRINTAT      DISPLAY OUTPUT           **    GO    **
000074 //SYSABOUT DD  SYSOUT=&PRINTAT      ABEND INFO               **          **
000075 //SYSDBOUT DD  SYSOUT=&PRINTAT      FDUMP INFO               **          **
000076 //SORTWK01 DD  UNIT=VIO,SPACE=(TRK,5)                         **          **
000077 //SORTWK02 DD  UNIT=VIO,SPACE=(TRK,5)                         **          **
000078 //SORTWK03 DD  UNIT=VIO,SPACE=(TRK,5)                         **          **
000079 //     ENDIF  ***********************************************************
```

Link edit only if compile was successful
"Go" only if compile and link edit successful

Figure 2.9 Typical Use of Compound Relation Conditions in a Modern Compile/Link/Go Cataloged Procedure

2.13 IF/ELSE "Blanket" Coding Analogous to COND=(4,LT)

By common convention, a COND CODE of 0000 means successful program execution, and 0004 means acceptable execution with informational messages. COND CODE values higher than 0004 usually indicate a serious problem. Suppose you wanted to arrange your JCL to shut off the execution of subsequent steps as soon as any step issued a COND CODE greater than 4. With COND coding, you can omit a stepname and apply the COND test coded on a given EXEC to the COND CODE of all the prior steps. To use COND, you have to rephrase your requirement to say "if 4 is less than the COND CODE of any prior step, shut off this step." Job stream control like this is often necessary in production job streams when you have to plan recovery and restart actions for interrupted job streams, as I discuss in Chapter 7. But the reversal of your thought pattern needed to implement job stream control is confusing. Here is how the your EXEC statements might look with COND:

```
//STEP010    EXEC PGM=A111
   -
   -
//STEP020    EXEC PGM=B222,COND=(4,LT)
   -
   -
//STEP030    EXEC PGM=C333,COND=(4,LT)
   -
   -
//STEP040    EXEC PGM=D444,COND=(4,LT)
   -
   -
```

You can now code relational expressions with IF/ELSE to give the same "blanket" COND CODE testing effect, and the coding is again clearer than the analogous coding of the COND parameter. If you omit the stepname on a relational expression, the test is applied to the COND CODEs of all prior steps as shown in Figure 2.10. All prior COND CODEs must satisfy the relational condition in order for RC <= 4 to be true.

In Figure 2.10, two IDCAMS steps execute to set COND CODEs of 0008 and 0004, respectively. Both are retained by MVS. The relation condition before STEP030, at line 24, lacks reference to a specific stepname, so this test is applied to *all* prior COND CODEs.

Figure 2.11 shows you the MVS system output that results when I submit the JCL in Figure 2.10. Notice that the effect of the blanket IF RC <= 4 tests is an implied AND. Only one of the prior COND CODEs meets the condition of being equal to or less than 4 (the COND CODE of STEP020). STEP030, STEP040, and STEP050 do not execute because RC <= 4 says "if *all* of the COND CODEs of prior steps are <= 4, execute this step."

```
EDIT ---- CSCJGJ.ADV.CNTL(B4ANY) - 01.01 -------------------- COLUMNS 001 072
COMMAND ===>                                                  SCROLL ===> PAGE
****** ***************************** TOP OF DATA ******************************
000001 //CSCJGJA   JOB 1,                    ACCOUNTING INFORMATION
000002 //  'BIN 7--JANOSSY',                  PROGRAMMER NAME AND DELIVERY BIN
000003 //  CLASS=A,                           INPUT QUEUE CLASS
000004 //  MSGLEVEL=(1,1),                    HOW MUCH MVS SYSTEM PRINT DESIRED
000005 //  MSGCLASS=X,                        PRINT DESTINATION X A L N OR O
000006 //  TIME=(0,6),                        SAFETY LIMIT: RUN TIME UP TO 6 SECS
000007 //  REGION=2M,                         ALLOW UP TO 2 MEGS VIRTUAL MEMORY
000008 //* TYPRUN=SCAN,                       UNCOMMENT THIS LINE TO DO SCAN ONLY
000009 //  NOTIFY=CSCJGJ                      WHO TO TELL WHEN JOB IS DONE
000010 //*
000011 //* DEMONSTRATE IF/THEN IN MULTIPLE STEPS
000012 //* THIS JCL IS STORED AT CSCJGJ.ADV.CNTL(B4ANY)
000013 //*-----------------------------------------------------------------
000014 //STEP010  EXEC  PGM=IDCAMS
000015 //SYSPRINT   DD  SYSOUT=*
000016 //SYSIN      DD  *
000017      SET LASTCC = 8
000018 //*-----------------------------------------------------------------
000019 //STEP020  EXEC  PGM=IDCAMS
000020 //SYSPRINT   DD  SYSOUT=*
000021 //SYSIN      DD  *
000022      SET LASTCC = 4
000023 //*-----------------------------------
000024 //      IF ( RC <= 4 ) THEN         ** IF **
000025 //STEP030  EXEC  PGM=IDCAMS
000026 //SYSPRINT   DD  SYSOUT=*
000027 //SYSIN      DD  *
000028      SET LASTCC = 0
000029 //      ENDIF                       ** ENDIF **
000030 //*-----------------------------------
000031 //      IF ( RC <= 4 ) THEN         ** IF **
000032 //STEP040  EXEC  PGM=IDCAMS
000033 //SYSPRINT   DD  SYSOUT=*
000034 //SYSIN      DD  *
000035      SET LASTCC = 0
000036 //      ENDIF                       ** ENDIF **
000037 //*-----------------------------------
000038 //      IF ( RC <= 4 ) THEN         ** IF **
000039 //STEP050  EXEC  PGM=IDCAMS
000040 //SYSPRINT   DD  SYSOUT=*
000041 //SYSIN      DD  *
000042      SET LASTCC = 0
000043 //      ENDIF                       ** ENDIF **
000044 //
```

Sets COND CODE **0008**

Sets COND CODE **0004**

These three steps do not execute because the **RC < = 4** relational expressions are false. Without a stepname the expression is applied to *all* of the prior steps, implying AND compound tests.

Figure 2.10 IF/THEN/ELSE Coding Equivalent to Older COND=(4,LT) Coding (last three steps shut off if any COND CODE > 4)

2.14 Coding an IF/ELSE Against a Step in a Proc

You can code a relational expression that involves a COND CODE from a step within a proc that your job stream has executed. This coding becomes especially important with MVS/ESA Version 4, because, as I explain in Chapter 5, you can now nest procs (that is, you can now create procs that can themselves invoke other procs).

To code a relational expression against the COND CODE set by a prior step within a proc, code the RC part of the expression as stepname.procstepname.RC. "Stepname" is the stepname at which you have

```
 8 //      IF ( RC <= 4 ) THEN
 9 //STEP030  EXEC  PGM=IDCAMS
10 //SYSPRINT   DD  SYSOUT=*
11 //SYSIN      DD  *
12 //      ENDIF
   //*-----------------------------------
13 //      IF ( RC <= 4 ) THEN
14 //STEP040  EXEC  PGM=IDCAMS
15 //SYSPRINT   DD  SYSOUT=*
16 //SYSIN      DD  *
17 //      ENDIF
   //*-----------------------------------
18 //      IF ( RC <= 4 ) THEN
19 //STEP050  EXEC  PGM=IDCAMS
20 //SYSPRINT   DD  SYSOUT=*
21 //SYSIN      DD  *
22 //      ENDIF
```

```
  -
  -
  -
ICH70001I CSCJGJ   LAST ACCESS AT 14:44:11 ON SATURDAY, AUGUST 14, 1993

IEF236I ALLOC. FOR CSCJGJA STEP010
IEF237I JES2 ALLOCATED TO SYSPRINT
IEF237I JES2 ALLOCATED TO SYSIN
IEF142I CSCJGJA STEP010 - STEP WAS EXECUTED - COND CODE 0008
IEF285I   CSCJGJ.CSCJGJA.JOB00437.D0000106.?           SYSOUT
IEF285I   CSCJGJ.CSCJGJA.JOB00437.D0000101.?           SYSIN
IEF373I STEP /STEP010 / START 93226.1449
IEF374I STEP /STEP010 / STOP  93226.1449 CPU    0MIN 00.13SEC

IEF236I ALLOC. FOR CSCJGJA STEP020
IEF237I JES2 ALLOCATED TO SYSPRINT
IEF237I JES2 ALLOCATED TO SYSIN
IEF142I CSCJGJA STEP020 - STEP WAS EXECUTED - COND CODE 0004
IEF285I   CSCJGJ.CSCJGJA.JOB00437.D0000107.?           SYSOUT
IEF285I   CSCJGJ.CSCJGJA.JOB00437.D0000102.?           SYSIN
IEF373I STEP /STEP020 / START 93226.1449
IEF374I STEP /STEP020 / STOP  93226.1449 CPU    0MIN 00.13SEC

IEF206I CSCJGJA STEP030 - STEP WAS NOT RUN BECAUSE OF CONDITIONAL EXPRESSION ON STATEMENT 8
IEF272I CSCJGJA STEP030 - STEP WAS NOT EXECUTED.
IEF373I STEP /STEP030 / START 93226.1449
IEF374I STEP /STEP030 / STOP  93226.1449 CPU    0MIN 00.00SEC

IEF206I CSCJGJA STEP040 - STEP WAS NOT RUN BECAUSE OF CONDITIONAL EXPRESSION ON STATEMENT 13
IEF272I CSCJGJA STEP040 - STEP WAS NOT EXECUTED.
IEF373I STEP /STEP040 / START 93226.1449
IEF374I STEP /STEP040 / STOP  93226.1449 CPU    0MIN 00.00SEC

IEF206I CSCJGJA STEP050 - STEP WAS NOT RUN BECAUSE OF CONDITIONAL EXPRESSION ON STATEMENT 18
IEF272I CSCJGJA STEP050 - STEP WAS NOT EXECUTED.
IEF373I STEP /STEP050 / START 93226.1449
IEF374I STEP /STEP050 / STOP  93226.1449 CPU    0MIN 00.00SEC

IEF375I  JOB /CSCJGJA / START 93226.1449
IEF376I  JOB /CSCJGJA / STOP  93226.1449 CPU    0MIN 00.26SEC
```

Statement numbers are not line numbers; you can't relate this message to the JCL as it appears on a TSO screen!

Figure 2.11 MVS System Reporting Shows Assigned JCL Statement Numbers, Not Original TSO-Applied Line Numbers

invoked the proc in your job stream. Procstepname is the name of the step within the proc where the program being executed is invoked. For example, here is part of a proc named B4PROC:

```
//B4PROC     PROC
//PS010      EXEC PGM=BETA4
   -
   -
//PS020      EXEC PGM=GAMMA8
   -
   -
   -
   -
   -
```

PS020 is the procstepname, that is, the name of the step within the proc

Following are the EXEC statements of a job stream that will execute program ALPHA, then proc B4PROC, and then another program named DELTA. The normal sequence of program executions caused by this job stream will thus be:

```
//STEPA EXEC PGM=ALPHA
//STEPB EXEC B4PROC
//STEPC EXEC PGM=DELTA
```

executes — Program BETA4, Program GAMMA8

But I want to execute program DELTA only if program GAMMA within the proc sets a COND CODE less than or equal to 0004. I can code my JCL to execute the programs and the proc in this way:

```
//CSCJGJA  JOB . . .
//STEPA     EXEC   PGM=ALPHA
   -
   -
//STEPB     EXEC   B4PROC
   -
//      IF ( STEPB.PS020.RC <= 4 ) THEN
//STEPC     EXEC   PGM=DELTA
   -
   -
//      ENDIF
//
```

STEPB is the stepname

I have left many lines out of this initial illustration to better highlight that the relational expression following the IF never does mention the name of the proc itself. The JCL also does not mention the name of program GAMMA, which is executed within the proc at step PS020, and which is responsible for setting the COND CODE to be tested.

2.15 Trying Out IF/ELSE and RC Testing Against a Proc Step

Proc execution is very much the "on-the-job" type of JCL usage that this book is about. But fragmentary illustrations such as those preceding are typical of JCL manuals, and they don't really give you much of a concrete coding example. Sometimes you simply have to run an example for yourself before a JCL feature makes sense.

I actually coded a series of small "do nothing" VS COBOL II programs named ALPHA, BETA, GAMMA, and DELTA to be able to demonstrate how IF/ELSE is handled by MVS/ESA. Each program simply moves 0000 to RETURN-CODE to leave behind a COND CODE of 0000, as shown by the source code of program ALPHA in Figure 2.12. Companion programs named ALPHA4, BETA4, GAMMA4, and DELTA4 are similar but set COND CODE 0004, and programs named ALPHA8, BETA8, GAMMA8, and DELTA8 set COND CODE 0008. You might want to create, as I did, load modules for a series of programs such as this so that you can readily experiment with IF/ELSE coding in MVS/ESA Version 4 JCL. Figure 2.13 shows you my

```
EDIT ---- CSCJGJ.ADV.COBOL(ALPHA) - 01.01 -------------------- COLUMNS 007 078
COMMAND ===>                                                  SCROLL ===> PAGE
****** ****************************** TOP OF DATA ******************************
000100  ID DIVISION.
000200  PROGRAM-ID. ALPHA.
000300  PROCEDURE DIVISION.
000400       MOVE 0 TO RETURN-CODE.
000500       STOP RUN.
```

```
EDIT ---- CSCJGJ.ADV.COBOL(GAMMA8) - 01.01 ------------------- COLUMNS 007 078
COMMAND ===>                                                  SCROLL ===> PAGE
****** ****************************** TOP OF DATA ******************************
000100  ID DIVISION.
000200  PROGRAM-ID. GAMMA8.
000300  PROCEDURE DIVISION.
000400       MOVE 8 TO RETURN-CODE.
000500       STOP RUN.
```

These are tiny VS COBOL II programs that simply MOVE a value to **RETURN-CODE** to leave behind that value as the COND COND. *Any COBOL program can set its COND CODE in this way.* You don't need to code ENVIRONMENT DIVISION or DATA DIVISION in VS COBOL II if those divisions are empty.

Figure 2.12 Examples of VS COBOL II Programs That You Can Use to Experiment with MVS/ESA Version 4 IF/THEN/ELSE Coding

```
EDIT ---- CSCJGJ.ADV.CNTL(B4PROC) - 01.05 ------------------- COLUMNS 001 072
COMMAND ===>                                                  SCROLL ===> PAGE
****** ******************************* TOP OF DATA ******************************
000001 //**********************************************************************
000002 //*  C4PROC   DEMONSTRATION PROC FOR IF/ELSE CODING               -JGJ- *
000003 //*  COPYRIGHT 1993 JAMES JANOSSY  ALL RIGHTS RESERVED                  *
000004 //**********************************************************************
000005 //B4PROC    PROC
000006 //PS010     EXEC  PGM=BETA4
000007 //STEPLIB     DD  DSN=CSCJGJ.ADV.LOADLIB,DISP=SHR      PRIVATE LOAD LIB
000008 //            DD  DSN=SYS1.COB2LIB,DISP=SHR            COBOL II LOADLIB
000009 //*
000010 //PS020     EXEC  PGM=GAMMA8
000011 //STEPLIB     DD  DSN=CSCJGJ.ADV.LOADLIB,DISP=SHR      PRIVATE LOAD LIB
000012 //            DD  DSN=SYS1.COB2LIB,DISP=SHR            COBOL II LOADLIB
```

My //STEPLIB DD statements point MVS to the private load module library I have used to house the machine language for these programs. SYS1.COB2LIB is a load module library where various modules used by the VS COBOL II compiler are stored.

Figure 2.13 B4PROC, A Small Proc Invoked by B5JOB to Demonstrate IF/THEN/ELSE Testing Against a Procedure

actual JCL for B4PROC for the example discussed in the preceding section. Figure 2.14 shows you the JCL for the job stream, and Figure 2.15 illustrates the system output generated by MVS from a test run of it.

The type of MVS system reporting in Figure 2.15 is easiest to read if you establish and follow a different step naming convention for your execution JCL (the JCL with the JOB statement) and for the JCL within your procs. Using different naming conventions for procs and execution JCL helps you quickly distinguish between stepnames within procs (such as PS020 in B4PROC) and stepnames within execution JCL (such as STEP010 in my JCL named B5JOB in Figure 2.14). In Chapter 5, I'll point out how such naming conventions become especially important if you use nested procs.

```
EDIT ---- CSCJGJ.ADV.CNTL(B5JOB) - 01.04 -------------------- COLUMNS 001 072
COMMAND ===>                                                  SCROLL ===> PAGE
****** ***************************** TOP OF DATA ******************************
000001 //CSCJGJA   JOB 1,                        ACCOUNTING INFORMATION
000002 //   'BIN 7--JANOSSY',                    PROGRAMMER NAME AND DELIVERY BIN
000003 //   CLASS=A,                             INPUT QUEUE CLASS
000004 //   MSGLEVEL=(1,1),                      HOW MUCH MVS SYSTEM PRINT DESIRED
000005 //   MSGCLASS=X,                          PRINT DESTINATION X A L N OR O
000006 //   TIME=(0,6),                          SAFETY LIMIT: RUN TIME UP TO 6 SECS
000007 //   REGION=2M,                           ALLOW UP TO 2 MEGS VIRTUAL MEMORY
000008 //*  TYPRUN=SCAN,                         UNCOMMENT THIS LINE TO DO SCAN ONLY
000009 //   NOTIFY=CSCJGJ                        WHO TO TELL WHEN JOB IS DONE
000010 //*
000011 //        JCLLIB  ORDER=(CSCJGJ.ADV.CNTL)          PRIVATE PROC LIB
000012 //*
000013 //* DEMONSTRATE IF/ELSE WITH PROC INVOCATION
000014 //* THIS JCL IS STORED AT CSCJGJ.ADV.CNTL(B5JOB)
000015 //*-----------------------------------------------------------------
000016 //STEP010  EXEC  PGM=ALPHA
000017 //STEPLIB    DD  DSN=CSCJGJ.ADV.LOADLIB,DISP=SHR      PRIVATE LOAD LIB
000018 //           DD  DSN=SYS1.COB2LIB,DISP=SHR            COBOL II LOADLIB
000019 //*-----------------------------------------------------------------
000020 //STEP020  EXEC  B4PROC
000021 //*-----------------------------------------------------------------
000022 //     IF ( STEP020.PS020.RC <= 4 ) THEN
000023 //STEP030  EXEC  PGM=DELTA
000024 //STEPLIB    DD  DSN=CSCJGJ.ADV.LOADLIB,DISP=SHR
000025 //           DD  DSN=SYS1.COB2LIB,DISP=SHR
000026 //     ENDIF
000027 //
```

This is how to code a test on the COND CODE set by a step within a proc

Figure 2.14 B5JOB, JCL That Shows You How to Code Stepname.Procstepname in an IF/THEN/ELSE Test

```
                 J E S 2  J O B  L O G  --  S Y S T E M  I B M 1  --  N O D E  N 1
11.56.31 JOB03924  IRR010I  USERID CSCJGJ   IS ASSIGNED TO THIS JOB.
11.56.32 JOB03924  ICH70001I CSCJGJ   LAST ACCESS AT 11:55:10 ON SUNDAY, JUNE 27, 1993
11.56.32 JOB03924  $HASP373 CSCJGJA  STARTED - INIT  1 - CLASS A - SYS IBM1
11.56.35 JOB03924  $HASP395 CSCJGJA  ENDED

------ JES2 JOB STATISTICS ------
  27 JUN 93 JOB EXECUTION DATE
         26 CARDS READ
         90 SYSOUT PRINT RECORDS
          0 SYSOUT PUNCH RECORDS
          5 SYSOUT SPOOL KBYTES
       0.05 MINUTES EXECUTION TIME

        1 //CSCJGJA   JOB 1,                 ACCOUNTING INFORMATION             JOB03924
          //  'BIN 7--JANOSSY',              PROGRAMMER NAME AND DELIVERY BIN
          //  CLASS=A,                       INPUT QUEUE CLASS
          //  MSGLEVEL=(1,1),                HOW MUCH MVS SYSTEM PRINT DESIRED
          //  MSGCLASS=X,                    PRINT DESTINATION X A L N OR O
          //  TIME=(0,6),                    SAFETY LIMIT: RUN TIME UP TO 6 SECS
          //  REGION=2M,                     ALLOW UP TO 2 MEGS VIRTUAL MEMORY
          //* TYPRUN=SCAN,                   UNCOMMENT THIS LINE TO DO SCAN ONLY
          //  NOTIFY=CSCJGJ                  WHO TO TELL WHEN JOB IS DONE
          //*
        2 //       JCLLIB  ORDER=(CSCJGJ.ADV.CNTL)          PRIVATE PROC LIB
          //*
          //* DEMONSTRATE IF/ELSE WITH PROC INVOCATION
          //* THIS JCL IS STORED AT CSCJGJ.ADV.CNTL(B5JOB)
          //*-----------------------------------------------------------------
        3 //STEP010  EXEC  PGM=ALPHA
        4 //STEPLIB    DD  DSN=CSCJGJ.ADV.LOADLIB,DISP=SHR     PRIVATE LOAD LIB
        5 //           DD  DSN=SYS1.COB2LIB,DISP=SHR           COBOL II LOADLIB
          //*-----------------------------------------------------------------
        6 //STEP020  EXEC  B4PROC
          XX*****************************************************************
          XX*  B4PROC   DEMONSTRATION PROC FOR IF/ELSE CODING          -JGJ- *
          XX*  COPYRIGHT 1993 JAMES JANOSSY  ALL RIGHTS RESERVED             *
          XX*****************************************************************
        7 XXB4PROC    PROC
        8 XXPS010     EXEC  PGM=BETA4
        9 XXSTEPLIB    DD  DSN=CSCJGJ.ADV.LOADLIB,DISP=SHR    PRIVATE LOAD LIB
       10 XX           DD  DSN=SYS1.COB2LIB,DISP=SHR          COBOL II LOADLIB
```

MVS/ESA Version 4 now makes it easy to create your own proc library. I show you how to use the new JCLLIB statement in Chapter 4!

Figure 2.15 MVS System Reporting Indicates a Procstepname.Stepname, the Reverse of How You Code Your JCL!

```
        XX*
     11 XXPS020     EXEC  PGM=GAMMA8
     12 XXSTEPLIB     DD  DSN=CSCJGJ.ADV.LOADLIB,DISP=SHR     PRIVATE LOAD LIB
     13 XX            DD  DSN=SYS1.COB2LIB,DISP=SHR           COBOL II LOADLIB
        //*-----------------------------------------
     14 //     IF ( STEP020.PS020.RC <= 4 ) THEN
     15 //STEP030   EXEC  PGM=DELTA
     16 //STEPLIB     DD  DSN=CSCJGJ.ADV.LOADLIB,DISP=SHR       PRIVATE LOAD LIB
     17 //            DD  DSN=SYS1.COB2LIB,DISP=SHR             COBOL II LOADLIB
     18 //       ENDIF

 STMT NO. MESSAGE
      6 IEFC001I PROCEDURE C4PROC WAS EXPANDED USING PRIVATE LIBRARY CSCJGJ.ADV.CNTL

ICH70001I CSCJGJ   LAST ACCESS AT 11:55:10 ON SUNDAY, JUNE 27, 1993

IEF236I ALLOC. FOR CSCJGJA STEP010
IEF237I 117  ALLOCATED TO STEPLIB
IEF237I 110  ALLOCATED TO
IEF142I CSCJGJA STEP010 - STEP WAS EXECUTED - COND CODE 0000
IEF285I   CSCJGJ.ADV.LOADLIB                          KEPT
IEF285I   VOL SER NOS= USER03.
IEF285I   SYS1.COB2LIB                                KEPT
IEF285I   VOL SER NOS= ACSRES.
IEF373I STEP /STEP010 / START 93178.1156
IEF374I STEP /STEP010 / STOP  93178.1156 CPU    0MIN 00.09SEC

IEF236I ALLOC. FOR CSCJGJA PS010 STEP020
IEF237I 117  ALLOCATED TO STEPLIB
IEF237I 110  ALLOCATED TO
IEF142I CSCJGJA PS010 STEP020 - STEP WAS EXECUTED - COND CODE 0004
IEF285I   CSCJGJ.ADV.LOADLIB                          KEPT
IEF285I   VOL SER NOS= USER03.
IEF285I   SYS1.COB2LIB                                KEPT
IEF285I   VOL SER NOS= ACSRES.
IEF373I STEP /PS010    / START      .1156
IEF374I STEP /PS010    / STOP       .1156 CPU    0MIN 00.08SEC SRB

IEF236I ALLOC. FOR CSCJGJA PS020 STEP020
IEF237I 117  ALLOCATED TO STEPLIB
IEF237I 110  ALLOCATED TO
IEF142I CSCJGJA PS020 STEP020 - STEP WAS EXECUTED - COND CODE 0008
IEF285I   CSCJGJ.ADV.LOADLIB                          KEPT
```

You code ***stepname.procstepname*** in your JCL to base a relational test on the COND CODE set by a step within a proc. You code the step name at which the proc is invoked (stepname) and the name of the step within the proc (procstepname).

MVS/ESA reports program execution status by ***job name, procstepname,*** and ***stepname,*** which is the reverse of how you code stepname and procstepname. It's important to use a different naming convention for steps within procs than for job stream execution JCL so that you can more readily understand MVS/ESA system output.

Figure 2.15 (continued)

```
IEF285I   VOL SER NOS= USER03.
IEF285I   SYS1.COB2LIB                                     KEPT
IEF285I   VOL SER NOS= ACSRES.
IEF373I STEP /PS020   / START 93178.1156
IEF374I STEP /PS020   / STOP  93178.1156 CPU    0MIN 00.08SEC SRB    0MIN 00.02SEC VIRT   268K SYS   192K EXT       4K SYS    9032K

IEF206I CSCJGJA STEP030 - STEP WAS NOT RUN BECAUSE OF CONDITIONAL EXPRESSION ON STATEMENT 14
IEF272I CSCJGJA STEP030 - STEP WAS NOT EXECUTED.
IEF373I STEP /STEP030 / START 93178.1156
IEF374I STEP /STEP030 / STOP  93178.1156 CPU    0MIN 00.00SEC SRB    0MIN 00.00SEC VIRT     0K SYS     0K EXT       0K SYS       0K

IEF375I  JOB /CSCJGJA / START 93178.1156
IEF376I  JOB /CSCJGJA / STOP  93178.1156 CPU    0MIN 00.25SEC SRB    0MIN 00.05SEC
```

The relational expression at statement 14 is:

IF (STEP020.PS020.RC < = 4)

In my naming convention, STEP020 is a name in the execution JCL for the job stream, while PS020 means "procstep" 020, a step coded *within* the proc. If you follow a naming convention like this, MVS system output is easier to read. This becomes especially important if you use MVS/ESA Version 4 capabilities to nest procs, as I show you in Chapter 5!

Figure 2.15 (continued)

3

IF/THEN/ELSE Tests for System and User Abends

3.1 Production Job Streams and Abends

3.2 MVS/ESA Program Loading and Execution

3.3 Normal Step Execution and MVS/ESA Reporting

3.4 System Abends and User Abends

3.5 System Abend: System Completion Code

3.6 User Abend: User Completion Code

3.7 Consequences of Step Execution on Subsequent Steps

3.8 Effects of a System Abend

3.9 Effects of a User Abend

3.10 A New Feature? "Unintentional" User Abends

3.11 Recognizing Unintentional User Abends

3.12 Making Steps Execute After an Abend with COND=EVEN

3.13 Making Steps Execute After an Abend with COND=ONLY

3.14 Making a Step Execute After an Abend with IF ABEND

3.15 Using IF ABEND in Production Job Streams

3.16 Testing a Prior Step to See If It Executed (IF RUN)

3.17 Nonnested ABEND Coding Variations

3.18 Nested IF/THEN/ELSE Coding

3.1 Production Job Streams and Abends

Job control language was designed to orchestrate the execution of programs in a business data processing "production" environment. In production environments, successful and effective information processing is critical to the organization's business. Hundreds or thousands of production batch jobs, originally designed and coded by programmers, are submitted each day by personnel other than programmers. These jobs must execute without attention or intervention. Production job streams must operate as intended, or clearly inform personnel when a problem has been encountered: The failure of any job step has to be automatically detected, recognized, and reported.

In this chapter, I describe how MVS/ESA supports the recognition of job step abends (abnormal endings). I'll also show you how to initiate a user abend generating a user completion code, and why you will find it especially useful to know about user abends if you use VS COBOL II or COBOL/370. Finally, I'll demonstrate how to override the inclination of MVS/ESA to stop executing steps following an abended step, and how you can code an IF/THEN/ELSE test to determine if a step has successfully run (executed).

The examples you see in this chapter illustrate JCL building blocks. I put these building blocks to further use in the examples of recoverable job streams in Chapter 7. I arranged this chapter in what strikes me as the most commonsense way. After the background you need to understand in order to put MVS/ESA Version 4 enhancements into perspective, I demonstrate convenient abend testing syntax first and show you how to use it to meet production job stream requirements. I reserved for the last part of the chapter the less useful and more redundant alternative syntax elements and coding.

3.2 MVS/ESA Program Loading and Execution

A program executable by MVS/ESA is actually machine language stored in a partitioned data set as a member. As I describe in Chapter 16 of my introductory book on MVS/ESA, *Practical MVS JCL Examples* (John Wiley & Sons, Inc., 1993), such a member is called a *load module* and the partitioned data set a *load module library*. You code the load module member name (the program name) in the EXEC statement that invokes the program. MVS/ESA assumes an installation default as the name of the partitioned data set housing the program (member), such as SYS1.LINKLIB, unless you code JOBLIB or STEPLIB to indicate a specific "private" program:

```
//CSCJGJA   JOB ...
//JOBLIB      DD DSN=CSCJGJ.CSC.LOADLIB,DISP=SHR
//STEP010  EXEC PGM=ABCD1234
    -
    -
```

or

```
//CSCJGJA   JOB ...
//STEP010  EXEC PGM=ABCD1234
//STEPLIB     DD DSN=CSCJGJ.CSC.LOADLIB,DISP=SHR
    -
    -
```

To execute a program, MVS/ESA finds the program load module, examines it to learn its execution memory and data set requirements, allocates the amount of computer memory the program requires to be housed for execution, and copies the load module to that memory. After data set allocation activities, MVS/ESA gives control of the computer's central processing unit (CPU) to the program by putting the address of the load module's first instruction into the CPU.

Several points of vulnerability exist in the process of loading a program to memory, executing it, and cleaning up after it. A step can either process successfully, or end in one or another form of failure. MVS/ESA defines two categories of step failure: system abend (abnormal ending) or user abend. For this reason there are three potential outcomes for the execution of any job stream step, and a unique form of system reporting for each, as shown in this chart:

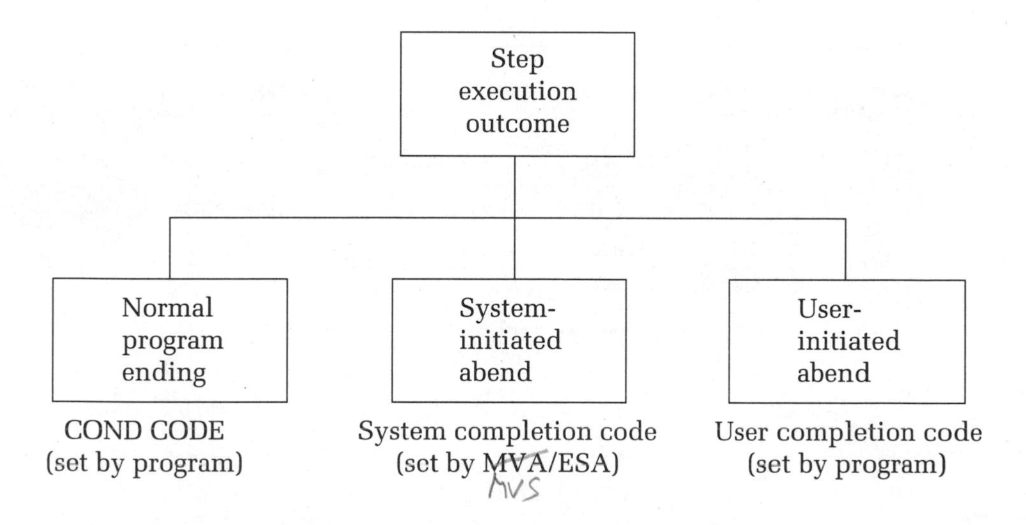

I have listed an example of the MVS/ESA system reporting for each of these three possible program outcomes in Figure 3.1. I'll explain each of the three possible step outcomes in detail because you need to know about them to build robust job streams.

3.3 Normal Step Execution and MVS/ESA Reporting

Any program executed under MVS/ESA—that is, any step of a job stream—has the potential to end execution normally by gracefully returning control to the operating system. The completion of a program that ended normally is reported by MVS/ESA with a COND CODE message line as shown at the top of Figure 3.1.

A program can use the COND CODE to provide a numeric indication of the "condition" of its operation. A nonzero COND CODE has a meaning specific to the program, and you have to examine the program's documentation or the program itself to know what a given COND CODE value means. IBM's own utility programs consistently use a value of 0000 to indicate entirely successful operation, 0004 to indicate that minor errors were encountered, and 0008 and higher to indicate other types of more serious errors.

```
SDSF OUTPUT DISPLAY CSCJGJA  JOB07991  DSID    4 LINE 1       COLUMNS 02- 81
COMMAND INPUT ===>                                            SCROLL ===> PAGE

IEF236I ALLOC. FOR CSCJGJA STEP010
IEF237I JES2 ALLOCATED TO SYSPRINT
IEF237I JES2 ALLOCATED TO SYSIN
IEF142I CSCJGJA STEP010 - STEP WAS EXECUTED - COND CODE 0004
IEF285I   CSCJGJ.CSCJGJA.JOB07991.D0000102.?
IEF285I   CSCJGJ.CSCJGJA.JOB07991.D0000101.?
IEF373I STEP /STEP010 / START 93211.1514
IEF374I STEP /STEP010 / STOP  93211.1514 CPU    0MIN 00.13SEC
        -
        -
```

Allocation — *Execution* — *Deallocation*

COND CODE: normal program ending, ***program*** sets it

```
SDSF OUTPUT DISPLAY CSCJGJA  JOB07996  DSID    4 LINE 28      COLUMNS 02- 81
COMMAND INPUT ===>                                            SCROLL ===> PAGE

IEF236I ALLOC. FOR CSCJGJA STEP010
IEF237I 111  ALLOCATED TO STEPLIB
IEF237I 110  ALLOCATED TO
IEF472I CSCJGJA STEP010 - COMPLETION CODE - SYSTEM=0C7 USER=0000
IEF285I   CSCJGJ.CSC.LOADLIB
IEF285I   VOL SER NOS= USER00.
IEF285I   SYS1.COB2LIB
IEF285I   VOL SER NOS= ACSRES.
IEF373I STEP /STEP010 / START 93244.1141
IEF374I STEP /STEP010 / STOP  93244.1141 CPU    0MIN 00.17SEC
        -
        -
```

Allocation — ***Abend*** — *Deallocation*

System completion code: program abends, ***MVS*** sets it

```
SDSF OUTPUT DISPLAY CSCJGJA  JOB07998  DSID    4 LINE 32      COLUMNS 02- 81
COMMAND INPUT ===>                                            SCROLL ===> PAGE

IEF236I ALLOC. FOR CSCJGJA STEP010
IEF237I 111  ALLOCATED TO STEPLIB
IEF237I 110  ALLOCATED TO
IEF472I CSCJGJA STEP010 - COMPLETION CODE - SYSTEM=000 USER=3401
IEF285I   CSCJGJ.CSC.LOADLIB
IEF285I   VOL SER NOS= USER00.
IEF285I   SYS1.COB2LIB
IEF285I   VOL SER NOS= ACSRES.
IEF373I STEP /STEP010 / START 93244.1141
IEF374I STEP /STEP010 / STOP  93244.1141 CPU    0MIN 00.17SEC
        -
        -
```

Allocation — ***Abend*** — *Deallocation*

User completion code: program abends, ***program*** sets it

Figure 3.1 Program and MVS/ESA Communication from a Job Step

IBM provides separate documentation for each of its own utility programs, such as DFSORT (the sort utility), and IDCAMS (which supports Virtual Storage Access Method). For your convenience, I have listed and described most of the IBM utility programs and each of the COND CODEs (return codes) generated by them in Appendix D of this book and in an appendix of the same name in my introductory book, *Practical MVS JCL Examples* (John Wiley & Sons, Inc., 1993).

In Chapter 2, I showed you how to test the COND CODE of a prior step with coding such as STEP020.RC <= 4 or RC <= 4. If you focus on the "RC" in that MVS/ESA Version 4 coding (which stands for "return code"), you may detect that COND CODE is very much of a misnomer in MVS/ESA reporting and labeling. COND CODE should actually be called RETURN CODE, a coded value "returned" by a program after its normal completion of execution. If COND CODE were actually labeled RETURN CODE, MVS/ESA reporting and your use of MVS/ESA relational test coding in the form IF STEP020.RC <= 4 would make more sense.

3.4 System Abends and User Abends

Two types of step abends are recognized and processed by MVS/ESA: system abends and user abends. The MVS/ESA system reporting associated with abends is shown in the middle and bottom parts of Figure 3.1.

System abends are abends that are initiated by MVS/ESA itself. These are not caused intentionally by a program, but occur due to program logic errors or device failures. System abends are reported by MVS/ESA using *system completion codes.*

User abends are intentionally triggered by a program itself, in a special way that communicates to MVS/ESA that an abend condition is desired. User abends are associated with a *user completion code* set by the program and are one way of reporting exceptional conditions detected by a program.

Although system and user abends are triggered by different factors, both are recognized by MVS/ESA as signifying an unusual, abnormal status for a job stream. MVS/ESA gives you a way to test, at the second and subsequent steps of a job stream, for system or user abend conditions in a prior step.

3.5 System Abend: System Completion Code

Most programs have the potential to "offend" MVS/ESA in some way, ending execution ungracefully by abending or "blowing up." When a step unintentionally abends, the cause can also be a failure external to a program, recognized by MVS/ESA during its program loading, during data set allocation actions, during program execution, or during deallocation activities. Unintentional abends are reported by MVS/ESA using a completion code message line as shown in the middle of Figure 3.1, and a system completion code prefaced by SYSTEM=. When a system completion code is issued, the USER=0000 that follows it is simply default printing and does not report that the program set a return code (COND CODE) of zero.

Allocation errors that can cause a step to abend include being unable to find the program named on the EXEC, lacking sufficient memory to load it for execution, inability to find data sets that the program attempts to open, or an equipment failure in input/output processing. For example, not being able to find the program load module named on the EXEC causes a system completion code of 806. IBM's message code manuals list each system completion code and discuss potential causes for their issuance. For your convenience, I have listed all the common system completion codes you may encounter in Appendix E in this book and in an appendix of the same name in my introductory book, *Practical MVS JCL Examples.*

Errors in program execution include logic errors that lead to an attempt to access a location in memory that the program is not authorized to use (0C4), arithmetic operations on nonnumeric data (0C7), the computation of values too large or too small to be represented, such as result from a divide by zero (0CB), running out of disk space (B37, D37, or E37), writing too many lines of print (722), or other similar problems. You can recognize the system completion code shown in the middle of Figure 3.1 as one of the most common of these.

Equipment, tape, or disk failures are often the cause of errors detected in end-of-program or deallocation actions. Data set labeling errors detected by a disk or tape drive, a dirty, damaged, or magnetically corrupted tape, a corrupted VSAM data set, and similar failures can lead to to a step abend during deallocation. As Appendix E shows you, system completion codes of 614, 714, 717, and 737 are among those associated with end-of-program or deallocation errors.

3.6 User Abend: User Completion Code

The third category of program execution outcome—user initiated abends—has its own form of MVS/ESA system reporting. This category of abend is called a "user abend" in IBM literature and is associated with a *user completion code.* The bottom part of Figure 3.1 illustrates the form of the completion code message line generated by MVS/ESA when you force a user abend.

A user abend is intentionally triggered by a program itself, using a technique that tells MVS/ESA to terminate program execution. To cause a user abend, an assembler program passes control to an operating system supervisory call (SVC) known as SVC 13. Higher-level language programs can issue a CALL to a module named ILBOABN0 to invoke SVC 13, as I illustrate later in this chapter, or can pass control to another program of local origin that invokes SVC 13.

A user abend is processed by MVS/ESA similarly to a system abend, in that no COND CODE message line is printed in MVS/ESA system reporting. But as you can see from the bottom part of Figure 3.1, a user abend does not cause a system completion code to print in the completion code message line; "SYSTEM=000" is default printing. Instead, a "user completion code" is printed after USER=, as a four-digit decimal number easily confused with a COND CODE. The user completion code is not a COND CODE, and you can't test it as such. But, just as with a COND CODE, you can make it any value from 0000 through 4095, to serve as communication from the program initiating the abend to the person reading the MVS/ESA system reporting.

3.7 Consequences of Step Execution on Subsequent Steps

A step that terminated either normally or with an abend has consequences for the way MVS/ESA treats the steps that follow. Figure 3.2 summarizes MVS/ESA treatment for these subsequent steps using two columns. The first column shows subsequent step treatment if no step has abended, whereas the second column shows you how MVS/ESA acts once a step has abended with either a system or user abend. I have labeled each of the six boxes in Figure 3.2 with a number from 1 to 6 to make it easier to refer to it as we consider it here.

A job stream always begins processing in a status known as normal processing mode. In *normal processing mode,* MVS/ESA is prepared to perform program loading, data set allocation, program execution, and data set deallocation activities for each step. As long as no step incurs either a system or user abend, the job stream remains in normal processing mode. In

	If the job is now in normal processing mode:	If the job is now in abnormal termination mode:
No COND test, COND test for condition code only, or an IF test based on condition code only (except IF ABEND)	1 Step is processed, COND tests based on condition code can shut off the EXEC; IF tests are made and take effect.	4 Step is acknowledged by MVS/ESA but EXEC is not processed.
COND=EVEN is coded on the EXEC or IF (ABEND OR NOT ABEND) THEN is coded before the EXEC	2 Step is processed, COND tests based on condition code can shut off the EXEC; IF tests are compounded with ABEND are made.	5 Step is processed, COND tests based on condition code can shut off the EXEC; IF tests are compounded with ABEND are made.
COND=ONLY is coded on the EXEC or IF ABEND THEN is coded before the EXEC	3 Step is acknowledged by MVS/ESA but EXEC is not processed.	6 Step is processed, COND tests based on condition code can shut off the EXEC; IF tests compounded with ABEND are made.

Figure 3.2 Consequences of Step Execution on Subsequent Steps

this mode, boxes 1, 2, and 3 in Figure 3.2 apply. If a step abends, however, issuing either a system completion code or a user completion code, MVS/ESA switches the processing mode of the remaining steps of the job stream to *abnormal termination mode,* represented by the second column of Figure 3.2. In this processing mode, boxes 4, 5, and 6 of Figure 3.2 depict the treatment MVS/ESA will give to remaining steps.

It's vital for you to understand MVS/ESA normal processing mode and abnormal termination mode, because you can't design and build robust job streams without this knowledge. Many MVS/ESA Version 4 enhancements are aimed at giving you greater capability to recognize what processing mode a job stream is in at any point, so that you can deal with most types of job step failure. To best explain how these MVS/ESA Version 4 features operate, I've created several programs and job streams that demonstrate them.

3.8 Effects of a System Abend

One reason a step can abend is illustrated by the small program in Figure 3.3. My program named EXPLODE attempts to add to an uninitialized counter field. Since the uninitialized counter field (WS-COUNT) contains nonnumeric data in the form of LOW-VALUES (hexadecimal X'00'), the program will fail. Its failure will be detected by MVS/ESA, and a system-initiated abend will be generated. As you can see in Appendix E, MVS/ESA will issue a system completion code of 0C7 for this type of failure. I compiled and link edited the EXPLODE program, and put its machine language into a load module library named CSCJGJ.ADV.LOADLIB, as described in Chapter 16 of my introductory book on MVS/ESA, *Practical MVS JCL Examples.*

```
EDIT ---- CSCJGJ.ADV.COBOL(EXPLODE) - 01.01 ----------------- COLUMNS 007 078
COMMAND ===>                                                  SCROLL ===> PAGE
****** ****************************** TOP OF DATA ******************************
000100  ID DIVISION.
000200  PROGRAM-ID. EXPLODE.
000300 *
000400  DATA DIVISION.
000500  WORKING-STORAGE SECTION.
000600  01  WS-COUNT            PIC 9(5).
000700 *
000800  PROCEDURE DIVISION.
000900  0000-MAINLINE.
001000      MOVE 1234 TO RETURN CODE.
001100      ADD 1 TO WS-COUNT.
001200      STOP RUN.
```

This VS COBOL II program adds to an uninitialized counter field and blows up with an 0C7 **system completion code.** Is the 1234 reported as a COND CODE?

Figure 3.3 A Program That Causes an Abend (abnormal ending)

The job stream stored at C1ABEND and shown in Figure 3.4 executes several programs discussed in Chapter 2, named ALPHA, BETA8, GAMMA, BETA4, and DELTA (you can see representative source codes for these small programs in Figure 2.12). Each of these programs leaves behind a COND CODE (return code) of 0000, 0004, or 0008; you can tell from the program name the COND CODE it leaves behind. The machine language (load modules) for these programs are also in my load module library.

As you can see in Figure 3.4, job stream C1ABEND executes the EXPLODE program, at STEP040. Prior to this step, the job stream will be in normal processing mode, and box 1 of Figure 3.2 applies. You can see from the message at the bottom of the TSO/ISPF screen in Figure 3.4 that the job quickly abended after submission. After the abending step, MVS/ESA put the job stream into abnormal termination mode. This switched the job stream to the second column of Figure 3.2, and box 4 of the chart in Figure 3.2 applies to the treatment of subsequent steps.

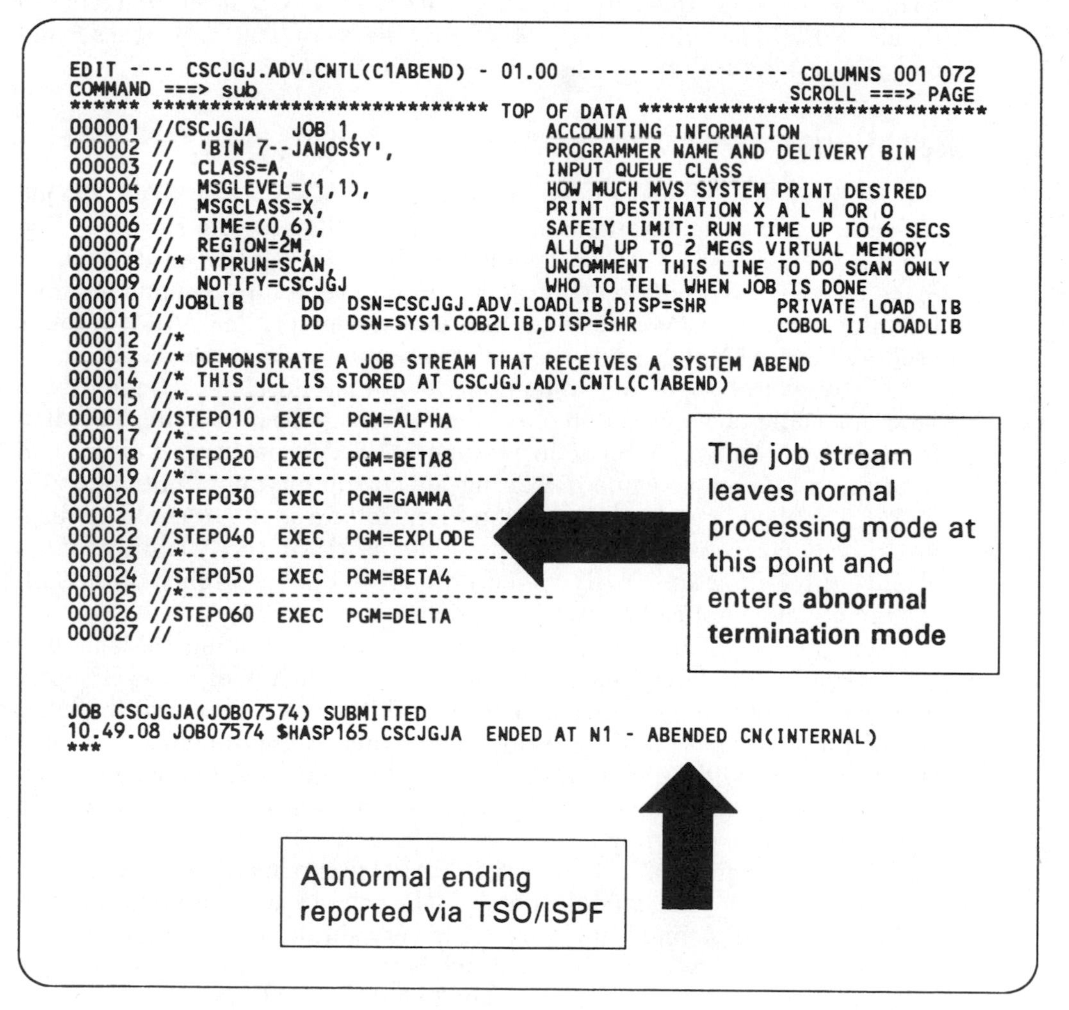

```
EDIT ---- CSCJGJ.ADV.CNTL(C1ABEND) - 01.00 ------------------- COLUMNS 001 072
COMMAND ===> sub                                               SCROLL ===> PAGE
****** ***************************** TOP OF DATA ******************************
000001 //CSCJGJA   JOB 1,                   ACCOUNTING INFORMATION
000002 //   'BIN 7--JANOSSY',               PROGRAMMER NAME AND DELIVERY BIN
000003 //   CLASS=A,                        INPUT QUEUE CLASS
000004 //   MSGLEVEL=(1,1),                 HOW MUCH MVS SYSTEM PRINT DESIRED
000005 //   MSGCLASS=X,                     PRINT DESTINATION X A L N OR O
000006 //   TIME=(0,6),                     SAFETY LIMIT: RUN TIME UP TO 6 SECS
000007 //   REGION=2M,                      ALLOW UP TO 2 MEGS VIRTUAL MEMORY
000008 //*  TYPRUN=SCAN,                    UNCOMMENT THIS LINE TO DO SCAN ONLY
000009 //   NOTIFY=CSCJGJ                   WHO TO TELL WHEN JOB IS DONE
000010 //JOBLIB      DD  DSN=CSCJGJ.ADV.LOADLIB,DISP=SHR       PRIVATE LOAD LIB
000011 //            DD  DSN=SYS1.COB2LIB,DISP=SHR             COBOL II LOADLIB
000012 //*
000013 //* DEMONSTRATE A JOB STREAM THAT RECEIVES A SYSTEM ABEND
000014 //* THIS JCL IS STORED AT CSCJGJ.ADV.CNTL(C1ABEND)
000015 //*-------------------------------
000016 //STEP010  EXEC  PGM=ALPHA
000017 //*-------------------------------
000018 //STEP020  EXEC  PGM=BETA8
000019 //*-------------------------------
000020 //STEP030  EXEC  PGM=GAMMA
000021 //*-------------------------------
000022 //STEP040  EXEC  PGM=EXPLODE
000023 //*-------------------------------
000024 //STEP050  EXEC  PGM=BETA4
000025 //*-------------------------------
000026 //STEP060  EXEC  PGM=DELTA
000027 //

JOB CSCJGJA(JOB07574) SUBMITTED
10.49.08 JOB07574 $HASP165 CSCJGJA  ENDED AT N1 - ABENDED CN(INTERNAL)
***
```

The job stream leaves normal processing mode at this point and enters abnormal termination mode
Abnormal ending reported via TSO/ISPF

Figure 3.4 Job Stream C1ABEND, Demonstrating MVS/ESA Systems Reporting for a System Abend

Figure 3.5 shows you the MVS/ESA system reporting generated by the C1ABEND job stream. I have annotated this output to highlight the fact that the first three steps have run and caused COND CODEs to be listed. Since the first three steps (programs ALPHA, BETA8, and GAMMA) all ended normally, the job stream remained in normal processing mode. The COND CODE 0008 of program BETA8 is just communication from the program to the outside world. It does not trigger any system abend by MVS/ESA.

STEP040 in job stream C1ABEND "blows up" as predicted. You see the 0C7 system completion code assigned by MVS/ESA to this at the top of the MVS/ESA system reporting, and in the main body of step reporting. Notice the messages for STEP050 and STEP060 on the last page of the system reporting. These steps were not executed because the job stream was in abnormal termination mode after the abend in STEP040, as indicated in box 4 of Figure 3.2.

You can force MVS/ESA to consider steps such as STEP050 and STEP060 for execution by coding COND=EVEN, COND=ONLY, or an IF/THEN/ELSE test involving the word ABEND, as indicated by boxes 5 and 6 in Figure 3.2. I'll show you how to do that in section 3.14.

3.9 Effects of a User Abend

A user abend arises when a program explicitly tells MVS/ESA to put the job stream into abnormal termination mode. I wrote the program shown in Figure 3.6, named USERABN, to demonstrate how a program can do this. To make USERABN more interesting and useful, I coded it to accept a parameter value via the PARM feature of the EXEC statement. The PARM value is used by USERABN to become the user completion code of the abend.

Why would a program intentionally initiate an abend? Generally, a program would take this action only when it detected a processing error that it could not resolve. A program reading a VSAM file, for example, and receiving a File Status value indicating file corruption might initiate a user abend. The abend would call attention to the failure so that it could be diagnosed and corrected as soon as possible. Without the visibility of an abend—if the program simply ended normally—the occurrence of the failure might not be noticed for too long a time.

Program USERABN triggers a user abend by CALLing IBM module ILBOABN0. I think this name is troublesome because it does not spell a pronounceable word, and it's usually hard to tell if the name contains the letter "o" or the number zero. I put a note about this in Figure 3.6 to help you avoid problems with it. By CALLing ILBOABN0 and passing it a value, you can have it put the value into the completion code field that appears in MVS/ESA system reporting.

I compiled and link edited my USERABN program and put its machine language into my load module library. The job stream stored as member C2ABEND and illustrated in Figure 3.7 is very similar to the C1ABEND job stream in Figure 3.4. The only difference is that at STEP040, I now execute program USERABN, instead of program EXPLODE, and I use PARM to pass it the value 3401 to set as a user completion code. The value 3401 means nothing in particular. I could just as well have used 2392, 3005, or another

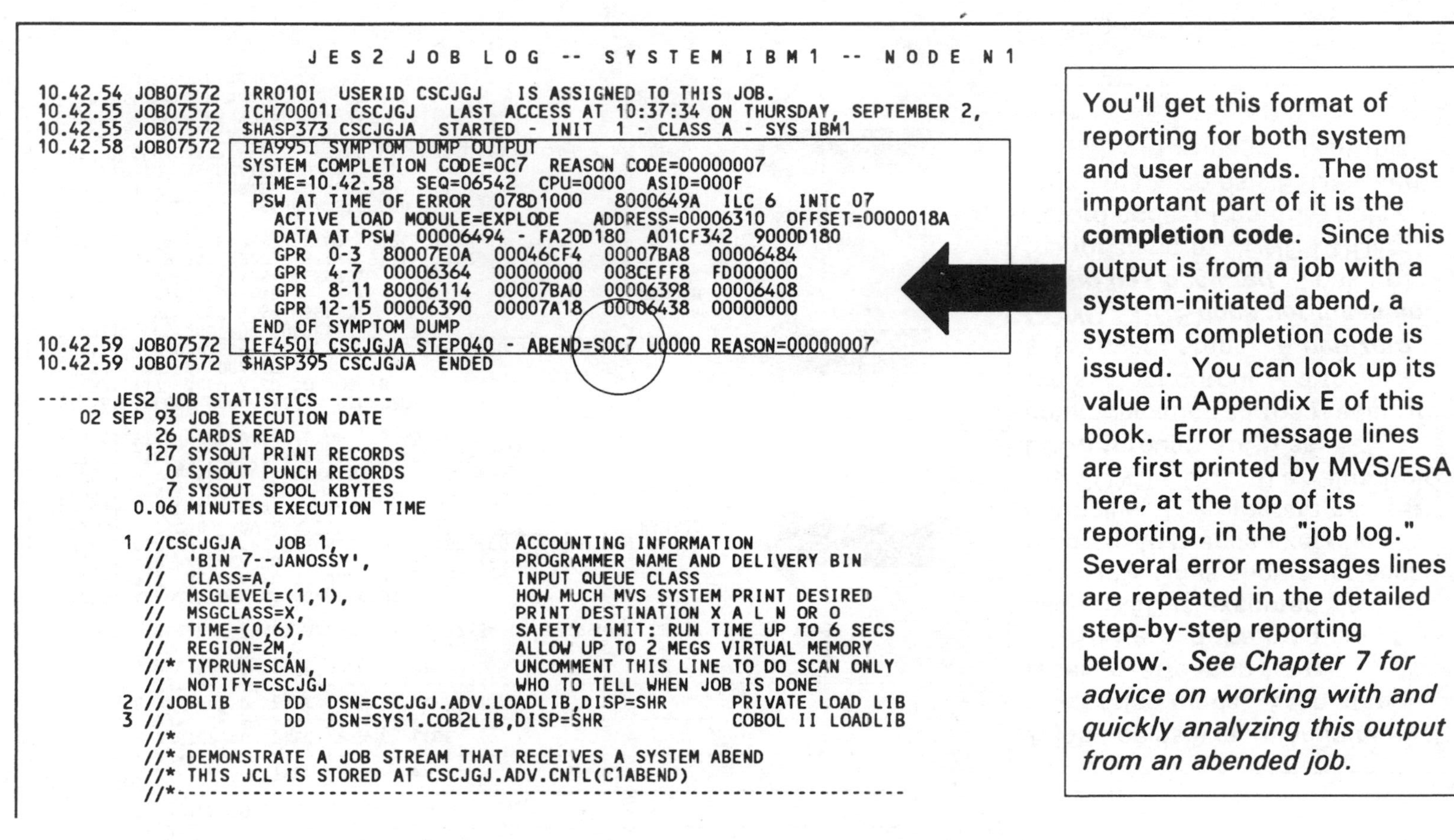

```
                     J E S 2  J O B  L O G  --  S Y S T E M  I B M 1  --  N O D E  N 1

10.42.54 JOB07572  IRR010I  USERID CSCJGJ    IS ASSIGNED TO THIS JOB.
10.42.55 JOB07572  ICH70001I CSCJGJ    LAST ACCESS AT 10:37:34 ON THURSDAY, SEPTEMBER 2,
10.42.55 JOB07572  $HASP373 CSCJGJA  STARTED - INIT  1 - CLASS A - SYS IBM1
10.42.58 JOB07572  IEA995I SYMPTOM DUMP OUTPUT
                   SYSTEM COMPLETION CODE=0C7  REASON CODE=00000007
                    TIME=10.42.58  SEQ=06542  CPU=0000  ASID=000F
                    PSW AT TIME OF ERROR  078D1000   8000649A  ILC 6  INTC 07
                      ACTIVE LOAD MODULE=EXPLODE    ADDRESS=00006310  OFFSET=0000018A
                      DATA AT PSW  00006494 - FA20D180  A01CF342  9000D180
                      GPR  0-3  80007E0A  00046CF4  00007BA8  00006484
                      GPR  4-7  00006364  00000000  008CEFF8  FD000000
                      GPR  8-11 80006114  00007BA0  00006398  00006408
                      GPR 12-15 00006390  00007A18  00006438  00000000
                    END OF SYMPTOM DUMP
10.42.59 JOB07572  IEF450I CSCJGJA STEP040 - ABEND=S0C7 U0000 REASON=00000007
10.42.59 JOB07572  $HASP395 CSCJGJA  ENDED

------ JES2 JOB STATISTICS ------
    02 SEP 93 JOB EXECUTION DATE
           26 CARDS READ
          127 SYSOUT PRINT RECORDS
            0 SYSOUT PUNCH RECORDS
            7 SYSOUT SPOOL KBYTES
         0.06 MINUTES EXECUTION TIME

         1 //CSCJGJA   JOB 1,                   ACCOUNTING INFORMATION
           //   'BIN 7--JANOSSY',               PROGRAMMER NAME AND DELIVERY BIN
           //   CLASS=A,                        INPUT QUEUE CLASS
           //   MSGLEVEL=(1,1),                 HOW MUCH MVS SYSTEM PRINT DESIRED
           //   MSGCLASS=X,                     PRINT DESTINATION X A L N OR O
           //   TIME=(0,6),                     SAFETY LIMIT: RUN TIME UP TO 6 SECS
           //   REGION=2M,                      ALLOW UP TO 2 MEGS VIRTUAL MEMORY
           //*  TYPRUN=SCAN,                    UNCOMMENT THIS LINE TO DO SCAN ONLY
           //   NOTIFY=CSCJGJ                   WHO TO TELL WHEN JOB IS DONE
         2 //JOBLIB      DD  DSN=CSCJGJ.ADV.LOADLIB,DISP=SHR       PRIVATE LOAD LIB
         3 //            DD  DSN=SYS1.COB2LIB,DISP=SHR             COBOL II LOADLIB
           //*
           //* DEMONSTRATE A JOB STREAM THAT RECEIVES A SYSTEM ABEND
           //* THIS JCL IS STORED AT CSCJGJ.ADV.CNTL(C1ABEND)
           //*-----------------------------------------------------------------
```

You'll get this format of reporting for both system and user abends. The most important part of it is the **completion code**. Since this output is from a job with a system-initiated abend, a system completion code is issued. You can look up its value in Appendix E of this book. Error message lines are first printed by MVS/ESA here, at the top of its reporting, in the "job log." Several error messages lines are repeated in the detailed step-by-step reporting below. *See Chapter 7 for advice on working with and quickly analyzing this output from an abended job.*

Figure 3.5 MVS/ESA System Reporting for a System Abend

```
        4 //STEP010  EXEC  PGM=ALPHA
          //*-----------------------------------------------------------------
        5 //STEP020  EXEC  PGM=BETA8
          //*-----------------------------------------------------------------
        6 //STEP030  EXEC  PGM=GAMMA
          //*-----------------------------------------------------------------
        7 //STEP040  EXEC  PGM=EXPLODE
          //*-----------------------------------------------------------------
        8 //STEP050  EXEC  PGM=BETA4
          //*-----------------------------------------------------------------
        9 //STEP060  EXEC  PGM=DELTA

ICH70001I CSCJGJ   LAST ACCESS AT 10:37:34 ON THURSDAY, SEPTEMBER 2, 1993

IEF236I ALLOC. FOR CSCJGJA STEP010
IEF237I 117  ALLOCATED TO JOBLIB
IEF237I 110  ALLOCATED TO
IEF142I CSCJGJA STEP010 - STEP WAS EXECUTED - COND CODE 0000
IEF285I   CSCJGJ.ADV.LOADLIB                                PASSED
IEF285I   VOL SER NOS= USER03.
IEF285I   SYS1.COB2LIB                                      PASSED
IEF285I   VOL SER NOS= ACSRES.
IEF373I STEP /STEP010 / START 93245.1042
IEF374I STEP /STEP010 / STOP  93245.1042

IEF236I ALLOC. FOR CSCJGJA STEP020
IEF237I 117  ALLOCATED TO JOBLIB
IEF237I 110  ALLOCATED TO
IEF142I CSCJGJA STEP020 - STEP WAS EXECUTED - COND CODE 0008
IEF285I   CSCJGJ.ADV.LOADLIB
IEF285I   VOL SER NOS= USER03.
IEF285I   SYS1.COB2LIB                                      PASSED
IEF285I   VOL SER NOS= ACSRES.
IEF373I STEP /STEP020 / START 93245.1042
IEF374I STEP /STEP020 / STOP  93245.1042

IEF236I ALLOC. FOR CSCJGJA STEP030
IEF237I 117  ALLOCATED TO JOBLIB
IEF237I 110  ALLOCATED TO
IEF142I CSCJGJA STEP030 - STEP WAS EXECUTED - COND CODE 0000
IEF285I   CSCJGJ.ADV.LOADLIB                                PASSED
IEF285I   VOL SER NOS= USER03.
IEF285I   SYS1.COB2LIB                                      PASSED
```

A job begins execution in **normal processing mode**. Each step receives attention from MVS/ESA and the program at each EXEC is executed. A COND CODE is shown for each program that ends execution normally. The program can set the COND CODE to a value from 0000 through 4095 as communication to the reader of the system output and to subsequent steps. ***A non-zero COND CODE does not mean an abend has occurred.*** Look up the meaning of COND CODEs (return codes) from IBM utility programs such as DFSORT and IDCAMS in Appendix D of this book.

Figure 3.5 (continued)

```
IEF285I   VOL SER NOS= ACSRES.
IEF373I STEP /STEP030 / START 93245.1042
IEF374I STEP /STEP030 / STOP  93245.1042

IEF236I ALLOC. FOR CSCJGJA STEP040
IEF237I 117  ALLOCATED TO JOBLIB
IEF237I 110  ALLOCATED TO
IEA995I SYMPTOM DUMP OUTPUT
SYSTEM COMPLETION CODE=0C7  REASON CODE=00000007
 TIME=10.42.58  SEQ=06542  CPU=0000  ASID=000F
 PSW AT TIME OF ERROR  078D1000   8000649A  ILC 6  INTC 07
   ACTIVE LOAD MODULE=EXPLODE    ADDRESS=00006310  OFFSET=0000018A
   DATA AT PSW  00006494 - FA20D180  A01CF342  9000D180
   GPR  0-3  80007E0A  00046CF4  00007BA8  00006484
   GPR  4-7  00006364  00000000  008CEFF8  FD000000
   GPR  8-11 80006114  00007BA0  00006398  00006408
   GPR 12-15 00006390  00007A18  00006438  00000000
 END OF SYMPTOM DUMP
IEF472I CSCJGJA STEP040 - COMPLETION CODE - SYSTEM=0C7 USER=0000
IEF285I   CSCJGJ.ADV.LOADLIB                            PASSED
IEF285I   VOL SER NOS= USER03.
IEF285I   SYS1.COB2LIB                                  PASSED
IEF285I   VOL SER NOS= ACSRES.
IEF373I STEP /STEP040 / START 93245.1042
IEF374I STEP /STEP040 / STOP  93245.1042

IEF272I CSCJGJA STEP050 - STEP WAS NOT EXECUTED.
IEF373I STEP /STEP050 / START 93245.1042
IEF374I STEP /STEP050 / STOP  93245.1042

IEF272I CSCJGJA STEP060 - STEP WAS NOT EXECUTED.
IEF373I STEP /STEP060 / START 93245.1042
IEF374I STEP /STEP060 / STOP  93245.1042

IEF285I   CSCJGJ.ADV.LOADLIB                            KEPT
IEF285I   VOL SER NOS= USER03.
IEF285I   SYS1.COB2LIB                                  KEPT
IEF285I   VOL SER NOS= ACSRES.
IEF375I  JOB /CSCJGJA / START 93245.1042
IEF376I  JOB /CSCJGJA / STOP  93245.1042
```

STEP040 executes program EXPLODE, which violates ES/9000 processing requirements by attempting to add to an uninitialized counter field (an uninitialized field that contains non-numeric data). This is an **unintentional abend** forced by MVS/ESA, and a system completion code is issued. The reporting here is identical to that in the job log at the top of MVS/ESA system reporting. ***At this point, the job stream enters abnormal termination mode.***

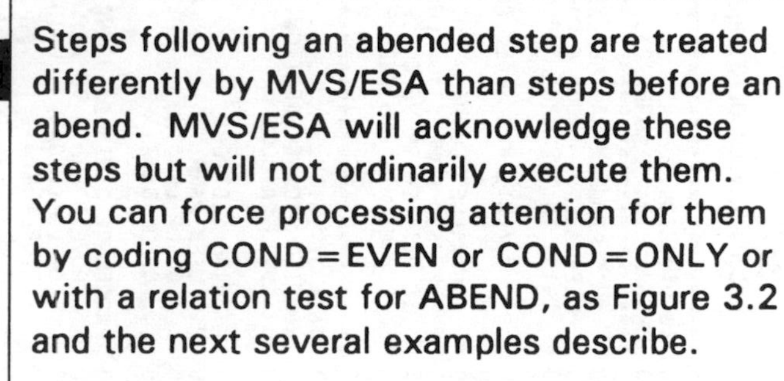

Steps following an abended step are treated differently by MVS/ESA than steps before an abend. MVS/ESA will acknowledge these steps but will not ordinarily execute them. You can force processing attention for them by coding COND=EVEN or COND=ONLY or with a relation test for ABEND, as Figure 3.2 and the next several examples describe.

Figure 3.5 (continued)

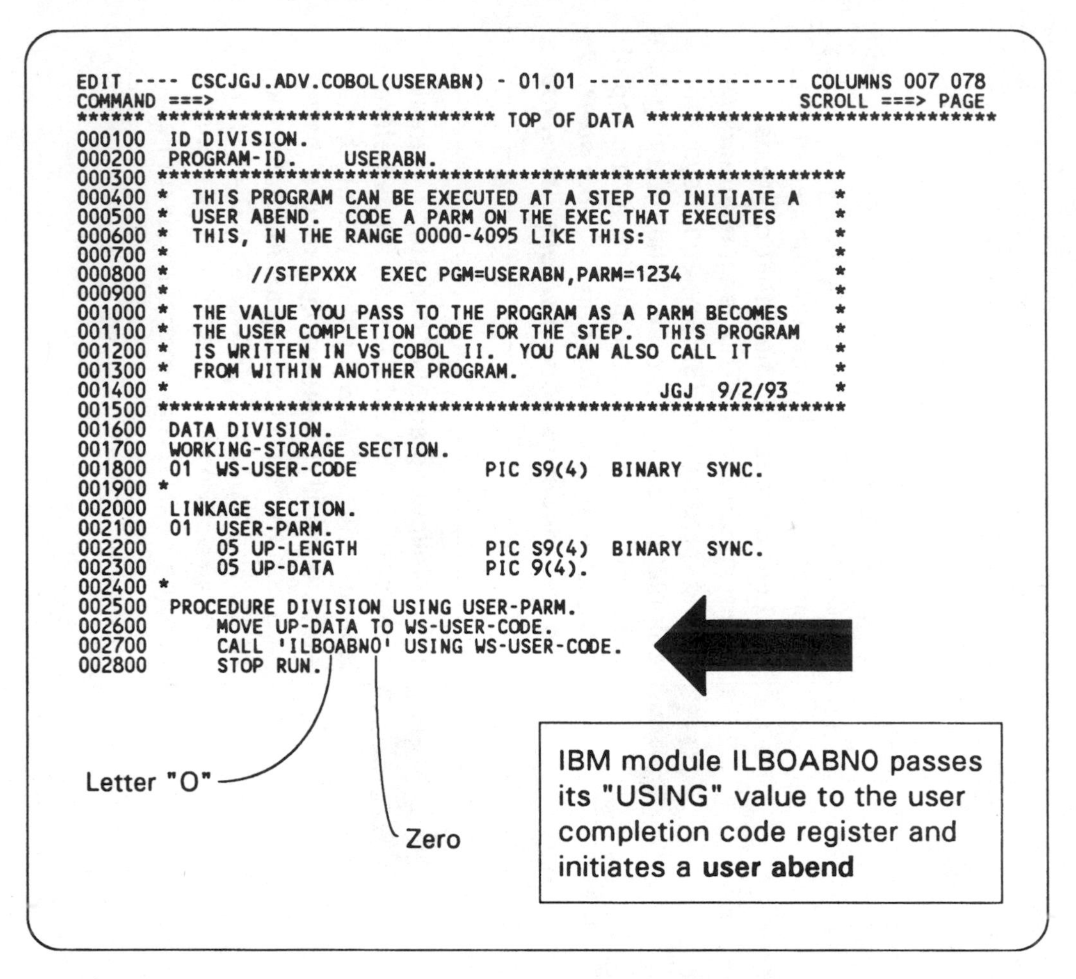

```
EDIT ---- CSCJGJ.ADV.COBOL(USERABN) - 01.01 ------------------ COLUMNS 007 078
COMMAND ===>                                                  SCROLL ===> PAGE
****** ****************************** TOP OF DATA ******************************
000100  ID DIVISION.
000200  PROGRAM-ID.    USERABN.
000300 **************************************************************
000400 *  THIS PROGRAM CAN BE EXECUTED AT A STEP TO INITIATE A      *
000500 *  USER ABEND.  CODE A PARM ON THE EXEC THAT EXECUTES        *
000600 *  THIS, IN THE RANGE 0000-4095 LIKE THIS:                   *
000700 *                                                            *
000800 *       //STEPXXX  EXEC PGM=USERABN,PARM=1234                *
000900 *                                                            *
001000 *  THE VALUE YOU PASS TO THE PROGRAM AS A PARM BECOMES       *
001100 *  THE USER COMPLETION CODE FOR THE STEP.  THIS PROGRAM      *
001200 *  IS WRITTEN IN VS COBOL II.  YOU CAN ALSO CALL IT          *
001300 *  FROM WITHIN ANOTHER PROGRAM.                              *
001400 *                                            JGJ  9/2/93     *
001500 **************************************************************
001600  DATA DIVISION.
001700  WORKING-STORAGE SECTION.
001800  01  WS-USER-CODE              PIC S9(4)  BINARY  SYNC.
001900 *
002000  LINKAGE SECTION.
002100  01  USER-PARM.
002200      05 UP-LENGTH              PIC S9(4)  BINARY  SYNC.
002300      05 UP-DATA                PIC 9(4).
002400 *
002500  PROCEDURE DIVISION USING USER-PARM.
002600      MOVE UP-DATA TO WS-USER-CODE.
002700      CALL 'ILBOABNO' USING WS-USER-CODE.
002800      STOP RUN.
```

Letter "O"
Zero
IBM module ILBOABNO passes its "USING" value to the user completion code register and initiates a **user abend**

Figure 3.6 USERABN Program to Intentionally Generate a User Abend

number between 0000 and 0999, or between 2000 and 4095. (Why not a number in the range 1000 to 1999? VS COBOL II lays claim to those values for user completion code abends it builds into its load modules. It's now a good idea to avoid using values in this range as return codes.)

Compare the MVS/ESA system output for C2ABEND, shown in Figure 3.8, with the output for C1ABEND shown in Figure 3.5. You'll note plenty of similarities, including the switch by MVS/ESA from normal processing mode to abnormal termination mode at STEP040. But notice that the job log now states "U3401" at the abend message line, and USER=3401 at the completion code message line in the allocations/deallocations. The effect of the intentional user abend is identical to a system abend, except that we get the ability to communicate, via the user completion code, a specific meaning to the reader of the MVS/ESA reporting.

3.10 A New Feature? "Unintentional" User Abends

The discussion I have conducted in the previous sections provides the most orderly presentation I can give you about the way MVS/ESA handles job

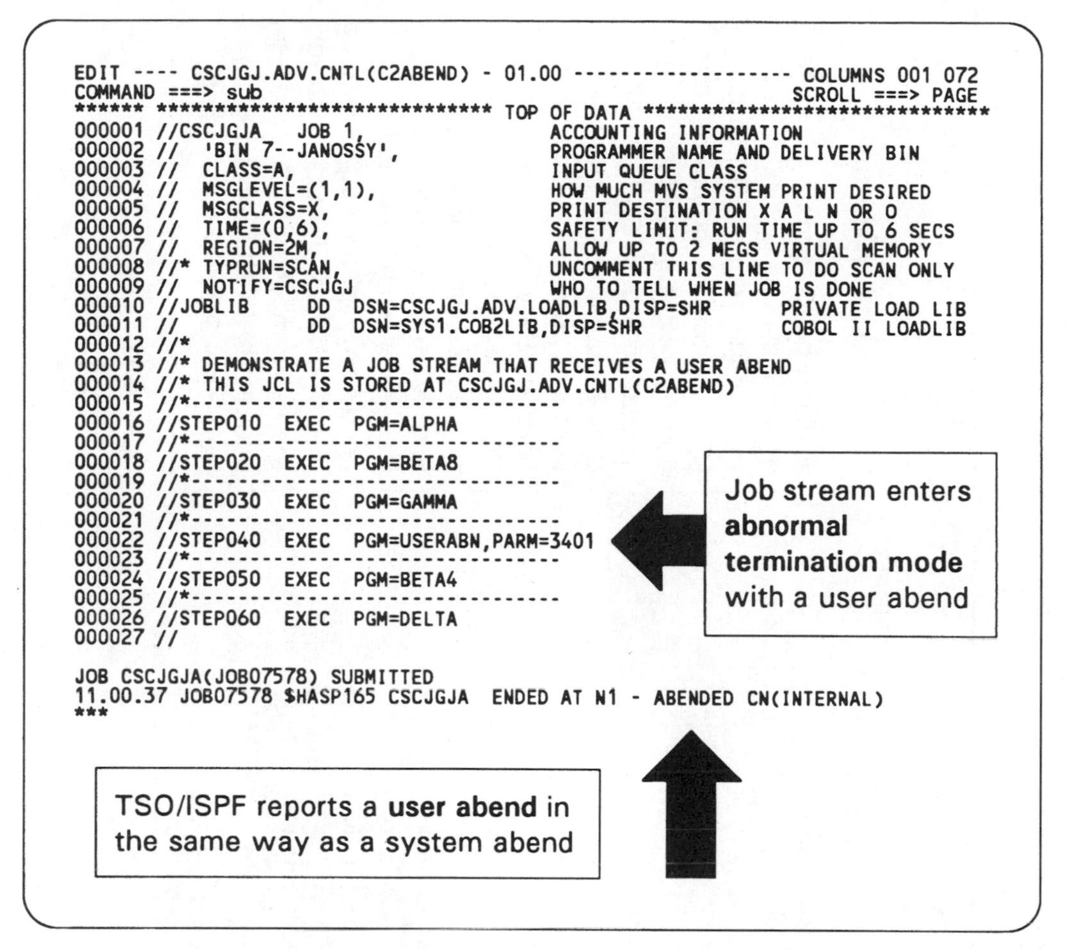
```
EDIT ---- CSCJGJ.ADV.CNTL(C2ABEND) - 01.00 ------------------ COLUMNS 001 072
COMMAND ===> sub                                               SCROLL ===> PAGE
****** ***************************** TOP OF DATA ******************************
000001 //CSCJGJA   JOB 1,                   ACCOUNTING INFORMATION
000002 //   'BIN 7--JANOSSY',               PROGRAMMER NAME AND DELIVERY BIN
000003 //   CLASS=A,                        INPUT QUEUE CLASS
000004 //   MSGLEVEL=(1,1),                 HOW MUCH MVS SYSTEM PRINT DESIRED
000005 //   MSGCLASS=X,                     PRINT DESTINATION X A L N OR O
000006 //   TIME=(0,6),                     SAFETY LIMIT: RUN TIME UP TO 6 SECS
000007 //   REGION=2M,                      ALLOW UP TO 2 MEGS VIRTUAL MEMORY
000008 //*  TYPRUN=SCAN,                    UNCOMMENT THIS LINE TO DO SCAN ONLY
000009 //   NOTIFY=CSCJGJ                   WHO TO TELL WHEN JOB IS DONE
000010 //JOBLIB     DD  DSN=CSCJGJ.ADV.LOADLIB,DISP=SHR      PRIVATE LOAD LIB
000011 //           DD  DSN=SYS1.COB2LIB,DISP=SHR            COBOL II LOADLIB
000012 //*
000013 //* DEMONSTRATE A JOB STREAM THAT RECEIVES A USER ABEND
000014 //* THIS JCL IS STORED AT CSCJGJ.ADV.CNTL(C2ABEND)
000015 //*-------------------------------
000016 //STEP010  EXEC  PGM=ALPHA
000017 //*-------------------------------
000018 //STEP020  EXEC  PGM=BETA8
000019 //*-------------------------------
000020 //STEP030  EXEC  PGM=GAMMA
000021 //*-------------------------------
000022 //STEP040  EXEC  PGM=USERABN,PARM=3401
000023 //*-------------------------------
000024 //STEP050  EXEC  PGM=BETA4
000025 //*-------------------------------
000026 //STEP060  EXEC  PGM=DELTA
000027 //

JOB CSCJGJA(JOB07578) SUBMITTED
11.00.37 JOB07578 $HASP165 CSCJGJA  ENDED AT N1 - ABENDED CN(INTERNAL)
***
```
Job stream enters **abnormal termination mode** with a user abend
TSO/ISPF reports a **user abend** in the same way as a system abend

Figure 3.7 Job Stream C2ABEND Demonstrating an Intentional User Abend

stream execution. Now, before I show you the capability MVS/ESA provides to test for and detect successful step operation as well as abends, I have to describe another aspect of modern mainframe program execution that may seem confusing.

As a whole I call system abends "unintentional" and user abends "intentional" because this distinction has traditionally applied. You get system completion codes from system abends without asking for them. You get user completion codes from user abends because you asked for them. But now you will also get user completion codes from user abends because IBM's compilers and utilities are being made to detect and report on errors previously left to MVS/ESA to detect and report on.

In developing its new compilers such as VS COBOL II and COBOL/370, IBM has begun shifting the location of some error detection from the operating system to program software products. In the past, for example, a compiler would allow MVS/ESA to report a problem such as not finding the source code member you wished to compile, and you would receive a system completion code of 013-18 for this problem. Now, the compiler itself reports this serious problem with a COND CODE 0012. Whether

```
                     J E S 2  J O B  L O G -- S Y S T E M  I B M 1 -- N O D E  N 1

11.00.33 JOB07578  IRR010I  USERID CSCJGJ   IS ASSIGNED TO THIS JOB.
11.00.33 JOB07578  ICH70001I CSCJGJ   LAST ACCESS AT 11:00:15 ON THURSDAY, SEPTEMBER
11.00.33 JOB07578  $HASP373 CSCJGJA  STARTED - INIT  1 - CLASS A - SYS IBM1
11.00.37 JOB07578  IEA995I SYMPTOM DUMP OUTPUT
                     USER COMPLETION CODE=3401
                    TIME=11.00.36  SEQ=06550  CPU=0000  ASID=000F
                    PSW AT TIME OF ERROR  078D1000   83600FFC  ILC 2  INTC 0D
                      ACTIVE LOAD MODULE=ILBOABN    ADDRESS=03600F48  OFFSET=000000B4
                      DATA AT PSW  03600FF6 - 00181610  0A0D0000  0000****
                      GPR  0-3  80000000  80000D49  00005219  00006180
                      GPR  4-7  00006260  00048038  00048038  83600F4A
                      GPR  8-11 800165A0  00007A08  00047CC0  83600F4A
                      GPR 12-15 80016022  00047E80  8001659E  83600F54
                    END OF SYMPTOM DUMP
11.00.37 JOB07578  IEF450I CSCJGJA STEP040 - ABEND=S000 U3401
11.00.37 JOB07578  $HASP395 CSCJGJA  ENDED

------ JES2 JOB STATISTICS ------
    02 SEP 93 JOB EXECUTION DATE
           26 CARDS READ
          127 SYSOUT PRINT RECORDS
            0 SYSOUT PUNCH RECORDS
            7 SYSOUT SPOOL KBYTES
         0.06 MINUTES EXECUTION TIME

        1 //CSCJGJA   JOB 1,                ACCOUNTING INFORMATION
          //  'BIN 7--JANOSSY',             PROGRAMMER NAME AND DELIVERY BIN
          //  CLASS=A,                      INPUT QUEUE CLASS
          //  MSGLEVEL=(1,1),               HOW MUCH MVS SYSTEM PRINT DESIRED
          //  MSGCLASS=X,                   PRINT DESTINATION X A L N OR O
          //  TIME=(0,6),                   SAFETY LIMIT: RUN TIME UP TO 6 SECS
          //  REGION=2M,                    ALLOW UP TO 2 MEGS VIRTUAL MEMORY
          //* TYPRUN=SCAN,                  UNCOMMENT THIS LINE TO DO SCAN ONLY
          //  NOTIFY=CSCJGJ                 WHO TO TELL WHEN JOB IS DONE
        2 //JOBLIB      DD  DSN=CSCJGJ.ADV.LOADLIB,DISP=SHR       PRIVATE LOAD LIB
        3 //            DD  DSN=SYS1.COB2LIB,DISP=SHR             COBOL II LOADLIB
          //*
          //* DEMONSTRATE A JOB STREAM THAT RECEIVES A USER ABEND
          //* THIS JCL IS STORED AT CSCJGJ.ADV.CNTL(C2ABEND)
          //*-----------------------------------------------------------------
```

User Abend

A user abend sends a job stream down in flames just as does a system-initiated abend, causing MVS system reporting that can quickly be recognized as indicating a problem. User-initiated abend steps are useful in production job streams because they can be triggered by COND or IF/THEN/ELSE tests of prior steps, and a user abend with a *unique* completion code issued for each abnormal condition. I show you how to do that in Chapter 7, but I illustrate the basic mechanism here in connection with MVS/ESA Version 4 **ABEND** test coding.

Figure 3.8 MVS/ESA System Reporting for a User Abend

```
        4 //STEP010  EXEC  PGM=ALPHA
          //*-------------------------------------------------------------
        5 //STEP020  EXEC  PGM=BETA8
          //*-------------------------------------------------------------
        6 //STEP030  EXEC  PGM=GAMMA
          //*-------------------------------------------------------------
        7 //STEP040  EXEC  PGM=USERABN,PARM=3401
          //*-------------------------------------------------------------
        8 //STEP050  EXEC  PGM=BETA4
          //*-------------------------------------------------------------
        9 //STEP060  EXEC  PGM=DELTA

ICH70001I CSCJGJ   LAST ACCESS AT 11:00:15 ON THURSDAY, SEPTEMBER 2, 1993

IEF236I ALLOC. FOR CSCJGJA STEP010
IEF237I 117  ALLOCATED TO JOBLIB
IEF237I 110  ALLOCATED TO
IEF142I CSCJGJA STEP010 - STEP WAS EXECUTED - COND CODE 0000
IEF285I   CSCJGJ.ADV.LOADLIB                               PASSED
IEF285I   VOL SER NOS= USER03.
IEF285I   SYS1.COB2LIB                                     PASSED
IEF285I   VOL SER NOS= ACSRES.
IEF373I STEP /STEP010 / START 93245.1100
IEF374I STEP /STEP010 / STOP  93245.1100

IEF236I ALLOC. FOR CSCJGJA STEP020
IEF237I 117  ALLOCATED TO JOBLIB
IEF237I 110  ALLOCATED TO
IEF142I CSCJGJA STEP020 - STEP WAS EXECUTED - COND CODE 0008
IEF285I   CSCJGJ.ADV.LOADLIB                               PASSED
IEF285I   VOL SER NOS= USER03.
IEF285I   SYS1.COB2LIB                                     PASSED
IEF285I   VOL SER NOS= ACSRES.
IEF373I STEP /STEP020 / START 93245.1100
IEF374I STEP /STEP020 / STOP  93245.1100

IEF236I ALLOC. FOR CSCJGJA STEP030
IEF237I 117  ALLOCATED TO JOBLIB
IEF237I 110  ALLOCATED TO
IEF142I CSCJGJA STEP030 - STEP WAS EXECUTED - COND CODE 0000
IEF285I   CSCJGJ.ADV.LOADLIB                               PASSED
IEF285I   VOL SER NOS= USER03.
IEF285I   SYS1.COB2LIB                                     PASSED
```

These steps executed and have each set a COND CODE. Different COND CODE values can mean different things, but as far as MVS is concerned, these programs all ended normally. The job stream began in normal processing mode, and it continues to be in normal processing mode here.

Figure 3.8 (continued)

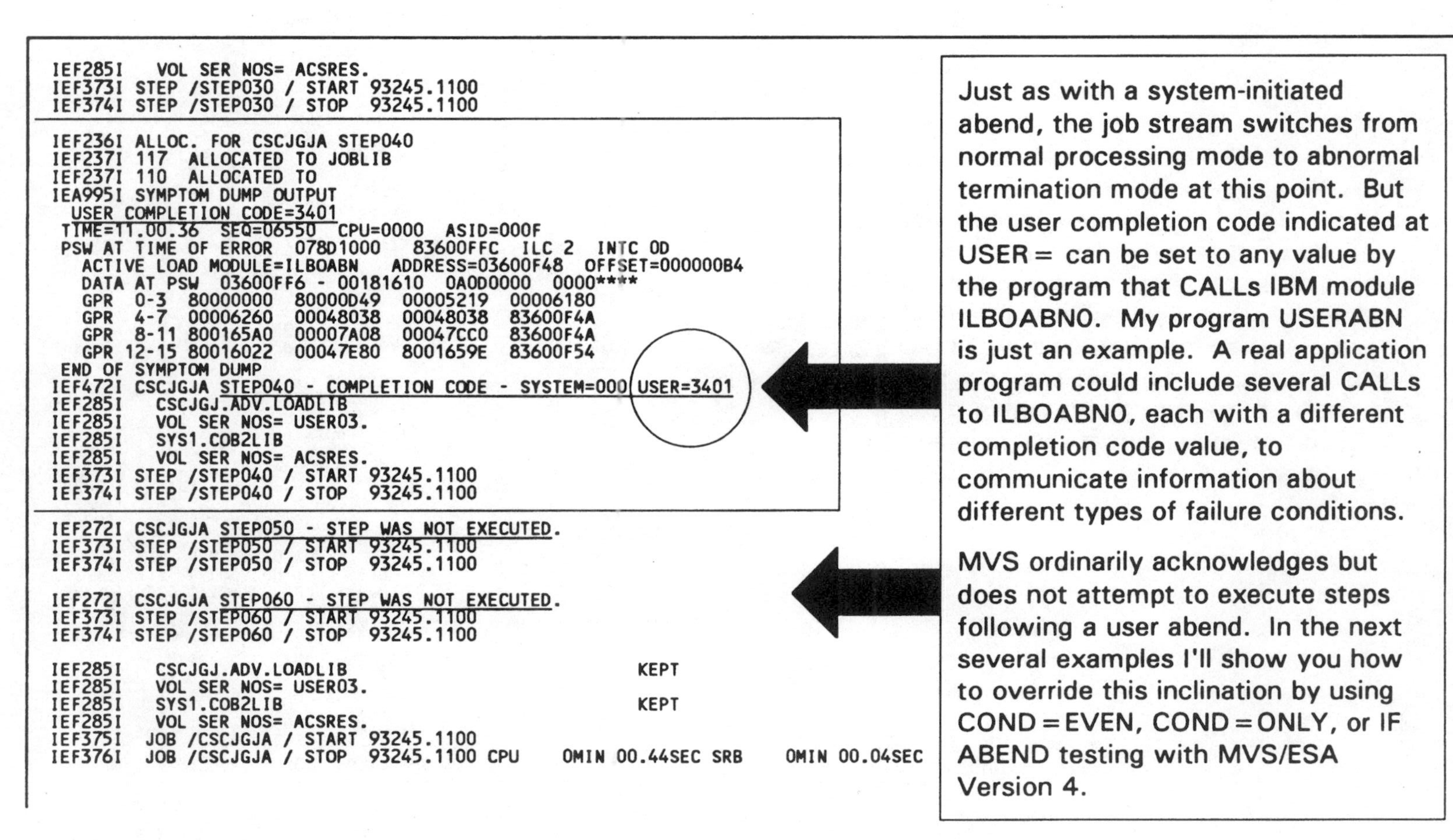

```
IEF285I   VOL SER NOS= ACSRES.
IEF373I STEP /STEP030 / START 93245.1100
IEF374I STEP /STEP030 / STOP  93245.1100

IEF236I ALLOC. FOR CSCJGJA STEP040
IEF237I 117  ALLOCATED TO JOBLIB
IEF237I 110  ALLOCATED TO
IEA995I SYMPTOM DUMP OUTPUT
 USER COMPLETION CODE=3401
 TIME=11.00.36  SEQ=06550  CPU=0000  ASID=000F
 PSW AT TIME OF ERROR  078D1000   83600FFC  ILC 2  INTC 0D
   ACTIVE LOAD MODULE=ILBOABN   ADDRESS=03600F48  OFFSET=000000B4
   DATA AT PSW  03600FF6 - 00181610  0A0D0000  0000****
   GPR  0-3  80000000  80000D49  00005219  00006180
   GPR  4-7  00006260  00048038  00048038  83600F4A
   GPR  8-11 800165A0  00007A08  00047CC0  83600F4A
   GPR 12-15 80016022  00047E80  8001659E  83600F54
 END OF SYMPTOM DUMP
IEF472I CSCJGJA STEP040 - COMPLETION CODE - SYSTEM=000 USER=3401
IEF285I   CSCJGJ.ADV.LOADLIB
IEF285I   VOL SER NOS= USER03.
IEF285I   SYS1.COB2LIB
IEF285I   VOL SER NOS= ACSRES.
IEF373I STEP /STEP040 / START 93245.1100
IEF374I STEP /STEP040 / STOP  93245.1100

IEF272I CSCJGJA STEP050 - STEP WAS NOT EXECUTED.
IEF373I STEP /STEP050 / START 93245.1100
IEF374I STEP /STEP050 / STOP  93245.1100

IEF272I CSCJGJA STEP060 - STEP WAS NOT EXECUTED.
IEF373I STEP /STEP060 / START 93245.1100
IEF374I STEP /STEP060 / STOP  93245.1100

IEF285I   CSCJGJ.ADV.LOADLIB                         KEPT
IEF285I   VOL SER NOS= USER03.
IEF285I   SYS1.COB2LIB                               KEPT
IEF285I   VOL SER NOS= ACSRES.
IEF375I  JOB /CSCJGJA / START 93245.1100
IEF376I  JOB /CSCJGJA / STOP  93245.1100 CPU    0MIN 00.44SEC SRB    0MIN 00.04SEC
```

Just as with a system-initiated abend, the job stream switches from normal processing mode to abnormal termination mode at this point. But the user completion code indicated at USER = can be set to any value by the program that CALLs IBM module ILBOABNO. My program USERABN is just an example. A real application program could include several CALLs to ILBOABNO, each with a different completion code value, to communicate information about different types of failure conditions.
MVS ordinarily acknowledges but does not attempt to execute steps following a user abend. In the next several examples I'll show you how to override this inclination by using COND=EVEN, COND=ONLY, or IF ABEND testing with MVS/ESA Version 4.

Figure 3.8 (continued)

IBM's shift in error detection emphasis and reporting is a blessing or nuisance is subject to debate, but this shift forces you to make some changes in the way you work.

Because some compilers and utilities are now in charge of detecting and reporting on certain errors, you now need to look in program documentation when some abends occur, instead of looking up a system completion code. More importantly, you *need to understand that now, programs written in VS COBOL II and COBOL/370 can, on their own, initiate user abends for some types of runtime problems that in the past were reported with system abends.* I call this class of abends "unintentional user abends" because you, as the program author, do not intentionally include logic in your programs or JCL to produce them. I'll demonstrate one for you, so that you can see precisely how significant this change is to the production environment.

3.11 Recognizing Unintentional User Abends

The small VS COBOL II program named B1OLDRC in Figure 3.9 appears in *VS COBOL II Highlights and Techniques* (Janossy, John Wiley & Sons, Inc., 1992). It demonstrates how this new compiler, typical of IBM's current crop of system software, introduces a major change in error reporting in the mainframe environment.

Program B1OLDRC uses a PERFORM verb to invoke a paragraph named 1000-ROUTINE. Nowhere within the program do I include logic to cause a user abend. But the logic in 1000-ROUTINE violates an important programming principle. It does an unconditional branch out of a PERFORMed paragraph, causing a loss of control. Although the program is syntactically correct and compiles with no problem, it will fail in operation. But how will the failure be reported at runtime?

I compiled and link edited B1OLDRC and put its machine language in my load module library. I then used the JCL in Figure 3.10 to run it. You can see from this JCL that I have not coded anything in the JCL to invoke a user abend. But when you examine the output from this job, shown in Figure 3.11, you will note that the job has received a user abend!

The annotations on Figure 3.11 explain why a user abend 1037 has occurred in my running of program B1OLDRC. If your shop, like many other mainframe installations, relies heavily on COBOL programs, you are either using VS COBOL II or COBOL/370 now or will be in the near future. As of 1994, IBM abandoned support for earlier versions of COBOL, such as VS COBOL. You need to understand how this class of unintentional user abends works, and how to anticipate and provide adequate visibility in your job streams for abends in general.

3.12 Making Steps Execute After an Abend with COND=EVEN

The EXEC statement COND parameter values EVEN and ONLY (coded as COND=EVEN or COND=ONLY) exist in JCL primarily to let you recognize when a prior step has abended, and to deal with this in whatever way is appropriate to the job. You can code neither, or one or the other, but not both on a given step. You can't predict at what step in a job stream a failure

```
EDIT ---- CSCJGJ.ADV.COBOL(B1OLDRC) - 01.00 ----------------- COLUMNS 007 078
COMMAND ===>                                                  SCROLL ===> PAGE
****** ******************************* TOP OF DATA ******************************
000100  IDENTIFICATION DIVISION.
000200  PROGRAM-ID.    B1OLDRC.
000300  AUTHOR.        J JANOSSY.
000400  INSTALLATION.  DEPAUL UNIVERSITY.
000500  DATE-WRITTEN.  SEP 1986.
000600  DATE-COMPILED.
000700 *REMARKS.       THIS PROGRAM JUMPS OUT OF A PERFORMED ROUTINE
000800 *               TO DEMONSTRATE A VS COBOL USER 0519 ERROR
000900 *               FOR COMPUTER CAREER PROGRAM TRAINING PURPOSES.
001000 *
001100  ENVIRONMENT DIVISION.
001200 *
001300  DATA DIVISION.
001400  WORKING-STORAGE SECTION.
001500  01  WS-START-MSG               PIC X(11)  VALUE 'HERE IS WS!'.
001600  01  WS-HERE-IS-DISPLAY-NUM     PIC 9(3)   VALUE 0.
001700  01  WS-HERE-IS-PACKED-NUM      PIC S9(5)  COMP-3  VALUE +0.
001800 *
001900  PROCEDURE DIVISION.
002000  0000-MAINLINE.
002100      MOVE 123         TO WS-HERE-IS-DISPLAY-NUM.
002200      MOVE +98765      TO WS-HERE-IS-PACKED-NUM.
002300      DISPLAY '**1** B1OLDRC PROGRAM STARTING ***'.
002400      PERFORM 1000-ROUTINE.
002500      STOP RUN.
002600 *
002700 *
002800  1000-ROUTINE.
002900      DISPLAY '**2** WE GOT TO THE 1000-ROUTINE ***'.
003000      GO TO 1000-EXIT.
003100 *
003200 *
003300 * I DID NOT PERFORM "THRU" 1000-EXIT SO BRANCHING HERE IS WRONG.
003400 * THE PROGRAM WILL LOSE CONTROL AS A RESULT:
003500 *
003600  1000-EXIT.  EXIT.
```

This program jumps out of a performed paragraph and "falls out the bottom." This is one of many potential execution errors that VS COBOL II uses hidden logic to automatically intercept.

Figure 3.9 B1OLDRC, A Program That Generates a VS COBOL II "Unintentional" User Abend

will occur in a given run, or if a failure will occur at all. COND=EVEN, COND=ONLY, the new MVS/ESA Version 4 IF ABEND test, and a new IF RUN test are the building blocks of robust job streams. I show you examples of their use here to demonstrate their syntax. I'll then show you a useful model for production job failure detection, and demonstrate it in typical job streams in Chapter 7.

An abend of any type at a step puts your job stream into abnormal termination mode and ordinarily causes the remaining steps to be acknowledged but not processed by MVS/ESA. You can code COND=EVEN or COND=ONLY to have the steps after an abend be given MVS/ESA attention

```
EDIT ---- CSCJGJ.ADV.CNTL(B1OLDRC) - 01.00 ------------------ COLUMNS 001 072
COMMAND ===>                                                  SCROLL ===> PAGE
****** ***************************** TOP OF DATA ******************************
000001 //CSCJGJA    JOB 1,               ACCOUNTING INFORMATION
000002 //  'BIN 7--JANOSSY',              PROGRAMMER NAME AND DELIVERY BIN
000003 //  CLASS=A,                      INPUT QUEUE CLASS
000004 //  MSGLEVEL=(1,1),               HOW MUCH MVS SYSTEM PRINT DESIRED
000005 //  MSGCLASS=X,                   PRINT DESTINATION X A L N OR O
000006 //* TYPRUN=SCAN,                  UNCOMMENT IF WANT ONLY A JCL SCAN
000007 //  NOTIFY=CSCJGJ                 WHO TO TELL WHEN JOB IS DONE
000008 //*
000009 //*******************************************************************
000010 //* B1OLDRC    RUN B1OLDRC PROGRAM                                    *
000011 //*******************************************************************
000012 //STEP010   EXEC  PGM=B1OLDRC
000013 //STEPLIB     DD  DSN=CSCJGJ.ADV.LOADLIB,DISP=SHR
000014 //            DD  DSN=SYS1.COB2LIB,DISP=SHR
000015 //SYSOUT      DD  SYSOUT=*
000016 //
```

This JCL executes an already-compiled load module, prepared using VS COBOL II, from my own load module library. Notice that I have not indicated any intention to cause a user abend.

Figure 3.10 JCL to Execute the Load Module of the B1OLDRC Program

as usual. This use of COND is very different from using coding like COND=(4,LT,STEP010) to shut off a step. (The overuse of the word COND is one confusing aspect of pre–MVS/ESA Version 4 JCL, which the new version helps eliminate.)

Figure 3.12 illustrates both the JCL submitted for a six-step job stream named C3EVEN and the MVS/ESA system reporting associated with each of its steps. You saw the initial version of this job stream, in Figure 3.4 as C1ABEND. In this job stream, STEP040 causes a system abend, which puts the job into abnormal termination mode. As an exercise, let's locate the step treatment box in which each step falls on the chart in Figure 3.2:

1. Steps STEP010 and STEP020 of the job stream in Figure 3.12 enjoy normal processing mode treatment, and fall into box 1 of Figure 3.2.

2. COND=EVEN is coded on the EXEC in STEP030. This allows it MVS/ESA processing consideration in boxes 2 and 5 of Figure 3.2. Since the job stream is in normal processing mode when STEP030 is reached, it is treated according to box 2 in Figure 3.2 and executes.

3. STEP040 begins processing in normal processing mode, but the program abends and puts the job stream into abnormal termination mode, the second column of Figure 3.2. This step receives a system completion code for an unintentional system abend.

4. STEP050 begins with the job stream in abnormal termination mode. Ordi-

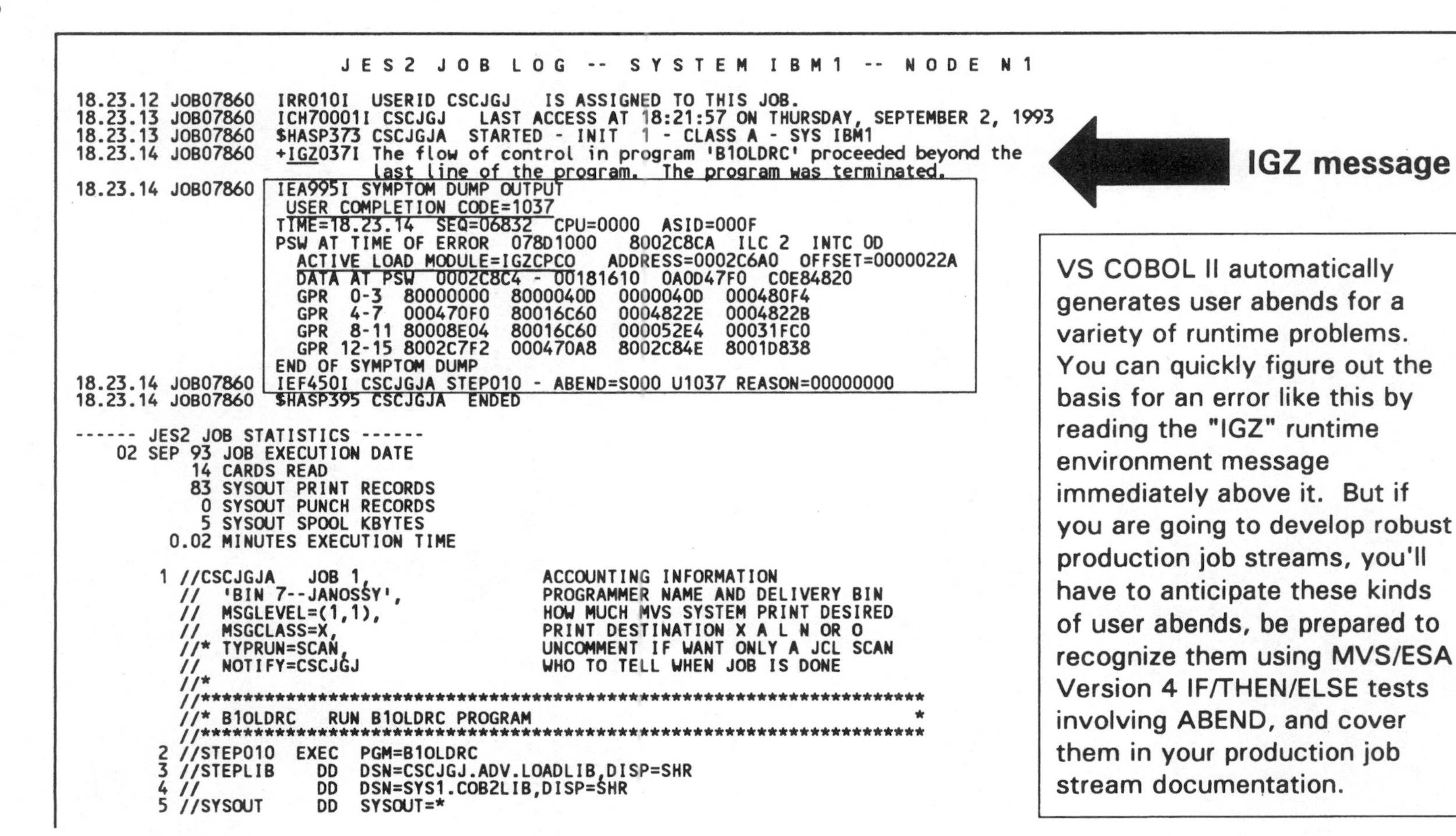

```
                    J E S 2  J O B  L O G  --  S Y S T E M  I B M 1  --  N O D E  N 1

18.23.12 JOB07860  IRR010I  USERID CSCJGJ   IS ASSIGNED TO THIS JOB.
18.23.13 JOB07860  ICH70001I CSCJGJ   LAST ACCESS AT 18:21:57 ON THURSDAY, SEPTEMBER 2, 1993
18.23.13 JOB07860  $HASP373 CSCJGJA  STARTED - INIT  1 - CLASS A - SYS IBM1
18.23.14 JOB07860  +IGZ037I The flow of control in program 'B1OLDRC' proceeded beyond the
                            last line of the program.  The program was terminated.
18.23.14 JOB07860  IEA995I SYMPTOM DUMP OUTPUT
                    USER COMPLETION CODE=1037
                   TIME=18.23.14  SEQ=06832  CPU=0000  ASID=000F
                   PSW AT TIME OF ERROR  078D1000   8002C8CA  ILC 2  INTC 0D
                     ACTIVE LOAD MODULE=IGZCPCO    ADDRESS=0002C6A0  OFFSET=0000022A
                     DATA AT PSW  0002C8C4 - 00181610  0A0D47F0  C0E84820
                     GPR  0-3  80000000  8000040D  0000040D  000480F4
                     GPR  4-7  000470F0  80016C60  0004822E  0004822B
                     GPR  8-11 80008E04  80016C60  000052E4  00031FC0
                     GPR 12-15 8002C7F2  000470A8  8002C84E  8001D838
                   END OF SYMPTOM DUMP
18.23.14 JOB07860  IEF450I CSCJGJA STEP010 - ABEND=S000 U1037 REASON=00000000
18.23.14 JOB07860  $HASP395 CSCJGJA  ENDED

------ JES2 JOB STATISTICS ------
   02 SEP 93 JOB EXECUTION DATE
          14 CARDS READ
          83 SYSOUT PRINT RECORDS
           0 SYSOUT PUNCH RECORDS
           5 SYSOUT SPOOL KBYTES
        0.02 MINUTES EXECUTION TIME

        1 //CSCJGJA   JOB 1,                      ACCOUNTING INFORMATION
          //  'BIN 7--JANOSSY',                   PROGRAMMER NAME AND DELIVERY BIN
          //  MSGLEVEL=(1,1),                     HOW MUCH MVS SYSTEM PRINT DESIRED
          //  MSGCLASS=X,                         PRINT DESTINATION X A L N OR O
          //* TYPRUN=SCAN,                        UNCOMMENT IF WANT ONLY A JCL SCAN
          //  NOTIFY=CSCJGJ                       WHO TO TELL WHEN JOB IS DONE
          //*
          //*******************************************************************
          //* B1OLDRC   RUN B1OLDRC PROGRAM                                     *
          //*******************************************************************
        2 //STEP010  EXEC  PGM=B1OLDRC
        3 //STEPLIB    DD  DSN=CSCJGJ.ADV.LOADLIB,DISP=SHR
        4 //           DD  DSN=SYS1.COB2LIB,DISP=SHR
        5 //SYSOUT     DD  SYSOUT=*
```

IGZ message
VS COBOL II automatically generates user abends for a variety of runtime problems. You can quickly figure out the basis for an error like this by reading the "IGZ" runtime environment message immediately above it. But if you are going to develop robust production job streams, you'll have to anticipate these kinds of user abends, be prepared to recognize them using MVS/ESA Version 4 IF/THEN/ELSE tests involving ABEND, and cover them in your production job stream documentation.

Figure 3.11 MVS/ESA System Reporting for a VS COBOL II "Unintentional" User Abend

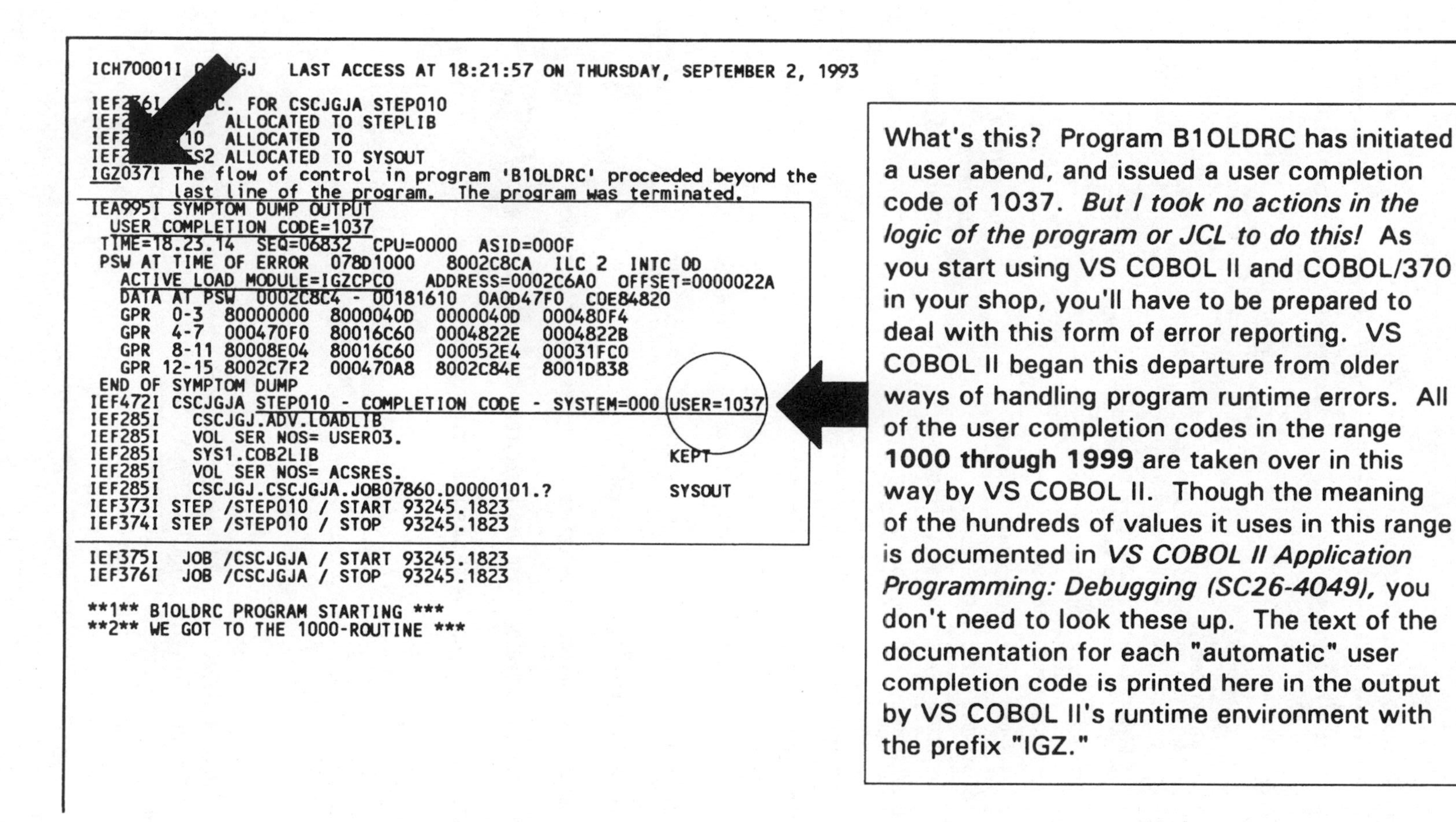

```
ICH70001I C  GJ    LAST ACCESS AT 18:21:57 ON THURSDAY, SEPTEMBER 2, 1993

IEF2 6I     C. FOR CSCJGJA STEP010
IEF2      7  ALLOCATED TO STEPLIB
IEF2     10  ALLOCATED TO
IEF2     S2 ALLOCATED TO SYSOUT
IGZ037I The flow of control in program 'B1OLDRC' proceeded beyond the
        last line of the program.  The program was terminated.
IEA995I SYMPTOM DUMP OUTPUT
  USER COMPLETION CODE=1037
 TIME=18.23.14  SEQ=06832  CPU=0000  ASID=000F
 PSW AT TIME OF ERROR  078D1000   8002C8CA  ILC 2  INTC 0D
   ACTIVE LOAD MODULE=IGZCPCO   ADDRESS=0002C6A0  OFFSET=0000022A
   DATA AT PSW  0002C8C4 - 00181610  0A0D47F0  C0E84820
   GPR  0-3  80000000  8000040D  0000040D  000480F4
   GPR  4-7  000470F0  80016C60  0004822E  0004822B
   GPR  8-11 80008E04  80016C60  000052E4  00031FC0
   GPR 12-15 8002C7F2  000470A8  8002C84E  8001D838
 END OF SYMPTOM DUMP
IEF472I CSCJGJA STEP010 - COMPLETION CODE - SYSTEM=000 USER=1037
IEF285I   CSCJGJ.ADV.LOADLIB
IEF285I   VOL SER NOS= USER03.
IEF285I   SYS1.COB2LIB                                  KEPT
IEF285I   VOL SER NOS= ACSRES.
IEF285I   CSCJGJ.CSCJGJA.JOB07860.D0000101.?            SYSOUT
IEF373I STEP /STEP010 / START 93245.1823
IEF374I STEP /STEP010 / STOP  93245.1823

IEF375I  JOB /CSCJGJA / START 93245.1823
IEF376I  JOB /CSCJGJA / STOP  93245.1823

**1** B1OLDRC PROGRAM STARTING ***
**2** WE GOT TO THE 1000-ROUTINE ***
```

What's this? Program B1OLDRC has initiated a user abend, and issued a user completion code of 1037. *But I took no actions in the logic of the program or JCL to do this!* As you start using VS COBOL II and COBOL/370 in your shop, you'll have to be prepared to deal with this form of error reporting. VS COBOL II began this departure from older ways of handling program runtime errors. All of the user completion codes in the range **1000 through 1999** are taken over in this way by VS COBOL II. Though the meaning of the hundreds of values it uses in this range is documented in *VS COBOL II Application Programming: Debugging (SC26-4049),* you don't need to look these up. The text of the documentation for each "automatic" user completion code is printed here in the output by VS COBOL II's runtime environment with the prefix "IGZ."

Figure 3.11 *(continued)*

```
EDIT ---- CSCJGJ.ADV.CNTL(C3EVEN) - 01.00 -------------------- COLUMNS 001 072
COMMAND ===>                                                  SCROLL ===> PAGE
****** ****************************** TOP OF DATA *******************************
000001 //CSCJGJA   JOB 1,                  ACCOUNTING INFORMATION
000002 //  'BIN 7--JANOSSY',               PROGRAMMER NAME AND DELIVERY BIN
000003 //  CLASS=A,                        INPUT QUEUE CLASS
000004 //  MSGLEVEL=(1,1),                 HOW MUCH MVS SYSTEM PRINT DESIRED
000005 //  MSGCLASS=X,                     PRINT DESTINATION X A L N OR O
000006 //  TIME=(0,6),                     SAFETY LIMIT: RUN TIME UP TO 6 SECS
000007 //  REGION=2M,                      ALLOW UP TO 2 MEGS VIRTUAL MEMORY
000008 //* TYPRUN=SCAN,                    UNCOMMENT THIS LINE TO DO SCAN ONLY
000009 //  NOTIFY=CSCJGJ                   WHO TO TELL WHEN JOB IS DONE
000010 //JOBLIB     DD  DSN=CSCJGJ.ADV.LOADLIB,DISP=SHR       PRIVATE LOAD LIB
000011 //           DD  DSN=SYS1.COB2LIB,DISP=SHR             COBOL II LOADLIB
000012 //*
000013 //* DEMONSTRATE HOW COND=EVEN WORKS
000014 //* THIS JCL IS STORED AT CSCJGJ.ADV.CNTL(C3EVEN)
000015 //*-----------------------------------------------------------------------
000016 //STEP010  EXEC  PGM=ALPHA
000017 //*-----------------------------------------------------------------------
000018 //STEP020  EXEC  PGM=BETA8
000019 //*--------------------------------------
000020 //STEP030  EXEC  PGM=GAMMA,COND=EVEN
000021 //*--------------------------------------
000022 //STEP040  EXEC  PGM=EXPLODE
000023 //*--------------------------------------
000024 //STEP050  EXEC  PGM=BETA4,COND=EVEN
000025 //*--------------------------------------
000026 //STEP060  EXEC  PGM=DELTA
000027 //
```

This step causes a system abend

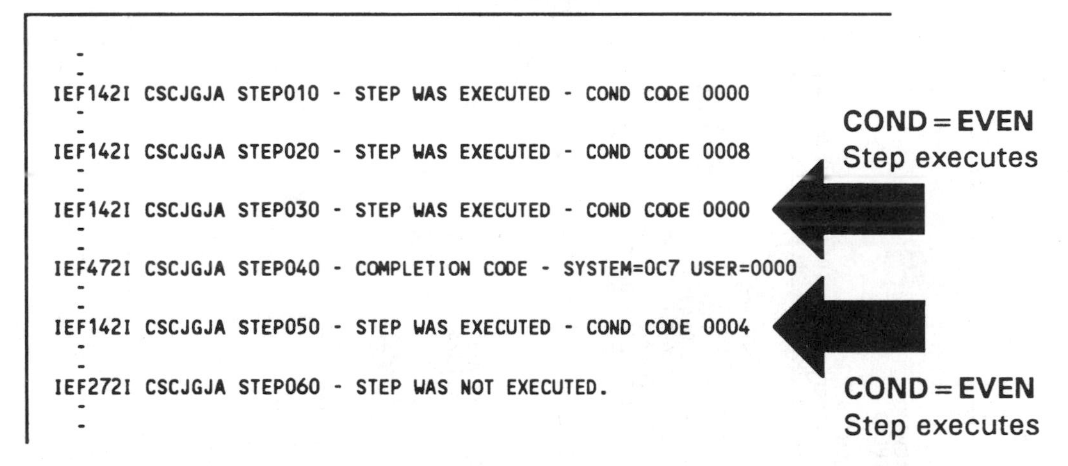

```
IEF142I CSCJGJA STEP010 - STEP WAS EXECUTED - COND CODE 0000

IEF142I CSCJGJA STEP020 - STEP WAS EXECUTED - COND CODE 0008

IEF142I CSCJGJA STEP030 - STEP WAS EXECUTED - COND CODE 0000

IEF472I CSCJGJA STEP040 - COMPLETION CODE - SYSTEM=0C7 USER=0000

IEF142I CSCJGJA STEP050 - STEP WAS EXECUTED - COND CODE 0004

IEF272I CSCJGJA STEP060 - STEP WAS NOT EXECUTED.
```


Figure 3.12 JCL and Extracted MVS/ESA System Reporting for Job Stream C3EVEN, Demonstrating the Effect of COND=EVEN on Step Execution with a System Abend

narily, MVS/ESA would acknowledge the presence of this step, but not process it. The syntax of COND=EVEN means “process this step EVEN if an abend has occurred.” With COND=EVEN coded on an EXEC, the step gets the treatment indicated in boxes 2 and 5 of Figure 3.2. Box 5 is in the abnormal termination mode column. As a result, this step is given normal processing attention by MVS/ESA even though a prior step in the job stream has abended!

5. STEP060 begins with the job stream in abnormal termination mode. Ordinarily, MVS/ESA would acknowledge its presence, but not process it. This is exactly what happens here. There is nothing to tell MVS/ESA to process STEP060 in spite of an abend in progress, and the step is treated according to box 4 of Figure 3.2.

As you can see in the example of Figure 3.12, putting COND=EVEN on a step gains the broadest possible execution consideration for it. Boxes 2 and 5 in Figure 3.2 straddle both the normal processing mode and abnormal termination columns, and a step coded this way *always* gains MVS/ESA processing attention.

3.13 Making Steps Execute After an Abend with COND=ONLY

COND=ONLY is similar to COND=EVEN for any steps following an abend, because it means "process this step ONLY if an abend has occurred." But as you might guess, ONLY does not give the same treatment as COND=EVEN when it is present on steps that are reached in normal processing mode.

Figure 3.13 shows you a job stream stored as member C4ONLY. This is identical to job stream C3EVEN in Figure 3.12, except that I have coded COND=ONLY at STEP030 and STEP050. As you can see at the bottom of Figure 3.13, the single difference between the outputs of C3EVEN and C4ONLY is that STEP030 is not run, due to the presence of COND=ONLY on its EXEC statement. STEP030 of job stream C4ONLY falls into processing box 6 in the chart in Figure 3.2, which is in the abnormal termination mode column. Since the job stream is not in abnormal termination mode when STEP030 is reached, MVS/ESA does not give STEP030 the chance to run.

COND=EVEN and COND=ONLY will work exactly the same way for intentional and unintentional user abends as you see demonstrated in Figures 3.12 and 3.13 for system abends. Figure 3.14 shows a job stream stored as member C5ONLY, which demonstrates how COND=ONLY works, for example, when a user abend instead of a system abend occurs at STEP040.

COND=ONLY will only execute a step after a system or user abend. But in some job streams, receiving a COND CODE greater than 4 may also mean that a serious error condition has arisen. COND=ONLY is not sufficient, by itself, to cause execution of a job step designed to flag or correct an error denoted by a COND CODE. To see how you can do this, look at section 3.15. In Chapter 8, I show you how to code EXEC statements to run a "cleanup" step that can delete files created during a run to facilitate one form of job stream recovery action.

3.14 Making a Step Execute After an Abend with IF ABEND

MVS/ESA Version 4 provides syntax much clearer than COND for the control of job stream execution. I showed you the IF/THEN/ELSE construct in Chapter 2, in connection with COND CODE testing. I'll now demonstrate how you can use IF/THEN/ELSE to make an ABEND test and control the execution of steps based on a prior abend in a positive way that is easier and more convenient to use than COND=EVEN or COND=ONLY.

```
EDIT ---- CSCJGJ.ADV.CNTL(C4ONLY) - 01.00 ------------------- COLUMNS 001 072
COMMAND ===>                                                  SCROLL ===> PAGE
****** ***************************** TOP OF DATA ******************************
000001 //CSCJGJA   JOB 1,                ACCOUNTING INFORMATION
000002 //  'BIN 7--JANOSSY',              PROGRAMMER NAME AND DELIVERY BIN
000003 //  CLASS=A,                      INPUT QUEUE CLASS
000004 //  MSGLEVEL=(1,1),               HOW MUCH MVS SYSTEM PRINT DESIRED
000005 //  MSGCLASS=X,                   PRINT DESTINATION X A L N OR O
000006 //  TIME=(0,6),                   SAFETY LIMIT: RUN TIME UP TO 6 SECS
000007 //  REGION=2M,                    ALLOW UP TO 2 MEGS VIRTUAL MEMORY
000008 //* TYPRUN=SCAN,                  UNCOMMENT THIS LINE TO DO SCAN ONLY
000009 //  NOTIFY=CSCJGJ                 WHO TO TELL WHEN JOB IS DONE
000010 //JOBLIB     DD  DSN=CSCJGJ.ADV.LOADLIB,DISP=SHR       PRIVATE LOAD LIB
000011 //           DD  DSN=SYS1.COB2LIB,DISP=SHR             COBOL II LOADLIB
000012 //*
000013 //* DEMONSTRATE HOW COND=ONLY WORKS
000014 //* THIS JCL IS STORED AT CSCJGJ.ADV.CNTL(C4ONLY)
000015 //*-------------------------------------------------------------------
000016 //STEP010  EXEC  PGM=ALPHA
000017 //*-------------------------------------------------------------------
000018 //STEP020  EXEC  PGM=BETA8
000019 //*-----------------------------------
000020 //STEP030  EXEC  PGM=GAMMA,COND=ONLY
000021 //*-----------------------------------
000022 //STEP040  EXEC  PGM=EXPLODE
000023 //*-----------------------------------
000024 //STEP050  EXEC  PGM=BETA4,COND=ONLY
000025 //*-----------------------------------
000026 //STEP060  EXEC  PGM=DELTA
000027 //
```

This step causes a system abend

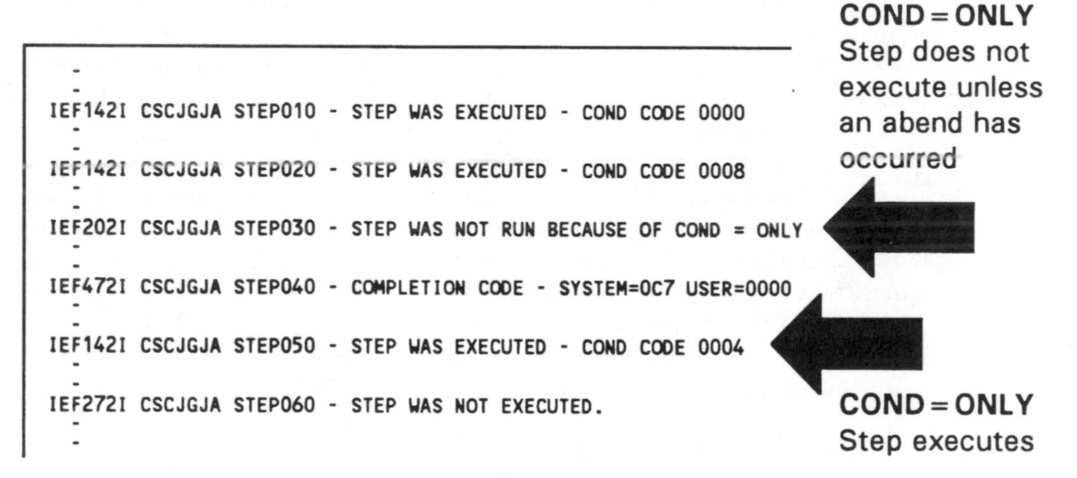

```
-
-
IEF142I CSCJGJA STEP010 - STEP WAS EXECUTED - COND CODE 0000
-
-
IEF142I CSCJGJA STEP020 - STEP WAS EXECUTED - COND CODE 0008
-
-
IEF202I CSCJGJA STEP030 - STEP WAS NOT RUN BECAUSE OF COND = ONLY
-
-
IEF472I CSCJGJA STEP040 - COMPLETION CODE - SYSTEM=0C7 USER=0000
-
-
IEF142I CSCJGJA STEP050 - STEP WAS EXECUTED - COND CODE 0004
-
-
IEF272I CSCJGJA STEP060 - STEP WAS NOT EXECUTED.
-
-
```

COND = ONLY
Step does not execute unless an abend has occurred
COND = ONLY
Step executes

Figure 3.13 JCL and Extracted MVS/ESA System Reporting for Job Stream C4ONLY, Demonstrating the Effect of COND=ONLY on Step Execution with a System Abend

Figure 3.15 shows you IF ABEND THEN coded (at its line 24), with syntax that is very straightforward:

```
//    IF ABEND THEN
//STEP050   EXEC   PGM=BETA4
//    ELSE
//STEP060   EXEC   PGM=DELTA8
//    ENDIF
```

```
EDIT ---- CSCJGJ.ADV.CNTL(C5ONLY) - 01.00 ------------------- COLUMNS 001 072
COMMAND ===>                                                  SCROLL ===> PAGE
****** ****************************** TOP OF DATA ******************************
000001 //CSCJGJA   JOB 1,                     ACCOUNTING INFORMATION
000002 //  'BIN 7--JANOSSY',                  PROGRAMMER NAME AND DELIVERY BIN
000003 //  CLASS=A,                           INPUT QUEUE CLASS
000004 //  MSGLEVEL=(1,1),                    HOW MUCH MVS SYSTEM PRINT DESIRED
000005 //  MSGCLASS=X,                        PRINT DESTINATION X A L N OR O
000006 //  TIME=(0,6),                        SAFETY LIMIT: RUN TIME UP TO 6 SECS
000007 //  REGION=2M,                         ALLOW UP TO 2 MEGS VIRTUAL MEMORY
000008 //* TYPRUN=SCAN,                       UNCOMMENT THIS LINE TO DO SCAN ONLY
000009 //  NOTIFY=CSCJGJ                      WHO TO TELL WHEN JOB IS DONE
000010 //JOBLIB    DD  DSN=CSCJGJ.ADV.LOADLIB,DISP=SHR      PRIVATE LOAD LIB
000011 //          DD  DSN=SYS1.COB2LIB,DISP=SHR            COBOL II LOADLIB
000012 //*
000013 //* DEMONSTRATE HOW COND=ONLY WORKS WITH A USER ABEND
000014 //* THIS JCL IS STORED AT CSCJGJ.ADV.CNTL(C5ONLY)
000015 //*-----------------------------------------------------------------
000016 //STEP010  EXEC  PGM=ALPHA
000017 //*-----------------------------------------------------------------
000018 //STEP020  EXEC  PGM=BETA8
000019 //*-----------------------------------
000020 //STEP030  EXEC  PGM=GAMMA,COND=ONLY
000021 //*-----------------------------------
000022 //STEP040  EXEC  PGM=USERABN,PARM=3756
000023 //*-----------------------------------
000024 //STEP050  EXEC  PGM=BETA4,COND=ONLY
000025 //*-----------------------------------
000026 //STEP060  EXEC  PGM=DELTA
000027 //
```

This step causes a user abend

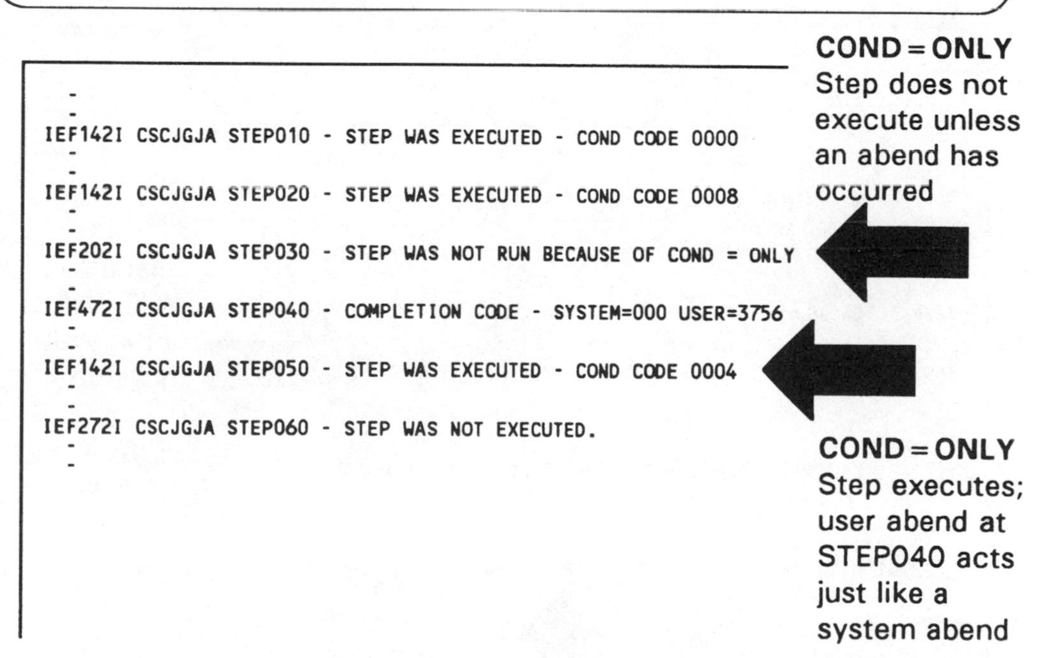

```
   -
   -
IEF142I CSCJGJA STEP010 - STEP WAS EXECUTED - COND CODE 0000
   -
   -
IEF142I CSCJGJA STEP020 - STEP WAS EXECUTED - COND CODE 0008
   -
   -
IEF202I CSCJGJA STEP030 - STEP WAS NOT RUN BECAUSE OF COND = ONLY
   -
   -
IEF472I CSCJGJA STEP040 - COMPLETION CODE - SYSTEM=000 USER=3756
   -
   -
IEF142I CSCJGJA STEP050 - STEP WAS EXECUTED - COND CODE 0004
   -
   -
IEF272I CSCJGJA STEP060 - STEP WAS NOT EXECUTED.
   -
   -
```

COND=ONLY
Step does not execute unless an abend has occurred
COND=ONLY
Step executes; user abend at STEP040 acts just like a system abend

Figure 3.14 JCL and Extracted MVS/ESA System Reporting for Job Stream C5ONLY, Demonstrating the Effect of COND=ONLY on Step Execution with a User Abend

STEP050 will be executed if a prior step has abended (the job stream is in abnormal termination mode), otherwise STEP060 will be executed. The extracted MVS/ESA system reporting at the bottom of Figure 3.15 confirms that this happens, since STEP030 executes the EXPLODE program and abends.

```
EDIT ---- CSCJGJ.ADV.CNTL(C6IFABN) - 01.00 ------------------ COLUMNS 001 072
COMMAND ===>                                                  SCROLL ===> PAGE
****** ****************************** TOP OF DATA *******************************
000001 //CSCJGJA   JOB 1,                    ACCOUNTING INFORMATION
000002 //  'BIN 7--JANOSSY',                  PROGRAMMER NAME AND DELIVERY BIN
000003 //  CLASS=A,                          INPUT QUEUE CLASS
000004 //  MSGLEVEL=(1,1),                   HOW MUCH MVS SYSTEM PRINT DESIRED
000005 //  MSGCLASS=X,                       PRINT DESTINATION X A L N OR O
000006 //  TIME=(0,6),                       SAFETY LIMIT: RUN TIME UP TO 6 SECS
000007 //  REGION=2M,                        ALLOW UP TO 2 MEGS VIRTUAL MEMORY
000008 //* TYPRUN=SCAN,                      UNCOMMENT THIS LINE TO DO SCAN ONLY
000009 //  NOTIFY=CSCJGJ                     WHO TO TELL WHEN JOB IS DONE
000010 //JOBLIB    DD  DSN=CSCJGJ.ADV.LOADLIB,DISP=SHR      PRIVATE LOAD LIB
000011 //          DD  DSN=SYS1.COB2LIB,DISP=SHR            COBOL II LOADLIB
000012 //*
000013 //* DEMONSTRATE HOW IF ABEND WORKS
000014 //* THIS JCL IS STORED AT CSCJGJ.ADV.CNTL(C6IFABN)
000015 //*-----------------------------------------------------------------
000016 //STEP010  EXEC  PGM=ALPHA
000017 //*-----------------------------------
000018 //STEP020  EXEC  PGM=BETA
000019 //*-----------------------------------
000020 //STEP030  EXEC  PGM=EXPLODE
000021 //*-----------------------------------
000022 //STEP040  EXEC  PGM=GAMMA
000023 //*-----------------------------------
000024 //   IF ABEND THEN
000025 //STEP050  EXEC  PGM=BETA4       true
000026 //   ELSE
000027 //STEP060  EXEC  PGM=DELTA8      false
000028 //   ENDIF
000029 //
```

This step causes a system abend

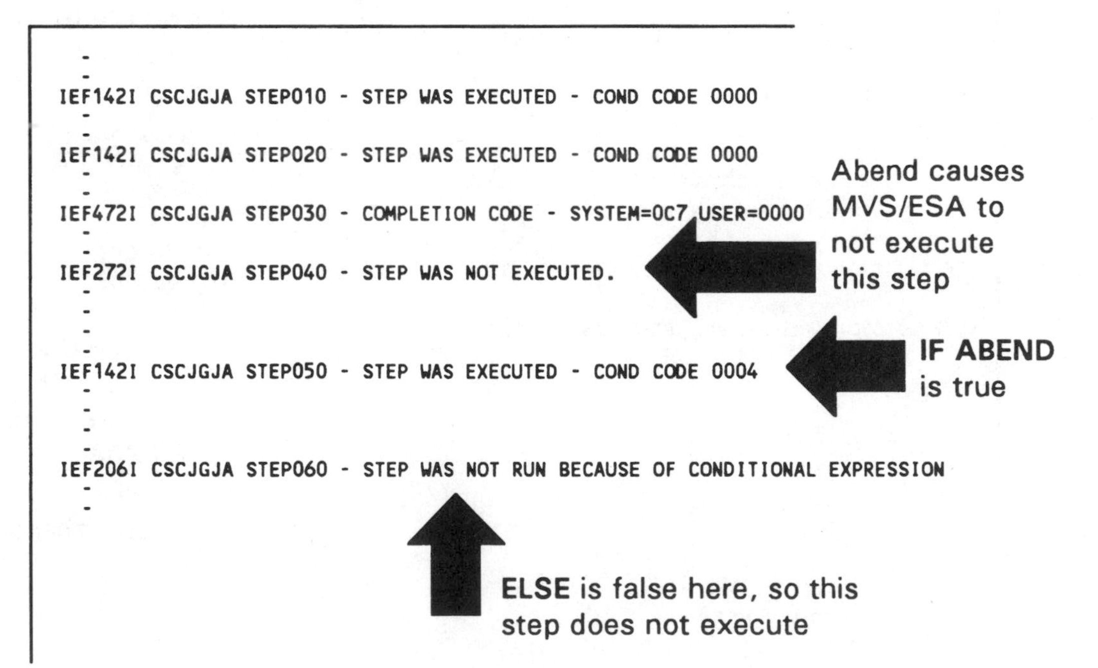

```
   -
   -
IEF142I CSCJGJA STEP010 - STEP WAS EXECUTED - COND CODE 0000
   -
IEF142I CSCJGJA STEP020 - STEP WAS EXECUTED - COND CODE 0000
   -
IEF472I CSCJGJA STEP030 - COMPLETION CODE - SYSTEM=0C7 USER=0000
   -
   -
IEF272I CSCJGJA STEP040 - STEP WAS NOT EXECUTED.
   -
   -
   -
   -
IEF142I CSCJGJA STEP050 - STEP WAS EXECUTED - COND CODE 0004
   -
   -
   -
   -
IEF206I CSCJGJA STEP060 - STEP WAS NOT RUN BECAUSE OF CONDITIONAL EXPRESSION
   -
   -
```

Abend causes MVS/ESA to not execute this step
IF ABEND is true
ELSE is false here, so this step does not execute

Figure 3.15 Simple Demonstration of IF ABEND Relational Test Coding and Its Effect

You can also negate the effect of the IF ABEND test by using the word NOT before ABEND. In the following example, STEP050 will execute if the job stream is in normal processing mode, and STEP060 will execute if the job stream is in abnormal termination mode:

```
//    IF NOT ABEND THEN
//STEP050   EXEC   PGM=BETA4
//    ELSE
//STEP060   EXEC   PGM=DELTA8
//    ENDIF
```

IF ABEND and IF NOT ABEND are the simplest but most useful forms of MVS/ESA Version 4 abend testing. I'll demonstrate how to use them to form a standard, productive model for job stream coding that lets you anticipate potential job stream failures and make any job failure highly conspicuous.

3.15 Using IF ABEND in Production Job Streams

Real-life job streams are designed to meet real-life processing requirements. Although specific program execution requirements vary from one production job stream to another, performance criteria such as these apply to most production job streams:

1. Job steps following an abended step or a step that returns a "problem" COND CODE should not be executed, to avoid time wasted on potentially flawed outputs.

2. A production job stream should make any problem or failure in its running highly visible, so that corrective action can be applied as soon as possible to achieve successful processing.

3. Depending on how an installation handles the recovery of a failed job stream, it may be desirable to automatically delete data sets created up to the point of failure, to expedite the process of rerunning the job. This is not desirable if a "step restart" is to be attempted to complete the work of the job stream, as discussed in Chapter 7.

You can address these criteria using IF ABEND coding in a standard pattern. The example of "problem anticipation" coding that follows demonstrates how to meet criteria 1 and 2. I'll extend the standard pattern to meet criteria 3 in Chapter 8.

Figure 3.16 shows you a job stream with seven steps. This job stream assumes that a step that has successfully executed will not have abended and will have returned a COND CODE less than or equal to 0004. As long as these conditions are met, subsequent steps can be executed. As soon as a step either abends or issues a COND CODE greater than 0004, execution of steps will stop (except for a flagging step), and the job stream will incur a user abend with a recognizable completion code, in this case 3333. This

```
EDIT ---- CSCJGJ.ADV.CNTL(C7REAL) - 01.03 -------------------- COLUMNS 001 072
COMMAND ===>                                                  SCROLL ===> PAGE
****** ******************************* TOP OF DATA ******************************
000001 //CSCJGJA   JOB 1,                  ACCOUNTING INFORMATION
000002 //  'BIN 7--JANOSSY',               PROGRAMMER NAME AND DELIVERY BIN
000003 //  CLASS=A,                        INPUT QUEUE CLASS
000004 //  MSGLEVEL=(1,1),                 HOW MUCH MVS SYSTEM PRINT DESIRED
000005 //  MSGCLASS=X,                     PRINT DESTINATION X A L N OR O
000006 //  TIME=(0,6),                     SAFETY LIMIT: RUN TIME UP TO 6 SECS
000007 //  REGION=2M,                      ALLOW UP TO 2 MEGS VIRTUAL MEMORY
000008 //* TYPRUN=SCAN,                    UNCOMMENT THIS LINE TO DO SCAN ONLY
000009 //  NOTIFY=CSCJGJ                   WHO TO TELL WHEN JOB IS DONE
000010 //JOBLIB     DD  DSN=CSCJGJ.ADV.LOADLIB,DISP=SHR      PRIVATE LOAD LIB
000011 //           DD  DSN=SYS1.COB2LIB,DISP=SHR            COBOL II LOADLIB
000012 //*
000013 //* DEMONSTRATE A SIMPLE JOB STREAM WITH PROBLEM ANTICIPATION
000014 //* THIS JCL IS STORED AT CSCJGJ.ADV.CNTL(C7REAL)
000015 //*-------------------------------------
000016 //STEP010  EXEC  PGM=ALPHA
000017 //*-------------------------------------
000018 //    IF ( NOT ABEND AND RC <= 4 ) THEN
000019 //STEP020  EXEC  PGM=BETA
000020 //    ENDIF
000021 //*-------------------------------------
000022 //    IF ( NOT ABEND AND RC <= 4 ) THEN
000023 //STEP030  EXEC  PGM=GAMMA4
000024 //    ENDIF
000025 //*-------------------------------------
000026 //    IF ( NOT ABEND AND RC <= 4 ) THEN
000027 //STEP040  EXEC  PGM=DELTA
000028 //    ENDIF
000029 //*-------------------------------------
000030 //    IF ( NOT ABEND AND RC <= 4 ) THEN
000031 //STEP050  EXEC  PGM=BETA
000032 //    ENDIF
000033 //*-------------------------------------
000034 //    IF ( NOT ABEND AND RC <= 4 ) THEN
000035 //STEP060  EXEC  PGM=DELTA
000036 //    ENDIF
000037 //*-------------------------------------
000038 //    IF ( ABEND OR RC > 4 ) THEN
000039 //STEP999  EXEC  PGM=USERABN,PARM=3333
000040 //    ENDIF
000041 //
```

Each step runs only if no prior step has abended or issued a COND CODE for a serious problem.

Final user abend step runs if any step has abended or returned a "problem" COND CODE.

```
  -
  -
IEF142I CSCJGJA STEP010 - STEP WAS EXECUTED - COND CODE 0000
  -
  -
IEF142I CSCJGJA STEP020 - STEP WAS EXECUTED - COND CODE 0000
  -
  -
IEF142I CSCJGJA STEP030 - STEP WAS EXECUTED - COND CODE 0004
  -
  -
IEF142I CSCJGJA STEP040 - STEP WAS EXECUTED - COND CODE 0000
  -
  -
IEF142I CSCJGJA STEP050 - STEP WAS EXECUTED - COND CODE 0000
  -
  -
IEF142I CSCJGJA STEP060 - STEP WAS EXECUTED - COND CODE 0000
  -
  -
IEF206I CSCJGJA STEP999 - STEP WAS NOT RUN BECAUSE OF CONDITIONAL EXPRESSION
  -
  -
```

0004 does not stop remaining steps

Final step does not run because no step abended or detected a serious problem

Figure 3.16 Job Stream C7REAL: How a Robust Job Stream Acts When No Errors Occurred During the Run

makes the job stream failure highly visible at the computer console and to anyone examining the MVS/ESA system reporting.

To meet my objectives for job stream problem anticipation, I coded this compound IF test before the second and all following job steps:

```
IF ( NOT ABEND AND RC <= 4 ) THEN
```

This states quite plainly, in a positive way, the conditions under which I want each step to be executed. In addition, I coded an attention-gaining "flagging" step STEP999 at the end of the job stream. This final step will, if executed, initiate a user abend with completion code 3333. The IF test before STEP999 is coded like this:

```
IF ( ABEND OR RC > 4 ) THEN
```

which also plainly states when I want the flagging step to be executed.

The bottom part of Figure 3.16 illustrates how this standard model for job stream control operates in a job stream stored as member C7REAL when no job step abends or issues a COND CODE greater than 4. Each step is executed, the final flagging step does not execute, and the outcome is normal.

Figure 3.17 shows you a job stream stored as member C8REAL. Here, you see how the standard model operates when a program issues a "problem" COND CODE (any code greater than 0004 is taken to represent a problem in job stream C8REAL). Since STEP040 issued COND CODE 0008, STEP050 and STEP060 did not execute. But attention-getting flagging step STEP999 executed and initiated a user abend. Figure 3.18 illustrates the first page of the MVS/ESA system output for this failed job. It would be hard to miss the fact that something has gone drastically wrong in this job. Attention could quickly be directed to determine the origin of the problem.

You see a job stream stored as member C9REAL in Figure 3.19. This job stream is identical to C7REAL and C8REAL, except that I have executed program EXPLODE at STEP030 to demonstrate handling of a system abend by this standard job stream model. STEP040, STEP050, and STEP060 do not execute, but once again the final flagging step does execute. The first page of the MVS/ESA system output in Figure 3.20 shows you how two step abends are now reported: the system abend, and the "flagging" user abend at STEP999. *Since it is individual steps that abend, and not job streams, it is possible to encounter more than one system or user completion code in a given job stream as you see here.*

The standard model for production job stream coding readily accommodates "cleanup" data set deletions in cases of job stream failure. You could accomplish data set deletions at STEP999 simply by coding appropriate DD statements or by coding additional EXECs within the scope of the final IF test. Those additional EXECs could invoke the IDCAMS utility, procs, or other utility programs used locally to handle data set deletions, as I illustrate in Chapter 8.

```
EDIT ---- CSCJGJ.ADV.CNTL(C8REAL) - 01.00 ------------------- COLUMNS 001 072
COMMAND ===> sub                                               SCROLL ===> PAGE
****** ***************************** TOP OF DATA ******************************
000001 //CSCJGJA   JOB 1,                  ACCOUNTING INFORMATION
000002 //  'BIN 7--JANOSSY',               PROGRAMMER NAME AND DELIVERY BIN
000003 //  CLASS=A,                        INPUT QUEUE CLASS
000004 //  MSGLEVEL=(1,1),                 HOW MUCH MVS SYSTEM PRINT DESIRED
000005 //  MSGCLASS=X,                     PRINT DESTINATION X A L N OR O
000006 //  TIME=(0,6),                     SAFETY LIMIT: RUN TIME UP TO 6 SECS
000007 //  REGION=2M,                      ALLOW UP TO 2 MEGS VIRTUAL MEMORY
000008 //* TYPRUN=SCAN,                    UNCOMMENT THIS LINE TO DO SCAN ONLY
000009 //  NOTIFY=CSCJGJ                   WHO TO TELL WHEN JOB IS DONE
000010 //JOBLIB     DD  DSN=CSCJGJ.ADV.LOADLIB,DISP=SHR       PRIVATE LOAD LIB
000011 //           DD  DSN=SYS1.COB2LIB,DISP=SHR             COBOL II LOADLIB
000012 //*
000013 //* DEMONSTRATE A SIMPLE JOB STREAM WITH PROBLEM ANTICIPATION
000014 //* THIS JCL IS STORED AT CSCJGJ.ADV.CNTL(C8REAL)
000015 //*-----------------------------------
000016 //STEP010  EXEC  PGM=ALPHA
000017 //*-----------------------------------
000018 //    IF ( NOT ABEND AND RC <= 4 ) THEN
000019 //STEP020  EXEC  PGM=BETA
000020 //    ENDIF
000021 //*-----------------------------------
000022 //    IF ( NOT ABEND AND RC <= 4 ) THEN
000023 //STEP030  EXEC  PGM=GAMMA4
000024 //    ENDIF
000025 //*-----------------------------------
000026 //    IF ( NOT ABEND AND RC <= 4 ) THEN
000027 //STEP040  EXEC  PGM=DELTA8
000028 //    ENDIF
000029 //*-----------------------------------
000030 //    IF ( NOT ABEND AND RC <= 4 ) THEN
000031 //STEP050  EXEC  PGM=BETA
000032 //    ENDIF
000033 //*-----------------------------------
000034 //    IF ( NOT ABEND AND RC <= 4 ) THEN
000035 //STEP060  EXEC  PGM=DELTA
000036 //    ENDIF
000037 //*-----------------------------------
000038 //    IF ( ABEND OR RC > 4 ) THEN
000039 //STEP999  EXEC  PGM=USERABN,PARM=3333
000040 //    ENDIF
000041 //

JOB CSCJGJA(JOB08220) SUBMITTED
11.12.39 JOB08220 $HASP165 CSCJGJA  ENDED AT N1 - ABENDED CN(INTERNAL)
***
```

Program DELTA8 sets COND CODE 0008

Final step executes and initiates user abend

```
 -
 -
IEF142I CSCJGJA STEP010 - STEP WAS EXECUTED - COND CODE 0000
 -
 -
IEF142I CSCJGJA STEP020 - STEP WAS EXECUTED - COND CODE 0000
 -
 -
IEF142I CSCJGJA STEP030 - STEP WAS EXECUTED - COND CODE 0004
 -
 -
IEF142I CSCJGJA STEP040 - STEP WAS EXECUTED - COND CODE 0008
 -
 -
IEF206I CSCJGJA STEP050 - STEP WAS NOT RUN BECAUSE OF CONDITIONAL EXPRESSION
 -
 -
IEF206I CSCJGJA STEP060 - STEP WAS NOT RUN BECAUSE OF CONDITIONAL EXPRESSION
 -
 -
IEF472I CSCJGJA STEP999 - COMPLETION CODE - SYSTEM=000 USER=3333
 -
 -
```

STEP050 and STEP060 are not allowed to run because of the "problem" COND CODE 0008

Final step executes and issues a user completion code that documentation could state signifies a particular type of problem for this run

Figure 3.17 Job Stream C8REAL: How a Robust Job Stream Acts When a COND CODE Error Occurred During the Run

```
                    J E S 2  J O B  L O G  --  S Y S T E M  I B M 1  --  N O D E  N 1

11.12.33 JOB08220  IRR010I  USERID CSCJGJ   IS ASSIGNED TO THIS JOB.
11.12.34 JOB08220  ICH70001I CSCJGJ   LAST ACCESS AT 11:11:39 ON FRIDAY, SEPTEMBER 3, 1993
11.12.34 JOB08220  $HASP373 CSCJGJA  STARTED - INIT  1 - CLASS A - SYS IBM1

11.12.39 JOB08220  IEA995I SYMPTOM DUMP OUTPUT
                     USER COMPLETION CODE=3333
                    TIME=11.12.38  SEQ=07398  CPU=
                    PSW AT TIME OF ERROR  078D1000   83600FFC  ILC 2  INTC OD
                      ACTIVE LOAD MODULE=ILBOABN     ADDRESS=03600F48  OFFSET=000000B4
                      DATA AT PSW  03600FF6 - 00181610  0A0D0000  0000****
                      GPR  0-3  80000000  80000D05  00005219  00006180
                      GPR  4-7  00006260  00048038  00048038  83600F4A
                      GPR  8-11 800165A0  00007A08  00047CC0  83600F4A
                      GPR 12-15 80016022  00047E80  8001659E  83600F5
                    END OF SYMPTOM DUMP
11.12.39 JOB08220  IEF450I CSCJGJA STEP999 - ABEND=S000 U3333

11.12.39 JOB08220  $HASP395 CSCJGJA  ENDED

------ JES2 JOB STATISTICS ------
    03 SEP 93 JOB EXECUTION DATE
           40 CARDS READ
          153 SYSOUT PRINT RECORDS
            0 SYSOUT PUNCH RECORDS
            9 SYSOUT SPOOL KBYTES
         0.08 MINUTES EXECUTION TIME

        1 //CSCJGJA   JOB 1,                  ACCOUNTING INFORMATION
          //   'BIN 7--JANOSSY',              PROGRAMMER NAME AND DELIVERY BIN
          //   CLASS=A,                       INPUT QUEUE CLASS
          //   MSGLEVEL=(1,1),                HOW MUCH MVS SYSTEM PRINT DESIRED
          //   MSGCLASS=X,                    PRINT DESTINATION X A L N OR O
          //   TIME=(0,6),                    SAFETY LIMIT: RUN TIME UP TO 6 SECS
          //   REGION=2M,                     ALLOW UP TO 2 MEGS VIRTUAL MEMORY
          //*  TYPRUN=SCAN,                   UNCOMMENT THIS LINE TO DO SCAN ONLY
          //   NOTIFY=CSCJGJ                  WHO TO TELL WHEN JOB IS DONE
        2 //JOBLIB      DD  DSN=CSCJGJ.ADV.LOADLIB,DISP=SHR        PRIVATE LOAD LIB
        3 //            DD  DSN=SYS1.COB2LIB,DISP=SHR              COBOL II LOADLIB
          //*
          //* DEMONSTRATE A SIMPLE JOB STREAM WITH PROBLEM ANTICIPATION
```

This is the first page of MVS/ESA system output for job stream C8REAL. STEP040 set COND CODE 0008, which would not have caused MVS/ESA to withhold execution of the following steps, and would not have provided conspicuous notice of job failure. By coding standard IF tests before each step, involving both NOT ABEND and a general RC test, you can shut off steps no matter which step encounters a "problem" COND CODE. By including a final step like STEP999, you can initiate a user abend for a situation like this, providing a very visible user completion code that requires immediate attention.

Figure 3.18 First Page of MVS/ESA System Reporting for the C8REAL Job Stream

```
EDIT ---- CSCJGJ.ADV.CNTL(C9REAL) - 01.00 -------------------- COLUMNS 001 072
COMMAND ===> sub                                               SCROLL ===> PAGE
****** ***************************** TOP OF DATA ******************************
000001 //CSCJGJA   JOB 1,                    ACCOUNTING INFORMATION
000002 //  'BIN 7--JANOSSY',                 PROGRAMMER NAME AND DELIVERY BIN
000003 //  CLASS=A,                          INPUT QUEUE CLASS
000004 //  MSGLEVEL=(1,1),                   HOW MUCH MVS SYSTEM PRINT DESIRED
000005 //  MSGCLASS=X,                       PRINT DESTINATION X A L N OR O
000006 //  TIME=(0,6),                       SAFETY LIMIT: RUN TIME UP TO 6 SECS
000007 //  REGION=2M,                        ALLOW UP TO 2 MEGS VIRTUAL MEMORY
000008 //* TYPRUN=SCAN,                      UNCOMMENT THIS LINE TO DO SCAN ONLY
000009 //  NOTIFY=CSCJGJ                     WHO TO TELL WHEN JOB IS DONE
000010 //JOBLIB     DD  DSN=CSCJGJ.ADV.LOADLIB,DISP=SHR      PRIVATE LOAD LIB
000011 //           DD  DSN=SYS1.COB2LIB,DISP=SHR            COBOL II LOADLIB
000012 //*
000013 //* DEMONSTRATE A SIMPLE JOB STREAM WITH PROBLEM ANTICIPATION
000014 //* THIS JCL IS STORED AT CSCJGJ.ADV.CNTL(C9REAL)
000015 //*-----------------------------------
000016 //STEP010  EXEC  PGM=ALPHA
000017 //*-----------------------------------
000018 //    IF ( NOT ABEND AND RC <= 4 ) THEN
000019 //STEP020  EXEC  PGM=BETA
000020 //    ENDIF
000021 //*-----------------------------------
000022 //    IF ( NOT ABEND AND RC <= 4 ) THEN
000023 //STEP030  EXEC  PGM=EXPLODE
000024 //    ENDIF
000025 //*-----------------------------------
000026 //    IF ( NOT ABEND AND RC <= 4 ) THEN
000027 //STEP040  EXEC  PGM=DELTA
000028 //    ENDIF
000029 //*-----------------------------------
000030 //    IF ( NOT ABEND AND RC <= 4 ) THEN
000031 //STEP050  EXEC  PGM=BETA
000032 //    ENDIF
000033 //*-----------------------------------
000034 //    IF ( NOT ABEND AND RC <= 4 ) THEN
000035 //STEP060  EXEC  PGM=DELTA
000036 //    ENDIF
000037 //*-----------------------------------
000038 //    IF ( ABEND OR RC > 4 ) THEN
000039 //STEP999  EXEC  PGM=USERABN,PARM=3333
000040 //    ENDIF
000041 //

JOB CSCJGJA(JOB08222) SUBMITTED
11.16.10 JOB08222 $HASP165 CSCJGJA  ENDED AT N1 - ABENDED CN(INTERNAL)
***
```

This step blows up and causes a **system abend**

Final step executes and also initiates **user abend**

```
 -
 -
IEF142I CSCJGJA STEP010 - STEP WAS EXECUTED - COND CODE 0000
 -
 -
IEF142I CSCJGJA STEP020 - STEP WAS EXECUTED - COND CODE 0000
 -
 -
IEF472I CSCJGJA STEP030 - COMPLETION CODE - SYSTEM=0C7 USER=0000
 -
 -
IEF206I CSCJGJA STEP040 - STEP WAS NOT RUN BECAUSE OF CONDITIONAL EXPRESSION
 -
 -
IEF206I CSCJGJA STEP050 - STEP WAS NOT RUN BECAUSE OF CONDITIONAL EXPRESSION
 -
 -
IEF206I CSCJGJA STEP060 - STEP WAS NOT RUN BECAUSE OF CONDITIONAL EXPRESSION
 -
 -
IEF472I CSCJGJA STEP999 - COMPLETION CODE - SYSTEM=000 USER=3333
 -
 -
```

Steps after the abend do not run

Final step executes and issues a user completion code. This is a consistent indicator that the job encountered a problem.

Figure 3.19 Job Stream C9REAL: How a Robust Job Stream Acts When a System Abend Occurred During the Run

```
                      J E S 2   J O B   L O G  --  S Y S T E M   I B M 1  --  N O D E  N 1

11.16.06 JOB08222  IRR010I  USERID CSCJGJ    IS ASSIGNED TO THIS JOB.
11.16.06 JOB08222  ICH70001I CSCJGJ    LAST ACCESS AT 11:15:46 ON FRIDAY, SEPTEMBER 3, 1993
11.16.06 JOB08222  $HASP373 CSCJGJA  STARTED - INIT  1 - CLASS A - SYS IBM1

11.16.09 JOB08222  IEA995I SYMPTOM DUMP OUTPUT
                   SYSTEM COMPLETION CODE=0C7
                    TIME=11.16.08  SEQ=07406  CPU=0000  ASID=000F
                    PSW AT TIME OF ERROR  078D1000   8000649A  ILC 6  INTC 07
                      ACTIVE LOAD MODULE=EXPLODE    ADDRESS=00006310  OFFSET=0000018A
                      DATA AT PSW  00006494 - FA20D180  A01CF342  9000D180
                      GPR  0-3  80007E0A  00046CF4  00007BA8  00006484
                      GPR  4-7  00006364  00000000  008CEFF8  FD000000
                      GPR  8-11 80006114  00007BA0  00006398  00006408
                      GPR 12-15 00006390  00007A18  00006438  0000000
                    END OF SYMPTOM DUMP
11.16.09 JOB08222  IEF450I CSCJGJA STEP030 - ABEND=S0C7 U0000

11.16.10 JOB08222  IEA995I SYMPTOM DUMP OUTPUT
                    USER COMPLETION CODE=3333
                    TIME=11.16.09  SEQ=07409  CPU=0000  ASID=000F
                    PSW AT TIME OF ERROR  078D1000   83600FFC  ILC 2  INTC 0D
                      ACTIVE LOAD MODULE=ILBOABN    ADDRESS=03600F48  OFFSET=000000B4
                      DATA AT PSW  03600FF6 - 00181610  0A0D0000  0000****
                      GPR  0-3  80000000  80000D05  00005219  00006180
                      GPR  4-7  00006260  00048038  00048038  83600F4A
                      GPR  8-11 800165A0  00007A08  00047CC0  83600F4A
                      GPR 12-15 80016022  00047E80  8001659E  83600F5
                    END OF SYMPTOM DUMP
11.16.10 JOB08222  IEF450I CSCJGJA STEP999 - ABEND=S000 U3333

11.16.10 JOB08222  $HASP395 CSCJGJA  ENDED

------ JES2 JOB STATISTICS ------
   03 SEP 93 JOB EXECUTION DATE
          40 CARDS READ
         182 SYSOUT PRINT RECORDS
           0 SYSOUT PUNCH RECORDS
          11 SYSOUT SPOOL KBYTES
        0.07 MINUTES EXECUTION TIME
```

MVS/ESA system output for job stream C9REAL. STEP030 of this job stream invoked program EXPLODE, which abended with a system completion code of 0C7. The general purpose "IF ABEND and RC" model followed in the job stream leads to *two abends* in cases of a system abend. The first abend is the exceptional case, such as 0C7 here. The second abend is the "flagging" final step STEP999, which invokes a user abend for any run of this job stream that fails.

Figure 3.20 First Page of MVS/ESA System Reporting for the C9REAL Job Stream

3.16 Testing a Prior Step to See If It Executed (IF RUN)

You can code an IF/THEN/ELSE test to determine if a prior step has run. Look at the job stream stored as member C10RUN, illustrated in Figure 3.21. Its STEP030 does not execute, because of the IF test based on the COND CODE of STEP010 coded before it. At line 26, I make this second IF test:

```
EDIT ---- CSCJGJ.ADV.CNTL(C10RUN) - 01.01 -------------------- COLUMNS 001 072
COMMAND ===>                                                   SCROLL ===> PAGE
****** ****************************** TOP OF DATA ******************************
000001 //CSCJGJA   JOB 1,                   ACCOUNTING INFORMATION
000002 //   'BIN 7--JANOSSY',               PROGRAMMER NAME AND DELIVERY BIN
000003 //   CLASS=A,                        INPUT QUEUE CLASS
000004 //   MSGLEVEL=(1,1),                 HOW MUCH MVS SYSTEM PRINT DESIRED
000005 //   MSGCLASS=X,                     PRINT DESTINATION X A L N OR O
000006 //   TIME=(0,6),                     SAFETY LIMIT: RUN TIME UP TO 6 SECS
000007 //   REGION=2M,                      ALLOW UP TO 2 MEGS VIRTUAL MEMORY
000008 //*  TYPRUN=SCAN,                    UNCOMMENT THIS LINE TO DO SCAN ONLY
000009 //   NOTIFY=CSCJGJ                   WHO TO TELL WHEN JOB IS DONE
000010 //JOBLIB     DD  DSN=CSCJGJ.ADV.LOADLIB,DISP=SHR     PRIVATE LOAD LIB
000011 //           DD  DSN=SYS1.COB2LIB,DISP=SHR           COBOL II LOADLIB
000012 //*
000013 //* DEMONSTRATE IF/ELSE WITH RUN TESTING
000014 //* THIS JCL IS STORED AT CSCJGJ.ADV.CNTL(C10RUN)
000015 //*-----------------------------------
000016 //STEP010  EXEC  PGM=ALPHA
000017 //*-----------------------------------
000018 //STEP020  EXEC  PGM=ALPHA8
000019 //*-----------------------------------
000020 //     IF ( STEP010.RC > 0 ) THEN
000021 //STEP030  EXEC  PGM=BETA
000022 //     ELSE
000023 //STEP040  EXEC  PGM=BETA4
000024 //     ENDIF
000025 //*-----------------------------------
000026 //     IF STEP030.RUN THEN
000027 //STEP050  EXEC  PGM=GAMMA
000028 //     ELSE
000029 //STEP060  EXEC  PGM=GAMMA4
000030 //     ENDIF
000031 //
```

STEP010 sets COND CODE 0000 so this test proves false. STEP030 is not run.

STEP060 executes since the RUN test proves false

```
  -
  -
IEF142I CSCJGJA STEP010 - STEP WAS EXECUTED - COND CODE 0000
  -
  -
IEF142I CSCJGJA STEP020 - STEP WAS EXECUTED - COND CODE 0008
  -
  -
IEF206I CSCJGJA STEP030 - STEP WAS NOT RUN BECAUSE OF CONDITIONAL EXPRESSION
  -
  -
IEF142I CSCJGJA STEP040 - STEP WAS EXECUTED - COND CODE 0004
  -
  -
IEF206I CSCJGJA STEP050 - STEP WAS NOT RUN BECAUSE OF CONDITIONAL EXPRESSION
  -
  -
IEF142I CSCJGJA STEP060 - STEP WAS EXECUTED - COND CODE 0004
  -
  -
  -
```

Figure 3.21 Job Stream C10RUN: How to Test to See If a Step Has Received Control to Run

```
//    IF STEP030.RUN THEN
//STEP050   EXEC PGM=GAMMA
//    ELSE
//STEP060   EXEC PGM=GAMMA4
//    ENDIF
//
```

When you test the run status in this way, you are really testing to see if the step you have named in the test received control from MVS to execute, not whether the step ran successfully (more about this in Figure 3.24!). You can only test the run status of a specific prior step. That is, you can't test to see if any prior step ran by coding just the word RUN, as you can with ABEND. A "generic" RUN test would be meaningless because it would always be true; your first step always receives control from MVS/ESA to execute.

Testing for the run status of a step that may have abended may seem like a potentially useful action. But an IF STEPxxx.RUN test alone is not a viable way to determine if a step started to run and abended. I make such a test in the example job stream stored as member C11RUN in Figure 3.22. Notice that all of the steps following the abend, including the steps involved in the IF STEPxxx.RUN test, are acknowledged but not given execution consideration by MVS/ESA in abend termination mode. My IF STEP010.RUN test is ignored. Negating the run test by coding IF NOT STEPxxx.RUN, as shown in a job stream stored as member C12RUN in Figure 3.23, is similarly meaningless.

Does a step that begins execution but abends make a RUN test true or false? Examine job stream C13RUN in Figure 3.24. In this example I test for both ABEND and STEPxxx.RUN before STEP050, giving STEP050 or STEP060 the chance to execute based on the truth value of the RUN test:

```
//     IF ( ABEND AND STEP020.RUN ) THEN
//STEP050   EXEC   PGM=GAMMA
//     ELSE
//STEP060   EXEC   PGM=GAMMA4
//     ENDIF
```

As you can see from the bottom of Figure 3.24, STEP050 executes, even though the program at STEP020 (EXPLODE) abended. *To MVS/ESA, "run" is true if a program received control from MVS to execute. You cannot depend on "run" being true to mean that a program ran successfully.*

3.17 Nonnested ABEND Coding Variations

I used simple and direct ABEND coding in the model for robust job stream design illustrated in section 3.15. But MVS/ESA Version 4 provides alternative codings for abend tests in addition to IF ABEND. I included these alternatives in the summary chart in Figure 2.8. Yet I find these alternative forms less straightforward or simply more wordy, and for these reasons I have given them less attention here at the end of Chapter 3. You should be aware

```
EDIT ---- CSCJGJ.ADV.CNTL(C11RUN) - 01.00 -------------------- COLUMNS 001 072
COMMAND ===>                                                  SCROLL ===> PAGE
****** ***************************** TOP OF DATA ******************************
000001 //CSCJGJA   JOB 1,                    ACCOUNTING INFORMATION
000002 //  'BIN 7--JANOSSY',                 PROGRAMMER NAME AND DELIVERY BIN
000003 //  CLASS=A,                          INPUT QUEUE CLASS
000004 //  MSGLEVEL=(1,1),                   HOW MUCH MVS SYSTEM PRINT DESIRED
000005 //  MSGCLASS=X,                       PRINT DESTINATION X A L N OR O
000006 //  TIME=(0,6),                       SAFETY LIMIT: RUN TIME UP TO 6 SECS
000007 //  REGION=2M,                        ALLOW UP TO 2 MEGS VIRTUAL MEMORY
000008 //* TYPRUN=SCAN,                      UNCOMMENT THIS LINE TO DO SCAN ONLY
000009 //  NOTIFY=CSCJGJ                     WHO TO TELL WHEN JOB IS DONE
000010 //JOBLIB     DD  DSN=CSCJGJ.ADV.LOADLIB,DISP=SHR      PRIVATE LOAD LIB
000011 //           DD  DSN=SYS1.COB2LIB,DISP=SHR           COBOL II LOADLIB
000012 //*
000013 //* DEMONSTRATE IF/ELSE WITH RUN TESTING
000014 //* THIS JCL IS STORED AT CSCJGJ.ADV.CNTL
000015 //*-------------------------------------
000016 //STEP010  EXEC  PGM=ALPHA
000017 //*-------------------------------------
000018 //STEP020  EXEC  PGM=EXPLODE
000019 //*-------------------------------------
000020 //STEP030  EXEC  PGM=BETA
000021 //*-------------------------------------
000022 //STEP040  EXEC  PGM=BETA4
000023 //*-------------------------------------
000024 //     IF STEP020.RUN THEN
000025 //STEP050  EXEC  PGM=GAMMA
000026 //     ELSE
000027 //STEP060  EXEC  PGM=GAMMA4
000028 //     ENDIF
000029 //
```

This step incurs a system abend, which puts the job stream into abnormal termination mode. All of the following steps are acknowledged but not processed.

```
   -
   -
IEF142I CSCJGJA STEP010 - STEP WAS EXECUTED - COND CODE 0000
   -
   -
IEF472I CSCJGJA STEP020 - COMPLETION CODE - SYSTEM=0C7 USER=0000
   -
   -
IEF272I CSCJGJA STEP030 - STEP WAS NOT EXECUTED.
   -
   -
IEF272I CSCJGJA STEP040 - STEP WAS NOT EXECUTED.
   -
   -
IEF272I CSCJGJA STEP050 - STEP WAS NOT EXECUTED.
   -
   -
IEF272I CSCJGJA STEP060 - STEP WAS NOT EXECUTED.
   -
   -
```

Neither STEP050 or STEP060 is run due to the abend; the RUN test based on STEP020 is ignored.

Figure 3.22 Job Stream C11RUN: RUN Tests Are Ignored When a Job Enters Abnormal Termination Mode

that these alternative forms of the IF test are supported by MVS/ESA Version 4, but you will probably find them of limited usefulness.

You can code a general abend test in the following alternative form. This syntax involves more keystrokes than simply coding IF ABEND, and does not really introduce additional clarity, so I don't see much to recommend it:

```
EDIT ---- CSCJGJ.ADV.CNTL(C12RUN) - 01.00 -------------------- COLUMNS 001 072
COMMAND ===>                                                   SCROLL ===> PAGE
****** ****************************** TOP OF DATA ******************************
000001 //CSCJGJA   JOB 1,                  ACCOUNTING INFORMATION
000002 //  'BIN 7--JANOSSY',               PROGRAMMER NAME AND DELIVERY BIN
000003 //  CLASS=A,                        INPUT QUEUE CLASS
000004 //  MSGLEVEL=(1,1),                 HOW MUCH MVS SYSTEM PRINT DESIRED
000005 //  MSGCLASS=X,                     PRINT DESTINATION X A L N OR O
000006 //  TIME=(0,6),                     SAFETY LIMIT: RUN TIME UP TO 6 SECS
000007 //  REGION=2M,                      ALLOW UP TO 2 MEGS VIRTUAL MEMORY
000008 //* TYPRUN=SCAN,                    UNCOMMENT THIS LINE TO DO SCAN ONLY
000009 //  NOTIFY=CSCJGJ                   WHO TO TELL WHEN JOB IS DONE
000010 //JOBLIB      DD  DSN=CSCJGJ.ADV.LOADLIB,DISP=SHR      PRIVATE LOAD LIB
000011 //            DD  DSN=SYS1.COB2LIB,DISP=SHR            COBOL II LOADLIB
000012 //*
000013 //* EXPERIMENT WITH RUN CODING AFTER AN ABEND
000014 //* THIS JCL IS STORED AT CSCJGJ.ADV.CNTL(C12RUN)
000015 //*-----------------------------------------
000016 //STEP010  EXEC  PGM=ALPHA
000017 //*-----------------------------------------
000018 //STEP020  EXEC  PGM=EXPLODE
000019 //*-----------------------------------------
000020 //STEP030  EXEC  PGM=BETA
000021 //*-----------------------------------------
000022 //STEP040  EXEC  PGM=BETA4
000023 //*-----------------------------------------
000024 //     IF NOT STEP020.RUN THEN
000025 //STEP050  EXEC  PGM=GAMMA
000026 //     ELSE
000027 //STEP060  EXEC  PGM=GAMMA4
000028 //     ENDIF
000029 //
```

System abend

NOT STEP020.RUN has no effect because steps are not processed after an abend

```
  -
  -
IEF142I CSCJGJA STEP010 - STEP WAS EXECUTED - COND CODE 0000
  -
  -
IEF472I CSCJGJA STEP020 - COMPLETION CODE - SYSTEM=0C7 USER=0000
  -
  -
IEF272I CSCJGJA STEP030 - STEP WAS NOT EXECUTED.
  -
  -
IEF272I CSCJGJA STEP040 - STEP WAS NOT EXECUTED.
  -
  -
IEF272I CSCJGJA STEP050 - STEP WAS NOT EXECUTED.
  -
  -
IEF272I CSCJGJA STEP060 - STEP WAS NOT EXECUTED.
  -
  -
```

None of these steps are processed

Figure 3.23 Job Stream C12RUN: NOT RUN Tests Are Ignored When a Job Enters Abnormal Termination Mode

```
//     IF ( ABEND = TRUE ) THEN
//STEP050   EXEC   PGM=BETA4
//     ELSE
//STEP060   EXEC   PGM=DELTA8
//     ENDIF
```

```
EDIT ---- CSCJGJ.ADV.CNTL(C13RUN) - 01.00 ------------------- COLUMNS 001 072
COMMAND ===>                                                  SCROLL ===> PAGE
****** ****************************** TOP OF DATA ******************************
000001 //CSCJGJA   JOB 1,                       ACCOUNTING INFORMATION
000002 //  'BIN 7--JANOSSY',                    PROGRAMMER NAME AND DELIVERY BIN
000003 //  CLASS=A,                             INPUT QUEUE CLASS
000004 //  MSGLEVEL=(1,1),                      HOW MUCH MVS SYSTEM PRINT DESIRED
000005 //  MSGCLASS=X,                          PRINT DESTINATION X A L N OR O
000006 //  TIME=(0,6),                          SAFETY LIMIT: RUN TIME UP TO 6 SECS
000007 //  REGION=2M,                           ALLOW UP TO 2 MEGS VIRTUAL MEMORY
000008 //* TYPRUN=SCAN,                         UNCOMMENT THIS LINE TO DO SCAN ONLY
000009 //  NOTIFY=CSCJGJ                        WHO TO TELL WHEN JOB IS DONE
000010 //JOBLIB   DD  DSN=CSCJGJ.ADV.LOADLIB,DISP=SHR       PRIVATE LOAD LIB
000011 //         DD  DSN=SYS1.COB2LIB,DISP=SHR             COBOL II LOADLIB
000012 //*
000013 //* EXPERIMENT WITH RUN CODING AFTER AN ABEND
000014 //* THIS JCL IS STORED AT CSCJGJ.ADV.CNTL(C13RUN)
000015 //*-----------------------------------------
000016 //STEP010  EXEC  PGM=ALPHA
000017 //*-----------------------------------------
000018 //STEP020  EXEC  PGM=EXPLODE
000019 //*-----------------------------------------
000020 //STEP030  EXEC  PGM=BETA
000021 //*-----------------------------------------
000022 //STEP040  EXEC  PGM=BETA4
000023 //*-----------------------------------------
000024 //    IF ( ABEND AND STEP020.RUN ) THEN
000025 //STEP050  EXEC  PGM=GAMMA
000026 //    ELSE
000027 //STEP060  EXEC  PGM=GAMMA4
000028 //    ENDIF
000029 //
```

Abend
ABEND with RUN allows processing even after an abend. *STEP050 executes because STEP020 started running.*

```
 -
 -
IEF142I CSCJGJA STEP010 - STEP WAS EXECUTED - COND CODE 0000
 -
 -
IEF472I CSCJGJA STEP020 - COMPLETION CODE - SYSTEM=0C7 USER=0000
 -
 -
IEF272I CSCJGJA STEP030 - STEP WAS NOT EXECUTED.
 -
 -
IEF272I CSCJGJA STEP040 - STEP WAS NOT EXECUTED.
 -
 -
IEF142I CSCJGJA STEP050 - STEP WAS EXECUTED - COND CODE 0000
 -
 -
IEF206I CSCJGJA STEP060 - STEP WAS NOT RUN BECAUSE OF CONDITIONAL EXPRESSION
 -
 -
```

STEP050 processed because both the **ABEND** and **RUN** tests were true

Figure 3.24 Job Stream C13RUN: A Step That Has Started Execution But Abends Is Considered to Have "RUN"

You can also reverse an abend test using the word FALSE instead of TRUE:

```
//   IF  ( ABEND = FALSE ) THEN
//STEP050   EXEC   PGM=BETA4
//   ELSE
//STEP060  EXEC  PGM=DELTA8
//   ENDIF
```

When you code IF ABEND without reference to a specific step, as I have done above, it applies to all prior steps. If any prior step has abended, an IF ABEND test produces a result of "true." You can limit an ABEND test to just a single step by coding IF stepname.ABEND, as in this example:

```
//   IF STEP040.ABEND THEN
//STEP050 EXEC PGM=BETA4
//   ELSE
//STEP060 EXEC PGM=DELTA8
//   ENDIF
```

or

```
//   IF STEP040.ABEND = TRUE THEN
//STEP050 EXEC PGM=BETA4
//   ELSE
//STEP060 EXEC PGM=DELTA8
//   ENDIF
```

You can also make ABEND testing specific to a particular user completion code or system completion code. To do this, you code ABENDCC=Sxxx or ABENDCC=Unnnn. I find the use of "CC" in this syntax confusing, because it's very easy to get the impression that CC stands for COND CODE; CC actually stands for "completion code." This JCL tests for a system completion code of 0C7 in any prior step:

```
//   IF ABENDCC=S0C7 THEN
//STEP050 EXEC PGM=BETA4
//   ELSE
//STEP060 EXEC PGM=DELTA8
//   ENDIF
```

This tests for a user completion code of 1234 in any prior step:

```
//   IF ABENDCC=U1234 THEN
//STEP050 EXEC PGM=BETA4
//   ELSE
//STEP060 EXEC PGM=DELTA8
//   ENDIF
```

You can make an abend test specific to both step *and* system or user completion code. You may find user abend testing like this of limited use:

```
//   IF STEP040.ABENDCC=S0C7 THEN
//STEP050 EXEC PGM=BETA4
//   ELSE
//STEP060 EXEC PGM=DELTA8
//   ENDIF
```

or

```
//   IF STEP040.ABENDCC=U1234 THEN
//STEP050 EXEC PGM=BETA4
//   ELSE
//STEP060 EXEC PGM=DELTA8
//   ENDIF
```

Finally, you can make any of these forms of coding apply to a a step within a proc that you are executing by coding the abend test as:

```
//STEP020 IF stepname.procstepname.ABENDCC=Sxxx THEN
```

or

```
//STEP020 IF stepname.procstepname.ABENDCC=Unnnn THEN
```

where *stepname* is the name of a prior step in the job stream, and *procstepname* is a name of a step within the proc executed at the prior step. Notice that you do not code the name of the proc itself in this form of the IF/THEN test, and that a separate naming convention for proc steps and job stream steps is vital for clarity.

3.18 Nested IF/THEN/ELSE Coding

You can nest IF/THEN/ELSE tests up to 15 levels deep. This means that you can imbed an IF/THEN/ELSE/ENDIF structure within an IF/THEN/ELSE/ENDIF. Frankly, I see little practical use for this capability, and a great deal of potential for it to cause confusion and illegibility. I constructed the example job stream stored as member C14NEST, shown in Figure 3.25, to demonstrate how nested IF tests work. I suggest that you examine the extracted MVS/ESA system reporting at the bottom of Figure 3.25 to see if you can readily understand why the steps that executed did so. The output is correct, but confirming this will give you an appreciation of the obfuscatory power of nested IF tests in MVS/ESA JCL.

If you think you have found a purpose to be served by nested IF coding in your JCL, reconsider what you are trying to accomplish in the job stream. You may be trying to do too much in one job stream or proc. Try grouping your program executions into separate procs to be invoked from a main proc, much like controlling detailed logical functions from a mainline in a program. This is possible with MVS/ESA Version 4, since it supports nested proc execution, as I demonstrate in Chapter 5. If you still think you need to use nested IF tests in your JCL, consider the following suggestions for their coding:

- Indent IF, ELSE, and ENDIF in a consistent way to show your intended nesting.
- Include same-line vertical comment bars as I have shown in Figure 3.25,

```
EDIT ---- CSCJGJ.ADV.CNTL(C14NEST) - 01.03 ------------------ COLUMNS 001 072
COMMAND ===>                                                  SCROLL ===> PAGE
****** ****************************** TOP OF DATA ******************************
000001 //CSCJGJA   JOB 1,                    ACCOUNTING INFORMATION
000002 //   'BIN 7--JANOSSY',                PROGRAMMER NAME AND DELIVERY BIN
000003 //   CLASS=A,                         INPUT QUEUE CLASS
000004 //   MSGLEVEL=(1,1),                  HOW MUCH MVS SYSTEM PRINT DESIRED
000005 //   MSGCLASS=X,                      PRINT DESTINATION X A L N OR O
000006 //   TIME=(0,6),                      SAFETY LIMIT: RUN TIME UP TO 6 SECS
000007 //   REGION=2M,                       ALLOW UP TO 2 MEGS VIRTUAL MEMORY
000008 //*  TYPRUN=SCAN,                     UNCOMMENT THIS LINE TO DO SCAN ONLY
000009 //   NOTIFY=CSCJGJ                    WHO TO TELL WHEN JOB IS DONE
000010 //JOBLIB     DD  DSN=CSCJGJ.ADV.LOADLIB,DISP=SHR      PRIVATE LOAD LIB
000011 //           DD  DSN=SYS1.COB2LIB,DISP=SHR            COBOL II LOADLIB
000012 //*
000013 //* DEMONSTRATE NESTED IF/ELSE
000014 //* THIS JCL IS STORED AT CSCJGJ.ADV.CNTL
000015 //*-----------------------------------
000016 //STEP010  EXEC  PGM=ALPHA
000017 //*-----------------------------------
000018 //STEP020  EXEC  PGM=ALPHA4
000019 //*-----------------------------------
000020 //STEP030  EXEC  PGM=ALPHA
000021 //*-----------------------------------
000022 //     IF ( STEP020.RC > 0 ) THEN        X
000023 //STEP040  EXEC  PGM=IEFBR14             !
000024 //STEP050  EXEC  PGM=IEFBR14             !
000025 //        IF ( STEP030.RC > 0 ) THEN X    !
000026 //STEP060  EXEC  PGM=IEFBR14        !    !
000027 //        ELSE                       !    !
000028 //STEP070  EXEC  PGM=IEFBR14        !    !
000029 //        ENDIF                      X    !
000030 //     ELSE                               !
000031 //STEP080  EXEC  PGM=IEFBR14             !
000032 //STEP090  EXEC  PGM=IEFBR14             !
000033 //     ENDIF                              X
000034 //
```

You can nest IF tests up to 15 levels deep. But even one nested level is difficult to interpret! Here is JCL I submitted and its ES/9000 system output. Confirm for yourself why these steps executed before you try to use nested IFs in your MVS/ESA Version 4 JCL!

```
   -
   -
IEF142I CSCJGJA STEP010 - STEP WAS EXECUTED - COND CODE 0000
   -
   -
IEF142I CSCJGJA STEP020 - STEP WAS EXECUTED - COND CODE 0004
   -
   -
IEF142I CSCJGJA STEP030 - STEP WAS EXECUTED - COND CODE 0000
   -
   -
IEF142I CSCJGJA STEP040 - STEP WAS EXECUTED - COND CODE 0000
   -
   -
IEF142I CSCJGJA STEP050 - STEP WAS EXECUTED - COND CODE 0000
   -
   -
IEF206I CSCJGJA STEP060 - STEP WAS NOT RUN BECAUSE OF CONDITIONAL EXPRESSION
   -
   -
IEF142I CSCJGJA STEP070 - STEP WAS EXECUTED - COND CODE 0000
   -
   -
IEF206I CSCJGJA STEP080 - STEP WAS NOT RUN BECAUSE OF CONDITIONAL EXPRESSION
   -
   -
IEF206I CSCJGJA STEP090 - STEP WAS NOT RUN BECAUSE OF CONDITIONAL EXPRESSION
   -
   -
```

?

Figure 3.25 Job Stream C14NEST: How to Nest IF/THEN/ELSE Relation Tests

bracketing each nested IF/THEN/ELSE/ENDIF structure, as a second form of documentation to aid later understanding.

- Insert a comment line of hyphens between IF/THEN/ELSE/ENDIF structures and other steps to visually segregate them into meaningful groups, as I have done in Figure 3.25 at lines 15, 17, and 21.

4

JCLLIB: Private Proc and JCL Libraries

4.1 JCLLIB: An Important New JCL Statement
4.2 Some Important Background
4.3 Starting with a Simple Example
4.4 Continuing JCLLIB Statements and Concatenating Proc Libraries
4.5 Introducing the INCLUDE and SET Statements
4.6 Using SET in Proc Development
4.7 A Realistic Example of a JCL Processing Requirement
4.8 First Steps in Developing the Job Stream
4.9 Using SET in the Example Job Stream
4.10 Converting SET to PROC
4.11 Proc Execution JCL
4.12 An Important SET Limitation
4.13 Summary of JCLLIB Statement Rules
4.14 Summary of INCLUDE Statement Rules
4.15 Summary of SET Statement Rules

4.1 JCLLIB: An Important New JCL Statement

Under MVS/ESA, a "library" can be a partitioned data set (often referred to as a PDS) or a partitioned data set extended (PDSE, or DSNTYPE=LIBRARY), a new form of data set described in Chapter 12. Libraries of either type contain members. Library members can be program source code, machine language, data, or job control language. As a programmer or end user you can have your own libraries of all of these types. But as a person invoking JCL and executing programs, you have always had less access to the "production" library where your installation's cataloged procedures—its "canned JCL" members—are stored. The main such library is named SYS1.PROCLIB. Most personnel can execute JCL from this library, but they can't put new procs into it and may not even be able to browse it, due to security restrictions.

"Private" proc libraries are handy for final testing of new procs and to house the procs of different work groups. MVS/ESA Version 4 provides a convenient way for you to create and access private proc libraries, using the new JCLLIB statement, as shown in Figure 4.1. Although private proc libraries have been supported by IBM under earlier releases of MVS, that support has involved the use of JES2 or JES3 control statements *and* the

Private proc library in MVS/ESA Version 4:

```
EDIT ---- A1092JJ.LIB.JCL(SORTEXEC) - 01.04 ----------------- COLUMNS 001 072
COMMAND ===>                                                  SCROLL ===> PAGE
****** ****************************** TOP OF DATA ******************************
000100 //A1092JJA  JOB  (1092,COB2),'JANOSSY',CLASS=A,MSGCLASS=X,
000200 //  NOTIFY=A1092JJ
000300 //       JCLLIB  ORDER=(A1092JJ.LIB.JCL)
000400 //*
000500 //*   THIS JCL IS STORED AT A1092JJ.LIB.JCL(SORTEXEC)
000600 //*
000700 //STEPA     EXEC  SORTLIST,
000800 //  INDATA='A1092JJ.LIB.JCL(WORKERS)'
000900 //
```

This is the new JCLLIB statement

Private proc library before Version 4, under JES2:

```
EDIT ---- A1092JJ.LIB.JCL(SORTEXEC) - 01.04 ----------------- COLUMNS 001 072
COMMAND ===>                                                  SCROLL ===> PAGE
****** ****************************** TOP OF DATA ******************************
000100 //A1092JJA  JOB  (1092,COB2),'JANOSSY',CLASS=A,MSGCLASS=X,
000200 //  NOTIFY=A1092JJ
000300 /*JOBPARM PROCLIB=PROC08
000400 //*
000500 //*   THIS JCL IS STORED AT A1092JJ.LIB.CNTL(SORTEXEC)
000600 //*
000700 //STEPA     EXEC  SORTLIST,
000800 //  INDATA='A1092JJ.LIB.JCL(WORKERS)'
000900 //
```

Private proc library before Version 4, under JES3:

```
EDIT ---- A1092JJ.LIB.JCL(SORTEXEC) - 01.04 ----------------- COLUMNS 001 072
COMMAND ===>                                                  SCROLL ===> PAGE
****** ****************************** TOP OF DATA ******************************
000100 //A1092JJA  JOB  (1092,COB2),'JANOSSY',CLASS=A,MSGCLASS=X,
000200 //  NOTIFY=A1092JJ
000300 //*MAIN PROC=08
000400 //*
000500 //*   THIS JCL IS STORED AT A1092JJ.LIB.JCL(SORTEXEC)
000600 //*
000700 //STEPA     EXEC  SORTLIST,
000800 //  INDATA='A1092JJ.LIB.JCL(WORKERS)'
000900 //
```

Figure 4.1 Private JCL (Proc) Library Support Varies in Different MVS Versions

involvement of a systems programmer to establish the names coded on these control statements. Using the new JCLLIB statement, you can create and access a private proc library entirely on your own. And unlike the JOBPARM and MAIN statement codings shown in Figure 4.1, JCLLIB works the same in the JES2 and JES3 environments.

You code the JCLLIB statement much differently than JOBLIB and STEPLIB, which perform a similar function for private program libraries. In this chapter, I'll show you how to code and use the JCLLIB statement. I'll also show you how another new JCL feature, the INCLUDE statement, draws ordinary, nonproc JCL from such a library. Finally, I'll demonstrate how you can use the new keyword SET to assign symbolic parameter values in ordinary JCL similar to the way EXEC assigns values to the symbolic parameters of a proc.

4.2 Some Important Background

Since its invention, the primary statements of job control language have been JOB, EXEC, and DD. With only these three statement types, you can tell MVS/ESA the essentials of any batch processing:

1. What programs you want to execute
2. What data sets the programs will access
3. What you want to do with the data sets after programs use them

And even now, you can still build large and elegant job streams using just JOB, EXEC, and DD statements. Using JCL effectively still means understanding the most important parameters of these three statement types, and how to use //* and same-line comments to make your JCL readable and understandable.

PROC and PEND are two other traditional JCL statement types. Both of these, however, are useful only when you already know how to use JOB, EXEC, and DD statements, because you use PROC and PEND statements to package JCL into procedures. A *cataloged procedure* (proc) is "canned JCL" that is stored as a member of a library. When you execute a proc, you cause MVS/ESA to bring in a copy of the proc and meld it with your JCL, forming a composite job stream.

The main "proc" library is SYS1.PROCLIB, a JCL library that MVS/ESA automatically knows about. Installations usually establish other similar default JCL libraries for their own locally developed job streams and inform MVS/ESA about them. Most installations limit access to proc libraries such as these, to safeguard important JCL from unintended alteration or deletion. When you develop a new proc, you can't test it by installing it in one of these libraries. Instead, you have traditionally used PROC and PEND to form an *instream proc* that you could test.

Under MVS/ESA Version 4, you can abandon use of the PEND statement and instream procs. MVS/ESA Version 4 gives you a new statement type named JCLLIB. JCLLIB indicates the name of one or more job control language libraries from which procs or other JCL can be obtained by

MVS/ESA. Using JCLLIB, you can completely simulate the production installation of a proc for your final testing, and even for production execution. Unlike JOBLIB and STEPLIB, which are forms of DD statements, JCLLIB is a completely new JCL statement type, a "peer" to JOB, EXEC, and DD.

4.3 Starting with a Simple Example

I created the illustrations in Figures 4.2 through 4.6 to focus on JCLLIB and related topics using a fully executable but concise example. These examples also involve a small program named CCPGM that you may find useful in your own job streams. You can get a quick overview of JCLLIB just by looking at these figures and the annotations I put on them.

Figure 4.2 shows you a small job stream named D1LIB, which has two steps. The purpose of this job stream is simple: to dump up to 50 records from a data set named CSCJGJ.CSC.WORKERS, shown in Figure 4.3. The job stream dumps (prints) record contents from this data set in character and hexadecimal form for analysis. The IDCAMS utility does a credible job of dumping data, and my job stream executes it in STEP010. But why is STEP010 present, invoking a proc named CCMAKER?

Proc CCMAKER at STEP010 is named as "control card maker." This step is present in my D1LIB job stream to meet the control card requirement of IDCAMS in a handy way. The IDCAMS utility needs a control statement—"control card"—like this to tell it to dump a data set:

```
PRINT INFILE(DD1) COUNT(50) DUMP
```

This indicates that IDCAMS should invoke its PRINT function, reading the file coded at DD statement DD1, and DUMP up to 50 records. IDCAMS must read this control statement at its //SYSIN input. I could have coded this control statement in STEP020 as instream data:

```
//SYSIN  DD *
  PRINT  INFILE(DD1) COUNT(50) DUMP
//
```

But you can't code instream data in a cataloged proc, and much of my most useful JCL (and yours) will eventually have to be packaged as procs. Both for demonstration purposes and for actual use, I developed proc CCMAKER, executing program CCPGM, to get around the awkwardness of instream control card data.

I could have put the IDCAMS control statement to dump up to 50 records of data into a JCL or other library as a hardcoded member, a very common practice. But that would mean I couldn't see the control statement directly in the JCL. I chose instead to convey the control card to IDCAMS via a program that puts it into a temporary data set, which the IDCAMS //SYSIN DD statement refers back to in line 34 of the D1LIB job stream. This way, I can still see the control statement in my JCL, and it is "living documentation." That is, the value at line 24 is not only visible in the JCL, it

```
EDIT ---- CSCJGJ.ADV.CNTL(D1LIB) - 01.17 --------------------- COLUMNS 001 072
COMMAND ===>                                                  SCROLL ===> PAGE
****** ***************************** TOP OF DATA ******************************
000001 //CSCJGJA   JOB 1,                    ACCOUNTING INFORMATION
000002 //   'BIN 7--JANOSSY',                PROGRAMMER NAME AND DELIVERY BIN
000003 //   CLASS=A,                         INPUT QUEUE CLASS
000004 //   MSGLEVEL=(1,1),                  HOW MUCH MVS SYSTEM PRINT DESIRED
000005 //   MSGCLASS=X,                      PRINT DESTINATION X A L N OR O
000006 //   TIME=(0,6),                      SAFETY LIMIT: RUN TIME UP TO 6 SECS
000007 //   REGION=2M,                       ALLOW UP TO 2 MEGS VIRTUAL MEMORY
000008 //*  TYPRUN=SCAN,                     UNCOMMENT THIS LINE TO DO SCAN ONLY
000009 //   NOTIFY=CSCJGJ                    WHO TO TELL WHEN JOB IS DONE
000010 //*
000011 //         JCLLIB  ORDER=(CSCJGJ.ADV.PROCLIB1)          PRIVATE PROC LIB
000012 //JOBLIB      DD   DSN=CSCJGJ.ADV.LOADLIB,DISP=SHR      PRIVATE LOAD LIB
000013 //            DD   DSN=SYS1.COB2LIB,DISP=SHR            COBOL II LOADLIB
000014 //*
000015 //* DEMONSTRATE USE OF JCLLIB AND CONTROL CARD MAKER PROGRAM
000016 //* THIS JCL IS STORED AT CSCJGJ.ADV.CNTL(D1LIB)
000017 //*
000018 //*****************************************************************
000019 //*                                                               *
000020 //* CREATE CONTROL CARD TELLING IDCAMS TO DUMP DATA SET AT DD1     *
000021 //*                                                               *
000022 //*****************************************************************
000023 //STEP010  EXEC  CCMAKER,
000024 //   CCIN='PRINT INFILE(DD1) COUNT(50) DUMP'
000025 //*
000026 //*****************************************************************
000027 //*                                                               *
000028 //* DUMP THE WORKERS DATA SET                                      *
000029 //*                                                               *
000030 //*****************************************************************
000031 //STEP020  EXEC  PGM=IDCAMS
000032 //SYSPRINT   DD  SYSOUT=*
000033 //DD1        DD  DSN=CSCJGJ.CSC.WORKERS,DISP=SHR
000034 //SYSIN      DD  DSN=*.STEP010.CCSTEP.CCOUT,DISP=(OLD,DELETE)
000035 //
```

STEP010 invokes job control language "canned" in a proc named CCMAKER. The proc is housed in private proc library CSCJGJ.ADV.PROCLIB1. The JCLLIB statement here points to this private proc library. Although JCLLIB serves the same purpose for a private proc library as JOBLIB does for a private load module library, the coding for these statements is radically different. In this case CSCJGJ.ADV.PROCLIB1 will be searched by MVS/ESA for procs invoked in the job stream. Procs invoked but not found in CSCJGJ.ADV.PROCLIB1 will be searched for in default proc libraries such as SYS1.PROCLIB.

Figure 4.2 D1LIB, A Job Stream Using the JCLLIB Statement

really is fed to the program that conveys it to IDCAMS. If I change the control statement at line 24 in my D1LIB job stream, the changed control statement will be the one IDCAMS receives.

Figure 4.4 shows you the CCMAKER proc. It executes just one program, CCPGM. I have already compiled and link edited CCPGM and put its machine language into my load module library, CSCJGJ.ADV.LOADLIB.

```
EDIT --- CSCJGJ.CSC.WORKERS -------------------------------- COLUMNS 001 072
COMMAND ===>                                                 SCROLL ===> PAGE
****** ***************************** TOP OF DATA ******************************
=COLS> ----+----1----+----2----+----3----+----4----+----5----+----6----+----7--
000002 21256 NILLY      WILLY     402CASHIERS OFFICE
000003 21257 IPPI       MRS.      378PHOTO DEPARTMENT
000004 21260 MALLOW     MARSHA    390KITCHEN APPLIANCES
000005 21307 WARE       DELLA     246FURNITURE
000006 21310 SHAW       ARKAN     300HARDWARE
000007 21574 AH         GEORGE    400PHOTO DEPARTMENT
000008 21668 ZOORI      MOE       179PLUMBING SUPPLIES
000009 25112 CABOOSE    LUCE      305FURNITURE
000010 25189 HOW        IDA       005SUITCASES AND BAGS
000011 33102 IFORNIA    CAL       200TRAVEL DEPARTMENT
000012 33261 CANNON     LUCE      316TOYS
000013 33377 WHIZ       G.        357PERSONAL COMPUTERS
000014 33480 TOUR       D.        160WOMENS CLOTHING
000015 33483 INA        CAROL     530REMODELING SUPPLIES
000016 39321 ABAMA      AL        420WOMENS CLOTHING
000017 39322 TUCKY      KEN       350HARDWARE
****** **************************** BOTTOM OF DATA ****************************
```

This test data has five fields of information for each employee in a small department store: employee number, last name, first name, hours worked during the last week (in hours and tenths, such as 40.2 for Willy Nilly), and department name.

Figure 4.3 Data Set to Be Dumped by the D1LIB Job Stream

CCPGM is named as my "control card program." It accepts a line of input using a PARM value on an EXEC statement, which the CCMAKER proc's symbolic parameter CCIN ("control card in") identifies. CCPGM opens a small disk data set at CCOUT ("control card out"), which the CCMAKER proc assigns to UNIT=VIO, the mainframe equivalent of a RAM disk (more about that in Chapter 6 on proc tuning). STEP020 (line 34) of the D1LIB job stream refers back to this temporary data set but could just as well access it using its temporary data set name, &&TEMPCARD.

Figure 4.5 shows you the CCPGM program itself, comprised of only 41 lines of VS COBOL II code. For robustness, I included logic in CCPGM to check if it received PARM data. If it didn't (for example, if I executed CCMAKER and didn't supply any control card data at CCIN) the CCPGM program will invoke a user abend with a completion code of 4095 by CALLing ILBOABN0. I showed you this technique of problem anticipation and conspicuous error reporting in Chapter 3.

Figure 4.6 shows you the complete MVS/ESA system output for a run of my D1LIB job stream. Rather than repeat information here and in the annotations on Figure 4.6, refer to it now for the most concise overview I can provide about JCLLIB.

```
EDIT ---- CSCJGJ.ADV.PROCLIB1(CCMAKER) - 01.06 --------------- COLUMNS 001 072
COMMAND ===>                                                   SCROLL ===> PAGE
****** ***************************** TOP OF DATA ******************************
000001 //CCMAKER  PROC  CCIN=
000002 //CCSTEP   EXEC  PGM=CCPGM,PARM='&CCIN'
000003 //STEPLIB    DD  DSN=CSCJGJ.ADV.LOADLIB,DISP=SHR         PRIVATE LOAD LIB
000004 //           DD  DSN=SYS1.COB2LIB,DISP=SHR               COBOL II LOADLIB
000005 //CCOUT      DD  DSN=&&TEMPCARD,
000006 //  DISP=(NEW,PASS,DELETE),
000007 //  UNIT=VIO,
000008 //  RECFM=FB,
000009 //  LRECL=80,
000010 //  BLKSIZE=3120,
000011 //  SPACE=(TRK,1)
```

Proc CCMAKER executes my small CCPGM, which takes a PARM value given to it and writes it out as a record in a temporary data set. I use this to pass a single-line control card needed by IDCAMS to it from the JCL in the D1LIB job stream in Figure 4.2. CCIN= on the PROC statement is a default for the symbolic parameter &CCIN and sets it to a null value if no value is provided for CCIN in the JCL invoking this proc. The temporary data set created by this proc and PASSed to following steps is written to UNIT=VIO, which is analogous to "ram disk" on a microcomputer. See proc output in Figure 4.6.

Figure 4.4 CCMAKER Proc, Invoked by the D1LIB Job Stream

4.4 Continuing JCLLIB Statements and Concatenating Proc Libraries

You may want to list more than one JCL library on a JCLLIB statement, to have MVS/ESA use procs or JCL from different sources. You can do this by continuing the JCLLIB statement as shown in Figure 4.7. You can continue JCLLIB to any number of lines using this pattern.

Figure 4.7 shows you a job stream named D2CAT, a seven-step job stream that uses procs from six private libraries and from SYS1.PROCLIB, the default proc library. I listed six private libraries on the JCLLIB statement; MVS/ESA will automatically search SYS1.PROCLIB if it is directed to execute a proc it cannot find in the private libraries listed on the JCLLIB statement. (Proc DEALLOC will come from SYS1.PROCLIB, since it is not in any of the private libraries I coded on JCLLIB, but is in SYS1.PROCLIB.) The procs invoked by job stream D2CAT are listed in Figure 4.8. You can see that each is trivial and just invokes one of the tiny COND CODE-setting programs I described in Chapters 2 and 3. I made up these procs simply to be able to run this complete example.

Figure 4.9 shows you the top of the MVS/ESA system reporting produced when I ran job stream D2CAT. I created this example to show you how MVS/ESA reports the use of multiple JCL libraries, as you can see after

```
EDIT ---- CSCJGJ.ADV.COBOL(CCPGM) - 01.06 -------------------- COLUMNS 007 078
COMMAND ===>                                                   SCROLL ===> PAGE
****** ****************************** TOP OF DATA ******************************
000100  ID DIVISION.
000200  PROGRAM-ID. CCPGM.
000300 *************************************************************
000400 *   PROGRAM TO READ A PARM VALUE AND WRITE IT TO A          *
000500 *   TEMPORARY FILE FOR USE AS A CONTROL CARD FOR A          *
000600 *   UTILITY PROGRAM (VS COBOL II)     J JANOSSY  9/3/93     *
000700 *************************************************************
000800  ENVIRONMENT DIVISION.
000900  INPUT-OUTPUT SECTION.
001000  FILE-CONTROL.
001100      SELECT CONTROL-CARD-FILE    ASSIGN TO CCOUT.
001200 *
001300  DATA DIVISION.
001400  FILE SECTION.
001500  FD  CONTROL-CARD-FILE
001600      BLOCK CONTAINS 0 RECORDS
001700      RECORD CONTAINS 80 CHARACTERS.
001800  01  CONTROL-CARD-RECORD.
001900      05                          PIC X(3).
002000      05 CC-TEXT                  PIC X(77).
002100 *
002200  WORKING-STORAGE SECTION.
002300  01  WS-NO-PARM-DATA-ABEND       PIC S9(4) BINARY VALUE +4095.
002400  LINKAGE SECTION.
002500  01  USER-PARM.
002600      05 UP-LENGTH                PIC S9(4) BINARY.
002700      05 UP-DATA.
002800         10 UP-DATA-BYTE  OCCURS 1 TO 100 TIMES
002900                          DEPENDING ON UP-LENGTH
003000                                  PIC X(1).
003100 /
003200  PROCEDURE DIVISION USING USER-PARM.
003300  0000-MAINLINE.
003400      IF UP-LENGTH = 0
003500         CALL 'ILBOABNO' USING WS-NO-PARM-DATA-ABEND.
003600      OPEN  OUTPUT  CONTROL-CARD-FILE.
003700      MOVE SPACES TO CONTROL-CARD-RECORD.
003800      MOVE UP-DATA TO CC-TEXT.
003900      WRITE CONTROL-CARD-RECORD.
004000      CLOSE CONTROL-CARD-FILE.
004100      STOP RUN.
```

This VS COBOL II program expects to receive a PARM value up to 77 bytes in length, which it puts into positions 3 through 80 of a single record it writes to DDname CCOUT. If it receives no PARM data, UP-LENGTH is zero and it initiates a user abend with completion code 4095. Note that the value passed to ILBOABNO as the user completion code must be two bytes, signed binary, coded here as PIC S9(4) BINARY.

Figure 4.5 CCPGM Program, Executed by the CCMAKER Proc

the expanded JCL in the second part of Figure 4.9. Note that the third proc (DEALLOC) is reported to have come from "system" library SYS1.PROCLIB, whereas the other procs were each found in a "private" library. I condensed the bottom of Figure 4.9 leaving only the COND CODE message lines to confirm the operation of this job stream to you.

```
                    J E S 2  J O B  L O G  --  S Y S T E M  I B M 1  --  N O D E  N 1

01.26.38 JOB09357  IRR010I  USERID CSCJGJ   IS ASSIGNED TO THIS JOB.
01.26.39 JOB09357  ICH70001I CSCJGJ   LAST ACCESS AT 01:25:53 ON SUNDAY, SEPTEMBER
01.26.39 JOB09357  $HASP373 CSCJGJA  STARTED - INIT  1 - CLASS A - SYS IBM1
01.26.41 JOB09357  $HASP395 CSCJGJA  ENDED

------ JES2 JOB STATISTICS ------
    05 SEP 93 JOB EXECUTION DATE
           34 CARDS READ
          198 SYSOUT PRINT RECORDS
            0 SYSOUT PUNCH RECORDS
           13 SYSOUT SPOOL KBYTES
         0.03 MINUTES EXECUTION TIME

        1 //CSCJGJA   JOB 1,                    ACCOUNTING INFORMATION
          //  'BIN 7--JANOSSY',                 PROGRAMMER NAME AND DELIVERY BIN
          //  CLASS=A,                          INPUT QUEUE CLASS
          //  MSGLEVEL=(1,1),                   HOW MUCH MVS SYSTEM PRINT DESIRED
          //  MSGCLASS=X,                       PRINT DESTINATION X A L N OR O
          //  TIME=(0,6),                       SAFETY LIMIT: RUN TIME UP TO 6 SECS
          //  REGION=2M,                        ALLOW UP TO 2 MEGS VIRTUAL MEMORY
          //* TYPRUN=SCAN,
          //  NOTIFY=CSCJGJ
          //*
        2 //        JCLLIB  ORDER=(CSCJGJ.ADV.PROCLIB1)
        3 //JOBLIB      DD  DSN=CSCJGJ.ADV.LOADLIB,DISP=SHR
        4 //            DD  DSN=SYS1.COB2LIB,DISP=SHR
          //*
          //* DEMONSTRATE USE OF JCLLIB AND CONTROL CARD MAKER PROGRAM
          //* THIS JCL IS STORED AT CSCJGJ.ADV.CNTL(D1LIB)
          //*
          //*******************************************************************
          //*                                                                 *
          //* CREATE CONTROL CARD TELLING IDCAMS TO DUMP DATA SET AT DD1      *
          //*                                                                 *
          //*******************************************************************
        5 //STEP010  EXEC  CCMAKER,
          //  CCIN='PRINT INFILE(DD1) COUNT(50) DUMP'
        6 XXCCMAKER  PROC
        7 XXCCSTEP   EXEC  PGM=CCPGM,PARM='&CCIN'
          IEFC653I SUBSTITUTION JCL - PRINT INFILE(DD1) COUNT(50) DUMP
```

JCLLIB is a new type of JCL statement, *not a ddname* as are //JOBLIB and //STEPLIB. You can code one JCLLIB statement following a JOB statement, before the first EXEC in the job stream. You must leave at least one space between the // and the word JCLLIB or MVS/ESA will assume it is a DDname. You can code a name on the JCLLIB statement, such as //**MYLIBS** JCLLIB ORDER=(...) but this is not necessary. First, MVS/ESA will search in the private proc libs you list on the JCLLIB statement for procs you invoke. It will then search your installation's default proc libs for procs not found.

Figure 4.6 Annotated MVS/ESA System Output Produced by the D1LIB Job Stream

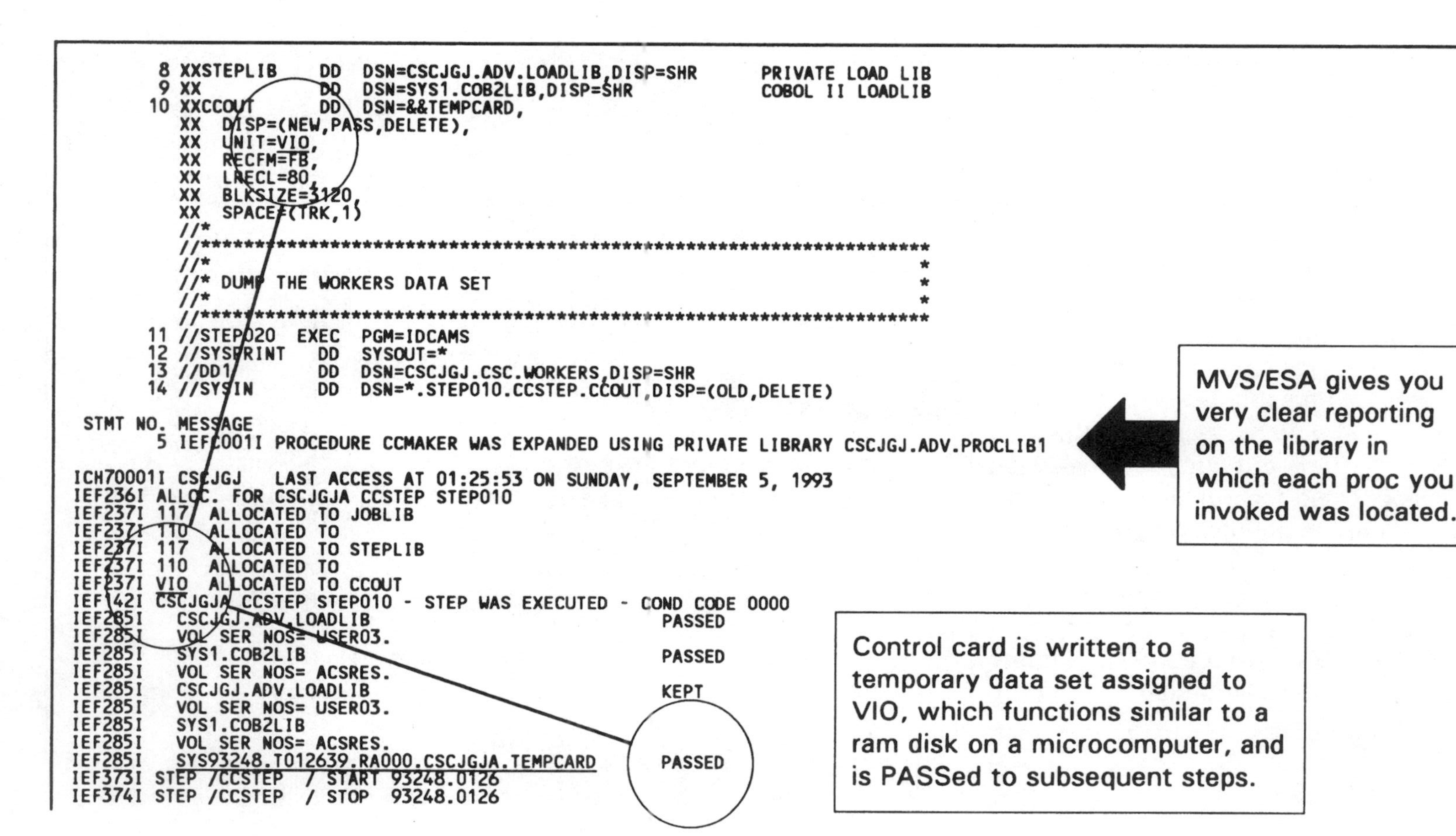

```
     8 XXSTEPLIB    DD  DSN=CSCJGJ.ADV.LOADLIB,DISP=SHR      PRIVATE LOAD LIB
     9 XX           DD  DSN=SYS1.COB2LIB,DISP=SHR            COBOL II LOADLIB
    10 XXCCOUT      DD  DSN=&&TEMPCARD,
       XX   DISP=(NEW,PASS,DELETE),
       XX   UNIT=VIO,
       XX   RECFM=FB,
       XX   LRECL=80,
       XX   BLKSIZE=3120,
       XX   SPACE=(TRK,1)
       //*
       //*********************************************************************
       //*                                                                   *
       //* DUMP THE WORKERS DATA SET                                         *
       //*                                                                   *
       //*********************************************************************
    11 //STEP020  EXEC  PGM=IDCAMS
    12 //SYSPRINT   DD  SYSOUT=*
    13 //DD1        DD  DSN=CSCJGJ.CSC.WORKERS,DISP=SHR
    14 //SYSIN      DD  DSN=*.STEP010.CCSTEP.CCOUT,DISP=(OLD,DELETE)

 STMT NO. MESSAGE
     5 IEFC001I PROCEDURE CCMAKER WAS EXPANDED USING PRIVATE LIBRARY CSCJGJ.ADV.PROCLIB1

ICH70001I CSCJGJ   LAST ACCESS AT 01:25:53 ON SUNDAY, SEPTEMBER 5, 1993
IEF236I ALLOC. FOR CSCJGJA CCSTEP STEP010
IEF237I 117  ALLOCATED TO JOBLIB
IEF237I 110  ALLOCATED TO
IEF237I 117  ALLOCATED TO STEPLIB
IEF237I 110  ALLOCATED TO
IEF237I VIO  ALLOCATED TO CCOUT
IEF142I CSCJGJA CCSTEP STEP010 - STEP WAS EXECUTED - COND CODE 0000
IEF285I   CSCJGJ.ADV.LOADLIB                              PASSED
IEF285I   VOL SER NOS= USER03.
IEF285I   SYS1.COB2LIB                                    PASSED
IEF285I   VOL SER NOS= ACSRES.
IEF285I   CSCJGJ.ADV.LOADLIB                              KEPT
IEF285I   VOL SER NOS= USER03.
IEF285I   SYS1.COB2LIB
IEF285I   VOL SER NOS= ACSRES.
IEF285I   SYS93248.T012639.RA000.CSCJGJA.TEMPCARD         PASSED
IEF373I STEP /CCSTEP  / START 93248.0126
IEF374I STEP /CCSTEP  / STOP  93248.0126
```

MVS/ESA gives you very clear reporting on the library in which each proc you invoked was located.
Control card is written to a temporary data set assigned to VIO, which functions similar to a ram disk on a microcomputer, and is PASSed to subsequent steps.

Figure 4.6 (continued)

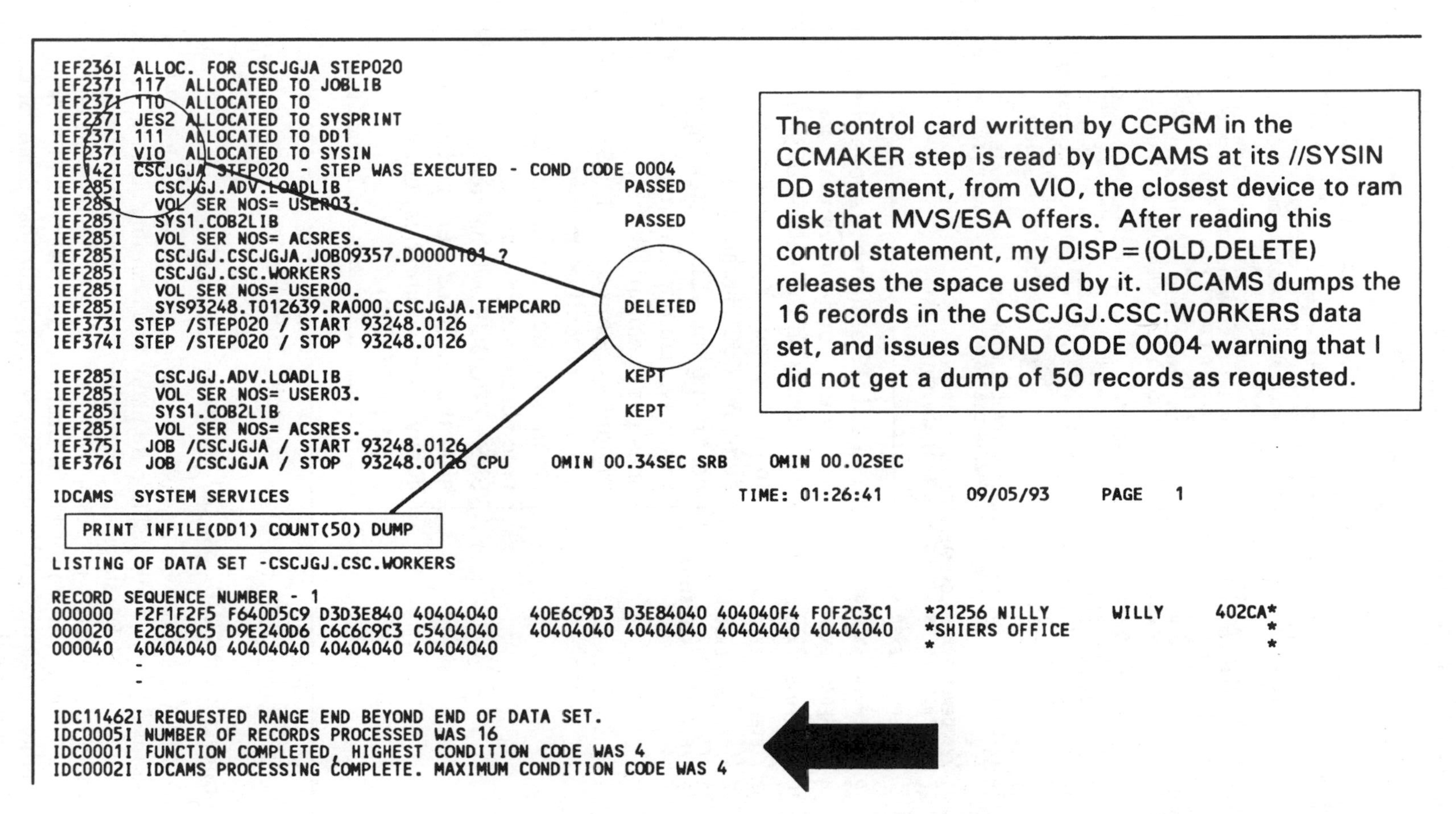

```
IEF236I ALLOC. FOR CSCJGJA STEP020
IEF237I 117  ALLOCATED TO JOBLIB
IEF237I 110  ALLOCATED TO
IEF237I JES2 ALLOCATED TO SYSPRINT
IEF237I 111  ALLOCATED TO DD1
IEF237I VIO  ALLOCATED TO SYSIN
IEF142I CSCJGJA STEP020 - STEP WAS EXECUTED - COND CODE 0004
IEF285I   CSCJGJ.ADV.LOADLIB                                 PASSED
IEF285I   VOL SER NOS= USER03.
IEF285I   SYS1.COB2LIB                                       PASSED
IEF285I   VOL SER NOS= ACSRES.
IEF285I   CSCJGJ.CSCJGJA.JOB09357.D0000101.?
IEF285I   CSCJGJ.CSC.WORKERS
IEF285I   VOL SER NOS= USER00.
IEF285I   SYS93248.T012639.RA000.CSCJGJA.TEMPCARD            DELETED
IEF373I STEP /STEP020 / START 93248.0126
IEF374I STEP /STEP020 / STOP  93248.0126

IEF285I   CSCJGJ.ADV.LOADLIB                                 KEPT
IEF285I   VOL SER NOS= USER03.
IEF285I   SYS1.COB2LIB                                       KEPT
IEF285I   VOL SER NOS= ACSRES.
IEF375I  JOB /CSCJGJA / START 93248.0126
IEF376I  JOB /CSCJGJA / STOP  93248.0126 CPU    0MIN 00.34SEC SRB    0MIN 00.02SEC

IDCAMS  SYSTEM SERVICES                                  TIME: 01:26:41        09/05/93     PAGE    1
  PRINT INFILE(DD1) COUNT(50) DUMP
LISTING OF DATA SET -CSCJGJ.CSC.WORKERS

RECORD SEQUENCE NUMBER - 1
000000  F2F1F2F5 F640D5C9 D3D3E840 40404040  40E6C9D3 D3E84040 404040F4 F0F2C3C1  *21256 NILLY      WILLY      402CA*
000020  E2C8C9C5 D9E240D6 C6C6C9C3 C5404040  40404040 40404040 40404040 40404040  *SHIERS OFFICE                   *
000040  40404040 40404040 40404040 40404040                                       *                                *
        -
        -

IDC11462I REQUESTED RANGE END BEYOND END OF DATA SET.
IDC0005I NUMBER OF RECORDS PROCESSED WAS 16
IDC0001I FUNCTION COMPLETED, HIGHEST CONDITION CODE WAS 4
IDC0002I IDCAMS PROCESSING COMPLETE. MAXIMUM CONDITION CODE WAS 4
```

The control card written by CCPGM in the CCMAKER step is read by IDCAMS at its //SYSIN DD statement, from VIO, the closest device to ram disk that MVS/ESA offers. After reading this control statement, my DISP=(OLD,DELETE) releases the space used by it. IDCAMS dumps the 16 records in the CSCJGJ.CSC.WORKERS data set, and issues COND CODE 0004 warning that I did not get a dump of 50 records as requested.

Figure 4.6 (continued)

```
EDIT ---- CSCJGJ.ADV.CNTL(D2CAT) - 01.01 --------------------- COLUMNS 001 072
COMMAND ===>                                                  SCROLL ===> PAGE
****** ***************************** TOP OF DATA ******************************
000001 //CSCJGJA   JOB 1,                  ACCOUNTING INFORMATION
000002 //   'BIN 7--JANOSSY',              PROGRAMMER NAME AND DELIVERY BIN
000003 //   CLASS=A,                       INPUT QUEUE CLASS
000004 //   MSGLEVEL=(1,1),                HOW MUCH MVS SYSTEM PRINT DESIRED
000005 //   MSGCLASS=X,                    PRINT DESTINATION X A L N OR O
000006 //   TIME=(0,6),                    SAFETY LIMIT: RUN TIME UP TO 6 SECS
000007 //   REGION=2M,                     ALLOW UP TO 2 MEGS VIRTUAL MEMORY
000008 //*  TYPRUN=SCAN,                   UNCOMMENT THIS LINE TO DO SCAN ONLY
000009 //   NOTIFY=CSCJGJ                  WHO TO TELL WHEN JOB IS DONE
000010 //*
000011 //   JCLLIB  ORDER=(CSCJGJ.ADV.PROCLIB1,       MY TESTING PROC LIBRARY
000012 //     CSCJGJ.ADV.PROCLIB2,                    MY "FINAL" PROC LIBRARY
000013 //     CSC.PROCLIB,                            DEPT. "FINAL" PROC LIB
000014 //     CSCJGJ.ADV.CNTL,                        MY ORDINARY JCL LIBRARY
000015 //     CSCJGJ.F92.CNTL,                        MY JCL LIB FOR PRIOR BOOK
000016 //     CSCJGJ.CSC.CNTL)                        "PUBLIC" JCL LIBRARY
000017 //*
000018 //JOBLIB     DD  DSN=CSCJGJ.ADV.LOADLIB,DISP=SHR      PRIVATE LOAD LIB
000019 //           DD  DSN=SYS1.COB2LIB,DISP=SHR            COBOL II LOADLIB
000020 //*
000021 //* DEMONSTRATE CONCATENATED PROC LIBRARIES
000022 //* THIS JCL IS STORED AT CSCJGJ.ADV.CNTL(D2CAT)
000023 //*
000024 //STEP010  EXEC ALPHA4
000025 //*
000026 //STEP020  EXEC BETA8
000027 //*
000028 //STEP030  EXEC DEALLOC
000029 //*
000030 //STEP040  EXEC DELTA
000031 //*
000032 //STEP050  EXEC GAMMA
000033 //*
000034 //STEP060  EXEC BETA
000035 //*
000036 //STEP070  EXEC ALPHA
000037 //
```

The JCLLIB statement above shows you how to code more than one JCL library as the source of procs to be invoked. You can list any number of JCL libraries by continuing the JCLLIB statement in this way. Do not start the indented lines past column 16 or they will be treated as comments. MVS/ESA will seek procs first in these libraries in the order listed. Default proc libraries such as SYS1.PROCLIB will be searched after these. (Proc DEALLOC is not in any of these libraries, but is in SYS1.PROCLIB.)

Figure 4.7 D2CAT Job Stream, Which Uses Multiple JCLLIB Libraries

4.5 Introducing the INCLUDE and SET Statements

MVS/ESA Version 4 gives you two new features related to JCLLIB. One of these is a "copy" facility similar to many programming languages and uses the new INCLUDE statement. The other new feature allows you to code symbolic parameters in ordinary JCL and relies on the new statement type SET. Figures 4.10 and 4.11 demonstrate INCLUDE and SET being used together. I'll show you additional examples later that demonstrate them used individually.

```
EDIT ---- CSCJGJ.ADV.PROCLIB1(ALPHA) - 01.00 ---------------- COLUMNS 001 072
COMMAND ===>                                                  SCROLL ===> PAGE
****** ****************************** TOP OF DATA ******************************
000001 //ALPHA    PROC
000002 //A1       EXEC  PGM=ALPHA
```

```
EDIT ---- CSCJGJ.ADV.PROCLIB2(BETA) - 01.00 ----------------- COLUMNS 001 072
COMMAND ===>                                                  SCROLL ===> PAGE
****** ****************************** TOP OF DATA ******************************
000001 //BETA     PROC
000002 //B1       EXEC  PGM=BETA
```

```
EDIT ---- CSC.PROCLIB(GAMMA) - 01.00 ------------------------ COLUMNS 001 072
COMMAND ===>                                                  SCROLL ===> PAGE
****** ****************************** TOP OF DATA ******************************
000001 //GAMMA    PROC
000002 //G1       EXEC  PGM=GAMMA
```

```
EDIT ---- CSCJGJ.ADV.CNTL(DELTA) - 01.00 -------------------- COLUMNS 001 072
COMMAND ===>                                                  SCROLL ===> PAGE
****** ****************************** TOP OF DATA ******************************
000001 //DELTA    PROC
000002 //D1       EXEC  PGM=DELTA
```

```
EDIT ---- CSCJGJ.F92.CNTL(ALPHA4) - 01.00 ------------------- COLUMNS 001 072
COMMAND ===>                                                  SCROLL ===> PAGE
****** ****************************** TOP OF DATA ******************************
000001 //ALPHA4   PROC
000002 //A4       EXEC  PGM=ALPHA4
```

```
EDIT ---- CSCJGJ.CSC.CNTL(BETA8) - 01.00 -------------------- COLUMNS 001 072
COMMAND ===>                                                  SCROLL ===> PAGE
****** ****************************** TOP OF DATA ******************************
000001 //BETA8    PROC
000002 //B8       EXEC  PGM=BETA8
```

I put these "do nothing" procs executing trivial programs into several different proc and JCL libraries so that I could give you an example of library concatenation using the JCLLIB statement, and to let you see how MVS/ESA reports on its access to multiple libraries. These procs just build my example. I don't recommend giving procs the same names as programs in your production work.

Figure 4.8 Various Procs Executed by the D2CAT Job Stream

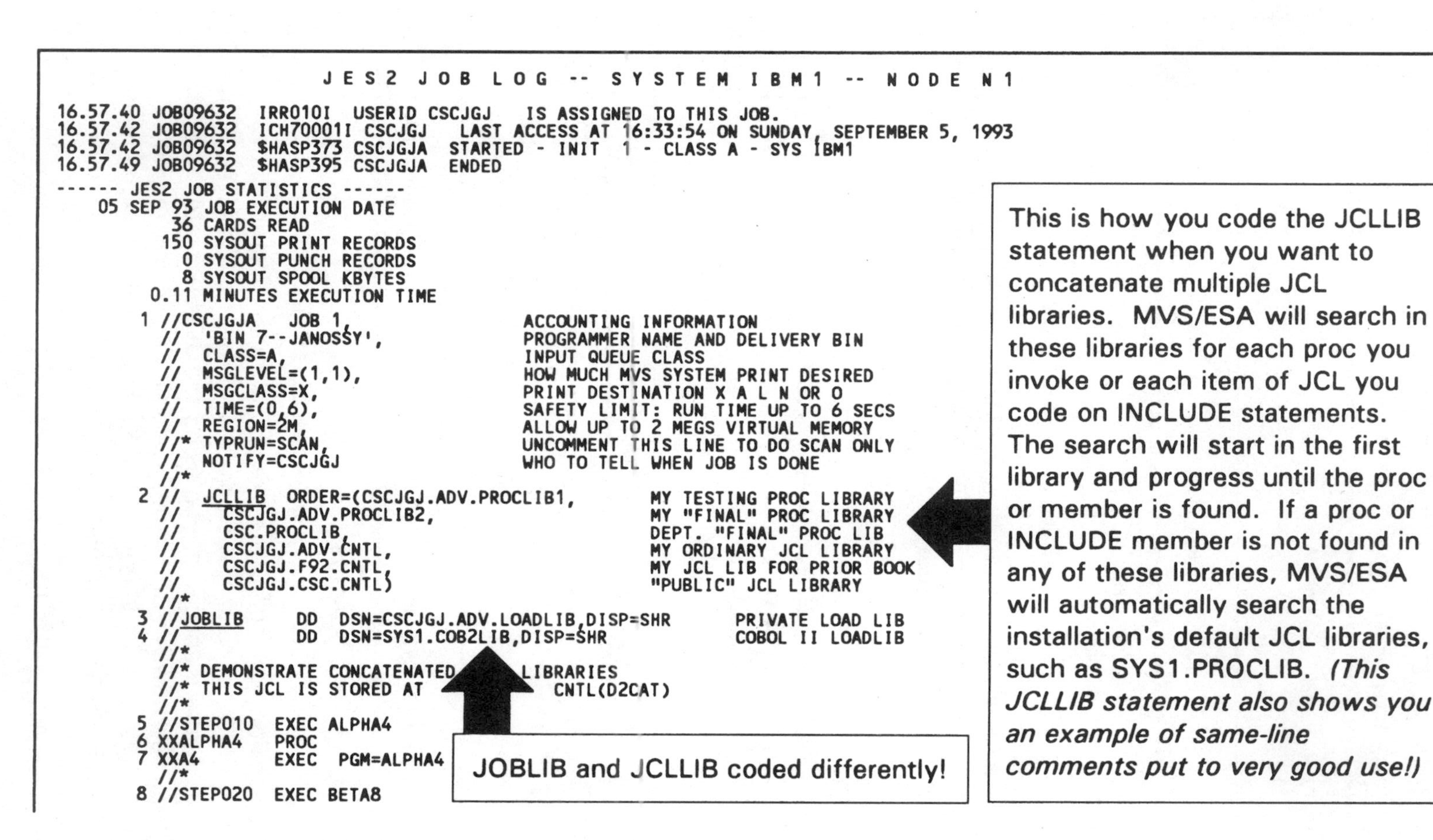

```
                    J E S 2  J O B  L O G  --  S Y S T E M  I B M 1  --  N O D E  N 1

16.57.40 JOB09632  IRR010I  USERID CSCJGJ   IS ASSIGNED TO THIS JOB.
16.57.42 JOB09632  ICH70001I CSCJGJ   LAST ACCESS AT 16:33:54 ON SUNDAY, SEPTEMBER 5, 1993
16.57.42 JOB09632  $HASP373 CSCJGJA  STARTED - INIT  1 - CLASS A - SYS IBM1
16.57.49 JOB09632  $HASP395 CSCJGJA  ENDED
------ JES2 JOB STATISTICS ------
    05 SEP 93 JOB EXECUTION DATE
           36 CARDS READ
          150 SYSOUT PRINT RECORDS
            0 SYSOUT PUNCH RECORDS
            8 SYSOUT SPOOL KBYTES
         0.11 MINUTES EXECUTION TIME
        1 //CSCJGJA   JOB 1,                        ACCOUNTING INFORMATION
          //  'BIN 7--JANOSSY',                     PROGRAMMER NAME AND DELIVERY BIN
          //  CLASS=A,                              INPUT QUEUE CLASS
          //  MSGLEVEL=(1,1),                       HOW MUCH MVS SYSTEM PRINT DESIRED
          //  MSGCLASS=X,                           PRINT DESTINATION X A L N OR O
          //  TIME=(0,6),                           SAFETY LIMIT: RUN TIME UP TO 6 SECS
          //  REGION=2M,                            ALLOW UP TO 2 MEGS VIRTUAL MEMORY
          //* TYPRUN=SCAN,                          UNCOMMENT THIS LINE TO DO SCAN ONLY
          //  NOTIFY=CSCJGJ                         WHO TO TELL WHEN JOB IS DONE
          //*
        2 //  JCLLIB  ORDER=(CSCJGJ.ADV.PROCLIB1,           MY TESTING PROC LIBRARY
          //     CSCJGJ.ADV.PROCLIB2,                       MY "FINAL" PROC LIBRARY
          //     CSC.PROCLIB,                               DEPT. "FINAL" PROC LIB
          //     CSCJGJ.ADV.CNTL,                           MY ORDINARY JCL LIBRARY
          //     CSCJGJ.F92.CNTL,                           MY JCL LIB FOR PRIOR BOOK
          //     CSCJGJ.CSC.CNTL)                           "PUBLIC" JCL LIBRARY
          //*
        3 //JOBLIB      DD  DSN=CSCJGJ.ADV.LOADLIB,DISP=SHR      PRIVATE LOAD LIB
        4 //            DD  DSN=SYS1.COB2LIB,DISP=SHR            COBOL II LOADLIB
          //*
          //* DEMONSTRATE CONCATENATED      LIBRARIES
          //* THIS JCL IS STORED AT            CNTL(D2CAT)
          //*
        5 //STEP010   EXEC ALPHA4
        6 XXALPHA4    PROC
        7 XXA4        EXEC  PGM=ALPHA4
          //*
        8 //STEP020   EXEC BETA8
```


Figure 4.9 Annotated MVS/ESA System Output Produced by the D2CAT Job Stream

```
       9 XXBETA8    PROC
      10 XXB8       EXEC  PGM=BETA8
         //*
      11 //STEP030  EXEC DEALLOC
      12 XXDEALLOC EXEC PGM=IEFBR14
         //*
      13 //STEP040  EXEC DELTA
      14 XXDELTA    PROC
      15 XXD1       EXEC  PGM=DELTA
         //*
      16 //STEP050  EXEC GAMMA
      17 XXGAMMA    PROC
      18 XXG1       EXEC  PGM=GAMMA
         //*
      19 //STEP060  EXEC BETA
      20 XXBETA     PROC
      21 XXB1       EXEC  PGM=BETA
         //*
      22 //STEP070  EXEC ALPHA
      23 XXALPHA    PROC
      24 XXA1       EXEC  PGM=ALPHA

 STMT NO. MESSAGE
       5 IEFC001I PROCEDURE ALPHA4 WAS EXPANDED USING PRIVATE LIBRARY CSCJGJ.F92.CNTL
       8 IEFC001I PROCEDURE BETA8 WAS EXPANDED USING PRIVATE LIBRARY CSCJGJ.CSC.CNTL
      11 IEFC001I PROCEDURE DEALLOC WAS EXPANDED USING SYSTEM LIBRARY SYS1.PROCLIB
      13 IEFC001I PROCEDURE DELTA WAS EXPANDED USING PRIVATE LIBRARY CSCJGJ.ADV.CNTL
      16 IEFC001I PROCEDURE GAMMA WAS EXPANDED USING PRIVATE LIBRARY CSC.PROCLIB
      19 IEFC001I PROCEDURE BETA WAS EXPANDED USING PRIVATE LIBRARY CSCJGJ.ADV.PROCLIB2
      22 IEFC001I PROCEDURE ALPHA WAS EXPANDED USING PRIVATE LIBRARY CSCJGJ.ADV.PROCLIB1

IEF142I CSCJGJA A4 STEP010 - STEP WAS EXECUTED - COND CODE 0004
IEF142I CSCJGJA B8 STEP020 - STEP WAS EXECUTED - COND CODE 0008
IEF142I CSCJGJA DEALLOC STEP030 - STEP WAS EXECUTED - COND CODE 0000
IEF142I CSCJGJA D1 STEP040 - STEP WAS EXECUTED - COND CODE 0000
IEF142I CSCJGJA G1 STEP050 - STEP WAS EXECUTED - COND CODE 0000
IEF142I CSCJGJA B1 STEP060 - STEP WAS EXECUTED - COND CODE 0000
IEF142I CSCJGJA A1 STEP070 - STEP WAS EXECUTED - COND CODE 0000
```

MVS/ESA lists the library in which it finds each proc or INCLUDEd item of JCL. This is not merely a restatement of JCLLIB statement coding; each message as you see here is specific to a particular EXEC or INCLUDE statement. One of the procs I listed, named DEALLOC, is not in any of the private proc libraries I coded on the JCLLIB statement, so MVS/ESA seeks it (and finds it) in default JCL library SYS1.PROCLIB.

Figure 4.9 (continued)

```
EDIT ---- CSCJGJ.ADV.CNTL(D3INCLU) - 01.02 ------------------ COLUMNS 001 072
COMMAND ===>                                                  SCROLL ===> PAGE
****** ***************************** TOP OF DATA ******************************
000001 //CSCJGJA   JOB 1,                   ACCOUNTING INFORMATION
000002 //  'BIN 7--JANOSSY',                PROGRAMMER NAME AND DELIVERY BIN
000003 //  CLASS=A,                         INPUT QUEUE CLASS
000004 //  MSGLEVEL=(1,1),                  HOW MUCH MVS SYSTEM PRINT DESIRED
000005 //  MSGCLASS=X,                      PRINT DESTINATION X A L N OR O
000006 //  TIME=(0,6),                      SAFETY LIMIT: RUN TIME UP TO 6 SECS
000007 //  REGION=2M,                       ALLOW UP TO 2 MEGS VIRTUAL MEMORY
000008 //* TYPRUN=SCAN,                     UNCOMMENT THIS LINE TO DO SCAN ONLY
000009 //  NOTIFY=CSCJGJ                    WHO TO TELL WHEN JOB IS DONE
000010 //*
000011 //        JCLLIB  ORDER=(CSCJGJ.ADV.PROCLIB1)         PRIVATE PROC LIB
000012 //JOBLIB      DD  DSN=CSCJGJ.ADV.LOADLIB,DISP=SHR      PRIVATE LOAD LIB
000013 //            DD  DSN=SYS1.COB2LIB,DISP=SHR            COBOL II LOADLIB
000014 //*
000015 //* DEMONSTRATE THE "INCLUDE" STATEMENT
000016 //* THIS JCL IS STORED AT CSCJGJ.ADV.CNTL(D3INCLU)
000017 //*
000018 //*
000019 //*****************************************************************
000020 //*                                                               *
000021 //* CREATE CONTROL CARD TELLING IDCAMS TO DUMP DATA SET AT DD1     *
000022 //*                                                               *
000023 //*****************************************************************
000024 //          SET   CCIN='PRINT INFILE(DD1) COUNT(50) DUMP'
000025 //      INCLUDE   MEMBER=CCMAKERI
000026 //*
000027 //*****************************************************************
000028 //*                                                               *
000029 //* DUMP THE WORKERS DATA SET                                     *
000030 //*                                                               *
000031 //*****************************************************************
000032 //STEP020  EXEC  PGM=IDCAMS
000033 //SYSPRINT   DD  SYSOUT=*
000034 //DD1        DD  DSN=CSCJGJ.CSC.WORKERS,DISP=SHR
000035 //SYSIN      DD  DSN=*.CCSTEP.CCOUT,DISP=(OLD,DELETE)
000036 //
```

The INCLUDE statement copies in JCL contained in the member name coded on it. The library from which the JCL is copied in is the first one in the JCLLIB statement that contains it, or a default library searched by MVS/ESA after the libraries indicated on JCLLIB have been searched. SET has no connection with INCLUDE but can be coded in combination with it. SET assigns values to symbolic parameters in ordinary (nonproc) JCL.

Figure 4.10 D3INCLU Job Stream Demonstrating Use of the SET and INCLUDE Statements

In Figure 4.2, you saw a two-step job stream that executed a proc named CCMAKER to form a control card for the IDCAMS utility, and a second step to execute IDCAMS to dump records from a data set named CSCJGJ.CSC.WORKERS. Job stream D3INCLU in Figure 4.10 does the same thing, but it does not invoke a proc in its first step. Instead, it INCLUDEs the JCL shown in Figure 4.11. The INCLUDE is coded at line 25 and draws in member CCMAKERI. CCMAKERI will come from the JCL library named on the JCLLIB statement at line 11, that is, CSCJGJ.ADV.PROCLIB1.

```
EDIT ---- CSCJGJ.ADV.PROCLIB1(CCMAKERI) - 01.00 ------------- COLUMNS 001 072
COMMAND ===>                                                  SCROLL ===> PAGE
****** ******************************** TOP OF DATA ********************************

000001 //*----- START OF JCL MEMBER CCMAKERI ----- J. JANOSSY  9/5/93 -----
000002 //CCSTEP   EXEC  PGM=CCPGM,PARM='&CCIN'
000003 //STEPLIB    DD  DSN=CSCJGJ.ADV.LOADLIB,DISP=SHR       PRIVATE LOAD LIB
000004 //           DD  DSN=SYS1.COB2LIB,DISP=SHR             COBOL II LOADLIB
000005 //CCOUT      DD  DSN=&&TEMPCARD,
000006 //   DISP=(NEW,PASS,DELETE),
000007 //   UNIT=VIO,
000008 //   RECFM=FB,
000009 //   LRECL=80,
000010 //   BLKSIZE=3120,
000011 //   SPACE=(TRK,1)
000012 //*------- END OF JCL MEMBER CCMAKERI ----- J. JANOSSY  9/5/93 -----
```

This is JCL that I will copy into a job stream using the new INCLUDE feature. If you compare this to the CCMAKER proc in Figure 4.4 you'll notice that while this is similar, there is no PROC statement here. When I bring this JCL into a job stream with INCLUDE, it is copied in similar to a copy or "include" in a programming language. It would be an error to code a proc statement at the beginning of this JCL.

Figure 4.11 JCL "Include Group" CCMAKERI, a Nonproc Version of the CCMAKER Proc

Compare the JCL named CCMAKERI in Figure 4.11 with proc CCMAKER in Figure 4.4, and you'll see that they are the same, except that there is no PROC statement in Figure 4.11. The PROC statement in CCMAKER provided the default value for symbolic paramater CCIN, the text of the control card required by IDCAMS to dump data: It nullified it, giving no PARM to CCMAKER by default. Since there is no PROC statement in CCMAKERI in Figure 4.11, but the symbolic parameter &CCIN still exists in it at its line 2, I have used the SET statement in the D3INCLU job stream to give CCIN a value.

The MVS/ESA system output shown in Figure 4.12 shows you the final job stream as brought together by MVS/ESA. You can see in this reporting that MVS/ESA has substituted the value from the SET statement into the symbolic parameter of the INCLUDEd JCL, just as it has always done for symbolic parameters in procs. JCL copied in with an INCLUDE statement is called an *include group*. MVS/ESA reports the originating library of include groups just as it reports this for procs that you invoke.

This example may give you the impression that SET and INCLUDE must work together, but they can actually be coded independently of one another. With some exceptions, which I cover in the summaries at the end of this chapter, you can house any of your standard job control language statements separately, as members, in a JCL library, and INCLUDE them at

```
                     J E S 2  J O B  L O G  --  S Y S T E M  I B M 1  --  N O D E  N 1

17.12.29 JOB09641  IRR010I  USERID CSCJGJ   IS ASSIGNED TO THIS JOB.
17.12.29 JOB09641  ICH70001I CSCJGJ   LAST ACCESS AT 16:57:42 ON SUNDAY, SEPTEMBER 5, 1993
17.12.29 JOB09641  $HASP373 CSCJGJA  STARTED - INIT  1 - CLASS A - SYS IBM1
17.12.32 JOB09641  $HASP395 CSCJGJA  ENDED

------ JES2 JOB STATISTICS ------
  05 SEP 93 JOB EXECUTION DATE
         35 CARDS READ
        200 SYSOUT PRINT RECORDS
          0 SYSOUT PUNCH RECORDS
         13 SYSOUT SPOOL KBYTES
       0.04 MINUTES EXECUTION TIME

        1 //CSCJGJA   JOB 1,                  ACCOUNTING INFORMATION
          //  'BIN 7--JANOSSY',               PROGRAMMER NAME AND DELIVERY BIN
          //  CLASS=A,                        INPUT QUEUE CLASS
          //  MSGLEVEL=(1,1),                 HOW MUCH MVS SYSTEM PRINT DESIRED
          //  MSGCLASS=X,                     PRINT DESTINATION X A L N OR O
          //  TIME=(0,6),                     SAFETY LIMIT: RUN TIME UP TO 6 SECS
          //  REGION=2M,                      ALLOW UP TO 2 MEGS VIRTUAL MEMORY
          //* TYPRUN=SCAN,                    UNCOMMENT THIS LINE TO DO SCAN ONLY
          //  NOTIFY=CSCJGJ                   WHO TO TELL WHEN JOB IS DONE
          //*
        2 //        JCLLIB  ORDER=(CSCJGJ.ADV.PROCLIB1)          PRIVATE PROC LIB
        3 //JOBLIB     DD  DSN=CSCJGJ.ADV.LOADLIB,DISP=SHR      PRIVATE LOAD LIB
        4 //           DD  DSN=SYS1.COB2LIB,DISP=SHR            COBOL II LOADLIB
          //*
          //* DEMONSTRATE THE "INCLUDE" STATEMENT
          //* THIS JCL IS STORED AT CSCJGJ.ADV.CNTL(D3INCLU)
          //*
          //*********************************************************************
          //*                                                                   *
          //* CREATE CONTROL CARD TELLING IDCAMS TO DUMP DATA SET AT DD1        *
          //*                                                                   *
          //*********************************************************************
        5 //          SET   CCIN='PRINT INFILE(DD1) COUNT(50) DUMP'
        6 //      INCLUDE   MEMBER=CCMAKERI
          XX*----- START OF JCL MEMBER CCMAKERI ----- J. JANOSSY  9/5/93 ---
        7 XXCCSTEP   EXEC  PGM=CCPGM,PARM='&CCIN'
          IEFC653I SUBSTITUTION JCL - PRINT INFILE(DD1) COUNT(50) DUMP
```

> The INCLUDE statement *copies JCL into a job stream* from a JCL library such as SYS1.PROCLIB or a private library you name on a JCLLIB statement. In the D3INCLU job stream, I use INCLUDE to copy in JCL almost identical to the CCMAKER proc, except lacking a PROC statement. Here you see the SET statement used to assign values to the symbolic parameter &CCIN. MVS/ESA reports the values assigned by SET in the same way as it reports symbolic parameter substitutions when you invoke a PROC.

Figure 4.12 Annotated MVS/ESA System Output Produced by the D3INCLU Job Stream

```
       8 XXSTEPLIB    DD  DSN=CSCJGJ.ADV.LOADLIB,DISP=SHR      PRIVATE LOAD LIB
       9 XX           DD  DSN=SYS1.COB2LIB,DISP=SHR            COBOL II LOADLIB
      10 XXCCOUT      DD  DSN=&&TEMPCARD,
         XX  DISP=(NEW,PASS,DELETE),
         XX  UNIT=VIO,
         XX  RECFM=FB,
         XX  LRECL=80,
         XX  BLKSIZE=3120,
         XX  SPACE=(TRK,1)
         XX*------- END OF JCL MEMBER CCMAKERI ----- J. JANOSSY  9/5/93 -----
         //*
         //*******************************************************************
         //*                                                                 *
         //* DUMP THE WORKERS DATA SET                                       *
         //*                                                                 *
         //*******************************************************************
      11 //STEP020  EXEC  PGM=IDCAMS
      12 //SYSPRINT   DD  SYSOUT=*
      13 //DD1        DD  DSN=CSCJGJ.CSC.WORKERS,DISP=SHR
      14 //SYSIN      DD  DSN=*.CCSTEP.CCOUT,DISP=(OLD,DELETE)

 STMT NO. MESSAGE
       6 IEFC002I INCLUDE GROUP CCMAKERI WAS EXPANDED USING PRIVATE LIBRARY CSCJGJ.ADV.PROCLIB1

ICH70001I CSCJGJ   LAST ACCESS AT 16:57:42 ON SUNDAY, SEPTEMBER 5, 1993
IEF236I ALLOC. FOR CSCJGJA CCSTEP
IEF237I 117  ALLOCATED TO JOBLIB
IEF237I 110  ALLOCATED TO
IEF237I 117  ALLOCATED TO STEPLIB
IEF237I 110  ALLOCATED TO
IEF237I VIO  ALLOCATED TO CCOUT
IEF142I CSCJGJA CCSTEP - STEP WAS EXECUTED - COND CODE 0000
IEF285I   CSCJGJ.ADV.LOADLIB                           PASSED
IEF285I   VOL SER NOS= USER03.
IEF285I   SYS1.COB2LIB                                 PASSED
IEF285I   VOL SER NOS= ACSRES.
IEF285I   CSCJGJ.ADV.LOADLIB                           KEPT
IEF285I   VOL SER NOS= USER03.
IEF285I   SYS1.COB2LIB                                 KEPT
IEF285I   VOL SER NOS= ACSRES.
IEF285I   SYS93248.T171229.RA000.CSCJGJA.TEMPCARD      PASSED
IEF373I STEP /CCSTEP  / START 93248.1712
```

JCL lines brought in by INCLUDE are identified by XX at the beginning, just as are cataloged procedure JCL lines when you EXECute a proc.

MVS/ESA reports the name of the library from which it copied in the JCL that the INCLUDE statement indicated. An "include group" is simply the group of JCL lines brought in by the INCLUDE statement.

Figure 4.12 (continued)

whatever points are appropriate in any job stream. Some likely candidates for this form of standardization are common OUTPUT JCL statements and DD statements.

4.6 Using SET in Proc Development

SET gives you the ability to introduce a new stage into your method for evolving production JCL. You can start with ordinary JCL and test it. Then you can introduce symbolic parameters, use SET to assign values to them, and test your JCL. As a third step, you can convert the SET statement into a PROC statement, put the new proc into a JCL library, and give a final test to the proc simulating actual production use. The advantage of using SET in this intermediate stage is that your JCL is still all in one place, making it easier to adjust and finalize. I have composed a full-scale example to illustrate this productive method. It's described in the next several sections.

4.7 A Realistic Example of a JCL Processing Requirement

Let's talk about a typical job stream. Suppose I need a job stream to compare two data sets and produce different printed outputs for analysis depending on whether the data sets are identical or different. If the data sets are identical, I need to print either one using IEBGENER (they are the same, so printing one is the same as printing the other). If the data sets are not the same, I need to dump each one in character and hexadecimal format for detailed analysis. Some other criteria that must be met: This job stream needs to be runnable by end users, using simple execution JCL. The only thing that the end user must be concerned about is supplying two data set names and submitting the job; this must initiate all necessary processing. And further, the end user can't reliably edit or submit a raw JCL job stream.

Figure 4.13 shows you the contents of three data sets, named CSCJGJ.ADV.APPLES, CSCJGJ.ADV.ORANGES, and CSCJGJ.ADV.POMMES. These will be the first of hundreds of data sets the user wants to compare in pairs. Comparing these three data sets alone will take three separate runs of the job you create:

`CSCJGJ.ADV.APPLES` compared to `CSCJGJ.ADV.ORANGES`
`CSCJGJ.ADV.APPLES` compared to `CSCJGJ.ADV.POMMES`
`CSCJGJ.ADV.ORANGES` compared to `CSCJGJ.ADV.POMMES`

("Pommes" means apples in French, so you have a hint about how this particular test data will compare.) How would you handle this JCL processing requirement?

4.8 First Steps in Developing the Job Stream

You can handle the JCL processing requirement described in section 4.7 by creating a proc to do the necessary comparison and print or dumps, and giving the end user JCL to invoke the proc. To develop such a proc, you'll find it expeditious to follow these steps:

```
EDIT ---- CSCJGJ.ADV.APPLES ---------------------------- COLUMNS 001 072
COMMAND ===>                                             SCROLL ===> PAGE
****** *************************** TOP OF DATA ****************************
000001 THE TIME HAS COME,
000002 THE WALRUS SAID,
000003 TO TALK OF MANY THINGS.
000004 SAILING SHIPS,
000005 AND SEALING WAX,
000006 AND CABBAGES AND KINGS.
```

Data set named
CSCJGJ.ADV.APPLES

```
EDIT ---- CSCJGJ.ADV.ORANGES --------------------------- COLUMNS 001 072
COMMAND ===>                                             SCROLL ===> PAGE
****** *************************** TOP OF DATA ****************************
000001 THE TIME HAS COME,
000002 THE WALRUS SAID,
000003 TO TALK OF MANY THINGS.
000004 SAILING SHIPS,
000005 AND CEILING WAX,
000006 AND CABBAGES AND KINGS.
```

?

Data set named
CSCJGJ.ADV.ORANGES

```
EDIT ---- CSCJGJ.ADV.POMMES ---------------------------- COLUMNS 001 072
COMMAND ===>                                             SCROLL ===> PAGE
****** *************************** TOP OF DATA ****************************
000001 THE TIME HAS COME,
000002 THE WALRUS SAID,
000003 TO TALK OF MANY THINGS.
000004 SAILING SHIPS,
000005 AND SEALING WAX,
000006 AND CABBAGES AND KINGS.
```

?

Data set named
CSCJGJ.ADV.POMMES

Figure 4.13 Three Data Sets to Be Compared (in pairs) by the D4COMPR Job Stream; Which Is Different from the First?

1. Design a job stream using the box (process), disk or tape data set, and report flowcharting symbols.
2. Build a raw JCL job stream from the flowchart to accomplish the necessary processing, and test it.
3. Introduce appropriate symbolic parameters into your job stream, and test it using SET.
4. Convert the SET statement in your job stream into a PROC statement, install the new proc into a private proc library, and test it using a JCLLIB statement in the execution JCL.
5. Install the proc into a production JCL library, and give the user the execution JCL, minus the JCLLIB statement.

Figure 4.14 shows you a flowcharted design for the job stream. This job stream uses the IBM utility programs IEBCOMPR, IEBGENER, and IDCAMS.

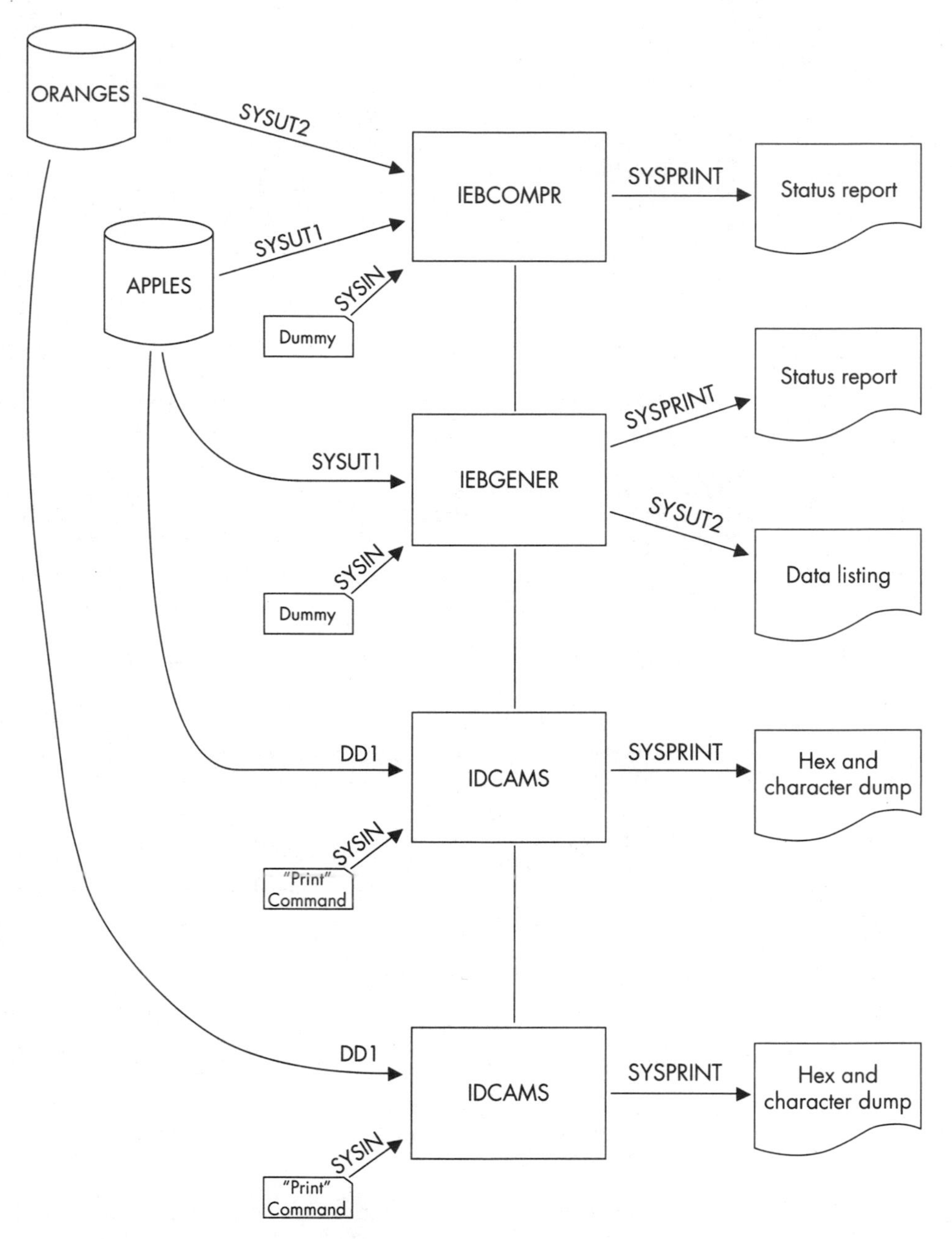

Figure 4.14 Flow-Charted Design for a Data Set Comparison Job Stream Using the IEBCOMPR Utility Program

IEBCOMPR compares data sets and sets COND CODE 0000 if they are identical, or COND CODE 0008 or 0012 if they are different (see Appendix D to learn the distinction between these COND CODE values for IEBCOMPR).

Figure 4.15 depicts a job stream named D4COMPR, which implements my flow-charted design meeting the data set comparison processing require-

```
EDIT ---- CSCJGJ.ADV.CNTL(D4COMPR) - 01.01 ------------------ COLUMNS 001 072
COMMAND ===>                                                 SCROLL ===> PAGE
****** ***************************** TOP OF DATA ******************************
000001 //CSCJGJA   JOB 1,                    ACCOUNTING INFORMATION
000002 //  'BIN 7--JANOSSY',                 PROGRAMMER NAME AND DELIVERY BIN
000003 //  CLASS=A,                          INPUT QUEUE CLASS
000004 //  MSGLEVEL=(1,1),                   HOW MUCH MVS SYSTEM PRINT DESIRED
000005 //  MSGCLASS=X,                       PRINT DESTINATION X A L N OR O
000006 //  TIME=(0,6),                       SAFETY LIMIT: RUN TIME UP TO 6 SECS
000007 //  REGION=2M,                        ALLOW UP TO 2 MEGS VIRTUAL MEMORY
000008 //* TYPRUN=SCAN,                      UNCOMMENT THIS LINE TO DO SCAN ONLY
000009 //  NOTIFY=CSCJGJ                     WHO TO TELL WHEN JOB IS DONE
000010 //*
000011 //* COMPARE TWO DATA SETS, PRINT IF SAME, DUMP IF DIFFERENT
000012 //* THIS JCL IS STORED AT CSCJGJ.ADV.CNTL(D4COMPR)
000013 //*
000014 //*****************************************************
000015 //*                                                   *
000016 //*    COMPARE ITEMS USING IEBCOMPR                   *
000017 //*    COND CODE 0000 MEANS THEY ARE THE SAME         *
000018 //*    COND CODE > 0000 MEANS THEY ARE DIFFERENT      *
000019 //*                                                   *
000020 //*****************************************************
000021 //STEP010  EXEC  PGM=IEBCOMPR
000022 //SYSPRINT   DD  SYSOUT=*
000023 //SYSIN      DD  DUMMY
000024 //SYSUT1     DD  DSN=CSCJGJ.ADV.APPLES,DISP=SHR
000025 //SYSUT2     DD  DSN=CSCJGJ.ADV.ORANGES,DISP=SHR
000026 //*
000027 //*****************************************************
000028 //*                                                   *
000029 //*    IF ITEMS THE SAME, PRINT ONE                   *
000030 //*                                                   *
000031 //*****************************************************
000032 //       IF ( STEP010.RC = 0 ) THEN                     X
000033 //STEP020  EXEC  PGM=IEBGENER                           !
000034 //SYSPRINT   DD  SYSOUT=*                               ! IF
000035 //SYSIN      DD  DUMMY                                  ! ENDIF
000036 //SYSUT1     DD  DSN=*.STEP010.SYSUT1,DISP=SHR          !
000037 //SYSUT2     DD  SYSOUT=*                               !
000038 //       ENDIF                                          X
000039 //*
000040 //*****************************************************
000041 //*                                                   *
000042 //*    IF ITEMS DIFFERENT, DUMP THE FIRST ONE         *
000043 //*                                                   *
000044 //*****************************************************
000045 //       IF ( STEP010.RC > 0 ) THEN                     X
000046 //STEP030  EXEC  PGM=IDCAMS                             !
000047 //SYSPRINT   DD  SYSOUT=*                               !
000048 //DD1        DD  DSN=*.STEP010.SYSUT1,DISP=SHR          !
000049 //SYSIN      DD  *                                      !
000050    PRINT INFILE(DD1) COUNT(50) DUMP
000051 //*                                                    !
000052 //*****************************************************! IF
000053 //*                                                   *! ENDIF
000054 //*    IF ITEMS DIFFERENT, DUMP THE SECOND ONE        *!
000055 //*                                                   *!
000056 //*****************************************************!
000057 //STEP040  EXEC  PGM=IDCAMS                             !
000058 //SYSPRINT   DD  SYSOUT=*                               !
000059 //DD1        DD  DSN=*.STEP010.SYSUT2,DISP=SHR          !
000060 //SYSIN      DD  *                                      !
000061    PRINT INFILE(DD1) COUNT(50) DUMP
000062 //       ENDIF                                          X
000063 //
```

This is ordinary, nonproc JCL to execute the IEBCOMPR utility, which compares the data sets it reads at its //SYSUT1 and //SYSUT2 inputs. If the data sets are identical, IEBCOMPR sets COND CODE 0000, otherwise a nonzero COND CODE. If IEBCOMPR "says" that the data sets are identical, this job stream prints one using IEBGENER at STEP020, otherwise it dumps each data set using IDCAMS at STEP030 and STEP040.

Figure 4.15 D4COMPR Job Stream, a First Step Toward a Comparison Proc

ment. The job stream uses IF/THEN/ENDIF tests to take appropriate processing actions based on the COND CODE set by IEBCOMPR. I also used data set name referbacks in STEP020, STEP030, and STEP040 for reliability, so that these steps would always process the same data set names as coded at STEP010.

Figure 4.16 show the MVS/ESA system output from a run of D4COMPAR comparing APPLES and ORANGES. The job stream works. Apparently these data sets have differing contents, because both were dumped.

4.9 Using SET in the Example Job Stream

Since my D4COMPAR job stream in Figure 4.15 works, I have taken the next step and installed symbolic parameters in it, creating job stream D5COMPAR, which you can see in Figure 4.17. It made sense to replace hardcoded data set names with symbolic parameters, since these names will change from run to run. I called one data set to be compared &ITEM1 and the other &ITEM2. These symbolic parameters exist at a total of five places in the job stream and allow me to replace three data set name referbacks in the original job stream.

Figure 4.18 provides the MVS/ESA system output from a run of my D5COMPAR job stream. You can see at the bottom of the first page of this output that symbolic parameter values have been substituted into the job stream from the SET statement just as these substitutions have traditionally been processed with proc execution. The hard part of getting the JCL into the form of a proc is now done, yet I still have the convenience of seeing it all in one place as ordinary JCL.

4.10 Converting SET to PROC

Figure 4.19 illustrates two elements of MVS/ESA JCL syntax that have a bearing on converting a job stream that uses SET with symbolic parameters into a proc. The symbolic parameter value assignments on the SET have to be converted into appropriate default values for the proc that will house the JCL. The SET statement is eliminated by this conversion.

I extracted Figure 4.19 from the actual proc I arrived at when I converted D5COMPAR into D6PROC. D6PROC is listed in Figure 4.20. The third symbolic parameter default at its beginning is for CCIN, which provides the text of the IDCAMS control card formed by the CCPGM program in the first step. You'll note that I removed the instream data from the job stream to finalize the proc, since procs cannot (even under MVS/ESA Version 4) contain instream data.

4.11 Proc Execution JCL

Figure 4.21 shows you the execution JCL for the D6PROC data set comparison proc, set up to compare CSCJGJ.ADV.APPLES with CSCJGJ.ADV.POMMES. This execution JCL fulfills the criteria of limiting the end user's concern to just the names of the data sets to be compared. None of the details of the job control language necessary to accomplish the

```
                    J E S 2  J O B  L O G  --  S Y S T E M  I B M 1  --  N O D E  N 1

11.49.27 JOB00030  IRR010I  USERID CSCJGJ   IS ASSIGNED TO THIS JOB.
11.49.28 JOB00030  ICH70001I CSCJGJ   LAST ACCESS AT 11:42:56 ON MONDAY, SEPTEMBER 6, 1993
11.49.28 JOB00030  $HASP373 CSCJGJA  STARTED - INIT  1 - CLASS A - SYS IBM1
11.49.29 JOB00030  $HASP395 CSCJGJA  ENDED

------ JES2 JOB STATISTICS ------
    06 SEP 93 JOB EXECUTION DATE
           62 CARDS READ
          208 SYSOUT PRINT RECORDS
            0 SYSOUT PUNCH RECORDS
           14 SYSOUT SPOOL KBYTES
         0.02 MINUTES EXECUTION TIME

        1 //CSCJGJA   JOB 1,                  ACCOUNTING INFORMATION
          //  'BIN 7--JANOSSY',               PROGRAMMER NAME AND DELIVERY BIN
          //  CLASS=A,                        INPUT QUEUE CLASS
          //  MSGLEVEL=(1,1),                 HOW MUCH MVS SYSTEM PRINT DESIRED
          //  MSGCLASS=X,                     PRINT DESTINATION X A L N OR O
          //  TIME=(0,6),                     SAFETY LIMIT: RUN TIME UP TO 6 SECS
          //  REGION=2M,                      ALLOW UP TO 2 MEGS VIRTUAL MEMORY
          //* TYPRUN=SCAN,                    UNCOMMENT THIS LINE TO DO SCAN ONLY
          //  NOTIFY=CSCJGJ                   WHO TO TELL WHEN JOB IS DONE
          //*
          //* COMPARE TWO DATA SETS, PRINT IF SAME, DUMP IF DIFFERENT
          //* THIS JCL IS STORED AT CSCJGJ.ADV.CNTL(D4COMPR)
          //*
          //*****************************************************
          //*                                                   *
          //*   COMPARE ITEMS USING IEBCOMPR                    *
          //*   COND CODE 0000 MEANS THEY ARE THE SAME          *
          //*   COND CODE > 0000 MEANS THEY ARE DIFFERENT       *
          //*                                                   *
          //*****************************************************
        2 //STEP010   EXEC  PGM=IEBCOMPR
        3 //SYSPRINT   DD   SYSOUT=*
        4 //SYSIN      DD   DUMMY
        5 //SYSUT1     DD   DSN=CSCJGJ.ADV.APPLES,DISP=SHR
        6 //SYSUT2     DD   DSN=CSCJGJ.ADV.ORANGES,DISP=SHR
          //*
```

Raw JCL Execution

The MVS/ESA system output from the D4COMPRO job stream shows // at the beginning of each line of JCL listed, because the job stream did not invoke any procs and did not use the INCLUDE statement to copy in any JCL. The names of the data sets to be compared and processed in the job stream are hardcoded at the inputs to the IEBCOMPR utility (SYSUT1 and SYSUT2). Data set name referbacks at lines 11, 17, and 21 will access these same data set names.

Figure 4.16 Annotated MVS/ESA System Output Produced by the D4COMPR Job Stream

```
        //*****************************************************
        //*                                                   *
        //*   IF ITEMS THE SAME, PRINT ONE                    *
        //*                                                   *
        //*****************************************************
      7 //       IF ( STEP010.RC = 0 ) THEN                     X
      8 //STEP020   EXEC  PGM=IEBGENER                          !
      9 //SYSPRINT    DD  SYSOUT=*                              ! IF
     10 //SYSIN       DD  DUMMY                                 ! ENDIF
     11 //SYSUT1      DD  DSN=*.STEP010.SYSUT1,DISP=SHR         !
     12 //SYSUT2      DD  SYSOUT=*                              !
     13 //       ENDIF                                          X
        //*
        //*****************************************************
        //*                                                   *
        //*   IF ITEMS DIFFERENT, DUMP THE FIRST ONE          *
        //*                                                   *
        //*****************************************************
     14 //       IF ( STEP010.RC > 0 ) THEN                     X
     15 //STEP030   EXEC  PGM=IDCAMS                            !
     16 //SYSPRINT    DD  SYSOUT=*                              !
     17 //DD1         DD  DSN=*.STEP010.SYSUT1,DISP=SHR         !
     18 //SYSIN       DD  *                                     !
        //*                                                     !
        //***************************************************** ! IF
        //*                                                   * ! ENDIF
        //*   IF ITEMS DIFFERENT, DUMP THE SECOND ONE         * !
        //*                                                   * !
        //***************************************************** !
     19 //STEP040   EXEC  PGM=IDCAMS                            !
     20 //SYSPRINT    DD  SYSOUT=*                              !
     21 //DD1         DD  DSN=*.STEP010.SYSUT2,DISP=SHR         !
     22 //SYSIN       DD  *                                     !
     23 //       ENDIF                                          X
ICH70001I CSCJGJ   LAST ACCESS AT 11:42:56 ON MONDAY, SEPTEMBER 6, 1993

IEF236I ALLOC. FOR CSCJGJA STEP010
IEF237I JES2 ALLOCATED TO SYSPRINT
IEF237I DMY  ALLOCATED TO SYSIN
IEF237I 117  ALLOCATED TO SYSUT1
IEF237I 117  ALLOCATED TO SYSUT2
```

This step will execute if IEBCOMPR leaves behind a COND CODE of 0000, indicating that the data sets compared are identical.

These steps will execute if IEBCOMPR leaves behind a nonzero COND CODE, indicating that the data sets are different. The IF test at statement 14 could have been coded as an ELSE in this job stream, and the ENDIF at statement 13 eliminated.

Figure 4.16 (continued)

```
IEF142I CSCJGJA STEP010 - STEP WAS EXECUTED - COND CODE 0008
IEF285I   CSCJGJ.CSCJGJA.JOB00030.D0000103.?            SYSOUT
IEF285I   CSCJGJ.ADV.APPLES                             KEPT
IEF285I   VOL SER NOS= USER03.
IEF285I   CSCJGJ.ADV.ORANGES                            KEPT
IEF285I   VOL SER NOS= USER03.
IEF373I STEP /STEP010 / START 93249.1149
IEF374I STEP /STEP010 / STOP  93249.1149

IEF206I CSCJGJA STEP020 - STEP WAS NOT RUN BECAUSE OF CONDITIONAL EXPRESSION ON STATEMENT 7
IEF272I CSCJGJA STEP020 - STEP WAS NOT EXECUTED.
IEF373I STEP /STEP020 / START 93249.1149
IEF374I STEP /STEP020 / STOP  93249.1149

IEF236I ALLOC. FOR CSCJGJA STEP030
IEF237I JES2 ALLOCATED TO SYSPRINT
IEF237I 117  ALLOCATED TO DD1
IEF237I JES2 ALLOCATED TO SYSIN
IEF142I CSCJGJA STEP030 - STEP WAS EXECUTED - COND CODE 0004
IEF285I   CSCJGJ.CSCJGJA.JOB00030.D0000106.?            SYSOUT
IEF285I   CSCJGJ.ADV.APPLES                             KEPT
IEF285I   VOL SER NOS= USER03.
IEF285I   CSCJGJ.CSCJGJA.JOB00030.D0000101.?            SYSIN
IEF373I STEP /STEP030 / START 93249.1149
IEF374I STEP /STEP030 / STOP  93249.1149

IEF236I ALLOC. FOR CSCJGJA STEP040
IEF237I JES2 ALLOCATED TO SYSPRINT
IEF237I 117  ALLOCATED TO DD1
IEF237I JES2 ALLOCATED TO SYSIN
IEF142I CSCJGJA STEP040 - STEP WAS EXECUTED - COND CODE 0004
IEF285I   CSCJGJ.CSCJGJA.JOB00030.D0000107.?            SYSOUT
IEF285I   CSCJGJ.ADV.ORANGES                            KEPT
IEF285I   VOL SER NOS= USER03.
IEF285I   CSCJGJ.CSCJGJA.JOB00030.D0000102.?            SYSIN
IEF373I STEP /STEP040 / START 93249.1149
IEF374I STEP /STEP040 / STOP  93249.1149

IEF375I  JOB /CSCJGJA / START 93249.1149
IEF376I  JOB /CSCJGJA / STOP  93249.1149
```

IEBCOMPR indicates that the data sets are different

IEBGENER step does not execute when the data sets are different

Both data sets are dumped in individual IDCAMS steps when the data sets are different. These dumps could have been done in one IDCAMS step by coding both DUMP commands there, but I wanted to build an example that used multiple steps to better demonstrate the scope of IF tests.

Figure 4.16 (continued)

```
                                        COMPARE UTILITY                                 PAGE 0001
IEB221I    RECORDS ARE NOT EQUAL

    DDNAME = SYSUT1
    PHYSICAL RECORD NUMBER = 00000001  LOGICAL RECORD NUMBER WITHIN PHYSICAL RECORD = 00000005
C1D5C440E2C5C1D3C9D5C740E6C1E76B40404040404040404040404040404040404040404040404040404040404040404040404040404040404040404040
4040404040404040404040404040404040404040

    DDNAME = SYSUT2
    PHYSICAL RECORD NUMBER = 00000001  LOGICAL RECORD NUMBER WITHIN PHYSICAL RECORD = 00000005
C1D5C440C3C5C9D3C9D5C740E6C1E76B40404040404040404040404040404040404040404040404040404040404040404040404040404040404040404040
4040404040404040404040404040404040404040

    END OF JOB-TOTAL NUMBER OF RECORDS COMPARED = 00000006
```

This is the simple report produced by IEBCOMPR when the data sets compared are different

```
IDCAMS  SYSTEM SERVICES                                  TIME: 11:49:28       09/06/93     PAGE    1

   PRINT INFILE(DD1) COUNT(50) DUMP

LISTING OF DATA SET -CSCJGJ.ADV.APPLES

RECORD SEQUENCE NUMBER - 1
000000  E3C8C540 E3C9D4C5 40C8C1E2 40C3D6D4   C56B4040 40404040 40404040 40404040   *THE TIME HAS COME,              *
000020  40404040 40404040 40404040 40404040   40404040 40404040 40404040 40404040   *                                *
000040  40404040 40404040 40404040 40404040                                         *                                *

RECORD SEQUENCE NUMBER - 2
000000  E3C8C540 E6C1D3D9 E4E240E2 C1C9C46B   40404040 40404040 40404040 40404040   *THE WALRUS SAID,                *
000020  40404040 40404040 40404040 40404040   40404040 40404040 40404040 40404040   *                                *
000040  40404040 40404040 40404040 40404040                                         *                                *
    -
    -

IDC11462I REQUESTED RANGE END BEYOND END OF DATA SET.
IDC0005I NUMBER OF RECORDS PROCESSED WAS 6
IDC0001I FUNCTION COMPLETED, HIGHEST CONDITION CODE WAS 4
    -
```

IDCAMS produces this standard format of dump showing data in both hexadecimal and character representations

Figure 4.16 (continued)

```
EDIT ---- CSCJGJ.ADV.CNTL(D5COMPR) - 01.01 ------------------ COLUMNS 001 072
COMMAND ===>                                                  SCROLL ===> PAGE
****** ***************************** TOP OF DATA ******************************
000001 //CSCJGJA   JOB 1,                   ACCOUNTING INFORMATION
000002 //   'BIN 7--JANOSSY',               PROGRAMMER NAME AND DELIVERY BIN
000003 //   CLASS=A,                        INPUT QUEUE CLASS
000004 //   MSGLEVEL=(1,1),                 HOW MUCH MVS SYSTEM PRINT DESIRED
000005 //   MSGCLASS=X,                     PRINT DESTINATION X A L N OR O
000006 //   TIME=(0,6),                     SAFETY LIMIT: RUN TIME UP TO 6 SECS
000007 //   REGION=2M,                      ALLOW UP TO 2 MEGS VIRTUAL MEMORY
000008 //*  TYPRUN=SCAN,                    UNCOMMENT THIS LINE TO DO SCAN ONLY
000009 //   NOTIFY=CSCJGJ                   WHO TO TELL WHEN JOB IS DONE
000010 //*
000011 //* DEMONSTRATE HOW THE NEW "SET" OPERATOR WORKS IN MVS JCL
000012 //* THIS JCL IS STORED AT CSCJGJ.ADV.CNTL(D5COMPR)
000013 //*
000014 //     SET  ITEM1='CSCJGJ.ADV.APPLES',     ONE DATA SET TO COMPARE
000015 //          ITEM2='CSCJGJ.ADV.ORANGES'     OTHER DATA SET TO COMPARE
000016 //*
000017 //*****************************************************
000018 //*                                                   *
000019 //*    COMPARE ITEMS USING THE IEBCOMPR UTILITY       *
000020 //*    COND CODE 0000 MEANS THEY ARE THE SAME         *
000021 //*    COND CODE > 0000 MEANS THEY ARE DIFFERENT      *
000022 //*                                                   *
000023 //*****************************************************
000024 //STEP010  EXEC  PGM=IEBCOMPR
000025 //SYSPRINT   DD  SYSOUT=*
000026 //SYSIN      DD  DUMMY
000027 //SYSUT1     DD  DSN=&ITEM1,DISP=SHR
000028 //SYSUT2     DD  DSN=&ITEM2,DISP=SHR
000029 //*
000030 //*****************************************************
000031 //*                                                   *
000032 //*    IF ITEMS THE SAME, PRINT ONE                   *
000033 //*                                                   *
000034 //*****************************************************
000035 //       IF ( STEP010.RC = 0 ) THEN                      X
000036 //STEP020  EXEC  PGM=IEBGENER                            !
000037 //SYSPRINT   DD  SYSOUT=*                                ! IF
000038 //SYSIN      DD  DUMMY                                   ! ENDIF
000039 //SYSUT1     DD  DSN=&ITEM1,DISP=SHR                     !
000040 //SYSUT2     DD  SYSOUT=*                                !
000041 //       ENDIF                                           X
000042 //*
000043 //*****************************************************
000044 //*                                                   *
000045 //*    IF ITEMS DIFFERENT, DUMP THE FIRST ONE         *
000046 //*                                                   *
000047 //*****************************************************
000048 //       IF ( STEP010.RC > 0 ) THEN                      X
000049 //STEP030  EXEC  PGM=IDCAMS                              !
000050 //SYSPRINT   DD  SYSOUT=*                                !
000051 //DD1        DD  DSN=&ITEM1,DISP=SHR                     !
000052 //SYSIN      DD  *                                       !
000053    PRINT INFILE(DD1) COUNT(50) DUMP
000054 //*                                                     !
000055 //***************************************************** ! IF
000056 //*                                                   * ! ENDIF
000057 //*    IF ITEMS DIFFERENT, DUMP THE SECOND ONE        * !
000058 //*                                                   * !
000059 //***************************************************** !
000060 //STEP040  EXEC  PGM=IDCAMS                              !
000061 //SYSPRINT   DD  SYSOUT=*                                !
000062 //DD1        DD  DSN=&ITEM2,DISP=SHR                     !
000063 //SYSIN      DD  *                                       !
000064    PRINT INFILE(DD1) COUNT(50) DUMP
000065 //       ENDIF                                           X
000066 //
```

I have taken the first step toward making the "compare" job stream into a proc. This is ordinary JCL but I installed symbolic parameters to replace the names of the data sets to be compared, naming them &ITEM1 and &ITEM2 at lines 27, 28, 39, 51, and 62. The SET statement assigns the symbolic parameters actual values.

Figure 4.17 D5COMPR Raw JCL Job Stream Showing Use of SET to Give Values to Symbolic Parameters

```
                  J E S 2  J O B  L O G  --  S Y S T E M  I B M 1  --  N O D E  N 1

11.53.22 JOB00033  IRR010I  USERID CSCJGJ   IS ASSIGNED TO THIS JOB.
11.53.23 JOB00033  ICH70001I CSCJGJ   LAST ACCESS AT 11:49:28 ON MONDAY, SEPTEMBER 6, 1993
11.53.23 JOB00033  $HASP373 CSCJGJA  STARTED - INIT  1 - CLASS A - SYS IBM1
11.53.24 JOB00033  $HASP395 CSCJGJA  ENDED
------ JES2 JOB STATISTICS ------
   06 SEP 93 JOB EXECUTION DATE
          65 CARDS READ
         216 SYSOUT PRINT RECORDS
           0 SYSOUT PUNCH RECORDS
          14 SYSOUT SPOOL KBYTES
        0.02 MINUTES EXECUTION TIME
        1 //CSCJGJA   JOB 1,                  ACCOUNTING INFORMATION
          //  'BIN 7--JANOSSY',               PROGRAMMER NAME AND DELIVERY BIN
          //  CLASS=A,                        INPUT QUEUE CLASS
          //  MSGLEVEL=(1,1),                 HOW MUCH MVS SYSTEM PRINT DESIRED
          //  MSGCLASS=X,                     PRINT DESTINATION X A L N OR O
          //  TIME=(0,6),                     SAFETY LIMIT: RUN TIME UP TO 6 SECS
          //  REGION=2M,                      ALLOW UP TO 2 MEGS VIRTUAL MEMORY
          //* TYPRUN=SCAN,                    UNCOMMENT THIS LINE TO DO SCAN ONLY
          //  NOTIFY=CSCJGJ                   WHO TO TELL WHEN JOB IS DONE
          //*
          //* DEMONSTRATE HOW THE NEW "SET" OPERATOR WORKS IN MVS JCL
          //* THIS JCL IS STORED AT CSCJGJ.ADV.CNTL(D5COMPR)
          //*
        2 //    SET  ITEM1='CSCJGJ.ADV.APPLES',         ONE DATA SET TO COMPARE
          //         ITEM2='CSCJGJ.ADV.ORANGES'         OTHER DATA SET TO COMPARE
          //*
          //*****************************************************
          //*                                                   *
          //*   COMPARE ITEMS USING THE IEBCOMPR UTILITY        *
          //*   COND CODE 0000 MEANS THEY ARE THE SAME          *
          //*   COND CODE > 0000 MEANS THEY ARE DIFFERENT       *
          //*                                                   *
          //*****************************************************
        3 //STEP010   EXEC  PGM=IEBCOMPR
        4 //SYSPRINT   DD   SYSOUT=*
        5 //SYSIN      DD   DUMMY
        6 //SYSUT1     DD   DSN=&ITEM1,DISP=SHR
          IEFC653I SUBSTITUTION JCL - DSN=CSCJGJ.ADV.APPLES,DISP=SHR
```

Using SET to Start New Proc Testing

SET substitutes actual values for symbolic parameters even though I am executing ordinary, nonproc JCL here. The JCL is all in one place rather than being housed as either an instream proc or a proc in a private JCL library. You can test your JCL this way with MVS/ESA Version 4, and refine your use of symbolic parameters, before taking the final step of housing a new proc separate from your execution JCL.

Figure 4.18 Annotated MVS/ESA System Output Produced by the D5COMPR Job Stream (SET and Symbolic Parameter Substitutions)

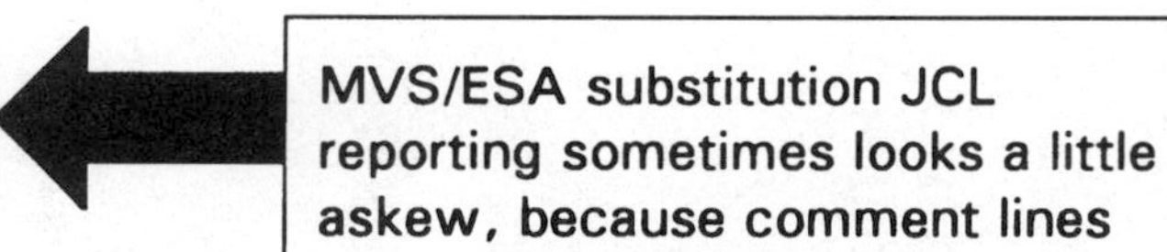

```
  7 //SYSUT2     DD  DSN=&ITEM2,DISP=SHR
    //*
    //*****************************************************
    //*                                                   *
    //*   IF ITEMS THE SAME, PRINT ONE                    *
    //*                                                   *
    //*****************************************************
    IEFC653I SUBSTITUTION JCL - DSN=CSCJGJ.ADV.ORANGES,DISP=SHR
  8 //       IF ( STEP010.RC = 0 ) THEN                    X
  9 //STEP020  EXEC  PGM=IEBGENER                          !
 10 //SYSPRINT   DD  SYSOUT=*                              !  IF
 11 //SYSIN      DD  DUMMY                                 !  ENDIF
 12 //SYSUT1     DD  DSN=&ITEM1,DISP=SHR                   !
    IEFC653I SUBSTITUTION JCL - DSN=CSCJGJ.ADV.APPLES,DISP=SHR
 13 //SYSUT2     DD  SYSOUT=*                              !
 14 //       ENDIF                                         X
    //*
    //*****************************************************
    //*                                                   *
    //*   IF ITEMS DIFFERENT, DUMP THE FIRST ONE          *
    //*                                                   *
    //*****************************************************
 15 //       IF ( STEP010.RC > 0 ) THEN                    X
 16 //STEP030  EXEC  PGM=IDCAMS                            !
 17 //SYSPRINT   DD  SYSOUT=*                              !
 18 //DD1        DD  DSN=&ITEM1,DISP=SHR                   !
    IEFC653I SUBSTITUTION JCL - DSN=CSCJGJ.ADV.APPLES,DISP=SHR
 19 //SYSIN      DD  *                                     !
    //*                                                    !
    //*****************************************************  !  IF
    //*                                                   *  !  ENDIF
    //*   IF ITEMS DIFFERENT, DUMP THE SECOND ONE         *  !
    //*                                                   *  !
    //*****************************************************  !
 20 //STEP040  EXEC  PGM=IDCAMS                            !
 21 //SYSPRINT   DD  SYSOUT=*                              !
 22 //DD1        DD  DSN=&ITEM2,DISP=SHR                   !
    IEFC653I SUBSTITUTION JCL - DSN=CSCJGJ.ADV.ORANGES,DISP=SHR
 23 //SYSIN      DD  *                                     !
 24 //       ENDIF                                         X

ICH70001I CSCJGJ   LAST ACCESS AT 11:49:28 ON MONDAY, SEPTEMBER 6, 1993
```

MVS/ESA substitution JCL reporting sometimes looks a little askew, because comment lines are passed over differently by different modules of system software. Here you see the substitution JCL values reported *after* the comment lines that follow the location of the symbolic parameter &ITEM2. There is no problem here, but at first glance you might think that the symbolic parameter substitution had not occurred.

Figure 4.18 (continued)

```
000014 //    SET   ITEM1='CSCJGJ.ADV.APPLES',
000015 //          ITEM2='CSCJGJ.ADV.ORANGES'
```

```
000001 //D6PROC   PROC  ITEM1='***',
000002 //   ITEM2='***',
000003 //   CCIN='PRINT INFILE(DD1) COUNT(50) DUMP'
```

Figure 4.19 Converting a SET Statement to a PROC Statement

comparison and printing or dumping actions is visible to the end user of this execution JCL. If you want to think about it that way, you can also envision that the EXEC statement in this JCL was built from the SET statement in Figure 4.19.

The output received by the end user from submission of the execution JCL is shown in Figure 4.22. The symbolic parameter substitutions are reported as expected. The IF/THEN/ELSE tests cause STEP020 to be executed, but not STEP030 and STEP040. The single printed copy of a data set in plain text at the end of the job stream indicates that APPLES and POMMES are the same. And so they are.

4.12 An Important SET Limitation

Figure 4.23 shows you a variation of proc execution that might occur to you, and it reveals several interesting things about SET and symbolic parameter substitution. In this case, I have coded SET to try to supply values to symbolic parameters while executing a proc. This will not be successful because D6PROC, like any modern proc coded for ease of maintenance, includes defaults (coded on the PROC statement) for all symbolic parameters.

Submitting the execution JCL in Figure 4.23 generates a JCL error and produces the MVS/ESA system output shown in Figure 4.24. Here's what it reveals about SET and good proc practice:

1. SET cannot override symbolic parameter defaults coded within a proc. The symbolic parameter substitutions made in this run are those carried on the PROC statement, not those on the SET statement.

2. Although there is no reasonable default value for &ITEM1 and &ITEM2 in this proc (these are the names of data sets to be compared), assigning patently invalid default values, such as '***' on the PROC statement, when a symbolic parameter is used for DSN, provides two benefits. For one thing, it documents the existence of the symbolic parameters at the PROC state-

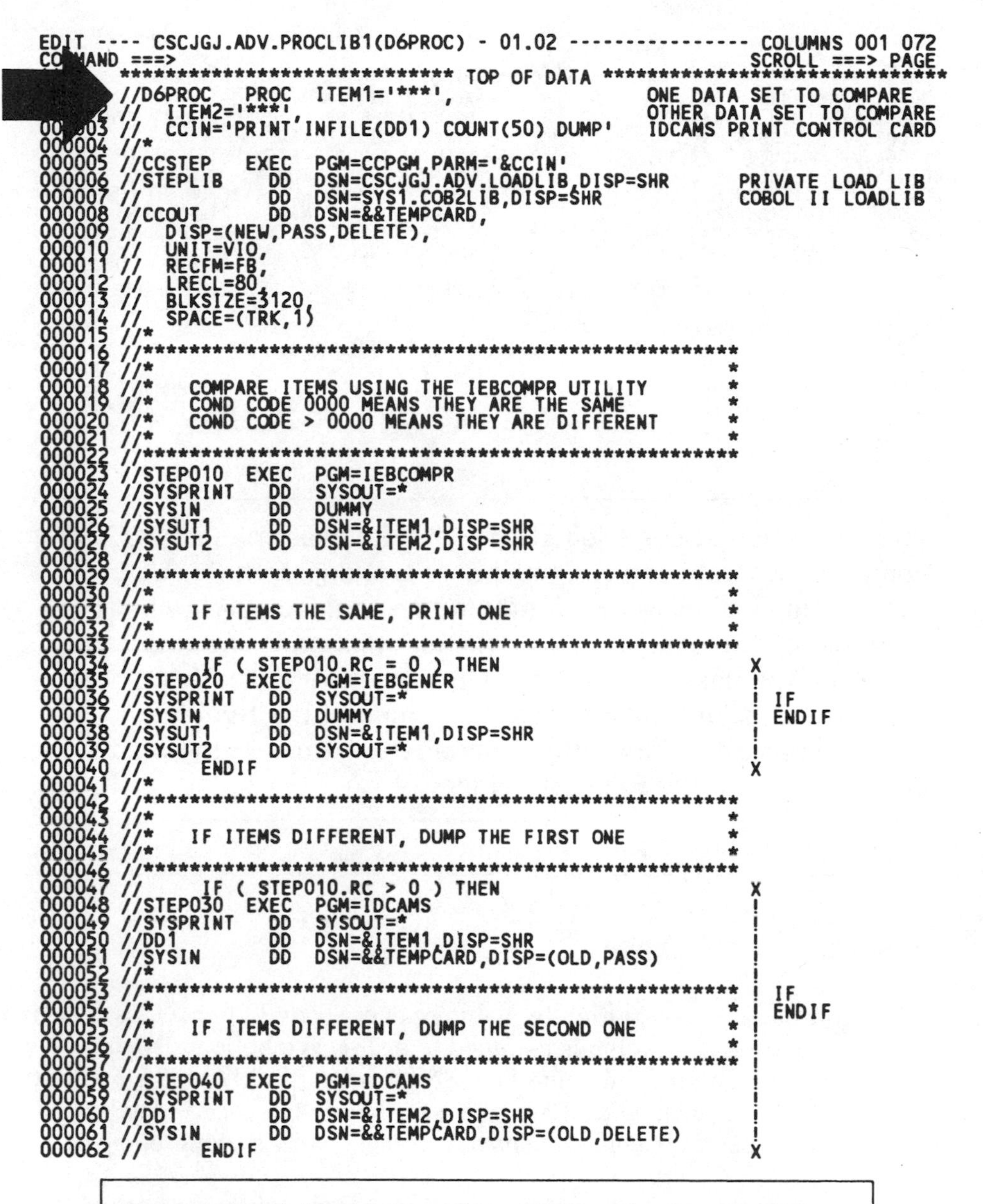

```
EDIT ---- CSCJGJ.ADV.PROCLIB1(D6PROC) - 01.02 --------------- COLUMNS 001 072
CO  AND ===>                                                  SCROLL ===> PAGE
       ****************************** TOP OF DATA ******************************
       //D6PROC   PROC  ITEM1='***',                    ONE DATA SET TO COMPARE
       //  ITEM2='***',                                 OTHER DATA SET TO COMPARE
00  03 //  CCIN='PRINT INFILE(DD1) COUNT(50) DUMP'      IDCAMS PRINT CONTROL CARD
000004 //*
000005 //CCSTEP   EXEC  PGM=CCPGM,PARM='&CCIN'
000006 //STEPLIB   DD   DSN=CSCJGJ.ADV.LOADLIB,DISP=SHR        PRIVATE LOAD LIB
000007 //          DD   DSN=SYS1.COB2LIB,DISP=SHR              COBOL II LOADLIB
000008 //CCOUT     DD   DSN=&&TEMPCARD,
000009 //  DISP=(NEW,PASS,DELETE),
000010 //  UNIT=VIO,
000011 //  RECFM=FB,
000012 //  LRECL=80,
000013 //  BLKSIZE=3120,
000014 //  SPACE=(TRK,1)
000015 //*
000016 //*****************************************************
000017 //*                                                   *
000018 //*    COMPARE ITEMS USING THE IEBCOMPR UTILITY       *
000019 //*    COND CODE 0000 MEANS THEY ARE THE SAME         *
000020 //*    COND CODE > 0000 MEANS THEY ARE DIFFERENT      *
000021 //*                                                   *
000022 //*****************************************************
000023 //STEP010  EXEC  PGM=IEBCOMPR
000024 //SYSPRINT  DD   SYSOUT=*
000025 //SYSIN     DD   DUMMY
000026 //SYSUT1    DD   DSN=&ITEM1,DISP=SHR
000027 //SYSUT2    DD   DSN=&ITEM2,DISP=SHR
000028 //*
000029 //*****************************************************
000030 //*                                                   *
000031 //*    IF ITEMS THE SAME, PRINT ONE                   *
000032 //*                                                   *
000033 //*****************************************************
000034 //       IF ( STEP010.RC = 0 ) THEN                       X
000035 //STEP020  EXEC  PGM=IEBGENER                             !
000036 //SYSPRINT  DD   SYSOUT=*                                 ! IF
000037 //SYSIN     DD   DUMMY                                    ! ENDIF
000038 //SYSUT1    DD   DSN=&ITEM1,DISP=SHR                      !
000039 //SYSUT2    DD   SYSOUT=*                                 !
000040 //       ENDIF                                            X
000041 //*
000042 //*****************************************************
000043 //*                                                   *
000044 //*    IF ITEMS DIFFERENT, DUMP THE FIRST ONE         *
000045 //*                                                   *
000046 //*****************************************************
000047 //       IF ( STEP010.RC > 0 ) THEN                       X
000048 //STEP030  EXEC  PGM=IDCAMS                               !
000049 //SYSPRINT  DD   SYSOUT=*                                 !
000050 //DD1       DD   DSN=&ITEM1,DISP=SHR                      !
000051 //SYSIN     DD   DSN=&&TEMPCARD,DISP=(OLD,PASS)           !
000052 //*                                                      !
000053 //***************************************************** ! IF
000054 //*                                                   * ! ENDIF
000055 //*    IF ITEMS DIFFERENT, DUMP THE SECOND ONE        * !
000056 //*                                                   * !
000057 //***************************************************** !
000058 //STEP040  EXEC  PGM=IDCAMS                               !
000059 //SYSPRINT  DD   SYSOUT=*                                 !
000060 //DD1       DD   DSN=&ITEM2,DISP=SHR                      !
000061 //SYSIN     DD   DSN=&&TEMPCARD,DISP=(OLD,DELETE)         !
000062 //       ENDIF                                            X
```

This is the finished "compare" proc. I converted the SET statement into a PROC statement and named the proc D6PROC. Invalid defaults for data set name document symbolic parameters ITEM1 and ITEM2. I used CCPGM to form the IDCAMS control statement from a PARM that receives a symbolic parameter default, since instream data can't be put into a proc.

Figure 4.20 Completed D6PROC Proc to Do Data Set Comparisons

```
EDIT ---- CSCJGJ.ADV.CNTL(D6EXJCL) - 01.01 ------------------- COLUMNS 001 072
COMMAND ===>                                                  SCROLL ===> PAGE
****** ****************************** TOP OF DATA ******************************
000001 //CSCJGJA   JOB 1,                  ACCOUNTING INFORMATION
000002 //   'BIN 7--JANOSSY',              PROGRAMMER NAME AND DELIVERY BIN
000003 //   CLASS=A,                       INPUT QUEUE CLASS
000004 //   MSGLEVEL=(1,1),                HOW MUCH MVS SYSTEM PRINT DESIRED
000005 //   MSGCLASS=X,                    PRINT DESTINATION X A L N OR O
000006 //   TIME=(0,6),                    SAFETY LIMIT: RUN TIME UP TO 6 SECS
000007 //   REGION=2M,                     ALLOW UP TO 2 MEGS VIRTUAL MEMORY
000008 //*  TYPRUN=SCAN,                   UNCOMMENT THIS LINE TO DO SCAN ONLY
000009 //   NOTIFY=CSCJGJ                  WHO TO TELL WHEN JOB IS DONE
000010 //*
000011 //        JCLLIB  ORDER=(CSCJGJ.ADV.PROCLIB1)          PRIVATE PROC LIB
000012 //*
000013 //* JCL TO EXECUTE D6PROC
000014 //* THIS JCL IS STORED AT CSCJGJ.ADV.CNTL(D6EXJCL)
000015 //*
000016 //STEPA    EXEC  D6PROC,
000017 //   ITEM1='CSCJGJ.ADV.APPLES',                 ONE DATA SET TO COMPARE
000018 //   ITEM2='CSCJGJ.ADV.POMME'                   OTHER DATA SET TO COMPARE
000019 //
```

This execution JCL is a job stream that invokes the D6PROC to compare two data sets. An end user working with this JCL has to supply a minimum of information to accomplish all of the work needed to compare two data sets and print or dump one or both. The user supplies the JOB statement indicating global factors that affect the job, and the names of the two data sets to be compared. The symbolic parameter values in the proc are assigned via the EXEC statement.

Figure 4.21 D6EXJCL Job Stream Executing D6PROC to Compare "Apples" and "Pommes" Data Sets

ment, for ease of recognition in maintenance. Second, it provides very clear error reporting if no value is assigned to a DSN symbolic parameter. (If you did not assign an invalid value for DSN as a default, MVS/ESA would treat data set names such as &ITEM1 and &ITEM2 as temporary data set names and issue potentially confusing error messages in its system reporting.)

I recap this and other SET limitations, along with those of the JCLLIB and INCLUDE statements, in the summary sections that follow.

4.13 Summary of JCLLIB Statement Rules

The JCLLIB statement is one of the biggest improvements provided by MVS/ESA Version 4. You use the JCLLIB statement to name private libraries (not individual JCL member names) that MVS/ESA will use for a job:

```
//      JCLLIB ORDER=(name1,name2,          comment
//          name3,                          comment
//          name4)                          comment
```

```
                    J E S 2  J O B  L O G  --  S Y S T E M  I B M 1  --  N O D E  N 1

12.10.46 JOB00054  IRR010I  USERID CSCJGJ   IS ASSIGNED TO THIS JOB.
12.10.46 JOB00054  ICH70001I CSCJGJ   LAST ACCESS AT 12:06:08 ON MONDAY, SEPTEMBER 6, 1993
12.10.46 JOB00054  $HASP373 CSCJGJA  STARTED - INIT  1 - CLASS A - SYS IBM1
12.10.49 JOB00054  $HASP395 CSCJGJA  ENDED

------ JES2 JOB STATISTICS ------
   06 SEP 93 JOB EXECUTION DATE
          18 CARDS READ
         162 SYSOUT PRINT RECORDS
           0 SYSOUT PUNCH RECORDS
          10 SYSOUT SPOOL KBYTES
        0.04 MINUTES EXECUTION TIME

         1 //CSCJGJA   JOB 1,                      ACCOUNTING INFORMATION
           //   'BIN 7--JANOSSY',                  PROGRAMMER NAME AND DELIVERY BIN
           //   CLASS=A,                           INPUT QUEUE CLASS
           //   MSGLEVEL=(1,1),                    HOW MUCH MVS SYSTEM PRINT DESIRED
           //   MSGCLASS=X,                        PRINT DESTINATION X A L N OR O
           //   TIME=(0,6),                        SAFETY LIMIT: RUN TIME UP TO 6 SECS
           //   REGION=2M,                         ALLOW UP TO 2 MEGS VIRTUAL MEMORY
           //*  TYPRUN=SCAN,                       UNCOMMENT THIS LINE TO DO SCAN ONLY
           //   NOTIFY=CSCJGJ                      WHO TO TELL WHEN JOB IS DONE
           //*
         2 //        JCLLIB  ORDER=(CSCJGJ.ADV.PROCLIB1)         PRIVATE PROC LIB
           //*
           //* JCL TO EXECUTE D6PROC
           //* THIS JCL IS STORED AT CSCJGJ.ADV.CNTL(D6EXJCL)
           //*
         3 //STEPA     EXEC  D6PROC,
           //   ITEM1='CSCJGJ.ADV.APPLES',                ONE DATA SET TO COMPARE
           //   ITEM2='CSCJGJ.ADV.POMMES'                 OTHER DATA SET TO COMPARE
         4 XXD6PROC    PROC  ITEM1='***',                  ONE DATA SET TO COMPARE
           XX   ITEM2='***',                               OTHER DATA SET TO COMPARE
           XX   CCIN='PRINT INFILE(DD1) COUNT(50) DUMP'    IDCAMS PRINT CONTROL CARD
           XX*
         5 XXCCSTEP    EXEC  PGM=CCPGM,PARM='&CCIN'
           IEFC653I SUBSTITUTION JCL - PRINT INFILE(DD1) COUNT(50) DUMP
         6 XXSTEPLIB     DD  DSN=CSCJGJ.ADV.LOADLIB,DISP=SHR         PRIVATE LOAD LIB
         7 XX            DD  DSN=SYS1.COB2LIB,DISP=SHR               COBOL II LOADLIB
         8 XXCCOUT       DD  DSN=&&TEMPCARD,
```

Testing the New Proc

I moved the actual symbolic parameter values for the data set names to be compared, previously assigned by the SET statement of the D5COMPR job stream, to an EXEC statement in the execution JCL named D6EXJCL. Here you see how this execution JCL invokes D6PROC, the completed proc built from D5COMPR. The symbolic parameter value substitutions now include a value for CCIN, which is not coded on the EXEC statement, but is supplied by a default coded on the D6PROC statement.

Figure 4.22 Annotated MVS/ESA System Output Produced by the D6EXJCL Job Stream, Which Invokes the D6PROC Proc

```
          XX  DISP=(NEW,PASS,DELETE),
          XX  UNIT=VIO,
          XX  RECFM=FB,
          XX  LRECL=80,
          XX  BLKSIZE=3120,
          XX  SPACE=(TRK,1)
          XX*
          XX*******************************************************
          XX*                                                     *
          XX*   COMPARE ITEMS USING THE IEBCOMPR UTILITY          *
          XX*   COND CODE 0000 MEANS THEY ARE THE SAME            *
          XX*   COND CODE > 0000 MEANS THEY ARE DIFFERENT         *
          XX*                                                     *
          XX*******************************************************
        9 XXSTEP010   EXEC  PGM=IEBCOMPR
       10 XXSYSPRINT   DD   SYSOUT=*
       11 XXSYSIN      DD   DUMMY
       12 XXSYSUT1     DD   DSN=&ITEM1,DISP=SHR
          IEFC653I SUBSTITUTION JCL - DSN=CSCJGJ.ADV.APPLES,DISP=SHR
       13 XXSYSUT2     DD   DSN=&ITEM2,DISP=SHR
          XX*
          XX*******************************************************
          XX*                                                     *
          XX*   IF ITEMS THE SAME, PRINT ONE                      *
          XX*                                                     *
          XX*******************************************************
          IEFC653I SUBSTITUTION JCL - DSN=CSCJGJ.ADV.POMMES,DISP=SHR

       14 XX       IF ( STEP010.RC = 0 ) THEN                      X
       15 XXSTEP020  EXEC  PGM=IEBGENER                            !
       16 XXSYSPRINT   DD   SYSOUT=*                               ! IF
       17 XXSYSIN      DD   DUMMY                                  ! ENDIF
       18 XXSYSUT1     DD   DSN=&ITEM1,DISP=SHR                    !
          IEFC653I SUBSTITUTION JCL - DSN=CSCJGJ.ADV.APPLES,DISP=SHR
       19 XXSYSUT2     DD   SYSOUT=*                               !
       20 XX       ENDIF                                           X
          XX*
          XX*******************************************************
          XX*                                                     *
          XX*   IF ITEMS DIFFERENT, DUMP THE FIRST ONE            *
          XX*                                                     *
          XX*******************************************************
```

Symbolic parameter value substitutions

Figure 4.22 *(continued)*

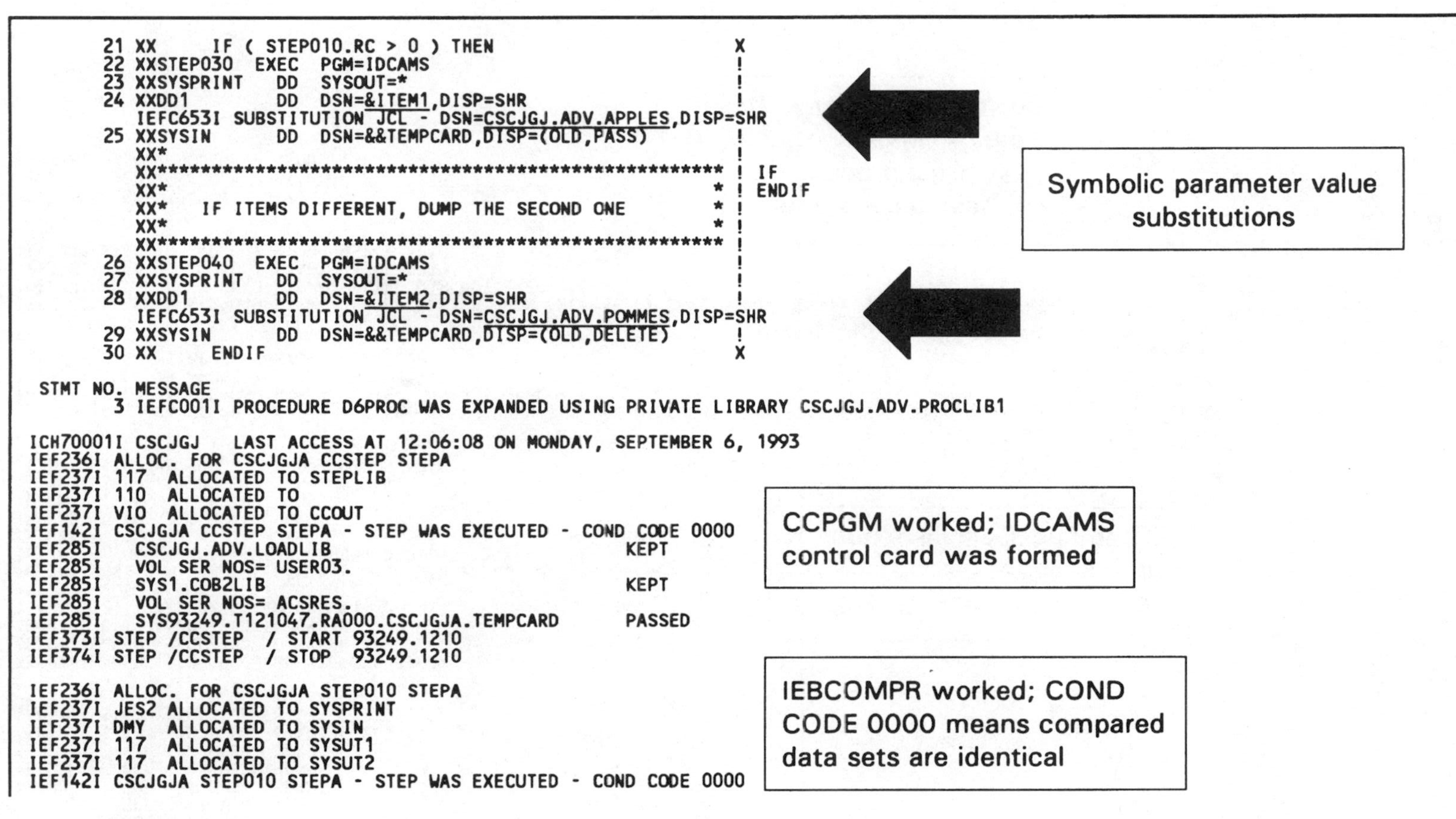

```
       21 XX       IF ( STEP010.RC > 0 ) THEN                         X
       22 XXSTEP030  EXEC  PGM=IDCAMS                                 !
       23 XXSYSPRINT   DD  SYSOUT=*                                   !
       24 XXDD1        DD  DSN=&ITEM1,DISP=SHR                        !
          IEFC653I SUBSTITUTION JCL - DSN=CSCJGJ.ADV.APPLES,DISP=SHR
       25 XXSYSIN      DD  DSN=&&TEMPCARD,DISP=(OLD,PASS)             !
          XX*                                                         !
          XX*******************************************************  ! IF
          XX*                                                      *  ! ENDIF
          XX*    IF ITEMS DIFFERENT, DUMP THE SECOND ONE            *  !
          XX*                                                      *  !
          XX*******************************************************  !
       26 XXSTEP040  EXEC  PGM=IDCAMS                                 !
       27 XXSYSPRINT   DD  SYSOUT=*                                   !
       28 XXDD1        DD  DSN=&ITEM2,DISP=SHR                        !
          IEFC653I SUBSTITUTION JCL - DSN=CSCJGJ.ADV.POMMES,DISP=SHR
       29 XXSYSIN      DD  DSN=&&TEMPCARD,DISP=(OLD,DELETE)           !
       30 XX       ENDIF                                              X

 STMT NO. MESSAGE
        3 IEFC001I PROCEDURE D6PROC WAS EXPANDED USING PRIVATE LIBRARY CSCJGJ.ADV.PROCLIB1

ICH70001I CSCJGJ   LAST ACCESS AT 12:06:08 ON MONDAY, SEPTEMBER 6, 1993
IEF236I ALLOC. FOR CSCJGJA CCSTEP STEPA
IEF237I 117  ALLOCATED TO STEPLIB
IEF237I 110  ALLOCATED TO
IEF237I VIO  ALLOCATED TO CCOUT
IEF142I CSCJGJA CCSTEP STEPA - STEP WAS EXECUTED - COND CODE 0000
IEF285I   CSCJGJ.ADV.LOADLIB                           KEPT
IEF285I   VOL SER NOS= USER03.
IEF285I   SYS1.COB2LIB                                 KEPT
IEF285I   VOL SER NOS= ACSRES.
IEF285I   SYS93249.T121047.RA000.CSCJGJA.TEMPCARD      PASSED
IEF373I STEP /CCSTEP  / START 93249.1210
IEF374I STEP /CCSTEP  / STOP  93249.1210

IEF236I ALLOC. FOR CSCJGJA STEP010 STEPA
IEF237I JES2 ALLOCATED TO SYSPRINT
IEF237I DMY  ALLOCATED TO SYSIN
IEF237I 117  ALLOCATED TO SYSUT1
IEF237I 117  ALLOCATED TO SYSUT2
IEF142I CSCJGJA STEP010 STEPA - STEP WAS EXECUTED - COND CODE 0000
```

Symbolic parameter value substitutions
CCPGM worked; IDCAMS control card was formed
IEBCOMPR worked; COND CODE 0000 means compared data sets are identical

Figure 4.22 (continued)

```
IEF285I   CSCJGJ.CSCJGJA.JOB00054.D0000101.?          SYSOUT
IEF285I   CSCJGJ.ADV.APPLES                           KEPT
IEF285I   VOL SER NOS= USER03.
IEF285I   CSCJGJ.ADV.POMMES                           KEPT
IEF285I   VOL SER NOS= USER03.
IEF373I STEP /STEP010 / START 93249.1210
IEF374I STEP /STEP010 / STOP  93249.1210

IEF236I ALLOC. FOR CSCJGJA STEP020 STEPA
IEF237I JES2 ALLOCATED TO SYSPRINT
IEF237I DMY  ALLOCATED TO SYSIN
IEF237I 117  ALLOCATED TO SYSUT1
IEF237I JES2 ALLOCATED TO SYSUT2
IEF142I CSCJGJA STEP020 STEPA - STEP WAS EXECUTED - COND CODE 0000
IEF285I   CSCJGJ.CSCJGJA.JOB00054.D0000102.?          SYSOUT
IEF285I   CSCJGJ.ADV.APPLES                           KEPT
IEF285I   VOL SER NOS= USER03.
IEF285I   CSCJGJ.CSCJGJA.JOB00054.D0000103.?          SYSOUT
IEF373I STEP /STEP020 / START 93249.1210
IEF374I STEP /STEP020 / STOP  93249.1210

IEF206I CSCJGJA STEP030 STEPA - STEP WAS NOT RUN BECAUSE OF CONDITIONAL EXPRESSION ON STATEMENT 21
IEF272I CSCJGJA STEP030 STEPA - STEP WAS NOT EXECUTED.
IEF373I STEP /STEP030 / START 93249.1210
IEF374I STEP /STEP030 / STOP  93249.1210

IEF206I CSCJGJA STEP040 STEPA - STEP WAS NOT RUN BECAUSE OF CONDITIONAL EXPRESSION ON STATEMENT 21
IEF272I CSCJGJA STEP040 STEPA - STEP WAS NOT EXECUTED.
IEF373I STEP /STEP040 / START 93249.1210
IEF374I STEP /STEP040 / STOP  93249.1210

IEF285I   SYS93249.T121047.RA000.CSCJGJA.TEMPCARD     DELETED
IEF375I  JOB /CSCJGJA / START 93249.1210
IEF376I  JOB /CSCJGJA / STOP  93249.1210
```

IEBGENER worked; one data set was copied to the printer to form a simple listing of it

The two IDCAMS dump steps did not execute; no need to dump the data sets since IEBCOMPR said they were identical!

Temporary data set containing the IDCAMS control card is deleted by MVS/ESA at job end

Figure 4.22 (continued)

```
                                        COMPARE UTILITY                                 PAGE 0001
    END OF JOB-TOTAL NUMBER OF RECORDS COMPARED = 00000006
```

IEBCOMPR report produced when compared data sets are identical

```
DATA SET UTILITY - GENERATE                                                             PAGE 0001
IEB352I WARNING : OUTPUT RECFM/LRECL COPIED FROM INPUT
PROCESSING ENDED AT EOD
```

IEBGENER's status report, produced at //SYSPRINT in STEP020 (the warning message can be ignored when IEBGENER is used to copy a data set to the printer)

```
THE TIME HAS COME,
THE WALRUS SAID,
TO TALK OF MANY THINGS.
SAILING SHIPS,
AND SEALING WAX,
AND CABBAGES AND KINGS.
```

Listing of one data set, produced at //SYSUT2 of STEP020

Figure 4.22 (continued)

```
EDIT ---- CSCJGJ.ADV.CNTL(D7SET) - 01.00 -------------------- COLUMNS 001 072
COMMAND ===>                                                  SCROLL ===> PAGE
****** ***************************** TOP OF DATA ******************************
000001 //CSCJGJA   JOB 1,                  ACCOUNTING INFORMATION
000002 //  'BIN 7--JANOSSY',               PROGRAMMER NAME AND DELIVERY BIN
000003 //  CLASS=A,                        INPUT QUEUE CLASS
000004 //  MSGLEVEL=(1,1),                 HOW MUCH MVS SYSTEM PRINT DESIRED
000005 //  MSGCLASS=X,                     PRINT DESTINATION X A L N OR O
000006 //  TIME=(0,6),                     SAFETY LIMIT: RUN TIME UP TO 6 SECS
000007 //  REGION=2M,                      ALLOW UP TO 2 MEGS VIRTUAL MEMORY
000008 //* TYPRUN=SCAN,                    UNCOMMENT THIS LINE TO DO SCAN ONLY
000009 //  NOTIFY=CSCJGJ                   WHO TO TELL WHEN JOB IS DONE
000010 //*
000011 //       JCLLIB  ORDER=(CSCJGJ.ADV.PROCLIB1)          PRIVATE PROC LIB
000012 //*
000013 //* JCL TO EXECUTE D6PROC USING "SET"
000014 //* THIS JCL IS STORED AT CSCJGJ.ADV.CNTL
000015 //*
000016 //   SET  ITEM1='CSCJGJ.ADV.APPLES',         ONE DATA SET TO COMPARE
000017 //        ITEM2='CSCJGJ.ADV.ORANGES'         OTHER DATA SET TO COMPARE
000018 //*
000019 //STEPA    EXEC  D6PROC
000020 //
```

You can't use SET to assign values to symbolic parameters within procs that have symbolic parameter defaults, because defaults coded on a PROC statement (within a proc) take precedence. Put another way, ***SET can't override proc defaults.***

Figure 4.23 D7SET Job Stream Demonstrating a SET Error; SET Cannot Override Proc Default Values for Symbolic Parameters

where *name1* and the other names shown are data set names such as CSCJGJ.ADV.PROCLIB1. You can continue a JCLLIB statement as shown, but as with any continued line, don't indent the continuations beyond column 16 or they will be ignored. You can put comments on the same line, abiding by customary JCL commenting rules.

You can put procs you want to invoke by name, and ordinary JCL that you want to obtain with INCLUDE, into the same or different JCL libraries. JCLLIB lets you execute procs and use INCLUDE even if you don't have security authorization to put procs and JCL into your installation's default (production) JCL libraries. Using JCLLIB, you can abandon instream procs completely and make your final job stream testing activities identical to "real" production job execution.

MVS/ESA searches the libraries you name on the JCLLIB statement in the order you code them after the ORDER parameter. If the same proc or JCL is in more than one of these libraries, MVS/ESA will use the first copy it finds. If MVS/ESA still has not found a proc or INCLUDE group after searching the libraries you name, it searches JCL libraries defined as a default by your installation. SYS1.PROCLIB is the single default JCL library defined to MVS/ESA as it is delivered by IBM, but your installation can define other default JCL libraries. If you don't use a JCLLIB statement, MVS/ESA looks only in the installation default JCL libraries for procs you execute or JCL you want to INCLUDE.

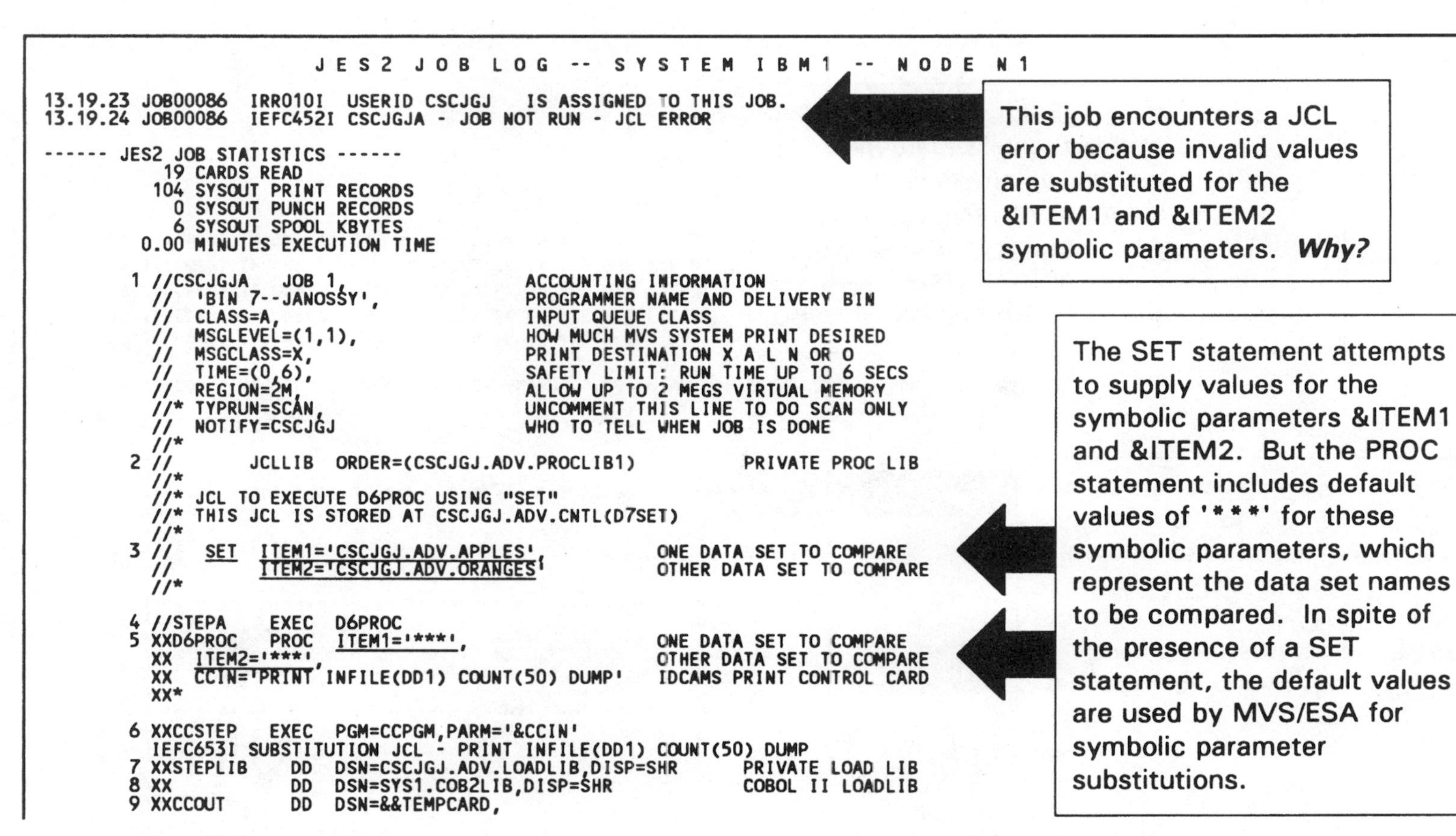

```
                    J E S 2   J O B   L O G  --  S Y S T E M   I B M 1  --  N O D E   N 1

13.19.23 JOB00086  IRR010I  USERID CSCJGJ   IS ASSIGNED TO THIS JOB.
13.19.24 JOB00086  IEFC452I CSCJGJA - JOB NOT RUN - JCL ERROR

------ JES2 JOB STATISTICS ------
       19 CARDS READ
      104 SYSOUT PRINT RECORDS
        0 SYSOUT PUNCH RECORDS
        6 SYSOUT SPOOL KBYTES
     0.00 MINUTES EXECUTION TIME

        1 //CSCJGJA   JOB 1,                  ACCOUNTING INFORMATION
          //  'BIN 7--JANOSSY',              PROGRAMMER NAME AND DELIVERY BIN
          //  CLASS=A,                       INPUT QUEUE CLASS
          //  MSGLEVEL=(1,1),                HOW MUCH MVS SYSTEM PRINT DESIRED
          //  MSGCLASS=X,                    PRINT DESTINATION X A L N OR O
          //  TIME=(0,6),                    SAFETY LIMIT: RUN TIME UP TO 6 SECS
          //  REGION=2M,                     ALLOW UP TO 2 MEGS VIRTUAL MEMORY
          //* TYPRUN=SCAN,                   UNCOMMENT THIS LINE TO DO SCAN ONLY
          //  NOTIFY=CSCJGJ                  WHO TO TELL WHEN JOB IS DONE
          //*
        2 //       JCLLIB  ORDER=(CSCJGJ.ADV.PROCLIB1)          PRIVATE PROC LIB
          //*
          //* JCL TO EXECUTE D6PROC USING "SET"
          //* THIS JCL IS STORED AT CSCJGJ.ADV.CNTL(D7SET)
          //*
        3 //   SET  ITEM1='CSCJGJ.ADV.APPLES',        ONE DATA SET TO COMPARE
          //        ITEM2='CSCJGJ.ADV.ORANGES'        OTHER DATA SET TO COMPARE
          //*

        4 //STEPA     EXEC  D6PROC
        5 XXD6PROC    PROC  ITEM1='***',                ONE DATA SET TO COMPARE
          XX  ITEM2='***',                              OTHER DATA SET TO COMPARE
          XX  CCIN='PRINT INFILE(DD1) COUNT(50) DUMP'   IDCAMS PRINT CONTROL CARD
          XX*

        6 XXCCSTEP    EXEC  PGM=CCPGM,PARM='&CCIN'
          IEFC653I SUBSTITUTION JCL - PRINT INFILE(DD1) COUNT(50) DUMP
        7 XXSTEPLIB     DD  DSN=CSCJGJ.ADV.LOADLIB,DISP=SHR      PRIVATE LOAD LIB
        8 XX            DD  DSN=SYS1.COB2LIB,DISP=SHR            COBOL II LOADLIB
        9 XXCCOUT       DD  DSN=&&TEMPCARD,
```

This job encounters a JCL error because invalid values are substituted for the &ITEM1 and &ITEM2 symbolic parameters. **Why?**
The SET statement attempts to supply values for the symbolic parameters &ITEM1 and &ITEM2. But the PROC statement includes default values of '***' for these symbolic parameters, which represent the data set names to be compared. In spite of the presence of a SET statement, the default values are used by MVS/ESA for symbolic parameter substitutions.

Figure 4.24 Annotated MVS/ESA System Output Produced by the D7SET Job Stream, Which Invokes the D6PROC Proc

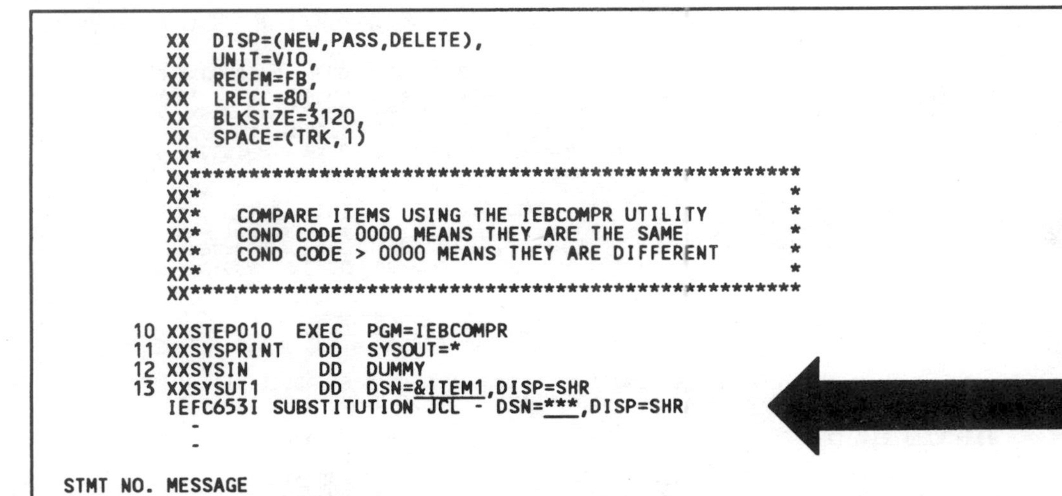

```
        XX  DISP=(NEW,PASS,DELETE),
        XX  UNIT=VIO,
        XX  RECFM=FB,
        XX  LRECL=80,
        XX  BLKSIZE=3120,
        XX  SPACE=(TRK,1)
        XX*
        XX*****************************************************
        XX*                                                   *
        XX*   COMPARE ITEMS USING THE IEBCOMPR UTILITY        *
        XX*   COND CODE 0000 MEANS THEY ARE THE SAME          *
        XX*   COND CODE > 0000 MEANS THEY ARE DIFFERENT       *
        XX*                                                   *
        XX*****************************************************

     10 XXSTEP010   EXEC   PGM=IEBCOMPR
     11 XXSYSPRINT    DD   SYSOUT=*
     12 XXSYSIN       DD   DUMMY
     13 XXSYSUT1      DD   DSN=&ITEM1,DISP=SHR
        IEFC653I SUBSTITUTION JCL - DSN=***,DISP=SHR
         -
         -

STMT NO. MESSAGE

      4 IEFC001I PROCEDURE D6PROC WAS EXPANDED USING PRIVATE LIBRARY CSCJGJ.ADV.PROCLIB1

     13 IEFC628I INCORRECT USE OF ASTERISK IN THE DSN FIELD
     14 IEFC628I INCORRECT USE OF ASTERISK IN THE DSN FIELD
     19 IEFC628I INCORRECT USE OF ASTERISK IN THE DSN FIELD
     25 IEFC628I INCORRECT USE OF ASTERISK IN THE DSN FIELD
     29 IEFC628I INCORRECT USE OF ASTERISK IN THE DSN FIELD
```

Here you see one of the symbolic parameter substitutions made by MVS/ESA. The default value '***' from the PROC statement is used for the substitution, not the value supplied by the SET statement.
These error messages document the five symbolic parameter substitutions made by MVS/ESA in the D6PROC for &ITEM1 and &ITEM2. All five substitutions cause errors, because the values coded on the SET statement cannot override the '***' default values on the PROC statement.

Figure 4.24 *(continued)*

JCLLIB serves a purpose for private procs and JCL similar to the service provided by JOBLIB and STEPLIB DD statements for private program load module (machine language) libraries. As with JCLLIB processing for proc libs, MVS/ESA searches default load module libraries such as SYS1.LINKLIB if the load module for the program you are trying to execute is not found in the libraries named on single or concatenated JOBLIB or STEPLIB statements.

JCLLIB coding do's and don'ts:

1. You can code only one JCLLIB statement per job.

2. If you use JCLLIB, you must code it after your JOB statement and any JES2 or JES3 control statements, before or after any any JOBLIB statement, and before your first EXEC statement.

3. You can create a JCL library (in which raw JCL, procs, and INCLUDE groups can be housed as members) as a PDS or PDSE ("LIBRARY") using TSO/ISPF function 3.2 or using JCL. You can define the attributes of JCL libraries as FB (fixed length records), LRECL=80 (80 byte records). In non-DFSMS environments, block a JCL library as appropriate for your disk devices (BLKSIZE=6160 is a good compromise block size); with DFSMS, MVS/ESA itself can compute the block size. Variable length record format also works for a JCL library, but using it is unusual and may impede concatenation of libraries.

4. You can mix references to JCL libraries housed as PDSs and JCL libraries housed as PDSEs in the JCLLIB statement.

5. You can catalog JCL libraries in the main system catalog only, and they have to be cataloged. You can't catalog them in private catalogs referred to only by JOBCAT or STEPCAT DD statements.

6. You can code a name such as //MYJCLLIB on the JCLLIB statement. But such a name is optional and serves no real purpose, since it is never referred to by other JCL statement coding or in MVS/ESA allocation/deallocation reporting. If you code such a name, it has to be no longer than eight characters, composed of uppercase letters or numbers or $, #, or @, and the first character has to be an uppercase letter or $, #, or @. You have to code a space after the name; if you don't code a name for the JCLLIB statement, column 3 of the statement has to contain a space.

7. You *can't* put a JCLLIB statement into an INCLUDE group (JCL copied in with the INCLUDE statement).

8. You *can't* specify temporary data set names, a partitioned data set member name, or a generation data set (GDS) as a JCL library on a JCLLIB statement.

9. You *can't* password protect JCL libraries.

4.14 Summary of INCLUDE Statement Rules

The INCLUDE statement is one of the minor new features of MVS/ESA Version 4. INCLUDE functions like a "copy" command to MVS/ESA to tell it to bring in the contents of the single member name you code after the parameter MEMBER:

```
//       INCLUDE MEMBER=abcdefgh          comments
//       INCLUDE MEMBER=stuvwxyz          comments
```

The member name such as *abcdefgh* represents a member in a JCL library. You can put comments on the same line as INCLUDE, abiding by customary JCL commenting rules. You can code only one member name on a given INCLUDE, but you can list INCLUDE statements one after another to copy in more than one member at a given place in JCL. The JCL statements in the member are known as an "INCLUDE group." MVS/ESA copies the member named on an INCLUDE statement from one of the libraries you have listed on the JCLLIB statement. If not found in one of those libraries, MVS/ESA then checks the system default libraries, such as SYS1.PROCLIB for the INCLUDE group. If you have not coded a JCLLIB statement, MVS/ESA looks only in the system default libraries. If the member exists in more than one of the libraries searched by MVS/ESA, it uses the first copy of the member that it finds.

If you adopt the use of INCLUDE groups in your JCL, your raw job streams and execution JCL can become harder to examine because parts of job streams will be located in different libraries. You'll find it convenient to use TYPRUN=SCAN on a JOB statement as a means of having MVS/ESA bring together all of the JCL in a job stream for your examination. MVS/ESA processes all of the INCLUDEs in a job stream as a part of the scanning process done by TYPRUN=SCAN. (I'd suggest coding a normally commented-out TYPRUN=SCAN parameter in your JOB statement, as shown in all of my examples. You can activate this parameter simply by removing the asterisk on that line and can replace the asterisk to again deactivate TYPRUN=SCAN.)

INCLUDE coding do's and don'ts:

1. You can code multiple INCLUDE statements in a job.

2. You can code INCLUDE after your JOB statement and after any JES control statements.

3. You can nest INCLUDE statements. That is, a member you INCLUDE can contain INCLUDE statements. You can do this to 15 levels deep, and the nested members can be in the same or different JCL libraries, since each is searched for independently. (Why you would want to do this is a good question; it seems like an invitation to an organizational nightmare, with the potential for unintended recursion!)

4. You can INCLUDE groups that contain EXEC statements, and the EXEC statements can invoke either programs or procs.

5. You can code DD statements and OUTPUT JCL statements in INCLUDE groups, to standardize these elements of JCL just as copy library (copy book) members can help standardize some aspects of program source code. But Storage Management Subsystem (DFSMS) represents a much more powerful standardizing mechanism for many of the specifications otherwise conveyed on DD statements.

6. You can code the SET statement in INCLUDE groups to assign values to symbolic parameters. If you code SET statements in an INCLUDE group, the values they give to symbolic parameters continue to be in effect for the JCL following the copied-in JCL in your job stream.

7. You can code a name such as //INCLUDE1 on the INCLUDE statement. But such a name is optional and serves no real purpose, since it is never referred to by other JCL statement coding or in MVS/ESA allocation/deallocation reporting. If you code such a name, it has to be no longer than eight characters, composed of uppercase letters or numbers or $, #, or @, and the first character has to be an uppercase letter or $, #, or @. You have to code a space after the name; if you don't code a name for the INCLUDE statement, column 3 of the statement has to contain a space.

8. You *can't* code these types of statements in an INCLUDE group:

   - JOB
   - PROC or PEND
   - JCLLIB
   - JES2 or JES3 control statements
   - instream data statements (DD * or DD DATA)

9. You *can't* copy in a regular proc using INCLUDE and successfully execute it, because the PROC statement on it will cause an error in the job stream. Invoke a proc using an EXEC statement, not an INCLUDE.

10. You *can't* code an INCLUDE between CNTL and ENDCNTL statements. (CNTL and ENDCNTL statements are a special purpose feature of MVS/ESA JCL. They define the beginning and end of control statements to IBM's Print Services Facility program in a way similar to instream data.)

4.15 Summary of SET Statement Rules

MVS/ESA Version 4 gives you the ability to install symbolic parameters in ordinary JCL, that is, JCL to be executed directly with a JOB statement rather than JCL that a job step invokes as a proc. The SET statement provides the way to assign values to these symbolic parameters:

```
//      SET ITEM1='CSCJGJ.ADV.APPLES',      ONE DATA SET
//          ITEM2='CSCJGJ.ADV.ORANGES'      OTHER DATA SET
```

The values carried on a SET are processed as characters and are used strictly for character string replacement in the text of your JCL before the JCL is given its final interpretation. For this reason it is always correct to enclose SET values in apostrophes. (I suggest you do this consistently, and not try to remember when you can omit the apostrophes.) You can code multiple symbolic parameter values on one SET statement and continue it as shown, but as with any continued line, don't indent the continuations beyond column 16 or they will be ignored. You can put comments on SET statement lines, abiding by customary JCL commenting rules.

Prior to the provision of SET, the only way you could use symbolic parameters was within procs. You traditionally assign actual values to symbolic parameter values within procs via defaults coded on the PROC statement or by coding values on the EXEC that invokes the proc. You can now use symbolic parameters in *any* JCL and use SET to assign actual values to them. Using SET in this way is like giving a commonly occurring value to a data field in a program, and using the data field name at various points in the program instead of using repeated hardcoded literal values. The advantage is that you can then make a change at one point to change the symbolic parameter value at every point where it occurs in the JCL statements after the SET.

SET is a fine idea, but not because it makes symbolic parameters practical in raw JCL. If you are simply working with raw JCL, you will be using an interactive editor like TSO/ISPF, and making mass changes to a value occurring in many places is easy and reliable using a "change all" command. The real benefit of SET is that it gives you a new way to begin building and testing JCL that you will eventually make into a proc. You can install symbolic parameters where you think they will be useful in your raw JCL. You can continue to have the JCL "all in one place" for initial testing, which may lead you to make adjustments in your symbolic parameter coding and default values. Once you are satisfied with your symbolic parameters and the default values carried on one or more SET statements, you can change the SET statement to a PROC statement, put the new proc into a JCL library (PDS or PDSE), and use JCL with a JCLLIB statement to give a final test to the new proc.

You can code SET anywhere in a job stream, and the values coded on it take effect from the location of the SET statement onward. You could, therefore, arrange to have a specific symbolic parameter be assigned one value up to a certain point in a job stream, and then, at a later point, use SET to either give it a new value or nullify it by coding the symbolic parameter name followed only by the equal sign, such as CCIN=. Though this is possible, I would not code a job stream using multiple SETs in this way. Changing a symbolic parameter value midway in a job stream seems like a tricky, overly clever, and fragile way to arrange things. Note that default symbolic parameter values coded within procs, or on EXEC statements invoking procs, override values assigned by SET as shown in Figure 4.24. This makes

SET less powerful than traditional ways to assign symbolic parameter values in procs.

SET coding do's and don'ts:

1. You can code SET anywhere after your JOB statement and any JES2 or JES3 control statements.

2. You can code multiple SET statements in a job stream for the same or different symbolic parameters.

3. You can code SET without any use of INCLUDE. While IBM documentation couples the use of these MVS/ESA Version 4 features, there is no necessary connection.

4. You can code one or more SET statements within an INCLUDE group.

5. You can code a name such as //MYSET1 on the SET statement. Such a name is optional and serves no real purpose, since it is never referred to by other JCL statement coding or in MVS/ESA allocation/deallocation reporting. If you code such a name, it has to be no longer than eight characters, composed of uppercase letters or numbers or $, #, or @, and the first character has to be an uppercase letter or $, #, or @. You have to code a space after the name; if you don't code a name for the JCLLIB statement, column 3 of the statement has to contain a space.

6. If you make a spelling error in the name of a symbolic parameter in a SET statement, it is not regarded as an error. In other words, MVS/ESA ignores your use of SET to assign values to symbolic parameters that are not coded in any of the JCL that follows. Whether this is a feature or deficiency is debatable. It is definitely different from the treatment of default values on a PROC statement, where MVS/ESA requires that only symbolic parameters that really exist are listed.

   If you misspell the name of symbolic parameter on a SET statement, you may or may not receive an error message in connection with the intended symbolic parameter, which will not receive the intended substitution value. You will not receive an error from MVS/ESA if the misspelled symbolic parameter name was passing a PARM value to a program or a data set name; instead, you may receive an error message or spurious output from the program being executed.

7. You can't conditionally assign values to symbolic parameters by putting SET within an IF/THEN/ELSE construct. The SET will be accepted by MVS/ESA, but SET is always processed regardless of the outcome of the IF/THEN/ELSE test. That is, the IF test is irrelevant to SET. The value(s) assigned by the SET statement(s) coded within an IF construct will always apply. This is not the way many other batch command languages work, and it limits your flexibility!

5

Nested Procs as Building Blocks

5.1 What Are Nested Procs?
5.2 A Simple Example Job Stream
5.3 The Example Job Stream as a Nonnested Proc
5.4 The Example Job Stream Using Nested Procs
5.5 XSORT: An Elementary Nested Proc Building Block
5.6 XCOPY Nested Proc: Another Building Block
5.7 Revised Naming Conventions for Nested Procs
5.8 Housing Nested Procs
5.9 System Reporting Step Labeling for Nested Procs
5.10 Additional Nested Proc Examples
5.11 Streamlining a Job Stream
5.12 Limitations of Nest Procs for Job Stream Streamlining
5.13 Overcoming Nested Proc Limitations
5.14 Problems with Recursion

5.1 What Are Nested Procs?

A "proc," or cataloged procedure, is a collection of job control language, containing one or more steps, that has been stored as a member of a PDS or PDSE. Procs are usually generalized by including symbolic parameters, so that other JCL streams can invoke the proc by name and easily change certain values within the proc.

Under MVS versions prior to MVS/ESA Version 4, you were prohibited from executing anything from within a proc except a program. What you could do under the older versions of MVS, and can continue to do under MVS/ESA, could be represented schematically like this:

```
    Execution JCL      Cataloged procedure
                     |
//STEPA EXEC ABCD  → //ABCD PROC
     -               | //STEP010 EXEC PGM=...
                     |     -
                     | //STEP020 EXEC PGM=...
                     |     -
                     | //STEP030 EXEC PGM=...
                     |     -
                     | //STEP040 EXEC PGM=...
```

Now, under MVS/ESA Version 4, it is possible for you to use an EXEC that executes a proc, within a proc. This is called "nesting" procs and looks schematically like this:

```
                                                              Nested
    Execution JCL         Cataloged procedure          cataloged procedure
                    |                            |
//STEPA  EXEC ABCD →  //ABCD      PROC           |
   -                |  //STEP010   EXEC PGM=...  |
                    |     -                      |
                    |  //STEP020   EXEC EFGH   →  //EFGH   PROC
                    |     -                      |  //STEP1  EXEC PGM=...
                    |  //STEP030   EXEC PGM=...  |     -
                    |     -                      |     -
                    |  //STEP040   EXEC PGM=...  |  //STEP2  EXEC PGM=...
```

This illustration shows nesting only to one level. Nesting can go further than depicted here; you can now nest procs to 15 levels deep. I will show you some examples where nesting makes it possible for you to create highly structured yet flexible job control language.

5.2 A Simple Example Job Stream

Figure 5.1 is a flowchart depicting a simple two-step job stream. In its first step, a sort utility reads the records in a data set named CSCJGJ.CSC.WORKERS and sorts them, putting the sorted records into a temporary data set. The second step executes the IEBGENER program to copy the contents of the temporary data set to the printer. This represents a trivial job stream, which is shown in coded form, as "raw" JCL, in Figure 5.2. I will build on this example to show it in proc form, and finally how it can appear with the use of nested procs.

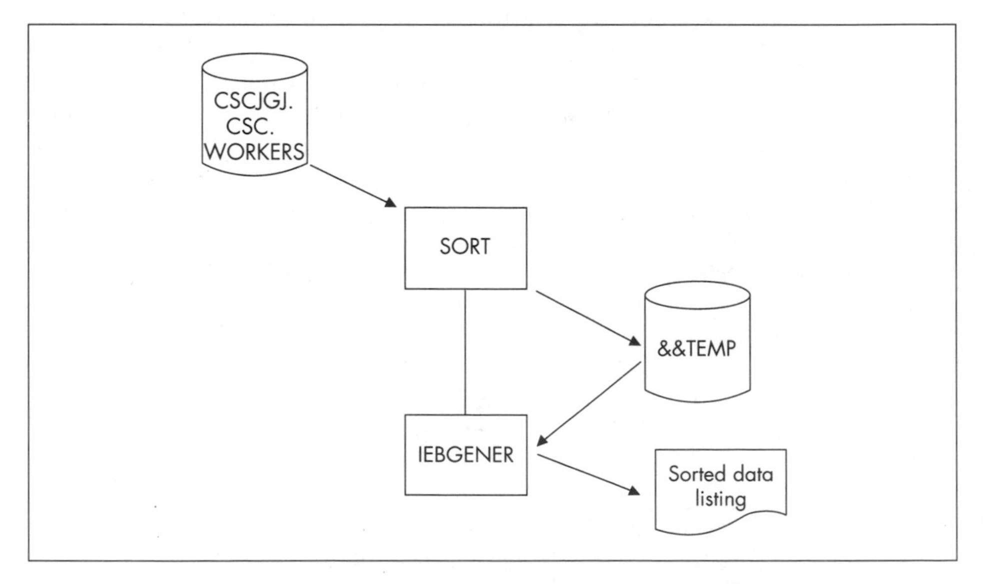

Figure 5.1 Job Stream Flowchart for a Simple Two-Step Example

```
EDIT ---- CSCJGJ.ADV.CNTL(E1RAWJCL) - 01.01 ----------------- COLUMNS 001 072
COMMAND ===>                                                  SCROLL ===> PAGE
****** ***************************** TOP OF DATA ******************************
000001 //CSCJGJA   JOB 1,                        ACCOUNTING INFORMATION
000002 //   'BIN 7--JANOSSY',                    PROGRAMMER NAME AND DELIVERY BIN
000003 //   CLASS=A,                             INPUT QUEUE CLASS
000004 //   MSGLEVEL=(1,1),                      HOW MUCH MVS SYSTEM PRINT DESIRED
000005 //   MSGCLASS=X,                          PRINT DESTINATION X A L N OR O
000006 //   TIME=(0,6),                          SAFETY LIMIT: RUN TIME UP TO 6 SECS
000007 //   REGION=2M,                           ALLOW UP TO 2 MEGS VIRTUAL MEMORY
000008 //*  TYPRUN=SCAN,                         UNCOMMENT THIS LINE TO DO SCAN ONLY
000009 //   NOTIFY=CSCJGJ                        WHO TO TELL WHEN JOB IS DONE
000010 //*
000011 //* RAW JCL TO SORT AND LIST THE "WORKERS" DATA SET
000012 //* THIS JCL IS STORED AT CSCJGJ.ADV.CNTL(E1RAWJCL)
000013 //*
000014 //*-----------------------------------------------------------------
000015 //* SORT WORKERS DATA
000016 //*-----------------------------------------------------------------
000017 //STEP010  EXEC  PGM=SORT
000018 //SYSOUT     DD  SYSOUT=*
000019 //SORTIN     DD  DSN=CSCJGJ.CSC.WORKERS,
000020 //   DISP=SHR
000021 //SORTOUT    DD  DSN=&&TEMP,
000022 //   DISP=(NEW,PASS,DELETE),
000023 //   UNIT=SYSDA,
000024 //   RECFM=FB,
000025 //   LRECL=80,
000026 //   BLKSIZE=3840,
000027 //   DSORG=PS,
000028 //   SPACE=(CYL,1)
000029 //SYSIN      DD  *
000030    SORT    FIELDS=(28,3,ZD,D)
000031    OPTION  EQUALS,FILSZ=E5000,DYNALLOC=(SYSDA,3),CHECK
000032 //*-----------------------------------------------------------------
000033 //* PRINT SORTED WORKERS DATA
000034 //*-----------------------------------------------------------------
000035 //STEP020  EXEC  PGM=IEBGENER
000036 //SYSPRINT   DD  SYSOUT=*
000037 //SYSUT1     DD  DSN=&&TEMP,
000038 //   DISP=(OLD,DELETE)
000039 //SYSUT2     DD  SYSOUT=*
000040 //SYSIN      DD  DUMMY
000041 //
```

Sort

Copy to printer

This raw job control language sorts a data set named CSCJGJ.CSC.WORKERS, creating a temporary data set named &&TEMP1. The second step then copies &&TEMP1 to the printer. This raw JCL establishes a baseline for the examples in this chapter. You'll see first how this JCL is represented as a traditional proc, and then how the same processing actions can be accomplished using nested proc "building blocks."

Figure 5.2 Raw Job Control Language Implementing the Processing Depicted in Figure 5.1

5.3 The Example Job Stream as a Nonnested Proc

Housing the two steps of JCL shown in Figure 5.2 as a cataloged procedure is warranted if it represents a job stream that will be used repeatedly for different input data sets. For repeated use, it's highly desirable to have to view only the bare minimum of JCL each time the job stream is submitted. The JCL in Figure 5.3 is "execution" JCL. Aside from the JOB statement and a JCLLIB statement pointing to a procedure library, this JCL contains only an EXEC statement. This EXEC invokes a procedure named E1PROC and cites the name of the data set to be processed by the sort/print job stream.

I can accomplish the intended processing by submitting the execution JCL in Figure 5.3 because I have packaged the actual JCL for the sort/print job stream as a member named E1PROC of a JCL library. The job control language in Figure 5.4 is much like the JCL in Figure 5.2. Now, I have converted the raw JCL into a proc and installed a symbolic parameter for the //SORTIN DD statement. I have also copied the instream data at //SYSIN in the first step into a member named CC1 of a library, since procs, even under MVS/ESA Version 4, cannot contain instream data. Figure 5.5 provides a thumbnail explanation of this modern coding of the control statement for the sort.

The system reporting from MVS/ESA Version 4 for the simple job stream submitted as a proc is shown in Figure 5.6. MVS/ESA labels step reporting by these three names:

Job name	CSCJGJ
Procstepname	STEP010 (name of step within the proc)
Stepname	STEPA (name of the execution JCL step)

```
EDIT ---- CSCJGJ.ADV.CNTL(E1EXJCL) - 01.00 ----------------- COLUMNS 001 072
COMMAND ===>                                                 SCROLL ===> PAGE
****** ****************************** TOP OF DATA ******************************
000001 //CSCJGJA   JOB 1,                  ACCOUNTING INFORMATION
000002 //   'BIN 7--JANOSSY',              PROGRAMMER NAME AND DELIVERY BIN
000003 //   CLASS=A,                       INPUT QUEUE CLASS
000004 //   MSGLEVEL=(1,1),                HOW MUCH MVS SYSTEM PRINT DESIRED
000005 //   MSGCLASS=X,                    PRINT DESTINATION X A L N OR O
000006 //   TIME=(0,6),                    SAFETY LIMIT: RUN TIME UP TO 6 SECS
000007 //   REGION=2M,                     ALLOW UP TO 2 MEGS VIRTUAL MEMORY
000008 //*  TYPRUN=SCAN,                   UNCOMMENT THIS LINE TO DO SCAN ONLY
000009 //   NOTIFY=CSCJGJ                  WHO TO TELL WHEN JOB IS DONE
000010 //*
000011 //   JCLLIB  ORDER=(CSCJGJ.ADV.PROCLIB1,      MY TESTING PROC LIBRARY
000012 //      CSCJGJ.ADV.PROCLIB2)                  MY "FINAL" PROC LIBRARY
000013 //*
000014 //* JCL TO EXECUTE E1PROC
000015 //* THIS JCL IS STORED AT CSCJGJ.ADV.CNTL(E1EXJCL)
000016 //*
000017 //STEPA    EXEC  E1PROC,
000018 //   INDATA='CSCJGJ.CSC.WORKERS'              DATA SET TO BE PROCESSED
000019 //
```

Figure 5.3 E1EXJCL, Execution JCL to Submit Proc E1PROC

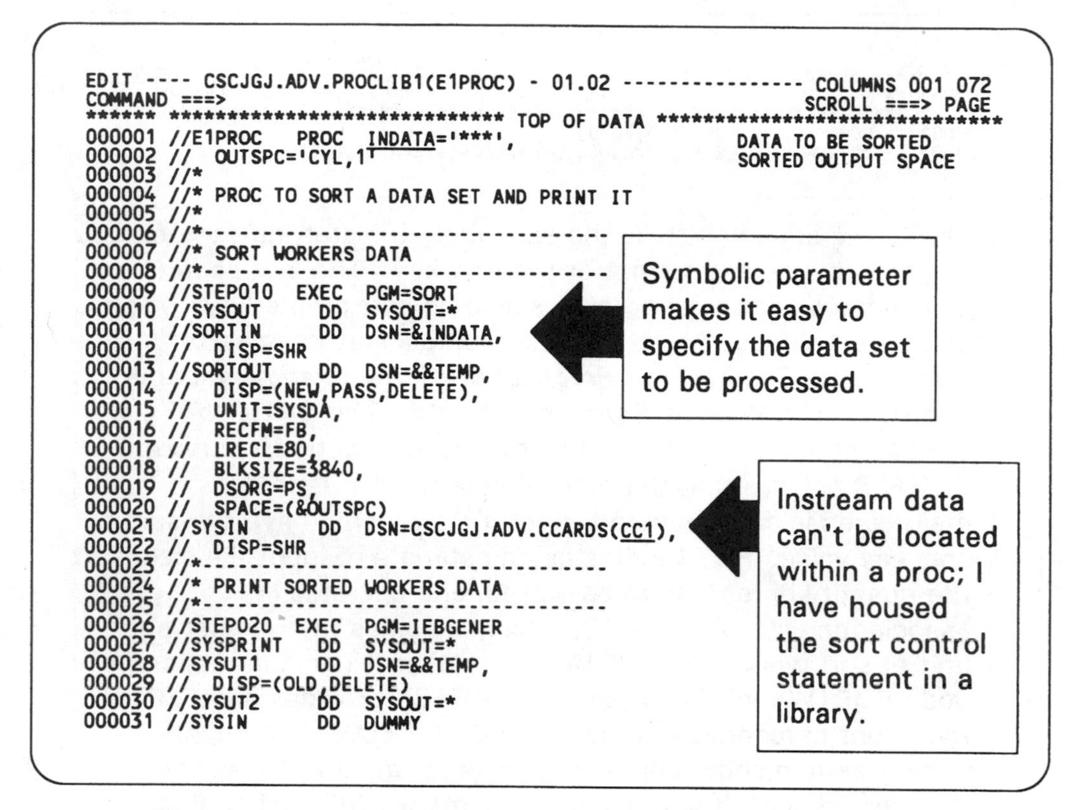

```
EDIT ---- CSCJGJ.ADV.PROCLIB1(E1PROC) - 01.02 ---------------- COLUMNS 001 072
COMMAND ===>                                                   SCROLL ===> PAGE
****** ****************************** TOP OF DATA ******************************
000001 //E1PROC   PROC  INDATA='***',                    DATA TO BE SORTED
000002 //  OUTSPC='CYL,1'                                 SORTED OUTPUT SPACE
000003 //*
000004 //* PROC TO SORT A DATA SET AND PRINT IT
000005 //*
000006 //*-----------------------------------
000007 //* SORT WORKERS DATA
000008 //*-----------------------------------
000009 //STEP010  EXEC  PGM=SORT
000010 //SYSOUT     DD  SYSOUT=*
000011 //SORTIN     DD  DSN=&INDATA,
000012 //  DISP=SHR
000013 //SORTOUT    DD  DSN=&&TEMP,
000014 //  DISP=(NEW,PASS,DELETE),
000015 //  UNIT=SYSDA,
000016 //  RECFM=FB,
000017 //  LRECL=80,
000018 //  BLKSIZE=3840,
000019 //  DSORG=PS,
000020 //  SPACE=(&OUTSPC)
000021 //SYSIN      DD  DSN=CSCJGJ.ADV.CCARDS(CC1),
000022 //  DISP=SHR
000023 //*-----------------------------------
000024 //* PRINT SORTED WORKERS DATA
000025 //*-----------------------------------
000026 //STEP020  EXEC  PGM=IEBGENER
000027 //SYSPRINT   DD  SYSOUT=*
000028 //SYSUT1     DD  DSN=&&TEMP,
000029 //  DISP=(OLD,DELETE)
000030 //SYSUT2     DD  SYSOUT=*
000031 //SYSIN      DD  DUMMY
```

Symbolic parameter makes it easy to specify the data set to be processed.
Instream data can't be located within a proc; I have housed the sort control statement in a library.

Figure 5.4 E1PROC, A Cataloged Procedure to Sort and List Data

It's critical that you understand how this labeling scheme works for MVS/ESA system reporting. The reporting shown in Figure 5.6 is your essential tool for determining if a run proceeded normally or experienced a problem at some point. If you don't understand how MVS/ESA labels its reporting for steps, you'll be unable to know if a job worked as it should have and will be hard put to fix it if it did not run successfully. And MVS/ESA step reporting gets more involved when you use nested procs!

5.4 The Example Job Stream Using Nested Procs

If it is structure and flexibility we seek in our execution JCL, the execution JCL shown in Figure 5.3 can hardly be improved upon. As it stands, it requires the bare essentials to be stated to initiate the example job stream. But we can now, under MVS/ESA Version 4, make some changes in the underlying proc to modularize it further than we could before.

Examine Figure 5.7, which lists a proc named E2PROC. Compare this with E1PROC in Figure 5.4. You will see that E2PROC itself invokes two procs, named XSORT and XCOPY. To understand E2PROC, you have to also look at Figures 5.8 and 5.9, which provide the JCL listings of the XSORT and XCOPY procs. Let's start by looking at these lowest-level procs and then see how E2PROC invokes them.

```
EDIT ---- CSCJGJ.ADV.CCARDS(CC1) - 01.01 -------------------- COLUMNS 001 072
COMMAND ===>                                                  SCROLL ===> PAGE
****** ****************************** TOP OF DATA ******************************
000001    SORT    FIELDS=(28,3,ZD,D)
000002    OPTION  EQUALS,FILSZ=E5000,DYNALLOC=(SYSDA,3),CHECK
```

The SORT statement tells the sort utility the starting position, length in bytes, and format of the sort key. The last code (A or D) indicates an ascending or descending sort on the keys. You can repeat the pattern to indicate multiple sort keys as illustrated in Chapter 4 of ***Practical MVS JCL Examples*** (James Janossy, John Wiley & Sons, Inc., 1993). The OPTION statement allows coding of several different optional services. **EQUALS** assures that the original sequence of records is maintained in cases where two or more records have the same sort key value. **FILSZ** indicates an estimate of input file size, the quantity of records to be sorted, and operates in association with DYNALLOC, which specifies the number and unit of sort work files. **DYNALLOC** makes it unnecessary to code SORTWKnn DD statements. **CHECK** provides a check of the count of records sorted. The SORT FIELDS statement coding pattern shown here is suitable for most applications. You should consult your local standards for OPTION coding, which varies according to local implementation of DFSMS and the sort utility in use.

Figure 5.5 Explanation of the Sort Control Statement Used in Cataloged Procedure E1PROC

5.5 XSORT: An Elementary Nested Proc Building Block

A good way to picture the purpose of the XSORT proc is to think of it as a shell. It serves as an interface between the program being executed (the sort utility) and the ddnames documented for its use. The ddnames coded into the sort program are, by modern standards, slightly arcane:

- SYSIN is the ddname at which the sort utility reads control statements telling it the sort keys and the sequence desired for the records to be sorted.
- SYSOUT is the ddname at which the printline records for the status report produced by the sort utility will emerge.
- SORTIN is the ddname for the input file to be sorted.
- SORTOUT is the ddname for the output file.

XSORT serves two purposes: It makes those ddnames that must be visible to a user more meaningful, and it "hides" details that can be taken care

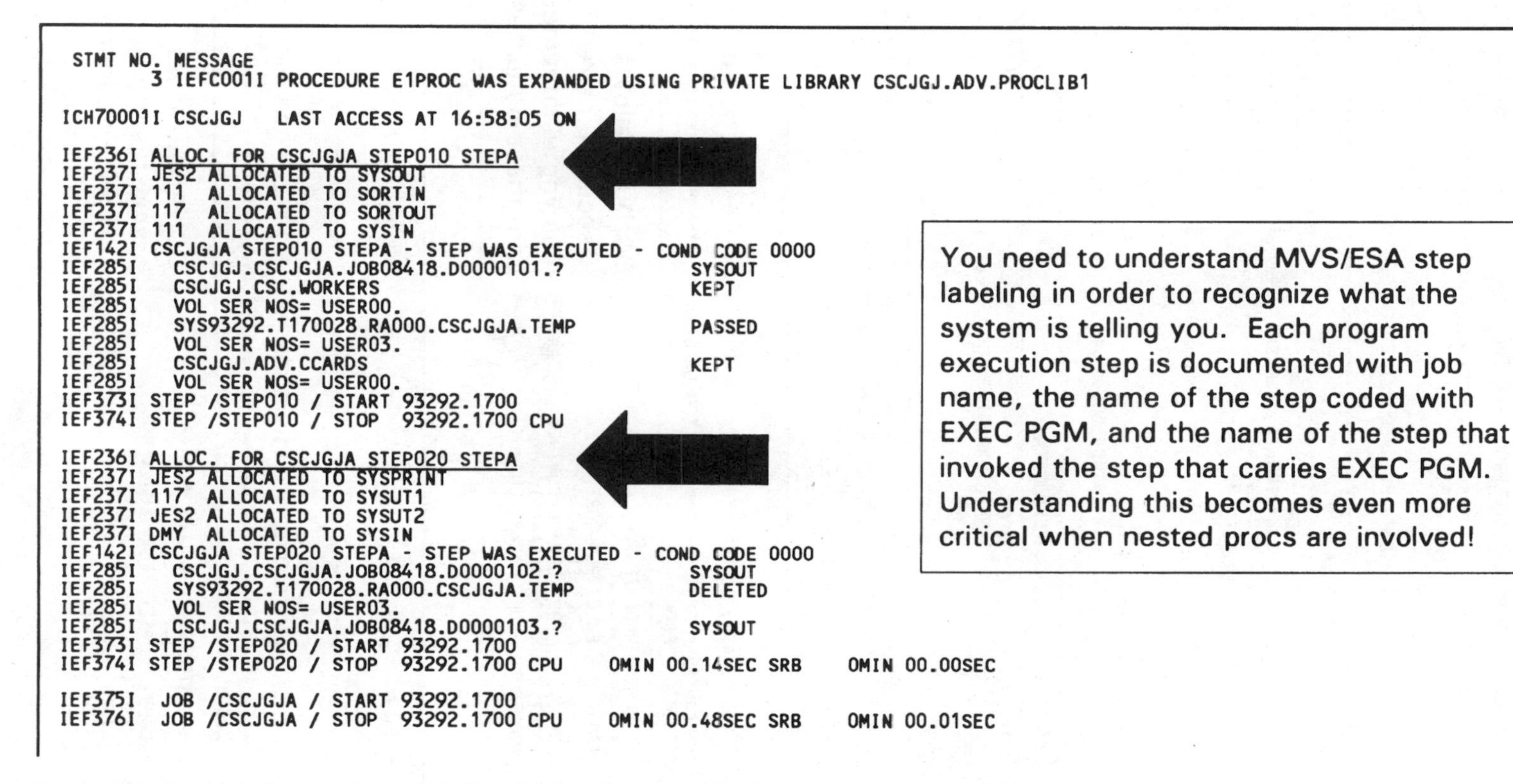

```
STMT NO. MESSAGE
       3 IEFC001I PROCEDURE E1PROC WAS EXPANDED USING PRIVATE LIBRARY CSCJGJ.ADV.PROCLIB1

ICH70001I CSCJGJ   LAST ACCESS AT 16:58:05 ON

IEF236I ALLOC. FOR CSCJGJA STEP010 STEPA
IEF237I JES2 ALLOCATED TO SYSOUT
IEF237I 111  ALLOCATED TO SORTIN
IEF237I 117  ALLOCATED TO SORTOUT
IEF237I 111  ALLOCATED TO SYSIN
IEF142I CSCJGJA STEP010 STEPA - STEP WAS EXECUTED - COND CODE 0000
IEF285I   CSCJGJ.CSCJGJA.JOB08418.D0000101.?            SYSOUT
IEF285I   CSCJGJ.CSC.WORKERS                            KEPT
IEF285I   VOL SER NOS= USER00.
IEF285I   SYS93292.T170028.RA000.CSCJGJA.TEMP           PASSED
IEF285I   VOL SER NOS= USER03.
IEF285I   CSCJGJ.ADV.CCARDS                             KEPT
IEF285I   VOL SER NOS= USER00.
IEF373I STEP /STEP010 / START 93292.1700
IEF374I STEP /STEP010 / STOP  93292.1700 CPU

IEF236I ALLOC. FOR CSCJGJA STEP020 STEPA
IEF237I JES2 ALLOCATED TO SYSPRINT
IEF237I 117  ALLOCATED TO SYSUT1
IEF237I JES2 ALLOCATED TO SYSUT2
IEF237I DMY  ALLOCATED TO SYSIN
IEF142I CSCJGJA STEP020 STEPA - STEP WAS EXECUTED - COND CODE 0000
IEF285I   CSCJGJ.CSCJGJA.JOB08418.D0000102.?            SYSOUT
IEF285I   SYS93292.T170028.RA000.CSCJGJA.TEMP           DELETED
IEF285I   VOL SER NOS= USER03.
IEF285I   CSCJGJ.CSCJGJA.JOB08418.D0000103.?            SYSOUT
IEF373I STEP /STEP020 / START 93292.1700
IEF374I STEP /STEP020 / STOP  93292.1700 CPU    0MIN 00.14SEC SRB    0MIN 00.00SEC

IEF375I  JOB /CSCJGJA / START 93292.1700
IEF376I  JOB /CSCJGJA / STOP  93292.1700 CPU    0MIN 00.48SEC SRB    0MIN 00.01SEC
```

You need to understand MVS/ESA step labeling in order to recognize what the system is telling you. Each program execution step is documented with job name, the name of the step coded with EXEC PGM, and the name of the step that invoked the step that carries EXEC PGM. Understanding this becomes even more critical when nested procs are involved!

Figure 5.6 Step Labeling Within MVS/ESA System Reporting for the E1PROC

```
EDIT ---- CSCJGJ.ADV.PROCLIB1(E2PROC) - 01.00 ---------------- COLUMNS 001 072
COMMAND ===>                                                  SCROLL ===> PAGE
****** ***************************** TOP OF DATA ******************************
000001 //E2PROC   PROC  INDATA='***',                          DATA TO BE SORTED
000002 //   OUTSPC='CYL,1'                                     SORTED OUTPUT SPACE
000003 //*
000004 //* PROC TO SORT A DATA SET AND PRINT IT USING NESTED PROCS
000005 //*
000006 //*-------------------------------------------------------------------
000007 //* SORT WORKERS DATA
000008 //*-------------------------------------------------------------------
000009 //PSTEP1      EXEC  XSORT
000010 //SORT.INPUT    DD  DSN=&INDATA,DISP=SHR
000011 //SORT.OUTPUT   DD  DSN=&&TEMP,
000012 //   DISP=(NEW,PASS,DELETE),
000013 //   UNIT=SYSDA,
000014 //   RECFM=FB,
000015 //   LRECL=80,
000016 //   BLKSIZE=3840,
000017 //   DSORG=PS,
000018 //   SPACE=(&OUTSPC)
000019 //SORT.CONTROL DD  DSN=CSCJGJ.ADV.CCARDS(CC1),DISP=SHR
000020 //*
000021 //*-------------------------------------------------------------------
000022 //* PRINT SORTED WORKERS DATA
000023 //*-------------------------------------------------------------------
000024 //PSTEP2      EXEC  XCOPY
000025 //COPY.IN       DD  DSN=&&TEMP,DISP=(OLD,DELETE)
000026 //COPY.OUT      DD  SYSOUT=*
```

The EXEC at line 9 invokes a nested proc, not a program!

Figure 5.7 E2PROC, A Cataloged Procedure That Uses Nested Procs (the EXECs invoke other procs, not programs)

```
EDIT ---- CSCJGJ.ADV.PROCLIB2(XSORT) - 01.00 ---------------- COLUMNS 001 072
COMMAND ===>                                                 SCROLL ===> PAGE
****** ***************************** TOP OF DATA ******************************
000001 //XSORT    PROC
000002 //*----------------------------------
000003 //* NESTED PROC TO SORT A DATA SET
000004 //*----------------------------------
000005 //SORT      EXEC  PGM=SORT
000006 //SYSOUT      DD  SYSOUT=*
000007 //SYSIN       DD  DDNAME=CONTROL
000008 //SORTIN      DD  DDNAME=INPUT
000009 //SORTOUT     DD  DDNAME=OUTPUT
```

DDNAME allows associating more meaningful ddnames with these ddnames

Figure 5.8 XSORT Nested Proc, a "Proc Building Block"

```
EDIT ---- CSCJGJ.ADV.PROCLIB2(XCOPY) - 01.00 ---------------- COLUMNS 001 072
COMMAND ===>                                                 SCROLL ===> PAGE
****** ***************************** TOP OF DATA ******************************
000001 //XCOPY    PROC
000002 //*----------------------------------
000003 //* NESTED PROC TO COPY A DATA SET
000004 //*----------------------------------
000005 //COPY      EXEC  PGM=IEBGENER
000006 //SYSPRINT    DD  SYSOUT=*
000007 //SYSIN       DD  DUMMY
000008 //SYSUT1      DD  DDNAME=IN
000009 //SYSUT2      DD  DDNAME=OUT
```

DDNAME allows associating more meaningful ddnames with these ddnames

Figure 5.9 XCOPY Nested Proc, a "Proc Building Block"

of without user involvement. To do this, XSORT uses the DDNAME facility, which associates a new ddname of your choosing with the original ddname. (A word of clarification is warranted here. I'll use the word "ddname" in lowercase letters to mean the label that immediately follows the slashes on a DD statement. DDNAME, on the other hand, is a DD statement parameter.) XSORT hides the details of sending the status report produced by the sort to the printer using an ordinary DD statement, so that the user need never code this (and never faces the risk of forgetting to code it, which would cause a sorting failure). For example, you can see this DD statement in Figure 5.8:

```
//SORT  EXEC  PGM=SORT
//SYSIN      DD   DDNAME=CONTROL
```

This makes it possible to provide an input to //SYSIN by referring to it as CONTROL. You see this statement in the E2PROC providing the sort control statement to the sort:

```
//SORT.CONTROL  DD  DSN=CSCJGJ.ADV.CCARDS(CC1),DISP=SHR
```

The word "SORT" in this statement is the name of the step within the nested proc XSORT; the word "CONTROL" is the new ddname for the sort control input.

Proc E2PROC is typical of JCL written locally to implement job streams. JCL like E2PROC is easier to compose and read when the ddnames used in it are meaningful. The nested proc XSORT, on the other hand, is an elementary JCL building block. Once built, installed, and documented, it would not ordinarily be changed.

Used this way, nested procs can provide a real advantage in legibility, but they can also streamline the process of replacing old software with new. If you wanted to replace the sort utility with another utility, such as an upgraded or revised release, you would only have to change the XSORT proc. All procs built using it, such as E2PROC here, would remain unchanged. This is one of the most powerful capabilities provided by the nested proc feature. It requires only one level of proc nesting, but it does change the appearance of MVS/ESA Version 4 system reporting.

5.6 XCOPY Nested Proc: Another Building Block

The XCOPY nested proc in Figure 5.9 provides even more JCL streamlining than does XSORT. It invokes the common utility program IEBGENER to copy the contents of a file, a PDS member, or a PDSE member to another location. XCOPY hides or renames the necessary but arcane DD statements IEBGENER requires. XCOPY sends the IEBGENER status report emerging at SYSPRINT to the printer, and it dummies out the little-used SYSIN DD statement at which IEBGENER could receive record reformatting instructions. XCOPY also renames the obtuse SYSUT1 used for input, and the equally obtuse SYSUT2 used for output, giving them the straightforward words IN and OUT. This makes it possible for the second step of E2PROC to concern itself only with DD statements citing the input and output, and to use readily understood names for these:

```
//PSTEP2      EXEC  XCOPY
//COPY.IN       DD  DSN=...
//COPY.OUT      DD  SYSOUT=*
```

For having developed and installed one XCOPY nested proc, *every* raw JCL job stream and proc coded thereafter could be streamlined in this way.

5.7 Revised Naming Conventions for Nested Procs

When you use nested procs with MVS/ESA Version 4, system reporting will look familiar, but it may be harder to decipher. To ease the burden of interpreting the step labeling in system reporting, you need to think through a meaningful naming convention. In particular, you need to establish three visibly different, but simple, formats for these types of stepnames:

- execution JCL stepnames, which I have coded as STEPA, STEPB, and so forth;
- top-level proc stepnames, for procs such as E2PROC, which are invoked by execution JCL; my examples code these stepnames as PSTEP1, PSTEP2, and so forth; and
- nested proc stepnames, which I have coded as functional names, such as SORT and COPY.

You may be free to choose your own naming conventions, or may inherit a convention. But if you do not use some consistent convention, you'll have a rough time being consistently correct in your interpretation of MVS/ESA Version 4 nested proc system reporting.

5.8 Housing Nested Procs

Nested procs can be housed in the same JCL library as the procs that invoke them. For example, I created a private proc library named CSCJGJ.ADV.PROCLIB1 to serve as a "home" for my proc examples for this book. You see a JCLLIB statement coded at the beginning of my execution JCL to reference this library. But for example purposes, I created a second JCL library named CSCJGJ.ADV.PROCLIB2 and have put my nested proc building blocks in it. As a result, you'll clearly see in Figure 5.10 how MVS/ESA indicates the origin of each proc and nested proc involved in a run.

5.9 System Reporting Step Labeling for Nested Procs

Figure 5.6 shows you MVS/ESA Version 4 system reporting step labeling when you do not use nested procs. You identify the start of system messages for each step by a line such as this:

```
IEF236I ALLOC. FOR CSCJGJA STEP010 STEPA
```

You might think that the list that starts with job name (CSCJGJA) and shows

```
                 J E S 2  J O B  L O G  --  S Y S T E M  I B M 1  --  N O D E  N 1

17.16.24 JOB08476  IRR010I  USERID CSCJGJ   IS ASSIGNED TO THIS JOB.
17.16.26 JOB08476  ICH70001I CSCJGJ   LAST ACCESS AT 17:00:28 ON TUESDAY, OCTOBER 19, 1993
17.16.26 JOB08476  $HASP373 CSCJGJA  STARTED - INIT  1 - CLASS A - SYS IBM1
17.16.30 JOB08476  $HASP395 CSCJGJA  ENDED

------ JES2 JOB STATISTICS ------
   19 OCT 93 JOB EXECUTION DATE
          18 CARDS READ
         154 SYSOUT PRINT RECORDS
           0 SYSOUT PUNCH RECORDS
           9 SYSOUT SPOOL KBYTES
        0.08 MINUTES EXECUTION TIME

        1 //CSCJGJA   JOB 1,                  ACCOUNTING INFORMATION              JOB08476
          //  'BIN 7--JANOSSY',               PROGRAMMER NAME AND DELIVERY BIN
          //  CLASS=A,                        INPUT QUEUE CLASS
          //  MSGLEVEL=(1,1),                 HOW MUCH MVS SYSTEM PRINT DESIRED
          //  MSGCLASS=X,                     PRINT DESTINATION X A L N OR O
          //  TIME=(0,6),                     SAFETY LIMIT: RUN TIME UP TO 6 SECS
          //  REGION=2M,                      ALLOW UP TO 2 MEGS VIRTUAL MEMORY
          //* TYPRUN=SCAN,                    UNCOMMENT THIS LINE TO DO SCAN ONLY
          //  NOTIFY=CSCJGJ                   WHO TO TELL WHEN JOB IS DONE
          //*
        2 //  JCLLIB  ORDER=(CSCJGJ.ADV.PROCLIB1,     MY TESTING PROC LIBRARY
          //     CSCJGJ.ADV.PROCLIB2)                 MY "FINAL" PROC LIBRARY
          //*
          //* JCL TO EXECUTE E2PROC TO DEMONSTRATE NESTED PROCS
          //* THIS JCL IS STORED AT CSCJGJ.ADV.CNTL(E2EXJCL)
          //*
        3 //STEPA    EXEC  E2PROC,
          //  INDATA='CSCJGJ.CSC.WORKERS'             DATA SET TO BE PROCESSED
        4 XXE2PROC   PROC  INDATA='***',                  DATA TO BE SORTED
          XX  OUTSPC='CYL,1'                              SORTED OUTPUT SPACE
          XX*
          XX* PROC TO SORT A DATA SET AND PRINT IT USING NESTED PROCS
          XX*
          XX*-------------------------------------------------------------------
          XX* SORT WORKERS DATA
          XX*-------------------------------------------------------------------
        5 XXPSTEP1     EXEC  XSORT
        6 XXXSORT    PROC
```

All JCL lines obtained from procs, whether nested or not, are listed in system reporting with XX replacing the original slashes //.

Figure 5.10 Step Labeling Within MVS/ESA System Reporting for the E2PROC, Involving Nested Procs

```
      XX*------------------------------------------------------------------------
      XX* NESTED PROC TO SORT A DATA SET
      XX*------------------------------------------------------------------------
    7 XXSORT      EXEC  PGM=SORT
    8 XXSYSOUT      DD  SYSOUT=*
    9 XXSYSIN       DD  DDNAME=CONTROL
   10 XXSORTIN      DD  DDNAME=INPUT
   11 XXSORTOUT     DD  DDNAME=OUTPUT
   12 XXSORT.INPUT    DD  DSN=&INDATA,DISP=SHR
      IEFC653I SUBSTITUTION JCL - DSN=CSCJGJ.CSC.WORKERS,DISP=SHR
   13 XXSORT.OUTPUT  DD  DSN=&&TEMP,
      XX  DISP=(NEW,PASS,DELETE),
      XX  UNIT=SYSDA,
      XX  RECFM=FB,
      XX  LRECL=80,
      XX  BLKSIZE=3840,
      XX  DSORG=PS,
      XX  SPACE=(&OUTSPC)
      IEFC653I SUBSTITUTION JCL - DSN=&TEMP,DISP=(NEW,PASS,DELETE),UNIT=SYSDA,RECFM=FB,LRECL=80,BLKSIZE=3840,
      DSORG=PS,SPACE=(CYL,1)
   14 XXSORT.CONTROL DD  DSN=CSCJGJ.ADV.CCARDS(CC1),DISP=SHR
      XX*
      XX*------------------------------------------------------------------------
      XX* PRINT SORTED WORKERS DATA
      XX*------------------------------------------------------------------------
   15 XXPSTEP2      EXEC  XCOPY
   16 XXXCOPY     PROC
      XX*------------------------------------------------------------------------
      XX* NESTED PROC TO COPY A DATA SET
      XX*------------------------------------------------------------------------
   17 XXCOPY      EXEC  PGM=IEBGENER
   18 XXSYSPRINT    DD  SYSOUT=*
   19 XXSYSIN       DD  DUMMY
   20 XXSYSUT1      DD  DDNAME=IN
   21 XXSYSUT2      DD  DDNAME=OUT
   22 XXCOPY.IN       DD  DSN=&TEMP,DISP=(OLD,DELETE)
   23 XXCOPY.OUT      DD  SYSOUT=*

STMT NO. MESSAGE
    3 IEFC001I PROCEDURE E2PROC WAS EXPANDED USING PRIVATE LIBRARY CSCJGJ.ADV.PROCLIB1
    5 IEFC001I PROCEDURE XSORT WAS EXPANDED USING PRIVATE LIBRARY CSCJGJ.ADV.PROCLIB2
   15 IEFC001I PROCEDURE XCOPY WAS EXPANDED USING PRIVATE LIBRARY CSCJGJ.ADV.PROCLIB2
```

DDNAME reporting shows the original DDname, then the DD statements that were supplied using the newly associated DDnames at the end of the step.

Origin of each proc and nested proc is reported

Figure 5.10 (continued)

```
ICH70001I CSCJGJ   LAST ACCESS AT 17:00:28 ON TUESDAY, OCTOBER 19, 1993

IEF236I ALLOC. FOR CSCJGJA SORT PSTEP1
IEF237I JES2 ALLOCATED TO SYSOUT
IEF237I 111  ALLOCATED TO SYSIN
IEF237I 111  ALLOCATED TO SORTIN
IEF237I 117  ALLOCATED TO SORTOUT
IEF142I CSCJGJA SORT PSTEP1 - STEP WAS EXECUTED - COND CODE 0000
IEF285I   CSCJGJ.CSCJGJA.JOB08476.D0000101.?             SYSOUT
IEF285I   CSCJGJ.ADV.CCARDS                              KEPT
IEF285I   VOL SER NOS= USER00.
IEF285I   CSCJGJ.CSC.WORKERS                             KEPT
IEF285I   VOL SER NOS= USER00.
IEF285I   SYS93292.T171626.RA000.CSCJGJA.TEMP            PASSED
IEF285I   VOL SER NOS= USER03.
IEF373I STEP /SORT    / START 93292.1716
IEF374I STEP /SORT    / STOP  93292.1716 CPU    0MIN 00.35SEC SRB    0MIN 00.01SEC

IEF236I ALLOC. FOR CSCJGJA COPY PSTEP2
IEF237I JES2 ALLOCATED TO SYSPRINT
IEF237I DMY  ALLOCATED TO SYSIN
IEF237I 117  ALLOCATED TO SYSUT1
IEF237I JES2 ALLOCATED TO SYSUT2
IEF142I CSCJGJA COPY PSTEP2 - STEP WAS EXECUTED - COND CODE 0000
IEF285I   CSCJGJ.CSCJGJA.JOB08476.D0000102.?             SYSOUT
IEF285I   SYS93292.T171626.RA000.CSCJGJA.TEMP            DELETED
IEF285I   VOL SER NOS= USER03.
IEF285I   CSCJGJ.CSCJGJA.JOB08476.D0000103.?             SYSOUT
IEF373I STEP /COPY    / START 93292.1716
IEF374I STEP /COPY    / STOP  93292.1716 CPU    0MIN 00.13SEC SRB    0MIN 00.01SEC
IEF375I  JOB /CSCJGJA / START 93292.1716
IEF376I  JOB /CSCJGJA / STOP  93292.1716 CPU    0MIN 00.48SEC SRB    0MIN 00.02SEC
```

Step labeling in MVS/ESA system reporting

Step labeling in MVS/ESA system reporting

Figure 5.10 (continued)

various stepnames would be longer when you use nested procs, but this is not the case. Even with nested procs, you will only see three names listed after "ALLOC. FOR" as you can see in Figure 5.10.

Figure 5.10 shows the MVS/ESA Version 4 system reporting produced when E2PROC is executed. (I made a copy of E1EXJCL in Figure 5.3, naming it E2EXJCL, and changed only the name of the proc being executed, from E1PROC to E2PROC.) Note that only three names are listed to label the message lines for each step. For example, the start of messages for the second step appears like this:

```
IEF236I ALLOC. FOR CSCJGJA COPY PSTEP2
```

You need to expand your thinking a bit to interpret what this labeling means, because it is actually a compromise. These reporting lines were designed for the nonnested proc environment. When you receive reporting dealing with the execution of nested procs, you will see only the *highest* level and the *lowest* level of names reported. For example, CSCJGJA in the preceding example is the job name. COPY is the stepname within the lowest-level proc being executed; it is the stepname that carries PGM=EXEC. PSTEP2 is the name of the step that invoked the lowest-level proc. You will not see any intermediate stepnames. In this instance, for example, you do not see the name STEPA anywhere in system reporting; it is the name of the JCL step that invoked E2PROC. A naming convention helps distinguish between the names, but the chart in Figure 5.11 will help clarify this labeling mechanism for you.

5.10 Additional Nested Proc Examples

Figures 5.12 and 5.13 show you two more nested proc building blocks, named XCOMPARE and XDUMP. Both of these accomplish the same type of packaging as XSORT and XCOPY did earlier. XCOMPARE packages the JCL to execute the IEBCOMPR utility to compare two data sets. XDUMP packages the JCL to use IDCAMS to produce a hex dump of a data set. Figure 5.14 shows you the simple control statement required by IDCAMS to produce a dump, which is housed as a member named CC2 in a library named CSCJGJ.ADV.CCARDS.

XCOMPARE and XDUMP both hide "housekeeping detail" DD statements and use DDNAME to provide clearer names for things like SYSUT1 and SYSUT2. I'll now use these additional nested proc building blocks to streamline a job stream you have already seen in Chapter 4.

5.11 Streamlining a Job Stream

You may recall a job stream depicted in the flowchart of Figure 4.14 in Chapter 4; if you don't recall it, please refer back to it now. This four-step job stream uses the IEBCOMPR program to compare two data sets. If the data sets are the same, one is printed in the second step using IEBGENER. If the data sets are different, each is dumped, separately, using IDCAMS at the third and fourth steps.

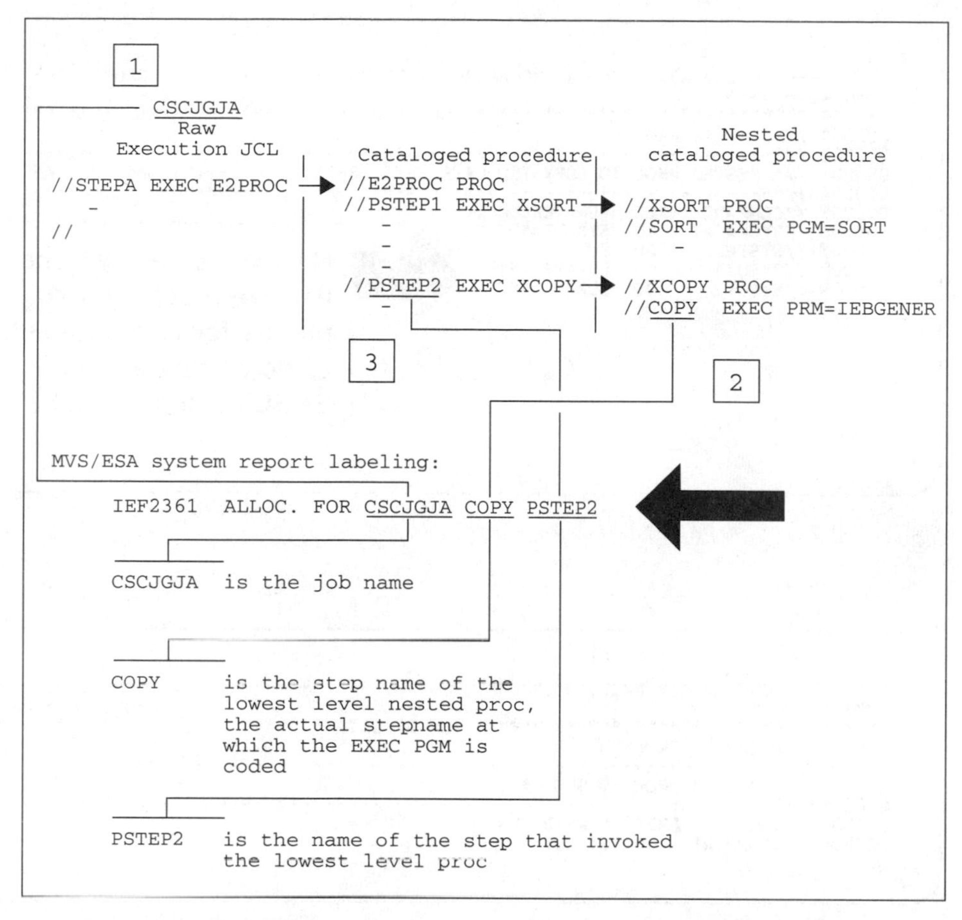

Figure 5.11 How MVS/ESA Forms Its Step Labeling in System Reporting

Figure 5.15 shows you the JCL to invoke a proc named E4PROC, to compare two data sets named CSCJGJ.ADV.APPLES and CSCJGJ.ADV.POMMES. Figure 5.16 shows you the proc itself, which I constructed using the nested proc building blocks. The nested proc technique has helped streamline this job stream, but if you look closely at Figure 5.16, you'll see some awkwardness. The syntax of JCL forces me to occasionally "look inside" a nested proc for stepnames and ddnames, which weakens the effectiveness of nested procs as a means of hiding detail.

5.12 Limitations of Nest Procs for Job Stream Streamlining

The use of nested proc building blocks in E4PROC in Figure 5.16 has allowed me to eliminate some low-level details in building a proc and to access more meaningful ddnames. But the syntax of JCL has forced me to pry into the nested procs I have invoked, in order to code these types of things:

- Data set name referbacks: These must refer back to the procstepname and actual ddname within the nested procs (see lines 24, 33, and 42 of

```
EDIT ---- CSCJGJ.ADV.PROCLIB2(XCOMPARE) - 01.00 -------------- COLUMNS 001 072
COMMAND ===>                                                  SCROLL ===> PAGE
****** ****************************** TOP OF DATA ******************************
000001 //XCOMPARE PROC
000002 //*-----------------------------------------------------------------
000003 //* NESTED PROC TO COPY TWO DATA SETS, SETS RC 0 IF IN1 AND IN2 SAME
000004 //*-----------------------------------------------------------------
000005 //COMPARE  EXEC  PGM=IEBCOMPR
000006 //SYSPRINT  DD   SYSOUT=*
000007 //SYSIN     DD   DUMMY
000008 //SYSUT1    DD   DDNAME=IN1
000009 //SYSUT2    DD   DDNAME=IN2
```

New ddnames IN1 and IN2 are much clearer names for two data sets to be compared than SYSUT1 and SYSUT2!

Figure 5.12 XCOMPARE Nested Proc

```
EDIT ---- CSCJGJ.ADV.PROCLIB2(XDUMP) - 01.00 ----------------- COLUMNS 001 072
COMMAND ===>                                                  SCROLL ===> PAGE
****** ****************************** TOP OF DATA ******************************
000001 //XDUMP    PROC
000002 //*-----------------------------------------------------------------
000003 //* NESTED PROC TO DUMP A DATA SET
000004 //*-----------------------------------------------------------------
000005 //DUMP     EXEC  PGM=IDCAMS
000006 //SYSPRINT  DD   SYSOUT=*
```

Figure 5.13 XDUMP Nested Proc

```
EDIT ---- CSCJGJ.ADV.CCARDS(CC2) - 01.00 --------------------- COLUMNS 001 072
COMMAND ===>                                                  SCROLL ===> PAGE
****** ****************************** TOP OF DATA ******************************
000001    PRINT INFILE(DD1) COUNT(50) DUMP
```

Figure 5.14 IDCAMS Control Card to Dump 50 Records from a Data Set

E4PROC). The associated DDNAME doesn't work when you use a data set name referback.

- Relational tests (return code tests): These must refer to stepnames within the nested procs (see line 22 of E4PROC).

It's unfortunate that the syntax of JCL makes these types of coding necessary, because it detracts from the "detail hiding" we are trying to accomplish in nesting procs.

```
EDIT ---- CSCJGJ.ADV.CNTL(E4EXJCL) - 01.01 ------------------ COLUMNS 001 072
COMMAND ===>                                                  SCROLL ===> PAGE
****** ***************************** TOP OF DATA ******************************
000001 //CSCJGJA    JOB 1,                     ACCOUNTING INFORMATION
000002 //   'BIN 7--JANOSSY',                  PROGRAMMER NAME AND DELIVERY BIN
000003 //   CLASS=A,                           INPUT QUEUE CLASS
000004 //   MSGLEVEL=(1,1),                    HOW MUCH MVS SYSTEM PRINT DESIRED
000005 //   MSGCLASS=X,                        PRINT DESTINATION X A L N OR O
000006 //   TIME=(0,6),                        SAFETY LIMIT: RUN TIME UP TO 6 SECS
000007 //   REGION=2M,                         ALLOW UP TO 2 MEGS VIRTUAL MEMORY
000008 //*  TYPRUN=SCAN,                       UNCOMMENT THIS LINE TO DO SCAN ONLY
000009 //   NOTIFY=CSCJGJ                      WHO TO TELL WHEN JOB IS DONE
000010 //*
000011 //   JCLLIB  ORDER=(CSCJGJ.ADV.PROCLIB1,        MY TESTING PROC LIBRARY
000012 //     CSCJGJ.ADV.PROCLIB2)                     MY "FINAL" PROC LIBRARY
000013 //*
000014 //* JCL TO EXECUTE E4PROC
000015 //* THIS JCL IS STORED AT CSCJGJ.ADV.CNTL(E4EXJCL)
000016 //*
000017 //STEPA     EXEC  E4PROC,
000018 //   ITEM1='CSCJGJ.ADV.APPLES',                 ONE DATA SET TO COMPARE
000019 //   ITEM2='CSCJGJ.ADV.POMMES'                  OTHER DATA SET TO COMPARE
000020 //
```

Figure 5.15 E4EXJCL, Execution JCL to Execute E4PROC to Compare Two Data Sets

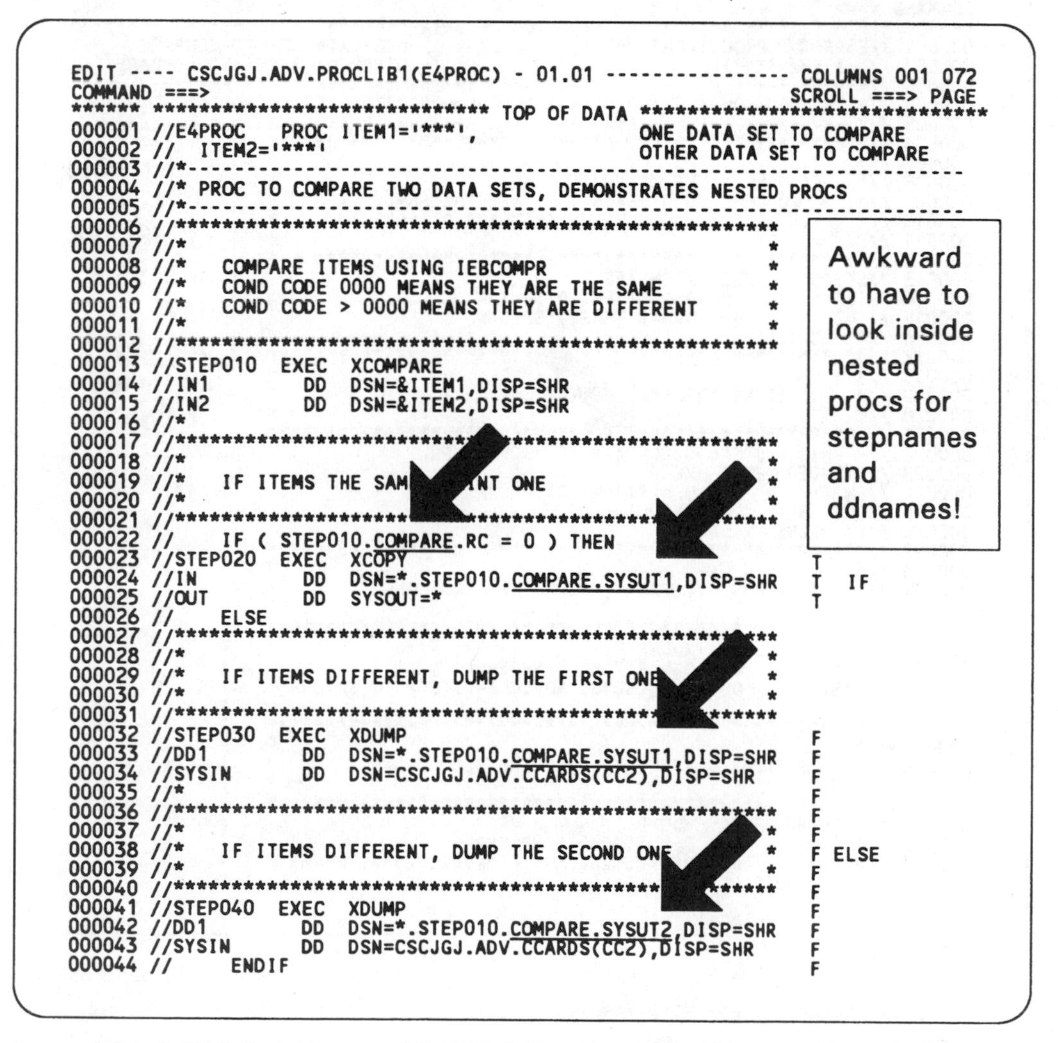

```
EDIT ---- CSCJGJ.ADV.PROCLIB1(E4PROC) - 01.01 --------------- COLUMNS 001 072
COMMAND ===>                                                  SCROLL ===> PAGE
****** ***************************** TOP OF DATA ******************************
000001 //E4PROC    PROC ITEM1='***',                ONE DATA SET TO COMPARE
000002 //   ITEM2='***'                             OTHER DATA SET TO COMPARE
000003 //*--------------------------------------------------------------------
000004 //* PROC TO COMPARE TWO DATA SETS, DEMONSTRATES NESTED PROCS
000005 //*--------------------------------------------------------------------
000006 //****************************************************
000007 //*                                                  *
000008 //*    COMPARE ITEMS USING IEBCOMPR                  *
000009 //*    COND CODE 0000 MEANS THEY ARE THE SAME        *
000010 //*    COND CODE > 0000 MEANS THEY ARE DIFFERENT     *
000011 //*                                                  *
000012 //****************************************************
000013 //STEP010  EXEC  XCOMPARE
000014 //IN1        DD  DSN=&ITEM1,DISP=SHR
000015 //IN2        DD  DSN=&ITEM2,DISP=SHR
000016 //*
000017 //****************************************************
000018 //*                                                  *
000019 //*    IF ITEMS THE SAM    INT ONE                   *
000020 //*                                                  *
000021 //****************************************************
000022 //     IF ( STEP010.COMPARE.RC = 0 ) THEN
000023 //STEP020  EXEC  XCOPY                                   T
000024 //IN         DD  DSN=*.STEP010.COMPARE.SYSUT1,DISP=SHR   T  IF
000025 //OUT        DD  SYSOUT=*                                T
000026 //     ELSE
000027 //****************************************************
000028 //*                                                  *
000029 //*    IF ITEMS DIFFERENT, DUMP THE FIRST ONE        *
000030 //*                                                  *
000031 //****************************************************
000032 //STEP030  EXEC  XDUMP                                   F
000033 //DD1        DD  DSN=*.STEP010.COMPARE.SYSUT1,DISP=SHR   F
000034 //SYSIN      DD  DSN=CSCJGJ.ADV.CCARDS(CC2),DISP=SHR     F
000035 //*                                                     F
000036 //****************************************************  F
000037 //*                                                  *  F
000038 //*    IF ITEMS DIFFERENT, DUMP THE SECOND ONE       *  F ELSE
000039 //*                                                  *  F
000040 //****************************************************  F
000041 //STEP040  EXEC  XDUMP                                   F
000042 //DD1        DD  DSN=*.STEP010.COMPARE.SYSUT2,DISP=SHR   F
000043 //SYSIN      DD  DSN=CSCJGJ.ADV.CCARDS(CC2),DISP=SHR     F
000044 //       ENDIF                                           F
```

Awkward to have to look inside nested procs for stepnames and ddnames!

Figure 5.16 E4PROC, A Version of D6PROC That Uses Nested Proc Building Blocks (refer also to Figure 4.20)

5.13 Overcoming Nested Proc Limitations

I can overcome at least some of the awkwardness of nested procs as a JCL streamlining device, demonstrated in E4PROC, by using symbolic parameters instead of data set name referbacks. I have changed lines 24, 33, and 42 of E4PROC in creating E5PROC in Figure 5.17. This eliminates three occasions, in this job stream, where I had previously found it necessary to delve into the nested proc building blocks for procstepnames and original ddnames.

I cannot overcome the need to "know" about what's inside of a proc to code IF/THEN/ELSE relational tests, as you see at line 22 in E5PROC (Figure 5.17). JCL syntax requires that when you test the return code of a step

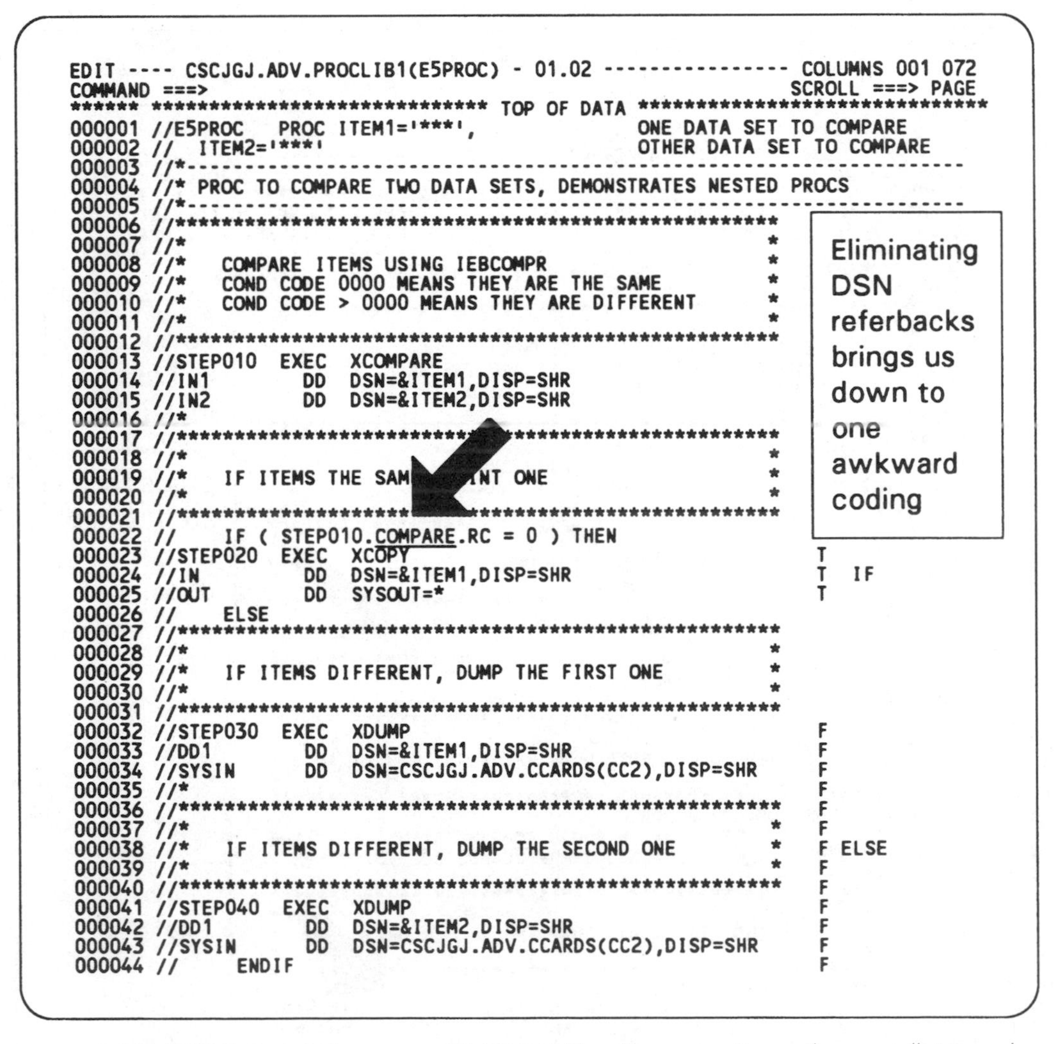

```
EDIT ---- CSCJGJ.ADV.PROCLIB1(E5PROC) - 01.02 --------------- COLUMNS 001 072
COMMAND ===>                                                  SCROLL ===> PAGE
****** ***************************** TOP OF DATA ******************************
000001 //E5PROC   PROC ITEM1='***',              ONE DATA SET TO COMPARE
000002 //   ITEM2='***'                          OTHER DATA SET TO COMPARE
000003 //*-------------------------------------------------------------------
000004 //* PROC TO COMPARE TWO DATA SETS, DEMONSTRATES NESTED PROCS
000005 //*-------------------------------------------------------------------
000006 //****************************************************
000007 //*                                                  *
000008 //*    COMPARE ITEMS USING IEBCOMPR                  *
000009 //*    COND CODE 0000 MEANS THEY ARE THE SAME        *
000010 //*    COND CODE > 0000 MEANS THEY ARE DIFFERENT     *
000011 //*                                                  *
000012 //****************************************************
000013 //STEP010  EXEC  XCOMPARE
000014 //IN1         DD  DSN=&ITEM1,DISP=SHR
000015 //IN2         DD  DSN=&ITEM2,DISP=SHR
000016 //*
000017 //****************************************************
000018 //*                                                  *
000019 //*    IF ITEMS THE SAM      INT ONE                 *
000020 //*                                                  *
000021 //****************************************************
000022 //     IF ( STEP010.COMPARE.RC = 0 ) THEN
000023 //STEP020  EXEC  XCOPY                                   T
000024 //IN          DD  DSN=&ITEM1,DISP=SHR                     T  IF
000025 //OUT         DD  SYSOUT=*                                T
000026 //     ELSE
000027 //****************************************************
000028 //*                                                  *
000029 //*    IF ITEMS DIFFERENT, DUMP THE FIRST ONE        *
000030 //*                                                  *
000031 //****************************************************
000032 //STEP030  EXEC  XDUMP                                   F
000033 //DD1         DD  DSN=&ITEM1,DISP=SHR                     F
000034 //SYSIN       DD  DSN=CSCJGJ.ADV.CCARDS(CC2),DISP=SHR     F
000035 //*                                                      F
000036 //****************************************************   F
000037 //*                                                  *   F
000038 //*    IF ITEMS DIFFERENT, DUMP THE SECOND ONE       *   F ELSE
000039 //*                                                  *   F
000040 //****************************************************   F
000041 //STEP040  EXEC  XDUMP                                   F
000042 //DD1         DD  DSN=&ITEM2,DISP=SHR                     F
000043 //SYSIN       DD  DSN=CSCJGJ.ADV.CCARDS(CC2),DISP=SHR     F
000044 //      ENDIF                                             F
```

Eliminating DSN referbacks brings us down to one awkward coding

Figure 5.17 E5PROC, A Refinement of E4PROC That Eliminates Some (but not all) Nested Proc Syntax Awkwardness

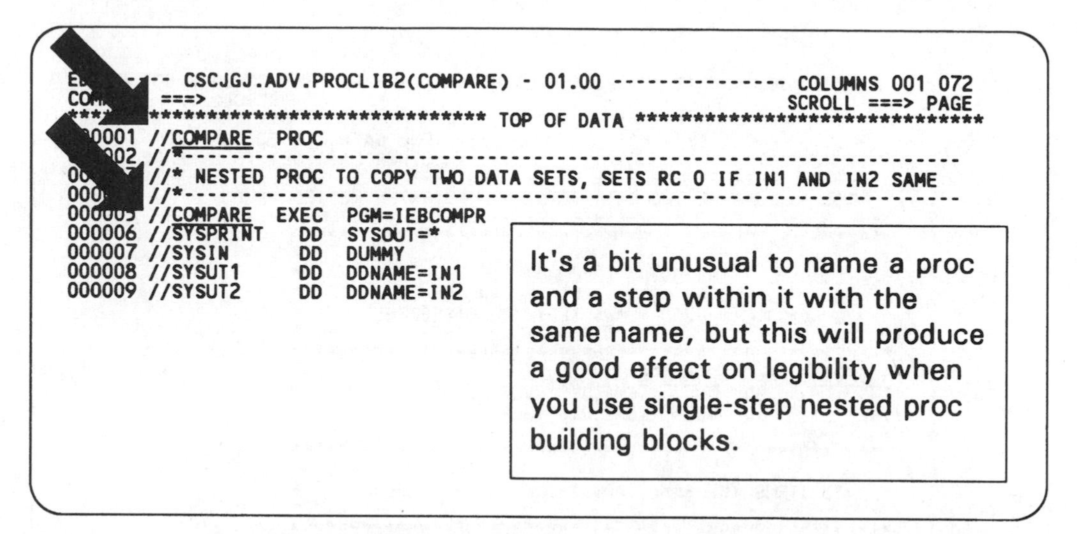

CSCJGJ.ADV.PROCLIB2(COMPARE) - 01.00 COLUMNS 001 072
===>
SCROLL ===> PAGE
TOP OF DATA
0001 //COMPARE PROC
//*--
//* NESTED PROC TO COPY TWO DATA SETS, SETS RC 0 IF IN1 AND IN2 SAME
//*--
//COMPARE EXEC PGM=IEBCOMPR
000006 //SYSPRINT DD SYSOUT=*
000007 //SYSIN DD DUMMY
000008 //SYSUT1 DD DDNAME=IN1
000009 //SYSUT2 DD DDNAME=IN2
It's a bit unusual to name a proc and a step within it with the same name, but this will produce a good effect on legibility when you use single-step nested proc building blocks.

Figure 5.18 Revised COMPARE Nested Proc Building Block That Overcomes Syntax Awkwardness in Return Code (RC) Testing for One-Step Nested Procs

coded within a proc, you refer to that step by name. In Figure 5.17, this occurs at line 22 and refers to something unseen in the E5PROC itself: the procstepname COMPARE, within the XCOMPARE proc.

One way around this final problem of nested proc awkwardness is to code one-step nested proc building blocks such as XCOMPARE with the procstepname identical to the proc name, as shown in Figure 5.18. There is no JCL syntax prohibition against doing this, but it may not be a common convention in your installation. With the COMPARE nested proc coded as shown in Figure 5.18, however, I can code the beginning of E5PROC as shown in Figure 5.19. The JCL reads better, because it appears that I am making, at line 22, a relational test of the return code set at STEP010 by the COMPARE program, and the value 0. In fact, line 22 is citing the procstepname, but since this and the proc name are the same, the appearance and readability of the invoking proc is improved. This is a convenient naming convention for nested proc building blocks, and I suggest you consider using it.

```
EDIT ---- CSCJGJ.ADV.PROCLIB1(E5PROC) - 01.02 ---------------- COLUMNS 001 072
COMMAND ===>                                                  SCROLL ===> PAGE
****** ******************************* TOP OF DATA ******************************
000001 //E5PROC   PROC ITEM1='***',               ONE DATA SET TO COMPARE
000002 //  ITEM2='***'                             OTHER DATA SET TO COMPARE
000003 //*-----------------------------------------------------------------------
000004 //* PROC TO COMPARE TWO DATA SETS, DEMONSTRATES NESTED PROCS
000005 //*-----------------------------------------------------------------------
000006 //*****************************************************
000007 //*                                                   *
000008 //*   COMPARE ITEMS USING IEBCOMPR                    *
000009 //*   COND CODE 0000 MEANS THEY ARE THE SAME          *
000010 //*   COND CODE > 0000 MEANS THEY ARE DIFFERENT       *
000011 //*                                                   *
000012 //*****************************************************
000013 //STEP010  EXEC  COMPARE
000014 //IN1         DD  DSN=&ITEM1,DISP=SHR
000015 //IN2         DD  DSN=&ITEM2,DISP=SHR
000016 //*
000017 //*****************************************************
000018 //*                                                   *
000019 //*   IF ITEMS THE SAME, PRINT ONE                    *
000020 //*                                                   *
000021 //*****************************************************
000022 //    IF ( STEP010.COMPARE.RC = 0 ) THEN
000023 //STEP020  EXEC  XCOPY                                         T
000024 //IN          DD  DSN=&ITEM1,DISP=SHR                         T  IF
000025 //OUT         DD  SYSOUT=*                                    T
000026 //    ELSE
          -
          -
          -
```

The coding of the relational test for STEP010 return code at line 22 now appears to be directly related to the coding at line 13. This makes the JCL in the proc very legible. Of course, it is a harmless illusion. STEP010.COMPARE.RC really refers to the unseen stepname within the COMPARE proc. But since the procname and the stepname are now the same in the nested proc COMPARE, it appears that all of our proc coding is completely external to nested proc details.

Figure 5.19 Revised Coding of Part of E5PROC, Showing Improved JCL Readability

5.14 Problems with Recursion

You can cause a problem for yourself if you introduce recursion into a job stream. You can make this happen by executing a proc that executes a proc that executes the original proc you execute, causing a "dog chasing its tail" situation. Figure 5.20 illustrates a proc named E6PROC that invokes itself, the worst case situation for recursion.

When I execute E6PROC, using JCL such as E6EXJCL shown in Figure 5.21, system reporting output as shown in Figure 5.22 is produced. MVS/ESA begins the task finding each nested proc within the proc libraries, but keeps track of how many apparent levels of nesting are encountered. It quits after 15 levels of nesting, as it clearly indicates.

The type of reporting you see in Figure 5.22 will almost always indicate a problem of recursion rather than any limitation of MVS/ESA to handle reasonable work. If you see this type of system output, check your procs carefully and you will almost certainly find an instance of a proc chaining back to invoke a proc that has invoked it!

```
EDIT ---- CSCJGJ.ADV.PROCLIB1(E6PROC) - 01.00 --------------- COLUMNS 001 072
COMMAND ===>                                                  SCROLL ===> PAGE
****** ***************************** TOP OF DATA ******************************
000001 //E6PROC   PROC
000002 //*-----------------------------------------------------------------
000003 //* THIS PROC ERRONEOUSLY INVOKES ITSELF TO DEMONSTRATE
000004 //* WHAT HAPPENS IF YOU UNINTENTIONALLY EXCEED THE MVS/ESA
000005 //* PROC NESTING LIMIT OF 15
000006 //*-----------------------------------------------------------------
000007 //STEP010  EXEC  E6PROC
```

Figure 5.20 E6PROC, Worst Case Recursion: A Proc That Invokes Itself!

```
EDIT ---- CSCJGJ.ADV.CNTL(E6EXJCL) - 01.00 ------------------ COLUMNS 001 072
COMMAND ===>                                                  SCROLL ===> PAGE
****** ***************************** TOP OF DATA ******************************
000001 //CSCJGJA   JOB 1,                      ACCOUNTING INFORMATION
000002 //   'BIN 7--JANOSSY',                  PROGRAMMER NAME AND DELIVERY BIN
000003 //   CLASS=A,                           INPUT QUEUE CLASS
000004 //   MSGLEVEL=(1,1),                    HOW MUCH MVS SYSTEM PRINT DESIRED
000005 //   MSGCLASS=X,                        PRINT DESTINATION X A L N OR O
000006 //   TIME=(0,6),                        SAFETY LIMIT: RUN TIME UP TO 6 SECS
000007 //   REGION=2M,                         ALLOW UP TO 2 MEGS VIRTUAL MEMORY
000008 //*  TYPRUN=SCAN,                       UNCOMMENT THIS LINE TO DO SCAN ONLY
000009 //   NOTIFY=CSCJGJ                      WHO TO TELL WHEN JOB IS DONE
000010 //*
000011 //   JCLLIB  ORDER=(CSCJGJ.ADV.PROCLIB1,        MY TESTING PROC LIBRARY
000012 //      CSCJGJ.ADV.PROCLIB2)                     MY "FINAL" PROC LIBRARY
000013 //*
000014 //* JCL TO EXECUTE E6PROC TO DEMONSTRATE UNINTENDED RECURSION
000015 //* THIS JCL IS STORED AT CSCJGJ.ADV.CNTL(E6EXJCL)
000016 //*
000017 //STEPA    EXEC  E6PROC
000018 //
```

Figure 5.21 E6EXJCL, Execution JCL to Invoke E6PROC

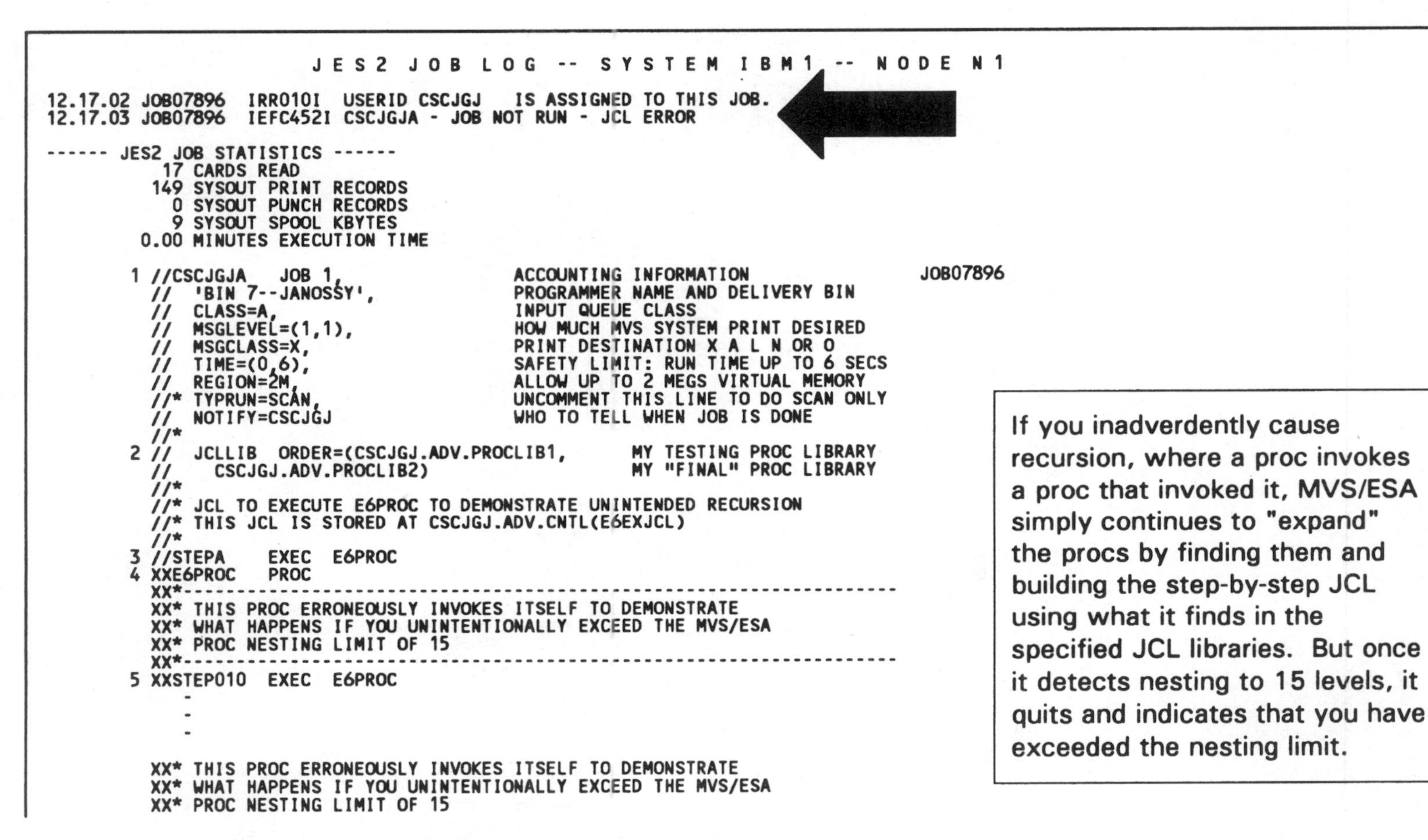

```
                  J E S 2  J O B  L O G  --  S Y S T E M  I B M 1  --  N O D E  N 1

12.17.02 JOB07896  IRR010I  USERID CSCJGJ   IS ASSIGNED TO THIS JOB.
12.17.03 JOB07896  IEFC452I CSCJGJA - JOB NOT RUN - JCL ERROR

------ JES2 JOB STATISTICS ------
      17 CARDS READ
     149 SYSOUT PRINT RECORDS
       0 SYSOUT PUNCH RECORDS
       9 SYSOUT SPOOL KBYTES
    0.00 MINUTES EXECUTION TIME

       1 //CSCJGJA   JOB 1,                 ACCOUNTING INFORMATION              JOB07896
         //  'BIN 7--JANOSSY',              PROGRAMMER NAME AND DELIVERY BIN
         //  CLASS=A,                       INPUT QUEUE CLASS
         //  MSGLEVEL=(1,1),                HOW MUCH MVS SYSTEM PRINT DESIRED
         //  MSGCLASS=X,                    PRINT DESTINATION X A L N OR O
         //  TIME=(0,6),                    SAFETY LIMIT: RUN TIME UP TO 6 SECS
         //  REGION=2M,                     ALLOW UP TO 2 MEGS VIRTUAL MEMORY
         //* TYPRUN=SCAN,                   UNCOMMENT THIS LINE TO DO SCAN ONLY
         //  NOTIFY=CSCJGJ                  WHO TO TELL WHEN JOB IS DONE
         //*
       2 //  JCLLIB  ORDER=(CSCJGJ.ADV.PROCLIB1,      MY TESTING PROC LIBRARY
         //    CSCJGJ.ADV.PROCLIB2)                   MY "FINAL" PROC LIBRARY
         //*
         //* JCL TO EXECUTE E6PROC TO DEMONSTRATE UNINTENDED RECURSION
         //* THIS JCL IS STORED AT CSCJGJ.ADV.CNTL(E6EXJCL)
         //*
       3 //STEPA     EXEC  E6PROC
       4 XXE6PROC    PROC
         XX*-----------------------------------------------------------------
         XX* THIS PROC ERRONEOUSLY INVOKES ITSELF TO DEMONSTRATE
         XX* WHAT HAPPENS IF YOU UNINTENTIONALLY EXCEED THE MVS/ESA
         XX* PROC NESTING LIMIT OF 15
         XX*-----------------------------------------------------------------
       5 XXSTEP010  EXEC  E6PROC
             -
             -
             -

         XX* THIS PROC ERRONEOUSLY INVOKES ITSELF TO DEMONSTRATE
         XX* WHAT HAPPENS IF YOU UNINTENTIONALLY EXCEED THE MVS/ESA
         XX* PROC NESTING LIMIT OF 15
```

If you inadverdently cause recursion, where a proc invokes a proc that invoked it, MVS/ESA simply continues to "expand" the procs by finding them and building the step-by-step JCL using what it finds in the specified JCL libraries. But once it detects nesting to 15 levels, it quits and indicates that you have exceeded the nesting limit.

Figure 5.22 MVS/ESA Version 4 System Reporting Typical of Proc Recursion

```
        XX*-------------------------------------------------------------------
     29 XXSTEP010  EXEC  E6PROC
     30 XXE6PROC   PROC
        XX*-------------------------------------------------------------------
        XX* THIS PROC ERRONEOUSLY INVOKES ITSELF TO DEMONSTRATE
        XX* WHAT HAPPENS IF YOU UNINTENTIONALLY EXCEED THE MVS/ESA
        XX* PROC NESTING LIMIT OF 15
        XX*-------------------------------------------------------------------
     31 XXSTEP010  EXEC  E6PROC
     32 XXE6PROC   PROC
        XX*-------------------------------------------------------------------
        XX* THIS PROC ERRONEOUSLY INVOKES ITSELF TO DEMONSTRATE
        XX* WHAT HAPPENS IF YOU UNINTENTIONALLY EXCEED THE MVS/ESA
        XX* PROC NESTING LIMIT OF 15
        XX*-------------------------------------------------------------------
     33 XXSTEP010  EXEC  E6PROC

STMT NO. MESSAGE
       3 IEFC001I PROCEDURE E6PROC WAS EXPANDED USING PRIVATE LIBRARY CSCJGJ.ADV.PROCLIB1
       5 IEFC001I PROCEDURE E6PROC WAS EXPANDED USING PRIVATE LIBRARY CSCJGJ.ADV.PROCLIB1
       7 IEFC001I PROCEDURE E6PROC WAS EXPANDED USING PRIVATE LIBRARY CSCJGJ.ADV.PROCLIB1
       9 IEFC001I PROCEDURE E6PROC WAS EXPANDED USING PRIVATE LIBRARY CSCJGJ.ADV.PROCLIB1
      11 IEFC001I PROCEDURE E6PROC WAS EXPANDED USING PRIVATE LIBRARY CSCJGJ.ADV.PROCLIB1
      13 IEFC001I PROCEDURE E6PROC WAS EXPANDED USING PRIVATE LIBRARY CSCJGJ.ADV.PROCLIB1
      15 IEFC001I PROCEDURE E6PROC WAS EXPANDED USING PRIVATE LIBRARY CSCJGJ.ADV.PROCLIB1
      17 IEFC001I PROCEDURE E6PROC WAS EXPANDED USING PRIVATE LIBRARY CSCJGJ.ADV.PROCLIB1
      19 IEFC001I PROCEDURE E6PROC WAS EXPANDED USING PRIVATE LIBRARY CSCJGJ.ADV.PROCLIB1
      21 IEFC001I PROCEDURE E6PROC WAS EXPANDED USING PRIVATE LIBRARY CSCJGJ.ADV.PROCLIB1
      23 IEFC001I PROCEDURE E6PROC WAS EXPANDED USING PRIVATE LIBRARY CSCJGJ.ADV.PROCLIB1
      25 IEFC001I PROCEDURE E6PROC WAS EXPANDED USING PRIVATE LIBRARY CSCJGJ.ADV.PROCLIB1
      27 IEFC001I PROCEDURE E6PROC WAS EXPANDED USING PRIVATE LIBRARY CSCJGJ.ADV.PROCLIB1
      29 IEFC001I PROCEDURE E6PROC WAS EXPANDED USING PRIVATE LIBRARY CSCJGJ.ADV.PROCLIB1
      31 IEFC001I PROCEDURE E6PROC WAS EXPANDED USING PRIVATE LIBRARY CSCJGJ.A
      33 IEFC011I MAXIMUM OF 15 LEVELS OF PROC STATEMENT NESTING EXCEEDED
```

The 15 level nesting limit was reached by recursion here, and MVS pulls the plug on the job! If you encounter this type of system reporting, look for more subtle recursion than simply a proc invoking itself.

Figure 5.22 (continued)

6

Tuning Up Old Procs

6.1 Poor JCL and Good JCL
6.2 What's Wrong with Some Older JCL?
6.3 Criteria for Improved JCL
6.4 Steps in Making Your Existing JCL Better
6.5 Milestone 1: List and Analyze
6.6 Milestone 2: Visually Separate Job Steps Within the JCL
6.7 Milestone 3: Reformat the JCL
6.8 Milestone 4: Flesh Out Parameter Defaults
6.9 Milestone 5: Use VIO, IF/ELSE, Same-Line Comments
6.10 Improvement Results
6.11 Locally Tuned Templates for Job Stream Construction
6.12 Conveying and Reinforcing Installation Standards Using Templates
6.13 A Caution About Comments!

6.1 Poor JCL and Good JCL

A lot of job control language now in place and running today's jobs in mainframe installations is poor in quality. I define "poor" JCL as JCL that consumes machine time in unproductive ways, is prone to failure, and/or presents a significant challenge for newcomers to deal with. Poor JCL can be improved at little cost. But why is it poor in the first place?

By nature, job control language looks terse and primitive, deals in labels no larger than eight characters, and provides short and choppy error reporting. This is no accident. When job control language was invented, most programmers worked in or had a functional knowledge of assembler language, to which JCL is similar. In the early days of the 1960s, mainframe computers were (by today's standards) tiny, yet information storage and processing demands were already large and growing. Assembler, which is essentially an abbreviation for the raw machine language instructions of the computer, is machine-efficient and powerful and was often employed to make processing practical at all. JCL was designed to complement assembler language in style. And, although neither assembler nor JCL purposely were designed to be unfriendly, both *were* designed to provide cryptic commands and syntax that would fit well on punched cards, the human/machine interface of the early days.

But we are no longer in the 1960s, most programmers no longer know much about assembler language, and we no longer use punched cards to convey JCL to the computer system. And—and this is a big and—we all have a lot more on our minds than one operating system and one type of software. This means we all have a lot less tolerance for things that take longer to understand than they should, such as old-style JCL from an earlier era. It makes a lot of sense to take a fresh look at how you code your JCL and to leave the past behind to build better, more efficient, and more readily maintained JCL suited to the modern environment rather than punched cards. I demonstrate a step-by-step method to do this in this chapter.

6.2 What's Wrong with Some Older JCL?

These are the kinds of things that you commonly find in older JCL, which detract from machine efficiency:

- *Extra steps that are no longer needed.* Some older JCL still contains steps to copy input punched cards to disk!
- *Inefficient, hardcoded block sizes.* These need to be respecified as a good compromise block size approaching 6233 bytes per block for disk or a more efficient value for your complement of disks, or changed to allow MVS/ESA to compute the block size, or changed to allow DFSMS to handle almost all storage allocation decisions.
- *The use of ordinary disk such as SYSDA for work files and temporary files as opposed to VIO.* VIO approximates on a mainframe the RAM disk of a PC.

Several other faults you'll find in older JCL detract from maintainability and waste personnel time—in using the JCL, in changing it as needed to recover from failures, and in adapting it to meet changing requirements:

- The use of arcane JCL defaults such as (,CATLG)
- The coding of too many parameters on a line, making the JCL hard to read and hard to change
- The lack of full-line comments to denote the start of each step
- The lack of same-line comments to plainly document DD statements (same-line comments can start on any JCL line after the JCL coding itself, as long as at least one space separates the beginning of the comment from the end of the JCL itself; IBM calls this variable-sized area the "comment field" in its documentation)
- Inconsistent or too-heavy indentation
- The use of cryptic stepnames, which makes system output needlessly difficult to read

Many of these faults in coding and naming result from the close association of JCL with assembler language and were actually helpful in the early days, but they have become much less so. For example, the name of the program IEFBR14 is really a benign inside joke among assembler programmers. As a "null" program, IEFBR14 actually does nothing; it merely receives control and stops, and provides an excuse to trigger MVS/ESA's data set allocation and deallocation activities. The humor results from the fact that "BR 14" is the assembler instruction to stop. The program name really says it all to someone who knows assembler, but the cleverness is lost on people who don't know assembler. This is certainly not a plea for programmers to learn assembler. It just makes the point that the assembler-oriented conventions of the 1960s become increasingly moot as time moves on.

6.3 Criteria for Improved JCL

You should consider how to "refurbish" older JCL for three reasons. First, refurbishing older JCL can provide improved machine efficiency, that is, less CPU time expended on computer runs. Second, learning what to look for and upgrade inherently leads to writing better job streams, so you don't perpetuate obsolete practices. Third, properly refurbished JCL is easier for others to understand and become comfortable with. It reduces JCL maintenance time, lessens the potential for coding errors as JCL is enhanced, speeds making JCL changes needed to recover from failed runs, and, in general, makes it easier for newcomers to become acclimated to your production runs.

To improve the quality of your JCL and increase the productivity of people who work with it, you need to aim at several improvements. You need to do these things in refurbishing JCL:

- Cut the tie to punched-card coding conventions designed purely to squeeze many parameters into the fewest number of punched cards; we no longer give prizes for the smallest decks of punched cards.
- Eliminate the use of arcane MVS/ESA defaults that force newcomers to guess about what JCL is doing; explicitly code what you want your JCL to tell MVS/ESA.
- Make your JCL consistent in format and as self-documenting as possible.

You can improve both the machine efficiency and productivity of personnel who work with your installation's job control language by following some simple steps. The steps described in the following sections form a series of actions that you can take in stages to make incremental improvements in JCL. Taken together, these actions can provide an improvement in machine efficiency as well as lessen the time needed for newcomers to become able to work with your JCL.

6.4 Steps in Making Your Existing JCL Better

One theory of program maintenance holds that every time you need to modify a program, you should also improve something in it. If you do this, your most heavily modified programs are improved more rapidly, allowing future modification to proceed faster and more reliably. This is a good theory, and, properly applied, leads to enhancement of your software portfolio rather than its deterioration over time.

```
EDIT ---- CSCJGJ.ADV.CNTL(DFHMAPS) - 01.00 ------------------ COLUMNS 001 072
COMMAND ===>                                                  SCROLL ===> PAGE
****** ****************************** TOP OF DATA ******************************
000110 //DFHMAP1 PROC INDEX='CICS330',
000120 //               MAPLIB='CCP.LOADLIB',
000130 //               DSCTLIB='CCP.MACLIB',
000140 //               MAPNAME=,
000150 //               A=,
000160 //               RMODE=24,
000170 //               ASMBLR=IEV90,
000180 //               REG=2048K,
000190 //               OUTC='*',
000191 //               WORK=SYSDA
000192 //COPY     EXEC PGM=IEBGENER
000193 //SYSPRINT DD SYSOUT=&OUTC
000194 //SYSUT2   DD DSN=&&TEMPM,UNIT=&WORK,DISP=(,PASS),
000195 //            DCB=(RECFM=FB,LRECL=80,BLKSIZE=400),
000196 //            SPACE=(400,(50,50))
000197 //SYSIN    DD DUMMY
000198 //* SYSUT1 DD * NEEDED FOR THE MAP SOURCE
000199 //ASMMAP   EXEC PGM=&ASMBLR,REGION=&REG,
000200 //  PARM='SYSPARM(&A.MAP),DECK,NOLOAD'
000201 //SYSPRINT DD SYSOUT=&OUTC
000202 //SYSLIB  DD DSN=&INDEX..SDFHMAC,DISP=SHR
000203 //          DD DSN=SYS1.MACLIB,DISP=SHR
000204 //SYSUT1  DD UNIT=&WORK,SPACE=(CYL,(5,5))
000205 //SYSUT2  DD UNIT=&WORK,SPACE=(CYL,(5,5))
000206 //SYSUT3  DD UNIT=&WORK,SPACE=(CYL,(5,5))
000207 //SYSPUNCH  DD DSN=&&MAP,DISP=(,PASS),UNIT=&WORK,
000208 //            DCB=(RECFM=FB,LRECL=80,BLKSIZE=400),
000209 //            SPACE=(400,(50,50))
000210 //SYSIN    DD DSN=&&TEMPM,DISP=(OLD,PASS)
000211 //LINKMAP  EXEC PGM=IEWL,PARM='LIST,LET,XREF,RMODE(&RMODE)'
000212 //SYSPRINT DD SYSOUT=&OUTC
000213 //SYSLMOD  DD DSN=&MAPLIB(&MAPNAME),DISP=SHR
000214 //SYSUT1  DD UNIT=&WORK,SPACE=(1024,(20,20))
000215 //SYSLIN  DD DSN=&&MAP,DISP=(OLD,DELETE)
000216 //ASMDSECT EXEC PGM=&ASMBLR,REGION=&REG,
000217 //  PARM='SYSPARM(&A.DSECT),DECK,NOLOAD'
000218 //SYSPRINT  DD SYSOUT=&OUTC
000219 //SYSLIB  DD DSN=&INDEX..SDFHMAC,DISP=SHR
000220 //         DD DSN=SYS1.MACLIB,DISP=SHR
000221 //SYSUT1   DD UNIT=&WORK,SPACE=(CYL,(5,5))
000222 //SYSUT2   DD UNIT=&WORK,SPACE=(CYL,(5,5))
000223 //SYSUT3   DD UNIT=&WORK,SPACE=(CYL,(5,5))
000224 //SYSPUNCH  DD DSN=&DSCTLIB(&MAPNAME),DISP=OLD
000225 //SYSIN  DD DSN=&&TEMPM,DISP=(OLD,DELETE)
```

This is an example of old JCL that can be improved to make it more efficient and easier to use. This is, frankly, an ugly, hard-to-read mess built long ago using punched cards!

Figure 6.1 DFHMAPS, A 1960s-Style Proc That Can Benefit from Refurbishing

You can apply the same maintenance theory to JCL. I've listed several "milestones" here that you can reach to enhance your investment in JCL. You need not reach all five milestones in one sitting; make progress in stages by reaching one milestone at a time, as you have time. For example purposes, I've applied these milestones to a job stream named DFHMAPS, a 1960s-vintage proc used to process screen coding into the physical and symbolic maps used by CICS programs. This JCL is shown in Figure 6.1. I have illustrated it as it appears in its original form. This proc works, but it can be made more efficient, more understandable, and more readily maintained.

6.5 Milestone 1: List and Analyze

List the JCL on paper and look over the whole job stream before trying to change it. Draw some horizontal lines as you figure out where each step ends and the next step (EXEC) begins. Number the steps (EXECs) 1, 2, 3, and so forth with handwritten comments. Do this yourself in this book with Figure 6.1 to demonstrate the effect.

6.6 Milestone 2: Visually Separate Job Steps Within the JCL

Make a copy of the JCL or proc under a slightly different name. I have called the copy DFHMAP2. Physically split this JCL up into steps by putting a full-line comment containing hyphens before each EXEC statement. This takes hardly any work at all and immediately makes examination of the JCL easier and faster. Then use TSO/ISPF's insert or delete features to align the EXEC and DD statements, and renumber the JCL or proc. I have done this in DFHMAP2 in Figure 6.2.

```
EDIT ---- CSCJGJ.ADV.CNTL(DFHMAP2) - 01.00 ------------------ COLUMNS 001 072
COMMAND ===>                                                  SCROLL ===> PAGE
****** ****************************** TOP OF DATA *******************************
000100 //DFHMAPS PROC INDEX='CICS330',
000200 //               MAPLIB='CCP.LOADLIB',
000300 //               DSCTLIB='CCP.MACLIB',
000400 //               MAPNAME=,
000500 //               A=,
000600 //               RMODE=24,
000700 //               ASMBLR=IEV90,
000800 //               REG=2048K,
000900 //               OUTC='*',
001000 //               WORK=SYSDA
001100 //*-------------------------------------------------------------------
001200 //COPY      EXEC PGM=IEBGENER
001300 //SYSPRINT DD SYSOUT=&OUTC
001400 //SYSUT2   DD DSN=&&TEMPM,UNIT=&WORK,DISP=(,PASS),
001500 //            DCB=(RECFM=FB,LRECL=80,BLKSIZE=400),
001600 //            SPACE=(400,(50,50))
001700 //SYSIN    DD DUMMY
001800 //* SYSUT1 DD * NEEDED FOR THE MAP SOURCE
001900 //*-----------------------------------------
002000 //ASMMAP   EXEC PGM=&ASMBLR,REGION=&REG,
002100 //   PARM='SYSPARM(&A.MAP),DECK,NOLOAD'
002200 //SYSPRINT DD SYSOUT=&OUTC
002300 //SYSLIB   DD DSN=&INDEX..SDFHMAC,DISP=SHR
002400 //         DD DSN=SYS1.MACLIB,DISP=SHR
002500 //SYSUT1   DD UNIT=&WORK,SPACE=(CYL,(5,5))
002600 //SYSUT2   DD UNIT=&WORK,SPACE=(CYL,(5,5))
002700 //SYSUT3   DD UNIT=&WORK,SPACE=(CYL,(5,5))
002800 //SYSPUNCH DD DSN=&&MAP,DISP=(,PASS),UNIT=&WORK,
002900 //            DCB=(RECFM=FB,LRECL=80,BLKSIZE=400),
003000 //            SPACE=(400,(50,50))
003100 //SYSIN    DD DSN=&&TEMPM,DISP=(OLD,PASS)
003200 //*-------------------------------------------------------------------
003300 //LINKMAP  EXEC PGM=IEWL,PARM='LIST,LET,XREF,RMODE(&RMODE)'
003400 //SYSPRINT DD SYSOUT=&OUTC
003500 //SYSLMOD  DD DSN=&MAPLIB(&MAPNAME),DISP=SHR
003600 //SYSUT1   DD UNIT=&WORK,SPACE=(1024,(20,20))
003700 //SYSLIN   DD DSN=&&MAP,DISP=(OLD,DELETE)
003800 //*-------------------------------------------------------------------
003900 //ASMDSECT EXEC PGM=&ASMBLR,REGION=&REG,
004000 //   PARM='SYSPARM(&A.DSECT),DECK,NOLOAD'
004100 //SYSPRINT DD SYSOUT=&OUTC
004200 //SYSLIB   DD DSN=&INDEX..SDFHMAC,DISP=SHR
004300 //         DD DSN=SYS1.MACLIB,DISP=SHR
004400 //SYSUT1   DD UNIT=&WORK,SPACE=(CYL,(5,5))
004500 //SYSUT2   DD UNIT=&WORK,SPACE=(CYL,(5,5))
004600 //SYSUT3   DD UNIT=&WORK,SPACE=(CYL,(5,5))
004700 //SYSPUNCH DD DSN=&DSCTLIB(&MAPNAME),DISP=OLD
004800 //SYSIN    DD DSN=&&TEMPM,DISP=(OLD,DELETE)
```

Start improving the JCL by separating steps visually, and aligning EXEC and DD statements.

Figure 6.2 DFHMAP2, Showing the First of Several Milestones of Improvement

6.7 Milestone 3: Reformat the JCL

Spread the coding of more involved JCL statements to multiple lines, coding only one JCL parameter per line. Any JOB, EXEC, or DD statement with three or more parameters warrants this type of treatment. For example, this is not a particularly involved DD statement, and I would leave it coded on one line:

```
EDIT ---- CSCJGJ.ADV.CNTL(DFHMAP3) - 01.00 ------------------ COLUMNS 001 072
COMMAND ===>                                                  SCROLL ===> PAGE
****** ***************************** TOP OF DATA ******************************
000100 //DFHMAPS PROC INDEX='CICS330',
000200 //              MAPLIB='CCP.LOADLIB',
000300 //              DSCTLIB='CCP.MACLIB',
000400 //              MAPNAME=,
000500 //              A=,
000600 //              RMODE=24,
000700 //              ASMBLR=IEV90,
000800 //              REG=2048K,
000900 //              OUTC='*',
001000 //              WORK=SYSDA
001100 //*-------------------------------------------------------------------
001200 //COPY      EXEC  PGM=IEBGENER
001300 //SYSPRINT   DD   SYSOUT=&OUTC
001400 //SYSUT2     DD   DSN=&&TEMPM,
001500 //  UNIT=&WORK,
001600 //  DISP=(,PASS),
001700 //  DCB=(RECFM=FB,LRECL=80,BLKSIZE=400),
001800 //  SPACE=(400,(50,50))
001900 //SYSIN    DD DUMMY
002000 //* SYSUT1 DD * NEEDED FOR THE MAP SOURCE
002100 //*---------------------------------------
002200 //ASMMAP    EXEC  PGM=&ASMBLR,
002300 //  REGION=&REG,
002400 //  PARM='SYSPARM(&A.MAP),DECK,NOLOAD'
002500 //SYSPRINT    DD   SYSOUT=&OUTC
002600 //SYSLIB      DD   DSN=&INDEX..SDFHMAC,DISP=SHR
002700 //            DD   DSN=SYS1.MACLIB,DISP=SHR
002800 //SYSUT1      DD   UNIT=&WORK,SPACE=(CYL,(5,5))
002900 //SYSUT2      DD   UNIT=&WORK,SPACE=(CYL,(5,5))
003000 //SYSUT3      DD   UNIT=&WORK,SPACE=(CYL,(5,5))
003100 //SYSPUNCH    DD   DSN=&&MAP,
003200 //  DISP=(,PASS),
003300 //  UNIT=&WORK,
003400 //  DCB=(RECFM=FB,LRECL=80,BLKSIZE=400),
003500 //  SPACE=(400,(50,50))
003600 //SYSIN       DD   DSN=&&TEMPM,DISP=(OLD,PASS)
003700 //*-------------------------------------------------------------------
003800 //LINKMAP  EXEC  PGM=IEWL,
003900 //  PARM='LIST,LET,XREF,RMODE(&RMODE)'
004000 //SYSPRINT    DD   SYSOUT=&OUTC
004100 //SYSLMOD     DD   DSN=&MAPLIB(&MAPNAME),DISP=SHR
004200 //SYSUT1      DD   UNIT=&WORK,SPACE=(1024,(20,20))
004300 //SYSLIN      DD   DSN=&&MAP,DISP=(OLD,DELETE)
004400 //*-------------------------------------------------------------------
004500 //ASMDSECT EXEC  PGM=&ASMBLR,REGION=&REG,
004600 //  PARM='SYSPARM(&A.DSECT),DECK,NOLOAD'
004700 //SYSPRINT    DD   SYSOUT=&OUTC
004800 //SYSLIB      DD   DSN=&INDEX..SDFHMAC,DISP=SHR
004900 //            DD   DSN=SYS1.MACLIB,DISP=SHR
005000 //SYSUT1      DD   UNIT=&WORK,SPACE=(CYL,(5,5))
005100 //SYSUT2      DD   UNIT=&WORK,SPACE=(CYL,(5,5))
005200 //SYSUT3      DD   UNIT=&WORK,SPACE=(CYL,(5,5))
005300 //SYSPUNCH    DD   DSN=&DSCTLIB(&MAPNAME),DISP=OLD
005400 //SYSIN       DD   DSN=&&TEMPM,DISP=(OLD,DELETE)
```

Reformatting lengthier EXEC and DD statements to put one parameter on each line improves legibility and makes room for the same-line comments we'll eventually apply.

Figure 6.3 DFHMAP3, Showing the Benefit of Reformatting with Parameters on Separate Lines

```
//SYSIN    DD DSN=&&TEMPM,DISP=(OLD,DELETE)
```

But I would certainly change this:

```
//SYSPUNCH DD DSN=&&MAP,DISP=(,PASS),UNIT=&WORK,
//            DCB=(RECFM=FB,LRECL=80,BLKSIZE=400),
//            SPACE=(400,(50,50))
```

to make it become:

```
//SYSPUNCH   DD  DSN=&&MAP,
//  DISP=(,PASS),
//  UNIT=&WORK,
//  DCB=(RECFM=FB,LRECL=80,BLKSIZE=400),
//  SPACE=(400,(50,50))
```

There is more work to do on the JCL beyond this, but I would suggest taking these reformatting actions without changing any of the parameters themselves. Reformatting in this way provides the room you need at the right side of each parameter to use same-line comments for documentation. I would suggest that you indent the continued JCL lines two spaces, not more, to leave the most room for same-line comments. If you take things one improvement at a time, you can more readily check your work by running the JCL to make sure your latest improvement has not adversely affected processing. I have applied these improvements to the map processing JCL to create DFHMAP3, shown in Figure 6.3.

6.8 Milestone 4: Flesh Out Parameter Defaults

This is the milestone where improvements really show themselves! The reformatting you have done up to this point sets the stage for making the JCL plainer to everyone who works with it, executes it, or reads the system output it produces. In working toward this milestone, you replace default-ridden parameters with explicitly coded parameters, eliminate the obsolete parameter SEP, simplify coding associated with the DCB parameter, and change disk block sizes to a value approximating 6233 (or another value stipulated by your installation as adequately efficient). You also install same-line comments to let the symbolic parameters in procs such as DFHMAPS explain themselves to everyone who uses the proc.

If you compare my DFHMAP4 JCL shown in Figure 6.4 with the DFHMAP3 JCL in Figure 6.3, you'll see that every occurrence of defaulted start-status DISP coding such as (,PASS) or (,CATLG) has been changed to a coding that carries all three parts of the DISP, such as (NEW,PASS,DELETE) or (NEW,CATLG,DELETE). There is really no excuse for perpetuating JCL that uses the start-status default of NEW, which forces everyone to remember trivia about this default, consult a reference book, or guess about what the JCL does.

Defaulted JCL was an idea of questionable benefit in 1964 but was provided to save a few columns on punch cards. The DISP defaults are now

```
EDIT ---- CSCJGJ.ADV.CNTL(DFHMAP4) - 01.00 ------------------ COLUMNS 001 072
COMMAND ===>                                                  SCROLL ===> PAGE
****** ***************************** TOP OF DATA ******************************
000100 //DFHMAPS PROC INDEX='CICS330',      CICS VERSION FOR SDFHMAC DSN
000200 //  MAPLIB='CCP.LOADLIB',            PHYSICAL MAP LIBRARY (A LOAD LIB)
000300 //  DSCTLIB='CCP.MACLIB',            SYMBOLIC MAP LIBRARY (COBOL CODE)
000400 //  MAPNAME=,                        INTENDED NAME OF PHYS AND SYM MAPS
000500 //  A=,                              A=A FOR ALIGNED MAP, ELSE NULL
000600 //  RMODE=24,                        24/ANY FOR PHY MAP RESIDENCE MODE
000700 //  ASMBLR=IEV90,                    ASSEMBLER PROGRAM NAME
000800 //  REG=2048K,                       MEMORY ALLOCATION FOR ASSEMBLER
000900 //  OUTC='*',                        PRINT SYSOUT CLASS
001000 //  WORK=SYSDA                       WORK FILE UNIT
001100 //*-----------------------------------------------------------------
001200 //COPY      EXEC  PGM=IEBGENER
001300 //SYSPRINT   DD  SYSOUT=&OUTC
001400 //* SYSUT1 DD * NEEDED FOR THE MAP SOURCE
001500 //SYSUT2     DD  DSN=&&TEMPM,
001600 //  DISP=(NEW,PASS,DELETE),
001700 //  UNIT=&WORK,
001800 //  RECFM=FB,
001900 //  LRECL=80,
002000 //  BLKSIZE=6160,
002100 //  SPACE=(6160,(10,10))
002200 //SYSIN    DD DUMMY
002300 //*----------------------------------------
002400 //ASMMAP   EXEC  PGM=&ASMBLR,
002500 //  REGION=&REG,
002600 //  PARM='SYSPARM(&A.MAP),DECK,NOLOAD'
002700 //SYSPRINT   DD  SYSOUT=&OUTC
002800 //SYSIN      DD  DSN=&&TEMPM,DISP=(OLD,PASS)
002900 //SYSLIB     DD  DSN=&INDEX..SDFHMAC,DISP=SHR
003000 //           DD  DSN=SYS1.MACLIB,DISP=SHR
003100 //SYSUT1     DD  UNIT=&WORK,SPACE=(CYL,(5,5))
003200 //SYSUT2     DD  UNIT=&WORK,SPACE=(CYL,(5,5))
003300 //SYSUT3     DD  UNIT=&WORK,SPACE=(CYL,(5,5))
003400 //SYSPUNCH   DD  DSN=&&MAP,
003500 //  DISP=(NEW,PASS,DELETE),
003600 //  UNIT=&WORK,
003700 //  RECFM=FB,
003800 //  LRECL=80,
003900 //  BLKSIZE=6160,
004000 //  SPACE=(6160,(10,10))
004100 //*-----------------------------------------------------------------
004200 //LINKMAP  EXEC  PGM=IEWL,
004300 //  PARM='LIST,LET,XREF,RMODE(&RMODE)'
004400 //SYSPRINT   DD  SYSOUT=&OUTC
004500 //SYSLIN     DD  DSN=&&MAP,DISP=(OLD,DELETE)
004600 //SYSUT1     DD  UNIT=&WORK,SPACE=(1024,(20,20))
004700 //SYSLMOD    DD  DSN=&MAPLIB(&MAPNAME),DISP=SHR
004800 //*-----------------------------------------------------------------
004900 //ASMDSECT EXEC  PGM=&ASMBLR,REGION=&REG,
005000 //  PARM='SYSPARM(&A.DSECT),DECK,NOLOAD'
005100 //SYSPRINT   DD  SYSOUT=&OUTC
005200 //SYSIN      DD  DSN=&&TEMPM,DISP=(OLD,DELETE)
005300 //SYSLIB     DD  DSN=&INDEX..SDFHMAC,DISP=SHR
005400 //           DD  DSN=SYS1.MACLIB,DISP=SHR
005500 //SYSUT1     DD  UNIT=&WORK,SPACE=(CYL,(5,5))
005600 //SYSUT2     DD  UNIT=&WORK,SPACE=(CYL,(5,5))
005700 //SYSUT3     DD  UNIT=&WORK,SPACE=(CYL,(5,5))
005800 //SYSPUNCH   DD  DSN=&DSCTLIB(&MAPNAME),DISP=SHR
```

Flesh out defaulted JCL for new data sets to explicitly specify their intended treatment. This makes the JCL much easier to understand. Use same-line comments to document symbolic parameter defaults.

Figure 6.4 DFHMAP4, With Defaulted Parameters Coded Explicitly, and Symbolic Parameter Documentation

more dangerous than beneficial to JCL maintenance, because fewer people who come in contact with JCL have the background or time to keep default meanings in mind. In fact, many people who code (,CATLG) probably don't even realize that this keeps and catalogs the remnant of a newly created data set if the step creating it abends, since it defaults to (NEW,CATLG,CATLG).

Code the full DISP parameter especially in the case of DD statements at which new data sets are created; change (,CATLG) and (,PASS) to what you really intend to have happen.

In revising the DCB parameter as you reach milestone 4, take the opportunity to eliminate the now-superfluous letters "DCB" and the parentheses around its subparameters. As I explained in Chapter 1, the DCB subparameters RECFM, LRECL, BLKSIZE have been "promoted" by IBM to become full-fledged parameters of their own. You can put RECFM, LRECL, BLKSIZE, and also any other DCB subparmeters on separate lines as freestanding parameters of the DD statement.

To reach this milestone, you should also revise block sizes that make no sense in the modern environment. Block sizes such as 400, coded at lines 1700 and 3400 in DFHMAP3, can be changed to higher values approximating the traditional "at least 90 percent efficient" value of 6233, to a higher value as appropriate to your complement of disk devices, or the block size can be omitted entirely to have MVS calculate it. My new values for these block sizes are coded on lines 2000 and 3900 in DFHMAP4, shown in Figure 6.4; in Figure 6.5, I eliminate block size entirely. (If you eliminate block size, you code SPACE in terms of physical quantities, such as tracks or cylinders, or use the new AVGREC parameter, described in Chapter 11, which becomes available if DFSMS is installed on your system.) You can also remove the obsolete JCL parameter SEP if you encounter it (it is now ignored).

6.9 Milestone 5: Use VIO, IF/ELSE, Same-Line Comments

The JCL shown in Figure 6.5, named DFHMAP5, again represents a major departure from the previous milestone. Follow these steps to learn how to revise a proc as I did to DFHMAP4 to arrive at DFHMAP5:

1. Install a comment block above each step, replacing the comment line of hyphens. Compose this comment as a single sentence that sums up what the step does.

2. Recognize and eliminate steps that are obsolete. For example, as I composed the comment to describe the COPY step in Figure 6.4, I realized that it was probably included more than 20 years ago to accept punched-card input and copy it to disk, so that the original ASMMAP and ASMDSECT steps could access it. I dropped this step because it, and its horribly inefficient original block size of 400, are now entirely obsolete.

3. Spread program parameters to separate lines and document them with same line comments. Doing this and documenting the controlling parms to the assembler program at lines 23, 24, and 25, the linkage editor at lines 46, 47, 48, and 49, and the assembler again at lines 63, 64, and 65 mean that no one else will have to be puzzled by what they mean.

4. Change the names of the steps to more modern conventions such as STEP010, STEP020, and so forth, replacing the cryptic older names such as ASMMAP and ASMDSECT, which convey little meaning to contemporary

```
EDIT ---- CSCJGJ.ADV.PROCLIB1(DFHMAP5) - 01.02 --------------- COLUMNS 001 072
COMMAND ===>                                                  SCROLL ===> PAGE
****** ***************************** TOP OF DATA ******************************
000001 //DFHMAP5 PROC   LIBRARY='***',       MAP SOURCE CODE LIBRARY
000002 //  MEMBER='***',                      MAP SOURCE CODE MEMBER NAME
000003 //  MAPNAME='***',                     INTENDED NAME OF PHYS AND SYM MAPS
000004 //  PHYLIB='CCP.LOADLIB',              PHYSICAL MAP LIBRARY (A LOAD LIB)
000005 //  SYMLIB='CCP.MACLIB',               SYMBOLIC MAP LIBRARY (COBOL CODE)
000006 //  INDEX='CICS330',                   CICS VERSION FOR SDFHMAC DSN
000007 //  ASMBLR='IEV90',                    ASSEMBLER PROGRAM NAME
000008 //  A=,                                A=A FOR ALIGNED MAP, ELSE NULL
000009 //  RMODE='ANY',                       24/ANY FOR PHY MAP RESIDENCE MODE
000010 //  REG='2M'                           MEMORY ALLOCATION FOR ASSEMBLER
000011 //*-----------------------------------------------------------------
000012 //*  PROC TO ASSEMBLE MAPSET SOURCE CODE INTO A PHYSICAL MAP
000013 //*  AND A SYMBOLIC MAP.               REVISED 11/93 BY J. JANOSSY
000014 //*-----------------------------------------------------------------
000015 //*
000016 //*****************************************************************
000017 //*
000018 //*  ASSEMBLE THE SOURCE CODE INTO A PHYSICAL MAP OBJECT FILE
000019 //*
000020 //*****************************************************************
000021 //STEP010  EXEC  PGM=&ASMBLR,
000022 //  REGION=&REG,
000023 //  PARM=('SYSPARM(&A.MAP)',                          PRODUCE PHYSICAL MAP
000024 //        'DECK',
000025 //        'NOLOAD')
000026 //SYSIN      DD  DSN=&LIBRARY(&MEMBER),DISP=SHR     MAP SOURCE CODE IN
000027 //SYSLIB     DD  DSN=&INDEX..SDFHMAC,DISP=SHR       SYSTEM LIBRARY
000028 //           DD  DSN=SYS1.MACLIB,DISP=SHR           SYSTEM LIBRARY
000029 //SYSUT1     DD  UNIT=VIO,SPACE=(CYL,(5,5))         WORK FILE
000030 //SYSUT2     DD  UNIT=VIO,SPACE=(CYL,(5,5))         WORK FILE
000031 //SYSUT3     DD  UNIT=VIO,SPACE=(CYL,(5,5))         WORK FILE
000032 //SYSPRINT   DD  SYSOUT=*                           SOURCE CODE LISTING
000033 //SYSPUNCH   DD  DSN=&&OBJECT,                      OBJECT FILE OUT
000034 //  DISP=(NEW,PASS),
000035 //  UNIT=VIO,
000036 //  RECFM=FB,
000037 //  LRECL=80,
000038 //  SPACE=(CYL,(1,1))
000039 //*****************************************************************
000040 //*
000041 //*  IF CODE OK, LINK EDIT THE OBJECT TO PRODUCE THE PHYSICAL MAP
000042 //*
000043 //*****************************************************************
000044 //    IF ( RC <= 4 ) THEN
000045 //STEP020  EXEC  PGM=IEWL,
000046 //  PARM=('LIST',                                     LIST CONTROL STATEMENTS
000047 //        'LET',                                      MINOR ERRORS OK
000048 //        'XREF',                                     CROSS REFERENCE
000049 //        'RMODE(&RMODE)')                            PHY MAP RES. MODE
000050 //SYSLIN     DD  DSN=&&OBJECT,DISP=(OLD,DELETE)     OBJECT FILE IN
000051 //SYSPRINT   DD  SYSOUT=*                           LINKAGE EDIT RPT
000052 //SYSUT1     DD  UNIT=VIO,SPACE=(CYL,(1,1))         WORK FILE
000053 //SYSLMOD    DD  DSN=&PHYLIB(&MAPNAME),DISP=SHR     PHYSICAL MAP OUT
000054 //    ENDIF
000055 //*****************************************************************
000056 //*
000057 //*  IF CODE OK, CONSTRUCT THE SYMBOLIC MAP (COBOL SOURCE CODE)
000058 //*
000059 //*****************************************************************
000060 //    IF ( RC <= 4 ) THEN
000061 //STEP030  EXEC  PGM=&ASMBLR,
000062 //  REGION=&REG,
000063 //  PARM=('SYSPARM(&A.DSECT)',                        PRODUCE COBOL CODE
000064 //        'DECK'
000065 //        'NOLOAD')
000066 //SYSIN      DD  DSN=&LIBRARY(&MEMBER),DISP=SHR     MAP SOURCE CODE IN
000067 //SYSLIB     DD  DSN=&INDEX..SDFHMAC,DISP=SHR       SYSTEM LIBRARY
000068 //           DD  DSN=SYS1.MACLIB,DISP=SHR           SYSTEM LIBRARY
000069 //SYSUT1     DD  UNIT=VIO,SPACE=(CYL,(5,5))         WORK FILE
000070 //SYSUT2     DD  UNIT=VIO,SPACE=(CYL,(5,5))         WORK FILE
000071 //SYSUT3     DD  UNIT=VIO,SPACE=(CYL,(5,5))         WORK FILE
000072 //SYSPRINT   DD  SYSOUT=*                           SOURCE CODE LISTING
000073 //SYSPUNCH   DD  DSN=&SYMLIB(&MAPNAME),DISP=SHR     SYMBOLIC MAP OUT
000074 //    ENDIF
```

Figure 6.5 DFHMAP5, A Refurbished Proc That Runs More Efficiently Than DFHMAPS and Is Easier to Learn

programmers and users. Stepnames such as ASMMAP make reading MVS/ESA system output more difficult, whereas lettered or numbered stepnames are easier to find in system output, especially for newcomers.

5. Change work files and temporary files from SYSDA or other ordinary disk devices to VIO, which stands for "virtual input/output." VIO is a much faster form of disk storage that you might think of much like RAM disk on microcomputers. It is the same high-speed storage used by MVS/ESA to swap parts of programs in and out of memory. You can't use VIO for permanent data storage, but you can benefit from using it for temporary storage within a job. *VIO is ideal for temporary passed files.*

6. Change COND coding for step control to IF/ELSE testing of COND CODEs, or (as in the case of the original DFHMAPS proc, which was completely deficient in this!) install job step control. I installed IF tests to allow STEP020 and STEP030 to execute only if STEP010 indicated that no problem existed in the map source code being processed.

7. Eliminate symbolic parameters that serve little or no purpose. Some symbolic parameters provide flexibility, but all symbolic parameters introduce more lines of print in the system output and make it harder to read. Eliminate any symbolic parameters that are rarely, if ever, changed. In DFHMAP5, I hardcoded the former WORK symbolic parameter as VIO at every occurrence and eliminated this symbolic parameter; this will not be changed from run to run. I also eliminated the symbolic parameter OUTC, which stood for output class, and simply coded each print output as SYSOUT=*, so that all print outputs go to the same message class as coded on MSGCLASS on the JOB statement that invokes this proc.

8. Rename any symbolic parameters with obscure names to give them names that mean something in the modern environment, and update default values. &MAPLIB was ambiguous as a symbolic parameter name (does it refer to the map source code, physical map, or symbolic map?). It actually referred to the physical map (machine language) library, so I named it &PHYLIB. &DSCTLIB refers to what we now call the symbolic map library, so I renamed this &SYMLIB. I changed the default for ® (the region parameter) to 2M, since this is the new coding for two megabytes, replacing the older specification 2048K.

9. Install new symbolic parameters that provide needed convenience. The original DFHMAPS proc did not provide a way to specify the location of the input map source code, forcing users to code a DD statement in their execution JCL. The map source code actually enters this proc at two places: SYSIN at line 26, and SYSIN at line 66. The map source code is usually stored as a member of a library. I therefore installed the symbolic parameters &LIBRARY and &MEMBER at lines 26 and 66, coded patently invalid defaults for them on the PROC statement that would draw attention to them if they were not specified when the proc was executed, and documented them with same-line comments.

10. Revise the JCL to eliminate block size completely for data sets being created, or, if your installation has installed and activated DFSMS, replace UNIT, RECFM, LRECL, and SPACE with the appropriate DATACLAS and STORCLAS (and possibly MGMTCLAS) parameters. If your installation has installed DFSMS, but you are creating data sets that will not be managed by it, use the AVGREC parameter and SPACE to make your space allocation by record count rather than by block count. (You can also use AVGREC and SPACE to override DATACLAS-supplied values for SMS-managed data sets.) If your installation is not using DFSMS yet, use the traditional block size value of 6233 as a target for block size, unless you are directed locally to use a different value known to be more efficient on the specific complement of disk devices in local use.

Test your revised proc before placing it back into production. You might want to record some timings for representative executions of the old and new proc version using the same inputs, to keep track of the improvement in processing time and time saved. Taking such timings, I quantified the improvement results described in the following section.

6.10 Improvement Results

In my work, I have been able to achieve between 8 percent and 12 percent runtime savings by aiming at the five milestones just described. For example, on a small model of ES/9000, with map source code defining a single CICS/BMS screen, a test run of the DFHMAPS proc required 3.07 seconds of CPU time. The revised DFHMAP5 proc required 2.70 seconds of CPU time. The difference of .37 seconds amounts to about 12 percent runtime reduction. Admittedly, this is a small job stream, but don't take the improvement lightly. Your actual cost for computer time may be about $3 per CPU second. It does not take much extrapolation to your "real" levels of production work to have a 12 percent reduction in cost amount to something significant. This level of savings on an annual CPU processing expense of a million dollars amounts to $120,000.

The machine time savings from job step elimination and input/output improvements is not the only benefit of refurbishing older JCL. Also significant is the time saved by newcomers to the JCL, in understanding it more more quickly, learning from the same-line documentation comments, and more rapidly becoming able to use and modify the JCL. With appropriate refurbishing, you can significantly enhance the level of productivity in your work group. And you well may find this improvement in productivity especially crucial, as the industry continues to restructure to meet competitive pressures!

6.11 Locally Tuned Templates for Job Stream Construction

When I conduct on-site training for personnel at corporations using mainframes, I always take the opportunity to explain how productivity-boosting templates can be built using the JCL improvements I've described here. I will explain the same thing to you.

```
EDIT ---- CSCJGJ.ADV.CNTL(IEBGENER) - 01.00 ----------------- COLUMNS 001 072
COMMAND ===>                                                  SCROLL ===> PAGE
****** ****************************** TOP OF DATA ******************************
000001 //******************************************************************
000002 //*                                                                *
000003 //*  COPY X------------------- TO Y-------------------             *
000004 //*                                                                *
000005 //******************************************************************
000006 //STEP      EXEC  PGM=IEBGENER
000007 //SYSPRINT    DD  SYSOUT=*                         STATUS REPORT
000008 //SYSIN       DD  DUMMY                            INSTRUCTIONS
000009 //SYSUT1      DD  DSN=X--------------------        INPUT
000010 //SYSUT2      DD  Y-------------------             OUTPUT
```

Figure 6.6 An Example of a JCL Template (this one is for the IEBGENER program)

A template is simply a start on the coding of the JCL needed to execute an individual program. You can create templates for your own use, and templates can be shared among a work group or others in an installation. A template provides the basic parts of the JCL needed to execute the program, with underscores at the places where coding is likely to be different from one use of the program to another. For example, Figure 6.6 shows a template for use of the common IEBGENER utility program (the "copy" program).

As the template in Figure 6.6 shows, the main work of IEBGENER is to copy the input provided at its SYSUT1 ddname to the ddname SYSUT2. You, of course, code the right side of the SYSUT1 and SYSUT2 DD statements to point to whatever the input is to be, and wherever the output is to go. But all of the precoded JCL in the template has to be present, and the template makes it unnecessary for anyone to recode any of that, including the descriptive comment box. To use the template, you simply copy it into a new job stream you are composing, or an existing job stream you are refurbishing, using TSO/ISPF, then finalize the coding.

Templates were not common in punched-card days, because they were physically hard to use; you had to feed a prepunched card into a card reader and hope to place new coding into the correct columns. But TSO/ISPF, as the modern-day "word processor for punched cards," makes JCL templates very easy to use. Figures 6.7 and 6.8 show you how you can use the TSO/ISPF external copy command to "reach out and grab something" (such as a template) to bring it into a new job stream, or a job stream being refurbished, and quickly modify it for use.

6.12 Conveying and Reinforcing Installation Standards Using Templates

In concluding this chapter, let me end where I began: This is the 1990s, not the 1960s. Much of what we have seen of job control language usage over the past 30 years reflects a world that is history. On the horizon, we can see a fragmentation of data processing and information handling techniques and technologies. For some smaller enterprises, mainframes and their JCL will become irrelevant. But for many larger organizations, with high-volume

```
EDIT ---- CSCJGJ.AD[obscured]IL(NUMAP) - 01.00 --------------------- COLUMNS 001 072
COMMAND ===> copy iebgener                                         SCROLL ===> PAGE
000065 //            'NOLOAD')
000066 //SYSIN        DD  DSN=&LIBRARY(&MEMBER),DISP=SHR    MAP SOURCE CODE IN
000067 //SYSLIB       DD  DSN=&INDEX..SDFHMAC,DISP=SHR      SYSTEM LIBRARY
000068 //             DD  DSN=SYS1.MACLIB,DISP=SHR          SYSTEM LIBRARY
000069 //SYSUT1       DD  UNIT=VIO,SPACE=(CYL,(5,5))        WORK FILE
00007[obscured]SYSUT2 DD  UNIT=VIO,SPACE=(CYL,(5,5))        WORK FILE
00007[obscured]/SYSUT3 DD UNIT=VIO,SPACE=(CYL,(5,5))        WORK FILE
00[obscured] //SYSPRINT DD SYSOUT=*                         SOURCE CODE LISTING
00[obscured] //SYSPUNCH DD DSN=&SYMLIB(&MAPNAME),DISP=SHR   SYMBOLIC MAP OUT
a      //    ENDIF
****** ***************************** BOTTOM OF DATA ******************************
```

The TSO/ISPF external copy command acts to "reach out and grab something." As long as you are copying something from within the same library, you can put COPY and the member name on the command line, and "a" (for "after") where you want the member you are copying in to reside. This copy command is very useful in bringing template JCL into a new or refurbished job stream.

Figure 6.7 Using the TSO/ISPF External Copy Command to Copy a JCL Template into a Job Stream

processing requirements and huge databases, mainframes will continue to be key elements of the equipment configuration. Personnel turnover and the absorption of newcomers into the workforce will make it necessary for all parties to know a greater variety of software products, do a wider variety of tasks effectively, and be able to quickly adapt to and understand a greater variety of things. And all of this will be expected to be done quickly and correctly.

Standards for implementing work on computers will become increasingly important as the processing environment changes, and as change accelerates. But standards don't have to be viewed or imposed as strictures. Some forms of job control language standards can be encouraged, or enforced, in a painless way by incorporating them into templates as described in this chapter.

I strongly suggest that as a programmer grappling with the intricacies of advanced MVS/ESA JCL usage, you begin now to form JCL templates for the most commonly executed software in the job streams that you deal with. You can form these templates by copying steps of job streams out to individual members in a JCL library. Separated from the job streams that use them, take the opportunity to clean these templates up, indenting continued lines moderately and including same-line comments to document each DD statement. Then refurbish steps of your job stream as time permits, installing templates into your actual JCL, to test the use of the templates you have created. Finally, place the templates into a centralized library and begin the

```
EDIT ---- CSCJGJ.ADV.CNTL(NUMAP) - 01.00 -------------------- COLUMNS 001 072
COMMAND ===>                                                  SCROLL ===> PAGE
000064 //             'DECK',
000065 //             'NOLOAD')
000066 //SYSIN      DD  DSN=&LIBRARY(&MEMBER),DISP=SHR   MAP SOURCE CODE IN
000067 //SYSLIB     DD  DSN=&INDEX..SDFHMAC,DISP=SHR     SYSTEM LIBRARY
000068 //           DD  DSN=SYS1.MACLIB,DISP=SHR         SYSTEM LIBRARY
000069 //SYSUT1     DD  UNIT=VIO,SPACE=(CYL,(5,5))       WORK FILE
000070 //SYSUT2     DD  UNIT=VIO,SPACE=(CYL,(5,5))       WORK FILE
000071 //SYSUT3     DD  UNIT=VIO,SPACE=(CYL,(5,5))       WORK FILE
000072 //SYSPRINT   DD  SYSOUT=*                         SOURCE CODE LISTING
000073 //SYSPUNCH   DD  DSN=&SYMLIB(&MAPNAME),DISP=SHR   SYMBOLIC MAP OUT
000074 //      ENDIF
000075 //*********************************************************************
000076 //*                                                                   *
000077 //*  COPY symbolic map-------- TO printer-------------                *
000078 //*                                                                   *
000079 //*********************************************************************
000080 //STEP040  EXEC  PGM=IEBGENER
000081 //SYSPRINT   DD  SYSOUT=*                         STATUS REPORT
000082 //SYSIN      DD  DUMMY                            INSTRUCTIONS
000083 //SYSUT1     DD  DSN=&symlib(&mapname),disp=shr   INPUT
000084 //SYSUT2     DD  sysout=*                         OUTPUT SCREEN DUMP
```

You "fill in the blanks" of the copied-in template JCL to use it. Here, you see my IEBGENER template copied in and the comment, input source, and output source filled in, but I have not yet pressed the <*Enter*> key. With well-formed templates, your JCL benefits from consistent commenting content, style, and indentation. Good templates automatically distribute and implement your installation standards.

Figure 6.8 A Copied-In JCL Template, and How You Complete It

process of making others aware of them. Encourage others in your work group to do the same thing, and begin making newcomers to your shop aware of the centralized library of JCL templates as a learning resource.

To the extent you can, make use of a template library a part of whatever formal or informal JCL training is conducted in your installation, so that newcomers can benefit to the maximum extent from these locally "tuned" templates. Following these steps can provide a solid base for the eventual movement of your installation to DFSMS, which introduces new, standard ways to simplify JCL and globally enhance system management of your data sets.

6.13 A Caution About Comments!

My emphasis in the chapter on the use of same-line comments as documentation warrants a caution to you if you are the recipient of JCL, or inherit it for maintenance purposes. It may or may not be obvious, but there is no inherent connection between what a comment says and what JCL actually does. As Hal Breitenberg, one of the very fine technical reviewers of this book pointed out, workplace deadlines, carelessness, and human error can cause erroneous comments to be placed into JCL, or accurate comments to be made inaccurate due to changes in JCL without corresponding changes in the comments. Comments can be incomplete, outdated, or simply misleading.

Consider treating comments that you find in JCL as an indication of what the JCL was *intended* to do, or descriptive of what the author or previous JCL maintainer *thought* the JCL did, while reserving judgment on what the JCL actually does at present. As Hal Breitenberg notes, JCL comments can be invaluable in documenting a job and an important tool that can aid in figuring out how a job runs, but only the JCL itself actually determines what happens at runtime. If you determine that a comment is wrong, and it's your job to maintain the JCL, correct the comment and make life easier for the next person who works with the JCL.

7

Handling Failed MVS/ESA Jobs

7.1 Jobs Will Fail
7.2 Context of an Example Job Stream
7.3 Overview: What the Job Stream Does
7.4 The Example Job Stream
7.5 Generation Data Set (GDS) Usage
7.6 Quick MVS/ESA System Reporting Analysis
7.7 Tutorial: Job Failure #1, a System Abend
7.8 Tutorial: Job Failure #2, Need for an Attention Grabber
7.9 Tutorial: Job Failure #3, a TSO/ISPF Diagnosis Method
7.10 Tutorial: Manipulating MVS/ESA System Reporting
7.11 Using the RESTART Parameter
7.12 Generation Data Sets and RESTART
7.13 Restarts and Job Stream Design
7.14 Checklist for Job Restarts
7.15 Typical Job Stream Recovery Instructions
7.16 The REG33UP1 Job Stream Packaged as a Procedure (Proc)
7.17 Executing Proc R33P1
7.18 Restarting a Proc at a Step
7.19 A Caution About Step Restarts and Reliability

7.1 Jobs Will Fail

Some of the jobs you submit for processing will fail. Why? As an old adage (often attributed to a certain Professor Murphy) goes, "anything that can go wrong will (sooner or later) go wrong." A job can fail because a disk unit lacks space to accommodate a file being created, a tape device encounters corrupted or damaged media, a program exceeds its memory or time allocation, a program commits a grievous logic error such as dividing by zero, or for any of scores of other reasons. When something goes drastically wrong with a job, MVS/ESA will issue reporting in the forms described in Chapters

2 and 3 of this book. What do you do about a job failure, and how do you complete the processing of the failed run?

If you have some experience with production JCL, you may have some answers to these questions. But if you lack experience in this area, or if you have not developed an organized approach to these situations, you will find this chapter of interest. In this chapter I discuss several aspects of handling failed jobs:

1. *Determining what MVS/ESA is telling you* the problem is
2. *Determining how to remedy the problem* (program logic, JCL, disk or tape error
3. *Creating the environment in which "recovery" of the failed job stream is possible* (to complete intended processing and production of the job outputs to the end user)
4. *Recovering the job*

The first step—determining what MVS/ESA is telling you—is not necessarily very easy in itself. I'll show you a simple, consistent on-line procedure using TSO/ISPF that gives you a method to do this.

Recovery of a failed job demands a strategy. After correcting the problem that caused the job to fail, will you attempt to pick up processing at the point of failure (*restart* the job), or will you attempt to repeat the job from the beginning (*rerun*)? In this chapter, I'll demonstrate the way to use the RESTART parameter of the JOB statement to continue processing, which involves some potentially subtle adjustments to the JCL involved. This is known formally as "deferred step restart." In Chapter 8, I'll show you how to design job streams to facilitate rerun-from-beginning as a recovery strategy, which, in many instances, is cost beneficial and more reliable than restarting a job.

In designing this book, one of the main criteria defining my goal was that examples should be full-length (within the limits of publishing practicality) and not just snippets of JCL coding. Both Chapters 7 and 8 focus on a modern, realistic eight-step job stream named REG33UP1, shown in Figures 7.1 and 7.2. I'll run this job stream first in Chapter 7 as ordinary JCL, then as a proc. In Chapter 8, I'll revise this proc for a recovery strategy based on job rerun and consider enhancements to it.

7.2 Context of an Example Job Stream

The diagram labeled Figure 7.1 provides an overview of an automated application in the administrative support area at a university. This application supports student enrollment, tuition payment, and related record keeping. The application involves three VSAM files (Key Sequenced Data Sets) that house data about students, courses, and registrations and tuition payments (accounts).

Figure 7.1 Overview of an Automated Application in the Administrative Support Area at a University (see facing page)

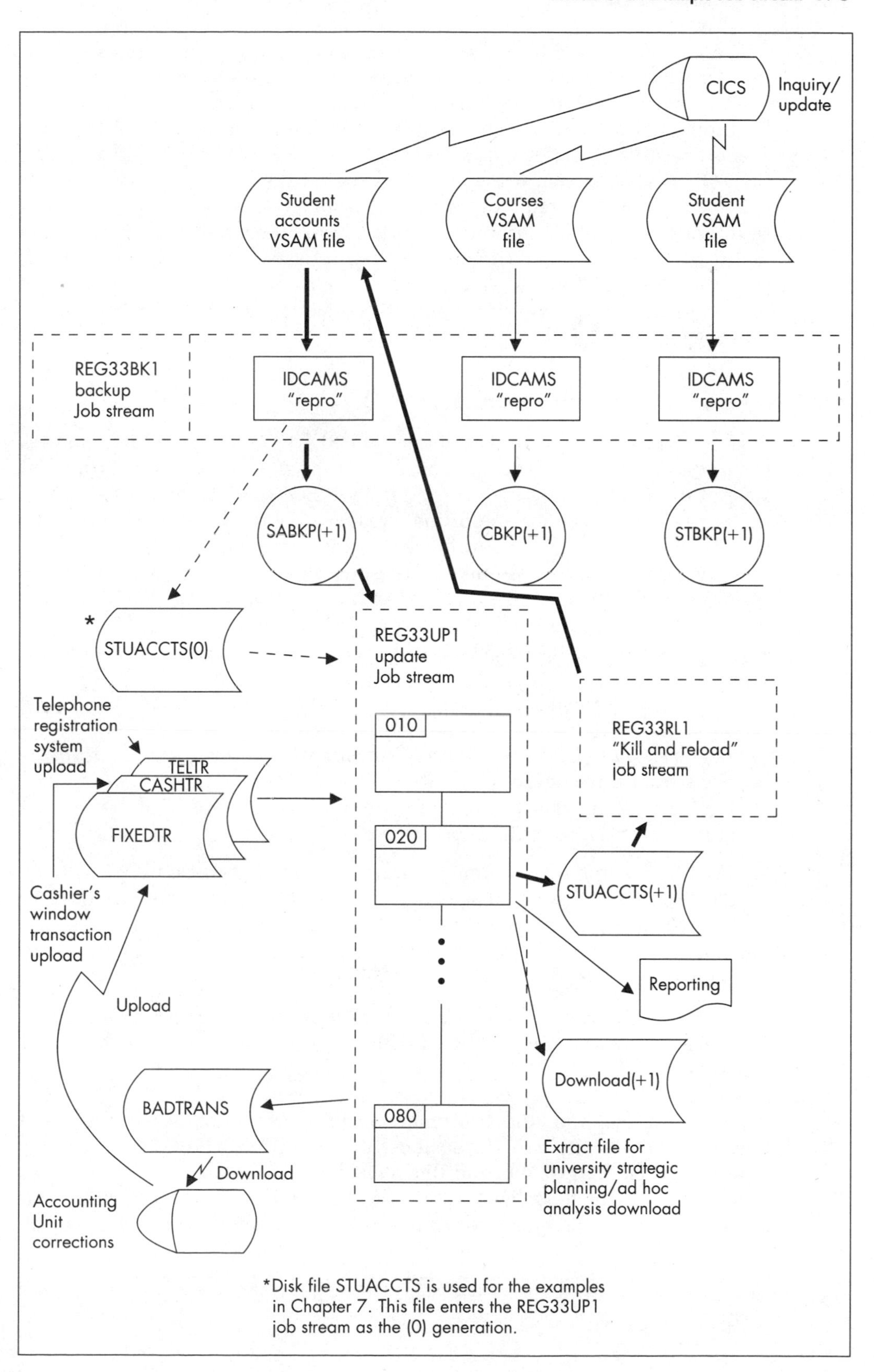
CICS
Inquiry/ update
Student accounts VSAM file
Courses VSAM file
Student VSAM file
REG33BK1 backup Job stream
IDCAMS "repro"
IDCAMS "repro"
IDCAMS "repro"
SABKP(+1)
CBKP(+1)
STBKP(+1)
*
STUACCTS(0)
REG33UP1 update Job stream
REG33RL1 "Kill and reload" job stream
Telephone registration system upload
TELTR
CASHTR
FIXEDTR
010
020
080
STUACCTS(+1)
Cashier's window transaction upload
Reporting
Upload
Download(+1)
BADTRANS
Download
Extract file for university strategic planning/ad hoc analysis download
Accounting Unit corrections
*Disk file STUACCTS is used for the examples in Chapter 7. This file enters the REG33UP1 job stream as the (0) generation.

Each of the files in the student accounts application is accessed on-line by CICS programs. During business hours, on-line access is used for information inquiry, to enroll new students, and to manage course meeting locations and schedules. Batch subsystems composed of JCL job streams executing utility programs back up each VSAM file nightly. Locally written VS COBOL II programs perform processing on the backups, such as high-volume file update based on transactions from mailed-in or telephone-input sources. Batch jobs also produce reporting and create files that exist on the mainframe for subsequent download by end users. Files updated by batch jobs are reloaded to VSAM storage before the next business day, so that the updated information exists in efficient, reorganized VSAM files for the on-line system.

7.3 Overview: What the Job Stream Does

Figure 7.2 provides a flowchart of the REG33UP1 job stream, which handles the updating of the student accounts file, "applying" transactions formed in several different processes during the day. REG33UP1 creates a backup of the transactions, produces reporting, creates a file of flawed transactions to be downloaded by the accounting group for correction and resubmission, and creates an extracted summary file from which university planning personnel can quickly download data for ad hoc analysis on PCs. The flowchart documents a multitude of files entering and leaving programs, but we can sum up the work of the REG33UP1 job stream by identifying its main purposes.

The three primary purposes served by the REG33UP1 job stream are:

1. *Receive, apply, and report on registration and tuition payment transactions* from three sources: cashier's window, telephone registration system, and erroneous transactions from previous runs that have been corrected and resubmitted for processing.

2. *Provide an updated student accounts master file* named CSCJGJ.REG.STUACCTS(+1), a member of a generation data set. (If you are unclear about what a generation data set is, you can learn how to create, use, and manage them in Chapter 17 of *Practical MVS JCL Examples* by James Janossy, published in 1993 by John Wiley & Sons, Inc.)

3. *Create a summary file for downloading,* named CSCJGJ.REG.DOWNLOAD(+1), containing extracted data available for download to a PC network.

As you can see from the flowchart, various sort steps are interspersed between the execution of three locally written VS COBOL II programs named REG3307, REG3308, and REG3350. The job stream executes them as documented in the flowchart, and we need not delve into their internal coding for the purposes of this discussion. (See Appendix F for information

Figure 7.2 Flowchart of the REG33UP1 Job Stream, Which Handles the Updating of the Student Accounts File (see facing page)

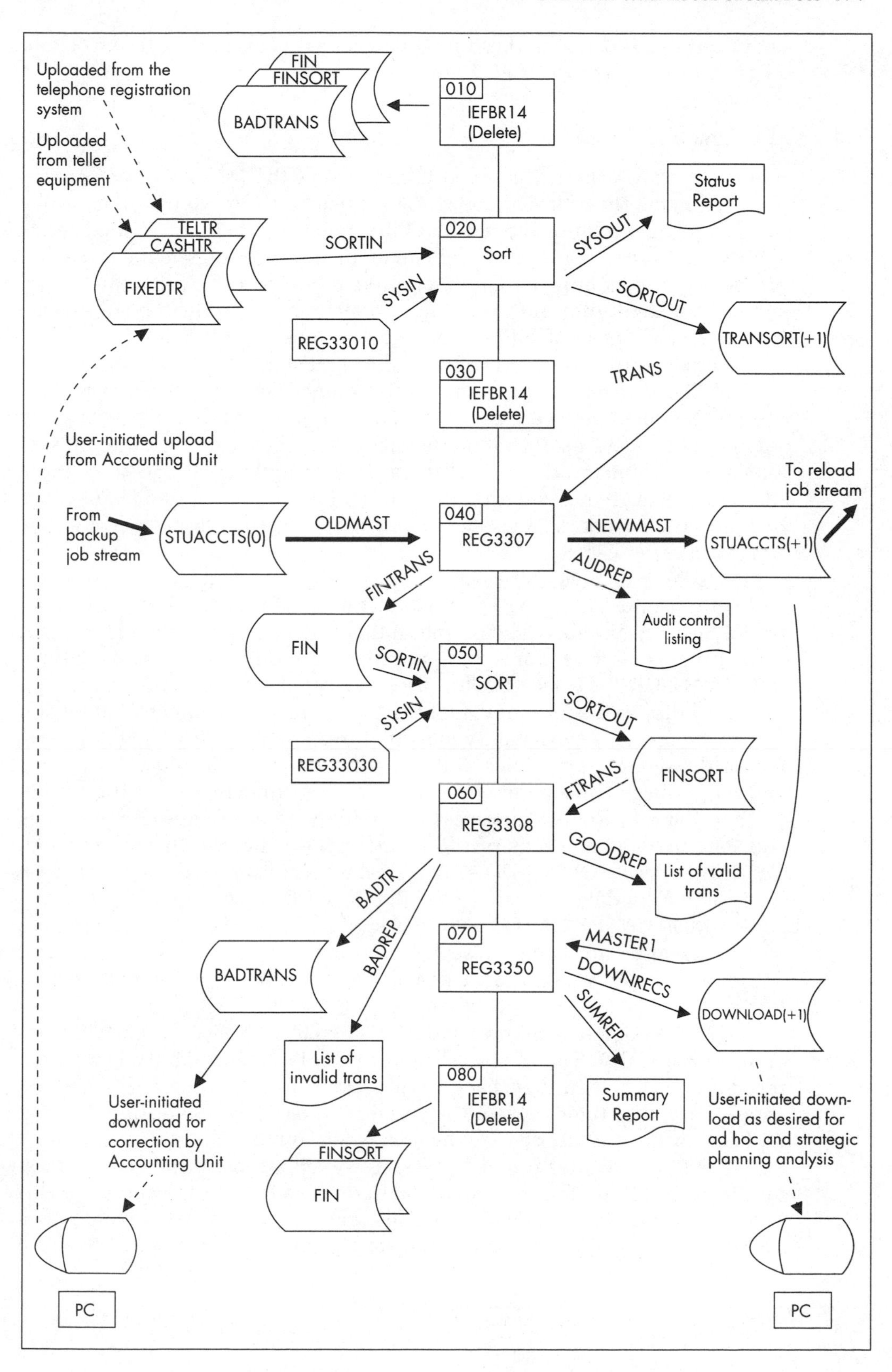

Uploaded from the telephone registration system
Uploaded from teller equipment
FIN
FINSORT
BADTRANS
010
IEFBR14 (Delete)
Status Report
TELTR
CASHTR
FIXEDTR
SORTIN
020
Sort
SYSOUT
SYSIN
SORTOUT
REG33010
TRANSORT(+1)
030
IEFBR14 (Delete)
TRANS
User-initiated upload from Accounting Unit
To reload job stream
From backup job stream
STUACCTS(0)
OLDMAST
040
REG3307
NEWMAST
STUACCTS(+1)
AUDREP
FINTRANS
Audit control listing
FIN
SORTIN
050
SORT
SYSIN
SORTOUT
REG33030
FINSORT
FTRANS
060
REG3308
GOODREP
List of valid trans
BADTR
BADREP
070
REG3350
MASTER1
DOWNRECS
BADTRANS
SUMREP
DOWNLOAD(+1)
List of invalid trans
080
IEFBR14 (Delete)
Summary Report
User-initiated download for correction by Accounting Unit
User-initiated down-load as desired for ad hoc and strategic planning analysis
FINSORT
FIN
PC
PC

about a diskette carrying these programs and JCL examples, if you would like to experiment with this JCL.)

7.4 The Example Job Stream

Figure 7.3 shows the JCL I coded to implement the REG33UP1 job stream depicted in the flowchart of Figure 7.2. Notice that each step is prefaced by the IF . . . THEN relational condition I illustrated in Chapter 3, which aborts processing in case of program problem or abend. This job stream is raw JCL on the way to becoming a production proc. It will be run by operations personnel, not the author of the JCL. If a problem arises in the job stream, the job stream itself has to facilitate corrective actions.

Here is a quick overview of what the eight steps of REG33UP1 do:

STEP010 executes program IEFBR14 and deletes intermediate files used to pass data between steps. Though temporary passed data sets using VIO could be used for these intermediate files, they would not be present after a failed run to allow restarting at intermediate steps. Some of these files are ordinarily deleted after they are no longer needed in STEP080, but they are deleted here if for some reason they are still present when a new run starts.

STEP020 receives transaction data from three concatenated sources and sorts it into ascending sequence of transaction key, which is student Social Security Number. The output of this step consists of the merged and sorted inputs and is housed in a generation data set named CSCJGJ.REG.TRANSORT(+1) as a backup. Here's a typical real-life quirk: some of the input files to the sort may not be present, since they are created by end users who may not consistently meet their responsibility to "feed" this system at the agreed-upon times. But this mainframe JCL has to work even if end users did not place one, two, or all of the input files onto the system prior to the run. Robust interfaces to a wide variety of end-user processes and data uploads are facts of life in the modern MVS/ESA environment. The JCL at the //SORTIN DD statement may seem unusual for a DD statement at which data sets are read. But this DD statement coding, using DISP=(MOD,CATLG,CATLG), UNIT, and SPACE, is tolerant of an input file being present or not being present. If all three inputs are missing, the run still proceeds, and we still get customary reporting and files ready for download.

STEP030 deletes the inputs to the STEP020 sort once the sort has executed successfully. The data sets input to STEP020 are like packages on a receiving dock. Once they have been picked up for processing, they are gone, preventing their repeated processing in cases where an input is not replaced by the end user before the next batch run.

STEP040 executes program REG3307, which updates the student master file. REG3307 performs a sequential update, so it reads the current generation of the student accounts master file and creates the next generation as the updated file. Since the key of the student master file is Social Security

Figure 7.3 REG33UP1, A Job Stream That Implements the Processing in the Flowchart of Figure 7.2 (see facing page)

```
EDIT ---- CSCJGJ.ADV.CNTL(REG33UP1) - 01.02 ----------------- COLUMNS 001 072
COMMAND ===>                                                  SCROLL ===> PAGE
****** ***************************** TOP OF DATA ******************************
000001 //CSCJGJA   JOB 1,                  ACCOUNTING INFORMATION
000002 //   'BIN 7--JANOSSY',              PROGRAMMER NAME AND DELIVERY BIN
000003 //   CLASS=A,                       INPUT QUEUE CLASS
000004 //   MSGLEVEL=(1,1),                HOW MUCH MVS SYSTEM PRINT DESIRED
000005 //   MSGCLASS=X,                    PRINT DESTINATION X A L N OR O
000006 //   TIME=(1,0),                    SAFETY LIMIT: RUN TIME UP TO 1 MINUTE
000007 //   REGION=3M,                     ALLOW UP TO 3 MEGS VIRTUAL MEMORY
000008 //*  TYPRUN=SCAN,                   UNCOMMENT THIS LINE TO DO SCAN ONLY
000009 //   NOTIFY=CSCJGJ                  WHO TO TELL WHEN JOB IS DONE
000010 //*
000011 //*  RUN THE REG33UP1 UPDATE JOB STREAM USING RAW JCL
000012 //*  THIS JCL IS STORED AT CSCJGJ.ADV.CNTL(REG33UP1)
000013 //*
000014 //*-----------------------------------------------------------------
000015 //*  CLEANUP: DELETE DATA SETS TO BE CREATED IN RUN
000016 //*-----------------------------------------------------------------
000017 //STEP010  EXEC  PGM=IEFBR14
000018 //DELETE1    DD  DSN=CSCJGJ.REG.FIN,                DATA SET TO BE
000019 //  DISP=(MOD,DELETE),                               RE-CREATED IN RUN
000020 //  UNIT=SYSDA,
000021 //  SPACE=(TRK,0)
000022 //DELETE2    DD  DSN=CSCJGJ.REG.FINSORT,            DATA SET TO BE
000023 //  DISP=(MOD,DELETE),                               RE-CREATED IN RUN
000024 //  UNIT=SYSDA,
000025 //  SPACE=(TRK,0)
000026 //DELETE3    DD  DSN=CSCJGJ.REG.BADTRANS,           DATA SET TO BE
000027 //  DISP=(MOD,DELETE),                               RE-CREATED IN RUN
000028 //  UNIT=SYSDA,
000029 //  SPACE=(TRK,0)
000030 //*-----------------------------------------------------------------
000031 //*  READ CONCATENATED TRANSACTION INPUTS, SORT THEM INTO ONE DATA SET
000032 //*-----------------------------------------------------------------
000033 //      IF ( NOT ABEND AND RC <= 4 ) THEN           NOTE: INPUTS TO
000034 //STEP020  EXEC  PGM=SORT                           THIS STEP ARE
000035 //SYSOUT     DD  SYSOUT=*                           UPLOADED BY USERS
000036 //*
000037 //SORTIN     DD  DSN=CSCJGJ.REG.TELTR,              TELEPHONE REGIS.
000038 //  DISP=(MOD,CATLG,CATLG),                          DATA SET MAY OR
000039 //  UNIT=SYSDA,                                      MAY NOT EXIST!
000040 //  DCB=(RECFM=FB,LRECL=68,BLKSIZE=22848),
000041 //  SPACE=(TRK,0)
000042 //*
000043 //           DD  DSN=CSCJGJ.REG.CASHTR,             CASHIER'S TRANS.
000044 //  DISP=(MOD,CATLG,CATLG),                          DATA SET MAY OR
000045 //  UNIT=SYSDA,                                      MAY NOT EXIST!
000046 //  DCB=(RECFM=FB,LRECL=68,BLKSIZE=22848),
000047 //  SPACE=(TRK,0)
000048 //*
000049 //           DD  DSN=CSCJGJ.REG.FIXEDTR,            CORRECTED TRANS.
000050 //  DISP=(MOD,CATLG,CATLG),                          DATA SET MAY OR
000051 //  UNIT=SYSDA,                                      MAY NOT EXIST!
000052 //  DCB=(RECFM=FB,LRECL=68,BLKSIZE=22848),
000053 //  SPACE=(TRK,0)
000054 //*
```

This job stream executes the programs that receive transactions, sort them, update the student accounts master file, produce reporting, and create files to be downloaded by end users. IF/THEN testing before each step aborts the execution of steps after an abend or receipt of a COND CODE greater than 4. I demonstrate restart recovery of this job stream in Chapter 7, and rerun recovery of a different version of it in Chapter 8. This JCL listing continues for two more pages and shows generation data set (GDS) creation.

GDS created

```
000055 //SORTOUT    DD  DSN=CSCJGJ.REG.TRANSORT(+1),       OUTPUT IS BACKUP,
000056 //  DISP=(NEW,CATLG,DELETE),                        GENERATION DATA SET
000057 //  UNIT=SYSDA,
000058 //  DCB=(CSCJGJ.CSC.MODEL,RECFM=FB,LRECL=68,BLKSIZE=22848),
000059 //  SPACE=(CYL,(2,1),RLSE)
000060 //*
000061 //SORTWK01   DD  UNIT=VIO,SPACE=(CYL,(1,1))
000062 //SORTWK02   DD  UNIT=VIO,SPACE=(CYL,(1,1))
000063 //SORTWK03   DD  UNIT=VIO,SPACE=(CYL,(1,1))
000064 //SYSIN      DD  DSN=CSCJGJ.CCARDS(REG33010),DISP=SHR
000065 //   ENDIF
000066 //*-----------------------------------------------------------------
000067 //*  DELETE INPUT DATA SETS AFTER SUCCESSFUL SORT
000068 //*-----------------------------------------------------------------
000069 //      IF ( NOT ABEND AND RC <= 4 ) THEN
000070 //STEP030  EXEC  PGM=IEFBR14
000071 //DELETE1    DD  DSN=CSCJGJ.REG.TELTR,              INPUT DELETED TO
000072 //  DISP=(MOD,DELETE),                             PREVENT REDUNDANT
000073 //  UNIT=SYSDA,                                    PROCESSING
000074 //  SPACE=(TRK,0)
000075 //DELETE2    DD  DSN=CSCJGJ.REG.CASHTR,             INPUT DELETED TO
000076 //  DISP=(MOD,DELETE),                             PREVENT REDUNDANT
000077 //  UNIT=SYSDA,                                    PROCESSING
000078 //  SPACE=(TRK,0)
000079 //DELETE3    DD  DSN=CSCJGJ.REG.FIXEDTR,            INPUT DELETED TO
000080 //  DISP=(MOD,DELETE),                             PREVENT REDUNDANT
000081 //  UNIT=SYSDA,                                    PROCESSING
000082 //  SPACE=(TRK,0)
000083 //      ENDIF
000084 //*-----------------------------------------------------------------
000085 //*  UPDATE THE STUACCTS MASTER FILE
000086 //*-----------------------------------------------------------------
000087 //      IF ( NOT ABEND AND RC <= 4 ) THEN
000088 //STEP040  EXEC  PGM=REG3307
000089 //STEPLIB    DD  DSN=CSCJGJ.ADV.LOADLIB,DISP=SHR
000090 //           DD  DSN=SYS1.COB2LIB,DISP=SHR
000091 //SYSOUT     DD  SYSOUT=*
000092 //TRANS      DD  DSN=CSCJGJ.REG.TRANSORT(+1),
000093 //  DISP=SHR
000094 //OLDMAST    DD  DSN=CSCJGJ.REG.STUACCTS(0),        OLD MASTER FILE
000095 //  DISP=SHR
000096 //NEWMAST    DD  DSN=CSCJGJ.REG.STUACCTS(+1),       NEW MASTER FILE
000097 //  DISP=(NEW,CATLG,DELETE),
000098 //  UNIT=SYSDA,
000099 //  DCB=(CSCJGJ.CSC.MODEL,RECFM=FB,LRECL=177,BLKSIZE=22833),
000100 //  SPACE=(CYL,(2,1),RLSE)
000101 //FINTRANS   DD  DSN=CSCJGJ.REG.FIN,                FINISHED TRANS
000102 //  DISP=(NEW,CATLG,DELETE),
000103 //  UNIT=SYSDA,
000104 //  RECFM=FB,
000105 //  LRECL=92,
000106 //  SPACE=(CYL,(1,1),RLSE)
000107 //AUDREP     DD  SYSOUT=*                           AUDIT REPORT
000108 //      ENDIF
000109 //*-----------------------------------------------------------------
000110 //*  SORT FINISHED TRANSACTIONS FOR DETAILED REPORTING
000111 //*-----------------------------------------------------------------
000112 //      IF ( NOT ABEND AND RC <= 4 ) THEN
000113 //STEP050  EXEC  PGM=SORT
000114 //SYSOUT     DD  SYSOUT=*
000115 //SORTIN     DD  DSN=CSCJGJ.REG.FIN,DISP=SHR
000116 //SORTOUT    DD  DSN=CSCJGJ.REG.FINSORT,            SORTED, FINISHED
000117 //  DISP=(NEW,CATLG,DELETE),                       TRANSACTIONS
000118 //  UNIT=SYSDA,
000119 //  RECFM=FB,
000120 //  LRECL=92,
000121 //  SPACE=(CYL,(2,1),RLSE)
000122 //SORTWK01   DD  UNIT=VIO,SPACE=(CYL,(1,1))
000123 //SORTWK02   DD  UNIT=VIO,SPACE=(CYL,(1,1))
000124 //SORTWK03   DD  UNIT=VIO,SPACE=(CYL,(1,1))
000125 //SYSIN      DD  DSN=CSCJGJ.CCARDS(REG33030),
000126 //  DISP=SHR
000127 //      ENDIF
```

GDS created

Figure 7.3 (continued)

```
000128 //*-----------------------------------------------------------------
000129 //*  PRODUCE ACCOUNTING, REGISTRAR RPTS AND "BAD TRANS" DOWNLOAD FILE
000130 //*-----------------------------------------------------------------
000131 //       IF ( NOT ABEND AND RC <= 4 ) THEN
000132 //STEP060  EXEC  PGM=REG3308
000133 //STEPLIB    DD  DSN=CSCJGJ.ADV.LOADLIB,DISP=SHR
000134 //           DD  DSN=SYS1.COB2LIB,DISP=SHR
000135 //SYSOUT     DD  SYSOUT=*
000136 //FTRANS     DD  DSN=CSCJGJ.REG.FINSORT,DISP=SHR
000137 //GOODREP    DD  SYSOUT=*,COPIES=2                TO ACCTNG, REGISTRAR
000138 //*
000139 //BADREP     DD  SYSOUT=*                         TO ACCTNG ONLY
000140 //*
000141 //BADTR      DD  DSN=CSCJGJ.REG.BADTRANS,         FOR ACCTNG DOWNLOAD,
000142 //  DISP=(NEW,CATLG,DELETE),                      CORRECTION, AND
000143 //  UNIT=SYSDA,                                   SUBSEQUENT UPLOAD
000144 //  RECFM=FB,                                     TO FIXEDTR FILE
000145 //  LRECL=68,                                     THAT IS INPUT TO
000146 //  SPACE=(CYL,(1,1),RLSE)                        A SUBSEQUENT RUN
000147 //       ENDIF
000148 //*-----------------------------------------------------------------
000149 //*  CREATE THE NEW DOWNLOAD SUMMARY FILE FOR UNIVERSITY PLANNING DIV.
000150 //*-----------------------------------------------------------------
000151 //       IF ( NOT ABEND AND RC <= 4 ) THEN
000152 //STEP070  EXEC  PGM=REG3350
000153 //STEPLIB    DD  DSN=CSCJGJ.ADV.LOADLIB,DISP=SHR
000154 //           DD  DSN=SYS1.COB2LIB,DISP=SHR
000155 //SYSOUT     DD  SYSOUT=*
000156 //SUMREP     DD  SYSOUT=*
000157 //MASTER1    DD  DSN=CSCJGJ.REG.STUACCTS(+1),     CURRENT MASTER FILE
000158 //  DISP=SHR
000159 //DOWNRECS   DD  DSN=CSCJGJ.REG.DOWNLOAD(+1),     NEW SUMMARY FILE
000160 //  DISP=(NEW,CATLG,DELETE),
000161 //  UNIT=SYSDA,
000162 //  DCB=(CSCJGJ.CSC.MODEL,RECFM=FB,LRECL=80,BLKSIZE=22880),
000163 //  SPACE=(TRK,(1,1),RLSE)
000164 //       ENDIF
000165 //*-----------------------------------------------------------------
000166 //*  CLEANUP: DELETE INTERMEDIATE DATA SETS TO BE CREATED IN RUN
000167 //*-----------------------------------------------------------------
000168 //       IF ( NOT ABEND AND RC <= 4 ) THEN
000169 //STEP080  EXEC  PGM=IEFBR14
000170 //DELETE1    DD  DSN=CSCJGJ.REG.FIN,              INTERMEDIATE
000171 //  DISP=(MOD,DELETE),                            DATA SET
000172 //  UNIT=SYSDA,
000173 //  SPACE=(TRK,0)
000174 //DELETE2    DD  DSN=CSCJGJ.REG.FINSORT,          INTERMEDIATE
000175 //  DISP=(MOD,DELETE),                            DATA SET
000176 //  UNIT=SYSDA,
000177 //  SPACE=(TRK,0)
000178 //       ENDIF
000179 //
```

GDS created

Figure 7.3 (continued)

Number, it enters the update in the same key sequence as the sorted transactions. Note that the current generation is really a backup of a VSAM file created just before this job by a previous job, as shown in Figure 7.1. The new (+1) generation of the master file becomes the current (0) generation after job stream REG33UP1 runs, and is used to reload the VSAM file, which then goes on-line, also as shown in Figure 7.1. The function of program REG3307 is updating, not reporting, and it does not include extensive reporting logic. It produces a simple listing of transactions processed, and also outputs a file of "finished" transactions consisting of the input records with appended disposition codes. A variety of reports from the update are produced in a different sort sequence by a subsequent step, using the finished transaction file.

This segregation of updating and reporting logic makes it possible to do flexible reporting using a fourth generation language if desired, while focusing more difficult VS COBOL II programming on the more intricate update logic.

STEP050 sorts the finished transaction records into student name sequence for reporting, creating an intermediate file named CSCJGJ.REG.FINSORT.

STEP060 executes program REG3308, which reads the data set of sorted, finished transactions. This program produces two reports: a list of all transactions, with disposition codes interpreted with plain-text messages, and a listing of bad (failed) transactions. The program also creates a file of failed transactions named CSCJGJ.REG.BADTRANS. The paper listing and failed transaction file are supplied to the accounting office for correction and reentry into the update cycle.

STEP070 executes program REG3350, which produces a summary data extract from the updated student master file. This program is typical of recent innovations in automated support. Staff analysts and managers now want to download data for analysis and manipulation on microcomputers to support enhanced decision making. Rather than downloading large volumes of data for summation on a PC, the REG33UP1 job stream uses a program to perform the bulk summarization of master file data into a few hundred records, which are "parked" in a file named CSCJGJ.REG.DOWNLOAD(+1). Planning analysts may or may not download data from any generation of this file on any given day. But since the summary data extract file is always present, planning analysts and corporate staff are free to download extracted data at any time through the local area network attached to the mainframe, without having to make any special run request of information services personnel. (We use Kermit software for mainframe and VAX data downloads, which—in addition to being easy to use—works superbly, is public-domain software, and, as such, is free of cost.)

STEP080 executes the IEFBR14 program and deletes the intermediate files used in the job stream to convey data between steps. These files are not deleted with (OLD,DELETE) in the last step accessing them, in order to make restart of the job stream possible for certain types of program failures. They can be deleted safely here in this last step because this step executes only if all of the prior steps ended successfully.

7.5 Generation Data Set (GDS) Usage

You will notice that data sets named CSCJGJ.REG.TRANSORT, CSCJGJ.REG.STUACCTS, and CSCJGJ.REG.DOWNLOAD in steps 020, 040, and 070 are generation data sets. JCL references to these data sets use (0) or (+1) to indicate the current or next generation of the data set. I assume that you are familiar with generation data sets, that you know how to establish them, and that you know the function of a model data set label such as CSCJGJ.CSC.MODEL referred to at lines 58, 99, and 162 in this job stream. If you *are* experienced with generation data sets, you can skip now to section 7.6.

In case you are not familiar with generation data sets, Figure 7.4 shows you the IDCAMS control statements and JCL I used to create the generation

```
EDIT ---- CSCJGJ.ADV.CNTL(K2BASE) - 01.05 ------------------- COLUMNS 001 072
COMMAND ===>                                                  SCROLL ===> HALF
****** ***************************** TOP OF DATA ******************************
000100 //CSCJGJA   JOB 1,'BIN 7 JANOSSY',CLASS=A,MSGCLASS=X,MSGLEVEL=(1,1),
000200 //  NOTIFY=CSCJGJ
000300 //*
000400 //*   THIS JCL IS STORED AT CSCJGJ.CSC.CNTL(K2BASE)
000500 //*
000600 //*******************************************************************
000700 //*                                                                 *
000800 //*   DEFINE A GENERATION DATA GROUP BASE USING IDCAMS              *
000900 //*                                                                 *
001000 //*******************************************************************
001100 //STEP010  EXEC  PGM=IDCAMS
001200 //SYSPRINT   DD  SYSOUT=*
001300 //SYSIN      DD  *
001400     DEFINE   GDG   (  NAME(CSCJGJ.REG.TRANSORT)  -
001500                       OWNER(CSCJGJ) -
001600                       FOR(9999) -
001700                       LIMIT(7) -
001800                       NOEMPTY -
001900                       SCRATCH                        )
002000 //
```

You can use JCL and IDCAMS control statements such as these to create a generation data set (GDS) base. If you need more information about generation data sets, see Chapter 17 of the introductory book, ***Practical MVS JCL Examples*** by James Janossy (John Wiley & Sons, Inc., 1993).

Figure 7.4 IDCAMS Control Statements and JCL to Create a Generation Data Set Base

data set "base," a system catalog entry, for one of the three GDSs used in this application. You can use separate, similar JCL one time each to establish each of the GDS bases before accessing any of them.

7.6 Quick MVS/ESA System Reporting Analysis

Job stream REG33UP1 usually executes successfully, with each step finishing and leaving behind a COND CODE of 0000 or 0004. I submitted the job stream as shown in Figure 7.5; after several seconds, I received the completion message shown at the bottom of the screen. The MVS/ESA system reporting for a successful run is shown in Figure 7.6. I have annotated it with some comments that point out interesting features.

The bulk of printlines produced by MVS/ESA for system reporting can obscure the important information needed to recognize what MVS is indicating about the outcome of a job. The most important lines of reporting that must be scanned quickly after a run are those indicating the outcome of each step. These lines indicate if the job progressed successfully or not, and if not, where a problem arose. Some installations enhance MVS/ESA reporting routines to extract information from these lines and print it at the top of the system reporting, near the job log. Not all installations, however, have

```
EDIT ---- CSCJGJ.ADV.CNTL(REG33UP1) - 01.09 ----------------- COLUMNS 001 072
COMMAND ===> sub                                              SCROLL ===> PAGE
****** ***************************** TOP OF DATA ******************************
000001 //CSCJGJA   JOB 1,                      ACCOUNTING INFORMATION
000002 //     'BIN 7--JANOSSY',                PROGRAMMER NAME AND DELIVERY BIN
000003 //     CLASS=A,                         INPUT QUEUE CLASS
000004 //     MSGLEVEL=(1,1),                  HOW MUCH MVS SYSTEM PRINT DESIRED
000005 //     MSGCLASS=X,                      PRINT DESTINATION X A L N OR O
000006 //     TIME=(1,0),                      SAFETY LIMIT: RUN TIME UP TO 1 MINUTE
000007 //     REGION=3M,                       ALLOW UP TO 3 MEGS VIRTUAL MEMORY
000008 //*    TYPRUN=SCAN,                     UNCOMMENT THIS LINE TO DO SCAN ONLY
000009 //     NOTIFY=CSCJGJ                    WHO TO TELL WHEN JOB IS DONE
000010 //*
000011 //*    RUN THE REG33UP1 UPDATE JOB STREAM USING RAW JCL
000012 //*    THIS JCL IS STORED AT CSCJGJ.ADV.CNTL(REG33UP1)
000013 //*
000014 //*-----------------------------------------------------------------
000015 //*    CLEANUP: DELETE DATA SETS TO BE CREATED IN RUN
000016 //*-----------------------------------------------------------------
000017 //STEP010  EXEC  PGM=IEFBR14

JOB CSCJGJA(JOB04818) SUBMITTED
13.43.32 JOB04818 $HASP165 CSCJGJA  ENDED AT N1 CN(INTERNAL)
***
```

Figure 7.5 Submission of Job Stream REG33UP1 and System Message Indicating Successful Completion

systems programmers do this. In my experience, some of the largest mainframe shops in existence run with exactly the same unenhanced format of system reporting shown in Figure 7.6.

It's patently unreliable and unproductive to have to manually scan the bulky MVS/ESA system reporting searching for COND CODE and completion code lines. Like a lot of other people, I suffered for many years as one of the cobbler's children who wore no shoes, a programmer who never found the time to automate the process of scanning MVS system reporting. I finally made the time to build such a tool, which I call SCANIT2.

SCANIT2 reads MVS/ESA system reporting you have captured to a file and produces a concise extract. I have used SCANIT2 to prepare several figures for this chapter because its extracts clearly show the reporting for various job stream run problems we'll discuss. Figure 7.7 shows you what the MVS/ESA system reporting of Figure 7.6 looks like when summarized by SCANIT2. As you can see, only the job number, COND CODE lines, and a summary message are produced. If the run had experienced a problem (which I'll demonstrate next) the SCANIT2 output would extract the best MVS/ESA reporting line for problem diagnosis.

MVS/ESA system reporting varies between JES2 and JES3 environments. I built SCANIT2 for the JES2 environment, and SCANIT3 for JES3 shops. I show the use of SCANIT2 here, but both programs are available to installations from Caliber Data Training, Inc., as described in Appendix F.

Figure 7.6 MVS/ESA System Reporting for a Successful Run of the REG33UP1 Job Stream (see facing page)

```
                    J E S 2   J O B   L O G  --  S Y S T E M   I B M 1

13.43.09 JOB04818  IRR010I  USERID CSCJGJ   IS ASSIGNED TO THIS JOB.
13.43.10 JOB04818  ICH70001I CSCJGJ   LAST ACCESS AT 13:40:05 ON THURSDAY, JANUARY
13.43.10 JOB04818  $HASP373 CSCJGJA  STARTED - INIT  1 - CLASS A - SYS IBM1
13.43.32 JOB04818  $HASP395 CSCJGJA  ENDED

------ JES2 JOB STATISTICS ------
    20 JAN 94 JOB EXECUTION DATE
          178 CARDS READ
        1,557 SYSOUT PRINT RECORDS
            0 SYSOUT PUNCH RECORDS
          180 SYSOUT SPOOL KBYTES
         0.35 MINUTES EXECUTION TIME
        1 //CSCJGJA   JOB 1,                 ACCOUNTING INFORMATION
          //    'BIN 7--JANOSSY',            PROGRAMMER NAME AND DELIVERY BIN
          //    CLASS=A,                     INPUT QUEUE CLASS
                -
                -
                -

ICH70001I CSCJGJ   LAST ACCESS AT 13:40:05 ON THURSDAY, JANUARY 20, 1994

IEF236I ALLOC. FOR CSCJGJA STEP010
IEF237I 111  ALLOCATED TO DELETE1
IEF237I 117  ALLOCATED TO DELETE2
IEF237I 116  ALLOCATED TO DELETE3
IEF142I CSCJGJA STEP010 - STEP WAS EXECUTED - COND CODE 0000
IEF285I   CSCJGJ.REG.FIN                                 DELETED
IEF285I   VOL SER NOS= USER00.
IEF285I   CSCJGJ.REG.FINSORT                             DELETED
IEF285I   VOL SER NOS= USER03.
IEF285I   CSCJGJ.REG.BADTRANS                            UNCATALOGED
IEF285I   VOL SER NOS= USER02.
IEF285I   CSCJGJ.REG.BADTRANS                            DELETED
IEF285I   VOL SER NOS= USER02.
IEF373I STEP /STEP010 / START 94020.1343
IEF374I STEP /STEP010 / STOP  94020.1343 CPU    0MIN 00.03SEC SRB    0MIN 00.00SEC

IEF236I ALLOC. FOR CSCJGJA STEP020
IEF237I JES2 ALLOCATED TO SYSOUT
IEF237I 115  ALLOCATED TO SORTIN
IEF237I 117  ALLOCATED TO
IEF237I 111  ALLOCATED TO
IEF237I 111  ALLOCATED TO SORTOUT
IEF237I VIO  ALLOCATED TO SORTWK01
IEF237I VIO  ALLOCATED TO SORTWK02
IEF237I VIO  ALLOCATED TO SORTWK03
IEF237I 116  ALLOCATED TO SYSIN
IEF142I CSCJGJA STEP020 - STEP WAS EXECUTED - COND CODE 0000
IEF285I   CSCJGJ.CSCJGJA.JOB04818.D0000101.?             SYSOUT
IEF287I   CSCJGJ.REG.TELTR                               NOT RECTLGD 2
IEF287I   VOL SER NOS= USER01.
IEF285I   CSCJGJ.REG.CASHTR                              CATALOGED
IEF285I   VOL SER NOS= USER03.
IEF287I   CSCJGJ.REG.FIXEDTR                             NOT RECTLGD 2
IEF287I   VOL SER NOS= USER00.
IEF285I   CSCJGJ.REG.TRANSORT.G0117V00                   CATALOGED
IEF285I   VOL SER NOS= USER00.
IEF285I   SYS94020.T134310.RA000.CSCJGJA.R0096025        DELETED
IEF285I   VOL SER NOS= USER03.
IEF285I   SYS94020.T134310.RA000.CSCJGJA.R0096026        DELETED
IEF285I   VOL SER NOS= USER00.
```

SCANIT2 extracts these lines

NOT RECATLG 2 indicates that the input data sets already existed; this is not an error.

The output from a run of the REG33UP1 job stream shows COND CODE lines and MVS/ESA data set disposition reporting. But it's not easy or reliable to manually search through all of this to see if the job ran successfully. Capture this output to a file, then run a program like SCANIT2 on it. The extracted output shows only the COND CODE or system completion code lines, as you can see in the next figure. (REG33UP1 output continues for two more pages.)

```
IEF285I   SYS94020.T134310.RA000.CSCJGJA.R0096027      DELETED
IEF285I   VOL SER NOS= USER03.
IEF285I   CSCJGJ.CCARDS                                KEPT
IEF285I   VOL SER NOS= USER02.
IEF373I STEP /STEP020 / START 94020.1343
IEF374I STEP /STEP020 / STOP  94020.1343 CPU    0MIN 00.57SEC SRB    0MIN 00.02SEC

IEF236I ALLOC. FOR CSCJGJA STEP030
IEF237I 115   ALLOCATED TO DELETE1
IEF237I 117   ALLOCATED TO DELETE2
IEF237I 111   ALLOCATED TO DELETE3
IEF142I CSCJGJA STEP030 - STEP WAS EXECUTED - COND CODE 0000
IEF285I   CSCJGJ.REG.TELTR                             UNCATALOGED
IEF285I   VOL SER NOS= USER01.
IEF285I   CSCJGJ.REG.TELTR                             DELETED
IEF285I   VOL SER NOS= USER01.
IEF285I   CSCJGJ.REG.CASHTR                            UNCATALOGED
IEF285I   VOL SER NOS= USER03.
IEF285I   CSCJGJ.REG.CASHTR                            DELETED
IEF285I   VOL SER NOS= USER03.
IEF285I   CSCJGJ.REG.FIXEDTR                           UNCATALOGED
IEF285I   VOL SER NOS= USER00.
IEF285I   CSCJGJ.REG.FIXEDTR                           DELETED
IEF285I   VOL SER NOS= USER00.
IEF373I STEP /STEP030 / START 94020.1343
IEF374I STEP /STEP030 / STOP  94020.1343 CPU    0MIN 00.03SEC SRB    0MIN 00.00SEC

IEF236I ALLOC. FOR CSCJGJA STEP040
IEF237I 117   ALLOCATED TO STEPLIB
IEF237I 110   ALLOCATED TO
IEF237I JES2 ALLOCATED TO SYSOUT
IEF237I 111   ALLOCATED TO TRANS
IEF237I 111   ALLOCATED TO OLDMAST
IEF237I 115   ALLOCATED TO NEWMAST
IEF237I 116   ALLOCATED TO FINTRANS
IEF237I JES2 ALLOCATED TO AUDREP
IEF142I CSCJGJA STEP040 - STEP WAS EXECUTED - COND CODE 0000
IEF285I   CSCJGJ.ADV.LOADLIB                           KEPT
IEF285I   VOL SER NOS= USER03.
IEF285I   SYS1.COB2LIB                                 KEPT
IEF285I   VOL SER NOS= ACSRES.
IEF285I   CSCJGJ.CSCJGJA.JOB04818.D0000102.?           SYSOUT
IEF285I   CSCJGJ.REG.TRANSORT.G0117V00                 KEPT
IEF285I   VOL SER NOS= USER00.
IEF285I   CSCJGJ.REG.STUACCTS.G0123V00                 KEPT
IEF285I   VOL SER NOS= USER00.
IEF285I   CSCJGJ.REG.STUACCTS.G0124V00                 CATALOGED
IEF285I   VOL SER NOS= USER01.
IEF285I   CSCJGJ.REG.FIN                               CATALOGED
IEF285I   VOL SER NOS= USER02.
IEF285I   CSCJGJ.CSCJGJA.JOB04818.D0000103.?           SYSOUT
IEF373I STEP /STEP040 / START 94020.1343
IEF374I STEP /STEP040 / STOP  94020.1343 CPU    0MIN 00.42SEC SRB    0MIN 00.04SEC

IEF236I ALLOC. FOR CSCJGJA STEP050
IEF237I JES2 ALLOCATED TO SYSOUT
IEF237I 116   ALLOCATED TO SORTIN
IEF237I 117   ALLOCATED TO SORTOUT
IEF237I VIO   ALLOCATED TO SORTWK01
IEF237I VIO   ALLOCATED TO SORTWK02
IEF237I VIO   ALLOCATED TO SORTWK03
IEF237I 116   ALLOCATED TO SYSIN
IEF142I CSCJGJA STEP050 - STEP WAS EXECUTED - COND CODE 0000
IEF285I   CSCJGJ.CSCJGJA.JOB04818.D0000104.?           SYSOUT
IEF285I   CSCJGJ.REG.FIN                               KEPT
IEF285I   VOL SER NOS= USER02.
IEF285I   CSCJGJ.REG.FINSORT                           CATALOGED
IEF285I   VOL SER NOS= USER03.
IEF285I   SYS94020.T134310.RA000.CSCJGJA.R0096028      DELETED
IEF285I   VOL SER NOS= USER00.
IEF285I   SYS94020.T134310.RA000.CSCJGJA.R0096029      DELETED
IEF285I   VOL SER NOS= USER01.
IEF285I   SYS94020.T134310.RA000.CSCJGJA.R0096030      DELETED
IEF285I   VOL SER NOS= USER03.
IEF285I   CSCJGJ.CCARDS                                KEPT
IEF285I   VOL SER NOS= USER02.
IEF373I STEP /STEP050 / START 94020.1343
IEF374I STEP /STEP050 / STOP  94020.1343 CPU    0MIN 00.45SEC SRB    0MIN 00.01SEC

IEF236I ALLOC. FOR CSCJGJA STEP060
IEF237I 117   ALLOCATED TO STEPLIB
IEF237I 110   ALLOCATED TO
```

The three input data sets are deleted

New generation of master file created

Temporary sort work files deleted

Figure 7.6 (continued)

```
IEF237I JES2 ALLOCATED TO SYSOUT
IEF237I 117  ALLOCATED TO FTRANS
IEF237I JES2 ALLOCATED TO GOODREP
IEF237I JES2 ALLOCATED TO BADREP
IEF237I 111  ALLOCATED TO BADTR
IEF142I CSCJGJA STEP060 - STEP WAS EXECUTED - COND CODE 0000
IEF285I   CSCJGJ.ADV.LOADLIB                              KEPT
IEF285I   VOL SER NOS= USER03.
IEF285I   SYS1.COB2LIB                                    KEPT
IEF285I   VOL SER NOS= ACSRES.
IEF285I   CSCJGJ.CSCJGJA.JOB04818.D0000105.?              SYSOUT
IEF285I   CSCJGJ.REG.FINSORT                              KEPT
IEF285I   VOL SER NOS= USER03.
IEF285I   CSCJGJ.CSCJGJA.JOB04818.D0000106.?              SYSOUT
IEF285I   CSCJGJ.CSCJGJA.JOB04818.D0000107.?              SYSOUT
IEF285I   CSCJGJ.REG.BADTRANS                             CATALOGED
IEF285I   VOL SER NOS= USER00.
IEF373I STEP /STEP060 / START 94020.1343
IEF374I STEP /STEP060 / STOP  94020.1343 CPU    0MIN 00.30SEC SRB    0MIN 00.04SEC

IEF236I ALLOC. FOR CSCJGJA STEP070
IEF237I 117  ALLOCATED TO STEPLIB
IEF237I 110  ALLOCATED TO
IEF237I JES2 ALLOCATED TO SYSOUT
IEF237I JES2 ALLOCATED TO SUMREP
IEF237I 115  ALLOCATED TO MASTER1
IEF237I 111  ALLOCATED TO DOWNRECS
IEF142I CSCJGJA STEP070 - STEP WAS EXECUTED - COND CODE 0000
IEF285I   CSCJGJ.ADV.LOADLIB                              KEPT
IEF285I   VOL SER NOS= USER03.
IEF285I   SYS1.COB2LIB                                    KEPT
IEF285I   VOL SER NOS= ACSRES.
IEF285I   CSCJGJ.CSCJGJA.JOB04818.D0000108.?              SYSOUT
IEF285I   CSCJGJ.CSCJGJA.JOB04818.D0000109.?              SYSOUT
IEF285I   CSCJGJ.REG.STUACCTS.G0124V00                    KEPT
IEF285I   VOL SER NOS= USER01.
IEF237I 116  ALLOCATED TO SYS00001
IEF285I   SYS94020.T134329.RA000.CSCJGJA.R0000001         KEPT
IEF285I   VOL SER NOS= USER02.
IEF285I   CSCJGJ.REG.DOWNLOAD.G0088V00                    CATALOGED
IEF285I   VOL SER NOS= USER00.
IEF373I STEP /STEP070 / START 94020.1343
IEF374I STEP /STEP070 / STOP  94020.1343 CPU    0MIN 00.24SEC SRB    0MIN 00.02SEC

IEF236I ALLOC. FOR CSCJGJA STEP080
IEF237I 116  ALLOCATED TO DELETE1
IEF237I 117  ALLOCATED TO DELETE2
IEF142I CSCJGJA STEP080 - STEP WAS EXECUTED - COND CODE 0000
IEF285I   CSCJGJ.REG.FIN                                  UNCATALOGED
IEF285I   VOL SER NOS= USER02.
IEF285I   CSCJGJ.REG.FIN                                  DELETED
IEF285I   VOL SER NOS= USER02.
IEF285I   CSCJGJ.REG.FINSORT                              UNCATALOGED
IEF285I   VOL SER NOS= USER03.
IEF285I   CSCJGJ.REG.FINSORT                              DELETED
IEF285I   VOL SER NOS= USER03.

IEF373I STEP /STEP080 / START 94020.1343
IEF374I STEP /STEP080 / STOP  94020.1343 CPU    0MIN 00.03SEC SRB    0MIN 00.00SEC

IEF375I  JOB /CSCJGJA / START 94020.1343
IEF376I  JOB /CSCJGJA / STOP  94020.1343 CPU    0MIN 02.07SEC SRB    0MIN 00.13SEC
```

Flawed transactions in file for end user downloading
Next generation of summary file for end user downloading
Intermediate files deleted; job finished successfully so these are not needed for recovery actions.

Figure 7.6 (continued)

```
*******************************************************************************
SCANIT2 HELPS YOU ANALYZE MVS/ESA JOB OUTPUT.  SEE MORE ABOUT THIS TOOL IN
"ADVANCED MVS JCL EXAMPLES" BY JIM JANOSSY (1994, JOHN WILEY & SONS, INC.)
*******************************************************************************

13.43.09 JOB04818  IRR010I  USERID CSCJGJ   IS ASSIGNED TO THIS JOB.
IEF142I CSCJGJA STEP010 - STEP WAS EXECUTED - COND CODE 0000
IEF142I CSCJGJA STEP020 - STEP WAS EXECUTED - COND CODE 0000
IEF142I CSCJGJA STEP030 - STEP WAS EXECUTED - COND CODE 0000
IEF142I CSCJGJA STEP040 - STEP WAS EXECUTED - COND CODE 0000
IEF142I CSCJGJA STEP050 - STEP WAS EXECUTED - COND CODE 0000
IEF142I CSCJGJA STEP060 - STEP WAS EXECUTED - COND CODE 0000
IEF142I CSCJGJA STEP070 - STEP WAS EXECUTED - COND CODE 0000
IEF142I CSCJGJA STEP080 - STEP WAS EXECUTED - COND CODE 0000

NO NON-ZERO SYSTEM COMPLETION CODE DETECTED
```

The SCANIT2 program extracts COND CODE and system completion code lines from the mass of MVS/ESA system reporting, giving you a quick way to see if a job executed successfully. Compare this output from a successful run with the SCANIT2 output of failed runs shown in other figures in this chapter.

Figure 7.7 MVS/ESA System Reporting for a Successful Run of REG33UP1 as Extracted by the SCANIT2 Program

7.7 Tutorial: Job Failure #1, a System Abend

On rare occasions, the REG33UP1 run encounters a problem and abends. The occurrence of one of these failures is shown in Figure 7.8. The JCL was submitted, and after a few seconds of operation, it concluded and an "abended" message was sent to my terminal. We must now investigate and find the cause of this failure.

Figure 7.9 shows you the critical lines of MVS/ESA system reporting produced by the failed REG33UP1 run. The complete "pile" of MVS/ESA system reporting for this run appears similar to Figure 7.6. Instead of reproducing all of those lines, however, I'm showing you here the extracted lines we need to examine. (I could have manually extracted these lines as I did in similar illustrations in Chapter 3, but I used SCANIT2, as described above, to provide this illustration.) Once these critical lines have been extracted, you can see the point of problem occurrence. By finding the system completion code, which is D37 in this case, and the related reporting for it, you can diagnose the problem. Look up D37 in Appendix E and you'll see it relates to a lack of disk space. The file involved was at the DD statement named FINTRANS in STEP040, and it appears to have been too big for the space allocation coded at line 106 in Figure 7.3.

In actuality, I simulated a problem situation to create this job failure. I reduced the disk space allocation for the file CSCJGJ.REG.FIN at STEP040's //FINTRAN DD statement and did not allow secondary space allocation. But

```
EDIT ---- CSCJGJ.ADV.CNTL(REG33UP1) - 01.03 ----------------- COLUMNS 001 072
COMMAND ===> sub                                              SCROLL ===> PAGE
****** ****************************** TOP OF DATA ******************************
000001 //CSCJGJA   JOB 1,                  ACCOUNTING INFORMATION
000002 //   'BIN 7--JANOSSY',              PROGRAMMER NAME AND DELIVERY BIN
000003 //   CLASS=A,                       INPUT QUEUE CLASS
000004 //   MSGLEVEL=(1,1),                HOW MUCH MVS SYSTEM PRINT DESIRED
000005 //   MSGCLASS=X,                    PRINT DESTINATION X A L N OR O
000006 //   TIME=(1,0),                    SAFETY LIMIT: RUN TIME UP TO 1 MINUTE
000007 //   REGION=3M,                     ALLOW UP TO 3 MEGS VIRTUAL MEMORY
000008 //*  TYPRUN=SCAN,                   UNCOMMENT THIS LINE TO DO SCAN ONLY
000009 //   NOTIFY=CSCJGJ                  WHO TO TELL WHEN JOB IS DONE
000010 //*
000011 //*  RUN THE REG33UP1 UPDATE JOB STREAM USING RAW JCL
000012 //*  THIS JCL IS STORED AT CSCJGJ.ADV.CNTL(REG33UP1)
000013 //*
000014 //*-------------------------------------------------------------------
000015 //*  CLEANUP: DELETE DATA SETS TO BE CREATED IN RUN
000016 //*-------------------------------------------------------------------
000017 //STEP010  EXEC  PGM=IEFBR14

JOB CSCJGJA(JOB05000) SUBMITTED
16.21.59 JOB05000 $HASP165 CSCJGJA  ENDED AT N1 - ABENDED CN(INTERNAL)
***
```

This run of REG33UP1 was submitted and progressed normally for a while, but then failed. **This immediately raises several questions.** *How will you diagnose the reason for the failure? What steps will you take to correct the problem?* And, finally, the most difficult question: *How will you arrange to deliver the work to be done by this job stream for the end user?* Will you attempt to restart the job at the point of failure, or will you arrange to rerun it completely? In this chapter I show you how to use the **RESTART** parameter of the JOB statement, which involves much more than simply putting it onto the JOB statement. In Chapter 8, I demonstrate how to use the rerun approach to recovery, setting in place the JCL to facilitate "rerun from the beginning" recovery.

Figure 7.8 Submission of Job Stream REG33UP1 and the System Message Indicating an Abend

running out of disk space is probably the most common cause for job failure. Although the cause of this type of problem might be a faulty program (which is looping and writing too much output), most often the problem is simply that the quantity of data being processed has increased beyond the amount the JCL was coded to allow. Unless the program being executed was recently modified and reinstalled without sufficient testing, the cure for this problem is almost always to increase the amount of disk space allowed for the file that experienced the problem.

Figure 7.9 actually shows you more than one important thing. It reveals that STEP040 failed, but it also shows you that steps 050, 060, 070, and 080 did not run. This means that the data sets to be produced by these latter steps were not created.

```
******************************************************************************
SCANIT2 HELPS YOU ANALYZE MVS/ESA JOB OUTPUT.  SEE MORE ABOUT THIS TOOL IN
"ADVANCED MVS JCL EXAMPLES" BY JIM JANOSSY (1994, JOHN WILEY & SONS, INC.)
******************************************************************************

 16.21.52 JOB05000  IRR010I  USERID CSCJGJ   IS ASSIGNED TO THIS JOB.
 IEF142I CSCJGJA STEP010 - STEP WAS EXECUTED - COND CODE 0000
 IEF142I CSCJGJA STEP020 - STEP WAS EXECUTED - COND CODE 0000
 IEF142I CSCJGJA STEP030 - STEP WAS EXECUTED - COND CODE 0000
 IEF472I CSCJGJA STEP040 - COMPLETION CODE - SYSTEM=D37 USER=0000 REASON=00000000
 IEF206I CSCJGJA STEP050 - STEP WAS NOT RUN BECAUSE OF CONDITIONAL EXPRESSION
 IEF206I CSCJGJA STEP060 - STEP WAS NOT RUN BECAUSE OF CONDITIONAL EXPRESSION
 IEF206I CSCJGJA STEP070 - STEP WAS NOT RUN BECAUSE OF CONDITIONAL EXPRESSION
 IEF206I CSCJGJA STEP080 - STEP WAS NOT RUN BECAUSE OF CONDITIONAL EXPRESSION

*** NON-ZERO SYSTEM COMPLETION CODE DETECTED! ***
    THE FOLLOWING LINE GIVES BEST INFORMATION.
    LOOK FOR INFORMATION ABOUT SYSTEM COMPLETION CODE D37 BELOW:

 16.22.10 JOB05000  IEC031I D37-04,IFG0554T,CSCJGJA,STEP040,FINTRANS,111,USER00,
```

In this SCANIT2 output you see the extracted reporting for a run of REG33UP1 that failed due to insufficient disk space in STEP040, at the FINTRANS DD statement. It's a lot easier to detect that something went wrong, and localize the problem, using an analysis tool such as SCANIT2, than to try to find these important lines in the full mass of MVS/ESA system reporting.

Figure 7.9 MVS/ESA System Reporting for an Abended Run as Extracted by the SCANIT2 Program

Since my recovery strategy in this chapter is to restart a failed run and not redo steps that already processed successfully, I'll use the RESTART parameter on the JOB statement to complete this run. But first, I want to show you a few more run failures and a simple but highly productive method for using TSO/ISPF to find information in MVS/ESA reporting.

7.8 Tutorial: Job Failure #2, Need for an Attention Grabber

Figure 7.10 shows you another submission of the REG33UP1 job stream, which receives an apparently normal completion message. But this run actually encountered a failure and did not complete successfully. Figure 7.11 shows you the extracted system reporting. This run failed due to a COND CODE greater than 4 posted by the program at STEP050. This form of failure was triggered by a program "complaining" via its return code, not by an MVS/ESA-issued system completion code. This causes subsequent steps to not run because of the IF . . . THEN relational tests I coded at the start of STEP020 and subsequent steps. In this job stream a COND CODE greater than 4 coming from a program indicates a problem that cannot be ignored.

Figures 7.10 and 7.11 reveal a serious shortcoming of my original eight-step JCL for job stream REG33UP1. It's too easy to overlook a run fail-

```
EDIT ---- CSCJGJ.ADV.CNTL(REG33UP1) - 01.09 ----------------- COLUMNS 001 072
COMMAND ===> sub                                              SCROLL ===> PAGE
****** ***************************** TOP OF DATA ******************************
000001 //CSCJGJA   JOB 1,                     ACCOUNTING INFORMATION
000002 //    'BIN 7--JANOSSY',                PROGRAMMER NAME AND DELIVERY BIN
000003 //    CLASS=A,                         INPUT QUEUE CLASS
000004 //    MSGLEVEL=(1,1),                  HOW MUCH MVS SYSTEM PRINT DESIRED
000005 //    MSGCLASS=X,                      PRINT DESTINATION X A L N OR O
000006 //    TIME=(1,0),                      SAFETY LIMIT: RUN TIME UP TO 1 MINUTE
000007 //    REGION=3M,                       ALLOW UP TO 3 MEGS VIRTUAL MEMORY
000008 //*   TYPRUN=SCAN,                     UNCOMMENT THIS LINE TO DO SCAN ONLY
000009 //    NOTIFY=CSCJGJ                    WHO TO TELL WHEN JOB IS DONE
000010 //*
000011 //*   RUN THE REG33UP1 UPDATE JOB STREAM USING RAW JCL
000012 //*   THIS JCL IS STORED AT CSCJGJ.ADV.CNTL(REG33UP1)
000013 //*
000014 //*--------------------------------------------------
000015 //*   CLEANUP: DELETE DATA SETS TO BE CREATED IN RUN
000016 //*--------------------------------------------------
000017 //STEP010  EXEC  PGM=IEFBR14

JOB CSCJGJA(JOB05032) SUBMITTED
16.35.44 JOB05032 $HASP165 CSCJGJA  ENDED AT N1 CN(INTERNAL)
***
```

Ended normally?

Figure 7.10 MVS/ESA System Reporting for a Run of the REG33UP1 Job Stream; Was the Run Successful or Not?

```
********************************************************************************
SCANIT2 HELPS YOU ANALYZE MVS/ESA JOB OUTPUT.  SEE MORE ABOUT THIS TOOL IN
"ADVANCED MVS JCL EXAMPLES" BY JIM JANOSSY (1994, JOHN WILEY & SONS, INC.)
********************************************************************************

 16.35.44 JOB05032  IRR010I  USERID CSCJGJ   IS ASSIGNED TO THIS JOB
 IEF142I CSCJGJA STEP010 - STEP WAS EXECUTED - COND CODE 0000
 IEF142I CSCJGJA STEP020 - STEP WAS EXECUTED - COND CODE 0000
 IEF142I CSCJGJA STEP030 - STEP WAS EXECUTED - COND CODE 0000
 IEF142I CSCJGJA STEP040 - STEP WAS EXECUTED - COND CODE 0000
 IEF142I CSCJGJA STEP050 - STEP WAS EXECUTED - COND CODE 0020
 IEF206I CSCJGJA STEP060 - STEP WAS NOT RUN BECAUSE OF CONDITIONAL EXPRESSION
 IEF206I CSCJGJA STEP070 - STEP WAS NOT RUN BECAUSE OF CONDITIONAL EXPRESSION
 IEF206I CSCJGJA STEP080 - STEP WAS NOT RUN BECAUSE OF CONDITIONAL EXPRESSION

NO NON-ZERO SYSTEM COMPLETION CODE DETECTED
```

The system reporting for the run of REG33UP1 extracted here shows cessation of processing after STEP050, which posted a COND CODE of 20. This is a good example showing why you need to include a final step to cause an intentional user abend when recovery actions are needed. A final step such as STEP999 in the C7REAL job stream shown in Figure 3.17 would call attention to this run by issuing an abend with an unusual user completion code. I've added that "attention getter" step to REG33UP1 for the illustration shown next.

Figure 7.11 MVS/ESA System Reporting for Run That Failed Without an Abend, Due to a COND CODE

ure due to a problem COND CODE. Since no system abend occurred, such a failing job does not "go down in flames"; rather, it dies with a whimper that may not be noticed right away. A better way to construct REG33UP1 would be to include a ninth step identical to the last step shown in Chapter 3 in Figure 3.17:

```
//* -----------------------------------------------------------
//*  ATTENTION GRABBER: ISSUE USER ABEND 3333 IF RUN FAILED
//* -----------------------------------------------------------
//      IF ( ABEND OR RC > 4 ) THEN
//STEP999 EXEC PGM=USERABN,PARM=3333
//STEPLIB   DD DSN=CSCJGJ.ADV.LOADLIB,DISP=SHR
//          DD DSN=SYS1.COB2LIB,DISP=SHR
//      ENDIF
```

This final step does not ordinarily execute. It executes only when a system abend has occurred *or* when any step leaves behind a COND CODE greater than 4. This step executes the program named USERABN, which I showed you in Chapter 3. USERABN does an intentional user abend, conveying whatever value you give it as a PARM (up to 4095) as a user completion code.

The net effect of this additional "attention getting" step becomes evident in Figures 7.12 and 7.13. This is the same job and same failure as shown in Figures 7.10 and 7.11. The job has been submitted as shown in Figure 7.12, but you will note that it now abends instead of apparently ending normally. This results in the ABENDED message at the bottom of the screen. Figure 7.13 represents the SCANIT2 output extracted from the MVS/ESA system reporting for this job. As in the prior run, real "worker" steps 060, 070, and 080 have not executed because of the problem. But now, STEP999 has executed and it's more evident that a problem has occurred because the job has died in a glorious blaze of fury. This failure causes MVS/ESA to issue a failure message on the computer operator's console—as all system and user completion codes do—and there is much more chance that the failure will be noticed and job recovery actions begun quickly.

What's the problem in this case? Since STEP050 executes the sort utility, look up COND CODE 0020 in Appendix D to see what the utility is telling you. (You'll find that I instigated this problem by removing the SYSOUT DD statement for the sort utility.) If the program issuing the COND CODE greater than 4 was not a utility, but was locally written, you would have to consult local documentation to determine the meaning of the COND CODE value.

```
EDIT ---- CSCJGJ.ADV.CNTL(REG33UP1) - 01.03 ------------------ COLUMNS 001 072
COMMAND ===> sub                                               SCROLL ===> PAGE
****** ***************************** TOP OF DATA ******************************
000001 //CSCJGJA   JOB 1,                  ACCOUNTING INFORMATION
000002 //    'BIN 7--JANOSSY',             PROGRAMMER NAME AND DELIVERY BIN
000003 //    CLASS=A,                      INPUT QUEUE CLASS
000004 //    MSGLEVEL=(1,1),               HOW MUCH MVS SYSTEM PRINT DESIRED
000005 //    MSGCLASS=X,                   PRINT DESTINATION X A L N OR O
000006 //    TIME=(1,0),                   SAFETY LIMIT: RUN TIME UP TO 1 MINUTE
000007 //    REGION=3M,                    ALLOW UP TO 3 MEGS VIRTUAL MEMORY
000008 //*   TYPRUN=SCAN,                  UNCOMMENT THIS LINE TO DO SCAN ONLY
000009 //    NOTIFY=CSCJGJ                 WHO TO TELL WHEN JOB IS DONE
000010 //*
000011 //*   RUN THE REG33UP1 UPDATE JOB STREAM USING RAW JCL
000012 //*   THIS JCL IS STORED AT CSCJGJ.ADV.CNTL(REG33UP1)
000013 //*
000014 //*-----------------------------------------------------------------
000015 //*   CLEANUP: DELETE DATA SETS TO BE CREATED IN RUN
000016 //*-----------------------------------------------------------------
000017 //STEP010  EXEC  PGM=IEFBR14

JOB CSCJGJA(JOB05091) SUBMITTED
18.05.06 JOB05091 $HASP165 CSCJGJA  ENDED AT N1 - ABENDED CN(INTERNAL)
***
```

Figure 7.12 Submission of Job Stream REG33UP1 and the System Message Indicating Another Abend

```
*****************************************************************************
SCANIT2 HELPS YOU ANALYZE MVS/ESA JOB OUTPUT.  SEE MORE ABOUT THIS TOOL IN
"ADVANCED MVS JCL EXAMPLES" BY JIM JANOSSY (1994, JOHN WILEY & SONS, INC.)
*****************************************************************************

 18.05.06 JOB05091  IRR010I  USERID CSCJGJ   IS ASSIGNED TO THIS JOB.
 IEF142I CSCJGJA STEP010 - STEP WAS EXECUTED - COND CODE 0000
 IEF142I CSCJGJA STEP020 - STEP WAS EXECUTED - COND CODE 0000
 IEF142I CSCJGJA STEP030 - STEP WAS EXECUTED - COND CODE 0000
 IEF142I CSCJGJA STEP040 - STEP WAS EXECUTED - COND CODE 0000
 IEF142I CSCJGJA STEP050 - STEP WAS EXECUTED - COND CODE 0020
 IEF206I CSCJGJA STEP060 - STEP WAS NOT RUN BECAUSE OF CONDITIONAL EXPRESSION
 IEF206I CSCJGJA STEP070 - STEP WAS NOT RUN BECAUSE OF CONDITIONAL EXPRESSION
 IEF206I CSCJGJA STEP080 - STEP WAS NOT RUN BECAUSE OF CONDITIONAL EXPRESSION
 IEF472I CSCJGJA STEP999 - COMPLETION CODE - SYSTEM=000 USER=3333 REASON=000000

NO NON-ZERO SYSTEM COMPLETION CODE DETECTED

*** USER ABEND DETECTED WITH USER COMPLETION CODE 3333
```

I added a ninth step named STEP999 to the REG33UP1 job stream, then ran it again with the error that caused STEP050 to issue COND CODE 20. The final "attention getter" step executed because its IF condition was coded

IF (ABEND OR RC > 4) THEN

STEP999 executes the USERABN program as shown in Chapter 3, Figure 3.17, passing it the parm 3333 to issue this as the user completion code. Here you see how SCANIT2 extracts and reports the result of the run.

Figure 7.13 Effect of Addition of an Attention Getter Step at the End of the REG33UP1 Job Stream

7.9 Tutorial: Job Failure #3, a TSO/ISPF Diagnosis Method

Figure 7.14 shows you yet another submission of the REG33UP1 job stream. Once again, this job has abended, as the message at the bottom of Figure 7.14 shows. You need to examine the output of this failed job to find the critical MVS/ESA system reporting printlines that reveal the location and nature of the problem. These lines present a mass of print, which often seem to be sheer gibberish to all but well-seasoned mainframe personnel. If you do not have access to a program such as SCANIT2 to extract and summarize these lines, you can follow a two-step method that uses TSO/ISPF as shown in Figure 7.15. I have not seen this method documented elsewhere, and it is only a commonsense combination of TSO/ISPF techniques. But it speeds up work quite a bit, especially for newcomers to the mainframe, and I'm describing it here for your benefit.

Figure 7.15 begins with viewing the output MVS/ESA system reporting for a failed job. The TSO/ISPF character string search facility works with SDSF, IBM's Spool Display and Search Facility, and within other similar products. Begin by viewing the top of the MVS/ESA system reporting. Use the "find" command to find the word ABEND. Immediately following this word will be the system completion code, as the first arrow in Figure 7.15 indicates. When you do this for the output of this failed run, you see ABEND=S013. The "013" is the system completion code you can look up in Appendix E.

But what's this? System completion code 013 is not specific enough! It is one of several system completion codes that have suffixes to denote specific problems. If the three-position system completion code you are looking up is similarly general, you need to take a second step, also using the "find" command.

```
EDIT ---- CSCJGJ.ADV.CNTL(REG33UP1) - 01.03 ----------------- COLUMNS 001 072
COMMAND ===> sub                                               SCROLL ===> PAGE
****** ***************************** TOP OF DATA ******************************
000001 //CSCJGJA   JOB 1,                     ACCOUNTING INFORMATION
000002 //     'BIN 7--JANOSSY',               PROGRAMMER NAME AND DELIVERY BIN
000003 //     CLASS=A,                        INPUT QUEUE CLASS
000004 //     MSGLEVEL=(1,1),                 HOW MUCH MVS SYSTEM PRINT DESIRED
000005 //     MSGCLASS=X,                     PRINT DESTINATION X A L N OR O
000006 //     TIME=(1,0),                     SAFETY LIMIT: RUN TIME UP TO 1 MINUTE
000007 //     REGION=3M,                      ALLOW UP TO 3 MEGS VIRTUAL MEMORY
000008 //*    TYPRUN=SCAN,                    UNCOMMENT THIS LINE TO DO SCAN ONLY
000009 //     NOTIFY=CSCJGJ                   WHO TO TELL WHEN JOB IS DONE
000010 //*
000011 //*  RUN THE REG33UP1 UPDATE JOB STREAM USING RAW JCL
000012 //*  THIS JCL IS STORED AT CSCJGJ.ADV.CNTL(REG33UP1)
000013 //*
000014 //*-----------------------------------------------------------------
000015 //*  CLEANUP: DELETE DATA SETS TO BE CREATED IN RUN
000016 //*-----------------------------------------------------------------
000017 //STEP010  EXEC  PGM=IEFBR14

JOB CSCJGJA(JOB09319) SUBMITTED
02.19.58 JOB09319 $HASP165 CSCJGJA  ENDED AT N1 - ABENDED CN(INTERNAL)
***
```

Figure 7.14 Submission of Job Stream REG33UP1 and the System Message Indicating Another Abend

Figure 7.15 Two-Step Method That Uses TSO/ISPF to Locate the System Completion Code in MVS/ESA System Reporting (see facing page)

```
SDSF OUTPUT DISPLAY CSCJGJA  JOB09319  DSID     2 LINE 0       COLUMNS 02- 81
COMMAND INPUT ===> find abend                                  SCROLL ===> PAGE
********************************** TOP OF DATA ***********************************
                  J E S 2  J O B  L O G  --  S Y S T E M  I B M 1  --  N

02.19.58 JOB09319  IRR010I  USERID CSCJGJ   IS ASSIGNED TO THIS JOB.
02.19.59 JOB09319  ICH70001I CSCJGJ   LAST ACCESS AT 02:13:11 ON SUNDAY, JANUARY
02.19.59 JOB09319  $HASP373 CSCJGJA  STARTED - INIT  1 - CLASS A - SYS IBM1
02.20.04 JOB09319  IEC141I 013-18,IGG0191B,CSCJGJA,STEP020,SYSIN,116,USER02,CSCJ
02.20.04 JOB09319  IEA995I SYMPTOM DUMP OUTPUT
                   SYSTEM COMPLETION CODE=013
                    TIME=02.20.03  SEQ=25286  CPU=0000  ASID=000F
                    PSW AT TIME OF ERROR  075C1000   00E8799C  ILC 2  INTC 0D
                      NO ACTIVE MODULE FOUND
                      DATA AT PSW  00E87996 - 4100395E  0A     E0  39025820
                      GPR  0-3  00E87B58  A0013000  0000      00E871FA
                      GPR  4-7  008D6740  008D6ED4  0      4  008D6ED8
                      GPR  8-11 008D6E5C  00FD6918      938  008D51AC
                      GPR 12-15 00000008  00000000      350  00000018
                    END OF SYMPTOM DUMP
02.20.05 JOB09319  IEF450I CSCJGJA STEP020 - ABEND=S013 U0000 REASON=00000000
02.20.09 JOB09319  IEA995I SYMPTOM DUMP OUTPUT
                     USER COMPLETION CODE=3333
                    TIME=02.20.08  SEQ=25289  CPU=0000  ASID=000F
```

A manual method exists to find the system completion code that reveals the reason for an abend. If you don't want to use SCANIT2, begin by viewing the MVS/ESA system output using SDSF, the "S" main menu selection; jump to view held output immediately with =S.H on the command line. If you are using a product other than SDSF to view output, go into it. **Use the TSO FIND command to find the character string ABEND.** Immediately after it will be a three-position code, such as S013. The "S" just stands for "system." You can look up the meaning of the code that follows "S" in Appendix E. Some codes have a suffix not shown in the ABEND line. Take the second step, shown below, to find complete information. **Put TOP on the command line.**

```
SDSF OUTPUT DISPLAY CSCJGJA  JOB09319  DSID     2 LINE 0       COLUMNS 02- 81
COMMAND INPUT ===> find '013-'                                 SCROLL ===> PAGE
********************************** TOP OF D     ***********************************
                  J E S 2  J O B      G  --  S Y S T E M  I B M 1  --  N

02.19.58 JOB09319  IRR010I  USERID             IS ASSIGNED TO THIS JOB.
02.19.59 JOB09319  ICH70001I CSCJGJ       ST ACCESS AT 02:13:11 ON SUNDAY, JANUARY
02.19.59 JOB09319  $HASP373 CSCJGJA       TED - INIT  1 - CLASS A - SYS IBM1
02.20.04 JOB09319  IEC141I 013-18,IGG0191B,CSCJGJA,STEP020,SYSIN,116,USER02,CSCJ
02.20.04 JOB09319  IEA995I SYMPTOM DUMP OUTPUT
                   SYSTEM COMPLETION CODE=013
                    TIME=02.20.03  SEQ=25286  CPU=0000  ASID=000F
                    PSW AT TIME OF ERROR  075C1000   00E8799C  ILC 2  INTC 0D
                      NO ACTIVE MODULE FOUND
                      DATA AT PSW  00E87996 - 4100395E  0A0D4DE0  39025820
```

Put TOP on the command line to return to the beginning. **Then do a FIND '013-' seeking the code you found above.** If the code has a suffix you will quickly find it. SCANIT2 does this for you.

As a second step, put "top" on the command line to bring the cursor to the top of the material you are viewing on the screen. Then do a second "find" command, this time seeking the three-position system completion code you found in the first step, followed immediately by a hyphen. For example, you see the command find '013-' in Figure 7.15. This will locate for you the full system completion code with its suffix, which is often physically listed by MVS/ESA *before* the ABEND message.

Following the simple method for this job failure, you find that this job failed in STEP020 with a system completion code of 013-18. What does this mean? Look it up in Appendix E. You'll find that I generated this problem by deleting member REG33010 in library CSCJGJ.CCARDS, the place where the sort control statement for the sort utility is stored. The line in MVS/ESA system reporting pointed to by the last arrow in Figure 7.15 indicates that this problem affects DD statement //SYSIN in STEP020.

SCANIT2 actually takes actions similar to those described above in summarizing the MVS/ESA reporting from this failed job. As you can see in Figure 7.16, SCANIT2 shows you all of the COND CODE and other step reporting lines, and picks out the most informative line for your convenience.

```
SDSF OUTPUT DISPLAY CSCJGJA  JOB09320  DSID   101 LINE 1       COLUMNS 02- 81
COMMAND INPUT ===>                                            SCROLL ===> PAGE
******************************************************************************
SCANIT2 HELPS YOU ANALYZE MVS/ESA JOB OUTPUT.  SEE MORE ABOUT THIS TOOL IN
"ADVANCED MVS JCL EXAMPLES" BY JIM JANOSSY (1994, JOHN WILEY & SONS, INC.)
******************************************************************************

02.19.58 JOB09319  IRR010I  USERID CSCJGJ   IS ASSIGNED TO THIS JOB.
IEF142I CSCJGJA STEP010 - STEP WAS EXECUTED - COND CODE 0000
IEF472I CSCJGJA STEP020 - COMPLETION CODE - SYSTEM=013 USER=0000 REASON=0000000
IEF206I CSCJGJA STEP030 - STEP WAS NOT RUN BECAUSE OF CONDITIONAL EXPRESSION
IEF206I CSCJGJA STEP040 - STEP WAS NOT RUN BECAUSE OF CONDITIONAL EXPRESSION
IEF206I CSCJGJA STEP050 - STEP WAS NOT RUN BECAUSE OF CONDITIONAL EXPRESSION
IEF206I CSCJGJA STEP060 - STEP WAS NOT RUN BECAUSE OF CONDITIONAL EXPRESSION
IEF206I CSCJGJA STEP070 - STEP WAS NOT RUN BECAUSE OF CONDITIONAL EXPRESSION
IEF206I CSCJGJA STEP080 - STEP WAS NOT RUN BECAUSE OF CONDITIONAL EXPRESSION
IEF472I CSCJGJA STEP999 - COMPLETION CODE - SYSTEM=000 USER=3333 REASON=0000000

*** NON-ZERO SYSTEM COMPLETION CODE DETECTED! ***
    THE FOLLOWING LINE GIVES BEST INFORMATION.
    LOOK FOR INFORMATION ABOUT SYSTEM COMPLETION CODE 013 BELOW:

02.20.04 JOB09319  IEC141I 013-18,IGG0191B,CSCJGJA,STEP020,SYSIN,116,USER02,CSC
```

SCANIT2 (or SCANIT3, for the JES3 environment) automates the data-gathering steps of the problem diagnosis process, extracting the most important lines of MVS/ESA reporting for a job. Here you see SCANIT2 output for job 9319, which the previous figure used to demonstrate the manual process for locating the system completion code.

Figure 7.16 MVS/ESA System Reporting for an Abended Run as Extracted by the SCANIT2 Program

7.10 Tutorial: Manipulating MVS/ESA System Reporting

You can actually take a copy of MVS/ESA system reporting printlines as a data set and process it in any way that you like, to analyze it. I will describe this process to you because it, like the use of the "find" command in examining system reporting on-line, is handy but not well documented. Knowing how to do this will make it possible for you to experiment with an analysis program such as SCANIT2, or with SCANIT2 itself should your installation license it as indicated in Appendix F.

In this discussion, I assume that you are using IBM's Spool Display and Search Facility to examine output. If you are using another product, such as Flasher or a locally programmed output viewing tool, you'll have to consult your installation's own documentation.

The first thing you need to do to capture MVS/ESA system reporting for a job is to allocate a data set to house these lines of print. Figure 7.17

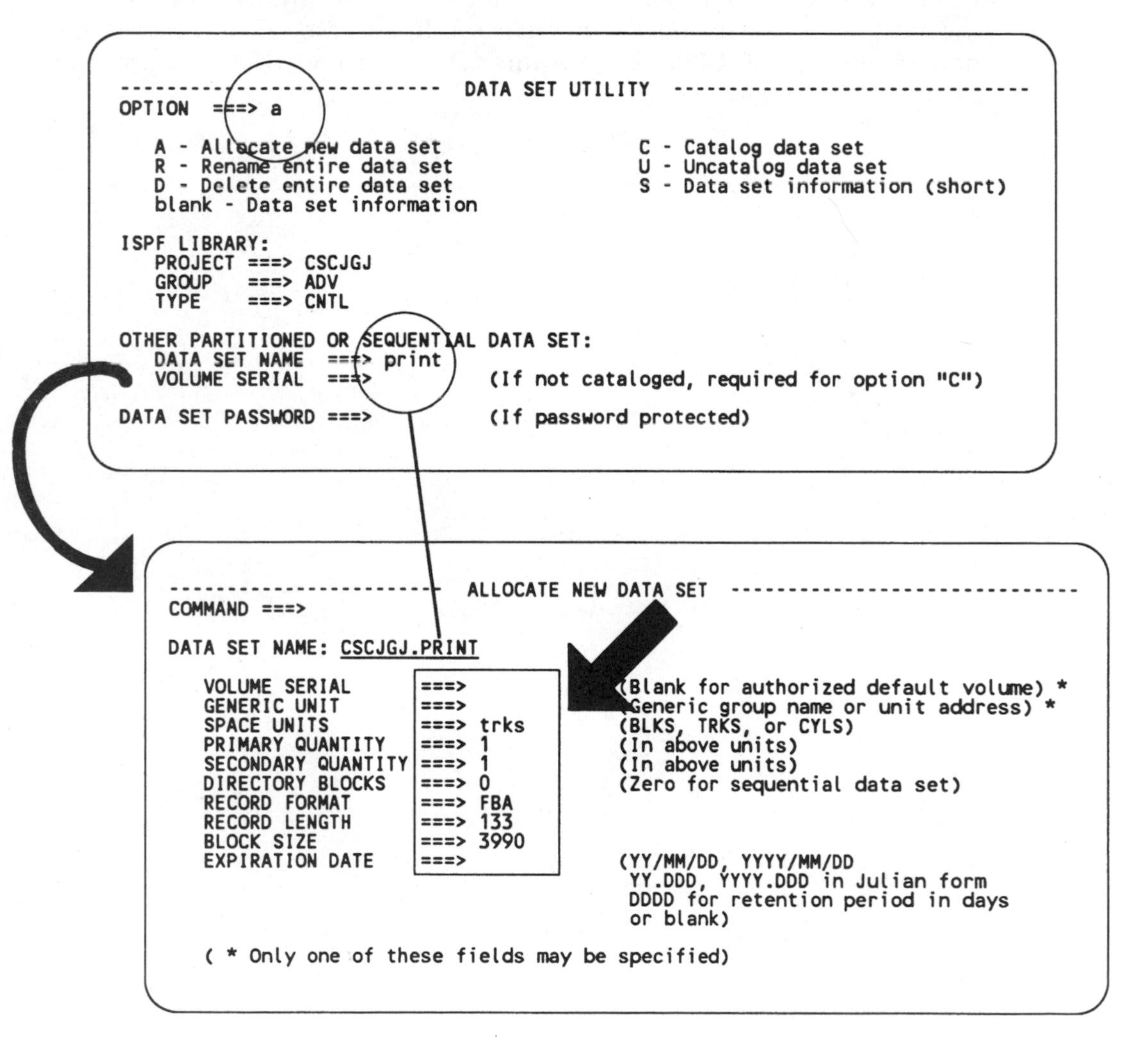

Figure 7.17 Allocating a Data Set to House a Copy of MVS/ESA System Reporting for Analysis

shows you how to use the TSO/ISPF 3.2 function to do this. I created a sequential data set named CSCJGJ.PRINT to house the system reporting printline output. You can create a partitioned data set (library) for this purpose if you wish, and store each set of output as a member, but I prefer using a sequential data set. You won't need to allocate a "print" data set again; one is enough.

Figure 7.18 shows you the sequence of actions within SDSF to capture MVS/ESA system reporting to the data set you just created. The three commands show here must be entered *when you are viewing the output:*

prt odsn print	*this opens data set name 'userid.print'*
prt	*this copies the lines being viewed to the data set that was opened*
prt close	*closes the data set*

After this sequence of actions, the printlines of the MVS/ESA system reporting exist as records in your "print" data set. In my case, since I created this data set named CSCJGJ.PRINT, it is this data set that my SCANIT2 program reads and processes.

Figure 7.18 Sequence of Actions Within SDSF to Capture MVS/ESA System Reporting to a Data Set (see facing page)

```
SDSF OUTPUT DISPLAY CSCJGJA  JOB04991  DSID     2 LINE 0       COLUMNS 02- 81
COMMAND INPUT ===> prt odsn print                               SCROLL ===> PAGE
********************************* TOP OF DATA **********************************
                           J E S 2  J O B  L O G  --  S Y S T E M  I B M 1  --  N

16.18.57 JOB04991  IRR010I  USERID CSCJGJ   IS ASSIGNED TO THIS JOB.
16.18.58 JOB04991  ICH70001I CSCJGJ   LAST ACCESS AT 16:15:34 ON THURSDAY, JANUA
16.18.58 JOB04991  $HASP373 CSCJGJA  STARTED - INIT  1 - CLASS A - SYS IBM1
16.19.36 JOB04991  $HASP395 CSCJGJA  ENDED
------ JES2 JOB STATISTICS ------
   20 JAN 94 JOB EXECUTION DATE
         178 CARDS READ
       1,549 SYSOUT PRINT RECORDS
           -
           -
           -
```

```
SDSF OUTPUT DISPLAY CSCJGJA  JOB04991  DSID     2 LINE  PRINT OPENED
COMMAND INPUT ===> prt                                          SCROLL ===> PAGE
********************************* TOP OF DATA **********************************
                           J E S 2  J O B  L O G  --  S Y S T E M  I B M 1  --  N

16.18.57 JOB04991  IRR010I  USERID CSCJGJ   IS ASSIGNED TO THIS JOB.
16.18.58 JOB04991  ICH70001I CSCJGJ   LAST ACCESS AT 16:15:34 ON THURSDAY, JANUA
16.18.58 JOB04991  $HASP373 CSCJGJA  STARTED - INIT  1 - CLASS A - SYS IBM1
16.19.36 JOB04991  $HASP395 CSCJGJA  ENDED
------ JES2 JOB STATISTICS ------
   20 JAN 94 JOB EXECUTION DATE
         178 CARDS READ
       1,549 SYSOUT PRINT RECORDS
           -
           -
           -
```

```
SDSF OUTPUT DISPLAY CSCJGJA  JOB04991  DSID     2 LINE      1,549 LINES PRINTED
COMMAND INPUT ===> prt close                                    SCROLL ===> PAGE
********************************* TOP OF DATA **********************************
                           J E S 2  J O B  L O G  --  S Y S T E M  I B M 1  --  N

16.18.57 JOB04991  IRR010I  USERID CSCJGJ   IS ASSIGNED TO THIS JOB.
16.18.58 JOB04991  ICH70001I CSCJGJ   LAST ACCESS AT 16:15:34 ON THURSDAY, JANUA
16.18.58 JOB04991  $HASP373 CSCJGJA  STARTED - INIT  1 - CLASS A - SYS IBM1
16.19.36 JOB04991  $HASP395 CSCJGJA  ENDED
------ JES2 JOB STATISTICS ------
   20 JAN 94 JOB EXECUTION DATE
         178 CARDS READ
       1,549 SYSOUT PRINT RECORDS
           -
           -
           -
```

```
SDSF OUTPUT DISPLAY CSCJGJA  JOB04991  DSID     2 LINE PRINT CLOSED  1,549 LINE
COMMAND INPUT ===>                                              SCROLL ===> PAGE
********************************* TOP OF DATA **********************************
                           J E S 2  J O B  L O G  --  S Y S T E M  I B M 1  --  N

16.18.57 JOB04991  IRR010I  USERID CSCJGJ   IS ASSIGNED TO THIS JOB.
16.18.58 JOB04991  ICH70001I CSCJGJ   LAST ACCESS AT 16:15:34 ON THURSDAY, JANUA
16.18.58 JOB04991  $HASP373 CSCJGJA
16.19.36 JOB04991  $HASP395 CSCJGJA
------ JES2 JOB STATISTICS ------
   20 JAN 94 JOB EXECUTION DATE
         178 CARDS READ
       1,549 SYSOUT PRINT RECORDS
           -
           -
           -

JOB CSCJGJA(JOB04998) SUBMITTED
***
```

With the submission of the SCANIT2 job assigned to the PF1 key, pressing it submits an execution of SCANIT2 reading the PRINT data set.

The last screen in Figure 7.18 shows how I submit the SCANIT2 job to analyze the captured MVS/ESA system reporting. I can press the <*PF1*> key to submit JCL to execute SCANIT2, because I have assigned the job submission command to this key using the KEYS command and screen. Figure 7.19 shows you how I made this assignment. Since the meaning of function keys within SDSF is stored apart from the meaning of PF keys outside of SDSF, using the <*PF1*> key in this way will not affect its use as the "help" key out-

```
 SDSF OUTPUT DISPLAY CSCJGJA  JOB04991  DSID     2 LINE PRINT CLOSED  1,549 LINE
 COMMAND INPUT ===> keys                                        SCROLL ===> PAGE
********************************* TOP OF DATA **********************************
                         J E S 2   J O B   L O G  --  S Y S T E M   I B M 1  --  N

16.18.57 JOB04991  IRR010I  USERID CSCJGJ    IS ASSIGNED TO THIS JOB.
16.18.58 JOB04991  ICH70001I CSCJGJ   LAST ACCESS AT 16:15:34 ON THURSDAY, JANUA
16.18.58 JOB04991  $HASP373 CSCJGJA  STARTED - INIT  1 - CLASS A - SYS IBM1
16.19.36 JOB04991  $HASP395 CSCJGJA  ENDED
------ JES2 JOB STATISTICS ------
    20 JAN 94 JOB EXECUTION DATE
          178 CARDS READ
        1,549 SYSOUT PRINT RECORDS
            0 SYSOUT PUNCH RECORDS
          179 SYSOUT SPOOL KBYTES
         0.62 MINUTES EXECUTION TIME
        1 //CSCJGJA   JOB 1,                      ACCOUNTING INFORMATION
          //    'BIN 7--JANOSSY',                 PROGRAMMER NAME AND DELIVERY BIN
          //    CLASS=A,                          INPUT QUEUE CLASS
          //    MSGLEVEL=(1,1),                   HOW MUCH MVS SYSTEM PRINT DESIRED
          //    MSGCLASS=X,                       PRINT DESTINATION X A L N OR O
          //    TIME=(1,0),                       SAFETY LIMIT: RUN TIME UP TO 1 MINUT
          //    REGION=3M,                        ALLOW UP TO 3 MEGS VIRTUAL MEMORY
          //*   TYPRUN=SCAN,                      UNCOMMENT THIS LINE TO DO SCAN ONLY
```

PF key for SDSF are stored apart from those in TSO/ISPF

```
---------------- PF KEY DEFINITIONS AND LABELS - ALTERNATE KEYS --------------
COMMAND ===>

NOTE: The definitions and labels below apply only to terminals with 24 PF keys.

PF1  ===> tso sub adv.cntl(scanit)
PF2  ===> SPLIT
PF3  ===> END
PF4  ===> RETURN
PF5  ===> IFIND
PF6  ===> FIND '- COND CODE'
PF7  ===> UP
PF8  ===> DOWN
PF9  ===> SWAP
PF10 ===> LEFT
PF11 ===> RIGHT
PF12 ===> RETRIEVE

PF1  LABEL ===>          PF2  LABEL ===>          PF3  LABEL ===>
PF4  LABEL ===>          PF5  LABEL ===>          PF6  LABEL ===>
PF7  LABEL ===>          PF8  LABEL ===>          PF9  LABEL ===>
PF10 LABEL ===>          PF11 LABEL ===>          PF12 LABEL ===>

Press ENTER key to display primary keys.  Enter END command to exit.
```

You can assign the submission of the SCANIT2 job to a program function key

Figure 7.19 Assigning the Submission of a System Reporting Analysis Job to a Program Function (PF) Key

side of SDSF. Once you do this key assignment, you need not do it again, since it will be retained.

The JCL to submit SCANIT2 is similar to the JCL you might use to submit any similar program to analyze stored printlines of MVS/ESA system reporting. Figure 7.20 shows you what my JCL looks like. This JCL need *not* be modified to use it repeatedly (that's why I always capture the MVS/ESA reporting to the same "print" data set).

As the ultimate in convenience, you can stack the SDSF printline capture commands and the SCANIT2 job submission command on the same key, such as *<PF1>*, as Figure 7.21 shows. By doing this, for example, I simply press *<PF1>* when viewing output to initiate a SCANIT2 analysis of it. The analysis appears as the output of a small job that I can also view while within SDSF. Use SCANIT2 or your own homegrown analysis program in the identical way. SCANIT2 (and SCANIT3 for the JES3 environment) are available from Caliber Data Training, Inc. as described in Appendix F.

```
EDIT ---- CSCJGJ.ADV.CNTL(SCANIT) - 01.00 ------------------- COLUMNS 001 072
COMMAND ===>                                                  SCROLL ===> PAGE
****** ***************************** TOP OF DATA ******************************
000001 //CSCJGJA   JOB 1,                     ACCOUNTING INFORMATION
000002 //   'BIN 7--JANOSSY',                 PROGRAMMER NAME AND DELIVERY BIN
000003 //   CLASS=A,                          INPUT QUEUE CLASS
000004 //   MSGLEVEL=(0,0),                   SHUT OFF SYSTEM MESSAGES
000005 //   MSGCLASS=X,                       PRINT DESTINATION X A L N OR O
000006 //*  TYPRUN=SCAN,                      UNCOMMENT IF WANT ONLY A JCL SCAN
000007 //   NOTIFY=CSCJGJ                     WHO TO TELL WHEN JOB IS DONE
000008 //*
000009 //*********************************************************************
000010 //* SCANIT  RUN THE SCANIT2 PROGRAM                                    *
000011 //*********************************************************************
000012 //STEP010  EXEC  PGM=SCANIT2
000013 //STEPLIB    DD  DSN=CSCJGJ.ADV.LOADLIB,DISP=SHR
000014 //           DD  DSN=SYS1.COB2LIB,DISP=SHR
000015 //INDD       DD  DSN=CSCJGJ.PRINT,DISP=SHR
000016 //OUTDD      DD  SYSOUT=*
000017 //
```

After compiling and link editing SCANIT2, its machine code resides in a load module library. This job control language executes SCANIT2, reading a file named CSCJGJ.PRINT for analysis. I use the SDSF "prt" command to copy system output to this file, then submit a run of SCANIT2 to extract the important lines from the system reporting.

Figure 7.20 JCL to Submit the SCANIT2 System Reporting Extraction Program

```
---------------- PF KEY DEFINITIONS AND LABELS - ALTERNATE KEYS ---------------
COMMAND ===>

NOTE: The definitions and labels below apply only to terminals with 24 PF keys.

PF1  ===> prt odsn print; prt; prt close; tso sub adv.cntl(scanit)
PF2  ===> SPLIT
PF3  ===> END
PF4  ===> RETURN
PF5  ===> IFIND
PF6  ===> FIND '- COND CODE'
PF7  ===> UP
PF8  ===> DOWN
PF9  ===> SWAP
PF10 ===> LEFT
PF11 ===> RIGHT
PF12 ===> RETRIEVE

PF1  LABEL ===>             PF2  LABEL ===>             PF3  LABEL ===>
PF4  LABEL ===>             PF5  LABEL ===>             PF6  LABEL ===>
PF7  LABEL ===>             PF8  LABEL ===>             PF9  LABEL ===>
PF10 LABEL ===>             PF11 LABEL ===>             PF12 LABEL ===>

Press ENTER key to display primary keys.  Enter END command to exit.
```

You can stack the SDSF "PRT" commands and job submission like this, so that MVS system reporting capture and SCANIT2 analysis take just a single keystroke. *Just remember to be viewing the output you want to analyze when you press the <PF1> key!*

Figure 7.21 Assigning "Stacked" TSO/ISPF Commands to a Program Function (PF) Key

7.11 Using the RESTART Parameter

In Figure 7.12 you saw an abend of the REG33UP1 job stream. Figure 7.13 presented the critical MVS/ESA system reporting lines that identified the nature and location of the problem, which was the lack of a //SYSOUT DD statement for the sort utility at STEP050. After correcting this problem, or any problem causing an abend, my recovery strategy in this chapter is to restart the job stream at the point that it failed, to have it continue and complete its work. How do I resume processing at STEP050 in the corrected job stream?

Figure 7.22 shows how I added the RESTART parameter to the JOB statement for the REG33UP1 job stream. For raw JCL, RESTART is coded simply as RESTART=stepname, in this case, RESTART=STEP050. If the JCL for job stream REG33UP1 were housed as a proc named REG33UP1, and I invoked it with an EXEC named //STEPA, I would have to code the RESTART as RESTART=*stepname.procstepname,* where *stepname* is the name of the step within my JCL that invokes the proc and *procstepname* is the name of the step within the proc at which I want execution to begin.

```
//CSCJGJA  JOB 1,                    ACCOUNTING INFORMATION
//    'BIN 7--JANOSSY',              PROGRAMMER NAME AND DELIVERY BIN
//    CLASS=A,                       INPUT QUEUE CLASS
//    MSGLEVEL=(1,1),                HOW MUCH MVS SYSTEM PRINT DESIRED
//    MSGCLASS=X,                    PRINT DESTINATION X A L N OR O
//    TIME=(1,0),                    SAFETY LIMIT: RUN TIME UP TO 1 MINUTE
//    REGION=3M,                     ALLOW UP TO 3 MEGS VIRTUAL MEMORY
//*   TYPRUN=SCAN,                   UNCOMMENT THIS LINE TO DO SCAN ONLY
//    RESTART=STEPA.STEP050,         RESTART JOB AT PROC'S STEP050
//    NOTIFY=CSCJGJ                  WHO TO TELL WHEN JOB IS DONE
//*
//*   RUN THE REG33UP1 UPDATE JOB STREAM USING A PROC
//*
//STEPA   EXEC R33P1
//
```

I actually demonstrate proc execution and restart in an example at the end of this chapter. Whether coded in raw JCL or in executing a proc, RESTART functions as simply a "GO TO" command at the point at which the JCL has been fully assembled, interpreted, and checked by MVS and is ready to be executed. If you have used INCLUDE statements in your JCL, they will have been processed before the action of the RESTART is attempted. In other words, RESTART acts on the completely assembled set of JCL you are invoking. It simply sends control to the location you have indicated rather than allowing JCL execution to begin at the first step.

But the system message at the bottom of the first screen in Figure 7.22 shows a puzzling problem! Apparently I have caused a JCL error in attempting my restart. How do I figure out what's going on? Well—it's back to the analysis of MVS/ESA system reporting!

The second screen in Figure 7.22 shows you the SCANIT2 extract of the restarted job. You would, of course, see these lines among all of the others if you examined the full extent of MVS/ESA system reporting. As you can see, the JCL error does not result from a simple error in inserting the RESTART parameter, as you might first assume. Things are more complicated than that. STEP050 did execute now, as did STEP060, but STEP070 failed. The last screen in Figure 7.22 shows you the detailed information about the reported JCL error. Why would the //MASTER1 DD statement in STEP070 incur a problem with data set name? To answer this question, you must examine Figure 7.23 as well as the flowchart of the job stream in Figure 7.2 and the original JCL of the REG33UP1 job stream in Figure 7.3.

```
EDIT ---- CSCJGJ.ADV.CNTL(REG33UP1) - 01.06 ------------------ COLUMNS 001 072
COMMAND ===> sub                                                SCROLL ===> PAGE
****** ***************************** TOP OF DATA ******************************
000001 //CSCJGJA   JOB 1,                   ACCOUNTING INFORMATION
000002 //    'BIN 7--JANOSSY',              PROGRAMMER NAME AND DELIVERY BIN
000003 //    CLASS=A,                       INPUT QUEUE CLASS
000004 //    MSGLEVEL=(1,1),                HOW MUCH MVS SYSTEM PRINT DESIRED
000005 //    MSGCLASS=X,                    PRINT DESTINATION X A L N OR O
000006 //    TIME=(1,0),                    SAFETY LIMIT: RUN TIME UP TO 1 MINUTE
000007 //    REGION=3M,                     ALLOW UP TO 3 MEGS VIRTUAL MEMORY
000008 //*   TYPRUN=SCAN,                   UNCOMMENT THIS LINE TO DO SCAN ONLY
000009 //    RESTART=STEP050,     <<<< STEP RESTART !
000010 //    NOTIFY=CSCJGJ                  WHO TO TELL WHEN JOB IS DONE
000011 //*
000012 //*   RUN THE REG33UP1 UPDATE JOB STREAM USING RAW JCL
000013 //*   THIS JCL IS STORED AT CSCJGJ.ADV.CNTL(REG33UP1)
000014 //*
000015 //*-----------------------------------------------------------
000016 //*   CLEANUP: DELETE DATA SETS TO BE CREATED IN RUN
000017 //*-----------------------------------------------------------

JOB CSCJGJA(JOB09338) SUBMITTED
02.36.44 JOB09338 $HASP165 CSCJGJA  ENDED AT N1 - JCL ERROR
***
```

Restart failed; why?

```
 SDSF OUTPUT DISPLAY CSCJGJA  JOB09339  DSID   101 LINE 1      COLUMNS 02- 81
 COMMAND INPUT ===>                                            SCROLL ===> PAGE
*****************************************************************************
SCANIT2 HELPS YOU ANALYZE MVS/ESA JOB OUTPUT.  SEE MORE ABOUT THIS TOOL IN
"ADVANCED MVS JCL EXAMPLES" BY JIM JANOSSY (1994, JOHN WILEY & SONS, INC.)
*****************************************************************************

 02.36.37 JOB09338  IRR010I  USERID CSCJGJ   IS ASSIGNED TO THIS JOB.
 IEF142I CSCJGJA STEP050 - STEP WAS EXECUTED - COND CODE 0000
 IEF142I CSCJGJA STEP060 - STEP WAS EXECUTED - COND CODE 0000
 IEF272I CSCJGJA STEP070 - STEP WAS NOT EXECUTED.

NO NON-ZERO SYSTEM COMPLETION CODE DETECTED
```

?

```
                        J E S 2  J O B  L O G  --  S Y S T E M  I B M 1

02.36.37 JOB09338  IRR010I  USERID CSCJGJ   IS ASSIGNED TO THIS JOB.
02.36.37 JOB09338  ICH70001I CSCJGJ   LAST ACCESS AT 02:35:14 ON SUNDAY, JANUARY
02.36.38 JOB09338  $HASP373 CSCJGJA  STARTED - INIT  1 - CLASS A - SYS IBM1
02.36.43 JOB09338  IEF453I CSCJGJA - JOB FAILED - JCL ERROR
02.36.43 JOB09338  $HASP395 CSCJGJA
------ JES2 JOB STATISTICS ------
    23 JAN 94 JOB EXECUTION DATE
          187 CARDS READ
          909 SYSOUT PRINT RECORDS
            0 SYSOUT PUNCH RECORDS
          102 SYSOUT SPOOL KBYTES
         0.10 MINUTES EXECUTION TIME
        1 //CSCJGJA   JOB 1,
          //    'BIN 7--JANOSSY',
          //    CLASS=A,
          //    MSGLEVEL=(1,1),
          //    MSGCLASS=X,
                -
                -
                -

IEF286I CSCJGJA STEP070 MASTER1 - DISP FIELD INCOMPATIBLE WITH DSNAME
IEF272I CSCJGJA STEP070 - STEP WAS NOT EXECUTED.
IEF373I STEP /STEP070 / START 94023.0236
IEF374I STEP /STEP070 / STOP  94023.0236 CPU    0MIN 00.00SEC SRB    0MIN 00.00SEC

IEF375I  JOB /CSCJGJA / START 94023.0236
IEF376I  JOB /CSCJGJA / STOP  94023.0236 CPU    0MIN 00.85SEC SRB    0MIN 00.05SEC
```

The restarted job failed in STEP070 where the new student accounts master file is referred to as the (+1) generation. This became the (0) generation when the original job ended. The JCL must be changed to do the restart!

7.12 Generation Data Sets and RESTART

If you examine Figure 7.2, you'll see that the new student account master file, a generation data set, is produced in STEP040 by program REG3307. As the next generation of the data set, the new master file is referred to as the (+1) generation at line 96 of the job stream in Figure 7.3. The new student accounts master file remains associated with the (+1) reference throughout the life of the job, and the program executed at STEP070 reads it as such at line 157. When the job ends, either normally or by failure at a subsequent step, the reference associated with the new generation of the student accounts master file "reverts" to (0). This reversion is handled automatically by MVS/ESA as it cleans up after the completed job.

By restarting the job at STEP050, I caused the JCL error in the restart when I did not change the reference to the "new" student accounts master file at line 157 from (+1) to (0). In fact, a better way to think about the file read at STEP070 is to think about it as the then "current" master file. Even in a normally functioning job, STEP070 processes the "current" master file, which happens (under normal circumstances) to be identified as the (+1) generation. But after the initial run of this job ceased, due to the failure that caused the abend, the current generation of the student accounts master file became the (0) generation.

To do a successful restart, I must temporarily change the reference at line 158 to (0) instead of (+1). (Note that line 157 became line 158 when I inserted the RESTART parameter on a line by itself in the JOB statement.) Changing the reference to (+0) is suitable as well, which is what I actually do in the first screen in Figure 7.23. To again attempt to recover this job, which has now run successfully through STEP060, I also have to change the RESTART to begin at STEP070. As you can see in the second screen in Figure 7.23, this second restart succeeds and the job ends normally. The third screen shows how I then must restore the JCL to its original form for future runs, again making the generation reference at line 158 be (+1). Figure 7.24 shows you a SCANIT2 extract of the MVS/ESA system output from the second restart. As you can see, steps 070, 080, and 090 have now executed normally, and the work of the job stream is (finally!) completed.

Figure 7.22 Submission of a Restarted Job That Ends with an Error (see facing page)

```
EDIT ---- CSCJGJ.ADV.CNTL(REG33UP1) - 01.07 ------------------ COLUMNS 001 072
COMMAND ===>                                                   SCROLL ===> PAGE
000157 //SUMREP     DD  SYSOUT=*
000158 //MASTER1    DD  DSN=CSCJGJ.REG.STUACCTS(+0),      CURRENT MASTER FILE
000159 //  DISP=SHR
000160 //DOWNRECS   DD  DSN=CSCJGJ.REG.DOWNLOAD(+1),      NEW SUMMARY FILE
000161 //  DISP=(NEW,CATLG,DELETE),
000162 //  UNIT=SYSDA,
000163 //  DCB=(CSCJGJ.CSC.MODEL,RECFM=FB,LRECL=80,BLKSIZE=22880),
```

The program at STEP070 reads the new (updated) student accounts file, the (+1) generation during the run. This reverts to the (0) generation when the job ends, regardless of whether it ends successfully or by failure. To do the restart, this reference must be changed to (0) or (+0).

```
EDIT ---- CSCJGJ.ADV.CNTL(REG33UP1) - 01.08 ------------------ COLUMNS 001 072
COMMAND ===> sub                                               SCROLL ===> PAGE
****** ***************************** TOP OF DATA ******************************
000001 //CSCJGJA   JOB 1,                   ACCOUNTING INFORMATION
000002 //   'BIN 7--JANOSSY',               PROGRAMMER NAME AND DELIVERY BIN
000003 //   CLASS=A,                        INPUT QUEUE CLASS
000004 //   MSGLEVEL=(1,1),                 HOW MUCH MVS SYSTEM PRINT DESIRED
000005 //   MSGCLASS=X,                     PRINT DESTINATION X A L N OR O
000006 //   TIME=(1,0),                     SAFETY LIMIT: RUN TIME UP TO 1 MINUTE
000007 //   REGION=3M,                      ALLOW UP TO 3 MEGS VIRTUAL MEMORY
000008 //*  TYPRUN=SCAN,                    UNCOMMENT THIS LINE TO DO SCAN ONLY
000009 //   RESTART=STEP070,     <<<< STEP RESTART !
000010 //   NOTIFY=CSCJGJ                   WHO TO TELL WHEN JOB IS DONE
000011 //*
000012 //*  RUN THE REG33UP1 UPDATE JOB STREAM USING RAW JCL
000013 //*  THIS JCL IS STORED AT CSCJGJ.ADV.CNTL(REG33UP1)
000014 //*
000015 //*-----------------------------------------------------------------
000016 //*  CLEANUP: DELETE DATA SETS TO BE CREATED IN RUN
000017 //*-----------------------------------------------------------------

JOB CSCJGJA(JOB09341) SUBMITTED
02.47.29 JOB09341 $HASP165 CSCJGJA  ENDED AT N1 CN(INTERNAL)
***
```

Job finished successfully!

```
EDIT ---- CSCJGJ.ADV.CNTL(REG33UP1) - 01.08 ------------------ COLUMNS 001 072
COMMAND ===>                                                   SCROLL ===> PAGE
000157 //SUMREP     DD  SYSOUT=*
000158 //MASTER1    DD  DSN=CSCJGJ.REG.STUACCTS(+1),      CURRENT MASTER FILE
000159 //  DISP=SHR
000160 //DOWNRECS   DD  DSN=CSCJGJ.REG.DOWNLOAD(+1),      NEW SUMMARY FILE
000161 //  DISP=(NEW,CATLG,DELETE),
000162 //  UNIT=SYSDA,
000163 //  DCB=(CSCJGJ.CSC.MODEL,RECFM=FB,LRECL=80,BLKS    880),
000164 //  SPACE=(TRK,(1,1),RLSE)
000165 //     ENDIF
        -
        -
        -
```

The job stream coding has to be returned to its original form after the restart, for future runs.

```
SDSF OUTPUT DISPLAY CSCJGJA  JOB09343  DSID   101 LINE 1      COLUMNS 02- 81
COMMAND INPUT ===>                                             SCROLL ===> PAGE
********************************************************************************
SCANIT2 HELPS YOU ANALYZE MVS/ESA JOB OUTPUT.  SEE MORE ABOUT THIS TOOL IN
"ADVANCED MVS JCL EXAMPLES" BY JIM JANOSSY (1994, JOHN WILEY & SONS, INC.)
********************************************************************************

02.47.24 JOB09341  IRR010I  USERID CSCJGJ   IS ASSIGNED TO THIS JOB.
IEF142I CSCJGJA STEP070 - STEP WAS EXECUTED - COND CODE 0000
IEF142I CSCJGJA STEP080 - STEP WAS EXECUTED - COND CODE 0000
IEF206I CSCJGJA STEP999 - STEP WAS NOT RUN BECAUSE OF CONDITIONAL EXPRESSION

NO NON-ZERO SYSTEM COMPLETION CODE DETECTED
```

The SCANIT2 extract of the second restart shows completion of job steps to finish the job. This output results from using RESTART=STEP070 after temporarily changing the reference to the student accounts file from (+1) to (+0). It would have been better to handle the recovery of the job in *one* restart rather than *two* by thoroughly understanding the actions needed to restart it after a failure. Documenting what to do to restart a job stream demands step-by-step consideration, documentation, and clear operational instructions!

Figure 7.24 MVS/ESA System Reporting for a Second Restart, Which Succeeded in Finishing the Job

7.13 Restarts and Job Stream Design

Restarts are one strategy of recovery from job failure. Job restarts work, but arranging for them demands a thorough understanding of what the failed job stream does, gained by experience with the job stream or from clear documentation about it. Restarts also demand several additional things:

- A working knowledge of JCL in general
- A degree of sophistication in recognizing how data sets are used to convey data from one step to another
- The authority and ability to change more than simply the JOB statement in a job stream to be restarted
- An understanding of how generation data sets and references to them are processed by MVS
- A job stream entirely free from passed temporary data sets, or, at least, the need to restart at a point where no temporary data set created before the point of failure is accessed at or beyond the point of restart. Since temporary data sets are deleted by MVS when a job ends normally or fails, they will not be present when a restart is initiated.

Figure 7.23 A RESTART That Requires Temporarily Changing Generation Data Set Reference *(see facing page)*

- A job stream that does not use PGM=*. . . referbacks on EXEC statements or VOL=REF=. . . referbacks on DD statements

If part of your responsibility is the design of job streams, you need to carefully plan how you will convey data from one job step to another, and arrange for data sets to be available, or deleted, for whatever job recovery strategy you intend to follow. This, of course, implies that one of your tasks as a job stream designer is to decide on the recovery strategy itself, *before or as you design the job stream,* not afterwards. I designed REG33UP1 as an example for this chapter, and the point here was to demonstrate restart as a recovery strategy. I therefore included STEP010, STEP030, and STEP080 to manage the deletion of data sets in such as way as to facilitate restarts.

7.14 Checklist for Job Restarts

It's critical to understand that you cannot do job restarts in a slapdash, cavalier, do-it-in-a-hurry manner. As I demonstrated with my REG33UP1 restart, it's possible for a poorly done restart to generate more job failures, and, even worse, to make a simple problem into a complicated mess. Here is a checklist that may help you in restarting a job that was intended, by design, to be restartable:

1. Read the MVS/ESA system reporting for the failed job to determine at what step it failed.
2. If the job failed due to a COND CODE rather than a system completion code, look in the appropriate documentation to see what the COND CODE indicates.
3. Read the operational documentation and recovery instructions associated with the step that failed.
4. Correct the program or JCL problem that caused the run to fail.
5. Read the MVS/ESA system reporting for the failed job and find out what data sets the job stream created up to the point of failure.
6. Read the MVS/ESA system reporting for the failed job and find out what data sets the job stream deleted, which might have to be re-created to serve as input for the steps to be executed in a restart.
7. Determine what data sets must be deleted, if any, for the restart to be successful.
8. Determine from the JCL what data sets the remaining steps in the job stream will access. If any of these are temporary data sets, realize that you will have to restart the job stream at a point earlier than the point of failure, in order to have these temporary data sets available for access.
9. If any of the data sets to be accessed in steps after the point of restart (which, according to the preceding point 3 might be earlier than the point of failure) are generation data sets, carefully modify the JCL to refer to (0) generations instead of (+1) generations where necessary.

10. Check the results of the restart carefully.

11. Don't forget to return the JCL to its original form after the restart!

Making temporary changes to a job stream is easier to arrange when job streams are housed as procedures (procs) rather than raw JCL. I'll show you how to arrange symbolic parameters for things such as generation data set references in procs later in this chapter.

7.15 Typical Job Stream Recovery Instructions

The designer of a job stream is the person who has the responsibility of identifying the recovery strategy intended for the job stream and of documenting recovery instructions. For a recovery strategy involving restart, this means explaining, step-by-step, what is to be done if each step fails. Operational documentation is incomplete if it lacks a clear statement of recovery strategy, and, for a restart strategy, step-by-step instructions.

This chapter would be incomplete if I did not show you what the recovery instructions for the REG33UP1 job stream should look like. To provide this, I have listed the recovery instructions in Figure 7.25, as they would appear in the paper or on-line "run book" for this production JCL. If I had read and followed these instructions, I would not have incurred a problem with my restart!

Preparing the documentation of the recovery actions indicated in Figure 7.25 involves the same thinking process demanded by automated job recovery and restart software. If your installation has acquired and uses job recovery software, you'll find that some of the actions indicated here are done by that software, but that thinking and planning is still required to produce robust and reliable job streams. You'll find that the same type of walk-through used in program logic development and coding provides significant benefits in job stream and recovery instruction design.

7.16 The REG33UP1 Job Stream Packaged as a Procedure (Proc)

Once a job stream such as REG33UP1 has been run and tested successfully as "raw" JCL, it's customary to package it as a procedure (proc) for production use. Figure 7.26 depicts the way that I housed this job stream in a proc named R33P1. As you can see from the annotations on Figure 7.26, I created symbolic parameters for six items and assigned default values for these on the PROC statement. The symbolic parameters I created fall into three categories, and all are designed to facilitate production operation.

Symbolic parameters DPRINT and UPRINT provide a means to separately assign the SYSOUT class for two different types of print, based on who usually gets it. DPRINT is print intended for technical personnel and is named for "display" print such as the output of the DISPLAY verb in COBOL programs. UPRINT is "user print," the reports and listings customarily directed to the nontechnical end users served by an automated application.

Symbolic parameters DSN1 and DSN2 carry the first and second parts of data set names. For testing purposes, for example, I assign the values

```
                    OPERATIONAL DOCUMENTATION

Job stream:      REG33UP1

Purpose:         Updates student accounts master file and
                 produces reports, download files for error
                 correction and university planning division

Recovery:        Step restart using following instructions:

If job
fails here:      Take these actions to restart and finish job:
-------------------------------------------------------------
STEP010          Submit the job again.  The only reason for a
                 failure at this step is a hardware problem with
                 the entire system, disk, or catalog failure.
-------------------------------------------------------------
STEP020          1. Determine cause of failure
                 2. Correct program or JCL error
                 3. Start job again at beginning (STEP010)
-------------------------------------------------------------
STEP030          1. Determine cause of failure
                 2. Correct program or JCL error
                 3. Restart job at STEP030
-------------------------------------------------------------
STEP040          1. Determine cause of failure
                 2. Correct program or JCL error
                 3. Change generation at STEP040 //TRANS to (0)
                 4. Restart job at STEP040
                 5. After run, change generation at STEP040
                    //TRANS back to (+1)
-------------------------------------------------------------
STEP050          1. Determine cause of failure
                 2. Correct program or JCL error
                 3. Change generation at STEP070 //MASTER1 to (0)
                 4. Restart job at STEP050
                 5. After run, change generation at STEP070
                    //MASTER1 back to (+1)
-------------------------------------------------------------
STEP060          1. Determine cause of failure
                 2. Correct program or JCL error
                 3. Change generation at STEP070 //MASTER1 to (0)
                 4. Restart job at STEP060
                 5. After run, change generation at STEP070
                    //MASTER1 back to (+1)
-------------------------------------------------------------
STEP070          1. Determine cause of failure
                 2. Correct program or JCL error
                 3. Change generation at STEP070 //MASTER1 to (0)
                 4. Restart job at STEP070
                 5. After run, change generation at STEP070
                    //MASTER1 back to (+1)
-------------------------------------------------------------
STEP080          Restart at STEP080.  The only reason for a
                 failure at this step is a hardware problem with
                 the entire system, disk, or catalog failure.
```

Figure 7.25 Example of Adequate Restart Instructions in Operational Documentation

---

Figure 7.26 The REG33UP1 Jobstream Packaged as Proc R33P1 with Symbolic Parameters and Defaults (see facing page)

```
EDIT ---- CSCJGJ.ADV.PROCLIB1(R33P1) - 01.09 ---------------- COLUMNS 001 072
COMMAND ===>                                                  SCROLL ===> PAGE
****** ****************************** TOP OF DATA ******************************
000001 //R33P1    PROC  DPRINT='*',       PRINT CLASS FOR DISPLAY, SYS OUTPUTS
000002 //*********************************************************************
000003 //*
000004 //*        UPDATE STUDENT ACCOUNTS MASTER FILE WITH TRANSACTIONS
000005 //*        FROM VARIOUS SOURCES, PRODUCE REPORTING AND DOWNLOAD FILES.
000006 //*        UPDATED MASTER FILE GENERATIONS ARE LATER RELOADED TO VSAM
000007 //*
000008 //******** PROC-SPECIFIC SYMBOLIC PARAMETER DOCUMENTATION: ***********
000009 //*
000010 //  UPRINT='L',                    PRINT CLASS FOR USER OUTPUTS
000011 //  DSN1='REGIS',                  FIRST PART OF DATA SET NAMES
000012 //  DSN2='APP33',                  SECOND PART OF DATA SET NAMES
000013 //  TRSGEN='+1',                   TRANSORT GENERATION
000014 //  STUGEN='+1'                    NEW STU ACCNTS MAST. FILE GENERATION
000015 //*-------------------------------------------------------------------
000016 //*  CLEANUP: DELETE DATA SETS TO BE CREATED IN RUN
000017 //*-------------------------------------------------------------------
000018 //STEP010  EXEC  PGM=IEFBR14
000019 //DELETE1    DD  DSN=&DSN1..&DSN2..FIN,            DATA SET TO BE
000020 //  DISP=(MOD,DELETE),                            RE-CREATED IN RUN
000021 //  UNIT=SYSDA,
000022 //  SPACE=(TRK,0)
000023 //DELETE2    DD  DSN=&DSN1..&DSN2..FINSORT,        DATA SET TO BE
000024 //  DISP=(MOD,DELETE),                            RE-CREATED IN RUN
000025 //  UNIT=SYSDA,
000026 //  SPACE=(TRK,0)
000027 //DELETE3    DD  DSN=&DSN1..&DSN2..BADTRANS,       DATA SET TO BE
000028 //  DISP=(MOD,DELETE),                            RE-CREATED IN RUN
000029 //  UNIT=SYSDA,
000030 //  SPACE=(TRK,0)
```

This is the REG33UP1 job stream housed as a procedure (proc). I have assigned symbolic parameters to several items to make them convenient to change. The same-line documentation describes these symbolic parameters. **DPRINT** and **UPRINT** segregate "display" output, such as DISPLAYs from COBOL programs and "system print" such as utility program messages, from print destined for end users. **DSN1** and **DSN2** give separate access to the first and second parts of all data set names in the proc. DSN1 and DSN2 make it easy to use test data sets for testing and maintenance, while using production data set names for production runs. **TRSGEN** and **STUGEN** give access to the generation number for the TRANSORT and STUACCNT generation data sets. These make it easier to change generation coding from (+1) to (0) as may be necessary for a restart of the job. The defaults shown for symbolic parameters are for a production run. The "execution deck" JCL shown in Figure 7.27 supplies some of these same values to the symbolic parameters but uses different ones for print destinations and DSN1 and DSN2. You can see the substitution of symbolic parameter values into the proc in the MVS/ESA system output shown in Figure 7.28. ***Note (on the third page of this proc) that there seems to be a bug in MVS/ESA Version 4. I found it necessary to code two ENDIFs at the last step to allow the proc to be accepted!***

```
000031 //*-------------------------------------------------------------------
000032 //*  READ CONCATENATED TRANSACTION INPUTS, SORT THEM INTO ONE DATA SET
000033 //*-------------------------------------------------------------------
000034 //       IF ( NOT ABEND AND RC <= 4 ) THEN           NOTE: INPUTS ARE
000035 //STEP020  EXEC  PGM=SORT                            UPLOADED BY USERS
000036 //SYSOUT     DD  SYSOUT=&DPRINT
000037 //*
000038 //SORTIN     DD  DSN=&DSN1..&DSN2..TELTR,
000039 //  DISP=(MOD,CATLG,CATLG),
000040 //  UNIT=SYSDA,
000041 //  DCB=(RECFM=FB,LRECL=68,BLKSIZE=22848),
000042 //  SPACE=(TRK,0)
000043 //*
000044 //           DD  DSN=&DSN1..&DSN2..CASHTR,
000045 //  DISP=(MOD,CATLG,CATLG),
000046 //  UNIT=SYSDA,
000047 //  DCB=(RECFM=FB,LRECL=68,BLKSIZE=22848),
000048 //  SPACE=(TRK,0)
000049 //*
000050 //           DD  DSN=&DSN1..&DSN2..FIXEDTR,
000051 //  DISP=(MOD,CATLG,CATLG),
000052 //  UNIT=SYSDA,
000053 //  DCB=(RECFM=FB,LRECL=68,BLKSIZE=22848),
000054 //  SPACE=(TRK,0)
000055 //*
000056 //SORTOUT    DD  DSN=&DSN1..&DSN2..TRANSORT(&TRSGEN),   OUTPUT IS
000057 //  DISP=(NEW,CATLG,DELETE),                            BACKUP, GDS
000058 //  UNIT=SYSDA,
000059 //  DCB=(CSCJGJ.CSC.MODEL,RECFM=FB,LRECL=68,BLKSIZE=22848),
000060 //  SPACE=(CYL,(2,1),RLSE)
000061 //*
000062 //SORTWK01   DD  UNIT=VIO,SPACE=(CYL,(1,1))
000063 //SORTWK02   DD  UNIT=VIO,SPACE=(CYL,(1,1))
000064 //SORTWK03   DD  UNIT=VIO,SPACE=(CYL,(1,1))
000065 //SYSIN      DD  DSN=CSCJGJ.CCARDS(REG33010),DISP=SHR
000066 //   ENDIF
000067 //*-------------------------------------------------------------------
000068 //*  DELETE INPUT DATA SETS AFTER SUCCESSFUL SORT
000069 //*-------------------------------------------------------------------
000070 //       IF ( NOT ABEND AND RC <= 4 ) THEN
000071 //STEP030  EXEC  PGM=IEFBR14
000072 //DELETE1    DD  DSN=&DSN1..&DSN2..TELTR,             INPUT DELETED TO
000073 //  DISP=(MOD,DELETE),                                PREVENT REDUNDANT
000074 //  UNIT=SYSDA,                                       PROCESSING
000075 //  SPACE=(TRK,0)
000076 //DELETE2    DD  DSN=&DSN1..&DSN2..CASHTR,            INPUT DELETED TO
000077 //  DISP=(MOD,DELETE),                                PREVENT REDUNDANT
000078 //  UNIT=SYSDA,                                       PROCESSING
000079 //  SPACE=(TRK,0)
000080 //DELETE3    DD  DSN=&DSN1..&DSN2..FIXEDTR,           INPUT DELETED TO
000081 //  DISP=(MOD,DELETE),                                PREVENT REDUNDANT
000082 //  UNIT=SYSDA,                                       PROCESSING
000083 //  SPACE=(TRK,0)
000084 //       ENDIF
000085 //*-------------------------------------------------------------------
000086 //*  UPDATE THE STUACCTS MASTER FILE
000087 //*-------------------------------------------------------------------
000088 //       IF ( NOT ABEND AND RC <= 4 ) THEN
000089 //STEP040  EXEC  PGM=REG3307
000090 //STEPLIB    DD  DSN=CSCJGJ.ADV.LOADLIB,DISP=SHR
000091 //           DD  DSN=SYS1.COB2LIB,DISP=SHR
000092 //SYSOUT     DD  SYSOUT=&DPRINT
000093 //TRANS      DD  DSN=&DSN1..&DSN2..TRANSORT(&TRSGEN),  NEW SORTED TRANS
000094 //  DISP=SHR
000095 //OLDMAST    DD  DSN=&DSN1..&DSN2..STUACCTS(0),        OLD MASTER FILE
000096 //  DISP=SHR
000097 //NEWMAST    DD  DSN=&DSN1..&DSN2..STUACCTS(&STUGEN),  NEW MASTER FILE
000098 //  DISP=(NEW,CATLG,DELETE),
000099 //  UNIT=SYSDA,
000100 //  DCB=(CSCJGJ.CSC.MODEL,RECFM=FB,LRECL=177,BLKSIZE=22833),
000101 //  SPACE=(CYL,(2,1),RLSE)
000102 //FINTRANS   DD  DSN=&DSN1..&DSN2..FIN,                FINISHED TRANS
000103 //  DISP=(NEW,CATLG,DELETE),
000104 //  UNIT=SYSDA,
000105 //  RECFM=FB,
000106 //  LRECL=92,
000107 //  SPACE=(CYL,(1,1),RLSE)
000108 //AUDREP     DD  SYSOUT=&UPRINT                          AUDIT REPORT
```

To use symbolic parameters for parts of data set name you must specify two periods between name parts.

Figure 7.26 (continued)

```
000109 //      ENDIF
000110 //*-----------------------------------------------------------------------
000111 //*  SORT FINISHED TRANSACTIONS FOR DETAILED REPORTING
000112 //*-----------------------------------------------------------------------
000113 //      IF ( NOT ABEND AND RC <= 4 ) THEN
000114 //STEP050  EXEC  PGM=SORT
000115 //SYSOUT     DD  SYSOUT=&DPRINT
000116 //SORTIN     DD  DSN=&DSN1..&DSN2..FIN,DISP=SHR
000117 //SORTOUT    DD  DSN=&DSN1..&DSN2..FINSORT,             SORTED, FINISHED
000118 //  DISP=(NEW,CATLG,DELETE),                              TRANSACTIONS
000119 //  UNIT=SYSDA,
000120 //  RECFM=FB,
000121 //  LRECL=92,
000122 //  SPACE=(CYL,(2,1),RLSE)
000123 //SORTWK01   DD  UNIT=VIO,SPACE=(CYL,(1,1))
000124 //SORTWK02   DD  UNIT=VIO,SPACE=(CYL,(1,1))
000125 //SORTWK03   DD  UNIT=VIO,SPACE=(CYL,(1,1))
000126 //SYSIN      DD  DSN=CSCJGJ.CCARDS(REG33030),
000127 //  DISP=SHR
000128 //      ENDIF
000129 //*-----------------------------------------------------------------------
000130 //*  PRODUCE ACCOUNTING, REGISTRAR RPTS AND "BAD TRANS" DOWNLOAD FILE
000131 //*-----------------------------------------------------------------------
000132 //      IF ( NOT ABEND AND RC <= 4 ) THEN
000133 //STEP060  EXEC  PGM=REG3308
000134 //STEPLIB    DD  DSN=CSCJGJ.ADV.LOADLIB,DISP=SHR
000135 //           DD  DSN=SYS1.COB2LIB,DISP=SHR
000136 //SYSOUT     DD  SYSOUT=&DPRINT
000137 //FTRANS     DD  DSN=&DSN1..&DSN2..FINSORT,DISP=SHR
000138 //GOODREP    DD  SYSOUT=&UPRINT,COPIES=2            TO ACCTNG, REGIS
000139 //*
000140 //BADREP     DD  SYSOUT=&UPRINT                     TO ACCTNG ONLY
000141 //*
000142 //BADTR      DD  DSN=&DSN1..&DSN2..BADTRANS,        FOR ACCTNG DOWNLOAD,
000143 //  DISP=(NEW,CATLG,DELETE),                         CORRECTION, AND
000144 //  UNIT=SYSDA,                                      SUBSEQUENT UPLOAD
000145 //  RECFM=FB,                                        TO FIXEDTR FILE
000146 //  LRECL=68,                                        THAT IS INPUT TO
000147 //  SPACE=(CYL,(1,1),RLSE)                           A SUBSEQUENT RUN
000148 //      ENDIF
000149 //*-----------------------------------------------------------------------
000150 //*  CREATE THE NEW DOWNLOAD SUMMARY FILE FOR UNIVERSITY PLANNING DIV.
000151 //*-----------------------------------------------------------------------
000152 //      IF ( NOT ABEND AND RC <= 4 ) THEN
000153 //STEP070  EXEC  PGM=REG3350
000154 //STEPLIB    DD  DSN=CSCJGJ.ADV.LOADLIB,DISP=SHR
000155 //           DD  DSN=SYS1.COB2LIB,DISP=SHR
000156 //SYSOUT     DD  SYSOUT=&DPRINT
000157 //SUMREP     DD  SYSOUT=&UPRINT
000158 //MASTER1    DD  DSN=&DSN1..&DSN2..STUACCTS(&STUGEN),  CUR MASTER FILE
000159 //  DISP=SHR
000160 //DOWNRECS   DD  DSN=&DSN1..&DSN2..DOWNLOAD(+1),       NEW SUMMARY FILE
000161 //  DISP=(NEW,CATLG,DELETE),
000162 //  UNIT=SYSDA,
000163 //  DCB=(CSCJGJ.CSC.MODEL,RECFM=FB,LRECL=80,BLKSIZE=22880),
000164 //  SPACE=(TRK,(1,1),RLSE)
000165 //      ENDIF
000166 //*-----------------------------------------------------------------------
000167 //*  CLEANUP: DELETE INTERMEDIATE DATA SETS TO BE CREATED IN RUN
000168 //*-----------------------------------------------------------------------
000169 //      IF ( NOT ABEND AND RC <= 4 ) THEN
000170 //STEP080  EXEC  PGM=IEFBR14
000171 //DELETE1    DD  DSN=&DSN1..&DSN2..FIN,             INTERMEDIATE
000172 //  DISP=(MOD,DELETE),                               DATA SET
000173 //  UNIT=SYSDA,
000174 //  SPACE=(TRK,0)
000175 //DELETE2    DD  DSN=&DSN1..&DSN2..FINSORT,         INTERMEDIATE
000176 //  DISP=(MOD,DELETE),                               DATA SET
000177 //  UNIT=SYSDA,
000178 //  SPACE=(TRK,0)
000179 //      ENDIF
000180 //*-----------------------------------------------------------------------
000181 //*  ATTENTION GRABBER: ISSUE USER ABEND 3333 IF RUN FAILED
000182 //*-----------------------------------------------------------------------
000183 //      IF ( ABEND OR RC > 4 ) THEN
000184 //STEP999  EXEC  PGM=USERABN,PARM=3333
000185 //STEPLIB    DD  DSN=CSCJGJ.ADV.LOADLIB,DISP=SHR
000186 //           DD  DSN=SYS1.COB2LIB,DISP=SHR
000187 //      ENDIF
000188 //      ENDIF
```

MVS/ESA bug! Need two ENDIFs at proc end?

Figure 7.26 (continued)

CSCJGJ and REG to these symbolic parameters, so all data sets referenced in the proc become CSCJGJ.REG.xxxxxxxx, where xxxxxxxxx is the unique part of the data set name hardcoded in the proc. A name such as CSCJGJ.REG.xxxxxxxx identifies (in my shop) a test data set, not a production "live data" data set. The proc default values for DSN1 and DSN2 are REGIS and APP33, which form a data set name such as REGIS.APP33. xxxxxxxx. This is a production data set name, to which different standards of access security and data integrity apply.

I used symbolic parameters named TSRGEN and STUGEN to carry the generation numbers used to access the TRANSORT and STUACCTS data sets. These symbolic parameters make it easier to change the generation numbers to '0' as appropriate for a restart, as documented in the recovery instructions shown in Figure 7.25. By default, both of these are assigned the value '+1' in the proc.

7.17 Executing Proc R33P1

Figure 7.27 shows you the "run" or execution deck (JCL) that will invoke the R33P1 proc, which I have stored as member XR33P1 (the "X" is my convention for "execution" JCL). The same-line comments clearly document the parameters that "feed" into the proc and summarize the restart instructions. Notice that in this submission of the proc for execution I have listed all six symbolic parameters, even though I am supplying some of the same values used in the proc as defaults. This causes no harm and makes all of the parameters accessible with very little modification of the execution JCL.

```
EDIT ---- CSCJGJ.EXEC.DECK(XR33P1) - 01.05 ------------------ COLUMNS 001 072
COMMAND ===>                                                  SCROLL ===> PAGE
****** ****************************** TOP OF DATA *******************************
000001 //CSCJGJA   JOB 1,                  ACCOUNTING INFORMATION
000002 //    'BIN 7--JANOSSY',             PROGRAMMER NAME AND DELIVERY BIN
000003 //    CLASS=A,                      INPUT QUEUE CLASS
000004 //    MSGLEVEL=(1,1),               HOW MUCH MVS SYSTEM PRINT DESIRED
000005 //    MSGCLASS=X,                   PRINT DESTINATION X A L N OR O
000006 //    TIME=(1,0),                   SAFETY LIMIT: RUN TIME UP TO 1 MINUTE
000007 //    REGION=3M,                    ALLOW UP TO 3 MEGS VIRTUAL MEMORY
000008 //*   TYPRUN=SCAN,                  UNCOMMENT THIS LINE TO DO SCAN ONLY
000009 //    NOTIFY=CSCJGJ                 WHO TO TELL WHEN JOB IS DONE
000010 //        JCLLIB  ORDER=('CSCJGJ.ADV.PROCLIB1')
000011 //*-------------------------------------------------------------
000012 //*   UPDATE THE STUDENT ACCNTS MASTER FILE, PRODUCE DOWNLOAD FILES
000013 //*   THIS JCL IS STORED AT CSCJGJ.EXEC.DECK(XR33P1)
000014 //*-------------------------------------------------------------
000015 //STEPA    EXEC  R33P1,
000016 //  UPRINT='*',           PRINT CLASS FOR USER OUTPUTS
000017 //  DPRINT='*',           PRINT CLASS FOR DISPLAY, SYS OUTPUTS
000018 //  DSN1='CSCJGJ',        FIRST PART OF DATA SET NAMES
000019 //  DSN2='REG',           SECOND PART OF DATA SET NAMES
000020 //*
000021 //  TRSGEN='+1',          TRANSORT GENERATION; MAKE '0' TO
000022 //*                      RECOVER AT STEP040
000023 //*
000024 //  STUGEN='+1'           NEW STU ACCNTS MAST. FILE GENERATION;
000025 //*                      MAKE '0' TO RECOVER AT STEP050 OR
000026 //*                      STEP060 OR STEP070
000027 //
```

Restart instructions

Figure 7.27 "Execution Deck" (Execution JCL) for the R33P1 Proc, Set for Proc Testing

```
                    J E S 2  J O B  L O G  --  S Y S T E M  I B M 1  --  N O D E  N 1

12.35.35 JOB04769  IRR010I  USERID CSCJGJ   IS ASSIGNED TO THIS JOB.
12.35.36 JOB04769  ICH70001I CSCJGJ   LAST ACCESS AT 12:31:05 ON THURSDAY, JANUARY 27, 1994
12.35.36 JOB04769  $HASP373 CSCJGJA  STARTED - INIT  1 - CLASS A - SYS IBM1
12.35.59 JOB04769  $HASP395 CSCJGJA  ENDED

------ JES2 JOB STATISTICS ------
  27 JAN 94 JOB EXECUTION DATE
         26 CARDS READ
      1,651 SYSOUT PRINT RECORDS
          0 SYSOUT PUNCH RECORDS
        186 SYSOUT SPOOL KBYTES
       0.37 MINUTES EXECUTION TIME

        1 //CSCJGJA   JOB 1,                   ACCOUNTING INFORMATION
          //    'BIN 7--JANOSSY',              PROGRAMMER NAME AND DELIVERY BIN
          //    CLASS=A,                       INPUT QUEUE CLASS
          //    MSGLEVEL=(1,1),                HOW MUCH MVS SYSTEM PRINT DESIRED
          //    MSGCLASS=X,                    PRINT DESTINATION X A L N OR O
          //    TIME=(1,0),                    SAFETY LIMIT: RUN TIME UP TO 1 MINUTE
          //    REGION=3M,                     ALLOW UP TO 3 MEGS VIRTUAL MEMORY
          //*   TYPRUN=SCAN,                   UNCOMMENT THIS LINE TO DO SCAN ONLY
          //    NOTIFY=CSCJGJ                  WHO TO TELL WHEN JOB IS DONE
        2 //       JCLLIB  ORDER=('CSCJGJ.ADV.PROCLIB1')
          //*-----------------------------------------------------------------
          //*   UPDATE THE STUDENT ACCNTS MASTER FILE, PRODUCE DOWNLOAD FILES
          //*   THIS JCL IS STORED AT CSCJGJ.EXEC.DECK(XR33P1)
          //*-----------------------------------------------------------------
        3 //STEPA     EXEC  R33P1,
          //  UPRINT='*',            PRINT CLASS FOR USER OUTPUTS
          //  DPRINT='*',            PRINT CLASS FOR DISPLAY, SYS OUTPUTS
          //  DSN1='CSCJGJ',         FIRST PART OF DATA SET NAMES
          //  DSN2='REG',            SECOND PART OF DATA SET NAMES
          //*
          //  TRSGEN='+1',           TRANSORT GENERATION; MAKE '0' TO
          //*                        RECOVER AT STEP040
          //*
          //  STUGEN='+1'            NEW STU ACCNTS MAST. FILE GENERATION;
        4 XXR33P1    PROC  DPRINT='*',      PRINT CLASS FOR DISPLAY, SYS OUTPUTS
          XX*****************************************************************
```

This is the MVS/ESA system output produced by submission of the execution JCL shown in Figure 7.27. I am running the proc R33P1 with "test" data set names formed with CSCJGJ and REG as the first and second parts. Execution JCL is listed with slashes in front, as it appears on the screen used to SUBmit it for processing. JCL brought into this job from the proc being invoked is listed by MVS/ESA with "XX" in front instead of "//".

Figure 7.28 MVS/ESA System Output for a Successful Run of the R33P1 Proc

```
     XX*
     XX*        UPDATE STUDENT ACCOUNTS MASTER FILE WITH TRANSACTIONS
     XX*        FROM VARIOUS SOURCES, PRODUCE REPORTING AND DOWNLOAD FILES.
     XX*        UPDATED MASTER FILE GENERATIONS ARE LATER RELOADED TO VSAM
     XX*
     XX******** PROC-SPECIFIC SYMBOLIC PARAMETER DOCUMENTATION: ***********
     XX*
     XX  UPRINT='L',                PRINT CLASS FOR USER OUTPUTS
     XX  DSN1='REGIS',              FIRST PART OF DATA SET NAMES
     XX  DSN2='APP33',              SECOND PART OF DATA SET NAMES
     XX  TRSGEN='+1',               TRANSORT GENERATION
     XX  STUGEN='+1'                NEW STU ACCNTS MAST. FILE GENERATION
     XX*-----------------------------------------------------------------
     XX*  CLEANUP: DELETE DATA SETS TO BE CREATED IN
     XX*-----------------------------------------------------------------
   5 XXSTEP010  EXEC  PGM=IEFBR14
   6 XXDELETE1    DD  DSN=&DSN1..&DSN2..FIN,               DATA SET TO BE
     XX  DISP=(MOD,DELETE),                                RE-CREATED IN RUN
     XX  UNIT=SYSDA,
     XX  SPACE=(TRK,0)
     IEFC653I SUBSTITUTION JCL - DSN=CSCJGJ.REG.FIN,DISP=(MOD,DELETE),UNIT=SYSDA,SPACE=(TRK,0)
   7 XXDELETE2    DD  DSN=&DSN1..&DSN2..FINSORT,           DATA SET TO BE
     XX  DISP=(MOD,DELETE),                                RE-CREATED IN RUN
     XX  UNIT=SYSDA,
     XX  SPACE=(TRK,0)
     IEFC653I SUBSTITUTION JCL - DSN=CSCJGJ.REG.FINSORT,DISP=(MOD,DELETE),UNIT=SYSDA,SPACE=(TRK,0)
   8 XXDELETE3    DD  DSN=&DSN1..&DSN2..BADTRANS,          DATA SET TO BE
     XX  DISP=(MOD,DELETE),                                RE-CREATED IN RUN
     XX  UNIT=SYSDA,
     XX  SPACE=(TRK,0)
     XX*-----------------------------------------------------------------
     XX*  READ CONCATENATED TRANSACTION INPUTS, SORT THEM INTO ONE DATA SET
     XX*-----------------------------------------------------------------
     IEFC653I SUBSTITUTION JCL - DSN=CSCJGJ.REG.BADTRANS,DISP=(MOD,DELETE),UNIT=SYSDA,SPACE=(TRK,0)
   9 XX      IF ( NOT ABEND AND RC <= 4 ) THEN             NOTE: INPUTS ARE
  10 XXSTEP020  EXEC  PGM=SORT                             UPLOADED BY USERS
  11 XXSYSOUT     DD  SYSOUT=&DPRINT
     XX*
     IEFC653I SUBSTITUTION JCL - SYSOUT=*
  12 XXSORTIN     DD  DSN=&DSN1..&DSN2..TELTR,             TELEPHONE REGIS.
     XX  DISP=(MOD,CATLG,CATLG),                           DATA SET MAY OR
     XX  UNIT=SYSDA,                                       MAY NOT EXIST!
     XX  DCB=(RECFM=FB,LRECL=68,BLKSIZE=22848),
```

Substitution of the symbolic parameters DSN1 and DSN2 form a data set name. The name consists of DSN1 and DSN2, to which is concatenated the third part of the data set name hardcoded in the proc. Using symbolic parameters like this is a reliable way to switch between "test" and "production" data set names.

Figure 7.28 (continued)

```
    XX  SPACE=(TRK,0)
    XX*
    IEFC653I SUBSTITUTION JCL - DSN=CSCJGJ.REG.TELTR,DISP=(MOD,CATLG,CATLG),UNIT=SYSDA,DCB=(RECFM=FB,LRECL=68,
    BLKSIZE=22848),SPACE=(TRK,0)
 13 XX            DD   DSN=&DSN1..&DSN2..CASHTR,          CASHIER'S TRANS.
    XX  DISP=(MOD,CATLG,CATLG),                          DATA SET MAY OR
    XX  UNIT=SYSDA,                                      MAY NOT EXIST!
    XX  DCB=(RECFM=FB,LRECL=68,BLKSIZE=22848),
    XX  SPACE=(TRK,0)
    XX*
    IEFC653I SUBSTITUTION JCL - DSN=CSCJGJ.REG.CASHTR,DISP=(MOD,CATLG,CATLG),UNIT=SYSDA,DCB=(RECFM=FB,LRECL=68,
    BLKSIZE=22848),SPACE=(TRK,0)
 14 XX            DD   DSN=&DSN1..&DSN2..FIXEDTR,         CORRECTED TRANS.
    XX  DISP=(MOD,CATLG,CATLG),                          DATA SET MAY OR
    XX  UNIT=SYSDA,                                      MAY NOT EXIST!
    XX  DCB=(RECFM=FB,LRECL=68,BLKSIZE=22848),
    XX  SPACE=(TRK,0)
    XX*
    IEFC653I SUBSTITUTION JCL - DSN=CSCJGJ.REG.FIXEDTR,DISP=(MOD,CATLG,
    BLKSIZE=22848),SPACE=(TRK,0)
 15 XXSORTOUT     DD   DSN=&DSN1..&DSN2..TRANSORT(&TRSGEN),  OUTPUT IS
    XX  DISP=(NEW,CATLG,DELETE),                             BACKUP, GDS
    XX  UNIT=SYSDA,
    XX  DCB=(CSCJGJ.CSC.MODEL,RECFM=FB,LRECL=68,BLKSIZE=22848),
    XX  SPACE=(CYL,(2,1),RLSE)
    XX*
    IEFC653I SUBSTITUTION JCL - DSN=CSCJGJ.REG.TRANSORT(+1),DISP=(NEW,CATLG,DELETE),UNIT=SYSDA,
    DCB=(CSCJGJ.CSC.MODEL,RECFM=FB,LRECL=68,BLKSIZE=22848),SPACE=(CYL,(2,1),RLSE)
 16 XXSORTWK01    DD   UNIT=VIO,SPACE=(CYL,(1,1))
 17 XXSORTWK02    DD   UNIT=VIO,SPACE=(CYL,(1,1))
 18 XXSORTWK03    DD   UNIT=VIO,SPACE=(CYL,(1,1))
 19 XXSYSIN       DD   DSN=CSCJGJ.CCARDS(REG33010),DISP=SHR
 20 XX    ENDIF
    XX*---------------------------------------------------------------------
    XX*  DELETE INPUT DATA SETS AFTER SUCCESSFUL SORT
    XX*---------------------------------------------------------------------
 21 XX      IF ( NOT ABEND AND RC <= 4 ) THEN
 22 XXSTEP030  EXEC  PGM=IEFBR14
 23 XXDELETE1     DD   DSN=&DSN1..&DSN2..TELTR,           INPUT DELETED TO
    XX  DISP=(MOD,DELETE),                               PREVENT REDUNDANT
    XX  UNIT=SYSDA,                                      PROCESSING
    XX  SPACE=(TRK,0)
    IEFC653I SUBSTITUTION JCL - DSN=CSCJGJ.REG.TELTR,DISP=(MOD,DELETE),UNIT=SYSDA,SPACE=(TRK,0)
```

Can't use VIO here because data sets may exist, and would be on a SYSDA or other physical device.

Figure 7.28 (continued)

```
24 XXDELETE2    DD  DSN=&DSN1..&DSN2..CASHTR,          INPUT DELETED TO
   XX  DISP=(MOD,DELETE),                              PREVENT REDUNDANT
   XX  UNIT=SYSDA,                                     PROCESSING
   XX  SPACE=(TRK,0)
   IEFC653I SUBSTITUTION JCL - DSN=CSCJGJ.REG.CASHTR,DISP=(MOD,DELETE),UNIT=SYSDA,SPACE=(TRK,0)
25 XXDELETE3    DD  DSN=&DSN1..&DSN2..FIXEDTR,         INPUT DELETED TO
   XX  DISP=(MOD,DELETE),                              PREVENT REDUNDANT
   XX  UNIT=SYSDA,                                     PROCESSING
   XX  SPACE=(TRK,0)
   IEFC653I SUBSTITUTION JCL - DSN=CSCJGJ.REG.FIXEDTR,DISP=(MOD,DELETE),UNIT=SYSDA,SPACE=(TRK,0)
26 XX     ENDIF
   XX*-------------------------------------------------------------------
   XX*  UPDATE THE STUACCTS MASTER FILE
   XX*-------------------------------------------------------------------
27 XX     IF ( NOT ABEND AND RC <= 4 ) THEN
28 XXSTEP040  EXEC  PGM=REG3307
29 XXSTEPLIB    DD  DSN=CSCJGJ.ADV.LOADLIB,DISP=SHR
30 XX           DD  DSN=SYS1.COB2LIB,DISP=SHR
31 XXSYSOUT     DD  SYSOUT=&DPRINT
   IEFC653I SUBSTITUTION JCL - SYSOUT=*
32 XXTRANS      DD  DSN=&DSN1..&DSN2..TRANSORT(&TRSGEN),  NEW SORTED TRANS
   XX  DISP=SHR
   IEFC653I SUBSTITUTION JCL - DSN=CSCJGJ.REG.TRANSORT(+1),DISP=SHR
33 XXOLDMAST    DD  DSN=&DSN1..&DSN2..STUACCTS(0),        OLD MASTER FILE
   XX  DISP=SHR
   IEFC653I SUBSTITUTION JCL - DSN=CSCJGJ.REG.STUACCTS(0),DISP=SHR
34 XXNEWMAST    DD  DSN=&DSN1..&DSN2..STUACCTS(&STUGEN),  NEW MASTER FILE
   XX  DISP=(NEW,CATLG,DELETE),
   XX  UNIT=SYSDA,
   XX  DCB=(CSCJGJ.CSC.MODEL,RECFM=FB,LRECL=177,BLKSIZE=22833),
   XX  SPACE=(CYL,(2,1),RLSE)
   IEFC653I SUBSTITUTION JCL - DSN=CSCJGJ.REG.STUACCTS(+1),DISP=(NEW,CATLG,DELETE),UNIT=SYSDA,
   DCB=(CSCJGJ.CSC.MODEL,RECFM=FB,LRECL=177,BLKSIZE=22833),SPACE=(CYL,(2,1),RLSE)
35 XXFINTRANS   DD  DSN=&DSN1..&DSN2..FIN,                FINISHED TRANS
   XX  DISP=(NEW,CATLG,DELETE),
   XX  UNIT=SYSDA,
   XX  RECFM=FB,
   XX  LRECL=92,
   XX  SPACE=(CYL,(1,1),RLSE)
   IEFC653I SUBSTITUTION JCL - DSN=CSCJGJ.REG.FIN,DISP=(NEW,CATLG,DELETE),UNIT=SYSDA,RECFM=FB,LRECL=92,
   SPACE=(CYL,(1,1),RLSE)
36 XXAUDREP     DD  SYSOUT=&UPRINT                             AUDIT REPORT
   XX     ENDIF
```

Substitution of the DSN1, DSN2, and TRSGEN symbolic parameters forms either a "test" or "production" data set name, with the generation number of the generation data set supplied by TRSGEN. This makes it easier to change the generation number for a restart in the execution JCL.

Figure 7.28 (continued)

```
   XX*-----------------------------------------------------------------
   XX*  SORT FINISHED TRANSACTIONS FOR DETAILED REPORTING
   XX*-----------------------------------------------------------------
   IEFC653I SUBSTITUTION JCL - SYSOUT=*
37 XX       IF ( NOT ABEND AND RC <= 4 ) THEN
38 XXSTEP050  EXEC  PGM=SORT
39 XXSYSOUT     DD  SYSOUT=&DPRINT
   IEFC653I SUBSTITUTION JCL - SYSOUT=*
40 XXSORTIN     DD  DSN=&DSN1..&DSN2..FIN,DISP=SHR
   IEFC653I SUBSTITUTION JCL - DSN=CSCJGJ.REG.FIN,DISP=SHR
41 XXSORTOUT    DD  DSN=&DSN1..&DSN2..FINSORT,           SORTED, FINISHED
   XX  DISP=(NEW,CATLG,DELETE),                           TRANSACTIONS
   XX  UNIT=SYSDA,
   XX  RECFM=FB,
   XX  LRECL=92,
   XX  SPACE=(CYL,(2,1),RLSE)
   IEFC653I SUBSTITUTION JCL - DSN=CSCJGJ.REG.FINSORT,DISP=(NEW,CATLG,DELETE),UNIT=SYSDA,RECFM=FB,LRECL=92,
   SPACE=(CYL,(2,1),RLSE)
42 XXSORTWK01   DD  UNIT=VIO,SPACE=(CYL,(1,1))
43 XXSORTWK02   DD  UNIT=VIO,SPACE=(CYL,(1,1))
44 XXSORTWK03   DD  UNIT=VIO,SPACE=(CYL,(1,1))
45 XXSYSIN      DD  DSN=CSCJGJ.CCARDS(REG33030),
   XX  DISP=SHR
46 XX      ENDIF
   XX*-----------------------------------------------------------------
   XX*  PRODUCE ACCOUNTING, REGISTRAR RPTS AND "BAD TRANS" DOWNLOAD FILE
   XX*-----------------------------------------------------------------
47 XX       IF ( NOT ABEND AND RC <= 4 ) THEN
48 XXSTEP060  EXEC  PGM=REG3308
49 XXSTEPLIB    DD  DSN=CSCJGJ.ADV.LOADLIB,DISP=SHR
50 XX           DD  DSN=SYS1.COB2LIB,DISP=SHR
51 XXSYSOUT     DD  SYSOUT=&DPRINT
   IEFC653I SUBSTITUTION JCL - SYSOUT=*
52 XXFTRANS     DD  DSN=&DSN1..&DSN2..FINSORT,DISP=SHR
   IEFC653I SUBSTITUTION JCL - DSN=CSCJGJ.REG.FINSORT,DISP=SHR
53 XXGOODREP    DD  SYSOUT=&UPRINT,COPIES=2           TO ACCTNG, REGIS
   XX*
   IEFC653I SUBSTITUTION JCL - SYSOUT=*,COPIES=2
54 XXBADREP     DD  SYSOUT=&UPRINT                    TO ACCTNG ONLY
   XX*
   IEFC653I SUBSTITUTION JCL - SYSOUT=*
55 XXBADTR      DD  DSN=&DSN1..&DSN2..BADTRANS,       FOR ACCTNG DOWNLOAD,
   XX  DISP=(NEW,CATLG,DELETE),                       CORRECTION, AND
```

This listing of your statement-numbered JCL, finalized for execution, is part of the MVS/ESA system reporting omitted by SCANIT2. While a program such as SCANIT2 can point you in the right direction concerning a run that has failed, *you can't avoid examining this part of system reporting in setting up a restart.*

Figure 7.28 (continued)

```
         XX  UNIT=SYSDA,                                      SUBSEQUENT UPLOAD
         XX  RECFM=FB,                                        TO FIXEDTR FILE
         XX  LRECL=68,                                        THAT IS INPUT TO
         XX  SPACE=(CYL,(1,1),RLSE)                           A SUBSEQUENT RUN
         IEFC653I SUBSTITUTION JCL - DSN=CSCJGJ.REG.BADTRANS,DISP=(NEW,CATLG,DELETE),UNIT=SYSDA,RECFM=FB,LRECL=68,
         SPACE=(CYL,(1,1),RLSE)
      56 XX      ENDIF
         XX*-------------------------------------------------------------
         XX*  CREATE THE NEW DOWNLOAD SUMMARY FILE FOR UNIVERSITY PLANNING DIV.
         XX*-------------------------------------------------------------
      57 XX      IF ( NOT ABEND AND RC <= 4 ) THEN
      58 XXSTEP070  EXEC  PGM=REG3350
      59 XXSTEPLIB    DD  DSN=CSCJGJ.ADV.LOADLIB,DISP=SHR
      60 XX           DD  DSN=SYS1.COB2LIB,DISP=SHR
      61 XXSYSOUT     DD  SYSOUT=&DPRINT
         IEFC653I SUBSTITUTION JCL - SYSOUT=*
      62 XXSUMREP     DD  SYSOUT=&UPRINT
         IEFC653I SUBSTITUTION JCL - SYSOUT=*
      63 XXMASTER1    DD  DSN=&DSN1..&DSN2..STUACCTS(&STUGEN),  CUR MASTER FILE
         XX  DISP=SHR
         IEFC653I SUBSTITUTION JCL - DSN=CSCJGJ.REG.STUACCTS(+1),DISP=SHR
      64 XXDOWNRECS   DD  DSN=&DSN1..&DSN2..DOWNLOAD(+1),       NEW SUMMARY FILE
         XX  DISP=(NEW,CATLG,DELETE),
         XX  UNIT=SYSDA,
         XX  DCB=(CSCJGJ.CSC.MODEL,RECFM=FB,LRECL=80,BLKSIZE=22880),
         XX  SPACE=(TRK,(1,1),RLSE)
         IEFC653I SUBSTITUTION JCL - DSN=CSCJGJ.REG.DOWNLOAD(+1),DISP=(NEW,CATLG,DELETE),UNIT=SYSDA,
         DCB=(CSCJGJ.CSC.MODEL,RECFM=FB,LRECL=80,BLKSIZE=22880),SPACE=(TRK,(1,1),RLSE)
      65 XX      ENDIF
         XX*-------------------------------------------------------------
         XX*  CLEANUP: DELETE INTERMEDIATE DATA SETS TO BE CREATED IN RUN
         XX*-------------------------------------------------------------
      66 XX      IF ( NOT ABEND AND RC <= 4 ) THEN
      67 XXSTEP080  EXEC  PGM=IEFBR14
      68 XXDELETE1    DD  DSN=&DSN1..&DSN2..FIN,            INTERMEDIATE
         XX  DISP=(MOD,DELETE),                             DATA SET
         XX  UNIT=SYSDA,
         XX  SPACE=(TRK,0)
         IEFC653I SUBSTITUTION JCL - DSN=CSCJGJ.REG.FIN,DISP=(MOD,DELETE),UNIT=SYSDA,SPACE=(TRK,0)
      69 XXDELETE2    DD  DSN=&DSN1..&DSN2..FINSORT,        INTERMEDIATE
         XX  DISP=(MOD,DELETE),                             DATA SET
         XX  UNIT=SYSDA,
         XX  SPACE=(TRK,0)
```

Figure 7.28 (continued)

```
        IEFC653I SUBSTITUTION JCL - DSN=CSCJGJ.REG.FINSORT,DISP=(MOD,DELETE),UNIT=SYSDA,SPACE=(TRK,0)
     70 XX      ENDIF
        XX*-------------------------------------------------------------------
        XX*  ATTENTION GRABBER: ISSUE USER ABEND 3333 IF RUN FAILED
        XX*-------------------------------------------------------------------
     71 XX      IF ( ABEND OR RC > 4 ) THEN
     72 XXSTEP999  EXEC  PGM=USERABN,PARM=3333
     73 XXSTEPLIB    DD  DSN=CSCJGJ.ADV.LOADLIB,DISP=SHR
     74 XX           DD  DSN=SYS1.COB2LIB,DISP=SHR
     75 XX      ENDIF
     76 XX      ENDIF
        //*                    MAKE '0' TO RECOVER AT STEP050 OR
        //*                    STEP060 OR STEP070

  STMT NO. MESSAGE

       3 IEFC001I PROCEDURE R33P1 WAS EXPANDED USING PRIVATE LIBRARY CSCJGJ.ADV.PROCLIB1

ICH70001I CSCJGJ   LAST ACCESS AT 12:31:05 ON THURSDAY, JANUARY 27, 1994
IEF236I ALLOC. FOR CSCJGJA STEP010 STEPA
IEF237I 117  ALLOCATED TO DELETE1
IEF237I 111  ALLOCATED TO DELETE2
IEF237I 116  ALLOCATED TO DELETE3
IEF142I CSCJGJA STEP010 STEPA - STEP WAS EXECUTED - COND CODE 0000
IEF285I   CSCJGJ.REG.FIN                                DELETED
IEF285I   VOL SER NOS= USER03.
          -
          -
          -
```

These comments in the execution JCL follow the last part of the continued EXEC statement. Notice that they appear in the JCL listing at the very end, which may be confusing.

MVS/ESA Version 4 seems to have a quirky bug. When I housed the REG33UP1 job stream as a proc, I repeatedly got error messages at the end of the JCL, which made it appear that the final ENDIF had not been recognized. I was able to overcome the problem by coding this ENDIF twice! I surmise that a problem exists in the MVS/ESA software that obtains JCL from a proc library, and that IBM will correct this problem in later MVS/ESA releases.

Figure 7.28 (continued)

```
SDSF OUTPUT DISPLAY CSCJGJA  JOB04770  DSID   101 LINE 1       COLUMNS 02- 81
COMMAND INPUT ===>                                             SCROLL ===> PAGE
*******************************************************************************
SCANIT2 HELPS YOU ANALYZE MVS/ESA JOB OUTPUT.  SEE MORE ABOUT THIS TOOL IN
"ADVANCED MVS JCL EXAMPLES" BY JIM JANOSSY (1994, JOHN WILEY & SONS, INC.)
*******************************************************************************

 12.35.35 JOB04769  IRR010I  USERID CSCJGJ   IS ASSIGNED TO THIS JOB.
 IEF142I CSCJGJA STEP010 STEPA - STEP WAS EXECUTED - COND CODE 0000
 IEF142I CSCJGJA STEP020 STEPA - STEP WAS EXECUTED - COND CODE 0000
 IEF142I CSCJGJA STEP030 STEPA - STEP WAS EXECUTED - COND CODE 0000
 IEF142I CSCJGJA STEP040 STEPA - STEP WAS EXECUTED - COND CODE 0000
 IEF142I CSCJGJA STEP050 STEPA - STEP WAS EXECUTED - COND CODE 0000
 IEF142I CSCJGJA STEP060 STEPA - STEP WAS EXECUTED - COND CODE 0000
 IEF142I CSCJGJA STEP070 STEPA - STEP WAS EXECUTED - COND CODE 0000
 IEF142I CSCJGJA STEP080 STEPA - STEP WAS EXECUTED - COND CODE 0000
 IEF206I CSCJGJA STEP999 STEPA - STEP WAS NOT RUN BECAUSE OF CONDITIONAL EXPRESS

NO NON-ZERO SYS... ...OMPLETIO... ...E DETECTED
```

STEPnnn is the step name within the proc

STEPA is the name of the step in the execution JCL that invoked the proc

Figure 7.29 MVS/ESA System Output for the R33P1 Proc as Extracted by the SCANIT2 Program

I have set, however, both DPRINT and UPRINT outputs to '*' so that they follow the MSGCLASS output to the held queue rather than going immediately to print.

Figure 7.28 shows you the complete MVS/ESA system output produced by the submission of the execution JCL. As this detailed output indicates, the run proceeded successfully. Read the annotations I have placed directly on the system output, and note how the DSN1 and DSN2 symbolic parameter substitutions correctly form the data set names throughout the job stream.

Figure 7.29 shows you the SCANIT2 output for the successful run of the R33P1 proc. SCANIT2 extracts the complete COND CODE or other step reporting lines. You can see that the step within the proc and the step at which the proc was invoked are both visible. Using a different naming convention for proc stepnames and invoking (execution JCL) stepnames, as I have suggested in earlier chapters, really helps makes system reporting easier to decipher.

7.18 Restarting a Proc at a Step

How would I restart the job stream at a step such as STEP040, if necessary, now that I have housed the JCL for the job stream as a proc? Figure 7.30 shows you another screen print of execution JCL XR33P1, with the RESTART parameter coded at line 8.

It's worthwhile to note an inconsistency in MVS/ESA system reporting and JCL coding. In system reporting, such as in Figure 7.29, you see job name, stepname, and procstepname one way, but when you code the RESTART parameter, you code the opposite:

```
CSCJGJA STEP040 STEPA - COMPLETION CODE - SYSTEM=D37 ...

RESTART=STEPA.STEP040
```

This inconsistency is unfortunate and can easily lead to incorrect coding of the RESTART parameter. It is unclear to me, even after more than two decades of experience with MVS, why it exhibits this arcane and troublesome type of inconsistency.

In Figure 7.30 you can see that I have followed the recovery instructions shown in Figure 7.25 (and also conveyed in the same-line comment at line 21 in the execution JCL itself) in setting up the restart of a job that previously failed at step 040. I have changed the value of the TRSGEN symbolic parameter from '+1' to '+0'. You can see the extracted lines of MVS/ESA system reporting for the restarted run in Figure 7.31, and note that the restart was successful. *Or was it?*

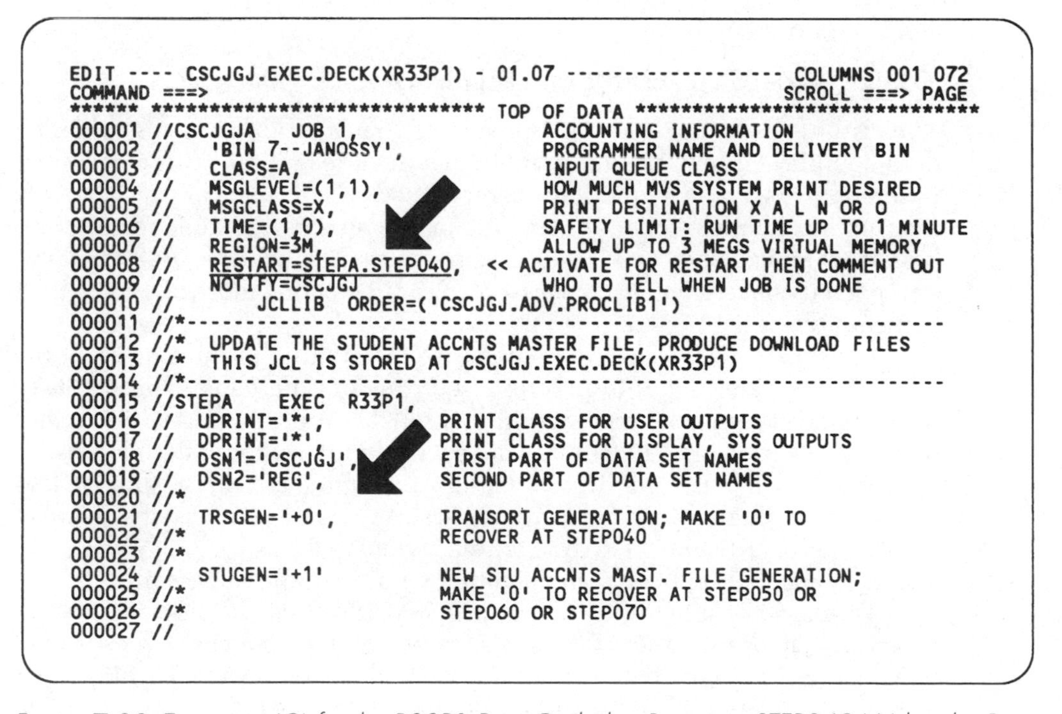

```
EDIT ---- CSCJGJ.EXEC.DECK(XR33P1) - 01.07 ------------------ COLUMNS 001 072
COMMAND ===>                                                  SCROLL ===> PAGE
****** ****************************** TOP OF DATA ******************************
000001 //CSCJGJA   JOB 1,                   ACCOUNTING INFORMATION
000002 //    'BIN 7--JANOSSY',              PROGRAMMER NAME AND DELIVERY BIN
000003 //    CLASS=A,                       INPUT QUEUE CLASS
000004 //    MSGLEVEL=(1,1),                HOW MUCH MVS SYSTEM PRINT DESIRED
000005 //    MSGCLASS=X,                    PRINT DESTINATION X A L N OR O
000006 //    TIME=(1,0),                    SAFETY LIMIT: RUN TIME UP TO 1 MINUTE
000007 //    REGION=3M,                     ALLOW UP TO 3 MEGS VIRTUAL MEMORY
000008 //    RESTART=STEPA.STEP040,  << ACTIVATE FOR RESTART THEN COMMENT OUT
000009 //    NOTIFY=CSCJGJ                  WHO TO TELL WHEN JOB IS DONE
000010 //        JCLLIB  ORDER=('CSCJGJ.ADV.PROCLIB1')
000011 //*-----------------------------------------------------------------
000012 //*  UPDATE THE STUDENT ACCNTS MASTER FILE, PRODUCE DOWNLOAD FILES
000013 //*  THIS JCL IS STORED AT CSCJGJ.EXEC.DECK(XR33P1)
000014 //*-----------------------------------------------------------------
000015 //STEPA     EXEC  R33P1,
000016 //  UPRINT='*',               PRINT CLASS FOR USER OUTPUTS
000017 //  DPRINT='*',               PRINT CLASS FOR DISPLAY, SYS OUTPUTS
000018 //  DSN1='CSCJGJ',            FIRST PART OF DATA SET NAMES
000019 //  DSN2='REG',               SECOND PART OF DATA SET NAMES
000020 //*
000021 //  TRSGEN='+0',              TRANSORT GENERATION; MAKE '0' TO
000022 //*                           RECOVER AT STEP040
000023 //*
000024 //  STUGEN='+1'               NEW STU ACCNTS MAST. FILE GENERATION;
000025 //*                           MAKE '0' TO RECOVER AT STEP050 OR
000026 //*                           STEP060 OR STEP070
000027 //
```

Figure 7.30 Execution JCL for the R33P1 Proc Coded to Restart at STEP040 Within the Proc

```
SDSF OUTPUT DISPLAY CSCJGJA  JOB04784  DSID   101 LINE 1       COLUMNS 02- 81
COMMAND INPUT ===>                                            SCROLL ===> PAGE
********************************************************************************
SCANIT2 HELPS YOU ANALYZE MVS/ESA JOB OUTPUT.  SEE MORE ABOUT THIS TOOL IN
"ADVANCED MVS JCL EXAMPLES" BY JIM JANOSSY (1994, JOHN WILEY & SONS, INC.)
********************************************************************************

 12.54.09 JOB04783  IRR010I  USERID CSCJGJ   IS ASSIGNED TO THIS JOB.
 IEF142I CSCJGJA STEP040 STEPA - STEP WAS EXECUTED - COND CODE 0000
 IEF142I CSCJGJA STEP050 STEPA - STEP WAS EXECUTED - COND CODE 0000
 IEF142I CSCJGJA STEP060 STEPA - STEP WAS EXECUTED - COND CODE 0000
 IEF142I CSCJGJA STEP070 STEPA - STEP WAS EXECUTED - COND CODE 0000
 IEF142I CSCJGJA STEP080 STEPA - STEP WAS EXECUTED - COND CODE 0000
 IEF206I CSCJGJA STEP999 STEPA - STEP WAS NOT RUN BECAUSE OF CONDITIONAL EXPRESS

NO NON-ZERO SYSTEM COMPLETION CODE DETECTED
```

Figure 7.31 MVS/ESA System Output for the Restarted R33P1 Proc as Extracted by the SCANIT2 Program

7.19 A Caution About Step Restarts and Reliability

The last thing anyone needs or appreciates when a production job has failed is to complicate the situation more by having a restart fail. But restarts are inherently fussy and potentially complicated. Clear and concise recovery instructions in operational documentation are an aid to reliable restart. Sufficient training, ready access to documentation, diligence, and a careful approach to the task are also necessary to avoid creating more of a mess than you started with.

Figure 7.32 illustrates the importance of carefully examining all of the MVS/ESA system output from a restarted run, after perhaps scanning it for the high-level summary provided in Figure 7.31. As it turns out, my restart of the R33P1 proc in STEP040 was not set up properly. I actually restarted it at STEP040, when the run did not require a restart at all; that is, the job had not failed in this step prior to my restart! As a consequence, the data set named CSCJGJ.REG.BADTRANS, ordinarily deleted in step 010, was still in existence when STEP060 created another data set of the same name.

Unlike some other operating systems, MVS/ESA will allow you to create more than one data set of the same name, but it cannot catalog more than one occurrence of the data set. Figure 7.32 shows one way that MVS/ESA reports that it has created but not cataloged a data set. Uncataloged data sets are dangerous because they are difficult to locate once the MVS/ESA system reporting for the job that created them is discarded.

```
SDSF OUTPUT DISPLAY CSCJGJA  JOB04783  DSID     2 LINE 0       COLUMNS 02- 81
COMMAND INPUT ===>                                             SCROLL ===> PAGE
*********************************** TOP OF DATA ***********************************
                         J E S 2  J O B  L O G  --  S Y S T E M  I B M 1  --  N

12.54.09 JOB04783  IRR010I  USERID CSCJGJ   IS ASSIGNED TO THIS JOB.
12.54.10 JOB04783  ICH70001I CSCJGJ   LAST ACCESS AT 12:47:25 ON THURSDAY, JANUA
12.54.10 JOB04783  $HASP373 CSCJGJA  STARTED - INIT  1 - CLASS A - SYS IBM1
12.54.20 JOB04783  IEF377I CSCJGJA STEP060 STEPA
                   CSCJGJ.REG.BADTRANS NOT CATLGD 2
12.54.23 JOB04783  $HASP395 CSCJGJA  ENDED
------ JES2 JOB STATISTICS ------
    27 JAN 94 JOB EXECUTION DATE
           26 CARDS READ
        1,558 SYSOUT PRINT RECORDS
            0 SYSOUT PUNCH RECORDS
          181 SYSOUT SPOOL KBYTES
         0.22 MINUTES EXECUTION TIME
```

This MVS/ESA system output indicates a problem with a restart. I submitted the JCL shown in Figure 7.30 to demonstrate how to code a restart at a step within a proc, but the job had not actually failed previously. Now the detailed system reporting for the restart shows that a second copy of a data set named CSCJGJ.REG.BADTRANS has been created. *More than one data set of the same name can exist on the mainframe, but only one occurrence can be cataloged.* This type of problem is only one of many that can arise with an incorrectly done restart. An alternative to step restart is complete rerun of a job from its beginning. I demonstrate that alternative recovery strategy in Chapter 8.

Figure 7.32 Typical MVS/ESA System Output for an Improperly Restarted Run

Failing in a restarted run is one potential outcome of restart as a recovery strategy. Succeeding in a restarted run, but inadvertently creating duplicate copies of data sets by restarting at the wrong step is another possible outcome. I demonstrate an alternative, less error prone recovery strategy in Chapter 8, that of a rerun from the beginning. Although rerun from the beginning does involve redoing some of the steps already completed successfully, its simplicity makes it an appealing choice for recovering failed small to moderately large runs.

8

Building Rerunnable MVS/ESA Jobstreams

8.1 Rerunnable Versus Restartable Job Streams

8.2 An Example Rerunnable Job Stream

8.3 Simple Rerunnability: Print Reruns

8.4 Recovery Rerunnability

8.5 Demonstrating a Successful Run

8.6 Demonstrating a Failed Run (System Completion Code)

8.7 Demonstrating a Failed Run (COND COND > 0004)

8.8 Demonstrating Print Rerun

8.1 Rerunnable Versus Restartable Job Streams

A *restartable* job stream is one that has been designed to retain data sets that pass information from one step to another. When a restartable job stream fails due to a program or data set problem, with careful attention its processing can be resumed using the RESTART parameter as described in Chapter 7. Restartable job streams represent one strategy for the completion of work, given the realization that problems will inevitably arise in a small proportion of runs.

Another strategy often used to ensure that the work of a job stream can be delivered regardless of problems involves rerunning a job stream from the beginning rather than restarting it. A *rerunnable* job stream is one that has been designed with exactly the opposite intention of a restartable job stream. A rerunnable job stream uses temporary data sets to pass information between steps, so that none linger beyond the active life of the job stream. In fact, we purposely include an extra final step in a rerunnable job stream to eliminate all new data sets created during the run, even data sets that are intended to remain as output of the job stream.

Both restartable and rerunnable job streams have their place in modern mainframe work. Generally speaking, rerunnable job streams are preferred for all but very lengthy-running job streams. Though rerunnable job streams do cause work done up to the point of failure to be repeated after problem correction, they offer ease and reliability of operation. Given that we do not anticipate a large number of run failures, the cost of repeating some processing in a rerun can be much lower than the cost, in both time and money, of fiddling with botched job restarts.

The choice of job stream design strategy—restartable job stream or rerunnable job stream—is significant but not the most important factor in "real world" JCL usage. The most important factor is realizing that you need to make a conscious job stream design choice in the first place! I have seen precious few published resources that actually explain this to people and so have developed Chapters 7 and 8 in this book to help fill that gap.

8.2 An Example Rerunnable Job Stream

Figure 8.1 depicts a variation of the job stream you have already seen in Chapter 7. This job stream is named REG33UP7. If you review Figure 7.1 in Chapter 7, you will see that this job stream fits into the same overall processing scheme of administrative support for university registration processing as job stream REG33UP1 in Figure 7.2. REG33UP7 is, in fact, a rerunnable version of the job stream and could be "plugged into" processing instead of REG33UP1. The JCL for REG33UP7 is listed in Figure 8.2.

Let's consider a thumbnail sketch of what the REG33UP7 job stream does. REG33UP7 accepts transactions from three different input data sets. One or more of these data sets may be placed on the system by end-user upload of data. The job stream sorts these input transactions together, and the REG3307 program uses them to update a backup copy of the student accounts file, which is then used (outside of this job stream) to reload the online student accounts file. The update produces a simple report, but its main reporting output is a file of "finished" transactions that carry disposition codes. The finished transactions are sorted and used by program REG3308 to produce end-user update reporting. The job stream also executes program REG3350, which extracts information for eventual download by end users in the university strategic planning office, and produces a simple report. Each of the steps at which these programs are executed, beginning with the second step, is "guarded" by a standard IF test that stops step execution if any program abends or issues a COND CODE greater than 4.

The activities just described account for only the first five steps of the REG33UP7 job stream. Steps 060, 070, 080, and 090, which represent almost half of the job stream, are present simply in the interest of rerunnability! Let's examine the two elements of rerunnability designed into this job stream.

8.3 Simple Rerunnability: Print Reruns

I designed the REG33UP7 job stream to meet a commonsense requirement that's easy to overlook. Sometimes it will be necessary to rerun work not because the job stream that was to accomplish it failed, but because someone lost his or her paper reports! Print outputs can be misplaced, damaged, or misrouted and not reach their destination. When an end user requires that another set of reports be produced, we should be able to accommodate the request without having to restore an entire set of master files to an earlier date and repeat updating work!

The JCL in job stream REG33UP7 that executes the REG3307 and REG3308 programs direct their print outputs into generation data sets, a separate GDS for each print output. You see these represented on the flowchart of Figure 8.1. Some of these reports are intended to be printed in one

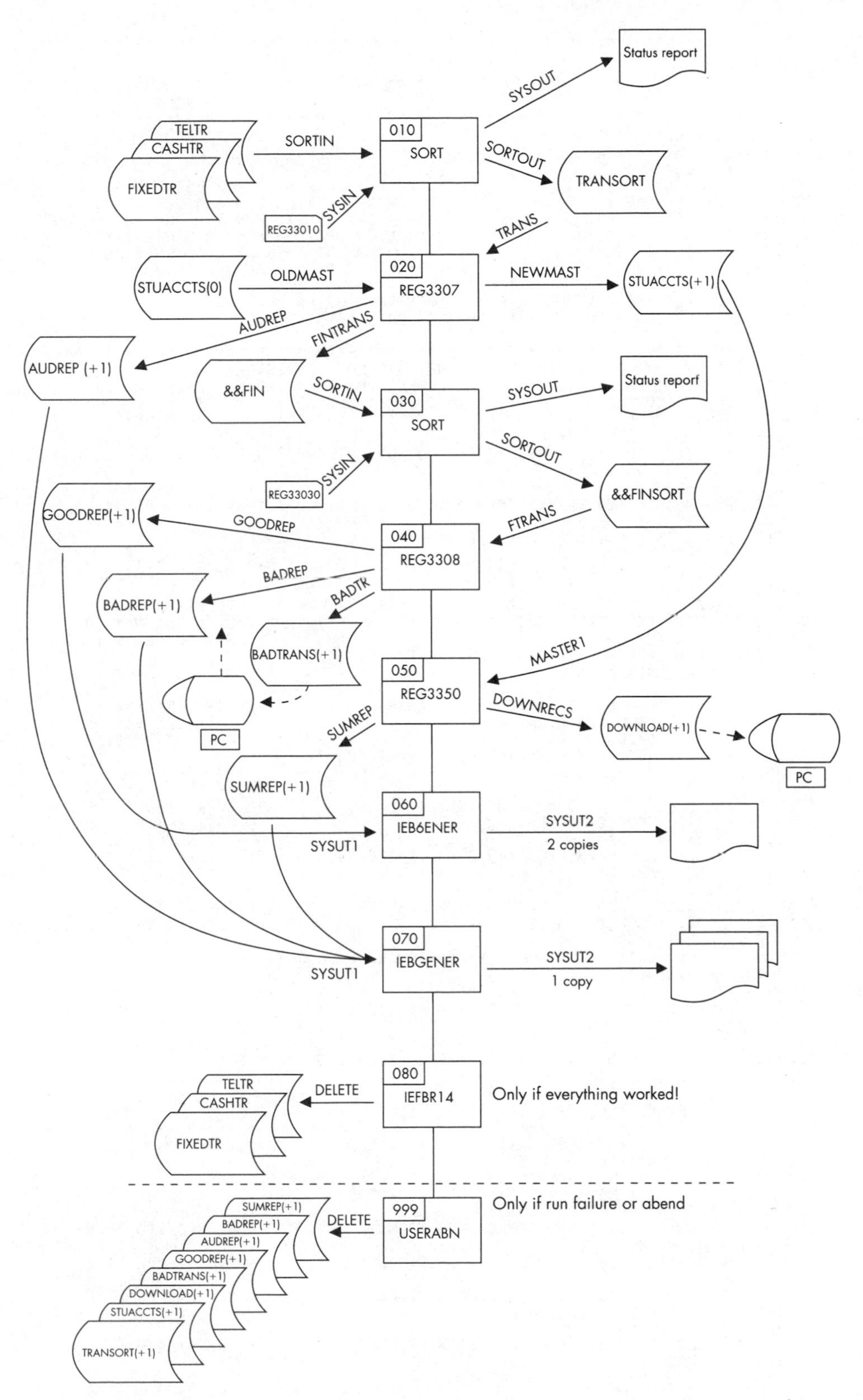

Figure 8.1 Flowchart of the Rerunnable REG33UP7 Job Stream, Which Handles the Updating of the Student Accounts File

```
EDIT ---- CSCJGJ.ADV.CNTL(REG33UP7) - 01.03 ------------------ COLUMNS 001 072
COMMAND ===>                                                  SCROLL ===> PAGE
****** ***************************** TOP OF DATA ******************************
000001 //CSCJGJA   JOB 1,                    ACCOUNTING INFORMATION
000002 //    'BIN 7--JANOSSY',               PROGRAMMER NAME AND DELIVERY BIN
000003 //    CLASS=A,                        INPUT QUEUE CLASS
000004 //    MSGLEVEL=(1,1),                 HOW MUCH MVS SYSTEM PRINT DESIRED
000005 //    MSGCLASS=X,                     PRINT DESTINATION X A L N OR O
000006 //    TIME=(1,0),                     SAFETY LIMIT: RUN TIME UP TO 1 MINUTE
000007 //    REGION=3M,                      ALLOW UP TO 3 MEGS VIRTUAL MEMORY
000008 //*   TYPRUN=SCAN,                    UNCOMMENT THIS LINE TO DO SCAN ONLY
000009 //    NOTIFY=CSCJGJ                   WHO TO TELL WHEN JOB IS DONE
000010 //*
000011 //*   RUN THE REG33UP7 UPDATE JOB STREAM USING RAW JCL
000012 //*   WRITES REPORTS TO GENERATION DATA SETS TO ALLOW REPRINTING
000013 //*
000014 //*   ***************************************************************
000015 //*   *  IN CASE OF FAILURE DO NOT ATTEMPT TO RESTART THIS JOB!      *
000016 //*   *  THIS JOB IS DESIGNED TO BE RERUN FROM THE BEGINNING AFTER   *
000017 //*   *  CORRECTION OF ANY PROBLEM THAT CAUSED A FAILURE             *
000018 //*   ***************************************************************
000019 //*
000020 //*   THIS JCL IS STORED AT CSCJGJ.ADV.CNTL(REG33UP7)
000021 //*
000022 //*-----------------------------------------------------------------
000023 //*   READ CONCATENATED TRANSACTION INPUTS, SORT THEM INTO ONE DATA SET
000024 //*-----------------------------------------------------------------
000025 //       IF ( NOT ABEND AND RC <= 4 ) THEN
000026 //STEP010  EXEC  PGM=SORT                           INPUT TO THIS STEP
000027 //SYSOUT     DD  SYSOUT=*                           UPLOADED BY USERS
000028 //*
000029 //SORTIN     DD  DSN=CSCJGJ.REG.TELTR,              TELEPHONE REGIS.
000030 //  DISP=(MOD,CATLG,CATLG),                         DATA SET MAY OR
000031 //  UNIT=SYSDA,                                     MAY NOT EXIST!
000032 //  DCB=(RECFM=FB,LRECL=68,BLKSIZE=22848),
000033 //  SPACE=(TRK,0)
000034 //*
000035 //            DD  DSN=CSCJGJ.REG.CASHTR,            CASHIER'S TRANS.
000036 //  DISP=(MOD,CATLG,CATLG),                         DATA SET MAY OR
000037 //  UNIT=SYSDA,                                     MAY NOT EXIST!
000038 //  DCB=(RECFM=FB,LRECL=68,BLKSIZE=22848),
000039 //  SPACE=(TRK,0)
000040 //*
000041 //            DD  DSN=CSCJGJ.REG.FIXEDTR,           CORRECTED TRANS.
000042 //  DISP=(MOD,CATLG,CATLG),                         DATA SET MAY OR
000043 //  UNIT=SYSDA,                                     MAY NOT EXIST!
000044 //  DCB=(RECFM=FB,LRECL=68,BLKSIZE=22848),
000045 //  SPACE=(TRK,0)
000046 //*
000047 //SORTOUT     DD  DSN=CSCJGJ.REG.TRANSORT(+1),      OUTPUT IS BACKUP,
000048 //  DISP=(NEW,CATLG,DELETE),                        GENERATION DATA SET
000049 //  UNIT=SYSDA,
000050 //  DCB=(CSCJGJ.CSC.MODEL,RECFM=FB,LRECL=68,BLKSIZE=22848),
000051 //  SPACE=(CYL,(2,1),RLSE)
000052 //*
000053 //SORTWK01   DD  UNIT=SYSDA,SPACE=(CYL,(1,1))
000054 //SORTWK02   DD  UNIT=SYSDA,SPACE=(CYL,(1,1))
000055 //SORTWK03   DD  UNIT=SYSDA,SPACE=(CYL,(1,1))
000056 //SYSIN      DD  DSN=CSCJGJ.CCARDS(REG33010),DISP=SHR
000057 //    ENDIF
000058 //*-----------------------------------------------------------------
000059 //*  UPDATE THE STUACCTS MASTER FILE
000060 //*-----------------------------------------------------------------
000061 //       IF ( NOT ABEND AND RC <= 4 ) THEN
000062 //STEP020  EXEC  PGM=REG3307
000063 //STEPLIB    DD  DSN=CSCJGJ.ADV.LOADLIB,DISP=SHR
000064 //           DD  DSN=SYS1.COB2LIB,DISP=SHR
000065 //SYSOUT     DD  SYSOUT=*
000066 //TRANS      DD  DSN=CSCJGJ.REG.TRANSORT(+1),       NEW SORTED TRANS
000067 //  DISP=SHR
000068 //OLDMAST    DD  DSN=CSCJGJ.REG.STUACCTS(0),        OLD MASTER FILE
000069 //  DISP=SHR
000070 //NEWMAST    DD  DSN=CSCJGJ.REG.STUACCTS(+1),       NEW MASTER FILE
000071 //  DISP=(NEW,CATLG,DELETE),
000072 //  UNIT=SYSDA,
000073 //  DCB=(CSCJGJ.CSC.MODEL,RECFM=FB,LRECL=177,BLKSIZE=22833),
000074 //  SPACE=(CYL,(2,1),RLSE)
```

Figure 8.2 REG33UP7, A Rerunnable Job Stream Coded from the Flowchart in Figure 8.1

```
000075 //FINTRANS   DD  DSN=&&FIN,                          FINISHED TRANS
000076 //  DISP=(NEW,PASS,DELETE),
000077 //  UNIT=VIO,
000078 //  RECFM=FB,
000079 //  LRECL=92,
000080 //  SPACE=(CYL,(1,1),RLSE)
000081 //AUDREP     DD  DSN=CSCJGJ.REG.AUDREP(+1),          AUDIT REPORT
000082 //  DISP=(NEW,CATLG,DELETE),
000083 //  UNIT=SYSDA,
000084 //  DCB=(CSCJGJ.CSC.MODEL,RECFM=FB,LRECL=133,BLKSIZE=22876),
000085 //  SPACE=(CYL,(2,1),RLSE)
000086 //      ENDIF
000087 //*---------------------------------------------------------------
000088 //*  SORT FINISHED TRANSACTIONS FOR DETAILED REPORTING
000089 //*---------------------------------------------------------------
000090 //      IF ( NOT ABEND AND RC <= 4 ) THEN
000091 //STEP030  EXEC  PGM=SORT
000092 //*YSOUT      DD  SYSOUT=*       FORCE 0012
000093 //SORTIN     DD  DSN=&&FIN,
000094 //  DISP=(OLD,DELETE)
000095 //SORTOUT    DD  DSN=&&FINSORT,                      SORTED, FINISHED
000096 //  DISP=(NEW,PASS,DELETE),                          TRANSACTIONS
000097 //  UNIT=VIO,
000098 //  RECFM=FB,
000099 //  LRECL=92,
000100 //  SPACE=(CYL,(2,1),RLSE)
000101 //SORTWK01   DD  UNIT=SYSDA,SPACE=(CYL,(1,1))
000102 //SORTWK02   DD  UNIT=SYSDA,SPACE=(CYL,(1,1))
000103 //SORTWK03   DD  UNIT=SYSDA,SPACE=(CYL,(1,1))
000104 //SYSIN      DD  DSN=CSCJGJ.CCARDS(REG33030),
000105 //  DISP=SHR
000106 //      ENDIF
000107 //*---------------------------------------------------------------
000108 //*  PRODUCE ACCOUNTING, REGISTRAR RPTS AND "BAD TRANS" DOWNLOAD FILE
000109 //*---------------------------------------------------------------
000110 //      IF ( NOT ABEND AND RC <= 4 ) THEN
000111 //STEP040  EXEC  PGM=REG3308
000112 //STEPLIB    DD  DSN=CSCJGJ.ADV.LOADLIB,DISP=SHR
000113 //           DD  DSN=SYS1.COB2LIB,DISP=SHR
000114 //SYSOUT     DD  SYSOUT=*
000115 //FTRANS     DD  DSN=&&FINSORT,
000116 //  DISP=(OLD,DELETE)
000117 //GOODREP    DD  DSN=CSCJGJ.REG.GOODREP(+1),         TO ACCTNG, REGISTRAR
000118 //  DISP=(NEW,CATLG,DELETE),
000119 //  UNIT=SYSDA,
000120 //  DCB=(CSCJGJ.CSC.MODEL,RECFM=FB,LRECL=133,BLKSIZE=22876),
000121 //  SPACE=(CYL,(2,1),RLSE)
000122 //*
000123 //BADREP     DD  DSN=CSCJGJ.REG.BADREP(+1),          TO ACCTNG ONLY
000124 //  DISP=(NEW,CATLG,DELETE),
000125 //  UNIT=SYSDA,
000126 //  DCB=(CSCJGJ.CSC.MODEL,RECFM=FB,LRECL=133,BLKSIZE=22876),
000127 //  SPACE=(CYL,(2,1),RLSE)
000128 //*
000129 //BADTR      DD  DSN=CSCJGJ.REG.BADTRANS(+1),        FOR ACCTNG DOWNLOAD,
000130 //  DISP=(NEW,CATLG,DELETE),                         CORRECTION, UPLOAD
000131 //  UNIT=SYSDA,
000132 //  DCB=(CSCJGJ.CSC.MODEL,RECFM=FB,LRECL=68,BLKSIZE=22848),
000133 //  SPACE=(CYL,(1,1),RLSE)
000134 //      ENDIF
000135 //*---------------------------------------------------------------
000136 //*  CREATE THE NEW DOWNLOAD SUMMARY FILE FOR UNIVERSITY PLANNING DIV.
000137 //*---------------------------------------------------------------
000138 //      IF ( NOT ABEND AND RC <= 4 ) THEN
000139 //STEP050  EXEC  PGM=REG3350
000140 //STEPLIB    DD  DSN=CSCJGJ.ADV.LOADLIB,DISP=SHR
000141 //           DD  DSN=SYS1.COB2LIB,DISP=SHR
000142 //SYSOUT     DD  SYSOUT=*
000143 //SUMREP     DD  DSN=CSCJGJ.REG.SUMREP(+1),
000144 //  DISP=(NEW,CATLG,DELETE),
000145 //  UNIT=SYSDA,
000146 //  DCB=(CSCJGJ.CSC.MODEL,RECFM=FB,LRECL=133,BLKSIZE=22876),
000147 //  SPACE=(CYL,(2,1),RLSE)
000148 //MASTER1    DD  DSN=CSCJGJ.REG.STUACCTS(+1),        CURRENT MASTER FILE
000149 //  DISP=SHR
000150 //DOWNRECS   DD  DSN=CSCJGJ.REG.DOWNLOAD(+1),        NEW SUMMARY FILE
```

Store printlines

Store printlines

Store printlines

Store printlines

Figure 8.2 (continued)

```
000151 //  DISP=(NEW,CATLG,DELETE),
000152 //  UNIT=SYSDA,
000153 //  DCB=(CSCJGJ.CSC.MODEL,RECFM=FB,LRECL=80,BLKSIZE=22880),
000154 //* SPACE=(TRK,0)      FORCE A D37
000155 //  SPACE=(TRK,(1,1),RLSE)
000156 //      ENDIF
000157 //*-----------------------------------------------------------------
000158 //*  PRINT 2-COPY REPORTS PRODUCED IN A SUCCESSFUL RUN
000159 //*-----------------------------------------------------------------
000160 //      IF ( NOT ABEND AND RC <= 4 ) THEN
000161 //STEP060  EXEC  PGM=IEBGENER                                   Copy
000162 //SYSPRINT   DD  SYSOUT=*                                       printlines
000163 //SYSIN      DD  DUMMY                                          to printer
000164 //SYSUT2     DD  SYSOUT=*,COPIES=2
000165 //SYSUT1     DD  DSN=CSCJGJ.REG.GOODREP(+1),DISP=SHR
000166 //      ENDIF
000167 //*-----------------------------------------------------------------
000168 //*  PRINT 1-COPY REPORTS PRODUCED IN A SUCCESSFUL RUN
000169 //*-----------------------------------------------------------------
000170 //      IF ( NOT ABEND AND RC <= 4 ) THEN
000171 //STEP070  EXEC  PGM=IEBGENER
000172 //SYSPRINT   DD  SYSOUT=*                                       Copy
000173 //SYSIN      DD  DUMMY                                          printlines
000174 //SYSUT2     DD  SYSOUT=*,COPIES=1                              to printer
000175 //SYSUT1     DD  DSN=CSCJGJ.REG.AUDREP(+1),DISP=SHR
000176 //           DD  DSN=CSCJGJ.REG.BADREP(+1),DISP=SHR
000177 //           DD  DSN=CSCJGJ.REG.SUMREP(+1),DISP=SHR
000178 //      ENDIF
000179 //*-----------------------------------------------------------------
000180 //*  DELETE INPUT DATA SETS IF RUN HAS BEEN SUCCESSFUL
000181 //*-----------------------------------------------------------------
000182 //      IF ( NOT ABEND AND RC <= 4 ) THEN
000183 //STEP080  EXEC  PGM=IEFBR14
000184 //DELETE1    DD  DSN=CSCJGJ.REG.TELTR,                 INPUT DELETED TO
000185 //  DISP=(MOD,DELETE),                                  PREVENT REDUNDANT
000186 //  UNIT=SYSDA,                                         PROCESSING
000187 //  SPACE=(TRK,0)
000188 //DELETE2    DD  DSN=CSCJGJ.REG.CASHTR,                INPUT DELETED TO
000189 //  DISP=(MOD,DELETE),                                  PREVENT REDUNDANT
000190 //  UNIT=SYSDA,                                         PROCESSING
000191 //  SPACE=(TRK,0)
000192 //DELETE3    DD  DSN=CSCJGJ.REG.FIXEDTR,               INPUT DELETED TO
000193 //  DISP=(MOD,DELETE),                                  PREVENT REDUNDANT
000194 //  UNIT=SYSDA,                                         PROCESSING
000195 //  SPACE=(TRK,0)
000196 //      ENDIF
000197 //*=================================================================
000198 //*
000199 //*  **  IF ABEND OR RUN FAILURE, CLEAR THE DECKS FOR A RERUN;   **
000200 //*  **  DELETE (+1) DATA SETS CREATED AND GO DOWN IN FLAMES!    **
000201 //*
000202 //*=================================================================
000203 //      IF ( ABEND OR RC > 4 ) THEN                             X
000204 //STEP999  EXEC  PGM=USERABN,PARM=3333                          !
000205 //STEPLIB    DD  DSN=CSCJGJ.ADV.LOADLIB,DISP=SHR                !
000206 //           DD  DSN=SYS1.COB2LIB,DISP=SHR                      !
000207 //*-----------------------------------                          !
000208 //* THE FOLLOWING DATA FILES ARE DELETED:                        !
000209 //*-----------------------------------                          !
000210 //SORTOUT    DD  DSN=CSCJGJ.REG.TRANSORT(+1),                   !
000211 //  DISP=(MOD,DELETE),                                          !
000212 //  UNIT=SYSDA,                                                 !
000213 //  DCB=(CSCJGJ.CSC.MODEL,RECFM=FB,LRECL=68,BLKSIZE=22848),     !
000214 //  SPACE=(TRK,0)                                               !
000215 //*                                                             !
000216 //NEWMAST    DD  DSN=CSCJGJ.REG.STUACCTS(+1),                   !
000217 //  DISP=(MOD,DELETE),                                          !
000218 //  UNIT=SYSDA,                                                 !
000219 //  DCB=(CSCJGJ.CSC.MODEL,RECFM=FB,LRECL=177,BLKSIZE=22833),    !
000220 //  SPACE=(TRK,0)                                               !
000221 //*                                                             !
000222 //DOWNRECS   DD  DSN=CSCJGJ.REG.DOWNLOAD(+1),                   !
000223 //  DISP=(MOD,DELETE),                                          !
000224 //  UNIT=SYSDA,                                                 !
000225 //  DCB=(CSCJGJ.CSC.MODEL,RECFM=FB,LRECL=80,BLKSIZE=22880),     !
000226 //  SPACE=(TRK,0)                                               !
000227 //*                                                             !
```

Figure 8.2 (continued)

```
000228 //BADTR       DD   DSN=CSCJGJ.REG.BADTRANS(+1),                          !
000229 //   DISP=(MOD,DELETE),                                                   !
000230 //   UNIT=SYSDA,                                                          !
000231 //   DCB=(CSCJGJ.CSC.MODEL,RECFM=FB,LRECL=68,BLKSIZE=22848),              !
000232 //   SPACE=(TRK,0)                                                        !
000233 //*-----------------------------------------                              !
000234 //* THE FOLLOWING PRINTLINE FILES ARE DELETED:                           !
000235 //*-----------------------------------------                              !
000236 //GOODREP     DD   DSN=CSCJGJ.REG.GOODREP(+1),                            !
000237 //   DISP=(MOD,DELETE),                                                   !
000238 //   UNIT=SYSDA,                                                          !
000239 //   DCB=(CSCJGJ.CSC.MODEL,RECFM=FB,LRECL=133,BLKSIZE=22876),             !
000240 //   SPACE=(TRK,0)                                                        !
000241 //*                                                                      !
000242 //AUDREP      DD   DSN=CSCJGJ.REG.AUDREP(+1),                             !
000243 //   DISP=(MOD,DELETE),                                                   !
000244 //   UNIT=SYSDA,                                                          !
000245 //   DCB=(CSCJGJ.CSC.MODEL,RECFM=FB,LRECL=133,BLKSIZE=22876),             !
000246 //   SPACE=(TRK,0)                                                        !
000247 //*                                                                      !
000248 //BADREP      DD   DSN=CSCJGJ.REG.BADREP(+1),                             !
000249 //   DISP=(MOD,DELETE),                                                   !
000250 //   UNIT=SYSDA,                                                          !
000251 //   DCB=(CSCJGJ.CSC.MODEL,RECFM=FB,LRECL=133,BLKSIZE=22876),             !
000252 //   SPACE=(TRK,0)                                                        !
000253 //*                                                                      !
000254 //SUMREP      DD   DSN=CSCJGJ.REG.SUMREP(+1),                             !
000255 //   DISP=(MOD,DELETE),                                                   !
000256 //   UNIT=SYSDA,                                                          !
000257 //   DCB=(CSCJGJ.CSC.MODEL,RECFM=FB,LRECL=133,BLKSIZE=22876),             !
000258 //   SPACE=(TRK,0)                                                        !
000259 //       ENDIF                                                            X
000260 //
```

Figure 8.2 (continued)

copy, and some in two copies. STEP060 copies the print data sets that require two-copy printing to the print queue, and STEP070 copies the print data sets that require one-copy printing to the print queue. If reports must be reprinted, a separate job stream with copies of just these steps can readily produce it. Later in this chapter, I'll show you a flexible way to arrange that "print rerun" job stream.

8.4 Recovery Rerunnability

Job stream recovery rerunnability is achieved in the REG33UP7 job stream by STEP080 and STEP090. Quite simply, both of these steps are "deletion" steps. Each eliminates particular data sets under different conditions.

STEP080 executes the null program, IEFBR14, simply as an excuse to have MVS act on the DD statements present at this step. DD statements are present to delete any data sets that should be eliminated after a successful run. In the case of REG33UP7, this includes the original transaction inputs to the update, which entered the sort utility at STEP010. Eliminating these ensures that they will not inadvertently be processed a second time. Since the sorted output of the sort at STEP010 is retained in a generation data set, we have a backup copy of these transactions should we need them for some purpose. STEP080 is guarded by the same IF test as preceding steps and executes if all programs executed normally. (If your installation uses a data set deletion method different from IEFBR14, you can code it at this step instead.)

STEP090 executes a forced user abend program named USERABN, shown in Figure 3.6 in Chapter 3. The IF test at this step executes the step only if a program has abended or issued a COND CODE greater than 4. This step accomplishes two important things:

- It issues a user condition code of 3333 and invokes an abend, which becomes very visible to the console operator, so that all job failures are readily detected.
- The DD statements at STEP090 are processed by MVS/ESA to delete the data sets named. A separate DD statement for each of the eight data sets created by the run in normal execution is present, including new generation data set generations.

A final step like STEP999 is almost always present in a rerunnable job stream. The role of this final step is to "clear the decks" for rerun of the job stream, by deleting all files created, so that no manual deletion actions are needed before rerun. Since this final step cannot "know" which step failed, and consequently which new files were created, it deletes all of them with the "permissive" DISP coding of MOD. MOD, unique among DISPosition coding, essentially says "I don't know if the data set named on this DD statement exists or not."

The print rerun facilitating steps 060 and 070 and the recovery rerunnability steps 080 and 090 work very well as intended, as you will see in the examples that follow.

8.5 Demonstrating a Successful Run

In Chapter 7 I described a program named SCANIT2, which I wrote to analyze and extract information from the voluminous MVS/ESA system reporting for a job. I used SCANIT2 to prepare several of the figures in this chapter, starting with Figure 8.3. You might want to review the discussion of SCANIT2 in Chapter 7, section 7.6, before you proceed.

Figure 8.3 shows you the output of the SCANIT2 program when it analyzed and extracted information from the MVS/ESA system reporting for a successful run of the REG33UP7 job stream. As you can see, all steps issued

```
SDSF OUTPUT DISPLAY CSCJGJA  JOB03634  DSID    101 LINE 1        COLUMNS 02- 81
 COMMAND INPUT ===>                                              SCROLL ===> PAGE
*************************************************************************
SCANIT2 HELPS YOU ANALYZE MVS/ESA JOB OUTPUT.  SEE MORE ABOUT THIS TOOL IN
"ADVANCED MVS JCL EXAMPLES" BY JIM JANOSSY (1994, JOHN WILEY & SONS, INC.)
*************************************************************************

 10.57.33 JOB03631   IRR010I  USERID CSCJGJ    IS ASSIGNED TO THIS JOB.
 IEF142I CSCJGJA STEP010 - STEP WAS EXECUTED - COND CODE 0000
 IEF142I CSCJGJA STEP020 - STEP WAS EXECUTED - COND CODE 0000
 IEF142I CSCJGJA STEP030 - STEP WAS EXECUTED - COND CODE 0000
 IEF142I CSCJGJA STEP040 - STEP WAS EXECUTED - COND CODE 0000
 IEF142I CSCJGJA STEP050 - STEP WAS EXECUTED - COND CODE 0000
 IEF142I CSCJGJA STEP060 - STEP WAS EXECUTED - COND CODE 0000
 IEF142I CSCJGJA STEP070 - STEP WAS EXECUTED - COND CODE 0000
 IEF142I CSCJGJA STEP080 - STEP WAS EXECUTED - COND CODE 0000
 IEF206I CSCJGJA STEP999 - STEP WAS NOT RUN BECAUSE OF CONDITIONAL EXPRESSION ON

NO NON-ZERO SYSTEM COMPLETION CODE DETECTED
```

This is output from a SCANIT2 analysis of the MVS/ESA system output of the good REG33UP7 run. (I described SCANIT2 in Chapter 7, as a tool for summarizing the result of a run.) Since all "worker" steps of the run executed successfully, STEP999, the data set cleanup step, did not execute.

Figure 8.3 MVS/ESA System Reporting for a Successful Run of REG33UP7, as Extracted by the SCANIT2 Program

COND CODE 0000, and the final rerun facilitating step, STEP999, did not execute. Figure 8.4 shows you a part of the actual MVS/ESA system reporting, which I have annotated to highlight the file deletions of STEP080. As this reporting indicates, the REG33UP7 run proceeded exactly as intended.

8.6 Demonstrating a Failed Run (System Completion Code)

Figure 8.5 shows you a SCANIT2 extract of a run of the REG33UP7 job stream that "blew up." The job stream failed in STEP050 with a D37 system completion code, which indicates insufficient disk space for a file (as you

```
                    J E S 2   J O B   L O G  --  S Y S T E M   I B M 1  --  N O D E

10.57.33 JOB03631  IRR010I  USERID CSCJGJ   IS ASSIGNED TO THIS JOB.
10.57.34 JOB03631  ICH70001I CSCJGJ   LAST ACCESS AT 10:54:49 ON SUNDAY, APRIL 10,
10.57.34 JOB03631  $HASP373 CSCJGJA  STARTED - INIT  1 - CLASS A - SYS IBM1
10.57.55 JOB03631  $HASP395 CSCJGJA  ENDED

------ JES2 JOB STATISTICS ------
    10 APR 94 JOB EXECUTION DATE
          258 CARDS READ
        1,647 SYSOUT PRINT RECORDS
            0 SYSOUT PUNCH RECORDS
          186 SYSOUT SPOOL KBYTES
         0.35 MINUTES EXECUTION TIME

        1 //CSCJGJA   JOB 1,                    ACCOUNTING INFORMATION
          //    'BIN 7--JANOSSY',               PROGRAMMER NAME AND DELIVERY BIN
          //    CLASS=A,                        INPUT QUEUE CLASS
          //    MSGLEVEL=(1,1),                 HOW MUCH MVS SYSTEM PRINT DESIRED
          //    MSGCLASS=X,                     PRINT DESTINATION X A L N OR O
          //    TIME=(1,0),                     SAFETY LIMIT: RUN TIME UP TO 1 MINUTE
          //    REGION=3M,                      ALLOW UP TO 3 MEGS VIRTUAL MEMORY
          //*   TYPRUN=SCAN,                    UNCOMMENT THIS LINE TO DO SCAN ONLY
          //    NOTIFY=CSCJGJ                   WHO TO TELL WHEN JOB IS DONE
          //*
          //*   RUN THE REG33UP7 UPDATE JOB STREAM USING RAW JCL
          //*   WRITES REPORTS TO GENERATION DATA SETS TO ALLOW REPRINTING
          //*
          //*   *****************************************************************
          //*   *  IN CASE OF FAILURE DO NOT ATTEMPT TO RESTART THIS JOB!      *
          //*   *  THIS JOB IS DESIGNED TO BE RERUN FROM THE BEGINNING AFTER   *
          //*   *  CORRECTION OF ANY PROBLEM THAT CAUSED A FAILURE              *
          //*   *****************************************************************
          //*
          //*   THIS JCL IS STORED AT CSCJGJ.ADV.CNTL(REG33UP7)
          //*
                -
                -

IEF236I ALLOC. FOR CSCJGJA STEP080
IEF237I 111  ALLOCATED TO DELETE1
IEF237I 115  ALLOCATED TO DELETE2
IEF237I 117  ALLOCATED TO DELETE3
IEF142I CSCJGJA STEP080 - STEP WAS EXECUTED - COND CODE 0000
IEF285I   CSCJGJ.REG.TELTR                                  UNCATALOGED
IEF285I   VOL SER NOS= USER00.
IEF285I   CSCJGJ.REG.TELTR                                  DELETED
IEF285I   VOL SER NOS= USER00.
IEF285I   CSCJGJ.REG.CASHTR                                 UNCATALOGED
IEF285I   VOL SER NOS= USER01.
IEF285I   CSCJGJ.REG.CASHTR                                 DELETED
IEF285I   VOL SER NOS= USER01.
IEF285I   CSCJGJ.REG.FIXEDTR                                UNCATALOGED
IEF285I   VOL SER NOS= USER03.
IEF285I   CSCJGJ.REG.FIXEDTR                                DELETED
IEF285I   VOL SER NOS= USER03.
IEF373I STEP /STEP080 / START 94100.1057
IEF374I STEP /STEP080 / STOP  94100.1057 CPU    0MIN 00.03SEC SRB    0MIN 00.00SEC

IEF206I CSCJGJA STEP999 - STEP WAS NOT RUN BECAUSE OF CONDITIONAL EXPRESSION ON 76
IEF272I CSCJGJA STEP999 - STEP WAS NOT EXECUTED.
IEF373I STEP /STEP999 / START 94100.1057
IEF374I STEP /STEP999 / STOP  94100.1057 CPU    0MIN 00.00SEC SRB    0MIN 00.00SEC

IEF375I  JOB /CSCJGJA / START 94100.1057
IEF376I  JOB /CSCJGJA / STOP  94100.1057 CPU    0MIN 02.60SEC SRB    0MIN 00.14SEC
```

Here you see the beginning and the ending of the MVS/ESA system reporting for a good run of the REG33UP7 job stream. The last two steps are in charge of normal and abnormal situation data sets deletions. The data sets deleted in STEP080 are the transaction inputs to the update, which have now been backed up to the next generation of CSCJGJ.REG.TRANSORT in STEP010. STEP999, the major failure cleanup step, has not executed.

Figure 8.4 MVS/ESA System Reporting for a Good Run

```
SDSF OUTPUT DISPLAY CSCJGJA  JOB03638  DSID   101 LINE 1        COLUMNS 02- 81
COMMAND INPUT ===>                                              SCROLL ===> PAGE
*****************************************************************************
SCANIT2 HELPS YOU ANALYZE MVS/ESA JOB OUTPUT.  SEE MORE ABOUT THIS TOOL IN
"ADVANCED MVS JCL EXAMPLES" BY JIM JANOSSY (1994, JOHN WILEY & SONS, INC.)
*****************************************************************************

 11.06.24 JOB03637  IRR010I  USERID CSCJGJ   IS ASSIGNED TO THIS JOB.
 IEF142I CSCJGJA STEP010 - STEP WAS EXECUTED - COND CODE 0000
 IEF142I CSCJGJA STEP020 - STEP WAS EXECUTED - COND CODE 0000
 IEF142I CSCJGJA STEP030 - STEP WAS EXECUTED - COND CODE 0000
 IEF142I CSCJGJA STEP040 - STEP WAS EXECUTED - COND CODE 0000
 IEF472I CSCJGJA STEP050 - COMPLETION CODE - SYSTEM=D37 USER=0000 REASON=0000000
 IEF206I CSCJGJA STEP060 - STEP WAS NOT RUN BECAUSE OF CONDITIONAL EXPRESSION ON
 IEF206I CSCJGJA STEP070 - STEP WAS NOT RUN BECAUSE OF CONDITIONAL EXPRESSION ON
 IEF206I CSCJGJA STEP080 - STEP WAS NOT RUN BECAUSE OF CONDITIONAL EXPRESSION ON
 IEF472I CSCJGJA STEP999 - COMPLETION CODE - SYSTEM=000 USER=3333 REASON=0000000

*** NON-ZERO SYSTEM COMPLETION CODE DETECTED! ***
    THE FOLLOWING LINE GIVES BEST INFORMATION.
    LOOK FOR INFORMATION ABOUT SYSTEM COMPLETION CODE D37 BELOW:

 11.06.46 JOB03637  IEC031I D37-04,IFG0554T,CSCJGJA,STEP050,DOWNRECS,111,USER00,
```

SCANIT2 analysis of the MVS/ESA system output of a failed REG33UP7 run makes the failure visible, pinpoints the location of the failure, and shows what steps were shut off. Notice that data set cleanup step STEP999 has executed to help clear the decks for rerun after problem correction.

Figure 8.5 MVS/ESA System Reporting for a Failed Run of REG33UP7, as Extracted by the SCANIT2 Program (system completion code failure)

can find out for yourself by consulting the system completion code reference in Appendix E!). As you can see in Figure 8.5, the steps following STEP050 were "shut off" by this event and did not execute. However, STEP999 did execute, *because* of the abend.

Figure 8.6 provides a partial listing of the MVS/ESA system reporting that SCANIT2 examined to produce the extract in Figure 8.5. I have annotated this listing to highlight the deletion actions of STEP999. Steps before STEP050 created new generations of generation data sets; these new generations are deleted. The DISP coding for new data sets within STEP050 is DISP=(NEW,CATLG,DELETE), so new data sets such as CSCJGJ.REG.SUM REP—generation 3—and CSCJGJ.REG.DOWNLOAD(+1)—generation 105—were already deleted within the failed step. These new data sets do not exist when STEP999 begins execution. The DISP=(MOD,DELETE) coding at STEP999, however, causes dummy data sets of these names to be created and deleted without any problem. STEP999 accomplishes what it is intended to do.

Had this run of REG33UP7 been more than a demonstration for a book, what would my next action be? Here is what I would do to repair the situation and achieve successful processing:

```
                 J E S 2  J O B  L O G -- S Y S T E M  I B M 1 -- N O D E

11.06.24 JOB03637  IRR010I  USERID CSCJGJ   IS ASSIGNED TO THIS JOB.
11.06.26 JOB03637  ICH70001I CSCJGJ   LAST ACCESS AT 11:04:18 ON SUNDAY, APRIL 10,
11.06.26 JOB03637  $HASP373 CSCJGJA  STARTED - INIT  2 - CLASS A - SYS IBM1
11.06.46 JOB03637  IEC031I D37-04,IFG0554T,CSCJGJA,STEP050,DOWNRECS,111,USER00,
11.06.46 JOB03637  IEC031I CSCJGJ.REG.DOWNLOAD.G0105V00
11.06.46 JOB03637  IEA995I SYMPTOM DUMP OUTPUT
                   SYSTEM COMPLETION CODE=D37
                    TIME=11.06.46  SEQ=18248  CPU=0000  ASID=0019
                    PSW AT TIME OF ERROR  075C1000   80E8AFEA  ILC 2  INTC 0D
                      NO ACTIVE MODULE FOUND
                      DATA AT PSW  00E8AFE4 - 41003802  0A0DB20A  00509808
                      GPR  0-3  00E8B1E4  A0D37000  000087D0  00E8A9E2
                      GPR  4-7  008D7928  00EA0000  008D7BC4  008D7C14
                      GPR  8-11 008D7BE4  008D76E8  00FC8618  008D5FF0
                      GPR 12-15 00000000  0003453C  00E8AF8E  00000004
                    END OF SYMPTOM DUMP
   -
   -
   -

IEF236I ALLOC. FOR CSCJGJA STEP050
IEF237I 117  ALLOCATED TO STEPLIB
IEF237I 110  ALLOCATED TO
IEF237I JES2 ALLOCATED TO SYSOUT
IEF237I 115  ALLOCATED TO SUMREP
IEF237I 116  ALLOCATED TO MASTER1
IEF237I 111  ALLOCATED TO DOWNRECS
IEC031I D37-04,IFG0554T,CSCJGJA,STEP050,DOWNRECS,111,USER00,
IEC031I CSCJGJ.REG.DOWNLOAD.G0105V00
IEA995I SYMPTOM DUMP OUTPUT
SYSTEM COMPLETION CODE=D37
 TIME=11.06.46  SEQ=18248  CPU=0000  ASID=0019
 PSW AT TIME OF ERROR  075C1000   80E8AFEA  ILC 2  INTC 0D
   NO ACTIVE MODULE FOUND
   DATA AT PSW  00E8AFE4 - 41003802  0A0DB20A  00509808
   GPR  0-3  00E8B1E4  A0D37000  000087D0  00E8A9E2
   GPR  4-7  008D7928  00EA0000  008D7BC4  008D7C14
   GPR  8-11 008D7BE4  008D76E8  00FC8618  008D5FF0
   GPR 12-15 00000000  0003453C  00E8AF8E  00000004
 END OF SYMPTOM DUMP
IEF472I CSCJGJA STEP050 - COMPLETION CODE - SYSTEM=D37 USER=0000 REASON=00000000
IEF285I   CSCJGJ.ADV.LOADLIB                                  KEPT
IEF285I   VOL SER NOS= USER03.
IEF285I   SYS1.COB2LIB                                        KEPT
IEF285I   VOL SER NOS= ACSRES.
IEF285I   CSCJGJ.CSCJGJA.JOB03637.D0000105.?                  SYSOUT
IEF285I   CSCJGJ.REG.SUMREP.G0003V00                          DELETED
IEF285I   VOL SER NOS= USER01.
IEF285I   CSCJGJ.REG.STUACCTS.G0148V00                        KEPT
IEF285I   VOL SER NOS= USER02.
IEF285I   CSCJGJ.REG.DOWNLOAD.G0105V00                        DELETED
IEF285I   VOL SER NOS= USER00.
IEF373I STEP /STEP050 / START 94100.1106
IEF374I STEP /STEP050 / STOP  94100.1106 CPU    0MIN 00.36

IEF206I CSCJGJA STEP060 - STEP WAS NOT RUN BECAUSE OF CONDITIONAL EXPRESSION ON 54
IEF272I CSCJGJA STEP060 - STEP WAS NOT EXECUTED.
IEF373I STEP /STEP060 / START 94100.1106
IEF374I STEP /STEP060 / STOP  94100.1106 CPU    0MIN 00.00

IEF206I CSCJGJA STEP070 - STEP WAS NOT RUN BECAUSE OF CONDITIONAL EXPRESSION ON 61
IEF272I CSCJGJA STEP070 - STEP WAS NOT EXECUTED.
IEF373I STEP /STEP070 / START 94100.1106
IEF374I STEP /STEP070 / STOP  94100.1106 CPU    0MIN 00.00

IEF206I CSCJGJA STEP080 - STEP WAS NOT RUN BECAUSE OF CONDITIONAL EXPRESSION ON 70
IEF272I CSCJGJA STEP080 - STEP WAS NOT EXECUTED.
IEF373I STEP /STEP080 / START 94100.1106
IEF374I STEP /STEP080 / STOP  94100.1106 CPU    0MIN 00.00
```

This run abends in STEP050 with system completion code D37. ***Does the automatic data set cleanup work?***

In-step deletes are a function of DISP on DD statements.

This run has failed, and the automatic data set deletions clean up after it. The next generation of the DOWNLOAD file (lower oval), generation 105, ran out of disk space. The cleanup at STEP999 makes error correction and then complete rerun possible.

Figure 8.6 MVS/ESA System Reporting for a Failed Run

```
IEF236I ALLOC. FOR CSCJGJA STEP999
IEF237I 117  ALLOCATED TO STEPLIB
IEF237I 110  ALLOCATED TO
IEF237I 111  ALLOCATED TO SORTOUT
IEF237I 116  ALLOCATED TO NEWMAST
IEF237I 117  ALLOCATED TO DOWNRECS
IEF237I 111  ALLOCATED TO BADTR
IEF237I 116  ALLOCATED TO GOODREP
IEF237I 115  ALLOCATED TO AUDREP
IEF237I 115  ALLOCATED TO BADREP
IEF237I 111  ALLOCATED TO SUMREP


IEA995I SYMPTOM DUMP OUTPUT
  USER COMPLETION CODE=3333
 TIME=11.06.50  SEQ=18250  CPU=0000  ASID=0019
 PSW AT TIME OF ERROR  078D1000   836000FC  ILC 2  INTC 0D
   ACTIVE LOAD MODULE=ILBOABN    ADDRESS=03600048  OFFSET=000000B4
   DATA AT PSW  036000F6 - 00181610  0A0D0000  000047F0
   GPR  0-3  80000000  80000D05  00005219  03600100
   GPR  4-7  036001E2  00046038  00046038  8360004A
   GPR  8-11 800145A0  03602028  00045CC0  8360004A
   GPR 12-15 80014022  00045E80  8001459E  83600054
 END OF SYMPTOM DUMP

IEF472I CSCJGJA STEP999 - COMPLETION CODE - SYSTEM=000 USER=3333 REASON=00000000
IEF285I   CSCJGJ.ADV.LOADLIB                            KEPT
IEF285I   VOL SER NOS= USER03.
IEF285I   SYS1.COB2LIB                                  KEPT
IEF285I   VOL SER NOS= ACSRES.
IEF285I   CSCJGJ.REG.TRANSORT.G0143V00                  UNCATALOGED
IEF285I   VOL SER NOS= USER00.
IEF285I   CSCJGJ.REG.TRANSORT.G0143V00                  DELETED
IEF285I   VOL SER NOS= USER00.
IEF285I   CSCJGJ.REG.STUACCTS.G0148V00                  UNCATALOGED
IEF285I   VOL SER NOS= USER02.
IEF285I   CSCJGJ.REG.STUACCTS.G0148V00                  DELETED
IEF285I   VOL SER NOS= USER02.
IEF285I   CSCJGJ.REG.DOWNLOAD.G0105V00                  DELETED
IEF285I   VOL SER NOS= USER03.
IEF285I   CSCJGJ.REG.BADTRANS.G0004V00                  UNCATALOGED
IEF285I   VOL SER NOS= USER00.
IEF285I   CSCJGJ.REG.BADTRANS.G0004V00                  DELETED
IEF285I   VOL SER NOS= USER00.
IEF285I   CSCJGJ.REG.GOODREP.G0003V00                   UNCATALOGED
IEF285I   VOL SER NOS= USER02.
IEF285I   CSCJGJ.REG.GOODREP.G0003V00                   DELETED
IEF285I   VOL SER NOS= USER02.
IEF285I   CSCJGJ.REG.AUDREP.G0003V00                    UNCATALOGED
IEF285I   VOL SER NOS= USER01.
IEF285I   CSCJGJ.REG.AUDREP.G0003V00                    DELETED
IEF285I   VOL SER NOS= USER01.
IEF285I   CSCJGJ.REG.BADREP.G0003V00                    UNCATALOGED
IEF285I   VOL SER NOS= USER01.
IEF285I   CSCJGJ.REG.BADREP.G0003V00                    DELETED
IEF285I   VOL SER NOS= USER01.
IEF285I   CSCJGJ.REG.SUMREP.G0003V00                    DELETED
IEF285I   VOL SER NOS= USER00.
IEF373I STEP /STEP999 / START 94100.1106
IEF374I STEP /STEP999 / STOP  94100.1106 CPU    0MIN 00.18SEC SRB    0MIN 00.02SEC

IEF375I  JOB /CSCJGJA / START 94100.1106
IEF376I  JOB /CSCJGJA / STOP  94100.1106 CPU    0MIN 02.33SEC SRB    0MIN 00.11SEC
```

STEP999 executes because run failure has been detected. It deletes any data sets created in the run, including (+1) generations of whatever generation data sets were created. The USERABN program at STEP999 issues user completion code 3333 to call attention to the failure.

Figure 8.6 (continued)

1. Figure out what caused the D37 abend at STEP050. To do this, I would have to examine the complete body of MVS/ESA system reporting, using the SCANIT2 output as a guide to home in at the right place.
2. Correct the space allocation problem that the D37 points to. This could be something as simple as an insufficient space allocation, or something as troublesome as an unintentional loop in a program involving a statement that writes to the file.

3. Submit the REG33UP7 job again.

After problem correction, the "cure" for a rerunnable job stream is always the same. You simply submit it again and rerun it from its start.

8.7 Demonstrating a Failed Run (COND COND > 0004)

My demonstration of a rerunnable job stream would be incomplete if I did not illustrate how the coding model I am describing handles a COND CODE problem. In my job stream design, a COND CODE problem is one in which a program issues a condition code greater than 4, since such a COND CODE by convention indicates an error.

Due to the IF test coding in the REG33UP7 job stream, it handles a COND CODE problem in exactly the same way that it handles an abend that results in a system completion code. Examine Figure 8.7 and you will see that a COND CODE 0020 at STEP030 causes subsequent "worker" steps to be shut off. Again, however, STEP999 executes, and clears away all data sets created in the run. The cause of the COND CODE 0020 can be investigated, a

```
 SDSF OUTPUT DISPLAY CSCJGJA  JOB03645  DSID    101 LINE 1       COLUMNS 02- 81
 COMMAND INPUT ===>                                             SCROLL ===> PAGE
********************************************************************************
SCANIT2 HELPS YOU ANALYZE MVS/ESA JOB OUTPUT.  SEE MORE ABOUT THIS TOOL IN
"ADVANCED MVS JCL EXAMPLES" BY JIM JANOSSY (1994, JOHN WILEY & SONS, INC.)
********************************************************************************

 11.15.15 JOB03644  IRR010I  USERID CSCJGJ   IS ASSIGNED TO THIS
 IEF142I CSCJGJA STEP010 - STEP WAS EXECUTED - COND CODE 0000
 IEF142I CSCJGJA STEP020 - STEP WAS EXECUTED - COND CODE 0000
 IEF142I CSCJGJA STEP030 - STEP WAS EXECUTED - COND CODE 0020
 IEF206I CSCJGJA STEP040 - STEP WAS NOT RUN BECAUSE OF CONDITIONAL EXPRESSION ON
 IEF206I CSCJGJA STEP050 - STEP WAS NOT RUN BECAUSE OF CONDITIONAL EXPRESSION ON
 IEF206I CSCJGJA STEP060 - STEP WAS NOT RUN BECAUSE OF CONDITIONAL EXPRESSION ON
 IEF206I CSCJGJA STEP070 - STEP WAS NOT RUN BECAUSE OF CONDITIONAL EXPRESSION ON
 IEF206I CSCJGJA STEP080 - STEP WAS NOT RUN BECAUSE OF CONDITIONAL EXPRESSION ON
 IEF472I CSCJGJA STEP999 - COMPLETION CODE - SYSTEM=000 USER=3333 REASON=0000000

NO NON-ZERO SYSTEM COMPLETION CODE DETECTED

*** USER ABEND DETECTED WITH USER COMPLETION CODE 3333
```

This is output from a SCANIT2 analysis of the MVS/ESA system output of an REG33UP7 run that failed in a subtle way. The program at STEP030 issued condition code 0020, which might easily have been overlooked. Because of the IF/ELSE testing in the REG33UP7 job stream, this occurrence shut off the subsequent steps and triggered STEP999 to do automatic data set cleanups. *The problem can be fixed and the job simply rerun from the start, without error-prone step restart actions.*

Figure 8.7 MVS/ESA System Reporting for a Failed Run of REG33UP7, as Extracted by the SCANIT2 Program (condition code failure)

correction made, and the job stream submitted again for rerun. What could be simpler? And with simplicity of recovery comes reliability.

8.8 Demonstrating Print Rerun

Figure 8.8 lists a simple job stream named REPRINT7, which I created to handle report reruns from REG33UP7. The two steps in the job stream were copied from STEP060 and STEP070 in REG33UP7. I installed a symbolic parameter named &GEN to conveniently specify the generation of the print-line data sets to be copied to the printer for a report rerun.

```
EDIT ---- CSCJGJ.ADV.CNTL(REPRINT7) - 01.01 ----------------- COLUMNS 001 072
COMMAND ===>                                                  SCROLL ===> PAGE
****** ****************************** TOP OF DATA ******************************
000001 //CSCJGJA   JOB 1,                  ACCOUNTING INFORMATION
000002 //    'BIN 7--JANOSSY',             PROGRAMMER NAME AND DELIVERY BIN
000003 //    CLASS=A,                      INPUT QUEUE CLASS
000004 //    MSGLEVEL=(1,1),               HOW MUCH MVS SYSTEM PRINT DESIRED
000005 //    MSGCLASS=X,                   PRINT DESTINATION X A L N OR O
000006 //    TIME=(1,0),                   SAFETY LIMIT: RUN TIME UP TO 1 MINUTE
000007 //    REGION=3M,                    ALLOW UP TO 3 MEGS VIRTUAL MEMORY
000008 //*   TYPRUN=SCAN,                  UNCOMMENT THIS LINE TO DO SCAN ONLY
000009 //    NOTIFY=CSCJGJ                 WHO TO TELL WHEN JOB IS DONE
000010 //*
000011 //*   REPRINT SELECTED GENERATION OF REG33UP7 REPORTS
000012 //*   THIS JCL IS STORED AT CSCJGJ.ADV.CNTL(REPRINT7)
000013 //*
000014 //    SET GEN='(+0)'     UNCOMMENT TO REPRINT MOST RECENT REPORT
000015 //*   SET GEN='(-1)'     UNCOMMENT TO REPRINT NEXT TO LAST REPORT
000016 //*   SET GEN=           UNCOMMENT TO REPORT ALL GENERATIONS OF REPORTS
000017 //*
000018 //*----------------------------------
000019 //*   REPRINT 2-COPY REPORTS
000020 //*----------------------------------
000021 //STEP060   EXEC  PGM=IEBGENER
000022 //SYSPRINT    DD  SYSOUT=*
000023 //SYSIN       DD  DUMMY
000024 //SYSUT2      DD  SYSOUT=*,COPIES=2
000025 //SYSUT1      DD  DSN=CSCJGJ.REG.GOODREP&GEN,DISP=SHR
000026 //*-------------------------------------------------------------------
000027 //*   REPRINT 1-COPY REPORTS
000028 //*-------------------------------------------------------------------
000029 //STEP070   EXEC  PGM=IEBGENER
000030 //SYSPRINT    DD  SYSOUT=*
000031 //SYSIN       DD  DUMMY
000032 //SYSUT2      DD  SYSOUT=*,COPIES=1
000033 //SYSUT1      DD  DSN=CSCJGJ.REG.AUDREP&GEN,DISP=SHR
000034 //            DD  DSN=CSCJGJ.REG.BADREP&GEN,DISP=SHR
000035 //            DD  DSN=CSCJGJ.REG.SUMREP&GEN,DISP=SHR
000036 //
```

This special job stream is designed to allow convenient reprint of the paper reports produced by the REG33UP7 job stream. It is really just an extract of STEP060 and STEP070 of the job stream, and I have left the same stepnames in place. The instructions indicate how to reprint the most recent copy of stored printlines, how to reprint earlier reports, and how to print ***all*** generations of reports.

Figure 8.8 REPRINT7, A Job Stream to Reprint End-User Reports Produced in a Prior REG33UP7 Run

```
                    J E S 2   J O B   L O G  --  S Y S T E M   I B M 1  --  N O D E

11.30.38 JOB03658  IRR010I  USERID CSCJGJ   IS ASSIGNED TO THIS JOB.
11.30.39 JOB03658  ICH70001I CSCJGJ   LAST ACCESS AT 11:24:52 ON SUNDAY, APRIL 10,
11.30.39 JOB03658  $HASP373 CSCJGJA  STARTED - INIT  1 - CLASS A - SYS IBM1
11.30.41 JOB03658  $HASP395 CSCJGJA  ENDED

------ JES2 JOB STATISTICS ------
    10 APR 94 JOB EXECUTION DATE
           35 CARDS READ
        1,239 SYSOUT PRINT RECORDS
            0 SYSOUT PUNCH RECORDS
          161 SYSOUT SPOOL KBYTES
         0.03 MINUTES EXECUTION TIME

        1 //CSCJGJA   JOB 1,                      ACCOUNTING INFORMATION
          //    'BIN 7--JANOSSY',                 PROGRAMMER NAME AND DELIVERY BIN
          //    CLASS=A,                          INPUT QUEUE CLASS
          //    MSGLEVEL=(1,1),                   HOW MUCH MVS SYSTEM PRINT DESIRED
          //    MSGCLASS=X,                       PRINT DESTINATION X A L N OR O
          //    TIME=(1,0),                       SAFETY LIMIT: RUN TIME UP TO 1 MINUTE
          //    REGION=3M,                        ALLOW UP TO 3 MEGS VIRTUAL MEMORY
          //*   TYPRUN=SCAN,                      UNCOMMENT THIS LINE TO DO SCAN ONLY
          //    NOTIFY=CSCJGJ                     WHO TO TELL WHEN JOB IS DONE
          //*
          //*   REPRINT SELECTED GENERATION OF REG33UP7 REPORTS
          //*   THIS JCL IS STORED AT CSCJGJ.ADV.CNTL(REPRINT7)
          //*
        2 //    SET GEN='(+0)'      UNCOMMENT TO REPRINT MOST RECENT REPORT
          //*   SET GEN='(-1)'      UNCOMMENT TO REPRINT NEXT TO LAST REPORT
          //*   SET GEN=            UNCOMMENT TO REPORT ALL GENERATIONS OF REPORTS
          //*
          //*-----------------------------------------------------------------
          //*   REPRINT 2-COPY REPORTS
          //*-----------------------------------------------------------------
        3 //STEP060   EXEC  PGM=IEBGENER
        4 //SYSPRINT    DD  SYSOUT=*
        5 //SYSIN       DD  DUMMY
        6 //SYSUT2      DD  SYSOUT=*,COPIES=2
        7 //SYSUT1      DD  DSN=CSCJGJ.REG.GOODREP&GEN,DISP=SHR
          //*-----------------------------------------------------------------
          //*   REPRINT 1-COPY REPORTS
          //*-----------------------------------------------------------------
          IEFC653I SUBSTITUTION JCL - DSN=CSCJGJ.REG.GOODREP(+0),DISP=SHR
        8 //STEP070   EXEC  PGM=IEBGENER
        9 //SYSPRINT    DD  SYSOUT=*
       10 //SYSIN       DD  DUMMY
       11 //SYSUT2      DD  SYSOUT=*,COPIES=1
       12 //SYSUT1      DD  DSN=CSCJGJ.REG.AUDREP&GEN,DISP=SHR
          IEFC653I SUBSTITUTION JCL - DSN=CSCJGJ.REG.AUDREP(+0),DISP=SHR
       13 //            DD  DSN=CSCJGJ.REG.BADREP&GEN,DISP=SHR
          IEFC653I SUBSTITUTION JCL - DSN=CSCJGJ.REG.BADREP(+0),DISP=SHR
       14 //            DD  DSN=CSCJGJ.REG.SUMREP&GEN,DISP=SHR
          IEFC653I SUBSTITUTION JCL - DSN=CSCJGJ.REG.SUMREP(+0),DISP=SHR

ICH70001I CSCJGJ   LAST ACCESS AT 11:24:52 ON SUNDAY, APRIL 10, 1994
```

This run reprinted the current generation of the update job stream reports. The SET statement that remains uncommented assigns the value '(+0)' to the symbolic parameter GEN, which sets the generation number for each of the printline data sets to be copied to the printer. This could also have been coded as '(0)'. Coding a job stream like this, with multiple variations of a SET already in place, make it as easy and reliable as possible to use the JCL. This consideration gets more and more important all the time, as the scope of everyone's work broadens to include support for multiple machine platforms such as PCs and Unix systems.

Figure 8.9 MVS/ESA System Reporting for a Run of the REPRINT7 Job Stream, as Set to Reprint the Most Recent Reports

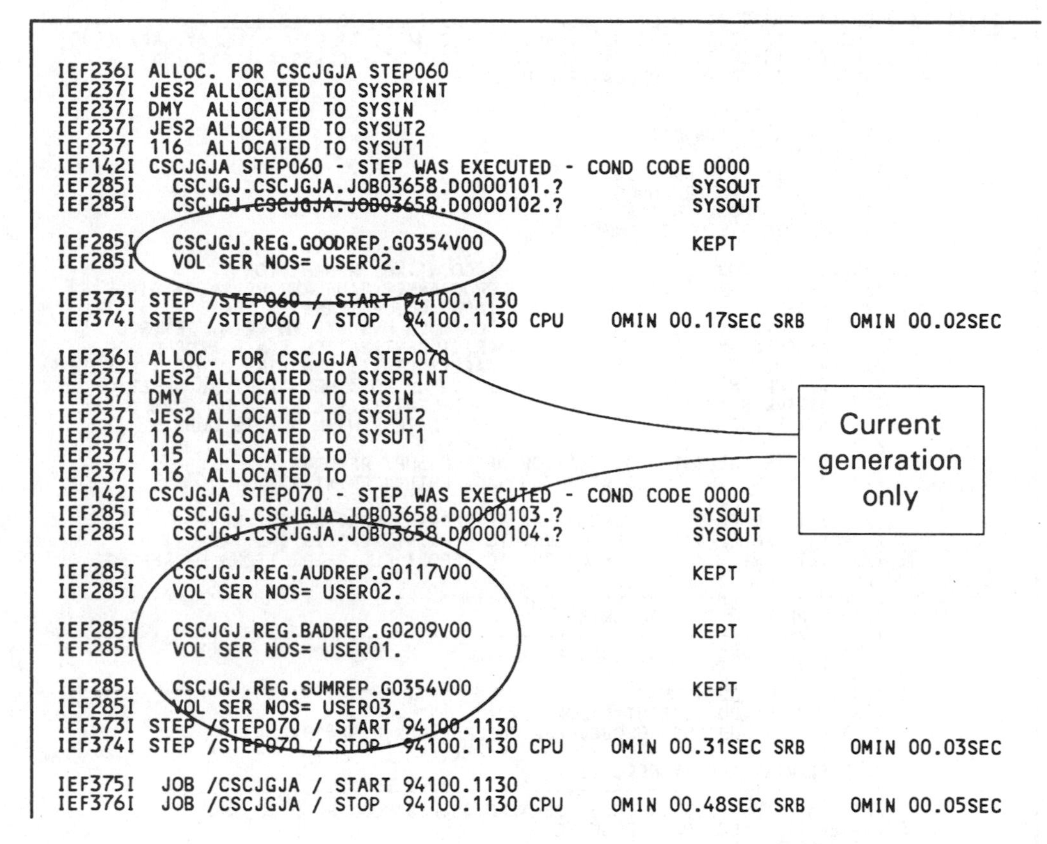

```
IEF236I ALLOC. FOR CSCJGJA STEP060
IEF237I JES2 ALLOCATED TO SYSPRINT
IEF237I DMY  ALLOCATED TO SYSIN
IEF237I JES2 ALLOCATED TO SYSUT2
IEF237I 116  ALLOCATED TO SYSUT1
IEF142I CSCJGJA STEP060 - STEP WAS EXECUTED - COND CODE 0000
IEF285I   CSCJGJ.CSCJGJA.JOB03658.D0000101.?                SYSOUT
IEF285I   CSCJGJ.CSCJGJA.JOB03658.D0000102.?                SYSOUT

IEF285I   CSCJGJ.REG.GOODREP.G0354V00                        KEPT
IEF285I   VOL SER NOS= USER02.

IEF373I STEP /STEP060 / START 94100.1130
IEF374I STEP /STEP060 / STOP  94100.1130 CPU    0MIN 00.17SEC SRB    0MIN 00.02SEC

IEF236I ALLOC. FOR CSCJGJA STEP070
IEF237I JES2 ALLOCATED TO SYSPRINT
IEF237I DMY  ALLOCATED TO SYSIN
IEF237I JES2 ALLOCATED TO SYSUT2
IEF237I 116  ALLOCATED TO SYSUT1
IEF237I 115  ALLOCATED TO
IEF237I 116  ALLOCATED TO
IEF142I CSCJGJA STEP070 - STEP WAS EXECUTED - COND CODE 0000
IEF285I   CSCJGJ.CSCJGJA.JOB03658.D0000103.?                SYSOUT
IEF285I   CSCJGJ.CSCJGJA.JOB03658.D0000104.?                SYSOUT

IEF285I   CSCJGJ.REG.AUDREP.G0117V00                         KEPT
IEF285I   VOL SER NOS= USER02.

IEF285I   CSCJGJ.REG.BADREP.G0209V00                         KEPT
IEF285I   VOL SER NOS= USER01.

IEF285I   CSCJGJ.REG.SUMREP.G0354V00                         KEPT
IEF285I   VOL SER NOS= USER03.
IEF373I STEP /STEP070 / START 94100.1130
IEF374I STEP /STEP070 / STOP  94100.1130 CPU    0MIN 00.31SEC SRB    0MIN 00.03SEC

IEF375I  JOB /CSCJGJA / START 94100.1130
IEF376I  JOB /CSCJGJA / STOP  94100.1130 CPU    0MIN 00.48SEC SRB    0MIN 00.05SEC
```


Figure 8.9 (continued)

As you can see in Figure 8.8, I coded three versions of the SET statement to assign values to the &GEN symbolic parameter. By commenting out two of them, and leaving one active, these different print reruns can be selected:

1. SET GEN='(+0)' specifies that the most recent, or "current," generation of printlines be printed. This could also have been coded as SET GEN='(0)' without the plus sign.
2. SET GEN='(−1) specifies that the second most recent (the penultimate) set of reports is to be printed.
3. SET GEN= nullifies the symbolic parameter, effectively eliminating it from the JCL. When you specify a generation data set name without a generation number, you are asking for "mass access" to all generations. Making this SET active will reprint *all* generations of the stored reports.

Figure 8.9 illustrates the MVS/ESA system reporting for a print rerun with SET GEN='(+0)'. You can see the absolute data set names of the most recent generations of the four printline data sets in this reporting.

```
                  J E S 2  J O B  L O G  --  S Y S T E M  I B M 1  --  N O D E

11.31.13 JOB03660  IRR010I  USERID CSCJGJ   IS ASSIGNED TO THIS JOB.
11.31.14 JOB03660  ICH70001I CSCJGJ   LAST ACCESS AT 11:31:01 ON SUNDAY, APRIL 10,
11.31.14 JOB03660  $HASP373 CSCJGJA  STARTED - INIT  1 - CLASS A - SYS IBM1
11.31.21 JOB03660  $HASP395 CSCJGJA  ENDED

------ JES2 JOB STATISTICS ------
  10 APR 94 JOB EXECUTION DATE
         35 CARDS READ
      2,397 SYSOUT PRINT RECORDS
          0 SYSOUT PUNCH RECORDS
        317 SYSOUT SPOOL KBYTES
       0.11 MINUTES EXECUTION TIME

        1 //CSCJGJA   JOB 1,                    ACCOUNTING INFORMATION
          //    'BIN 7--JANOSSY',                PROGRAMMER NAME AND DELIVERY BIN
          //    CLASS=A,                         INPUT QUEUE CLASS
          //    MSGLEVEL=(1,1),                  HOW MUCH MVS SYSTEM PRINT DESIRED
          //    MSGCLASS=X,                      PRINT DESTINATION X A L N OR O
          //    TIME=(1,0),                      SAFETY LIMIT: RUN TIME UP TO 1 MINUTE
          //    REGION=3M,                       ALLOW UP TO 3 MEGS VIRTUAL MEMORY
          //*   TYPRUN=SCAN,                     UNCOMMENT THIS LINE TO DO SCAN ONLY
          //    NOTIFY=CSCJGJ                    WHO TO TELL WHEN JOB IS DONE
          //*
          //*   REPRINT SELECTED GENERATION OF REG33UP7 REPORTS
          //*   THIS JCL IS STORED AT CSCJGJ.ADV.CNTL(REPRINT7)
          //*
          //*   SET GEN='(+0)'    UNCOMMENT TO REPRINT MOST RECENT REPORT
          //*   SET GEN='(-1)'    UNCOMMENT TO REPRINT NEXT TO LAST REPORT
        2 //    SET GEN=          UNCOMMENT TO REPORT ALL GENERATIONS OF REPORTS
          //*
          //*-----------------------------------------------------------------
          //*   REPRINT 2-COPY REPORTS
          //*-----------------------------------------------------------------
        3 //STEP060  EXEC  PGM=IEBGENER
        4 //SYSPRINT   DD  SYSOUT=*
        5 //SYSIN      DD  DUMMY
        6 //SYSUT2     DD  SYSOUT=*,COPIES=2
        7 //SYSUT1     DD  DSN=CSCJGJ.REG.GOODREP&GEN,DISP=SHR
          //*-----------------------------------------------------------------
          //*   REPRINT 1-COPY REPORTS
          //*-----------------------------------------------------------------
          IEFC653I SUBSTITUTION JCL - DSN=CSCJGJ.REG.GOODREP,DISP=SHR
        8 //STEP070  EXEC  PGM=IEBGENER
        9 //SYSPRINT   DD  SYSOUT=*
       10 //SYSIN      DD  DUMMY
       11 //SYSUT2     DD  SYSOUT=*,COPIES=1
       12 //SYSUT1     DD  DSN=CSCJGJ.REG.AUDREP&GEN,DISP=SHR
          IEFC653I SUBSTITUTION JCL - DSN=CSCJGJ.REG.AUDREP,DISP=SHR
       13 //           DD  DSN=CSCJGJ.REG.BADREP&GEN,DISP=SHR
          IEFC653I SUBSTITUTION JCL - DSN=CSCJGJ.REG.BADREP,DISP=SHR
       14 //           DD  DSN=CSCJGJ.REG.SUMREP&GEN,DISP=SHR
          IEFC653I SUBSTITUTION JCL - DSN=CSCJGJ.REG.SUMREP,DISP=SHR

ICH70001I CSCJGJ   LAST ACCESS AT 11:31:01 ON SUNDAY, APRIL 10, 1994
```

This run reprinted all existing generations of the update job stream reports, by nullifying the GEN symbolic parameter. I coded the symbolic parameter to include the parenthesis as well as the generation number to make this possible. This way, coding GEN= makes nothing appear after the data set name, and MVS/ESA sees this as a request to access all generations. The next page shows you how system reports indicates the absolute names of the data sets actually accessed. Reprinting all reports is a handy technique for instances where the reports are not overly large, and the end user can't seem to figure out *which* reports have been misplaced. (This technique can help preserve your sanity when dealing with particularly problematic end users.)

Figure 8.10 MVS/ESA System Reporting for a Run of the REPRINT7 Job Stream, as Set to Reprint All Generations of Reports

```
IEF236I ALLOC. FOR CSCJGJA STEP060
IEF237I JES2 ALLOCATED TO SYSPRINT
IEF237I DMY  ALLOCATED TO SYSIN
IEF237I JES2 ALLOCATED TO SYSUT2
IEF237I 116  ALLOCATED TO SYSUT1
IEF237I 111  ALLOCATED TO
IEF142I CSCJGJA STEP060 - STEP WAS EXECUTED - COND CODE 0000
IEF285I   CSCJGJ.CSCJGJA.JOB03660.D0000101.?              SYSOUT
IEF285I   CSCJGJ.CSCJGJA.JOB03660.D0000102.?              SYSOUT

IEF285I   CSCJGJ.REG.GOODREP.G0354V00                     KEPT
IEF285I   VOL SER NOS= USER02.
IEF285I   CSCJGJ.REG.GOODREP.G0353V00                     KEPT
IEF285I   VOL SER NOS= USER00.
IEF285I   CSCJGJ.REG.GOODREP.G0352V00                     KEPT
IEF285I   VOL SER NOS= USER00.

IEF373I STEP /STEP060 / START 94100.1131
IEF374I STEP /STEP060 / STOP  94100.1131 CPU    OMIN 00.25SEC SRB    OMIN 00.03SEC

IEF236I ALLOC. FOR CSCJGJA STEP070
IEF237I JES2 ALLOCATED TO SYSPRINT
IEF237I DMY  ALLOCATED TO SYSIN
IEF237I JES2 ALLOCATED TO SYSUT2
IEF237I 116  ALLOCATED TO SYSUT1
IEF237I 115  ALLOCATED TO
IEF237I 115  ALLOCATED TO
IEF237I 115  ALLOCATED TO
IEF237I 116  ALLOCATED TO
IEF237I 116  ALLOCATED TO
IEF142I CSCJGJA STEP070 - STEP WAS EXECUTED - COND CODE 0000
IEF285I   CSCJGJ.CSCJGJA.JOB03660.D0000103.?              SYSOUT
IEF285I   CSCJGJ.CSCJGJA.JOB03660.D0000104.?              SYSOUT

IEF285I   CSCJGJ.REG.AUDREP.G0117V00                      KEPT
IEF285I   VOL SER NOS= USER02.
IEF285I   CSCJGJ.REG.AUDREP.G0116V00                      KEPT
IEF285I   VOL SER NOS= USER01.
IEF285I   CSCJGJ.REG.AUDREP.G0115V00                      KEPT
IEF285I   VOL SER NOS= USER00.
IEF285I   CSCJGJ.REG.AUDREP.G0114V00                      KEPT
IEF285I   VOL SER NOS= USER01.

IEF285I   CSCJGJ.REG.BADREP.G0209V00                      KEPT
IEF285I   VOL SER NOS= USER01.
IEF285I   CSCJGJ.REG.BADREP.G0208V00                      KEPT
IEF285I   VOL SER NOS= USER00.
IEF285I   CSCJGJ.REG.BADREP.G0207V00                      KEPT
IEF285I   VOL SER NOS= USER02.

IEF285I   CSCJGJ.REG.SUMREP.G0354V00                      KEPT
IEF285I   VOL SER NOS= USER03.
IEF285I   CSCJGJ.REG.SUMREP.G0353V00                      KEPT
IEF285I   VOL SER NOS= USER01.
IEF285I   CSCJGJ.REG.SUMREP.G0352V00                      KEPT
IEF285I   VOL SER NOS= USER02.
IEF373I STEP /STEP070 / START 94100.1131
IEF374I STEP /STEP070 / STOP  94100.1131 CPU    OMIN 00.55SEC SRB    OMIN 00.06SEC

IEF375I  JOB /CSCJGJA / START 94100.1131
IEF376I  JOB /CSCJGJA / STOP  94100.1131 CPU    OMIN 00.80SEC SRB    OMIN 00.09SEC
```

Generations are accessed starting with the most recent and proceeding backward.

Figure 8.10 (continued)

Figure 8.10 shows you MVS/ESA system reporting for a run with SET GEN=. As you can see, the generations of each printline data set are accessed from the most recent to the oldest, working backward by generation number.

Based on my experience in commercial work, I think you'll occasionally find a complete report reprint a handy tool. If the bulk of reporting is small to moderate, reprinting all recent reports for a user who can't seem to specify what is missing is a lot easier than making multiple runs to try to fill a gap. I would not, however, suggest using this "shot gun" reprinting technique for large-volume reports for obvious reasons!

9

JCL for C, COBOL, and Assembler PARMs and Intercommunication

9.1 JCL and Programming Languages
9.2 An Example Scenario for PARM Usage
9.3 VS COBOL II Program Receiving a PARM
9.4 VS COBOL II Compile and Link
9.5 PARM Coding Complications
9.6 PARM Coding for Execution Within a Proc
9.7 PARM Coding for Runtime Environment Communication
9.8 Receiving a PARM in an Assembler Program
9.9 Assembling and Linking an Assembler Program
9.10 Executing an Assembler Program
9.11 Receiving a PARM in a C Program with argc and *argv[]
9.12 Trigraphs in Mainframe C Programs
9.13 Compiling and Linking a C/370 Program
9.14 Executing a C/370 Program
9.15 VS COBOL II CALLing a C/370 Subprogram
9.16 Passing Data Between COBOL and C
9.17 Static or Dynamic CALLs?
9.18 Compiling, Linking, and Running COBLMAIN and CSUB
9.19 RMODE and AMODE Considerations
9.20 C/370 Calling VS COBOL II
9.21 Compiling, Linking, and Running CMAIN and COBLSUB
9.22 C/370 Calling Assembler
9.23 Assembler Calling C/370

9.1 JCL and Programming Languages

When JCL was invented in the early 1960s, a number of factors made it appealing for many installations to use IBM's assembler language, also known as "Basic Assembly Language" or BAL. Essentially a mnemonic device to facilitate machine language programming, assembler can produce extremely efficient programs. Machines and storage devices of the early days were puny by today's standards, making machine efficiency of great concern. But assembler is very tedious to code and presents a great many opportunities to make logic and syntax errors.

In the 1970s, higher-level languages such as COBOL, Fortran, and PL/I became popular. These sacrificed machine efficiency and access to low-level features in the interest of coding ease, flexibility, and reliability. These higher-level languages can build assembler or machine language from symbolic source code when compiled. Now, the C language—already very popular with microcomputers and the Unix minicomputer environment—is gaining a following on mainframes because it provides high-level language features and convenience while also giving access to very low level facilities such as individual bit manipulations and dynamic memory allocation.

In this chapter we explore two advanced aspects of JCL usage in the MVS/ESA Version 4 environment. Programs are made more capable when they can be controlled by parameters using the PARM feature of the EXEC statement. We'll consider here how you can use PARM to feed controlling information into VS COBOL II, assembler, and C/370 programs. You'll see the JCL necessary to execute such programs, and also the program source code, JCL, and procs to prepare the programs themselves.

The programming language progression is bringing the need for *interlanguage communication* to the mainframe environment. Interlanguage communication occurs when a program in one language, such as VS COBOL II, CALLs a subprogram written in another language, such as C/370. In this chapter you will see complete program and JCL examples of COBOL calling C, C calling COBOL, C calling assembler, and assembler calling C. You can use these examples as a good first step and springboard to experimentation and implementation in your own installation.

I designed the C and assembler examples in this chapter and secured the assistance of Bob Narino, DePaul master's graduate and programmer analyst of Trans Union Corporation, Chicago, in preparing the actual C and assembler source code. Bob prepared the examples using C/370 on DePaul's IBM ES/9000 mainframe. C source code for SAS/C, another capable C compiler for IBM mainframes, would appear essentially identical to the source code you'll see here.

9.2 An Example Scenario for PARM Usage

Figure 9.1 shows you the content of a small data set containing payment records. Each record in this data set documents a mortgage payment made by a person to a lending institution. Each record appears like this:

```
112993 35256 WILLIE NILLY      089350
```

and contains these four fields:

```
EDIT ---- CSCJGJ.ADV.CNTL(PAYMENTS) - 01.00 ----------------- COLUMNS 001 072
COMMAND ===>                                                  SCROLL ===> PAGE
****** ***************************** TOP OF DATA ******************************
000001 112993 35256 WILLIE NILLY            089350
000002 112993 53257 MRS. IPPI               010550
000003 112993 61658 JERRY ATTRIC            036275
000004 112993 71860 MARSHA MALLOW           167380
000005 112993 31307 DELLA WARE              090815
000006 113093 64310 ARKAN SHAW              007620
000007 113093 75375 WILL B. DUNNE           120000
000008 113093 86447 T. TOTALLER             005023
000009 113093 22574 GEORGE AH               134575
000010 113093 36668 MOE ZOORI               010670
000011 113093 65778 R. U. SLEEPING          075430
000012 113093 20779 M. T. HEAD              005560
000013 113093 79112 LUCE CABOOSE            006123
000014 113093 43114 WILLIE MAKEIT           005950
000015 120193 64115 NOEY WOONT              029512
000016 120193 35189 IDA HOE                 000810
000017 120193 91190 VERN MONT               145640
000018 120193 43901 CANDI BARR              001615
000019 120193 33802 CAL IFORNIA             006824
000020 120193 66703 CRYSTAL SHANDELEER      098060
000021 120293 15661 LUCE CANNON             004072
000022 120293 28577 G. WHIZ                 038026
000023 120293 37230 D. TOUR                 003622
000024 120293 86583 CAROL INA               198543
000025 120393 61484 HARRY ZONA              013958
000026 120393 38507 MARGA RITA              014820
000027 120393 77257 O. FOOEY                145268
000028 120393 66521 AL ABAMA                127510
000029 120393 15322 KEN TUCKY               006865
000030 120493 08514 CHIC N. LITTLE          031960
```

The data read by program J1COBOL consists of payment records. Each record carries a payment date, shown by the arrow. The program will select and list only the payment records with the payment date specified in the **PARM** on the EXEC.

Figure 9.1 Payment Transactions to Be Read by COBOL, Assembler, and C programs Using a PARM for Demonstration Purposes

```
Date of payment     112993
Account number      35256
Name of payer       WILLIE NILLY
Amount of payment   089350        (This is 893.50)
```

Figure 9.1 depicts this data as it appears on a TSO/ISPF "edit" screen, with line numbers at the left. We'll use this data set as input to a program that selects records based on payment date and lists the selected records in a simple format. For example, for the date 12/01/93, the program would produce a listing such as this:

```
PARM DATA ENTERED = "120193"

REPORT WILL LIST A SELECTION OF RECORDS FOR 120193
120193 64115 NOEY WOONT                  295.12
120193 35189 IDA HOE                       8.10
120193 91190 VERN MONT                 1,456.40
120193 43901 CANDI BARR                   16.15
120193 33802 CAL IFORNIA                  68.24
120193 66703 CRYSTAL SHANDELEER          980.60
                                   $   2,824.61
```

```
TOTAL RECORDS READ       30
TOTAL RECORDS LISTED      6
```

PARM presents an excellent technique to control the listing program, so that it can be run, without recompiling, to produce different lists of selected records. We wish to execute and control programs written in VS COBOL II, assembler, and C with an exec statement that looks like this:

```
//STEP010   EXEC   PGM=J1COBOL,PARM='120193'
```

Figure 9.2 shows you the JCL to execute the first of the example PARM programs, a VS COBOL II program named J1COBOL. Figure 9.3 lists the MVS/ESA system output for a run of this program.

```
EDIT ---- CSCJGJ.ADV.CNTL(J1COBOL) - 01.03 ------------------- COLUMNS 001 072
COMMAND ===> sub                                               SCROLL ===> PAGE
****** ******************************* TOP OF DATA ******************************
000001 //CSCJGJA    JOB 1,                      ACCOUNTING INFORMATION
000002 //   'BIN 7--JANOSSY',                   PROGRAMMER NAME AND DELIVERY BIN
000003 //   MSGLEVEL=(1,1),                     HOW MUCH MVS SYSTEM PRINT DESIRED
000004 //   MSGCLASS=X,                         PRINT DESTINATION X A L N OR O
000005 //*  TYPRUN=SCAN,                        UNCOMMENT IF WANT ONLY A JCL SCAN
000006 //   NOTIFY=CSCJGJ                       WHO TO TELL WHEN JOB IS DONE
000007 //*
000008 //***********************************************************************
000009 //* J1COBOL   RUN J1COBOL PARM DEMO PROGRAM                              *
000010 //***********************************************************************
000011 //STEP010   EXEC   PGM=J1COBOL,PARM='120193'
000012 //STEPLIB     DD   DSN=CSCJGJ.ADV.LOADLIB,DISP=SHR
000013 //            DD   DSN=SYS1.COB2LIB,DISP=SHR
000014 //SYSOUT      DD   SYSOUT=*
000015 //PAYDAT      DD   DSN=CSCJGJ.ADV.CNTL(PAYMENTS),DISP=SHR
000016 //PAYLIST     DD   SYSOUT=*
000017 //
```

Coding **PARM** on an EXEC statement causes MVS to count the number of characters coded between the apostrophes. MVS puts this count into a two-byte binary field, followed by the up to 100 characters themselves. It then gives the program the address of this 102-byte block of memory. This is how **PARM** passes data into a program.

Figure 9.2 How You Code JCL to Execute a Program Passing a PARM

```
                    J E S 2  J O B  L O G  --  S Y S T E M  I B M 1  --  N O D E  N 1

20.01.30 JOB08151  IRR010I  USERID CSCJGJ   IS ASSIGNED TO THIS JOB.
20.01.30 JOB08151  ICH70001I CSCJGJ   LAST ACCESS AT 19:59:34 ON THURSDAY, JULY 8, 1993
20.01.30 JOB08151  $HASP373 CSCJGJA  STARTED - INIT  1 - CLASS A - SYS IBM1
20.01.33 JOB08151  $HASP395 CSCJGJA  ENDED

------ JES2 JOB STATISTICS ------
    08 JUL 93 JOB EXECUTION DATE
           16 CARDS READ
           61 SYSOUT PRINT RECORDS
            0 SYSOUT PUNCH RECORDS
            3 SYSOUT SPOOL KBYTES
         0.05 MINUTES EXECUTION TIME

        1 //CSCJGJA   JOB 1,                    ACCOUNTING INFORMATION          JOB08151
          //  'BIN 7--JANOSSY',                 PROGRAMMER NAME AND DELIVERY BIN
          //  MSGLEVEL=(1,1),                   HOW MUCH MVS SYSTEM PRINT DESIRED
          //  MSGCLASS=X,                       PRINT DESTINATION X A L N OR O
          //* TYPRUN=SCAN,                      UNCOMMENT IF WANT ONLY A JCL SCAN
          //  NOTIFY=CSCJGJ                     WHO TO TELL WHEN JOB IS DONE
          //*
          //*****************************************************************
          //* J1COBOL  RUN J1COBOL PARM DEMO PROGRAM
          //*****************************************************************
        2 //STEP010  EXEC  PGM=J1COBOL,PARM='120193'
        3 //STEPLIB    DD  DSN=CSCJGJ.ADV.LOADLIB,DISP=SHR
        4 //           DD  DSN=SYS1.COB2LIB,DISP=SHR
        5 //SYSOUT     DD  SYSOUT=*
        6 //PAYDAT     DD  DSN=CSCJGJ.ADV.CNTL(PAYMENTS),DISP=SHR
        7 //PAYLIST    DD  SYSOUT=*

ICH70001I CSCJGJ   LAST ACCESS AT 19:59:34 ON THURSDAY, JULY 8, 1993
```

PARM sends data into the program via JCL. In this case the data is a date that the program uses to select records for printing.

Figure 9.3 MVS/ESA System Output and Program Output from J1COBOL Selecting Records for December 1, 1993 with PARM='120193'

```
IEF236I ALLOC. FOR CSCJGJA STEP010
IEF237I 117  ALLOCATED TO STEPLIB
IEF237I 110  ALLOCATED TO
IEF237I JES2 ALLOCATED TO SYSOUT
IEF237I 111  ALLOCATED TO PAYDAT
IEF237I JES2 ALLOCATED TO PAYLIST
IEF142I CSCJGJA STEP010 - STEP WAS EXECUTED - COND CODE 0000
IEF285I   CSCJGJ.ADV.LOADLIB                           KEPT
IEF285I   VOL SER NOS= USER03.
IEF285I   SYS1.COB2LIB                                 KEPT
IEF285I   VOL SER NOS= ACSRES.
IEF285I   CSCJGJ.CSCJGJA.JOB08151.D0000101.?           SYSOUT
IEF285I   CSCJGJ.ADV.CNTL                              KEPT
IEF285I   VOL SER NOS= USER00.
IEF285I   CSCJGJ.CSCJGJA.JOB08151.D0000102.?           SYSOUT
IEF373I STEP /STEP010 / START 93189.2001
IEF374I STEP /STEP010 / STOP  93189.2001 CPU    0MIN 00.19SEC SRB    0MIN 00.02SEC VIRT   296K SYS   228K EXT       4K SYS    9040K

IEF375I  JOB /CSCJGJA / START 93189.2001
IEF376I  JOB /CSCJGJA / STOP  93189.2001 CPU    0MIN 00.19SEC SRB    0MIN 00.02SEC

PARM DATA ENTERED = "120193"

REPORT WILL LIST A SELECTION OF RECORDS FOR 120193
120193 64115 NOEY WOONT                295.12
120193 35189 IDA HOE                     8.10
120193 91190 VERN MONT               1,456.40
120193 43901 CANDI BARR                 16.15
120193 33802 CAL IFORNIA                68.24
120193 66703 CRYSTAL SHANDELEER        980.60
                                 $   2,824.61
TOTAL RECORDS READ      30
TOTAL RECORDS LISTED     6
```

Output of the program is controlled by the **PARM** value and is limited to the records that carry the date indicated. The **PARM** feature is very handy as a means to give programs flexibility.

Figure 9.3 (continued)

9.3 VS COBOL II Program Receiving a PARM

Figure 9.4 lists the VS COBOL II source code for J1COBOL. Follow the annotations on this figure to see how coding is arranged in a LINKAGE SECTION to acquire access to the up to 102-byte memory area that MVS/ESA creates when PARM is coded on an EXEC statement. In particular, note the PARM validation actions that you have to take before using the PARM value received for selection purposes. I coded J1COBOL using a modern streamlined coding style made possible by VS COBOL II and COBOL/370. If you need more information about these new coding constructs, such as omitted FILLER, NOT AT END, SET for condition names, and other features such as hex values, in-line PERFORMS, EVALUATE, INITIALIZE, user-defined data classes, and much more, see *VS COBOL II Highlights and Techniques* by James Janossy, published by John Wiley & Sons, Inc., in 1992.

9.4 VS COBOL II Compile and Link

The JCL in Figure 9.2 executes an already prepared load module for J1COBOL and so depicts very straightforward EXEC coding. To prepare this load module, I submitted the JCL named MYCL shown in Figure 9.5. MYCL stands for "my compile and link" and invokes a proc named COB2CLJ. This is our locally tuned copy of IBM's standard VS COBOL II COB2UCL proc, shown in Figure 9.6. If you review Chapter 6, you will see how I applied the advice I've given there to tuning up this proc, making it more efficient.

9.5 PARM Coding Complications

The EXEC statement PARM coding shown in Figure 9.2 is simple, but PARM coding sometimes becomes more complicated for two reasons. You need to code PARM differently when you feed a PARM to a program that you execute with a proc. In addition, some program language environments allow PARM to communicate with the program being executed or the runtime (support) environment. Let's consider each situation separately.

9.6 PARM Coding for Execution Within a Proc

You may prefer to compile, link, and run a program in one action using a proc such as COB2J, shown earlier in Figure 2.9 in Chapter 2. When you execute a program via a proc, and the program is intended to receive a PARM, you have to code PARM.stepname as shown in Figure 9.7. "Stepname" in this coding is the name of the step at which the program will be executed, which is GO in this case, so I coded PARM.GO=.

Notice that the coding of PARM for a program executed via a proc is exactly the opposite of the coding for DD statements intended for a program, which are coded with stepname first, such as GO.PAYDAT and GO.PAYLIST in Figure 9.7. Given the cryptic nature of JCL in general, this difference in coding often causes confusion and miscoding even for experienced JCL users.

```
EDIT ---- CSCJGJ.ADV.COBOL(J1COBOL) - 01.00 ------------------ COLUMNS 007 078
COMMAND ===>                                                  SCROLL ===> PAGE
****** ***************************** TOP OF DATA ******************************
000100 ID DIVISION.
000200 PROGRAM-ID.     J1COBOL.
000300 AUTHOR.         J JANOSSY.
000400 *
000500 *   LIST PAYMENT RECORDS SELECTING BY DATE VIA PARM
000600 *
000700 ENVIRONMENT DIVISION.
000800 INPUT-OUTPUT SECTION.
000900 FILE-CONTROL.
001000     SELECT PAYMENT-FILE           ASSIGN TO PAYDAT.
001200     SELECT PAYMENT-LISTING        ASSIGN TO PAYLIST.
001400
001500 DATA DIVISION.
001600 FILE SECTION.
001700
001800 FD  PAYMENT-FILE
001900     LABEL RECORDS ARE STANDARD
002000     BLOCK CONTAINS 0 RECORDS
002100     RECORD CONTAINS 80 CHARACTERS.
002200 01  PAYMENT-RECORD.
002300     05 PR-PAYMENT-DATE            PIC X(6).
002400     05                            PIC X(1).
002500     05 PR-PAYER-ID                PIC X(5).
002600     05                            PIC X(1).
002700     05 PR-PAYER-NAME              PIC X(20).
002800     05                            PIC X(1).
002900     05 PR-PAYMENT-AMOUNT          PIC 9(4)V99.
003000     05                            PIC X(40).
003100
003200 FD  PAYMENT-LISTING
003300     LABEL RECORDS ARE OMITTED
003400     BLOCK CONTAINS 0 RECORDS
003500     RECORD CONTAINS 75 CHARACTERS.
003600 01  PAYMENT-LISTING-RECORD        PIC X(75).
003700 /
003800 WORKING-STORAGE SECTION.
003900 01  PIC X(1)   VALUE 'M'.    88  END-OF-FILE  VALUE 'E'.
004000 01  WS-RECORDS-READ-COUNT         PIC 9(5)     VALUE 0.
004100 01  WS-RECORDS-LISTED-COUNT       PIC 9(5)     VALUE 0.
004200 01  WS-PAYMENT-AMT-TOTAL          PIC 9(7)V99  VALUE 0.
004300
004400 01  LISTING-PRINTLINE.
004500     05                            PIC X(1)  VALUE SPACE.
004600     05 LP-PAYMENT-DATE            PIC X(6).
004700     05                            PIC X(1)  VALUE SPACE.
004800     05 LP-PAYER-ID                PIC X(5).
004900     05                            PIC X(1)  VALUE SPACE.
005000     05 LP-PAYER-NAME              PIC X(21).
005100     05                            PIC X(1)  VALUE SPACE.
005200     05 LP-PAYMENT-AMOUNT          PIC Z,ZZZ.99.
005300
005400 01  GRAND-TOTAL-PRINTLINE.
005500     05                            PIC X(1)  VALUE SPACE.
005600     05                            PIC X(30) VALUE SPACES.
005700     05 GTP-PAYMENT-AMT-TOTAL      PIC $Z,ZZZ,ZZZ.99.
005800
005900 01  READ-COUNT-PRINTLINE.
006000     05                            PIC X(1)  VALUE SPACE.
006100     05            PIC X(21) VALUE 'TOTAL RECORDS READ   '.
006200     05 RCP-RECORDS-READ-COUNT     PIC ZZZZ9.
006300
006400 01  LISTED-COUNT-PRINTLINE.
006500     05                            PIC X(1)  VALUE SPACE.
006600     05            PIC X(21) VALUE 'TOTAL RECORDS LISTED '.
006700     05 LCP-RECORDS-LISTED-COUNT   PIC ZZZZ9.
006800
```

This is a VS COBOL II program and I have used several 1985 COBOL features in it, such as omitting FILLER coding and using SET with 88 level names.

Figure 9.4 VS COBOL II Source Code for the J1COBOL Program, Which Receives a PARM Value

```
006900  LINKAGE SECTION.
007000  01  USER-PARM.
007100      05 UP-LENGTH                  PIC S9(4) BINARY.
007200      05 UP-DATA.
007300         10 UP-DATA-BYTE  OCCURS 0 TO 100 TIMES
007400                          DEPENDING ON UP-LENGTH  PIC X(1).
007500 /
007600  PROCEDURE DIVISION USING USER-PARM.
007700  0000-MAINLINE.
007800      PERFORM 1000-BOJ.
007900      PERFORM 2000-PROCESS-A-RECORD  UNTIL END-OF-FILE.
008000      PERFORM 3000-EOJ.
008100      STOP RUN.
008200
008300  1000-BOJ.
008400      IF UP-LENGTH = 0
008500         DISPLAY '** ERROR ** NO DATE PARM ENTERED ON EXEC!'
008600         STOP RUN.
008700
008800      DISPLAY 'PARM DATA ENTERED = "', UP-DATA, '"'.
008900      IF UP-LENGTH NOT = 6
009000         DISPLAY '** ERROR ** INVALID DATE ENTERED ON EXEC!'
009100         STOP RUN.
009200
009300      IF UP-DATA NOT NUMERIC
009400         DISPLAY '** ERROR ** INVALID DATE ENTERED ON EXEC!'
009500         STOP RUN.
009600
009700      OPEN   INPUT  PAYMENT-FILE   OUTPUT  PAYMENT-LISTING.
009800
009900      STRING ' REPORT WILL LIST A SELECTION OF RECORDS FOR ',
010000         UP-DATA  DELIMITED BY SIZE
010100         INTO PAYMENT-LISTING-RECORD.
010200      WRITE PAYMENT-LISTING-RECORD
010300         AFTER ADVANCING 1 LINES.
010400
010500      PERFORM 2700-READ-A-RECORD.
010600
010700  2000-PROCESS-A-RECORD.
010800      IF PR-PAYMENT-DATE = UP-DATA
010900         PERFORM 2100-LIST-THE-RECORD.
011000      PERFORM 2700-READ-A-RECORD.
011100
011200  2100-LIST-THE-RECORD.
011300      MOVE PR-PAYMENT-DATE     TO  LP-PAYMENT-DATE.
011400      MOVE PR-PAYER-ID         TO  LP-PAYER-ID.
011500      MOVE PR-PAYER-NAME       TO  LP-PAYER-NAME.
011600      MOVE PR-PAYMENT-AMOUNT   TO  LP-PAYMENT-AMOUNT.
011700      WRITE PAYMENT-LISTING-RECORD
011800         FROM LISTING-PRINTLINE
011900         AFTER ADVANCING 1 LINES.
012000      ADD 1 TO WS-RECORDS-LISTED-COUNT.
012100      ADD PR-PAYMENT-AMOUNT TO WS-PAYMENT-AMT-TOTAL.
012200
012300  2700-READ-A-RECORD.
012400      READ PAYMENT-FILE
012500         AT END
012600            SET END-OF-FILE TO TRUE
012700         NOT AT END
012800            ADD 1 TO WS-RECORDS-READ-COUNT.
012900
013000  3000-EOJ.
013100      MOVE WS-PAYMENT-AMT-TOTAL TO GTP-PAYMENT-AMT-TOTAL.
013200      WRITE PAYMENT-LISTING-RECORD FROM GRAND-TOTAL-PRINTLINE
013300         AFTER ADVANCING 1 LINES.
013400
013500      MOVE WS-RECORDS-READ-COUNT TO RCP-RECORDS-READ-COUNT.
013600      WRITE PAYMENT-LISTING-RECORD FROM READ-COUNT-PRINTLINE
013700         AFTER ADVANCING 1 LINES.
013800
013900      MOVE WS-RECORDS-LISTED-COUNT TO LCP-RECORDS-LISTED-COUNT.
014000      WRITE PAYMENT-LISTING-RECORD FROM LISTED-COUNT-PRINTLINE
014100         AFTER ADVANCING 1 LINES.
014200      CLOSE  PAYMENT-FILE  PAYMENT-LISTING.
```

Coding to receive the **PARM**

Coding to validate the **PARM** before using it

Using the **PARM** data for record selection

Figure 9.4 (continued)

```
EDIT ---- CSCJGJ.ADV.CNTL(MYCL) - 01.76 --------------------- COLUMNS 001 072
COMMAND ===>                                                  SCROLL ===> PAGE
****** ***************************** TOP OF DATA ******************************
000001 //CSCJGJA   JOB 1,                 ACCOUNTING INFORMATION
000002 //   'BIN 7--JANOSSY',             PROGRAMMER NAME AND DELIVERY BIN
000003 //   CLASS=A,                      INPUT QUEUE CLASS
000004 //   MSGLEVEL=(1,1),               HOW MUCH MVS SYSTEM PRINT DESIRED
000005 //   MSGCLASS=X,                   PRINT DESTINATION X A L N OR O
000006 //   TIME=(0,6),                   SAFETY LIMIT: RUN TIME UP TO 6 SECS
000007 //   REGION=2M,                    ALLOW UP TO 2 MEGS VIRTUAL MEMORY
000008 //   NOTIFY=CSCJGJ                 WHO TO TELL WHEN JOB IS DONE
000009 //*
000010 //*******************************************************************
000011 //* COMPILE AND LINK USING VS COBOL II                               *
000012 //*******************************************************************
000013 //STEP010  EXEC  COB2CLJ,
000014 //       PDS='CSCJGJ.ADV.COBOL',
000015 //    MEMBER='J1COBOL',
000016 //   LOADLIB='CSCJGJ.ADV.LOADLIB'
000017 //
```

Prepare a load module from VS COBOL II source code

Figure 9.5 MYCL, JCL to Compile and Link VS COBOL II Program J1COBOL by Invoking the COB2CLJ Proc Shown in Figure 9.6

9.7 PARM Coding for Runtime Environment Communication

PARM coding becomes potentially more complicated for some language environments such as VS COBOL II, in which a runtime environment supports the execution of the program. Some of these environments can be informed to operate differently via a PARM on the EXEC statement for the program to be executed. If a program expects to receive its own PARM, and the runtime environment can also receive a PARM, how do you indicate which is which in your PARM coding?

Here is PARM coding to execute a VS COBOL II program such as J1COBOL, which expects to receive a PARM, and also communicate to the VS COBOL II runtime environment not to do subscript range checking, a runtime PARM (not actually relevant to what J1COBOL does!):

```
//STEP010   EXEC   PGM=J1COBOL,PARM='120193/NOSSRANGE'
```

The forward slash is a separator that delimits the program's PARM from the runtime environment PARM. The program will receive 120193. The runtime environment will receive NOSSRANGE. Neither will actually receive the "/" character.

Because "/" is treated in this special way, you cannot use it within a PARM value that is intended to be received by a program. For example, you

Figure 9.6 COB2CLJ, A Locally Customized Proc Based on IBM's Standard Proc COB2UCL, to Compile and Link a VS COBOL II Program (see facing page)

```
EDIT ---- CSC.PROCLIB(COB2CLJ) - 01.06 ----------------------- COLUMNS 001 072
COMMAND ===>                                                    SCROLL ===> PAGE
****** ******************************* TOP OF DATA ******************************
000100 //COB2CLJ  PROC PDS='***',      NAME OF SOURCE CODE LIBRARY
000200 //   MEMBER='***',              NAME OF PROGRAM MEMBER TO COMPILE
000300 //  PRINTAT='*',                PRINT DESTINATION
000400 //  LOADLIB='***'
000500 //*****************************************************************
000600 //*                                                               *
000700 //*  DEPAUL UNIVERSITY  DEPT OF COMPUTER SCIENCE AND INFO SYSTEMS  *
000800 //*  COMPILE AND LINK USING VS COBOL II                           *
000900 //*                                         JIM JANOSSY 9/06/92   *
001000 //*                                                               *
001100 //*****************************************************************
001200 //*
001300 //*  VS COBOL II COMPILE
001400 //*
001500 //COB2    EXEC PGM=IGYCRCTL,REGION=2048K,TIME=(,6), *****************
001600 //  PARM=('NOADV',              PGM RESERVES CC BYTE COL 1 **       **
001700 //        'NOCMPR2',            DON'T EMULATE RELEASE 2    **       **
001800 //        'NUMPROC(PFD)',       PREFERRED SIGN HANDLING    **       **
001900 //        'FLAG(I,E)',          ALL MSGS; IMBED ERROR MSGS **       **
002000 //        'DYN',                USE DYNAMIC LOADING        **       **
002100 //        'LANGUAGE(UE)',       HEADING/MSGS UPPERCASE     **       **
002200 //        'APOST',              USE APOSTROPHE AS QUOTE    **       **
002300 //        'FDUMP',              GIVE FORMATTED ABEND DUMP  **       **
002400 //        'LIB',                COPY LIBRARY OK            **       **
002500 //        'NOMAP',              NO IMBEDDED CELL REFS      **       **
002600 //        'OBJ',                PRODUCE OBJECT CODE        **       **
002700 //        'RES',                MAKE CODE DYN RESIDENT     **       **
002800 //        'RENT',               RES + RENT GIVES AMODE 31  **       **
002900 //        'NOOPT',              GIVES LINE # ON ABEND      ** COMPILE **
003000 //        'XREF')               PROVIDE IMBEDDED CROSS REF **       **
003100 //STEPLIB  DD  DSN=SYS1.COB2COMP,DISP=SHR                  **       **
003200 //SYSIN    DD  DSN=&PDS(&MEMBER),DISP=SHR                  **       **
003300 //SYSLIB   DD  DSN=&PDS,DISP=SHR                           **       **
003400 //SYSPRINT DD  SYSOUT=&PRINTAT                             **       **
003500 //SYSLIN   DD  DSN=&&LOADSET,                              **       **
003600 //  DISP=(NEW,PASS),                                        **       **
003700 //  UNIT=VIO,                                               **       **
003800 //  SPACE=(TRK,(3,3),RLSE),                                 **       **
003900 //  DCB=(RECFM=FB,LRECL=80,BLKSIZE=3120)                    **       **
004000 //SYSUT1   DD  UNIT=VIO,SPACE=(CYL,(1,1))                  **       **
004100 //SYSUT2   DD  UNIT=VIO,SPACE=(CYL,(1,1))                  **       **
004200 //SYSUT3   DD  UNIT=VIO,SPACE=(CYL,(1,1))                  **       **
004300 //SYSUT4   DD  UNIT=VIO,SPACE=(CYL,(1,1))                  **       **
004400 //SYSUT5   DD  UNIT=VIO,SPACE=(CYL,(1,1))                  **       **
004500 //SYSUT6   DD  UNIT=VIO,SPACE=(CYL,(1,1))                  **       **
004600 //SYSUT7   DD  UNIT=VIO,SPACE=(CYL,(1,1)) ***************************
004700 //*
004800 //*  LINK EDIT
004900 //*
005000 //LKED   EXEC  PGM=IEWL,                                   *************
005100 //  PARM=('SIZE=2048K'),                                    **       **
005200 //  TIME=(,6),                                              **       **
005300 //  COND=(4,LT,COB2)                                        **       **
005400 //SYSLIN   DD  DSN=&&LOADSET,DISP=(OLD,DELETE)             **  LINK  **
005500 //SYSLMOD  DD  DSN=&LOADLIB(&MEMBER),                      **       **
005600 //  DISP=SHR                                                **       **
005700 //SYSLIB   DD  DSN=SYS1.COB2LIB,DISP=SHR                   **       **
005800 //SYSUT1   DD  UNIT=VIO,SPACE=(CYL,(1,1))                  **       **
005900 //SYSPRINT DD  SYSOUT=&PRINTAT ***************************************
```

Here you see the COB2CLJ proc, which compiles and links a VS COBOL II program. I used this to prepare the load module for the COBLMAIN program. This proc is a locally tuned-up version of IBM's standard COB2UCL proc. If you compare this to Figure 2.9 in Chapter 2, you'll see that this is really just the first two steps of the COB2J compile/link/go proc. Review Chapter 6 to see the steps I followed to streamline this proc and increase its efficiency.

```
EDIT ---- CSCJGJ.ADV.CNTL(J1COBOLC) - 01.01 ----------------- COLUMNS 001 072
COMMAND ===>                                                  SCROLL ===> PAGE
****** ****************************** TOP OF DATA ******************************
000001 //CSCJGJA   JOB 1,                    ACCOUNTING INFORMATION
000002 //   'BIN 7--JANOSSY',                PROGRAMMER NAME AND DELIVERY BIN
000003 //   CLASS=A,                         INPUT QUEUE CLASS
000004 //   MSGLEVEL=(1,1),                  HOW MUCH MVS SYSTEM PRINT DESIRED
000005 //   MSGCLASS=X,                      PRINT DESTINATION X A L N OR O
000006 //   TIME=(0,6),                      SAFETY LIMIT: RUN TIME UP TO 6 SECS
000007 //   REGION=2M,                       ALLOW UP TO 2 MEGS VIRTUAL MEMORY
000008 //   NOTIFY=CSCJGJ                    WHO TO TELL WHEN JOB IS DONE
000009 //*
000010 //*********************************************
000011 //* COMPILE, LINK, AND GO USING VS COBOL
000012 //*********************************************
000013 //STEP010  EXEC  COB2J,PARM.GO='120193',
000014 //   PDS='CSCJGJ.ADV.COBOL',
000015 //   MEMBER='J1COBOL'
000016 //GO.PAYDAT  DD  DSN=CSCJGJ.ADV.CNTL(PAYMENTS),
000017 //   DISP=SHR
000018 //GO.PAYLIST DD  SYSOUT=*
000019 //
```

PARM.GO feeds data at the GO step when you use a compile, link, and go proc such as COB2J.

//GO. ... is needed for DD statements when using a compile, link, go proc to associate the statements with the GO step.

Figure 9.7 JCL to Compile, Link, and Run J1COBOL, Illustrating How to Pass a PARM to the Runtime Environment

could not arrange to code a date PARM such as 120193 as 12/01/93. You could, however, design it to be coded as 12-01-93 or 12 01 93 simply by changing the LINKAGE SECTION declarations in a program such as J1COBOL to allow for the "filler" positions between the parts of the date.

9.8 Receiving a PARM in an Assembler Program

Figure 9.8 presents the source code for program J1ASM, which accomplishes the same thing in System/370 assembler that J1COBOL does in VS COBOL II. Using standard IBM interlanguage calling conventions, the location of the 102-byte PARM string in memory is pointed to by register 1 as this program receives control. The location of the 102-byte PARM string in memory is copied into register 3 from register 1 as the program begins execution. The first two bytes contain a 16-bit binary number indicating the length of the PARM field coded on the EXEC. If no PARM was coded, this value is zero. The PARM data itself starts in the third position of the 102-byte memory area that holds the length and PARM. J1ASM validates the PARM value and uses it to select records from the payments file. Like J1COBOL, J1ASM produces a list of the selected records.

Figure 9.8 J1ASM, An Assembler Program That Reads a File and Selects and Prints Records from It Using a PARM Value (see facing page)

```
EDIT ---- CSCJGJ.ADV.ASM(J1ASM) - 01.00 --------------------- COLUMNS 001 072
COMMAND ===>                                                  SCROLL ===> PAGE
****** ***************************** TOP OF DATA ******************************
000001          PRINT NOGEN
000002 ***********************************************************************
000003 ** J1ASM   READS DATA, SELECTS BY PARM, LISTS                        **
000004 **         RECORDS TO PAPER PRODUCING A SIMPLE REPORT                **
000005 **         BOB NARINO, 9/93                                          **
000006 ***********************************************************************
000007 R0       EQU   00
000008 R1       EQU   01
000009 R2       EQU   02
000010 R3       EQU   03
000011 R4       EQU   04
000012 R5       EQU   05
000013 R6       EQU   06
000014 R7       EQU   07
000015 R8       EQU   08
000016 R9       EQU   09
000017 R10      EQU   10
000018 R11      EQU   11
000019 R12      EQU   12
000020 R13      EQU   13
000021 R14      EQU   14
000022 R15      EQU   15
000023          EJECT
000024 ***********************************************************************
000025 ** REGISTER USAGE:                                                   **
000026 **                                                                   **
000027 ** R0      LOCATION OF PAYMENT RECORD                                **
000028 ** R1      LOCATION OF READER DATA CONTROL BLOCK                     **
000029 ** R2      COUNT - NUMBER OF RECORDS READ                            **
000030 ** R3      COUNT - NUMBER OF RECORDS SELECTED                        **
000031 ** R4      LEN(PARM) AND POINTER TO INPUT PMENT REC                  **
000032 ** R5      LOCATION OF PARM-DATE STRING                              **
000033 ** R10     INTERNAL SUBROUTINE LINKAGE                               **
000034 ** R12     BASE REGISTER                                             **
000035 ** R13     LOCATION OF SAVE_AREA (CALLER'S REGISTERS)                **
000036 **                                                                   **
000037 ***********************************************************************
000038          SPACE 2
000039 J1ASM    CSECT
000040          DS    0H                           INITIALIZATION
000041          USING *,R15
000042          B     R14(,R15)
000043          DC    AL1(9),CL9'J1ASM'
000044          STM   R14,R12,12(R13)
000045          ST    R13,SAVEAREA+4
000046          LR    R12,R13
000047          LA    R13,SAVEAREA
000048          ST    R13,8(R12)
000049          BALR  R12,0
000050          DROP  R15
000051          USING *,R12
000052          SPACE
000053          L     R3,0(R1)                     R3 POINTS TO LOC W/PARM-LENGTH
000054          LH    R4,0(R3)                     R4 -> LENGTH(PARM-FIELD)
000055          SPACE
000056          OPEN  (CONSOLE,OUTPUT)             OPEN THE CONSOLE FILE
000057          OPEN  (READER,INPUT)               OPEN THE INPUT FILE
000058          OPEN  (PRINTER,OUTPUT)             OPEN THE OUTPUT FILE
000059          EJECT
000060          LTR   R4,R4                        PARM DATA ON EXEC CARD?
000061          BZ    PARMERR1                     NO,  REPORT MISSING PARM
000062          SPACE
```

These statements equate the labels R0 through R15 with the values 0 through 15 so that references to registers are clearer in the program.

This assembler program, named J1ASM, does the same processing as J1COBOL in Figure 9.4. J1ASM expects to receive a parameter from the EXEC statement that invokes it. It checks to see that the parameter value is present, that it is six bytes in length, and that it is numeric. If the PARM fails these tests, J1ASM issues a message and stops. If the PARM passes these tests, it is used to select, list, and total records from the payments file that carry the PARM value as the date of payment.

```
000063          C     R4,SIX                    PARM LENGTH = 6?
000064          BNE   PARMERR2                  NO,  REPORT MISSING PARM
000065          SPACE
000066          MVC   PARMDATE(6),2(R3)         COPY EXEC-PARM INTO STORAGE
000067          LA    R5,PARMDATE               R5 -> LOCATION OF PARM-DATE
000068 CHKPARM  DS    0H
000069          CLI   0(R5),C'0'                NUMERIC?
000070          BL    PARMERR3                  NO,  REPORT NON NUMERIC ERROR
000071          LA    R5,1(R5)                  INCREMENT POINTER BY ONE
000072          BCT   R4,CHKPARM                CONTINUE CHECK UNTIL R4 = 0
000073 *                                        OR ERROR CONDITION FOUND
000074          SPACE
000075 * REPORT THE PARM DATE
000076          MVC   PARM_MSG+22(L'PARMDATE),PARMDATE
000077          PUT   PRINTER,PARM_MSG
000078          SPACE
000079 * DISPLAY DATE SELECTION MESSAGE
000080          MVC   REPT_MSG+47(L'PARMDATE),PARMDATE
000081          PUT   PRINTER,REPT_MSG
000082          EJECT
000083          SR    R2,R2                     RECORDS_READ -> 0
000084          SR    R3,R3                     RECORDS_SELECTED -> 0
000085          ZAP   TOTPYAMT,=P'0'            TOTAL_LTSTED_AMOUNTS -> 0
000086          SPACE
000087          GET   READER,PAYRECD            READ FIRST RECORD
000088          LA    R4,PAYRECD                R4 -> LOCATION OF PAY RECORD
000089          USING PAYMENT,R4                SET UP LOGICAL TEMPLATE
000090          EJECT
000091 PROCESS  DS    0H
000092          A     R2,ONE                    R2 -> R2 + 1 (RECORDS READ)
000093          CLC   PAYRECD(6),PARMDATE       PAYMENT-DATE = PARM-DATE?
000094          BNE   READREC                   NO,  FETCH ANOTHER RECORD
000095          SPACE
000096          A     R3,ONE                    R3 -> R3 + 1 (RECORDS LISTED)
000097          PACK  WORKAMT(5),PR_AMT(6)
000098          AP    TOTPYAMT,WORKAMT
000099          MVI   PRNTLINE,C' '             OUTPUT THE PAY-RECORD
000100          MVC   PRNTLINE+1(132),PRNTLINE
000101          MVC   PRNTLINE+4(34),PAYRECD
000102          MVC   PRNTLINE+44(13),EDIT2
000103          ED    PRNTLINE+44(13),WORKAMT
000104          PUT   PRINTER,PRNTLINE          OUTPUT THE PAY-RECORD
000105          SPACE
000106 READREC  DS    0H
000107          GET   READER,PAYRECD            FETCH ANOTHER RECORD
000108          B     PROCESS                   NOT EOF? DO IT AGAIN
000109          SPACE
000110 PARMERR1 DS    0H
000111          PUT   CONSOLE,ERRMSG1           DISPLAY NO PARM ERROR
000112          B     CLSFILES                  CLOSE FILES
000113 PARMERR2 DS    0H
000114          PUT   CONSOLE,ERRMSG2           DISPLAY PARM LENGTH ERROR
000115          B     CLSFILES
000116 PARMERR3 DS    0H
000117          PUT   CONSOLE,ERRMSG3           DISPLAY PARM NOT NUMERIC
000118          B     CLSFILES
000119 EXIT     DS    0H
000120          MVI   PRNTLINE,C' '             OUTPUT TOTAL AMOUNT LISTED
000121          MVC   PRNTLINE+1(132),PRNTLINE
000122          MVI   PRNTLINE+33,C'$'
000123          MVC   PRNTLINE+44(13),EDIT2
000124          ED    PRNTLINE+44(13),TOTPYAMT
000125          PUT   PRINTER,PRNTLINE
000126          SPACE
000127          CVD   R2,DOUBLWRD               REPORT TOTAL RECORDS READ
000128          MVC   TOT_MSG+24(6),EDIT1       MOVE IN EDIT PATTERN
000129          ED    TOT_MSG+24(6),DOUBLWRD+5
000130          PUT   PRINTER,TOT_MSG
000131 *
000132          CVD   R3,DOUBLWRD               REPORT TOTAL RECORDS LISTED
000133          MVC   LST_MSG+24(6),EDIT1
000134          ED    LST_MSG+24(6),DOUBLWRD+5
000135          PUT   PRINTER,LST_MSG
000136 CLSFILES DS    0H
000137          CLOSE READER                    CLOSE INPUT FILE
000138          CLOSE PRINTER                   CLOSE OUTPUT FILE
000139          CLOSE CONSOLE                   CLOSE CONSOLE FILE
000140 *
000141          L     R13,SAVEAREA+4            RELOAD CONTENTS OF
000142          LM    R14,R12,12(R13)           CALLER'S REGISTERS
```

Figure 9.8 (continued)

```
000143          SR    R15,R15                     SET RETURN CODE
000144          BR    R14                         RETURN TO CALLER (OS)
000145          EJECT
000146 ******************************
000147 ***  SUBROUTINE(S)          ***
000148 ******************************
000149          SPACE
000150          EJECT
000151 ******************************
000152 ***  DATA CONTROL BLOCKS   ***
000153 ******************************
000154 READER   DCB   DSORG=PS,MACRF=GM,RECFM=FB,                        X
000155                DDNAME=PAYDAT,EODAD=EXIT
000156 *
000157 PRINTER  DCB   RECFM=FA,DSORG=PS,MACRF=PM,                        X
000158                DDNAME=PAYLIST
000159 *
000160 CONSOLE  DCB   RECFM=FA,DSORG=PS,MACRF=PM,LRECL=133,BLKSIZE=133,  X
000161                DDNAME=SYSOUT
000162          SPACE 2
000163 ******************************
000164 ***  DATA STORAGE AREA     ***
000165 ******************************
000166          DS    0H
000167 SAVEAREA DS    18F                         STORE CALLER'S REGISTERS
000168 INPARM   DS    F                           ADDRESS OF INPUT PARM
000169 PAYRECD  DS    CL80                        PARK THE PAY RECORD HERE
000170 PARMDATE DS    CL10                        PARM-DATE FROM EXEC CARD
000171 WORKAMT  DS    PL5                         TOTAL LISTED AMOUNTS PAID
000172 TOTPYAMT DS    PL5                         TOTAL LISTED AMOUNTS PAID
000173 DOUBLWRD DS    CL8                         WORK-AREA FOR CVD INSTRUCTION
000174 PRNTLINE DS    CL133                       OUTPUT BUFFER
000175 ******************************
000176 ***  CONSTANTS/MESSAGES    ***
000177 ******************************
000178 ONE      DC    F'1'
000179 SIX      DC    F'6'
000180 PCKD100  DC    X'100C'                     PACKED 100
000181 EDIT1    DC    X'402020202120'                   EDIT FOR INTEGERS
000182 EDIT2    DC    X'40206B2020206B2020214B2020' EDIT FOR AMOUNT (LINE)
000183 PARM_MSG DC    CL133'1 PARM DATA ENTERED '
000184 REPT_MSG DC    CL133'0 REPORT WILL LIST A SELECTION OF RECORDS FOR '
000185 TOT_MSG  DC    CL133'0 TOTAL RECORDS READ: '
000186 LST_MSG  DC    CL133'0 TOTAL RECORDS LISTED: '
000187 ERRMSG1  DC    CL133'0 NO PARAMETER ENTERED ON EXEC CARD,  RESUBMIT'
000188 ERRMSG2  DC    CL133'0 PARMETER LENGTH ON EXEC CARD NE 6, RESUBMIT'
000189 ERRMSG3  DC    CL133'0 EXEC PARAMETER MUST BE NUMERIC,  RESUBMIT'
000190          SPACE
000191 *
000192          LTORG
000193 ******************************
000194 ***  RECORD LAYOUT(S)      ***
000195 ******************************
000196 PAYMENT  DSECT                             LOGICAL PAY RECORD
000197 PR_DATE  DS    CL7                         PAYMENT DATE
000198 PR_ID    DS    CL6                         PAYER ID
000199 PR_NAME  DS    CL21                        PAYER NAME
000200 PR_AMT   DS    CL7                         PAYER AMOUNT
000201 FILLER   DS    CL39
000202          END   J1ASM
```

Program does not specify LRECL so the JCL must.

Figure 9.8 (continued)

9.9 Assembling and Linking an Assembler Program

Figure 9.9 lists the JCL I used to assemble and link the J1ASM program. Although I could have used a proc for this, I instead used raw JCL enhanced with symbolic parameters given values with SET. Lines 1 through 20 of ASMCL in Figure 9.9 are visible when I edit it, and I have the same convenience in using this JCL as I would with a proc.

9.10 Executing an Assembler Program

Executing an assembler program to test it should involve making sure that it does what is intended under error conditions. Testing has to confirm that a valid PARM value causes the appropriate action. But the program should also perform in a defined way if it is executed without a PARM value, with an invalid (in this case, nonnumeric) PARM, and with a PARM that is too short (or too long). The JCL in Figure 9.10 executes the load module for J1ASM four times, with PARM data variations for these conditions.

The annotated MVS/ESA system and program output shown in Figure 9.11 shows you what J1ASM produces in response to these PARM data values.

9.11 Receiving a PARM in a C Program with argc and *argv[]

You can arrange to receive a PARM value in a C program just as with a program written in COBOL or an assembler. The C program receives the PARM value in exactly the same way as a C program prepared and run on a PC receives command line arguments. This makes it especially appealing to develop C programs using a PC-based compiler, test them on the PC, then upload them for mainframe compiling and production execution. This is exactly how program J1C, shown in Figure 9.12, was prepared. We use PowerC, by Mix Software (1-800-333-0330), an outstanding value at $19.95—that's right, less than $20—including text and compiler. (Incidentally, when you call Mix Software, ask about their C/Utilities Toolchest, which will put a Unix emulator on your PC for $19.95 as well!)

In a C program, you use the parameters argc and *argv[] to receive parameters. Argc receives the number of command line arguments, while *argv[] is an array of strings that actually contains the command line arguments. When you execute a C program on a PC under DOS, more than one command line argument may be present. Under MVS, only one PARM is passed via the EXEC PARM parameter. Argc counts the program's name as the first argument, which occupies occurrence [0] in the *argv[] array. The first argument (the PARM value) is thus occurrence [1] within *argv[].

9.12 Trigraphs in Mainframe C Programs

Examine Figure 9.12 and you will see how mainframe C programming suffers from the lack of the square bracket symbols [and] on 3270 terminals. To encode these symbols, you must use "trigraphs," which consist of three characters.

```
EDIT ---- CSCJGJ.ADV.CNTL(ASMCL) - 01.09 -------------------- COLUMNS 001 072
COMMAND ===>                                                  SCROLL ===> PAGE
****** ***************************** TOP OF DATA ******************************
000001 //CSCJGJA   JOB 1,                  ACCOUNTING INFORMATION
000002 //  'BIN 7--NARINO',                 PROGRAMMER NAME AND DELIVERY BIN
000003 //  CLASS=A,                        INPUT QUEUE CLASS
000004 //  MSGLEVEL=(1,1),                 HOW MUCH MVS SYSTEM PRINT DESIRED
000005 //  MSGCLASS=X,                     PRINT DESTINATION X A L N OR O
000006 //  TIME=(0,6),                     SAFETY LIMIT: RUN TIME UP TO 6 SECS
000007 //  REGION=2M,                      ALLOW UP TO 2 MEGS VIRTUAL MEMORY
000008 //* TYPRUN=SCAN,                    UNCOMMENT THIS LINE TO DO SCAN ONLY
000009 //  NOTIFY=CSCJGJ                   WHO TO TELL WHEN JOB IS DONE
000010 //*--------------------------------------------------------------------
000011 //* ASSEMBLE AND LINK
000012 //* THIS JCL IS STORED AT CSCJGJ.ADV.CNTL(ASMCL)
000013 //*
000014 //* NOTE:  MACROS NEEDED FOR ASM TO C COMMUNICATION CAN FOUND IN
000015 //*        EDC.V2R1M0.SEDCMCLB
000016 //*
000017 //           SET  ASMPDS='CSCJGJ.ADV.ASM',      LIB WITH ASM SOURCE
000018 //  OBJPDS='CSCJGJ.ADV.OBJ',                   OBJECT LIBRARY
000019 // LOADPDS='CSCJGJ.ADV.LOADLIB',               LOAD MODULE LIBRARY
000020 //     PGM='J1ASM'                              PROGRAM NAME
000021 //*
000022 //*********************************************************************
000023 //* EXECUTE THE ASSEMBLER                                             *
000024 //*********************************************************************
000025 //ASM        EXEC  PGM=IEV90,
000026 //  PARM='NOESD,NORLD,NOXREF,OBJECT,NOALIGN'
000027 //SYSPRINT   DD  SYSOUT=*
000028 //SYSUT1     DD  UNIT=VIO                                 WORK FILE
000029 //SYSLIB     DD  DSN=SYS1.MODGEN,DISP=SHR
000030 //           DD  DSN=SYS1.MACLIB,DISP=SHR
000031 //           DD  DSN=EDC.V2R1M0.SEDCMCLB,DISP=SHR
000032 //SYSIN      DD  DSN=&ASMPDS(&PGM),                       SOURCE IN
000033 //  DISP=SHR
000034 //SYSLIN     DD  DSN=&OBJPDS(&PGM),                       OBJECT OUT
000035 //  DISP=SHR
000036 //SYSPUNCH   DD  DUMMY
000037 //*********************************************************************
000038 //* LINK OBJECT FILES INTO LOAD MODULE                                *
000039 //*********************************************************************
000040 //      IF (ASM.RC <= 4) THEN
000041 //LKED       EXEC  PGM=IEWL,
000042 //  PARM='NOXREF,NOLIST',
000043 //  REGION=2M
000044 //SYSPRINT   DD  SYSOUT=*
000045 //SYSLIN     DD  DSN=&OBJPDS(&PGM),DISP=SHR              OBJ FILE IN
000046 //SYSLIB     DD  DSN=EDC.V2R1M0.SEDCBASE,DISP=SHR        LIBRARIES
000047 //           DD  DSN=PLI.V2R3M0.SIBMBASE,DISP=SHR
000048 //SYSUT1     DD  UNIT=VIO,SPACE=(CYL,(1,1))              WORK FILE
000049 //SYSLMOD    DD  DSN=&LOADPDS(&PGM),DISP=SHR             LOAD MOD OUT
000050 //      ENDIF
000051 //
```

This is raw JCL to execute the assembler and the linkage editor. I built it from the standard ASMHCL proc, tuning it up as described in Chapter 6, and used the MVS/ESA Version 4 SET feature to install symbolic parameters for convenience.

Figure 9.9 JCL to Assemble and Link the J1ASM Program, Creating a Load Module

```
EDIT ---- CSCJGJ.ADV.CNTL(RUNJ1) - 01.08 -------------------- COLUMNS 001 072
COMMAND ===>                                                  SCROLL ===> PAGE
****** ***************************** TOP OF DATA ******************************
000001 //CSCJGJA   JOB 1,                    ACCOUNTING INFORMATION
000002 //   'BIN 7--NARINO',                 PROGRAMMER NAME AND DELIVERY BIN
000003 //   CLASS=A,                         INPUT QUEUE CLASS
000004 //   MSGLEVEL=(1,1),                  HOW MUCH MVS SYSTEM PRINT DESIRED
000005 //   MSGCLASS=X,                      PRINT DESTINATION X A L N OR O
000006 //   TIME=(0,6),                      SAFETY LIMIT: RUN TIME UP TO 6 SECS
000007 //   REGION=2M,                       ALLOW UP TO 2 MEGS VIRTUAL MEMORY
000008 //*  TYPRUN=SCAN,                     UNCOMMENT THIS LINE TO DO SCAN ONLY
000009 //   NOTIFY=CSCJGJ                    WHO TO TELL WHEN JOB IS DONE
000010 //*-----------------------------------------------------------------
000011 //* TEST THE J1ASM PROGRAM WITH VARIOUS PARM VALUES
000012 //* THIS JCL IS STORED AT CSCJGJ.ADV.CNTL(R   1)
000013 //*****************************************************************
000014 //* EXECUTE J1ASM WITH PARM                                       *
000015 //*****************************************************************
000016 //STEP010  EXEC  PGM=J1ASM,PARM='120193'
000017 //STEPLIB    DD  DSN=CSCJGJ.ADV.LOADLIB,DISP=SHR
000018 //           DD  DSN=SYS1.COB2LIB,DISP=SHR
000019 //PAYDAT     DD  DSN=CSCJGJ.ADV.CNTL(PAYMENTS),DISP=SHR
000020 //PAYLIST    DD  SYSOUT=*,RECFM=FBA,LRECL=133
000021 //SYSOUT     DD  SYSOUT=*
000022 //*
000023 //*****************************************************************
000024 //* EXECUTE J1ASM WITHOUT   RM VALUE ON EXEC                      *
000025 //*****************************************************************
000026 //STEP020  EXEC  PGM=J1ASM
000027 //STEPLIB    DD  DSN=CSCJGJ.ADV.LOADLIB,DISP=SHR
000028 //PAYDAT     DD  DSN=CSCJGJ.ADV.CNTL(PAYMENTS),DISP=SHR
000020 //PAYLIST    DD  SYSOUT=*,RECFM=FBA,LRECL=133
000030 //SYSOUT     DD  SYSOUT=*
000031 //*
000032 //*****************************************************************
000033 //* EXECUTE J1ASM BUT PARM IS NOT ALL N   IC                      *
000034 //*****************************************************************
000035 //STEP030  EXEC  PGM=J1ASM,PARM='12V393'
000036 //STEPLIB    DD  DSN=CSCJGJ.ADV.LOADLIB,DISP=SHR
000037 //PAYDAT     DD  DSN=CSCJGJ.ADV.CNTL(PAYMENTS),DISP=SHR
000020 //PAYLIST    DD  SYSOUT=*,RECFM=FBA,LRECL=133
000039 //SYSOUT     DD  SYSOUT=*
000040 //*
000041 //*****************************************************************
000042 //* EXECUTE J1ASM BUT PARM IS NOT PROP   ENGTH                    *
000043 //*****************************************************************
000044 //STEP040  EXEC  PGM=J1ASM,PARM='12393'
000045 //STEPLIB    DD  DSN=CSCJGJ.ADV.LOADLIB,DISP=SHR
000046 //PAYDAT     DD  DSN=CSCJGJ.ADV.CNTL(PAYMENTS),DISP=SHR
000020 //PAYLIST    DD  SYSOUT=*,RECFM=FBA,LRECL=133
000048 //SYSOUT     DD  SYSOUT=*
000049 //
```

> This JCL executes the J1ASM load module four times, to test it with various PARM values. The first PARM value, '120193', should select six records from the payments file and cause them to be listed and tabulated. The second PARM value is missing, the third PARM value is invalid, and the fourth PARM value is not the required six bytes in length. Does J1ASM work properly? See Figure 9.9 and see for yourself!

Figure 9.10 JCL to Test the J1ASM Load Module and Demonstrate Its PARM Validation Features

---

Figure 9.11 MVS/ESA System Output and Assembler Program Output from the J1ASM Test

```
                    J E S 2   J O B   L O G  --  S Y S T E M   I B M 1  --  N O D E   N 1

18.59.26 JOB08284  IRR010I  USERID CSCJGJ   IS ASSIGNED TO THIS JOB.
18.59.27 JOB08284  ICH70001I CSCJGJ   LAST ACCESS AT 18:58:14 ON TUESDAY, APRIL 5,
18.59.27 JOB08284  $HASP373 CSCJGJA  STARTED - INIT  1 - CLASS A - SYS IBM1
18.59.29 JOB08284  $HASP395 CSCJGJA  ENDED

------ JES2 JOB STATISTICS ------
    05 APR 94 JOB EXECUTION DATE
           48 CARDS READ
          137 SYSOUT PRINT RECORDS
            0 SYSOUT PUNCH RECORDS
            8 SYSOUT SPOOL KBYTES
         0.05 MINUTES EXECUTION TIME

        1 //CSCJGJA   JOB 1,                      ACCOUNTING INFORMATION
          //  'BIN 7--NARINO',                    PROGRAMMER NAME AND DELIVERY BIN
          //  CLASS=A,                            INPUT QUEUE CLASS
          //  MSGLEVEL=(1,1),                     HOW MUCH MVS SYSTEM PRINT DESIRED
          //  MSGCLASS=X,                         PRINT DESTINATION X A L N OR O
          //  TIME=(0,6),                         SAFETY LIMIT: RUN TIME UP TO 6 SECS
          //  REGION=2M,                          ALLOW UP TO 2 MEGS VIRTUAL MEMORY
          //* TYPRUN=SCAN,                        UNCOMMENT THIS LINE TO DO SCAN ONLY
          //  NOTIFY=CSCJGJ                       WHO TO TELL WHEN JOB IS DONE
          //*-------------------------------------------------------------------
          //* TEST THE J1ASM PROGRAM WITH VARIOUS PARM VALUES
          //* THIS JCL IS STORED AT CSCJGJ.ADV.CNTL(RUNJ1)
          //*******************************************************************
          //* EXECUTE J1ASM WITH PARM                                         *
          //*******************************************************************
        2 //STEP010  EXEC  PGM=J1ASM,PARM='120193'
        3 //STEPLIB    DD  DSN=CSCJGJ.ADV.LOADLIB,DISP=SHR
        4 //           DD  DSN=SYS1.COB2LIB,DISP=SHR
        5 //PAYDAT     DD  DSN=CSCJGJ.ADV.CNTL(PAYMENTS),DISP=SHR
        6 //PAYLIST    DD  SYSOUT=*,RECFM=FBA,LRECL=133
        7 //SYSOUT     DD  SYSOUT=*
          //*
          //*******************************************************************
          //* EXECUTE J1ASM WITHOUT A PARM VALUE ON EXEC                      *
          //*******************************************************************
        8 //STEP020  EXEC  PGM=J1ASM
        9 //STEPLIB    DD  DSN=CSCJGJ.ADV.LOADLIB,DISP=SHR
       10 //PAYDAT     DD  DSN=CSCJGJ.ADV.CNTL(PAYMENTS),DISP=SHR
       11 //PAYLIST    DD  SYSOUT=*,RECFM=FBA,LRECL=133
       12 //SYSOUT     DD  SYSOUT=*
          //*
          //*******************************************************************
          //* EXECUTE J1ASM BUT PARM IS NOT ALL NUMERIC                       *
          //*******************************************************************
       13 //STEP030  EXEC  PGM=J1ASM,PARM='12V393'
       14 //STEPLIB    DD  DSN=CSCJGJ.ADV.LOADLIB,DISP=SHR
       15 //PAYDAT     DD  DSN=CSCJGJ.ADV.CNTL(PAYMENTS),DISP=SHR
       16 //PAYLIST    DD  SYSOUT=*,RECFM=FBA,LRECL=133
       17 //SYSOUT     DD  SYSOUT=*
          //*
          //*******************************************************************
          //* EXECUTE J1ASM BUT PARM IS NOT PROPER LENGTH                     *
          //*******************************************************************
       18 //STEP040  EXEC  PGM=J1ASM,PARM='12393'
       19 //STEPLIB    DD  DSN=CSCJGJ.ADV.LOADLIB,DISP=SHR
       20 //PAYDAT     DD  DSN=CSCJGJ.ADV.CNTL(PAYMENTS),DISP=SHR
       21 //PAYLIST    DD  SYSOUT=*,RECFM=FBA,LRECL=133
       22 //SYSOUT     DD  SYSOUT=*

ICH70001I CSCJGJ   LAST ACCESS AT 18:58:14 ON TUESDAY, APRIL 5, 1994

IEF236I ALLOC. FOR CSCJGJA STEP010
IEF237I 117  ALLOCATED TO STEPLIB
IEF237I 110  ALLOCATED TO
IEF237I 111  ALLOCATED TO PAYDAT
IEF237I JES2 ALLOCATED TO PAYLIST
IEF237I JES2 ALLOCATED TO SYSOUT
IEF142I CSCJGJA STEP010 - STEP WAS EXECUTED - COND CODE 0000
IEF285I   CSCJGJ.ADV.LOADLIB                          KEPT
IEF285I   VOL SER NOS= USER03.
IEF285I   SYS1.COB2LIB                                KEPT
IEF285I   VOL SER NOS= ACSRES.
IEF285I   CSCJGJ.ADV.CNTL                             KEPT
IEF285I   VOL SER NOS= USER00.
IEF285I   CSCJGJ.CSCJGJA.JOB08284.D0000101.?          SYSOUT
IEF285I   CSCJGJ.CSCJGJA.JOB08284.D0000102.?          SYSOUT
IEF373I STEP /STEP010 / START 94095.1859
IEF374I STEP /STEP010 / STOP  94095.1859 CPU    0MIN 00.13SEC SRB    0MIN 00.00SEC
```

```
IEF236I ALLOC. FOR CSCJGJA STEP020
IEF237I 117  ALLOCATED TO STEPLIB
IEF237I 111  ALLOCATED TO PAYDAT
IEF237I JES2 ALLOCATED TO PAYLIST
IEF237I JES2 ALLOCATED TO SYSOUT
IEF142I CSCJGJA STEP020 - STEP WAS EXECUTED - COND CODE 0000
IEF285I   CSCJGJ.ADV.LOADLIB                         KEPT
IEF285I   VOL SER NOS= USER03.
IEF285I   CSCJGJ.ADV.CNTL                            KEPT
IEF285I   VOL SER NOS= USER00.
IEF285I   CSCJGJ.CSCJGJA.JOB08284.D0000103.?         SYSOUT
IEF285I   CSCJGJ.CSCJGJA.JOB08284.D0000104.?         SYSOUT
IEF373I STEP /STEP020 / START 94095.1859
IEF374I STEP /STEP020 / STOP  94095.1859 CPU    0MIN 00.12SEC SRB    0MIN 00.00SEC

IEF236I ALLOC. FOR CSCJGJA STEP030
IEF237I 117  ALLOCATED TO STEPLIB
IEF237I 111  ALLOCATED TO PAYDAT
IEF237I JES2 ALLOCATED TO PAYLIST
IEF237I JES2 ALLOCATED TO SYSOUT
IEF142I CSCJGJA STEP030 - STEP WAS EXECUTED - COND CODE 0000
IEF285I   CSCJGJ.ADV.LOADLIB                         KEPT
IEF285I   VOL SER NOS= USER03.
IEF285I   CSCJGJ.ADV.CNTL                            KEPT
IEF285I   VOL SER NOS= USER00.
IEF285I   CSCJGJ.CSCJGJA.JOB08284.D0000105.?         SYSOUT
IEF285I   CSCJGJ.CSCJGJA.JOB08284.D0000106.?         SYSOUT
IEF373I STEP /STEP030 / START 94095.1859
IEF374I STEP /STEP030 / STOP  94095.1859 CPU    0MIN 00.12SEC SRB    0MIN 00.00SEC
IEF236I ALLOC. FOR CSCJGJA STEP040
IEF237I 117  ALLOCATED TO STEPLIB
IEF237I 111  ALLOCATED TO PAYDAT
IEF237I JES2 ALLOCATED TO PAYLIST
IEF237I JES2 ALLOCATED TO SYSOUT
IEF142I CSCJGJA STEP040 - STEP WAS EXECUTED - COND CODE 0000
IEF285I   CSCJGJ.ADV.LOADLIB                         KEPT
IEF285I   VOL SER NOS= USER03.
IEF285I   CSCJGJ.ADV.CNTL                            KEPT
IEF285I   VOL SER NOS= USER00.
IEF285I   CSCJGJ.CSCJGJA.JOB08284.D0000107.?         SYSOUT
IEF285I   CSCJGJ.CSCJGJA.JOB08284.D0000108.?         SYSOUT
IEF373I STEP /STEP040 / START 94095.1859
IEF374I STEP /STEP040 / STOP  94095.1859 CPU    0MIN 00.12SEC
IEF375I  JOB /CSCJGJA / START 94095.1859
IEF376I  JOB /CSCJGJA / STOP  94095.1859 CPU    0MIN 00.49SEC

 PARM DATA ENTERED   120193
 REPORT WILL LIST A SELECTION OF RECORDS FOR  120193
   120193 64115 NOEY WOONT                          295.12
   120193 35189 IDA HOE                               8.10
   120193 91190 VERN MONT                         1,456.40
   120193 43901 CANDI BARR                           16.15
   120193 33802 CAL IFORNIA                          68.24
   120193 66703 CRYSTAL SHANDELEER                  980.60
                                  $               2,824.61
 TOTAL RECORDS READ:        30
 TOTAL RECORDS LISTED:       6
```

Output from first test; result valid

```
        8 //STEP020  EXEC  PGM=J1ASM

 NO PARAMETER ENTERED ON EXEC CARD,  RESUBMIT
```

Output from second test; missing PARM detected

```
       13 //STEP030  EXEC  PGM=J1ASM,PARM='12V393'

 EXEC PARAMETER MUST BE NUMERIC,  RESUBMIT
```

Output from third test; invalid PARM detected

```
       18 //STEP040  EXEC  PGM=J1ASM,PARM='12393'

 PARAMETER LENGTH ON EXEC CARD NE 6, RESUBMIT
```

Output from fourth test; short PARM detected

Figure 9.11 (continued)

Figure 9.12 J1C, A C Program That Reads a File and Selects and Prints Records from It Using a PARM Value *(see facing page)*

```
EDIT ---- CSCJGJ.ADV.ASM(J1C) - 01.00 ------------------------ COLUMNS 001 072
COMMAND ===>                                                   SCROLL ===> PAGE
****** ****************************** TOP OF DATA ******************************
000001 /*  This is a program in C/370 that accomplishes the same
000002  *  thing that the J1COBOL program does in VS COBOL II.
000003  *
000004  *  This program was written and tested using Mix Software's
000005  *  PowerC before being uploaded to an ES/9000 and compiled
000006  *  with C/370.  Trigraphs worked fine; no changes required
000007  *  except in the fopens for ddnames.
000008  *
000009  *  Bob Narino and Jim Janossy, March, 1993
000010  */
000011
000012 #pragma runopts( execops )
000013
000014 #include <stdio.h>
000015 #include <ctype.h>
000016 #include <string.h>
000017 #include <stdlib.h>
000018
000019 #define WRITE        "w"
000020 #define READ         "r"
000021
000022 /* ----- Function prototypes ----------------------------------*/
000023
000024 int  s1000_boj( int parms, char *parm_date );
000025 void s2000_process_records( char *parm_date );
000026 void s3000_eoj( void );
000027 double convert_pay_amount( char *orig_num );
000028
000029 /* ----- Global variables -------------------------------------*/
000030
000031 int  records_read = 0;
000032 int  recrds_listed = 0;
000033 double payment_amount_total = 0.0;
000034
000035 /* Note:  Within the IBM environment you must use the
000036           trigraph "??) ??)" symbols  for array notation.
000037           since 3270 keyboards don't have square brackets */
000038
000039 char    buffer??(80??);                  /* Output buffer */
000040
000041 FILE *pay_dat, *pay_list, *fopen();     /* File pointers */
000042
000043 /* -----------------------------------------------------------*/
000044
000045 int main( int argc,  char *argv??( ??) )
000046 {
000047  if ( s1000_boj( argc, argv??( 1 ??) ) )
000048  {
000049   s2000_process_records( argv??( 1 ??) );
000050   s3000_eoj();
000051   return ( 0 );
000052  }
000053  else
000054   return ( 12 );
000055 }
000056
000057 /* -----------------------------------------------------------*/
000058 /* s1000_boj is written in the style of an assembler programmer! */
000059 /* See if you can figure out why...                           */
000060 /* -----------------------------------------------------------*/
000061
000062 int s1000_boj( int parms, char *parm_date )
000063 {
000064  int result = 1;                 /* optimistic about the outcome  */
000065  int arg_length;                 /* size of the parm date         */
000066  short index;                    /* used for looping              */
000067
000068  if ( parms != 2 )               /* check number of parms entered */
000069  {
000070   puts( "** ERROR ** NO DATE PARM ENTERED ON EXEC!" );
000071   --result;
000072   goto boj_exit;
000073  }
000074
000075  printf( "??/nPARM DATA ENTERED =  %s.??/n", parm_date );
000076  arg_length = strlen( parm_date );
000077
000078  if ( arg_length != 6 )
000079  {
000080   puts( "** ERROR ** INVALID DATE ENTERED ON EXEC! (LENGTH NE 6)" );
```

argc and *argv??(??) receive the PARM

This value becomes the COND CODE

```
000081    --result;
000082    goto boj_exit;
000083   }
000084
000085  /*
000086   * Examine the parm-string character by character.
000087   * If the current character is a digit, i.e. 0 - 9,  keep looping.
000088   * Else note the failure and break out of the loop.
000089   */
000090
000091   for ( index = 0; index < 6; index++ )
000092   {
000093    if ( isdigit( *( parm_date + index )  ) )
000094     continue;
000095    else
000096    {
000097     --result;
000098     goto check_result;
000099    }
000100   }
000101
000102  /***************/
000103  check_result:
000104  /***************/
000105   if ( result < 1 )
000106   {
000107    puts( "** ERROR ** INVALID DATE ENTERED ON EXEC! (NOT NUMERIC)" );
000108    goto boj_exit;
000109   }
000110   pay_dat = fopen( "dd:paydat", READ );
000111   pay_list = fopen( "dd:paylist", WRITE );
000112   printf( "??/nREPORT WILL LIST RECORDS FOR %s", parm_date );
000113
000114  /***************/
000115  boj_exit:
000116  /***************/
000117   return ( result );
000118  }
000119
000120  /* ------------------------------------------------------------*/
000121
000122  void  s2000_process_records( char *parm_date  )
000123  {
000124   double employee_pay;
000125
000126   fgets( buffer, 80, pay_dat );
000127   while ( !feof( pay_dat ) )
000128   {
000129    records_read++;
000130    if ( strncmp( parm_date, buffer, 6 ) == 0 )
000131    {
000132     recrds_listed++;
000133     employee_pay = convert_pay_amount( buffer+34 );
000134     payment_amount_total += employee_pay;
000135     fputs( buffer, pay_list );
000136    }
000137    fgets( buffer, 80, pay_dat );
000138   }
000139  }
000140
000141  /* ------------------------------------------------------------*/
000142
000143  void  s3000_eoj( void )
000144  {
000145   printf( "??/nTOTAL AMOUNT PAID: %8.2f??/n", payment_amount_total );
000146   printf( "TOTAL RECORDS READ: %d??/n", records_read );
000147   printf( "TOTAL RECORDS LISTED: %d??/n", recrds_listed );
000148   fclose( pay_dat );
000149   fclose( pay_list );
000150  }
000151
000152  /* ------------------------------------------------------------*/
000153
000154  double  convert_pay_amount( char *orig_num )
000155  {
000156   char work_str??( 10 ??), *endptr;
000157   double temp;
000158
000159   strncpy( work_str, orig_num, 6 );
000160   temp = strtod( work_str, &endptr );
000161   return ( temp / 100.0  );
000162  }
```

For example, the left square bracket [is coded as ??(while the right square bracket] is coded as ??). Here is a list of trigraphs for graphic symbols and escape sequences:

codes as ??=

[codes as ??(

] codes as ??)

{ codes as ??<

} codes as ??>

\ codes as ??/

^ codes as ??'

| codes as ??!

~ codes as ??-

\a alert (beep)	codes as ??/a
\b backspace	codes as ??/b
\f new page	codes as ??/f
\n newline	codes as ??/n
\r carriage return	codes as ??/r
\t horizontal tab	codes as ??/t
\v vertical tab	codes as ??/v
\\ backslash	codes as ??//
\' single quote	codes as ??/'
\" double quote	codes as ??/"
\0 end-of-string (null)	codes as ??/0

The trigraphs for escape sequences are particularly important because C/370 does not recognize sequences such as \n even if they appear on your screen in programs developed on a PC and uploaded to your mainframe. Sequences such as \n are simply printed without causing the intended action. Trigraphs are recognized by Ansi-compliant C compilers. If you develop code on a PC for C/370 use, save yourself some grief by using them from the start.

Figure 9.12 (continued on facing page)

9.13 Compiling and Linking a C/370 Program

Figure 9.13 shows you the JCL we used to compile and link C/370 programs. This JCL executes a locally tuned proc named CCX4. This proc is based on IBM's standard proc EDCCLG. As with the COBOL procs and assembler JCL, I tuned this proc using the suggestions I discussed in Chapter 6. The CCX4 proc is listed in Figure 9.14. Complete MVS/ESA system output for the compile and link of the J1C program is shown in Figure 9.15. Examine the annotations I placed directly on Figure 9.15 for more information about compiling and linking C/370 programs.

```
EDIT ---- CSCJGJ.ADV.CNTL(J1C) - 01.01 ----------------------- COLUMNS 001 072
COMMAND ===>                                                  SCROLL ===> PAGE
****** ***************************** TOP OF DATA ******************************
000001 //CSCJGJA   JOB 1,                     ACCOUNTING INFORMATION
000002 //   'BIN 7--NARINO',                  PROGRAMMER NAME AND DELIVERY BIN
000003 //   CLASS=A,                          INPUT QUEUE CLASS
000004 //   MSGLEVEL=(1,1),                   HOW MUCH MVS SYSTEM PRINT DESIRED
000005 //   MSGCLASS=X,                       PRINT DESTINATION X A L N OR O
000006 //   TIME=(0,6),                       SAFETY LIMIT: RUN TIME UP TO 6 SECS
000007 //   REGION=2M,                        ALLOW UP TO 2 MEGS VIRTUAL MEMORY
000008 //*  TYPRUN=SCAN,                      UNCOMMENT THIS LINE TO DO SCAN ONLY
000009 //   NOTIFY=CSCJGJ                     WHO TO TELL WHEN JOB IS DONE
000010 //         JCLLIB  ORDER=(CSCJGJ.ADV.PROCLIB1)
000011 //*
000012 //* EXECUTE THE CCX4 PROC TO COMPILE AND LINK A C/370 PROGRAM
000013 //* THIS JCL IS STORED AT CSCJGJ.ADV.CNTL(J1C)
000014 //*-------------------------------------------------------------
000015 //STEP010  EXEC  CCX4,
000016 //     SRCLIB='CSCJGJ.ADV.ASM',
000017 //     MEMBER='J1C',
000018 //     OBJLIB='CSCJGJ.ADV.OBJ',
000019 //    LOADLIB='CSCJGJ.ADV.LOADLIB',
000020 //      CPARM='SOURCE,XREF,NOTERMINAL'
000021 //
```

Object file retained

Figure 9.13 JCL to Compile and Link the J1C Program Using a Proc Named CCX4

```
EDIT ---- CSCJGJ.ADV.PROCLIB1(CCX4) - 01.00 ----------------- COLUMNS 001 072
COMMAND ===>                                                  SCROLL ===> PAGE
****** ***************************** TOP OF DATA ******************************
000001 //*****************************************************************
000002 //*  CCX4    COMPILE AND LINK EDIT A C/370 PROGRAM                    *
000003 //*                                                                  *
000004 //*  COMPARE THIS PROC TO IBM'S EDCCLG, WHICH I USED AS A GUIDE      *
000005 //*  TO PREPARE IT.  THE VERSION OF A C COMPILE, LINK, AND GO        *
000006 //*  PROC YOU SEE HERE BENEFITS FROM THE TUNE-UPS I DESCRIBE         *
000007 //*  IN CHAPTER 6 OF ADVANCED MVS JCL EXAMPLES (WILEY, 1994) -JGJ-   *
000008 //*                                                                  *
000009 //*  NOTE: "EDC" IDENTIFIES IBM C/370 SOFTWARE AND MESSAGES          *
000010 //*****************************************************************
000011 //CCX4    PROC CREGSIZ='1536K',        COMPILER REGION SIZE
000012 //  SRCLIB=,                           SOURCE LIBRARY
000013 //  LOADLIB=,                          LOAD LIBRARY
000014 //  MEMBER=,                           PDS MEMBER
000015 //  OBJLIB=,                           OBJECT LIBRARY
000016 //  CPARM='SOURCE,XREF',               COMPILER PARM OPTIONS
000017 //  LPARM='AMODE=31,NONCAL',           LINKAGE EDITOR PARM OPTIONS
000018 //  VSCCHD='EDC',                      EDC SYSTEM FILES "PROJECT"
000019 //  COMHD='PLI',                       COMMON LIBRARY "PROJECT"
000020 //  COMVER='V2R3M0',                   COMMON LIBRARY "GROUP"
000021 //  CVER='V2R1M0',                     EDC COMPILER "GROUP"
000022 //  COMPL='SEDCCOMP',                  EDC COMPILER MODULES "TYPE"
000023 //  EDCMSGS='SEDCMSGS',                EDC COMPILER MESSAGES "TYPE"
000024 //  LANG='EDCMSGE',                    EDC COMPILER LANGUAGE MEMBER
000025 //  COMLINK='SIBMLINK',                DYN RUNTIME LIBRARY "TYPE"
000026 //  CLINK='SEDCLINK',                  EDC DYN RUNTIME LIB "TYPE"
000027 //  COMBASE='SIBMBASE',                EDC RUNTIME LIB STUBS "TYPE"
000028 //  CBASE='SEDCBASE',                  EDC LIBRARY STUBS "TYPE"
000029 //  EDCHDRS='SEDCHDRS',                EDC HEADER LIBRARY "TYPE"
000030 //  WORKDA='VIO',                      UNIT FOR WORK FILES
000031 //  WRKSPC='(32000,(30,30))',          SPACE QTY, WORK FILES (VIO)
000032 //  PR='*'                             SYSOUT CLASS
000033 //  DCB80='(RECFM=FB,LRECL=80,BLKSIZE=3200)',        SYNONYM
000034 //  DCB3200='(RECFM=FB,LRECL=3200,BLKSIZE=12800)'    SYNONYM
000035 //*----------------------------------------------------------------
000036 //* C/370 COMPILE
000037 //*----------------------------------------------------------------
000038 //CC      EXEC PGM=EDCCOMP,
000039 //  REGION=&CREGSIZ,
000040 //  PARM=('&CPARM')
000041 //STEPLIB  DD  DSN=&VSCCHD..&CVER..&CLINK,DISP=SHR          EDC RUNTIME
000042 //         DD  DSN=&COMHD..&COMVER..&COMLINK,DISP=SHR       COMMON RUNTIME
000043 //         DD  DSN=&VSCCHD..&CVER..&COMPL,DISP=SHR          EDC MODULES
000044 //SYSMSGS  DD  DSN=&VSCCHD..&CVER..&EDCMSGS(&LANG),         EDC MESSAGES
000045 //  DISP=SHR
000046 //SYSIN    DD  DSN=&SRCLIB(&MEMBER),                        SOURCE INPUT
000047 //  DISP=SHR
000048 //SYSLIB   DD  DSN=&VSCCHD..&CVER..&EDCHDRS,                EDC HDR LIB
000049 //  DISP=SHR
000050 //SYSUT1   DD  DSN=&&SYSUT1,                                WORK FILE
000051 //  DISP=(NEW,DELETE,DELETE),
000052 //  UNIT=&WORKDA,
000053 //  DCB=&DCB80,
000054 //  SPACE=&WRKSPC
```

This proc invokes the C/370 compiler to process your source code into an object file, then invokes the standard linkage editor to combine the object file with service routines housed in libraries to create a load module. Most of the symbolic parameters in this proc exist to make it easy for systems personnel to modify the proc as new releases of software are received. *As you can see in Figure 9.11, you need to access only five of these symbolic parameters to use this proc, which is a "tuned up" version of EDCCLG, IBM's standard C/370 compile and link proc.*

Figure 9.14 The CCX4 Proc, a Customized Version of the Standard EDCCLG Proc

```
000055 //SYSUT4   DD  DSN=&&SYSUT4,                           WORK FILE
000056 //  DISP=(NEW,DELETE,DELETE),
000057 //  UNIT=&WORKDA,
000058 //  SPACE=&WRKSPC,
000059 //  DCB=&DCB80
000060 //SYSUT5   DD  DSN=&&SYSUT5,                           WORK FILE
000061 //  DISP=(NEW,DELETE,DELETE),
000062 //  UNIT=&WORKDA,
000063 //  SPACE=&WRKSPC,
000064 //  DCB=&DCB3200
000065 //SYSUT6   DD  DSN=&&SYSUT6,                           WORK FILE
000066 //  DISP=(NEW,DELETE,DELETE),
000067 //  UNIT=&WORKDA,
000068 //  SPACE=&WRKSPC,
000069 //  DCB=&DCB3200
000070 //SYSUT7   DD  DSN=&&SYSUT7,                           WORK FILE
000071 //  UNIT=&WORKDA,
000072 //  DISP=(NEW,DELETE,DELETE),
000073 //  DCB=&DCB3200,
000074 //  SPACE=&WRKSPC
000075 //SYSUT8   DD  DSN=&&SYSUT8,                           WORK FILE
000076 //  DISP=(NEW,DELETE,DELETE),
000077 //  UNIT=&WORKDA,
000078 //  DCB=&DCB3200,
000079 //  SPACE=&WRKSPC
000080 //SYSUT9   DD  DSN=&&SYSUT9,                           WORK FILE
000081 //  DISP=(NEW,DELETE,DELETE),
000082 //  UNIT=&WORKDA,
000083 //  DCB=(RECFM=VB,LRECL=137,BLKSIZE=882),
000084 //  SPACE=&WRKSPC
000085 //SYSCPRT  DD  SYSOUT=&PR                              SOURCE LIST
000086 //SYSPRINT DD  SYSOUT=&PR                              ERROR MSGS
000087 //SYSUT10  DD  SYSOUT=&PR                              MISC MSGS
000088 //SYSLIN   DD  DSN=&OBJLIB(&MEMBER),DISP=SHR            OBJECT FILE
000089 //*------------------------------
000090 //* LINK EDIT
000091 //*------------------------------
000092 //      IF (CC.RC <= 4 ) THEN
000093 //LKED   EXEC  PGM=IEWL,
000094 //  PARM='&LPARM'
000095 //SYSLIB   DD  DSN=&VSCCHD..&CVER..&CBASE,DISP=SHR
000096 //         DD  DSN=&COMHD..&COMVER..&COMBASE,DISP=SHR
000097 //         DD  DSN=CSCJGJ.ADV.LOADLIB,DISP=SHR          CALLED PGMS
000098 //SYSLIN   DD  DSN=*.CC.SYSLIN,DISP=SHR                 OBJECT FILE IN
000099 //SYSLMOD  DD  DSN=&LOADLIB(&MEMBER),                   LOAD MODULE
000100 //  DISP=SHR
000101 //SYSUT1   DD  DSN=&&SYSUT1,                           WORK FILE
000102 //  DISP=(NEW,DELETE,DELETE),
000103 //  UNIT=&WORKDA,
000104 //  SPACE=&WRKSPC
000105 //SYSPRINT DD  SYSOUT=&PR                              LINK ED MSGS
000106 //      ENDIF
```

Subprogram load modules are available to linkage editor

Figure 9.14 (continued)

```
                  J E S 2  J O B  L O G  --  S Y S T E M  I B M 1  --  N O D E  N 1

14.34.54 JOB08030  IRR010I  USERID CSCJGJ   IS ASSIGNED TO THIS JOB.
14.34.55 JOB08030  ICH70001I CSCJGJ   LAST ACCESS AT 14:32:29 ON TUESDAY, APRIL 5, 1994
14.34.55 JOB08030  $HASP373 CSCJGJA  STARTED - INIT  1 - CLASS A - SYS IBM1
14.35.23 JOB08030  $HASP395 CSCJGJA  ENDED

------ JES2 JOB STATISTICS ------
    05 APR 94 JOB EXECUTION DATE
           20 CARDS READ
          792 SYSOUT PRINT RECORDS
            0 SYSOUT PUNCH RECORDS
           55 SYSOUT SPOOL KBYTES
         0.46 MINUTES EXECUTION TIME

        1 //CSCJGJA   JOB 1,                    ACCOUNTING INFORMATION
          //  'BIN 7--NARINO',                  PROGRAMMER NAME AND DELIVERY BIN
          //  CLASS=A,                          INPUT QUEUE CLASS
          //  MSGLEVEL=(1,1),                   HOW MUCH MVS SYSTEM PRINT DESIRED
          //  MSGCLASS=X,                       PRINT DESTINATION X A L N OR O
          //  TIME=(0,6),                       SAFETY LIMIT: RUN TIME UP TO 6 SECS
          //  REGION=2M,                        ALLOW UP TO 2 MEGS VIRTUAL MEMORY
          //* TYPRUN=SCAN,                      UNCOMMENT THIS LINE TO DO SCAN ONLY
          //  NOTIFY=CSCJGJ                     WHO TO TELL WHEN JOB IS DONE
        2 //       JCLLIB  ORDER=(CSCJGJ.ADV.PROCLIB1)
          //*
          //* EXECUTE THE CCX4 PROC TO COMPILE AND LINK A C/370 PROGRAM
          //* THIS JCL IS STORED AT CSCJGJ.ADV.CNTL(J1C)
          //*-------------------------------------------------------------------
        3 //STEP010  EXEC  CCX4,
          //   SRCLIB='CSCJGJ.ADV.ASM',
          //   MEMBER='J1C',
          //   OBJLIB='CSCJGJ.ADV.OBJ',
          //  LOADLIB='CSCJGJ.ADV.LOADLIB',
          //    CPARM='SOURCE,XREF,NOTERMINAL'
          XX*******************************************************************
          XX*  CCX4    COMPILE AND LINK EDIT A C/370 PROGRAM                   *
          XX*                                                                  *
          XX*  COMPARE THIS PROC TO IBM'S EDCCLG, WHICH I USED AS A GUIDE      *
          XX*  TO PREPARE IT.  THE VERSION OF A C COMPILE, LINK, AND GO        *
          XX*  PROC YOU SEE HERE BENEFITS FROM THE TUNE-UPS I DESCRIBE         *
```

A Complete C/370 Example

I have included here the entire body of MVS/ESA system output and the compiler listing, annotated with comments and advice, for the parm-driven C/370 program named J1C shown in Figure 9.12. I used the locally customized CCX4 proc to compile and link this program, so you can see exactly how it works. My annotations point to places where you might hit rough spots, as Bob Narino and I did, when we initially set up this example. The execution JCL for this program is shown in Figure 9.16, and its output is in Figure 9.17.

Figure 9.15 MVS/ESA System Output from C/370 Compile and Link, and C/370 Compiler Listing of the J1C Program

```
   XX*  IN CHAPTER 6 OF ADVANCED MVS JCL EXAMPLES (WILEY, 1994) -JGJ- *
   XX*                                                               *
   XX*  NOTE: "EDC" IDENTIFIES IBM C/370 SOFTWARE AND MESSAGES       *
   XX*****************************************************************
 4 XXCCX4    PROC CREGSIZ='1536K',        COMPILER REGION SIZE
   XX  SRCLIB=,                           SOURCE LIBRARY
   XX  LOADLIB=,                          LOAD LIBRARY
   XX  MEMBER=,                           PDS MEMBER
   XX  OBJLIB=,                           OBJECT LIBRARY
   XX  CPARM='SOURCE,XREF',               COMPILER PARM OPTIONS
   XX  LPARM='AMODE=31,NONCAL',           LINKAGE EDITOR PARM OPTIONS
   XX  VSCCHD='EDC',                      EDC SYSTEM FILES "PROJECT"
   XX  COMHD='PLI',                       COMMON LIBRARY "PROJECT"
   XX  COMVER='V2R3M0',                   COMMON LIBRARY "GROUP"
   XX  CVER='V2R1M0',                     EDC COMPILER "GROUP"
   XX  COMPL='SEDCCOMP',                  EDC COMPILER MODULES "TYPE"
   XX  EDCMSGS='SEDCMSGS',                EDC COMPILER MESSAGES "TYPE"
   XX  LANG='EDCMSGE',                    EDC COMPILER LANGUAGE MEMBER
   XX  COMLINK='SIBMLINK',                DYN RUNTIME LIBRARY "TYPE"
   XX  CLINK='SEDCLINK',                  EDC DYN RUNTIME LIB "TYPE"
   XX  COMBASE='SIBMBASE',                EDC RUNTIME LIB STUBS "TYPE"
   XX  CBASE='SEDCBASE',                  EDC LIBRARY STUBS "TYPE"
   XX  EDCHDRS='SEDCHDRS',                EDC HEADER LIBRARY "TYPE"
   XX  WORKDA='VIO',                      UNIT FOR WORK FILES
   XX  WRKSPC='(32000,(30,30))',          SPACE QTY, WORK FILES (VIO)
   XX  PR='*',                            SYSOUT CLASS
   XX  DCB80='(RECFM=FB,LRECL=80,BLKSIZE=3200)',        SYNONYM
   XX  DCB3200='(RECFM=FB,LRECL=3200,BLKSIZE=12800)'    SYNONYM
   XX*----------------------------------------------------------------
   XX* C/370 COMPILE
   XX*----------------------------------------------------------------
 5 XXCC      EXEC PGM=EDCCOMP,
   XX  REGION=&CREGSIZ,
   XX  PARM=('&CPARM')
   IEFC653I SUBSTITUTION JCL - PGM=EDCCOMP,REGION=1536K,PARM=('&CPARM')
   IEFC653I SUBSTITUTION JCL - SOURCE,XREF,NOTERMINAL
 6 XXSTEPLIB  DD  DSN=&VSCCHD..&CVER..&CLINK,DISP=SHR      EDC RUNTIME
   IEFC653I SUBSTITUTION JCL - DSN=EDC.V2R1M0.SEDCLINK,DISP=SHR
 7 XX         DD  DSN=&COMHD..&COMVER..&COMLINK,DISP=SHR   COMMON RUNTIME
   IEFC653I SUBSTITUTION JCL - DSN=PLI.V2R3M0.SIBMLINK,DISP=SHR
 8 XX         DD  DSN=&VSCCHD..&CVER..&COMPL,DISP=SHR      EDC MODULES
   IEFC653I SUBSTITUTION JCL - DSN=EDC.V2R1M0.SEDCCOMP,DISP=SHR
 9 XXSYSMSGS  DD  DSN=&VSCCHD..&CVER..&EDCMSGS(&LANG),     EDC MESSAGES
```

The LPARM symbolic parameter is part of the original EDCCLG proc and intended to make it convenient for you to specify the options that control the linkage editor program, which is named IEWL. The most important options for interlanguage communication are AMODE and RMODE, as discussed in this chapter. *But you will find LPARM troublesome, since these options require their own apostrophes around them, and the coding you see here doesn't work!* You'll see the problem this causes at the bottom of this listing, where AMODE=31 is not properly received by the linkage editor. I'd suggest you either hard code the critical linkage editor AMODE and RMODE settings in your proc, or create a separate symbolic parameter for each.

Figure 9.15 (continued)

```
        XX  DISP=SHR
        IEFC653I SUBSTITUTION JCL - DSN=EDC.V2R1M0.SEDCMSGS(EDCMSGE),DISP=SHR
     10 XXSYSIN     DD  DSN=&SRCLIB(&MEMBER),                   SOURCE INPUT
        XX  DISP=SHR
        IEFC653I SUBSTITUTION JCL - DSN=CSCJGJ.ADV.ASM(J1C),DISP=SHR
     11 XXSYSLIB    DD  DSN=&VSCCHD..&CVER..&EDCHDRS,           EDC HDR LIB
        XX  DISP=SHR
        IEFC653I SUBSTITUTION JCL - DSN=EDC.V2R1M0.SEDCHDRS,DISP=SHR
     12 XXSYSUT1    DD  DSN=&&SYSUT1,                           WORK FILE
        XX  DISP=(NEW,DELETE,DELETE),
        XX  UNIT=&WORKDA,
        XX  DCB=&DCB80,
        XX  SPACE=&WRKSPC
        IEFC653I SUBSTITUTION JCL - DSN=&SYSUT1,DISP=(NEW,DELETE,DELETE),UNIT=VIO,DCB=(RECFM=FB,LRECL=80,
        BLKSIZE=3200),SPACE=(32000,(30,30))
     13 XXSYSUT4    DD  DSN=&&SYSUT4,                           WORK FILE
        XX  DISP=(NEW,DELETE,DELETE),
        XX  UNIT=&WORKDA,
        XX  SPACE=&WRKSPC,
        XX  DCB=&DCB80
        IEFC653I SUBSTITUTION JCL - DSN=&SYSUT4,DISP=(NEW,DELETE,DELETE),UNIT=VIO,
        LRECL=80,BLKSIZE=3200)
     14 XXSYSUT5    DD  DSN=&&SYSUT5,                           WORK FILE
        XX  DISP=(NEW,DELETE,DELETE),
        XX  UNIT=&WORKDA,
        XX  SPACE=&WRKSPC,
        XX  DCB=&DCB3200
        IEFC653I SUBSTITUTION JCL - DSN=&SYSUT5,DISP=(NEW,DELETE,DELETE),UNIT=VIO,
        LRECL=3200,BLKSIZE=12800)
     15 XXSYSUT6    DD  DSN=&&SYSUT6,                           WORK FILE
        XX  DISP=(NEW,DELETE,DELETE),
        XX  UNIT=&WORKDA,
        XX  SPACE=&WRKSPC,
        XX  DCB=&DCB3200
        IEFC653I SUBSTITUTION JCL - DSN=&SYSUT6,DISP=(NEW,DELETE,DELETE),UNIT=VIO,
        LRECL=3200,BLKSIZE=12800)
     16 XXSYSUT7    DD  DSN=&&SYSUT7,                           WORK FILE
        XX  UNIT=&WORKDA,
        XX  DISP=(NEW,DELETE,DELETE),
        XX  DCB=&DCB3200,
        XX  SPACE=&WRKSPC
        IEFC653I SUBSTITUTION JCL - DSN=&SYSUT7,UNIT=VIO,DISP=(NEW,DELETE,DELETE),DCB=(RECFM=FB,LRECL=3200,
        BLKSIZE=12800),SPACE=(32000,(30,30))
```

I labeled the symbolic parameters DCB80 and DCB3200 as "synonyms" at the bottom of the symbolic parameter defaults at the PROC statement, since these are just a handy way to avoid lengthy repeated coding. LIKE, REFDD, and SMS give you additional capabilities to streamline your DD statements.

Figure 9.15 (continued)

```
17 XXSYSUT8    DD  DSN=&&SYSUT8,                              WORK FILE
   XX  DISP=(NEW,DELETE,DELETE),
   XX  UNIT=&WORKDA,
   XX  DCB=&DCB3200,
   XX  SPACE=&WRKSPC
   IEFC653I SUBSTITUTION JCL - DSN=&SYSUT8,DISP=(NEW,DELETE,DELETE),UNIT=VIO,DCB=(RECFM=FB,LRECL=3200,
   BLKSIZE=12800),SPACE=(32000,(30,30))
18 XXSYSUT9    DD  DSN=&&SYSUT9,                              WORK FILE
   XX  DISP=(NEW,DELETE,DELETE),
   XX  UNIT=&WORKDA,
   XX  DCB=(RECFM=VB,LRECL=137,BLKSIZE=882),
   XX  SPACE=&WRKSPC
   IEFC653I SUBSTITUTION JCL - DSN=&SYSUT9,DISP=(NEW,DELETE,DELETE),UNIT=VIO,DCB=(RECFM=VB,LRECL=137,
   BLKSIZE=882),SPACE=(32000,(30,30))
19 XXSYSCPRT  DD   SYSOUT=&PR                                 SOURCE LIST
   IEFC653I SUBSTITUTION JCL - SYSOUT=*
20 XXSYSPRINT DD   SYSOUT=&PR                                 ERROR MSGS
   IEFC653I SUBSTITUTION JCL - SYSOUT=*
21 XXSYSUT10  DD   SYSOUT=&PR                                 MISC MSGS
   IEFC653I SUBSTITUTION JCL - SYSOUT=*
22 XXSYSLIN    DD  DSN=&OBJLIB(&MEMBER),DISP=SHR              OBJECT FILE
   XX*-----------------------------------------------------------------
   XX* LINK EDIT
   XX*-----------------------------------------------------------------
   IEFC653I SUBSTITUTION JCL - DSN=CSCJGJ.ADV.OBJ(J1C),DISP=SHR
23 XX       IF (CC.RC <= 4 ) THEN
24 XXLKED    EXEC  PGM=IEWL,
   XX  PARM='&LPARM'
   IEFC653I SUBSTITUTION JCL - AMODE=31,NONCAL
25 XXSYSLIB    DD  DSN=&VSCCHD..&CVER..&CBASE,DISP=SHR
   IEFC653I SUBSTITUTION JCL - DSN=EDC.V2R1M0.SEDCBASE,DISP=SHR
26 XX          DD  DSN=&COMHD..&COMVER..&COMBASE,DISP=SHR
   IEFC653I SUBSTITUTION JCL - DSN=PLI.V2R3M0.SIBMBASE,DISP=SHR
27 XX          DD  DSN=CSCJJJ.CSC.LOADLIB,DISP=SHR
28 XXSYSLIN    DD  DSN=*.CC.SYSLIN,DISP=SHR                   OBJECT FILE IN
29 XXSYSLMOD   DD  DSN=&LOADLIB(&MEMBER),                     LOAD MODULE
   XX  DISP=SHR
   IEFC653I SUBSTITUTION JCL - DSN=CSCJGJ.ADV.LOADLIB(J1C),DISP=SHR
30 XXSYSUT1    DD  DSN=&&SYSUT1,                              WORK FILE
   XX  DISP=(NEW,DELETE,DELETE),
   XX  UNIT=&WORKDA,
   XX  SPACE=&WRKSPC
   IEFC653I SUBSTITUTION JCL - DSN=&SYSUT1,DISP=(NEW,DELETE,DELETE),UNIT=VIO,SPACE=(32000,(30,30))
```

Here it appears that the LPARM symbolic parameter has been successfully substituted. But AMODE=31 contains the "=" sign, which requires that the AMODE specification reach the linkage editor program as 'AMODE=31' with apostrophes. You see at the bottom of this listing that this parm has been rejected by the linkage editor as invalid. (Since our default for it is AMODE=31, I still got the same effect, however.)

Figure 9.15 (continued)

```
      31 XXSYSPRINT DD  SYSOUT=&PR                                   LINK ED MSGS
         IEFC653I SUBSTITUTION JCL - SYSOUT=*
      32 XX      ENDIF

 STMT NO. MESSAGE

       3 IEFC001I PROCEDURE CCX4 WAS EXPANDED USING PRIVATE LIBRARY CSCJGJ.ADV.PROCLIB1

ICH70001I CSCJGJ   LAST ACCESS AT 14:32:29 ON TUESDAY, APRIL 5, 1994

IEF236I ALLOC. FOR CSCJGJA CC STEP010
IEF237I 110  ALLOCATED TO STEPLIB
IEF237I 110  ALLOCATED TO
IEF237I 110  ALLOCATED TO
IEF237I 110  ALLOCATED TO SYSMSGS
IEF237I 117  ALLOCATED TO SYSIN
IEF237I 110  ALLOCATED TO SYSLIB
IEF237I VIO  ALLOCATED TO SYSUT1
IEF237I VIO  ALLOCATED TO SYSUT4
IEF237I VIO  ALLOCATED TO SYSUT5
IEF237I VIO  ALLOCATED TO SYSUT6
IEF237I VIO  ALLOCATED TO SYSUT7
IEF237I VIO  ALLOCATED TO SYSUT8
IEF237I VIO  ALLOCATED TO SYSUT9
IEF237I JES2 ALLOCATED TO SYSCPRT
IEF237I JES2 ALLOCATED TO SYSPRINT
IEF237I JES2 ALLOCATED TO SYSUT10
IEF237I 115  ALLOCATED TO SYSLIN
IEF142I CSCJGJA CC STEP010 - STEP WAS EXECUTED - COND CODE 0000
IEF285I   EDC.V2R1M0.SEDCLINK                          KEPT
IEF285I   VOL SER NOS= ACSRES.
IEF285I   PLI.V2R3M0.SIBMLINK                          KEPT
IEF285I   VOL SER NOS= ACSRES.
IEF285I   EDC.V2R1M0.SEDCCOMP                          KEPT
IEF285I   VOL SER NOS= ACSRES.
IEF285I   EDC.V2R1M0.SEDCMSGS                          KEPT
IEF285I   VOL SER NOS= ACSRES.
IEF285I   CSCJGJ.ADV.ASM                               KEPT
IEF285I   VOL SER NOS= USER03.
IEF285I   EDC.V2R1M0.SEDCHDRS                          KEPT
IEF285I   VOL SER NOS= ACSRES.
IEF285I   SYS94095.T143455.RA000.CSCJGJA.SYSUT1        DELETED
IEF285I   SYS94095.T143455.RA000.CSCJGJA.SYSUT4        DELETED
```

A private proc lib is handy for experimenting with your C/370 compile and link proc as you tune it up to suit local requirements.

I find that C/370 compiles take noticeably longer than either VS COBOL II compiles or assemblies. I suspect it has a lot to do with the number of work files that the EDCCOMP compiler accesses. Using VIO (virtual input/output) for these can help speed things up.

Figure 9.15 (continued)

```
IEF285I   SYS94095.T143455.RA000.CSCJGJA.SYSUT5        DELETED
IEF285I   SYS94095.T143455.RA000.CSCJGJA.SYSUT6        DELETED
IEF285I   SYS94095.T143455.RA000.CSCJGJA.SYSUT7        DELETED
IEF285I   SYS94095.T143455.RA000.CSCJGJA.SYSUT8        DELETED
IEF285I   SYS94095.T143455.RA000.CSCJGJA.SYSUT9        DELETED
IEF285I   CSCJGJ.CSCJGJA.JOB08030.D0000101.?           SYSOUT
IEF285I   CSCJGJ.CSCJGJA.JOB08030.D0000102.?           SYSOUT
IEF285I   CSCJGJ.CSCJGJA.JOB08030.D0000103.?           SYSOUT
IEF285I   CSCJGJ.ADV.OBJ                               KEPT
IEF285I   VOL SER NOS= USER01.
IEF373I STEP /CC      / START 94095.1434
IEF374I STEP /CC      / STOP  94095.1435 CPU    0MIN 02.03SEC SRB    0MIN 00.37SEC VIRT   168K SYS   244K EXT    1936K SYS    9152K

IEF236I ALLOC. FOR CSCJGJA LKED STEP010
IEF237I 110  ALLOCATED TO SYSLIB
IEF237I 110  ALLOCATED TO
IEF237I 111  ALLOCATED TO
IEF237I 115  ALLOCATED TO SYSLIN
IEF237I 117  ALLOCATED TO SYSLMOD
IEF237I VIO  ALLOCATED TO SYSUT1
IEF237I JES2 ALLOCATED TO SYSPRINT
IEF142I CSCJGJA LKED STEP010 - STEP WAS EXECUTED - COND CODE 0000
IEF285I   EDC.V2R1M0.SEDCBASE                          KEPT
IEF285I   VOL SER NOS= ACSRES.
IEF285I   PLI.V2R3M0.SIBMBASE                          KEPT
IEF285I   VOL SER NOS= ACSRES.
IEF285I   CSCJJJ.CSC.LOADLIB                           KEPT
IEF285I   VOL SER NOS= USER00.
IEF285I   CSCJGJ.ADV.OBJ                               KEPT
IEF285I   VOL SER NOS= USER01.
IEF285I   CSCJGJ.ADV.LOADLIB                           KEPT
IEF285I   VOL SER NOS= USER03.
IEF285I   SYS94095.T143455.RA000.CSCJGJA.SYSUT1        DELETED
IEF285I   CSCJGJ.CSCJGJA.JOB08030.D0000104.?           SYSOUT
IEF373I STEP /LKED    / START 94095.1435
IEF374I STEP /LKED    / STOP  94095.1435 CPU    0MIN 00.51SEC

IEF375I  JOB /CSCJGJA / START 94095.1434
IEF376I  JOB /CSCJGJA / STOP  94095.1435 CPU    0MIN 02.54SEC
```

Why not 0004?

The linkage editor worked fine and created a load module, but at the bottom of this listing indicates that the parm it received was invalid. The problem could have created the load module with AMODE=24 rather than AMODE=31, if AMODE=31 had not been the default. The reporting of warnings, which previously caused software to issue COND CODE 0004, is becoming inconsistent in some of IBM's software, complicating the task of determining if a run executed as desired. Modern software increasingly relies on user abend codes for problem indication, complicating documentation requirements.

Figure 9.15 (continued)

```
5688187 V2 R1 M00 IBM C/370                    CSCJGJ.ADV.ASM(J1C)                    04/05/94 14:35:01     Page     1

                                     * * * * *   P R O L O G   * * * * *

 Command options:
   Program name. . . . . . . . . : CSCJGJ.ADV.ASM(J1C)
   Compiler options. . . . . . . : *NOGONUMBER *NOALIAS    *NODECK     *NORENT     *NOTERMINAL *NOUPCONV   *SOURCE     *NOLIST
                                 : *XREF       *NOAGGR     *NOPPONLY   *NOEXPMAC   *NOSHOWINC  *NOOFFSET   *NOMEMORY   *NOSSCOMM
                                 : *NOCSECT    *NOLONGNAME *START
                                 : *TARGET()   *FLAG(I)    *NOTEST(SYM,BLOCK,LINE) *OPTIMIZE(0)*SPILL(128)
                                 : *NOINLINE(AUTO,NOREPORT,250,1000)
                                 : *NOCHECKOUT(NOPPTRACE,PPCHECK,GOTO,ACCURACY,PARM,NOENUM,
                                 : *           NOEXTERNAL,TRUNC,INIT,NOPORT,GENERAL)
                                 : *NOSEARCH
                                 : *NOLSEARCH
                                 : *OBJECT
   Language level. . . . . . . . : *EXTENDED
   Source margins. . . . . . . . :
     Varying length. . . . . . . : 1 - 32767
     Fixed length  . . . . . . . : 1 - 72
   Sequence columns. . . . . . . :
     Varying length. . . . . . . : none
     Fixed length. . . . . . . . : 73 - 80
5688187 V2 R1 M00 IBM C/370                    CSCJGJ.ADV.ASM(J1C)                    04/05/94 14:35:01     Page     2

                                       * * * * *   S O U R C E   * * * * *

 LINE  STMT                                                                                                     SEQNBR INCNO
             *...+....1....+....2....+....3....+....4....+....5....+....6....+....7....+....8....+....9......*
    1        |/*  This is a program in C/370 that accomplishes the same                                     |      1
    2        | *  thing that the J1COBOL program does in VS COBOL II.                                       |      2
    3        | *                                                                                            |      3
    4        | *  This program was written and tested using Mix Software's                                  |      4
    5        | *  PowerC before being uploaded to an ES/9000 and compiled                                   |      5
    6        | *  with C/370.  Trigraphs worked fine; no changes required                                   |      6
    7        | *  except in the fopens for ddnames.                                                         |      7
    8        | *                                                                                            |      8
    9        | *  Bob Narino and Jim Janossy, March, 1993                                                   |      9
   10        | */                                                                                           |     10
```

Figure 9.15 (continued)

```
11                                                                                   11
12          #pragma runopts( execops )                                               12
13                                                                                   13
14          #include <stdio.h>                                                       14
15          #include <ctype.h>                                                       15
16          #include <string.h>                                                      16
17          #include <stdlib.h>                                                      17
18                                                                                   18
19          #define WRITE       "w"                                                  19
20          #define READ        "r"                                                  20
21                                                                                   21
22          /* ----- Function prototypes ------------------------------------*/      22
23                                                                                   23
24          int  s1000_boj( int parms, char *parm_date );                            24
25          void s2000_process_records( char *parm_date );                           25
26          void s3000_eoj( void );                                                  26
27          double convert_pay_amount( char *orig_num );                             27
28                                                                                   28
29          /* ----- Global variables ---------------------------------------*/      29
30                                                                                   30
31          int  records_read = 0;                                                   31
32          int  recrds_listed = 0;                                                  32
33          double payment_amount_total = 0.0;                                       33
34                                                                                   34
35          /* Note:  Within the IBM environment you must use the                    35
36                    trigraph "??) ??)" symbols  for array notation.                36
37                    since 3270 keyboards don't have square brackets */             37
38                                                                                   38
39          char    buffer??(80??);                  /* Output buffer */             39
40                                                                                   40
41          FILE *pay_dat, *pay_list, *fopen();      /* File pointers */             41
42                                                                                   42
43          /* -------------------------------------------------------------*/      43
44                                                                                   44
45          int main( int argc,  char *argv??( ??) )                                 45
46          {                                                                        46
47     1     if ( s1000_boj( argc, argv??( 1 ??) ) )                                 47
48           {                                                                       48
49     2      s2000_process_records( argv??( 1 ??) );                                49
50     3      s3000_eoj();                                                           50
51     4      return ( 0 );                                                          51
52           }                                                                       52
53           else                                                                    53
```

Figure 9.15 (continued)

```
54   5     return ( 12 );
55        }
56
57        /* -------------------------------------------------------------*/
58        /* s1000_boj is written in the style of an assembler programmer! */
59        /* See if you can figure out why...                              */
60        /* -------------------------------------------------------------*/
61
62        int s1000_boj( int parms, char *parm_date )
63        {
64         int result = 1;                /* optimistic about the outcome  */
65         int arg_length;                /* size of the parm date         */
66         short index;                   /* used for looping              */
67
68   6     if ( parms != 2 )              /* check number of parms entered */
69         {
70   7      puts( "** ERROR ** NO DATE PARM ENTERED ON EXEC!" );
71   8      --result;
72   9      goto boj_exit;
73         }
74
75  10     printf( "??/nPARM DATA ENTERED =  %s.??/n", parm_date );
76  11     arg_length = strlen( parm_date );
77
78  12     if ( arg_length != 6 )
79         {
80  13      puts( "** ERROR ** INVALID DATE ENTERED ON EXEC! (LENGTH NE 6)" );
81  14      --result;
82  15      goto boj_exit;
83         }
84
85        /*
86         * Examine the parm-string character by character.
87         * If the current character is a digit, i.e. 0 - 9,  keep looping.
88         * Else note the failure and break out of the loop.
89         */
90
91  16     for ( index = 0; index < 6; index++ )
92         {
93  17      if ( isdigit( *( parm_date + index )  ) )
94  18       continue;
95          else
96          {
```

Figure 9.15 (continued)

```
 97   19 |    --result;
 98   20 |    goto check_result;
 99      |   }
100      |  }
101      |
102      | /***************/
103      | check_result:
104      | /***************/
105   21 |  if ( result < 1 )
106      |  {
107   22 |   puts( "** ERROR ** INVALID DATE ENTERED ON EXEC! (NOT NUMERIC)" );
108   23 |   goto boj_exit;
109      |  }
110   24 |  pay_dat = fopen( "dd:paydat", READ );
111   25 |  pay_list = fopen( "dd:paylist", WRITE );
112   26 |  printf( "??/nREPORT WILL LIST RECORDS FOR %s", parm_date );
113      |
114      | /***************/
115      | boj_exit:
116      | /***************/
117   27 |  return ( result );
118      | }
119      |
120      | /* ------------------------------------------------------------*/
121      |
122      | void  s2000_process_records( char *parm_date  )
123      | {
124      |  double employee_pay;
125      |
126   28 |  fgets( buffer, 80, pay_dat );
127   29 |  while ( !feof( pay_dat ) )
128      |  {
129   30 |   records_read++;
130   31 |   if ( strncmp( parm_date, buffer, 6 ) == 0 )
131      |   {
132   32 |    recrds_listed++;
133   33 |    employee_pay = convert_pay_amount( buffer+34 );
134   34 |    payment_amount_total += employee_pay;
135   35 |    fputs( buffer, pay_list );
136      |   }
137   36 |   fgets( buffer, 80, pay_dat );
138      |  }
139      | }
```

Figure 9.15 *(continued)*

```
 140         |                                                                      |  140
 141         | /* -----------------------------------------------------------------*/ |  141
 142         |                                                                      |  142
 143         | void  s3000_eoj( void )                                              |  143
 144         | {                                                                    |  144
 145    37   |  printf( "??/nTOTAL AMOUNT PAID: %8.2f??/n", payment_amount_total );  |  145
 146    38   |  printf( "TOTAL RECORDS READ: %d??/n", records_read );                |  146
 147    39   |  printf( "TOTAL RECORDS LISTED: %d\n", recrds_listed );               |  147
 148    40   |  fclose( pay_dat );                                                  |  148
 149    41   |  fclose( pay_list );                                                 |  149
 150         | }                                                                    |  150
 151         |                                                                      |  151
 152         | /* -----------------------------------------------------------------*/ |  152
 153         |                                                                      |  153
 154         | double  convert_pay_amount( char *orig_num )                         |  154
 155         | {                                                                    |  155
 156         |  char work_str??( 10 ??), *endptr;                                   |  156
 157         |  double temp;                                                        |  157
 158         |                                                                      |  158
 159    42   |  strncpy( work_str, orig_num, 6 );                                   |  159
 160    43   |  temp = strtod( work_str, &endptr );                                 |  160
 161    44   |  return ( temp / 100.0  );                                           |  161
 162         | }                                                                    |  162
                         * * * * *   E N D   O F   S O U R C E   * * * * *

        5688187 V2 R1 M00 IBM C/370                    CSCJGJ.ADV.ASM(J1C)                04/05/94 14:35:01
        Page     6

                  * * * * *   I N C L U D E S   * * * * *

 INCLUDE FILES  ---  FILE#   NAME
                       1     DD:SYSLIB(STDIO)
                       2     DD:SYSLIB(CTYPE)
                       3     DD:SYSLIB(STRING)
                       4     DD:SYSLIB(STDLIB)

                  * * * * *   E N D   O F   I N C L U D E S   * * * * *
```

Figure 9.15 (continued)

```
                      * * * * *  C R O S S   R E F E R E N C E   L I S T I N G  * * * * *

IDENTIFIER          DEFINITION      ATTRIBUTES
                                    <SEQNBR>-<FILE NO>:<FILE LINE NO>

___valist           14-1:81         typedef
                                    Type = array[2] of
                                             pointer to unsigned character

__amrc_ptr          14-1:387        typedef
                                    Type = pointer to structure with no tag

__amrc_type         14-1:383        typedef
                                    Type = structure with no tag

__cusp              14-1:125        typedef
                                    Type = pointer to  constant unsigned short integer

__ffile             14-1:41         Class = tag, Type = structure
                                    14-1:46, 14-1:47

work_str            156-0:156       Class = automatic, Length = 10,
                                    Type = array[10] of unsigned character
                                    159-0:159, 160-0:160

   -
   -
   -

FILE                14-1:46         typedef
                                    Type = structure __ffile
                  * * * * *  E N D   O F   C R O S S   R E F E R E N C E   L I S T I N G  * * * * *
```

Figure 9.15 (continued)

```
                    * * * * *  M E S S A G E   S U M M A R Y  * * * * *
    Total          Informational(00)          Warning(10)        Error(30)          Severe Error(40)
      0                   0                        0                 0                    0
                  * * * * *  E N D   O F   M E S S A G E   S U M M A R Y  * * * * *


                      * * * * *  S T O R A G E   O F F S E T   L I S T I N G  * * * * *
IDENTIFIER         DEFINITION      ATTRIBUTES
                                   <SEQNBR>-<FILE NO>:<FILE LINE NO>
arg_length         65-0:65         Class = automatic,           Offset = 144,        Length = 4
argc               45-0:45         Class = parameter,           Offset = 0,          Length = 4
argv               45-0:45         Class = parameter,           Offset = 4,          Length = 4
buffer             39-0:39         Class = external definition, Offset = 0,          Length = 80
employee_pay       124-0:124       Class = automatic,           Offset = 144,        Length = 8
endptr             156-0:156       Class = automatic,           Offset = 152,        Length = 4
index              66-0:66         Class = automatic,           Offset = 148,        Length = 2
orig_num           154-0:154       Class = parameter,           Offset = 0,          Length = 4
parm_date          62-0:62         Class = parameter,           Offset = 4,          Length = 4
parm_date          122-0:122       Class = parameter,           Offset = 0,          Length = 4
parms              62-0:62         Class = parameter,           Offset = 0,          Length = 4
pay_dat            41-0:41         Class = external definition, Offset = 0,          Length = 4
pay_list           41-0:41         Class = external definition, Offset = 0,          Length = 4
```

Figure 9.15 (continued)

```
payment_amount_total
                     33-0:33        Class = external definition, Offset = 0,        Length = 8
records_read         31-0:31        Class = external definition, Offset = 0,        Length = 4
recrds_listed        32-0:32        Class = external definition, Offset = 0,        Length = 4
result               64-0:64        Class = automatic,           Offset = 140,      Length = 4
temp                 157-0:157      Class = automatic,           Offset = 160,      Length = 8
work_str             156-0:156      Class = automatic,           Offset = 140,      Length = 10
                 * * * * *  E N D   O F   S T O R A G E   O F F S E T   L I S T I N G  * * * * *

                     * * * * *  E N D   O F   C O M P I L A T I O N  * * * * *
```

```
            MVS/DFP VERSION 3 RELEASE 3 LINKAGE EDITOR
JOB CSCJGJA     STEP STEP010     PROCEDURE LKED
INVOCATION PARAMETERS - AMODE=31,INVALID
ACTUAL SIZE=(317440,86016)
OUTPUT DATA SET CSCJGJ.ADV.LOADLIB IS ON VOLUME USER03

** J1C      REPLACED AND HAS AMODE 31
** LOAD MODULE HAS RMODE 24
** AUTHORIZATION CODE IS         0.
```

The linkage editor could not interpret what parm it was given, because it was not surrounded with apostrophes when it finally got it. *How did AMODE get set to 31 anyway?* It just happens to be our default for the linkage editor. If I had wanted AMODE=24 this would have been a problem. Adjust the coding of the symbolic parameter in the proc, or hard code the AMODE and RMODE parameters in your proc.

Figure 9.15 (continued)

9.14 Executing a C/370 Program

Figure 9.16 illustrates JCL to execute a load module prepared from C/370 source code. If you compare this with Figures 9.2 and 9.10, you'll see that it is essentially identical to the JCL to execute load modules prepared from COBOL or assembler source code. This makes sense: COBOL, assembler, and C are just three different ways to express logic that various compilers turn into machine language. (This is the same reason that interlanguage communication is possible.) The JCL in Figure 9.16, as that in Figure 9.10, executes the program with various good and invalid PARM values to test it.

You can see the result of our testing of the J1C program in the MVS/ESA system output of Figure 9.17. The PARM value of 120193 results in the selection of the same six records from the payments data set, which are printed. Totals are provided for the selection. In the case of invalid PARM values, J1C returns a value of 12, which is received by MVS/ESA as the COND CODE value you see in the system output.

9.15 VS COBOL II CALLing a C/370 Subprogram

A program written in VS COBOL II can CALL a subprogram written in C/370. The small program named COBLMAIN, shown in Figure 9.18, does precisely this in CALLing subprogram CSUB. As you can see from examining line 3000 of this program, the CALL is made in exactly the same way that it would be if CSUB had been written in COBOL.

Examine Figure 9.18 and you will see that COBLMAIN passes two integer values to subprogram CSUB, the source code for which is in Figure 9.19. CSUB adds the two integers it is given and provides the result in a third shared field, ANSWER. If you compare the source code for COBLMAIN and CSUB, you'll see that the shared fields are named differently in each. This is, of course, of no consequence since the main and subprograms interact only as machine language, not in source code form.

The COBLMAIN program groups the three fields it shares with CSUB into one record, named WS-PASSED-VALUES. The CALL it makes at line 3000 to CSUB passes just the address of the beginning of this record. The CSUB subprogram receives just this address and associates it with a data structure ("struct") it names "bucket." Figure 9.19 is an important model for COBOL/C interlanguage communication because you can see in it how "fields" in a structure are named and accessed. Note the use of this coding at the start of the CSUB subprogram:

```
#pragma linkage ( csub, COBOL )
```

This is a preprocessor directive that advises the C compiler that the load module should follow COBOL language conventions for data passing. The item named *parm in the csub function header is a pointer, the memory address of an instance of the struct named bucket. That memory address is what the subprogram receives from the CALL by COBMAIN.

```
EDIT ---- CSCJGJ.ADV.CNTL(RUNJ1C) - 01.05 ------------------- COLUMNS 001 072
COMMAND ===>                                                  SCROLL ===> PAGE
****** ***************************** TOP OF DATA ******************************
000001 //CSCJGJA   JOB 1,                    ACCOUNTING INFORMATION
000002 //  'BIN 7--NARINO',                   PROGRAMMER NAME AND DELIVERY BIN
000003 //  CLASS=A,                          INPUT QUEUE CLASS
000004 //  MSGLEVEL=(1,1),                   HOW MUCH MVS SYSTEM PRINT DESIRED
000005 //  MSGCLASS=X,                       PRINT DESTINATION X A L N OR O
000006 //  TIME=(0,6),                       SAFETY LIMIT: RUN TIME UP TO 6 SECS
000007 //  REGION=2M,                        ALLOW UP TO 2 MEGS VIRTUAL MEMORY
000008 //* TYPRUN=SCAN,                      UNCOMMENT THIS LINE TO DO SCAN ONLY
000009 //  NOTIFY=CSCJGJ                     WHO TO TELL WHEN JOB IS DONE
000010 //*-------------------------------------------------------------------
000011 //* TEST THE J1C PROGRAM WITH VARIOUS PARM VALUES
000012 //* THIS JCL IS STORED AT CSCJGJ.ADV.CNTL  NJ1C)
000013 //*******************************************************************
000014 //* EXECUTE J1C WITH PARM                                           *
000015 //*******************************************************************
000016 //STEP010  EXEC  PGM=J1C,PARM='120193'
000017 //STEPLIB    DD  DSN=CSCJGJ.ADV.LOADLIB,DISP=SHR
000018 //PAYDAT     DD  DSN=CSCJGJ.ADV.CNTL(PAYMENTS),DISP=SHR
000019 //PAYLIST    DD  SYSOUT=*
000020 //*
000021 //*******************************************************************
000022 //* EXECUTE J1C WITHOUT A   M VALUE ON EXEC                         *
000023 //*******************************************************************
000024 //STEP020  EXEC  PGM=J1C
000025 //STEPLIB    DD  DSN=CSCJGJ.ADV.LOADLIB,DISP=SHR
000026 //PAYDAT     DD  DSN=CSCJGJ.ADV.CNTL(PAYMENTS),DISP=SHR
000027 //PAYLIST    DD  SYSOUT=*
000028 //*
000029 //*******************************************************************
000030 //* EXECUTE J1C BUT PARM IS NOT ALL    RIC                          *
000031 //*******************************************************************
000032 //STEP030  EXEC  PGM=J1C,PARM='12GX93'
000033 //STEPLIB    DD  DSN=CSCJGJ.ADV.LOADLIB,DISP=SHR
000034 //PAYDAT     DD  DSN=CSCJGJ.ADV.CNTL(PAYMENTS),DISP=SHR
000035 //PAYLIST    DD  SYSOUT=*
000036 //*
000037 //*******************************************************************
000038 //* EXECUTE J1C BUT PARM IS NOT PR   LENGTH                         *
000039 //*******************************************************************
000040 //STEP040  EXEC  PGM=J1C,PARM='12093'
000041 //STEPLIB    DD  DSN=CSCJGJ.ADV.LOADLIB,DISP=SHR
000042 //PAYDAT     DD  DSN=CSCJGJ.ADV.CNTL(PAYMENTS),DISP=SHR
000043 //PAYLIST    DD  SYSOUT=*
000044 //
```

Exactly like the JCL in Figure 9.10, which executes the J1ASM load module, this JCL executes the C/370-produced J1C load module four times, to test it with various PARM values. The first PARM value, '120193', should select six records from the payments file and cause them to be listed and tabulated. The second PARM value is missing, the third PARM value is invalid, and the fourth PARM value is not the required six bytes in length. ***Does J1C work properly?*** See Figure 9.17 and see for yourself!

Figure 9.16 JCL to Test the J1C Load Module and Demonstrate Its PARM Validation Features

Figure 9.17 MVS/ESA System Output and C/370 Program Output from the J1C Test *(see facing page)*

```
                 J E S 2   J O B   L O G  --  S Y S T E M  I B M 1  --  N O D E
21.46.27 JOB08490  IRR010I  USERID CSCJGJ   IS ASSIGNED TO THIS JOB.
21.46.28 JOB08490  ICH70001I CSCJGJ   LAST ACCESS AT 21:42:09 ON TUESDAY, APRIL 5
21.46.28 JOB08490  $HASP373 CSCJGJA  STARTED - INIT  1 - CLASS A - SYS IBM1
21.46.32 JOB08490  $HASP395 CSCJGJA  ENDED

------ JES2 JOB STATISTICS ------
    05 APR 94 JOB EXECUTION DATE
           43 CARDS READ
          134 SYSOUT PRINT RECORDS
            0 SYSOUT PUNCH RECORDS
            8 SYSOUT SPOOL KBYTES
         0.08 MINUTES EXECUTION TIME

        1 //CSCJGJA   JOB 1,                   ACCOUNTING INFORMATION
          //  'BIN 7--NARINO',                 PROGRAMMER NAME AND DELIVERY BIN
          //  CLASS=A,                         INPUT QUEUE CLASS
          //  MSGLEVEL=(1,1),                  HOW MUCH MVS SYSTEM PRINT DESIRED
          //  MSGCLASS=X,                      PRINT DESTINATION X A L N OR O
          //  TIME=(0,6),                      SAFETY LIMIT: RUN TIME UP TO 6 SECS
          //  REGION=2M,                       ALLOW UP TO 2 MEGS VIRTUAL MEMORY
          //* TYPRUN=SCAN,                     UNCOMMENT THIS LINE TO DO SCAN ONLY
          //  NOTIFY=CSCJGJ                    WHO TO TELL WHEN JOB IS DONE
          //*---------------------------------------------------------------------
          //* TEST THE J1C PROGRAM WITH VARIOUS PARM VALUES
          //* THIS JCL IS STORED AT CSCJGJ.ADV.CNTL(RUNJ1C)
          //*********************************************************************
          //* EXECUTE J1C WITH PARM                                             *
          //*********************************************************************
        2 //STEP010  EXEC  PGM=J1C,PARM='120193'
        3 //STEPLIB    DD  DSN=CSCJGJ.ADV.LOADLIB,DISP=SHR
        4 //PAYDAT     DD  DSN=CSCJGJ.ADV.CNTL(PAYMENTS),DISP=SHR
        5 //PAYLIST    DD  SYSOUT=*
          //*
          //*********************************************************************
          //* EXECUTE J1C WITHOUT A PARM VALUE ON EXEC                          *
          //*********************************************************************
        6 //STEP020  EXEC  PGM=J1C
        7 //STEPLIB    DD  DSN=CSCJGJ.ADV.LOADLIB,DISP=SHR
        8 //PAYDAT     DD  DSN=CSCJGJ.ADV.CNTL(PAYMENTS),DISP=SHR
        9 //PAYLIST    DD  SYSOUT=*
          //*
          //*********************************************************************
          //* EXECUTE J1C BUT PARM IS NOT ALL NUMERIC                           *
          //*********************************************************************
       10 //STEP030  EXEC  PGM=J1C,PARM='12GX93'
       11 //STEPLIB    DD  DSN=CSCJGJ.ADV.LOADLIB,DISP=SHR
       12 //PAYDAT     DD  DSN=CSCJGJ.ADV.CNTL(PAYMENTS),DISP=SHR
       13 //PAYLIST    DD  SYSOUT=*
          //*
          //*********************************************************************
          //* EXECUTE J1C BUT PARM IS NOT PROPER LENGTH                         *
          //*********************************************************************
       14 //STEP040  EXEC  PGM=J1C,PARM='12093'
       15 //STEPLIB    DD  DSN=CSCJGJ.ADV.LOADLIB,DISP=SHR
       16 //PAYDAT     DD  DSN=CSCJGJ.ADV.CNTL(PAYMENTS),DISP=SHR
       17 //PAYLIST    DD  SYSOUT=*

ICH70001I CSCJGJ   LAST ACCESS AT 21:42:09 ON TUESDAY, APRIL 5, 1994

IEF236I ALLOC. FOR CSCJGJA STEP010
IEF237I 117  ALLOCATED TO STEPLIB
IEF237I 111  ALLOCATED TO PAYDAT
IEF237I JES2 ALLOCATED TO PAYLIST
IEF237I JES2 ALLOCATED TO SYS00001
IEF142I CSCJGJA STEP010 - STEP WAS EXECUTED - COND CODE 0000
IEF285I   CSCJGJ.ADV.LOADLIB                                  KEPT
IEF285I   VOL SER NOS= USER03.
IEF285I   CSCJGJ.ADV.CNTL                                     KEPT
IEF285I   VOL SER NOS= USER00.
IEF285I   CSCJGJ.CSCJGJA.JOB08490.D0000101.?                  SYSOUT
IEF285I   CSCJGJ.CSCJGJA.JOB08490.D0000105.?                  SYSOUT
IEF373I STEP /STEP010 / START 94095.2146
IEF374I STEP /STEP010 / STOP  94095.2146 CPU    0MIN 00.30SEC

IEF236I ALLOC. FOR CSCJGJA STEP020
IEF237I 117  ALLOCATED TO STEPLIB
IEF237I 111  ALLOCATED TO PAYDAT
IEF237I JES2 ALLOCATED TO PAYLIST
IEF237I JES2 ALLOCATED TO SYS00002
IEF142I CSCJGJA STEP020 - STEP WAS EXECUTED - COND CODE 0012
IEF285I   CSCJGJ.ADV.LOADLIB                                  KEPT
```

J1C sets **COND CODE 0000** when PARM was valid and sets **COND CODE 0012** if PARM was invalid.

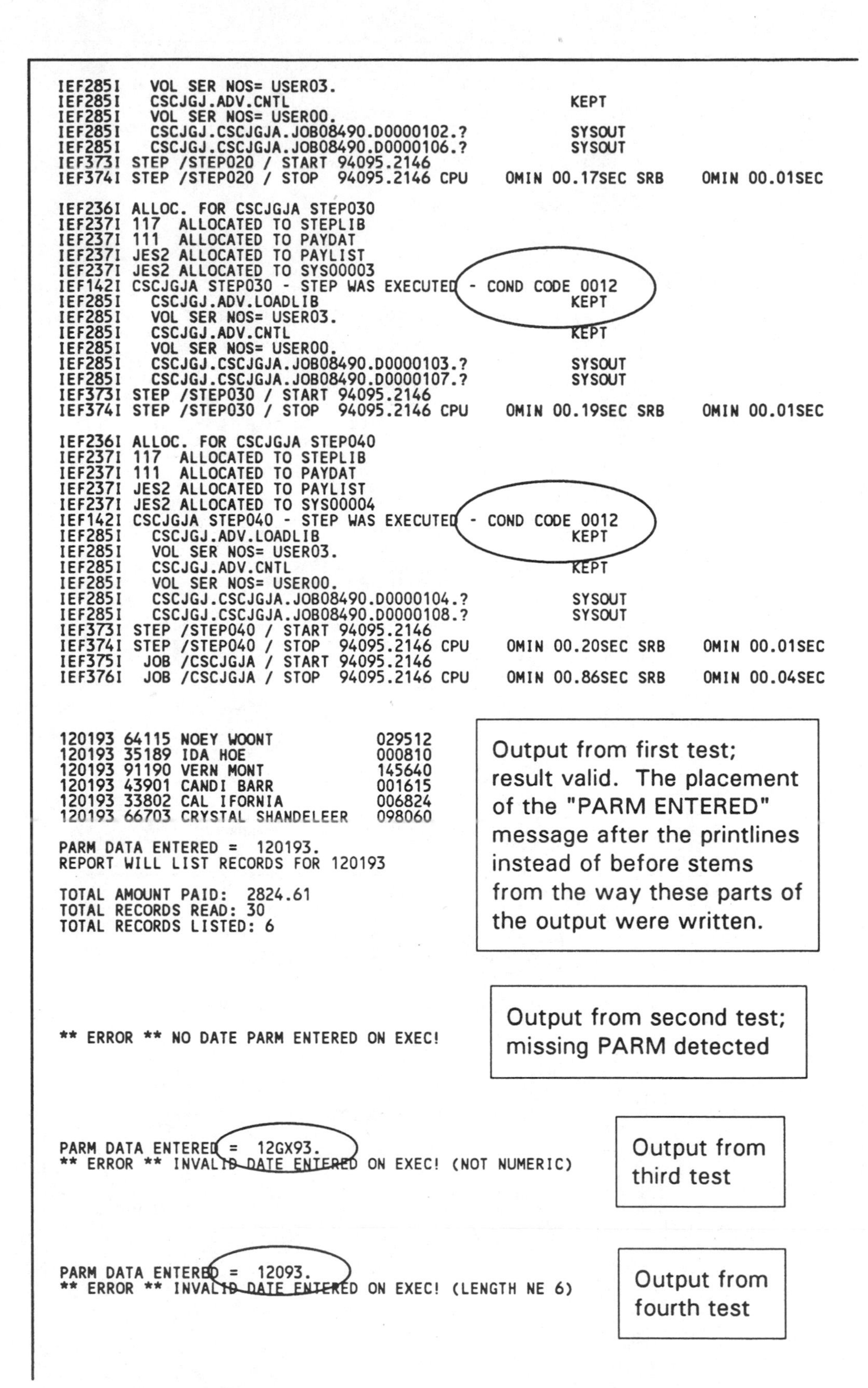

```
IEF285I   VOL SER NOS= USER03.
IEF285I   CSCJGJ.ADV.CNTL                                   KEPT
IEF285I   VOL SER NOS= USER00.
IEF285I   CSCJGJ.CSCJGJA.JOB08490.D0000102.?                SYSOUT
IEF285I   CSCJGJ.CSCJGJA.JOB08490.D0000106.?                SYSOUT
IEF373I STEP /STEP020 / START 94095.2146
IEF374I STEP /STEP020 / STOP  94095.2146 CPU    0MIN 00.17SEC SRB    0MIN 00.01SEC

IEF236I ALLOC. FOR CSCJGJA STEP030
IEF237I 117  ALLOCATED TO STEPLIB
IEF237I 111  ALLOCATED TO PAYDAT
IEF237I JES2 ALLOCATED TO PAYLIST
IEF237I JES2 ALLOCATED TO SYS00003
IEF142I CSCJGJA STEP030 - STEP WAS EXECUTED - COND CODE 0012
IEF285I   CSCJGJ.ADV.LOADLIB                                KEPT
IEF285I   VOL SER NOS= USER03.
IEF285I   CSCJGJ.ADV.CNTL                                   KEPT
IEF285I   VOL SER NOS= USER00.
IEF285I   CSCJGJ.CSCJGJA.JOB08490.D0000103.?                SYSOUT
IEF285I   CSCJGJ.CSCJGJA.JOB08490.D0000107.?                SYSOUT
IEF373I STEP /STEP030 / START 94095.2146
IEF374I STEP /STEP030 / STOP  94095.2146 CPU    0MIN 00.19SEC SRB    0MIN 00.01SEC

IEF236I ALLOC. FOR CSCJGJA STEP040
IEF237I 117  ALLOCATED TO STEPLIB
IEF237I 111  ALLOCATED TO PAYDAT
IEF237I JES2 ALLOCATED TO PAYLIST
IEF237I JES2 ALLOCATED TO SYS00004
IEF142I CSCJGJA STEP040 - STEP WAS EXECUTED - COND CODE 0012
IEF285I   CSCJGJ.ADV.LOADLIB                                KEPT
IEF285I   VOL SER NOS= USER03.
IEF285I   CSCJGJ.ADV.CNTL                                   KEPT
IEF285I   VOL SER NOS= USER00.
IEF285I   CSCJGJ.CSCJGJA.JOB08490.D0000104.?                SYSOUT
IEF285I   CSCJGJ.CSCJGJA.JOB08490.D0000108.?                SYSOUT
IEF373I STEP /STEP040 / START 94095.2146
IEF374I STEP /STEP040 / STOP  94095.2146 CPU    0MIN 00.20SEC SRB    0MIN 00.01SEC
IEF375I  JOB /CSCJGJA / START 94095.2146
IEF376I  JOB /CSCJGJA / STOP  94095.2146 CPU    0MIN 00.86SEC SRB    0MIN 00.04SEC


120193 64115 NOEY WOONT             029512
120193 35189 IDA HOE                000810
120193 91190 VERN MONT              145640
120193 43901 CANDI BARR             001615
120193 33802 CAL IFORNIA            006824
120193 66703 CRYSTAL SHANDELEER     098060

PARM DATA ENTERED =  120193.
REPORT WILL LIST RECORDS FOR 120193

TOTAL AMOUNT PAID:  2824.61
TOTAL RECORDS READ: 30
TOTAL RECORDS LISTED: 6


** ERROR ** NO DATE PARM ENTERED ON EXEC!


PARM DATA ENTERED =  12GX93.
** ERROR ** INVALID DATE ENTERED ON EXEC! (NOT NUMERIC)


PARM DATA ENTERED =  12093.
** ERROR ** INVALID DATE ENTERED ON EXEC! (LENGTH NE 6)
```

Output from first test; result valid. The placement of the "PARM ENTERED" message after the printlines instead of before stems from the way these parts of the output were written.
Output from second test; missing PARM detected
Output from third test
Output from fourth test

Figure 9.17 (continued)

```
EDIT ---- CSCJGJ.ADV.COBOL(COBLMAIN) - 01.03 ---------------- COLUMNS 007 078
COMMAND ===>                                                  SCROLL ===> PAGE
****** ***************************** TOP OF DATA ******************************
000100 ID DIVISION.
000200 PROGRAM-ID. COBLMAIN.
000300 AUTHOR.  ROBERT F. NARINO AND JIM JANOSSY.
000400
000500 * THIS PROGRAM DEMONSTRATES A CALL TO A SUBPROGRAM WRITTEN
000600 * IN C/370
000700
000800 DATA DIVISION.
000900 WORKING-STORAGE SECTION.
001000
001100 01  WS-VALUE1                   PIC 9(3)   VALUE 123.
001200 01  WS-VALUE2                   PIC 9(3)   VALUE 456.
001300 01  WS-VALUE3                   PIC 9(3)   VALUE 0.
001400
001500 01  WS-PASSED-VALUES.
001600     05 INTEGER-1                PIC S9(9)  BINARY.
001700     05 INTEGER-2                PIC S9(9)  BINARY.
001800     05 WS-ANSWER                PIC S9(9)  BINARY.
001900
002000 PROCEDURE DIVISION.
002100
002200     DISPLAY 'COBLMAIN PROGRAM STARTING'.
002300     DISPLAY 'VALUE OF WS-VALUE1 IS ', WS-VALUE1.
002400     DISPLAY 'VALUE OF WS-VALUE2 IS ', WS-VALUE2.
002500     DISPLAY 'VALUE OF WS-VALUE3 IS ', WS-VALUE3.
002600
002700     MOVE WS-VALUE1 TO INTEGER-1.
002800     MOVE WS-VALUE2 TO INTEGER-2.
002900     DISPLAY 'NOW CALLING CSUB C/370 SUBPROGRAM'.
003000     CALL 'CSUB' USING WS-PASSED-VALUES.
003100
003200     DISPLAY 'CONTROL HAS RETURNED FROM CSUB SUBPROGRAM'.
003300     MOVE INTEGER-1 TO WS-VALUE1.
003400     MOVE INTEGER-2 TO WS-VALUE2.
003500     MOVE WS-ANSWER TO WS-VALUE3.
003600     DISPLAY 'VALUE OF WS-VALUE1 IS ', WS-VALUE1.
003700     DISPLAY 'VALUE OF WS-VALUE2 IS ', WS-VALUE2.
003800     DISPLAY 'VALUE OF WS-VALUE3 IS ', WS-VALUE3.
003900     STOP RUN.
```

BINARY is the modern way to say COMP.

CALL

COBLMAIN is a main program. It CALLs CSUB, sharing WS-PASSED-VALUES with it. CSUB provides the service of summing the first two values, INTEGER-1 and INTEGER-2, and puts the result in WS-ANSWER. A COBOL-to-C CALL is one of the most common modern examples of interlanguage communication (ILC).

Figure 9.18 COBLMAIN, A VS COBOL II Program That CALLs a Subprogram Named CSUB, Written in C/370

9.16 Passing Data Between COBOL and C

In passing values between COBOL and C/370, both main and subprogram must "look" at shared memory in the same way. In COBLMAIN, all three shared fields are declared with PIC S9(9) BINARY. BINARY is the 1985 COBOL way of saying COMP; you can still code COMP if you like, as an

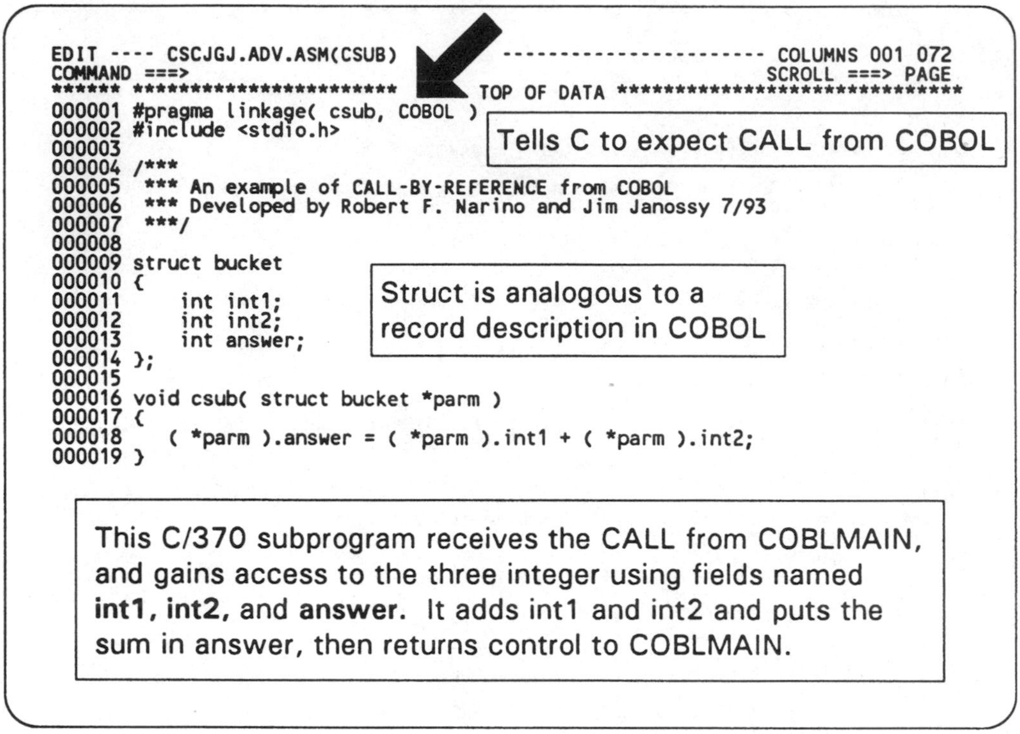

```
EDIT ---- CSCJGJ.ADV.ASM(CSUB)          ---------------------- COLUMNS 001 072
COMMAND ===>                                                  SCROLL ===> PAGE
****** ************************  TOP OF DATA *******************************
000001 #pragma linkage( csub, COBOL )
000002 #include <stdio.h>
000003
000004 /***
000005  *** An example of CALL-BY-REFERENCE from COBOL
000006  *** Developed by Robert F. Narino and Jim Janossy 7/93
000007  ***/
000008
000009 struct bucket
000010 {
000011     int int1;
000012     int int2;
000013     int answer;
000014 };
000015
000016 void csub( struct bucket *parm )
000017 {
000018    ( *parm ).answer = ( *parm ).int1 + ( *parm ).int2;
000019 }
```

Tells C to expect CALL from COBOL

Struct is analogous to a record description in COBOL

This C/370 subprogram receives the CALL from COBLMAIN, and gains access to the three integer using fields named **int1, int2,** and **answer.** It adds int1 and int2 and puts the sum in answer, then returns control to COBLMAIN.

Figure 9.19 CSUB, A Subprogram Written in C/370 to Receive a CALL from a VS COBOL II Program

indicator of binary. Only compatible data types can be passed between COBOL and C programs. Here is how COBOL and C declarations relate to one another:

C	COBOL	Size	Alignment
char	PIC X	1 byte	byte
signed int	PIC S9(9) BINARY	4 bytes	fullword
double	COMP-2	8 bytes	doubleword
struct	Record description with 01, 05, levels		
array	OCCURS clause		

If you pass a record from a COBOL program to a C program, you have to make sure that the fields are properly aligned on word boundaries through the use of slack (unused) bytes. You can use the VS COBOL II MAP option to see how your data structures are arranged in COBOL. The AGGR option of the C/370 compiler (not activated in Figure 9.15) gives you similar information about C structure declarations. ***Note that C does not directly deal with packed decimal data.***

9.17 Static or Dynamic CALLs?

A call from a COBOL program to a subprogram, developed in any language, can be accomplished in two different ways. These ways are named "static" and "dynamic" after the action that occurs when the main program is executed. The call can appear the same way in source code, although calling by literal program name usually implies a static call, whereas calling by variable name containing a program name must always be handled dynamically. The static or dynamic nature of a call is also affected by compiler and linkage editor parameter options.

A *static call* is actually more of a "logical" arrangement of function than a physical one. To arrange a static call, you compile main and subprograms separately, then run the linkage editor once, giving it instructions to prepare one physical load module that includes the machine language of the main and subprograms. The load module is given the name of the main program and is self-contained. That is, when loaded to memory, all of the logic of the main and subprograms is present.

In a *dynamic call,* main and subprograms are compiled *and* link edited separately. Machine language modules for each are prepared and exist as separate entities in a load module library. The main program is executed, and at the time it issues a CALL to a subprogram, MVS/ESA dynamically seeks and locates the subprogram load module, allocates memory for it, and "links" the main and subprograms together.

Static and dynamic calls each have strengths and weaknesses. A static call is faster and preferred for interactive programs, because the process of finding and loading a subprogram is eliminated. But static load modules are larger, since all code is present in one place. Dynamic calls offer more flexibility, since subprograms can be regarded as detachable parts that can be separately maintained and replaced. Dynamic calls are preferable for batch programs because they directly implement reusability at the machine language level; many batch programs can call the same subprogram, the load module of which is stored only once. The static or dynamic nature of calls is a factor even if you don't use CALLs within programs, since a load module "calls" upon service routines to accomplish input/output actions and other functions.

The JCL illustrated in the next figures prepares the CSUB subprogram as a dynamically callable module. Its load module is placed into a load module library, and COBLMAIN is compiled and linked separately. When COBLMAIN is executed, its CALL to CSUB is handled dynamically by MVS/ESA. You may have to experiment with static and dynamic CALLs between COBOL and C, because the type of call possible may be dictated by factors concerning the placement of support libraries in your installation, and the version of COBOL and C/370 you are using. As a suggestion, consider adjusting your compile and link procs to use a permanent object module library rather than a temporary one, so that you retain the object code from the compile even if you do not immediately require it. This would force a change at line 3500 in my COB2CLJ proc in Figure 9.6. The CCX4 proc, in Figure 9.14, already uses a permanent object library, accessed at lines 88 and 98.

9.18 Compiling, Linking, and Running COBLMAIN and CSUB

Figure 9.20 lists the JCL we used to compile and link the CSUB subprogram. Figure 9.21 lists the JCL we used to compile and link the COBLSUB main program. Both of these sets of JCL involve the same procs discussed and illustrated earlier in this chapter, namely CCX4 and COB2CLJ. With dynamic calling, it is convenient to be able to use the same processing procs for all programs, whether they invoke subprograms or not.

Figure 9.22 lists the JCL to execute the COBLMAIN program. You see this JCL restated in the MVS/ESA system output from a run, shown in Figure 9.23. The sum displayed at the end of this run, 579, has been developed by the CSUB program.

The type of C subprogram illustrated in this example is probably the handiest use you will find for interlanguage communication, at least to start with. A C subprogram may be more convenient for certain types of complex calculations and algorithms than a COBOL subprogram. With the model provided by COBLMAIN and CSUB, and the JCL to process them, you have a good start on this form of mainframe interlanguage communication.

```
EDIT ---- CSCJGJ.ADV.CNTL(CSUB) - 01.02 --------------------- COLUMNS 001 072
COMMAND ===>                                                  SCROLL ===> PAGE
****** ****************************** TOP OF DATA ******************************
000001 //CSCJGJA   JOB 1,                    ACCOUNTING INFORMATION
000002 //   'BIN 7--NARINO',                 PROGRAMMER NAME AND DELIVERY BIN
000003 //   CLASS=A,                         INPUT QUEUE CLASS
000004 //   MSGLEVEL=(1,1),                  HOW MUCH MVS SYSTEM PRINT DESIRED
000005 //   MSGCLASS=X,                      PRINT DESTINATION X A L N OR O
000006 //   TIME=(0,6),                      SAFETY LIMIT: RUN TIME UP TO 6 SECS
000007 //   REGION=2M,                       ALLOW UP TO 2 MEGS VIRTUAL MEMORY
000008 //*  TYPRUN=SCAN,                     UNCOMMENT THIS LINE TO DO SCAN ONLY
000009 //   NOTIFY=CSCJGJ                    WHO TO TELL WHEN JOB IS DONE
000010 //        JCLLIB   ORDER=(CSCJGJ.ADV.PROCLIB1)
000011 //*
000012 //* COMPILE AND LINK A C/370 PROGRAM, CREATING LOAD MODULE
000013 //* THIS JCL IS STORED AT CSCJGJ.ADV.CNTL(CSUB)
000014 //*-----------------------------------------------------------------
000015 //STEP010  EXEC  CCX4,
000016 //     SRCLIB='CSCJGJ.ADV.ASM',
000017 //     MEMBER='CSUB',
000018 //     OBJLIB='CSCJGJ.ADV.OBJ',
000019 //    LOADLIB='CSCJGJ.ADV.LOADLIB',
000020 //       CPARM='SOURCE,XREF,NOTERMINAL'
000021 //
```

This JCL compiles and links the CSUB subprogram. As you can see, this invokes the same CCX4 proc shown in Figure 9.14, which I previously used to compile and link the J1C program. CSUB will be dynamically callable, meaning that I can link edit it separately and put its load module into a load module library rather than "hard linking" CSUB and COBLMAIN into one load module.

Figure 9.20 JCL to Compile and Link the CSUB Subprogram Using a Proc Named CCX4 (compare this to Figure 9.13)

```
EDIT ---- CSCJGJ.ADV.CNTL(COBLMAIN) - 01.00 ------------------ COLUMNS 001 072
COMMAND ===>                                                  SCROLL ===> PAGE
****** ***************************** TOP OF DATA ******************************
000001 //CSCJGJA   JOB 1,                  ACCOUNTING INFORMATION
000002 //   'BIN 7--JANOSSY',              PROGRAMMER NAME AND DELIVERY BIN
000003 //  CLASS=A,                        INPUT QUEUE CLASS
000004 //  MSGLEVEL=(1,1),                 HOW MUCH MVS SYSTEM PRINT DESIRED
000005 //  MSGCLASS=X,                     PRINT DESTINATION X A L N OR O
000006 //  TIME=(0,6),                     SAFETY LIMIT: RUN TIME UP TO 6 SECS
000007 //  REGION=2M,                      ALLOW UP TO 2 MEGS VIRTUAL MEMORY
000008 //  NOTIFY=CSCJGJ                   WHO TO TELL WHEN JOB IS DONE
000009 //*
000010 //* COMPILE AND LINK USING VS COBOL II, PREPARES LOAD MODULE
000011 //* THIS JCL IS STORED AT CSCJGJ.ADV.CNTL(COBLMAIN)
000012 //*-----------------------------------------------------------------------
000013 //STEP010  EXEC  COB2CLJ,
000014 //        PDS='CSCJGJ.ADV.COBOL',
000015 //   MEMBER='COBLMAIN',
000016 //  LOADLIB='CSCJGJ.ADV.LOADLIB'
000017 //
```

Here I create the load module for the COBLMAIN program by executing a proc named COB2CLJ. The machine language for the program is placed into my load module library, CSCJGJ.ADV.LOADLIB.

Figure 9.21 JCL to Compile and Link the COBLMAIN Program Using the COB2CLJ Proc Shown in Figure 9.6

```
EDIT ---- CSCJGJ.ADV.CNTL(RUNCOBL) - 01.02 ------------------ COLUMNS 001 072
COMMAND ===>                                                  SCROLL ===> PAGE
****** ***************************** TOP OF DATA ******************************
000001 //CSCJGJA   JOB 1,                  ACCOUNTING INFORMATION
000002 //   'BIN 7--JANOSSY',              PROGRAMMER NAME AND DELIVERY BIN
000003 //  MSGLEVEL=(1,1),                 HOW MUCH MVS SYSTEM PRINT DESIRED
000004 //  MSGCLASS=X,                     PRINT DESTINATION X A L N OR O
000005 //* TYPRUN=SCAN,                    UNCOMMENT IF WANT ONLY A JCL SCAN
000006 //  NOTIFY=CSCJGJ                   WHO TO TELL WHEN JOB IS DONE
000007 //*
000008 //* EXECUTE THE COBLMAIN LOAD MODULE (IT CALLS CSUB)
000009 //* THIS JCL IS STORED AT CSCJGJ.ADV.CNTL(RUNCOBL)
000010 //*-----------------------------------------------------------------------
000011 //STEP010  EXEC  PGM=COBLMAIN
000012 //STEPLIB    DD  DSN=CSCJGJ.ADV.LOADLIB,DISP=SHR
000013 //           DD  DSN=SYS1.COB2LIB,DISP=SHR
000014 //SYSOUT     DD  SYSOUT=*
000015 //
```

This is straightforward JCL to execute the load module for COBLMAIN. This main program CALLs the CSUB subprogram, which was written in C/370.

Figure 9.22 JCL to Execute the COBLMAIN Main Program

```
                    J E S 2   J O B   L O G  --  S Y S T E M   I B M 1  --  N O D E

08.10.01 JOB09764  IRR010I  USERID CSCJGJ   IS ASSIGNED TO THIS JOB.
08.10.02 JOB09764  ICH70001I CSCJGJ   LAST ACCESS AT 08:09:26 ON THURSDAY, APRIL 7
08.10.02 JOB09764  $HASP373 CSCJGJA  STARTED - INIT  1 - CLASS A - SYS IBM1
08.10.04 JOB09764  $HASP395 CSCJGJA  ENDED

------ JES2 JOB STATISTICS ------
    07 APR 94 JOB EXECUTION DATE
           14 CARDS READ
           52 SYSOUT PRINT RECORDS
            0 SYSOUT PUNCH RECORDS
            3 SYSOUT SPOOL KBYTES
         0.02 MINUTES EXECUTION TIME

        1 //CSCJGJA   JOB 1,                      ACCOUNTING INFORMATION
          //   'BIN 7--JANOSSY',                  PROGRAMMER NAME AND DELIVERY BIN
          //  MSGLEVEL=(1,1),                     HOW MUCH MVS SYSTEM PRINT DESIRED
          //  MSGCLASS=X,                         PRINT DESTINATION X A L N OR O
          //* TYPRUN=SCAN,                        UNCOMMENT IF WANT ONLY A JCL SCAN
          //  NOTIFY=CSCJGJ                       WHO TO TELL WHEN JOB IS DONE
          //*
          //* EXECUTE THE COBLMAIN LOAD MODULE (IT CALLS CSUB)
          //* THIS JCL IS STORED AT CSCJGJ.ADV.CNTL(RUNCOBL)
          //*-----------------------------------------------------------------
        2 //STEP010  EXEC  PGM=COBLMAIN
        3 //STEPLIB    DD  DSN=CSCJGJ.ADV.LOADLIB,DISP=SHR
        4 //           DD  DSN=SYS1.COB2LIB,DISP=SHR
        5 //SYSOUT     DD  SYSOUT=*

ICH70001I CSCJGJ   LAST ACCESS AT 08:09:26 ON THURSDAY, APRIL 7, 1994

IEF236I ALLOC. FOR CSCJGJA STEP010
IEF237I 117  ALLOCATED TO STEPLIB
IEF237I 110  ALLOCATED TO
IEF237I JES2 ALLOCATED TO SYSOUT
IEF142I CSCJGJA STEP010 - STEP WAS EXECUTED - COND CODE 0000
IEF285I   CSCJGJ.ADV.LOADLIB                         KEPT
IEF285I   VOL SER NOS= USER03.
IEF285I   SYS1.COB2LIB                               KEPT
IEF285I   VOL SER NOS= ACSRES.
IEF285I   CSCJGJ.CSCJGJA.JOB09764.D0000101.?         SYSOUT
IEF373I STEP /STEP010 / START 94097.0810
IEF374I STEP /STEP010 / STOP  94097.0810 CPU    0MIN 00.18SEC SRB    0MIN 00.02SEC
IEF375I  JOB /CSCJGJA / START 94097.0810
IEF376I  JOB /CSCJGJA / STOP  94097.0810 CPU    0MIN 00.18SEC SRB    0MIN 00.02SEC

COBLMAIN PROGRAM STARTING

VALUE OF WS-VALUE1 IS 123
VALUE OF WS-VALUE2 IS 456
VALUE OF WS-VALUE3 IS 000

NOW CALLING CSUB C/370 SUBPROGRAM

CONTROL HAS RETURNED FROM CSUB SUBPROGRAM
VALUE OF WS-VALUE1 IS 123
VALUE OF WS-VALUE2 IS 456
VALUE OF WS-VALUE3 IS 579
```

This is the output from COBLMAIN. Here you can see the values sent to the CSUB subprogram before the CALL, and again after the CALL. The sum of 123 and 456 has been developed by CSUB as 579.

Figure 9.23 MVS/ESA System Output from the Execution of the COBLMAIN Program

9.19 RMODE and AMODE Considerations

As OS was originally implemented, it used 24-bit addresses, which could work with a maximum of 16 megabytes of memory. This amount of memory seemed huge in 1963, when OS was designed, because the magnetic core technology of the day constrained memory to a few megabytes for nearly all machines. When MVS/XA was introduced in the 1980s as an evolutionary step forward for MVS, it provided the ability to go beyond the limits of 24-bit memory addresses, providing 31-bit address capabilities. Though the increase in address size may seem small, 31-bit addresses can work with more than 2 billion bytes of memory! This development allowed mainframes to expand to memory sizes of 96 megabytes and well beyond, making good use of today's advanced semiconductor memory technology.

Two settings now exist that deal with aspects of memory addressing. Both of these are reported to you by the linkage editor in its brief summary reporting. One of these is AMODE, which can take the values 24, 31, or the word ANY. The other setting is RMODE, which can assume a value of 24 or ANY. The settings of AMODE and RMODE must be compatible for main and subprograms to operate correctly, both between the programs and between the programs and language libraries. You set AMODE and RMODE with compiler parameters or linkage editor parameters. Your installation determines how the language libraries are installed.

AMODE means addressing mode and dictates how the program expects to receive control. A program can either expect to deal with addresses as 24 bit, 31 bit, or either of these (ANY). AMODE must be the same for programs and subprograms.

RMODE means residency mode and indicates where in memory the program can be loaded. A value of 24 for RMODE means that the program must operate within the first 16 megabytes of memory, that is, under the 16-megabyte "line." The only other value RMODE can assume is ANY, which means that the program may reside above or below the 16-megabyte line.

Incompatible AMODE values can cause unusual errors and abends. If you get "strange" error messages such as IBM004I, indicating that a problem has been experienced during initialization, check that your compile and link edits have produced consistent AMODE and RMODE values for your programs and subprograms.

9.20 C/370 Calling VS COBOL II

Let's now consider how a main program written in C/370 can invoke a load module (subprogram) prepared using VS COBOL II source code. Such a main program, named CMAIN, is listed in Figure 9.24. CMAIN passes three integers to a COBOL subprogram named COBLSUB, which is listed in Figure 9.25.

```
EDIT ---- CSCJGJ.ADV.ASM(CMAIN) - 01.04 --------------------- COLUMNS 001 072
COMMAND ===>                                                   SCROLL ===> PAGE
****** ****************************** TOP OF DATA ******************************
000001 /***
000002  *** cmain - This C/370 program will pass three parameters to a
000003  ***         subprogram written in VS COBOL II.  The subprogram will
000004  ***         the first two parms and return the result in the third
000005  ***         cell.  Finally, cmain will display the result.
000006  ***         Bob Narino and Jim Janossy, Sept. 1993
000007  ***/
000008
000009 #pragma linkage( coblsub, OS )
000010
000011 #include <stdio.h>
000012
000013 void coblsub( int *, int *, int * );       /* function prototype */
000014
000015 int main( void )
000016 {
000017     int    int2 = 567,
                answer = 0,
                  int1 = 234;

           printf( "??/n cmain program starting" );
           printf( "??/n int1 + int2 = %d + %d = %d", int1, int2, answer );

           printf( "??/n now passing control to the COBOL subprogram" );
           coblsub( &int1, &int2, &answer );       /* call the subprogram */

000027     printf( "??/n control has returned from the subprogram" );
000028     printf( "??/n int1 + int2 = %d + %d = %d", int1, int2, answer );
000029     return ( 0 );
000030 }
```

Tells C it is the main program

You must use the ??/ trigraph instead of \n for printf formatting!

C "calls" COBOL

Figure 9.24 CMAIN, A C/370 Program That Invokes ("CALLs") a Subprogram Written in VS COBOL II

```
EDIT ---- CSCJGJ.ADV.COBOL(COBLSUB) - 01.02 ----------------- COLUMNS 007 078
COMMAND ===>                                                   SCROLL ===> PAGE
****** ****************************** TOP OF DATA ******************************
000100 ID DIVISION.
000200 PROGRAM-ID. COBLSUB.
000300 AUTHOR. ROBERT F. NARINO AND JIM JANOSSY.
000400 DATA DIVISION.
000500 LINKAGE SECTION.
000600 01  INTEGER-1    PIC S9(9) COMP.
000700 01  INTEGER-2    PIC S9(9) COMP.
000800 01  ANSWER       PIC S9(9) COMP.
000900
001000 PROCEDURE DIVISION USING INTEGER-1, INTEGER-2, ANSWER.
001100     COMPUTE ANSWER = INTEGER-1 + INTEGER-2.
001200     GOBACK.
```

COMP here is the older way to say "binary" storage

Figure 9.25 COBLSUB, A Subprogram Written in VS COBOL II to Receive a CALL from a C/370 Program

The CMAIN program invokes COBLSUB at its line 25, as it might any function:

```
coblsub( &int1, &int2, &answer );
```

Because of the #pragma coded in CMAIN, this causes the program to pass the addresses of the integers int1, int2, and answer to COBLSUB. Notice that we declared these integers in a different sequence at lines 17, 18, and 19, just to make the point that three separate addresses would be passed. COBLSUB declares these three fields in the sequence they are mentioned in line 25, not as they are declared at lines 17, 18, and 19.

COBLSUB receives three addresses from the call from CMAIN. It is prepared to accept these addresses because of the way its PROCEDURE DIVISION heading is coded:

```
PROCEDURE DIVISION USING INTEGER-1, INTEGER-2, ANSWER.
```

These addresses are associated with the fields defined in the LINKAGE SECTION at the time that the call is made by CMAIN.

9.21 Compiling, Linking, and Running CMAIN and COBLSUB

We compiled and linked CMAIN and COBLSUB using the same JCL as used earlier in this chapter for our examples, involving the procs CCX4 and COB2CLJ already illustrated. However, it's important to note that the sequence of these actions now becomes important, because the CMAIN program wishes to be compiled and linked statically. Because of the way libraries are concatenated in the CCX4 proc, this presents no problem. But the subprogram, COBLSUB, must be compiled and linked first, before the CMAIN program can be compiled and linked.

Review Figure 9.5 (line 16) and Figure 9.6 (line 5500) and you will see that when we compiled the COBLSUB subprogram using the COB2CLJ proc, its load module (machine language) was placed into a load module library named CSCJGJ.ADV.LOADLIB. Now review Figure 9.14 (line 97) and you will see that this library is concatenated at the //SYSLIB input to the linkage editor within the CCX4 proc. This means that the machine language of the COBLSUB load module is available to the linkage editor when it link edits the CMAIN program. CMAIN contains a static reference to COBLSUB, which the linkage editor resolves by including the machine language of COBLSUB within the CMAIN load module.

Figure 9.26 shows you the MVS/ESA system output produced when we execute the CMAIN program. The passed integers have been properly accessed by the COBLSUB subprogram, which computed the sum correctly. The result is made visible by the CMAIN program.

9.22 C/370 Calling Assembler

C is widely regarded as a "high-level portable assembler" because of its low-level bit-oriented capabilities. C is very nearly as machine efficient as assembler, yet more structured and easier to code. Shops with a large installed base of assembler programs will find it easiest to migrate from assembler to C gradually, a process that will often involve assembler and C intercommunication.

Figure 9.27 shows you the coding for a C/370 program named ADD2C that invokes an assembler subprogram named ASMSUM2. The ADD2C

```
                     J E S 2  J O B  L O G  --  S Y S T E M  I B M 1  --  N O D E

11.56.00 JOB09891  IRR010I  USERID CSCJGJ   IS ASSIGNED TO THIS JOB.
11.56.01 JOB09891  ICH70001I CSCJGJ   LAST ACCESS AT 11:55:47 ON THURSDAY, APRIL 7
11.56.01 JOB09891  $HASP373 CSCJGJA  STARTED - INIT  1 - CLASS A - SYS IBM1
11.56.03 JOB09891  $HASP395 CSCJGJA  ENDED

------ JES2 JOB STATISTICS ------
    07 APR 94 JOB EXECUTION DATE
           17 CARDS READ
           52 SYSOUT PRINT RECORDS
            0 SYSOUT PUNCH RECORDS
            3 SYSOUT SPOOL KBYTES
         0.03 MINUTES EXECUTION TIME

        1 //CSCJGJA   JOB 1,                       ACCOUNTING INFORMATION
          //  'BIN 7--NARINO',                      PROGRAMMER NAME AND DELIVERY BIN
          //  CLASS=A,                              INPUT QUEUE CLASS
          //  MSGLEVEL=(1,1),                       HOW MUCH MVS SYSTEM PRINT DESIRED
          //  MSGCLASS=X,                           PRINT DESTINATION X A L N OR O
          //  TIME=(0,6),                           SAFETY LIMIT: RUN TIME UP TO 6 SECS
          //  REGION=2M,                            ALLOW UP TO 2 MEGS VIRTUAL MEMORY
          //* TYPRUN=SCAN,                          UNCOMMENT THIS LINE TO DO SCAN ONLY
          //  NOTIFY=CSCJGJ                         WHO TO TELL WHEN JOB IS DONE
          //*
          //* EXECUTE THE CMAIN PROGRAM LOAD MODULE
          //* THIS JCL IS STORED AT CSCJGJ.ADV.CNTL(RUNCMAIN)
          //*-------------------------------------------------------------------
        2 //STEP010  EXEC  PGM=CMAIN
        3 //STEPLIB   DD   DSN=CSCJGJ.ADV.LOADLIB,DISP=SHR
        4 //          DD   DSN=SYS1.COB2LIB,DISP=SHR
        5 //SYSOUT    DD   SYSOUT=*

ICH70001I CSCJGJ   LAST ACCESS AT 11:55:47 ON THURSDAY, APRIL 7

IEF236I ALLOC. FOR CSCJGJA STEP010
IEF237I 117  ALLOCATED TO STEPLIB
IEF237I 110  ALLOCATED TO
IEF237I JES2 ALLOCATED TO SYSOUT
IEF237I JES2 ALLOCATED TO SYS00001
IEF142I CSCJGJA STEP010 - STEP WAS EXECUTED - COND CODE 0000
IEF285I   CSCJGJ.ADV.LOADLIB                           KEPT
IEF285I   VOL SER NOS= USER03.
IEF285I   SYS1.COB2LIB                                 KEPT
IEF285I   VOL SER NOS= ACSRES.
IEF285I   CSCJGJ.CSCJGJA.JOB09891.D0000101.?           SYSOUT
IEF285I   CSCJGJ.CSCJGJA.JOB09891.D0000102.?           SYSOUT
IEF373I STEP /STEP010 / START 94097.1156
IEF374I STEP /STEP010 / STOP  94097.1156 CPU    0MIN 00.21SEC SRB    0MIN 00.02SEC
IEF375I  JOB /CSCJGJA / START 94097.1156
IEF376I  JOB /CSCJGJA / STOP  94097.1156 CPU    0MIN 00.21SEC SRB    0MIN 00.02SEC

 cmain program starting
 int1 + int2 = 234 + 567 = 0

 now passing control to the COBOL subprogram

 control has returned from the subprogram
 int1 + int2 = 234 + 567 = 801
```

Need VS COBOL II library since a COBOL subprogram is involved

Figure 9.26 MVS/ESA System Output from the Execution of the CMAIN Program

program passes two integers to the assembler subprogram, which the subprogram adds together. The assembler subprogram, listed in Figure 9.28, returns the sum via register 15. The C program acquires the returned value as if it were returned by an ordinary C function. Here is the general pattern of register usage for assembler programs dealing with C:

	Communicating	At exit
R0	—	—
R1	address of parameter list	—
R2	—	restored
R3	—	restored
R4	—	restored
R5	—	restored
R6	—	restored
R7	—	restored
R8	—	restored
R9	—	restored
R10	—	restored
R11	—	restored
R12	control block address	restored
R13	DSA address	restored
R14	return address	—
R15	called program address	return value

Figure 9.29 shows the MVS/ESA system output and program output from a run of the ADD2C main program.

We compiled and linked the ADD2C C/370 program using the CCX4 proc, very similar to the way that the J1C program was compiled in Figure 9.13. We used the JCL shown in Figure 9.9, named ASMCL, to compile and link ASMSUM2. Of course, the compile and link for the ASMSUM2 subprogram must be done first, so that it exists in an accessible form when the static reference to it in the ADD2C main program is to be resolved by the linkage editor.

```
EDIT ---- CSCJGJ.ADV.ASM(ADD2C) - 01.01 ---------------------- COLUMNS 001 072
COMMAND ===>                                                  SCROLL ===> PAGE
****** ****************************** TOP OF DATA ******************************
000001 /***
000002  *** add2c - This C/370 program will pass two integers to a
000003  ***         subprogram written in BAL.  The subprogram will add
000004  ***         the two integers and provide the sum as the value
000005  ***         returned.  This program then prints the sum.
000006  ***/
000007
000008 #pragma linkage( asmsum2, OS )
000009
000010 #include <stdio.h>
000011
000012 int  asmsum2( int, int );                  /* function prototype */
000013
000014 int main( void )
000015 {
000016     int int1 = 123,
000017         int2 = 567,
000018       answer = 0;
000019
000020     printf( "??/n add2c program is now starting " );
000021     printf( "??/n call to asmsum2 will be made  " );
000022
000023     answer = asmsum2( int1, int2 );
000024
000025     printf( "??/n int1 + int2 = %d + %d = %d", int1, int2, answer );
000026     printf( "??/n add2c program ending " );
000027     return ( 0 );
000028 }
```

This C/370 program invokes an assembler program in exactly the same way as it would invoke an ordinary function. The assembler program, named **asmsum2**, adds the two numbers passed to it and returns the result by placing it in register 15. The C program receives it without having to "know" how it came back to it.

Figure 9.27 ADD2C, A C/370 Program That Invokes a Subprogram Written in System/370 Assembler Language (BAL)

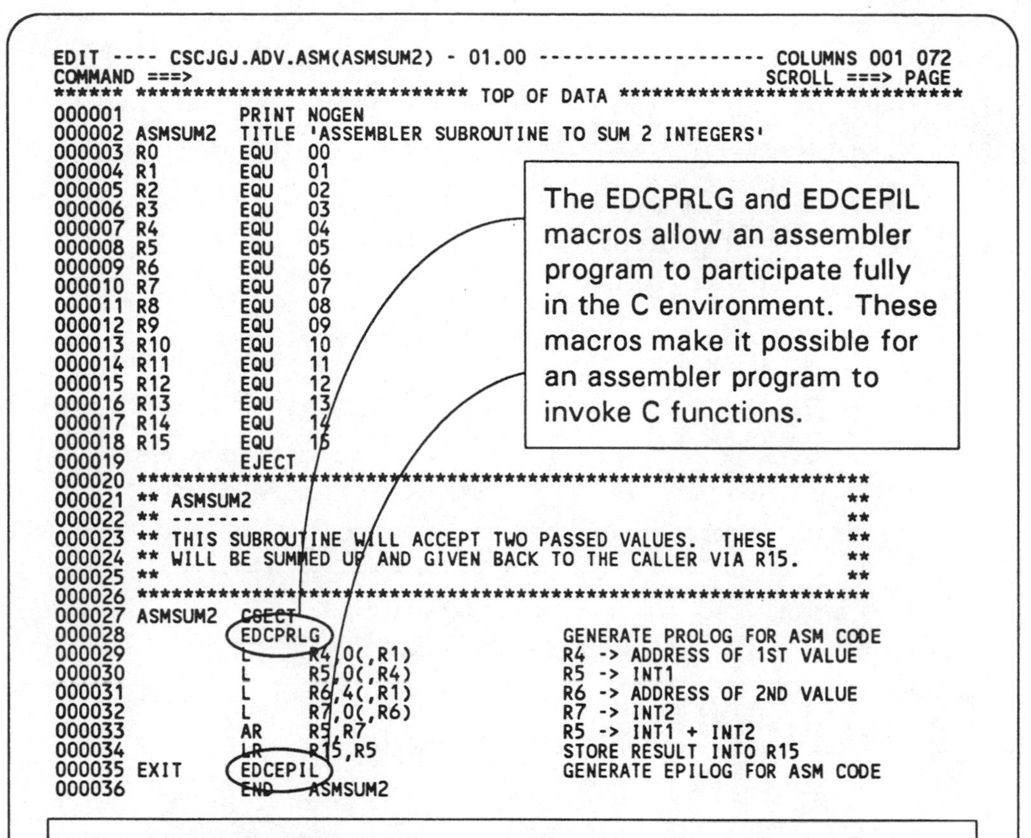

```
EDIT ---- CSCJGJ.ADV.ASM(ASMSUM2) - 01.00 ------------------- COLUMNS 001 072
COMMAND ===>                                                  SCROLL ===> PAGE
****** ***************************** TOP OF DATA ******************************
000001          PRINT NOGEN
000002 ASMSUM2  TITLE 'ASSEMBLER SUBROUTINE TO SUM 2 INTEGERS'
000003 R0       EQU   00
000004 R1       EQU   01
000005 R2       EQU   02
000006 R3       EQU   03
000007 R4       EQU   04
000008 R5       EQU   05
000009 R6       EQU   06
000010 R7       EQU   07
000011 R8       EQU   08
000012 R9       EQU   09
000013 R10      EQU   10
000014 R11      EQU   11
000015 R12      EQU   12
000016 R13      EQU   13
000017 R14      EQU   14
000018 R15      EQU   15
000019          EJECT
000020 *****************************************************************
000021 ** ASMSUM2                                                     **
000022 ** -------                                                     **
000023 ** THIS SUBROUTINE WILL ACCEPT TWO PASSED VALUES.  THESE       **
000024 ** WILL BE SUMMED UP AND GIVEN BACK TO THE CALLER VIA R15.     **
000025 **                                                             **
000026 *****************************************************************
000027 ASMSUM2  CSECT
000028          EDCPRLG                        GENERATE PROLOG FOR ASM CODE
000029          L     R4,0(,R1)                R4 -> ADDRESS OF 1ST VALUE
000030          L     R5,0(,R4)                R5 -> INT1
000031          L     R6,4(,R1)                R6 -> ADDRESS OF 2ND VALUE
000032          L     R7,0(,R6)                R7 -> INT2
000033          AR    R5,R7                    R5 -> INT1 + INT2
000034          LR    R15,R5                   STORE RESULT INTO R15
000035 EXIT     EDCEPIL                        GENERATE EPILOG FOR ASM CODE
000036          END   ASMSUM2
```

The EDCPRLG and EDCEPIL macros allow an assembler program to participate fully in the C environment. These macros make it possible for an assembler program to invoke C functions.

This System/370 assembler program receives two integers from a C/370 program, adds them, and returns the sum in register 15. This subprogram acts exactly like a C function, and is invoked by a C/370 program just as if it were a C function. See ***C/370 Programming Guide, Version 2, Release 1.0,*** *SC09-1384-00* for more information about the EDCPRLG and EDCEPIL macros.

Figure 9.28 ASMSUM2, A Subprogram Written in Assembler to Receive a CALL from a C/370 Program

```
                  J E S 2   J O B   L O G  --  S Y S T E M   I B M 1  --  N O D E

22.23.13 JOB01766  IRR010I  USERID CSCJGJ   IS ASSIGNED TO THIS JOB.
22.23.13 JOB01766  ICH70001I CSCJGJ   LAST ACCESS AT 22:22:20 ON FRIDAY, APRIL 8
22.23.13 JOB01766  $HASP373 CSCJGJA  STARTED - INIT  1 - CLASS A - SYS IBM1
22.23.14 JOB01766  $HASP395 CSCJGJA  ENDED

------ JES2 JOB STATISTICS ------
    08 APR 94 JOB EXECUTION DATE
           15 CARDS READ
           44 SYSOUT PRINT RECORDS
            0 SYSOUT PUNCH RECORDS
            2 SYSOUT SPOOL KBYTES
         0.01 MINUTES EXECUTION TIME

        1 //CSCJGJA   JOB 1,                        ACCOUNTING INFORMATION
          //  'BIN 7--NARINO',                      PROGRAMMER NAME AND DELIVERY BIN
          //  CLASS=A,                              INPUT QUEUE CLASS
          //  MSGLEVEL=(1,1),                       HOW MUCH MVS SYSTEM PRINT DESIRED
          //  MSGCLASS=X,                           PRINT DESTINATION X A L N OR O
          //  TIME=(0,6),                           SAFETY LIMIT: RUN TIME UP TO 6 SECS
          //  REGION=2M,                            ALLOW UP TO 2 MEGS VIRTUAL MEMORY
          //* TYPRUN=SCAN,                          UNCOMMENT THIS LINE TO DO SCAN ONLY
          //  NOTIFY=CSCJGJ                         WHO TO TELL WHEN JOB IS DONE
          //*
          //* RUN THE ADD2C PROGRAM; EXECUTES A C PROGRAM THAT CALLS BAL
          //* THIS JCL IS STORED AT CSCJGJ.ADV.CNTL(RUNADD2C)
          //*-------------------------------------------------------------
        2 //STEP010  EXEC  PGM=ADD2C
        3 //STEPLIB    DD  DSN=CSCJGJ.ADV.LOADLIB,DISP=SHR

 ICH70001I CSCJGJ   LAST ACCESS AT 22:22:20 ON FRIDAY, APRIL 8, 1994

 IEF236I ALLOC. FOR CSCJGJA STEP010
 IEF237I 117  ALLOCATED TO STEPLIB
 IEF237I JES2 ALLOCATED TO SYS00001
 IEF142I CSCJGJA STEP010 - STEP WAS EXECUTED - COND CODE 0000
 IEF285I   CSCJGJ.ADV.LOADLIB                           KEPT
 IEF285I   VOL SER NOS= USER03.
 IEF285I   CSCJGJ.CSCJGJA.JOB01766.D0000101.?           SYSOUT
 IEF373I STEP /STEP010 / START 94098.2223
 IEF374I STEP /STEP010 / STOP  94098.2223 CPU    0MIN 00.16SEC SRB    0MIN 00.01SEC
 IEF375I  JOB /CSCJGJA / START 94098.2223
 IEF376I  JOB /CSCJGJA / STOP  94098.2223 CPU    0MIN 00.16SEC SRB    0MIN 00.01SEC

  add2c program is now starting
  call to asmsum2 will be made
  int1 + int2 = 123 + 567 = 690
  add2c program ending
```

Figure 9.29 MVS/ESA System Output from the Execution of the ADD2C Program

9.23 Assembler Calling C/370

In this final example, we arranged for an assembler program named ADD2ASM to call a C/370 subprogram named CSUM2. The following illustrations are related to this example:

```
EDIT ---- CSCJGJ.ADV.ASM(CADD2ASM) - 01.00 ------------------ COLUMNS 001 072
COMMAND ===>                                                  SCROLL ===> PAGE
****** ***************************** TOP OF DATA ******************************
000001 /***
000002  *** This program will establish the C environment and invoke
000003  *** the C environment so it is established just once
000004  ***/
000005
000006 #pragma linkage( add2asm, OS )
000007
000008 int main( void )
000009 {
000010     add2asm();                 /* invoke the assembler routine */
000011     return ( 0 );
000012 }
```

This C/370 program will establish the C environment, and will then pass control to **add2asm,** written in assembler. Add2asm will behave as if it is the main program, and can invoke external C routines. This is the most efficient way for assembler programs to invoke C subprograms.

Figure 9.30 CADD2ASM, A C/370 Program Used to Create the C Environment Before Main Program ADD2ASM (Written in BAL) Executes

CADD2ASM	Initiating C program	Figure 9.30
ADD2ASM	Assembler "main" program	Figure 9.31
CSUM2	C/370 subprogram	Figure 9.32

Why the CADD2ASM "initiating" program? As you can see in Figure 9.30, this program is trivial and only serves to invoke the ADD2ASM main program. We execute it, rather than the assembler program directly, to establish the C runtime environment. Since it appears that a C program is already active, the C subprogram does not try to establish and then eliminate the C runtime environment each time it is called.

The assembler ADD2ASM program in Figure 9.31 passes two integers, in this case 321 and 654, to the CSUM2 subprogram. It does this by putting the starting address of those integers into register 1. The C/370 CSUM2 subprogram, listed in Figure 9.32, receives these parameters, sums

```
EDIT ---- CSCJGJ.ADV.ASM(ADD2ASM) - 01.01 ------------------- COLUMNS 001 072
COMMAND ===>                                                  SCROLL ===> PAGE
****** ***************************** TOP OF DATA ******************************
000001 ADD2ASM  TITLE 'ASSEMBLER TO C PGM DEMO'
000002          PRINT NOGEN
000003 R0       EQU   00
000004 R1       EQU   01
000005 R2       EQU   02
000006 R3       EQU   03
000007 R4       EQU   04
000008 R5       EQU   05
000009 R6       EQU   06
000010 R7       EQU   07
000011 R8       EQU   08
000012 R9       EQU   09
000013 R10      EQU   10
000014 R11      EQU   11
000015 R12      EQU   12
000016 R13      EQU   13
000017 R14      EQU   14
000018 R15      EQU   15
000019          EJECT
000020 *****************************************************************
000021 ** THIS ASSEMBLER ROUTINE WILL PASS TWO INTEGERS TO A PROGRAM **
000022 ** WRITTEN IN C/370.  THE CALLED C PGM WILL DISPLAY THE ARGS   **
000023 ** AND SUM OF THE ARGS                                         **
000024 *****************************************************************
000025 ADD2ASM  CSECT
000026          EDCPRLG                         GENERATE PROLOG FOR ASM CODE
000027          SPACE
000028          LA    R1,ADDR_BLK               R1 -> LOCATION OF PARM LIST
000029          L     R15,=V(CSUM2)             R15 -> LOCATION OF SUM 2 C-PGM
000030          BALR  R14,R15                   INVOKE C PGM
000031          EDCEPIL                         GENERATE EPILOG FOR ASM CODE
000032          EJECT
000033 *****************************
000034 ***  DATA STORAGE AREA    ***
000035 *****************************
000036          DS    0H
000037 SAVEAREA DS    18F                        STORE CALLER'S REGISTERS
000038 ADDR_BLK DS    0H
000039          DC    A(INT1)                    PARAMETER ADDRESS BLOCK
000040          DC    A(INT2)
000041 CABOOSE  DC    AL1(X'80')                 END OF PARM LIST
000042          DS    0F
000043 INT1     DC    F'321'
000044 INT2     DC    F'654'
000045          LTORG
000046          END   ADD2ASM
```

This assembler program invokes a C/370 subprogram named **csum2** to have it add to integers and provide the sum. The C/370 program itself will display the result.

Figure 9.31 ADD2ASM, A Program Written in Assembler (BAL) That CALLs a C/370 Program Named CSUM2

```
EDIT ---- CSCJGJ.ADV.ASM(CSUM2) - 01.02 --------------------- COLUMNS 001 072
COMMAND ===>                                                   SCROLL ===> PAGE
****** ***************************** TOP OF DATA ******************************
000001 /****
000002  **** csum2 -- This routine will accept two arguments (ints passed from
000003  ****           from an Assembler coded program),  sum them and display
000004  ****           the args and their result.
000005  ****           The result is returned via Register 15.
000006  ****/
000007
000008 #pragma linkage( csum2, OS )     /* function will be called from BAL */
000009
000010 #include <stdio.h>
000011
000012 int csum2( int num1, int num2 )
000013 {
000014  int result = num1 + num2;
000015
000016  printf( "??/n csum2 c subprogram starting" );
000017  printf( "??/n num1 + num2 = %d + %d = %d ", num1, num2, result );
000018  return ( result );
000019 }
```

This C/370 subprogram receives two integers passed to it by an assembler program, adds them together, and displays the result. The result is returned to the assembler program in register 15.

Figure 9.32 CSUM2, A Subprogram Written in C/370 to Receive a CALL from an Assembler (BAL) Program

them, and prints the result. The result is also received by the assembler program in register 15.

We compiled and linked the CSUM2 subprogram first, using the CCX4 proc, very similar to the way that the J1C program was compiled in Figure 9.13. We then assembled and linked the ADD2ASM main program using the ASMCL JCL shown in Figure 9.9. We compiled and linked the CADD2ASM C/370 program using the CCX4 proc, as in Figure 9.13. Finally, we ran this software by executing the CADD2ASM program. As you can see in the MVS/ESA system and program output in Figure 9.33, the result is as you would expect, with the correct sum at the end of the listing.

```
                 J E S 2   J O B   L O G  --  S Y S T E M   I B M 1  --  N O D E

23.08.35 JOB01828  IRR010I  USERID CSCJGJ   IS ASSIGNED TO THIS JOB.
23.08.36 JOB01828  ICH70001I CSCJGJ   LAST ACCESS AT 23:08:16 ON FRIDAY, APRIL 8
23.08.36 JOB01828  $HASP373 CSCJGJA  STARTED - INIT  1 - CLASS A - SYS IBM1
23.08.37 JOB01828  $HASP395 CSCJGJA  ENDED

------ JES2 JOB STATISTICS ------
    08 APR 94 JOB EXECUTION DATE
           16 CARDS READ
           45 SYSOUT PRINT RECORDS
            0 SYSOUT PUNCH RECORDS
            2 SYSOUT SPOOL KBYTES
         0.01 MINUTES EXECUTION TIME

        1 //CSCJGJA   JOB 1,                    ACCOUNTING INFORMATION
          //   'BIN 7--NARINO',                PROGRAMMER NAME AND DELIVERY BIN
          //   CLASS=A,                         INPUT QUEUE CLASS
          //   MSGLEVEL=(1,1),                  HOW MUCH MVS SYSTEM PRINT DESIRED
          //   MSGCLASS=X,                      PRINT DESTINATION X A L N OR O
          //   TIME=(0,6),                      SAFETY LIMIT: RUN TIME UP TO 6 SECS
          //   REGION=2M,                       ALLOW UP TO 2 MEGS VIRTUAL MEMORY
          //*  TYPRUN=SCAN,                     UNCOMMENT THIS LINE TO DO SCAN ONLY
          //   NOTIFY=CSCJGJ                    WHO TO TELL WHEN JOB IS DONE
          //*
          //* RUN THE CADD2ASM PROGRAM TO RUN AN ASM PROGRAM CALLING A
          //* THIS JCL IS STORED AT CSCJGJ.ADV.CNTL(RUNA2ASM)
          //*-------------------------------------------------------------
        2 //STEP010  EXEC  PGM=CADD2ASM
        3 //STEPLIB    DD  DSN=CSCJGJ.ADV.LOADLIB,DISP=SHR
        4 //SYSOUT     DD  SYSOUT=*

ICH70001I CSCJGJ   LAST ACCESS AT 23:08:16 ON FRIDAY, APRIL 8, 1994

IEF236I ALLOC. FOR CSCJGJA STEP010
IEF237I 117  ALLOCATED TO STEPLIB
IEF237I JES2 ALLOCATED TO SYSOUT
IEF237I JES2 ALLOCATED TO SYS00001
IEF142I CSCJGJA STEP010 - STEP WAS EXECUTED - COND CODE 0000
IEF285I   CSCJGJ.ADV.LOADLIB                         KEPT
IEF285I   VOL SER NOS= USER03.
IEF285I   CSCJGJ.CSCJGJA.JOB01828.D0000101.?         SYSOUT
IEF285I   CSCJGJ.CSCJGJA.JOB01828.D0000102.?         SYSOUT
IEF373I STEP /STEP010 / START 94098.2308
IEF374I STEP /STEP010 / STOP  94098.2308 CPU    0MIN 00.16SEC SRB    0MIN 00.01SEC
IEF375I  JOB /CSCJGJA / START 94098.2308
IEF376I  JOB /CSCJGJA / STOP  94098.2308 CPU    0MIN 00.16SEC SRB    0MIN 00.01SEC

 csum2 c subprogram starting
 num1 + num2 = 321 + 654 = 975
```

Figure 9.33 MVS/ESA System Output from the Execution of the ADD2ASM Program (Invoked by CADD2ASM Shown in Figure 9.30)

10

Introducing SMS: Storage Management Subsystem

10.1 What Is SMS?
10.2 Why SMS?
10.3 What SMS Manages
10.4 SMS Constructs
10.5 DATACLAS
10.6 STORCLAS
10.7 MGMTCLAS
10.8 Automatic Class Selection (ACS) Routines
10.9 Overriding SMS Constructs
10.10 How SMS Affects MVS/ESA System Reporting
10.11 Role and Use of ISMF
10.12 ISMF Data Class Application Selection Screen
10.13 ISMF STORCLAS Screens
10.14 ISMF MGMTCLAS Screens
10.15 ISMF Data Set Facility
10.16 ISMF On-Line Help
10.17 GDG Considerations Under SMS
10.18 VSAM Changes with SMS
10.19 Converting to SMS: Comments, Questions, Recommendations

With MVS/ESA Version 4, an additional subsystem can be acquired and installed to run as part of the operating system. This optional product, known as Data Facility Storage Management Subsystem, is commonly referred to as DFSMS or just plain "SMS." This chapter explains what SMS is and the effect it has or will have on your mainframe system and JCL. Included here you will find information about new MVS/ESA system output messages, the role of Automatic Class Selection (ACS) routines, the use of ISMF, the Interactive Storage Management Facility, the ISPF Data Set Utility option, SMS and GDGs, and the DFDSS utility. This chapter closes with some observations about the impact of converting to an SMS environment, including a list of questions you should ask of those responsible for implementing and maintaining SMS on your system.

SMS is a major new factor in IBM mainframe work, and the guided tour this chapter gives you through it required a major effort. I was fortunate to have enlisted the help of Hal Breitenberg in developing this chapter. In fact, after preliminary collaboration on the design of this chapter, Hal carried the ball on this chapter, in conjunction with Chris Robinson, who provided support in many areas of ISMF. You have here the best product of our joint efforts in explaining and illustrating the "whys" and "hows" of SMS and ISMF.

10.1 What Is SMS?

SMS is a name loosely used to refer to three related but different things:

- the concept of system-managed storage,
- the DFSMS product itself, and
- the Storage Management Subsystem as implemented, involving DFSMS and support utilities.

Although DFSMS (Data Facility Storage Management Subsystem) runs as part of MVS/ESA, other major utility subsystems are essential for its operation. These include DFHSM (Data Facility Hierarchical Storage Management), DFDSS (Data Facility Data Set Services), and ISMF (Interactive Storage Management Facility). DFHSM and DFDSS can be used either with or without SMS.

The actual name of the SMS software product is IGDZILLA. Following IBM's convention for identifying messages produced by its software, you will find the letter IGD prefacing any messages SMS issues. For example, new messages that will begin to appear in your MVS/ESA system reporting such as the following are generated by IGDZILLA, SMS:

```
IGD104I CSCJGJ.ADV.SHRSMS          RETAINED, DDNAME=SHRSMS
```

At least one prominent installation has taken to calling SMS "Godzilla" based on its name and the dominant role it is assuming in system management.

10.2 Why SMS?

SMS takes time, energy, and expense to install. There are many reasons why an installation may choose to commit the resources to install it. One compelling reason to implement SMS is the desire to give MVS/ESA greater control of data set management. This increased control can produce more efficient and reliable use of system resources, provide better custodianship of the vast quantities of data on a mainframe, and, in the long run, makes JCL coding simpler.

In addition, SMS moves toward the goal of supporting vastly different types of disk and optical storage, such as RAID (redundant array of inexpensive disks) that are now appearing on the horizon. These new forms of storage will present different storage formats that it would be unproductive to deal with directly. SMS is a buffer being set in place to shield and insulate applications from the potentially complex and changing hardware underbelly of mainframe data storage.

A major goal of SMS is to isolate logical data set requirements from physical ones, as much as possible, and thereby free programmers from some of the decisions and burdens associated with data set creation. Coding requirements from which you may be relieved include the need to code a new data set's block size, the need to explicitly code data set allocation attributes such as LRECL, RECFM, and SPACE, and the need to code UNIT and VOL=SER for new disk data sets. Simply stated, SMS allows you to think about the logical requirements for data storage, and lets the system worry about the physical arrangements needed to meet your logical requirements.

Another goal of SMS is to allow MVS/ESA to manage the backup, migration, and expiration of data sets based upon criteria assigned to each data set when it is created. Finally, performance and availability levels are associated with each system-managed data set when it is created.

All of these goals can be achieved for each system-managed data set. These goals may seem either simply "nice" to you, or wrapped up with distant concerns. But when Storage Management Subsystem is installed and activated on your system, it introduces a number of significant changes that affect how data sets are created and managed, it causes changes in your JCL, and it causes changes for other related mainframe software. If you code JCL you need to know about SMS and the changes that result from its advent. We have summarized several of the changes brought about by SMS in Figure 10.1.

10.3 What SMS Manages

SMS manages *individual* disk data sets. Existing components of MVS/ESA have always managed disk resources as a whole, by keeping track of disk space use and availability, and the MVS/ESA system catalog is oriented to managing the entire disk resources of the computer system. SMS, on the other hand, gets down to the level of individual data sets, and, depending on the various specifications it has been given about them, can treat different data sets quite differently. When SMS is installed, it is given control of one or more disk volumes (disk packs) by your systems programmers. Over time, it is likely that SMS will be given control of an increasing number of volumes. When SMS is fully implemented on a system, you may find that nearly all disk volumes are controlled by it.

MVS/ESA determines whether a given data set is to be SMS-managed when the data set is *created*; that is, when you allocate a new disk data set. Data sets that are to be system-managed are allocated to SMS-managed disk volumes when created and are referred to as SMS-managed data sets; data sets that are not system-managed are called non-SMS-managed data sets.

- SMS manages disk data sets only.
- SMS manages sequential, partitioned, VSAM, VIO, temporary, and generation data sets.
- SMS does not manage tape data sets, instream data, printed output, or ISAM data sets.
- With SMS the system, not the user, manages the location of system-managed data sets.
- All system-managed data sets are cataloged when they are created and cannot be uncataloged unless they are deleted.
- System-managed data sets can only be created on system-managed volumes.
- UNIT and VOL are not coded for system-managed data sets.
- Even DD statements used to create non-system-managed data sets can omit the UNIT parameter, if your installation has taken advantage of the SMS-provided capability to define a default symbolic device group name.
- Space for new disk data sets can be requested in terms of a data set's average record length using AVGREC.
- BLKSIZE can be omitted for new data sets, both disk and tape.
- Data set allocation attributes for new data sets, such as DCB and SPACE information, can be coded by the user, and obtained by the system, in several different ways.
- Users can select the most appropriate backup, migration, and expiration criteria for system-managed data sets when they are created.
- Users can select the most appropriate performance and availability criteria for system-managed data sets when they are created.
- A new format of MVS-ESA allocation messages are generated in job output listings for SMS-managed data sets.
- You can eliminate model data set control block (model DSCB) coding when allocating generation data sets.
- Certain DISP parameter values are interpreted differently.
- You cannot avoid the system catalog when accessing system-managed data sets; all SMS data sets are cataloged.
- JOBCAT and STEPCAT DD statements are not allowed.
- You can create VSAM data sets using JCL alone, and you can also create temporary VSAM data sets.

Figure 10.1 Highlights of Storage Management Subsystem (SMS) Operation

You may or may not have the latitude to choose whether SMS manages some or all of the data sets your JCL creates. A major new utility named DFDSS (Data Facility Data Set Services) can also convert existing data sets to SMS-managed status, or remove data sets from SMS management (DFDSS is introduced in Appendix A of this book).

- JOB statements
- EXEC statements (1)
- OUTPUT statements
- DD statements used to create non-SMS-managed disk data sets (2)
- DD statements used to define existing data sets (3)
- DD statements used to create tape data sets (4)
- DD statements used to produce printed output
- DD statements used with instream data
- PROC statements (1)

Notes:

1. The use of SMS may cause changes to DD statements within procs. Such changes may in turn necessitate changes to default symbolic parameter values coded on PROC statements and EXEC statements.
2. You can use new JCL features used for non-SMS-managed disk data sets, such as omission of BLKSIZE, use of DATACLAS, AVGREC, and promotion of DCB subparameters.
3. See the caution in section 10.18 about coding DISP=(OLD,DELETE) for VSAM data sets.
4. You can use some new JCL features when allocating tape data sets. These include system-determined block size, the DATACLAS parameter, and promoted DCB and LABEL keyword subparameters—LRECL, RECFM, EXPDT, and RETPD.

Figure 10.2 JCL Statements Not Affected by the Storage Management Subsystem

SMS changes primarily the way DD statements for new data sets work. JCL not affected by SMS is described in Figure 10.2.

10.4 SMS Constructs

SMS manages the treatment of each data set by associating each data set with up to three sets of criteria, called SMS "constructs," or "classes," named DATACLAS, STORCLAS, and MGMTCLAS. The criteria associated with these constructs include traditional data set characteristics, or "attributes," such as data set organization, record length, block size, and so forth, as well as new criteria that describe how fast data must be provided (in milliseconds), how often it is to be backed up, and how long it can remain on active disk storage before being automaticaly "migrated" to tape in compressed form or deleted. MVS/ESA keeps the attribute values associated with each construct in memory, so that it can obtain this information very quickly.

SMS constructs are created and maintained locally, not by IBM, but by systems programmers and data storage administration personnel. Since changes to class attributes affect not only new data sets but also all existing data sets associated with the class, alterations in constructs must be handled with great care. Storage administration personnel can create new SMS constructs as the need arises.

If your installation allows access to ISMF, you can use it to view the storage, management, and data classes available on your system and the attributes associated with each class. If you are unable to access ISMF, your storage administration personnel will have to provide documentation about the names of valid classes, and the attributes associated with each class name, to all system users who need to create data sets.

10.5 DATACLAS

DATACLAS is an SMS construct that you can code even if the data set you are creating is not to be managed by SMS. Think of the DATACLAS specification as a grouping of these ordinary data set characteristics:

RECFM	Record format
LRECL	Logical record length
SPACE	Disk space allocation
volume count	Limit of disk volumes allowed to be used
RETPD or EXPDT	Retention period or expiration date
AVGREC	New way to specify SPACE in records

as well as these VSAM data set characteristics:

KEYLEN	Key Sequenced Data Set key length
RECORG	Organization of VSAM data set
KEYOFF	Key offset (position)
IMBED	Placement of KSDS index
REPLICATE	Redundant storage of index (for access speed)
CISIZE	Control interval size
FREESPACE	Amount and placement of imbedded free space
SHAREOPTIONS	Settings controlling concurrent access

Each data class usually has values associated with some but not all possible attributes. For instance, data classes intended to be used for non-VSAM data sets will not have values assigned for VSAM-related attributes. And for tape data sets, the system can obtain only EXPDT, LRECL, RECFM, and RETPD from a data class.

If you specify an appropriate DATACLAS, you can potentially omit coding any of these characteristics in your JCL, and the data set will acquire them from SMS. If you code a characteristic such as LRELC in your JCL, and LRECL is also specified in the DATACLAS you coded or were assigned, your coding may override the coding in the DATACLAS.

As a programmer, you don't create DATACLAS groupings. Disk space management personnel create DATACLASs, and you find out about them from these personnel via documentation, or from the system directly using ISMF.

10.6 STORCLAS

Think of STORCLAS as a grouping of UNIT and VOL specifications. If you code STORCLAS, you do not have to code UNIT and VOL. ***But you must realize that coding STORCLAS makes a data set SMS-managed!***

Most storage class attributes are related to data set performance and availability levels. Performance means the speed with which MVS/ESA can read or write data to and from the data set. Availability means whether a data set is continuously available; that is, whether the system maintains dual copies of the data set at all times. (Dual copies are neither backup copies nor migrated data sets. They are real-time duplicates of data sets whose immediate availability is so critical to your organization that it is willing to dedicate the resources needed to maintain them.)

As with DATACLAS, programmers do not originate STORCLASs, they use the STORCLASs defined by disk space administrators. If your installation forces certain data sets to be SMS-managed, routines that analyze JCL as it is processed—named Automatic Class Selection (ACS) routines—may associate a STORCLAS with a new data set even if you did not code STORCLAS in your JCL yourself. STORCLAS attributes are more hardware-dependent than are data and management class attributes, and your storage administrator may be less inclined to make changes to existing storage classes or create new ones.

10.7 MGMTCLAS

SMS controls the backup, migration, and expiration (deletion) of data sets under its control. The criteria that control this aspect of its work are associated with a new keyword, MGMTCLAS. Unlike the characteristics grouped under DATACLAS and STORCLAS, however, the characteristics under MGMTCLAS have no analogous specifications in JCL. For example, EXPIRE NON USAGE is a MGMTCLAS specification, which indicates how long the data set can remain on disk after its most recent access.

MGMTCLAS data set management is accomplished by SMS in connection with DFHSM and DFDSS. Attributes associated with a management class specify the backup, migration, and expiration criteria for *all* data sets assigned to that management class. Backup information is used by MVS/ESA to determine the conditions under which DFHSM should make backup copies of a data set and the number, frequency, and length of time backup versions are retained.

MGMTCLAS attributes refer to "primary DASD," which is readily available, uncompressed disk storage, in connection with data set "migration." Migration attributes specify how long and under what circumstances a data set is to remain on primary DASD (also called migration level zero or ML0) before being migrated by DFHSM and stored in compressed format on migration level one (disk storage called ML1) or migrated further in compressed format to migration level two (tape storage called ML2). Each of these migrations preserves the data but makes it progressively slower to retrieve and access. To read from or write to migrated data sets, the system must first use DFHSM to migrate the data set back to primary DASD and in the process decompress it.

Expiration criteria determine how long a data set can exist on the system before it is available to be deleted by DFHSM. For instance, a management class can direct the system to expire a data set that has not been opened for seven days. In this context, days means calendar days, not 24-hour periods of time.

As with DATACLAS and STORCLAS criteria, MGMTCLAS criteria are maintained by disk space management personnel. MGMTCLASs are developed locally at each installation. A management class is assigned to an SMS-managed data set when the data set is created. You can request a management class for a data set by coding JCL's new MGMTCLAS parameter or the system can automatically assign a management class to an SMS-managed data set when it is created. Coding MGMTCLAS might be optional in your installation, or for given data sets. MGMTCLAS can only be coded for new SMS-managed data sets, hence it can only be coded in conjunction with STORCLAS.

10.8 Automatic Class Selection (ACS) Routines

Automatic class selection (ACS) routines are an important part of an SMS environment. ACS routines are written by systems programmers at each installation, in concert with storage administration personnel. These routines provide three important functions related to your use of JCL with SMS.

- ACS routines can select SMS constructs—storage, management, or data classes, or a combination of these—to be associated with a new data set.

- ACS routines can override STORCLAS, MGMTCLAS, or DATACLAS values coded in your JCL. Depending on the way in which SMS is installed and used, ACS routines can determine any combination of STORCLAS, MGMTCLAS, or DATACLAS values for some or all new disk data sets—based on criteria (including DSN and information coded on your JOB, EXEC, and DD statements) specified by the storage administrator.

- ACS routines can be configured to automatically supply class information for existing jobs while at the same time filtering out certain JCL parameters. If this is done, the JCL you code and the job that actually runs may significantly differ!

One installation may elect to take a rather aggressive approach to its use of ACS routines while another may decide to pursue a more conservative course. Thus, one location may let ACS routines automatically provide one, two, or three SMS constructs for some or all new disk data sets while another installation may require users to code STORCLAS, MGMTCLAS, or DATACLAS, or all three, for every new disk data set allocated. Check with your storage administrator to determine the conditions, if any, under which ACS routines will provide default classes. Storage administration personnel should also be able to tell you the conditions, if any, under which ACS routines will override classes coded in your JCL.

Quite the reverse of forcing the assignment of SMS classes on a new data set, your installation can use IBM's RACF security system or another security system to limit access to one or more storage and management classes.

10.9 Overriding SMS Constructs

By coding DATACLAS, you can simplify your JCL by allowing MVS/ESA to obtain data set allocation attributes from a data class. Assuming that data class FLATFILE has associated with it attributes corresponding to those required for a new data set, this DD statement could be coded for an SMS-managed data set:

```
//NEWFILE4    DD DSN=CSCJGJ.ADV.NEWFILE4,
//   DISP=(NEW,CATLG,DELETE),
//   DATACLAS=FLATFILE,
//   STORCLAS=DEFAULT,
//   MGMTCLAS=GENERIC
```

If the attributes associated with FLATFILE are not exactly the ones you want, you can code the specific attributes you do want, as ordinary JCL parameters, to override them. This allows you to use some but not all of a data class's attributes.

```
//NEWFILE5    DD DSN=CSCJGJ.ADV.NEWFILE5,
//   DISP=(NEW,CATLG,DELETE),
//   DATACLAS=FLATFILE,
//   LRECL=50,
//   STORCLAS=DEFAULT,
//   MGMTCLAS=GENERIC
```

If you override a data class's LRECL you may or may not need to override the space request. Override SPACE as well as LRECL if you think DATACLAS will not allocate enough space for the data set. Obviously, the need for both of these override actions requires that you have been informed about the specific attributes associated with the DATACLAS. Figure 10.3 summarizes SMS specifications and factors affecting overrrides.

Parameter	Use of Parameter Requires SMS to Be Active (1)	Use of Parameter Limited to SMS-managed Data Sets	If Omitted, Parameter Value Can Be Provided By	Value(s) Obtained from the Parameter Can Be Overridden
AVGREC	Yes	No	DATACLAS LIKE REFDD	NO (2)
BLKSIZE	No (3)	No	System-determined if omitted	Only if coded as zero
DATACLAS	Yes	No (4)	ACS routines	Yes (5, 6, & 7)
DSNTYPE	Yes	No	Variable (8)	No
EXPDT	No (9)	No	DATACLAS MGMTCLAS	Maybe (7)
KEYLEN	No	No	DATACLAS LIKE REFDD	No
KEYOFF	Yes	No	DATACLAS LIKE REFDD	No
LIKE	Yes	No	None	Yes (5 & 6)
LRECL	No (9)	No	DATACLAS LIKE REFDD	No
MGMTCLAS	Yes	Yes (10)	ACS routines	No (11)
RECFM	No (9)	No	DATACLAS LIKE REFDD	NO
RECORG	Yes	No	DATACLAS LIKE REFDD; if none of these, SMS assumes PS or PO DSORG	No
REFDD	Yes	No	None	Yes (5 & 6)
RETPD	No (9)	No	DATACLAS MGMTCLAS	Maybe (7)
SPACE	No	No	DATACLAS LIKE REFDD	No
STORCLAS	Yes	Yes (10)	ACS routines	No

Figure 10.3 Reference to Parameters Related to Data Set Allocation Under SMS (continued on facing page)

Notes:

1. Many parameters require SMS to be installed and active. If such parameters are coded on a system that either does not have SMS installed, or on which SMS is installed but not active, the system checks these parameters for syntax and then ignores them.
2. When SPACE is coded to override the SPACE value obtained from a DATACLAS, the DATACLAS's AVGREC value may also be overridden in the process.
3. If SMS is installed, active or not, you can omit BLKSIZE when creating a new data set, PDS, PDSE, or sequential; disk or tape. MVS will then obtain a system-determined block size for the new data set, based on the device type and other criteria. Coding BLKSIZE=0 produces the same result.
4. IF DATACLAS is coded for tape data set allocation, the system can only obtain EXPDT, LRECL, RECFM, and RETPD information from the DATACLAS.
5. If any parameter, whose value is obtained through DATACLAS, LIKE, or REFDD, is coded on the same DD statement as DATACLAS, LIKE, or REFDD, the coded parameter overrides the corresponding DATACLAS, LIKE, or REFDD value.
6. If LIKE or REFDD is coded along with DATACLAS, values obtained through LIKE or REFDD override all corresponding DATACLAS values.
7. An EXPDT or RETPD value may be obtained from the DATACLAS or MGMTCLAS coded or from the DATACLAS or MGMTCLAS provided by ACS routines. This is done through the DATACLAS "RETPD OR EXPDT" field and the MGMTCLAS "EXPIRE DATE/DAYS" field. Additionally, a MGMTCLAS can limit the EXPDT and RETPD values coded on a DD statement or obtained from a DATACLAS. To determine if this is the case, check the RET LIMIT value associated with the MGMTCLAS explicitly coded in your JCL or automatically assigned by ACS routines. If the RET LIMIT is zero, the system ignores any EXPDT or RETPD coded or obtained from a DATACLAS. If the RET LIMIT is greater than zero, you may code a EXPDT or RETPD, or obtain one from a DATACLAS, as long as the EXPDT or RETPD does not exceed this RET LIMIT. If the RET LIMIT is exceeded, the system overrides the EXPDT or RETPD coded or obtained from a DATACLAS with the value of the MGMTCLAS's RET LIMIT. You can use ISMF to determine the values assigned to the attributes associated with each DATACLAS and MGMTCLAS.
8. If the DSNTYPE parameter is not coded, the system determines the data set type through other means: by other criteria associated with the data set, by the DSNTYPE value obtained from a DATACLAS, or by a system default. You should consult with installation storage management personnel prior to allocating a PDSE, to find out if your system's SMS configuration supports PDSE allocations.
9. All DCB and LABEL keyword subparameters can be coded as stand-alone DD statement parameters under MVS/ESA; SMS is not required for this "promotion" of subparameters.
10. STORCLAS and MGMTCLAS access can be limited by RACF or other security systems.
11. STORCLAS and MGMTCLAS values cannot be overridden. The only possible exception is a MGMTCLAS's EXPIRE DATE/DAYS value. Coding EXPDT or RETPD, or obtaining one from a DATACLAS, can override a MGMTCLAS's EXPIRE DATE/DAYS value up to, but not in excess of, the MGMTCLAS's RET LIMIT value. See note 7 above.

10.10 How SMS Affects MVS/ESA System Reporting

Several new system messages are produced in MVS/ESA system reporting in an SMS environment. As with all such messages, you may not need to examine each of them with every job run, but at times it is crucial for you to know what they mean. This section discusses some of the more important system messages associated with data set allocation. It also considers changes to the way in which the system interprets the DISP parameter, since this has an impact on data set allocation.

The job shown in Figure 10.4 executes the do-nothing program, IEFBR14, for the purpose of generating system messages related to data set allocation. In the first job step two existing data sets are used (ddnames SHRSMS and DLTOLDSM), a new SMS-managed data set is created and cataloged (CATLGSMS), and another one is created and kept (KEEPSMS). The ddname PASSSMS is associated with a new temporary SMS-managed data set passed to the second step. WORKSMS refers to a new temporary SMS-managed data set created and deleted in the first step. Keep in mind that a temporary data set is one whose data set name begins with one or two ampersands—& or &&—regardless of the DISP value coded. The second step simply deletes the SMS-managed data set passed to it. Also notice the absence of UNIT, VOL, SPACE, and DCB parameters in this job. STORCLAS replaces UNIT and VOL for new SMS-managed data sets and DATACLAS provides data set allocation attributes for each new data set.

Since all new SMS-managed data sets are cataloged at allocation time, a message of CATALOGED would be rather redundant. As a result, a "RETAINED" message is produced for new SMS-managed data sets that are not passed or deleted. Also, since MVS/ESA cannot simply KEEP a new SMS-managed data set, MVS/ESA interprets DISP=(NEW,KEEP,. . .) as DISP=(NEW,CATLG,. . .) for all SMS-managed data sets that are not part of a GDG.

A job's allocation messages also list the class names assigned to a new data set when it is created. Messages for new SMS-managed data sets will specify the storage, management, and data class names associated with the data set. If the name field following a parameter is blank in a job's messages, it means that no class value was coded for that parameter. Keep in mind that MVS/ESA can be configured so that ACS routines provide default classes or override JCL class values coded in your job. Messages for new non-SMS-managed data sets that use DATACLAS will also show the data class name associated with the data set.

Figure 10.5 shows portions of the MVS/ESA system reporting for the job shown in Figure 10.4. Notice the allocation message returned for KEEPSMS, the new SMS-managed data set that had DISP=(NEW, KEEP,DELETE) coded. Also notice that the RETAINED message is associated with three different types of data sets: an existing SMS-managed data set, a new SMS-managed data set that had CATLG coded, and a new SMS-managed data set that had KEEP coded.

Most messages associated with non-SMS-managed data sets remain the same as they were prior to SMS. Figure 10.6 contains some of the most common system allocation messages encountered in job listings. As it shows, several different meanings are associated with the RETAINED message.

```
EDIT ---- CSCJGJ.ADV.CNTL(FIG1004) - 01.03 ------------------ COLUMNS 001 072
COMMAND ===>                                                  SCROLL ===> PAGE
****** ***************************** TOP OF DATA ******************************
000100 //CSCJGJA   JOB 1,                    ACCOUNTING INFORMATION
000200 //   'BIN 7--JANOSSY',                PROGRAMMER NAME AND DELIVERY BIN
000300 //   CLASS=A,                         INPUT QUEUE CLASS
000400 //   MSGLEVEL=(1,1),                  HOW MUCH MVS SYSTEM PRINT DESIRED
000500 //   MSGCLASS=X,                      PRINT DESTINATION X A L N OR O
000600 //   TIME=(1,0),                      SAFETY LIMIT: RUN TIME UP TO 1 MINUTE
000700 //   REGION=3M,                       ALLOW UP TO 3 MEGS VIRTUAL MEMORY
000800 //*  TYPRUN=SCAN,                     UNCOMMENT THIS LINE TO DO SCAN ONLY
000900 //   NOTIFY=CSCJGJ                    WHO TO TELL WHEN JOB IS DONE
001000 //*
001100 //*  DEMONSTRATE ACCESS TO NEW AND EXISTING SMS-MANAGED DATA SETS
001200 //*
001300 //*  THIS JCL IS STORED AT CSCJGJ.ADV.CNTL(FIG1004)
001400 //*
001500 //*-----------------------------------------------------------------
001600 //*  ACCESS DATA SETS
001700 //*-----------------------------------------------------------------
001800 //STEP010  EXEC  PGM=IEFBR14
001900 //*
002000 //SHRSMS      DD  DSN=CSCJGJ.ADV.SHRSMS,          KEEP EXIST. SMS DATA SET
002100 //  DISP=SHR
002200 //*
002300 //DLTOLDSM    DD  DSN=CSCJGJ.ADV.DLTOLDSM,        DELETE SMS DATA SET
002400 //  DISP=(OLD,DELETE,DELETE)
002500 //*
002600 //CATLGSMS    DD  DSN=CSCJGJ.ADV.CATLGSMS,        CATALOG NEW SMS D.S.
002700 //  DISP=(NEW,CATLG,DELETE),
002800 //  STORCLAS=FASTWRIT,
002900 //  MGMTCLAS=LONGTERM,
003000 //  DATACLAS=FLATFILE
003100 //*
003200 //KEEPSMS     DD  DSN=CSCJGJ.ADV.KEEPSMS,
003300 //  DISP=(NEW,KEEP,DELETE),
003400 //  STORCLAS=FASTREAD,
003500 //  MGMTCLAS=SHORTERM,
003600 //  DATACLAS=FLATFILE
003700 //*
003800 //PASSSMS     DD  DSN=&&TEMPSMS1,
003900 //  DISP=(NEW,PASS,DELETE),
004000 //  STORCLAS=ENHANCED,
004100 //  DATACLAS=FLATFILE
004200
004300 //WORKSMS     DD  DSN=&&WORKSMS1,                 CREATE AND DELETE
004400 //  DISP=(NEW,DELETE,DELETE),                     NEW SMS D.S. IN
004500 //  STORCLAS=ENHANCED,                            SAME STEP
004600 //  DATACLAS=FLATFILE,
004700 //  LRECL=220                                     OVERRIDE DATACLAS LRECL
004800 //*-----------------------------------------------------------------
004900 //*  NEXT STEP
005000 //*-----------------------------------------------------------------
005100 //STEP020  EXEC  PGM=IEFBR14                      DELETE PASSED TEMP D.S.
005200
005300 //PASSSMS     DD  DSN=&&TEMPSMS1,
005400 //  DISP=(OLD,DELETE,DELETE)
           -
           -
           -
```

ACS routines may assign MGMTCLAS if you omit coding it.

These typical DD statements access new or existing SMS-managed data sets. You omit UNIT, VOL, DCB, and SPACE parameters when you code DD statements for new SMS-managed data sets. If you code selected parameters like LRECL, they may override SMS-provided data set attributes.

Figure 10.4 JCL That Accesses New and Existing SMS-Managed Data Sets

```
   -
   -
   -
ICH70001I CSCJGJ   LAST ACCESS AT 16:22:56 ON MONDAY, NOVEMBER 15, 1993
IEF236I ALLOC. FOR CSCJGJA STEP010
IGD103I SMS ALLOCATED TO DDNAME SHRSMS
IGD103I SMS ALLOCATED TO DDNAME DLTOLDSM

IGD101I SMS ALLOCATED TO DDNAME (CATLGSMS)
        DSN (CSCJGJ.ADV.CATLGSMS                             )
        STORCLAS (FASTWRIT) MGMTCLAS (LONGTERM) DATACLAS (FLATFILE)
IGD101I VOL SER NOS= USER10

IGD101I SMS ALLOCATED TO DDNAME (KEEPSMS )
        DSN (CSCJGJ.ADV.KEEPSMS                              )
        STORCLAS (FASTREAD) MGMTCLAS (SHORTERM) DATACLAS (FLATFILE)
IGD101I VOL SER NOS= USER09

IGD101I SMS ALLOCATED TO DDNAME (PASSSMS )
        DSN (SYS93319.T162257.RA000.CSCJGJA.TEMPSMS1      )
        STORCLAS (ENHANCED) MGMTCLAS (         ) DATACLAS (FLATFILE)
IGD101I VOL SER NOS= VIO

IGD101I SMS ALLOCATED TO DDNAME (WORKSMS )
        DSN (SYS93319.T162257.RA000.CSCJGJA.WORKSMS1      )
        STORCLAS (ENHANCED) MGMTCLAS (         ) DATACLAS (FLATFILE)
IGD101I VOL SER NOS= VIO

IEF142I CSCJGJA STEP010 - STEP WAS EXECUTED - COND CODE 0000
IGD104I CSCJGJ.ADV.SHRSMS                           RETAINED,  DDNAME=SHRSMS
IGD105I CSCJGJ.ADV.DLTOLDSM                         DELETED,   DDNAME=DLTOLDSM
IGD104I CSCJGJ.ADV.CATLGSMS                         RETAINED,  DDNAME=CATLGSMS
IGD104I CSCJGJ.ADV.KEEPSMS                          RETAINED,  DDNAME=KEEPSMS
IGD106I SYS93319.T162257.RA000.CSCJGJA.TEMPSMS1     PASSED,    DDNAME=PASSSMS
IGD105I SYS93319.T162257.RA000.CSCJGJA.WORKSMS1     DELETED,   DDNAME=WORKSMS
IEF373I STEP /STEP010 / START 93319.1622
IEF374I STEP /STEP010 / STOP  93319.1623 CPU    OMIN 00.01SEC SRB    OMIN

IEF236I ALLOC. FOR CSCJGJA STEP020
IGD103I SMS ALLOCATED TO DDNAME PASSSMS
IEF142I CSCJGJA STEP020 - STEP WAS EXECUTED - COND CODE 0000
IGD105I SYS93319.T162257.RA000.CSCJGJA.TEMPSMS1     DELETED,   DDNAME=PASSSMS
IEF373I STEP /STEP020 / START 93319.1623
IEF374I STEP /STEP020 / STOP  93319.1623 CPU    OMIN 00.01SEC SRB    OMIN 00.00S
   -
   -
   -
```


Figure 10.5 MVS/ESA Deallocation Messages Produced Under Storage Management Subsystem

Note that since all SMS-managed data sets are cataloged at allocation time, you will no longer receive the message "NOT CATLGD 2." This message was often encountered when a job attempted to create and catalog a new data set when a cataloged data set of the same name already existed. When this happened prior to SMS, the system would often create a second data set with the same name but would be unable to catalog it at step termination. If you try to create an SMS-managed data set when a data set of the same name already exists and is cataloged on the system, the new data set will not be created and the job will fail.

Figure 10.6 Reference to MVS/ESA Data Set Allocation Messages Under MVS/ESA with SMS (see facing page)

Type of Data Set Allocation	Message Number	Message
New and old non-SMS-managed data sets	IEF285I	CATALOGED DELETED KEPT PASSED
New, non-SMS-managed data sets	IGD100I	xxx ALLOCATED TO DDNAME ddname DATACLAS (clasname)
New SMS-managed data sets	IGD101I	SMS ALLOCATED TO DDNAME (ddname) DSN (data set name STORCLAS (clasname) MGMTCLAS (clasname) DATACLAS (clasname)
Existing SMS-managed data sets	IGD103I	SMS ALLOCATED TO DDNAME ddname
New SMS-managed data sets that are not GDSs, not passed, and not deleted	IGD104I	data set name RETAINED, DDNAME=ddname Comment: This message is used in place of CATALOGED for new SMS-managed data sets, which are not part of a GDG, that are cataloged or kept.
Existing SMS-managed GDSs	IGD104I	data set name RETAINED, DDNAME=
New SMS-managed GDSs for which DISP=(NEW,KEEP, DELETE) was coded	IGD104I	data set name RETAINED, DDNAME-ddname Comment: Although this message is appropriate for new SMS-managed data sets (that are not GDSs) and for existing SMS-managed GDSs, new GDSs should rarely, if ever, be allocated with DISP=(NEW,KEEP,DELETE). Thus, when this message is associated with a new SMS-managed GDS, it may indicate potential problems.
Deleted SMS-managed data sets	IGD105I	data set name DELETED, DDNAME=ddname
Passed SMS-managed data sets	IGD106I	data set name PASSED, DDNAME=ddname
New SMS-managed GDSs for which DISP=(NEW,CATLG, DELETE) was coded	IGD107I	data set name ROLLED IN, DDNAME=ddname Comment: This is the desired message when allocating a new SMS-managed GDS, since all new GDSs should normally be allocated with DISP=(NEW,CATLG, DELETE)

Note: The RETAINED message (IGD104I) has different meanings depending on the JCL associated with the data set in question. This message can mean that a new SMS-managed data set (non-GDS) was allocated and cataloged, that an existing SMS-managed GDS was kept, or that a new SMS-managed GDS was retained but not rolled in at step termination.

```
                          ISMF PRIMARY OPTION MENU
ENTER SELECTION OR COMMAND ===> 4

SELECT ONE OF THE FOLLOWING:

 0  ISMF PROFILE        - Change ISMF user profile
 1  DATA SET            - Perform Functions Against Data Sets
 2  VOLUME              - Perform Functions Against Volumes
 3  MANAGEMENT CLASS    - Display Backup and Migration Criteria
 4  DATA CLASS          - Display Data Set Allocation Parameters
 5  STORAGE CLASS       - Display Performance and Availability Criteria
 L  LIST                - Perform Functions Against Saved ISMF Lists
 X  EXIT                - Terminate ISMF




USE HELP COMMAND FOR HELP; USE END COMMAND TO EXIT.
```

Figure 10.7 Interactive Storage Management Facility (ISMF) Primary Option Menu

10.11 Role and Use of ISMF

The Interactive Storage Management Facility (ISMF) is an IBM product that runs under ISPF. This powerful tool can be a valuable asset in an SMS environment: it is your "window" into DATACLASs, STORCLASs, and MGMT-CLASs. Used effectively, ISMF can provide an abundance of SMS-related information, ease users in converting to SMS, and simplify your work. ISMF can be used to perform a number of specific functions, but here we focus on two:

- providing information about available classes and their attributes, and
- displaying lists of data sets and data set information according to user-specified criteria.

Your installation determines if ISMF is available to its general programming community and, if so, the ISPF option through which ISMF is invoked.

Figure 10.7 shows ISMF's main menu screen. We'll use this screen to bring up the four options covered in this chapter—the DATA CLASS, STORAGE CLASS, and MANAGEMENT CLASS options (selection numbers 4, 5, and 3, respectively) and the DATA SET option (selection number 1).

10.12 ISMF Data Class Application Selection Screen

Figure 10.8 shows you the data class application selection screen. You use this screen to produce a list of all available data classes on the system. This screen is almost identical to the first screens generated under the STORAGE CLASS and MANAGEMENT CLASS options of ISMF; if you learn how the first DATA CLASS screen works you will also understand how to use the first STORAGE and MANAGEMENT CLASS screens.

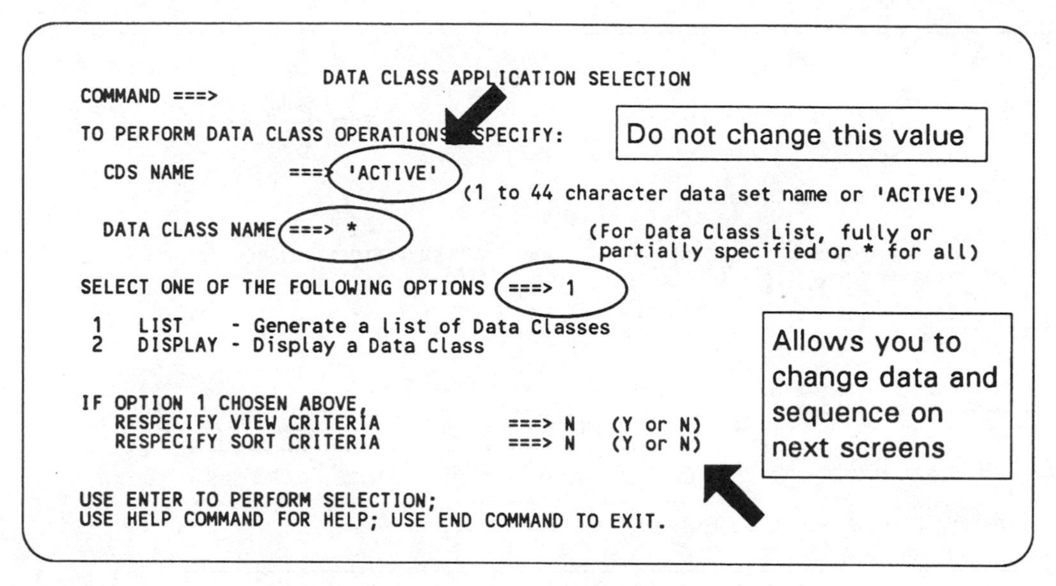

Figure 10.8 ISMF Data Class Application Selection Screen

The CDS NAME on the data class application selection screen specifies the name of the *control data set* whose contents we want listed. We use the "ACTIVE" control data set because it contains all data classes available to the general user community. Classes being tested by storage administration personnel for possible future use are not included in the ACTIVE list.

To generate a list of all available data classes, use an asterisk for the DATA CLASS NAME and code 1 for the SELECT ONE OF THE FOLLOWING OPTIONS value. If you know the name of the data class you wish to view, you can code its name in place of the asterisk and code "2" for the SELECT value (if you follow this procedure, ISMF will generate class information for only one data class, as shown in Figure 10.10).

Should you desire to change the order in which the attribute fields are listed on the screen generated with the LIST option (option 1), you can code "Y" in the RESPECIFY VIEW CRITERIA field. You can also change the order in which the classes are sorted by coding "Y" in the RESPECIFY SORT CRITERIA field. For instance, with a user-specified sort you can request ISMF to list data classes in ascending sequence according to their primary space allocation requests, as opposed to the alphabetical order in which data class names are usually listed. If you code "Y" for either of these RESPECIFY fields, ISMF will generate another screen on which you can enter your desired view and sort criteria.

Based on specifications coded on the DATA CLASS APPLICATION SELECTION screen, ISMF produces data class information in either list or display mode. Our request for a list of all data classes caused ISMF to produce the screen shown in Figure 10.9. In the upper right-hand corner of Figure 10.9 the SCROLL value is set to PAGE. This allows you to move ahead or back a full screen, just as in TSO/ISPF. Since the system on which this screen was generated has only seven active data classes, all seven entries

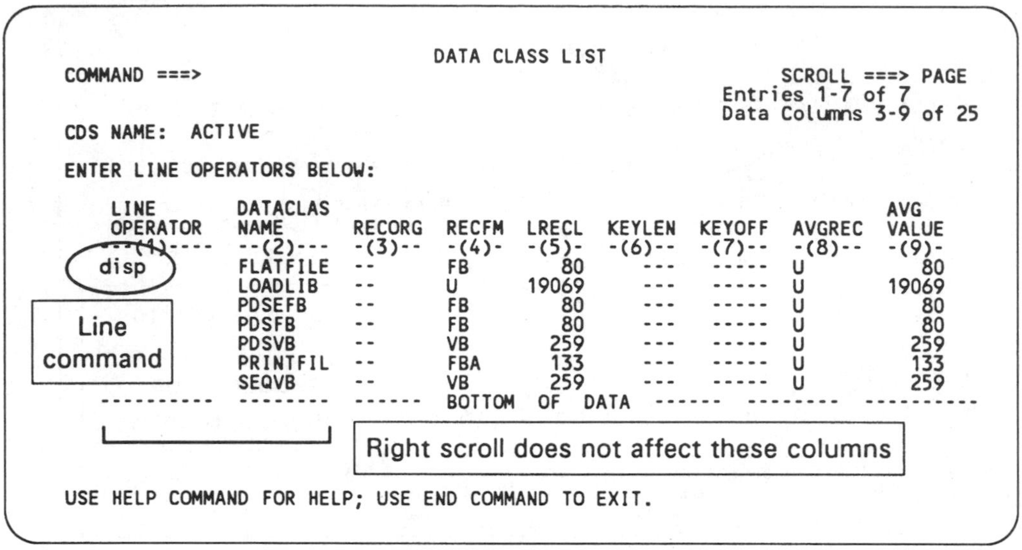

```
                                DATA CLASS LIST
COMMAND ===>                                                   SCROLL ===> PAGE
                                                            Entries 1-7 of 7
                                                            Data Columns 3-9 of 25
CDS NAME:  ACTIVE

ENTER LINE OPERATORS BELOW:

    LINE        DATACLAS                                                       AVG
    OPERATOR    NAME      RECORG  RECFM  LRECL  KEYLEN  KEYOFF  AVGREC  VALUE
    ---(1)----  --(2)---  -(3)--  -(4)-  -(5)-  -(6)--  -(7)--  -(8)--  -(9)-
    disp        FLATFILE  --      FB        80  ---     -----   U          80
                LOADLIB   --      U      19069  ---     -----   U       19069
                PDSEFB    --      FB        80  ---     -----   U          80
                PDSFB     --      FB        80  ---     -----   U          80
                PDSVB     --      VB       259  ---     -----   U         259
                PRINTFIL  --      FBA      133  ---     -----   U         133
                SEQVB     --      VB       259  ---     -----   U         259
    ----------  --------  ------  BOTTOM  OF  DATA  ------  --------  ---------

USE HELP COMMAND FOR HELP; USE END COMMAND TO EXIT.
```

Line command

Right scroll does not affect these columns

Figure 10.9 ISMF Data Class List, Available DATACLASs (horizontal list)

appear on this screen. If 20 data classes existed, we would have to page forward to see all of them.

ISMF can display only a portion of the 25 data columns associated with each data class on a single screen. The first screen shows data columns 3 to 9. To see all 25 columns you must scroll left and right using the appropriate PF keys. If you do so, the first two columns, LINE OPERATOR and DATACLAS NAME, remain fixed on the screen. You can see from Figure 10.9 that the data class named FLATFILE has no RECORG, KEYLEN, or KEYOFF information associated with it (since this class was not designed to be used with VSAM data sets), but it does have RECFM, LRECL, AVGREC, and AVG VALUE attributes.

Similarities exist between the lists of attributes produced by ISMF for data, storage, and management classes. Not all of the class attributes shown are values used by the system in the creation of data sets. For instance, one of the data columns (not shown on this screen) displays the date on which a class was last changed by storage administration personnel.

When you code a DATACLAS parameter in a DD statement, the DATACLAS must reference one of the data class names displayed on a list such as the one shown in Figure 10.9. You can override any of the attribute values used as data set allocation attributes obtained from a data class (for example, LRECL or RECFM). This lets you use a DATACLAS that is close to what you need, but not an exact match.

Class names and their attributes are installation-specific and thus unique. Your installation's class names and attribute values will differ from those shown in this book. Additionally, attribute values shown here should not be interpreted as recommendations for other installations. Their function is purely illustrative.

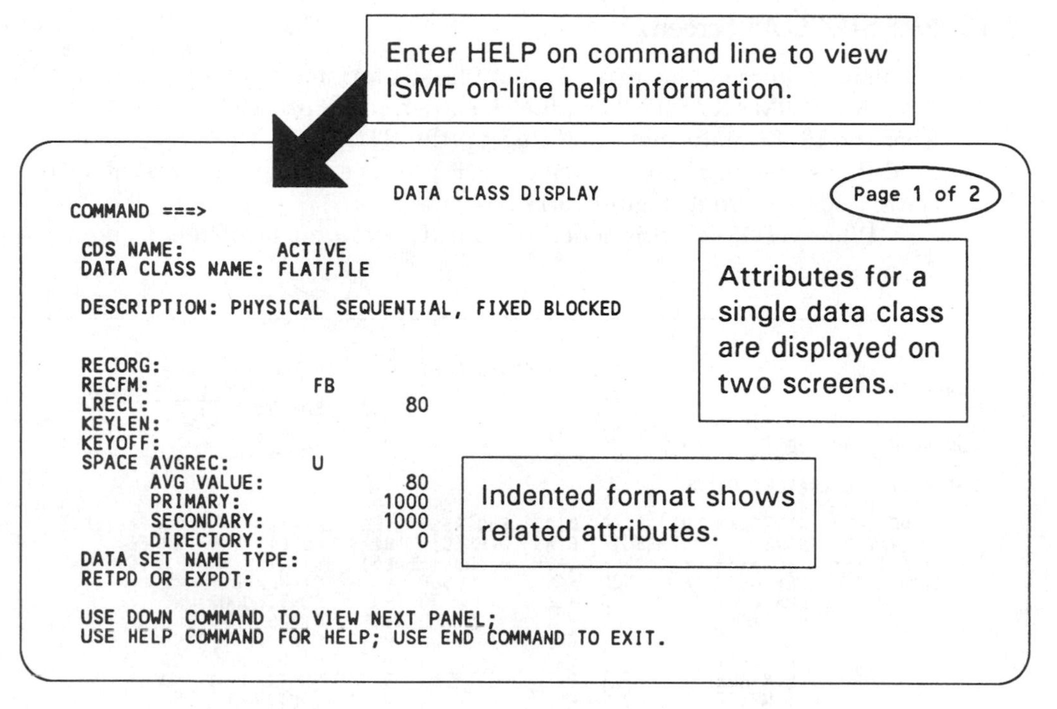

Figure 10.10 ISMF Data Class Display of a Single DATACLAS, First Screen (vertical list)

For demonstration purposes, we entered DISPLAY line command, abbreviated "disp," for the FLATFILE data class. This causes ISMF to display attribute information just for the FLATFILE data class and to do so in vertical format, as shown in Figure 10.10. The same vertical list would be produced if we had entered a DATA CLASS NAME of FLATFILE and a SELECT value of 2 instead of 1 on the screen shown in Figure 10.8.

Aside from the fact that ISMF's DISPLAY screen shows the information for a single data class on two vertical screens, the DISPLAY option has the added advantage of grouping and indenting related attribute information. Figure 10.10 shows that AVGREC, AVG VALUE, PRIMARY, SECONDARY, and DIRECTORY attributes are all related to SPACE. Although this relationship may seem obvious, relationships between other attributes associated with storage, management, and data classes are often not apparent except by this type of indentation.

By using the DISPLAY option, and by consulting the on-line help information (PF1) available for each data column, you can quickly learn some of the intricacies associated with SMS. For instance, with information provided by the help facility you could determine that AVG VALUE provides a number used as the first positional SPACE subparameter. The name "AVG VALUE" is an ISMF convention. IBM's JCL manuals refer to the first SPACE subparameter as "average record length" when used in conjunction with the AVGREC parameter, as described in Chapter 11.

10.13 ISMF STORCLAS Screens

To display storage and management class information you must return to the ISMF PRIMARY OPTION MENU, shown in Figure 10.7. Select option 5 from the ISMF main menu to bring up the STORAGE CLASS screens. We used this series of actions to have ISMF produce a list of all available storage classes, shown in Figure 10.11.

When STORCLAS is coded in your JCL, you must reference one of the

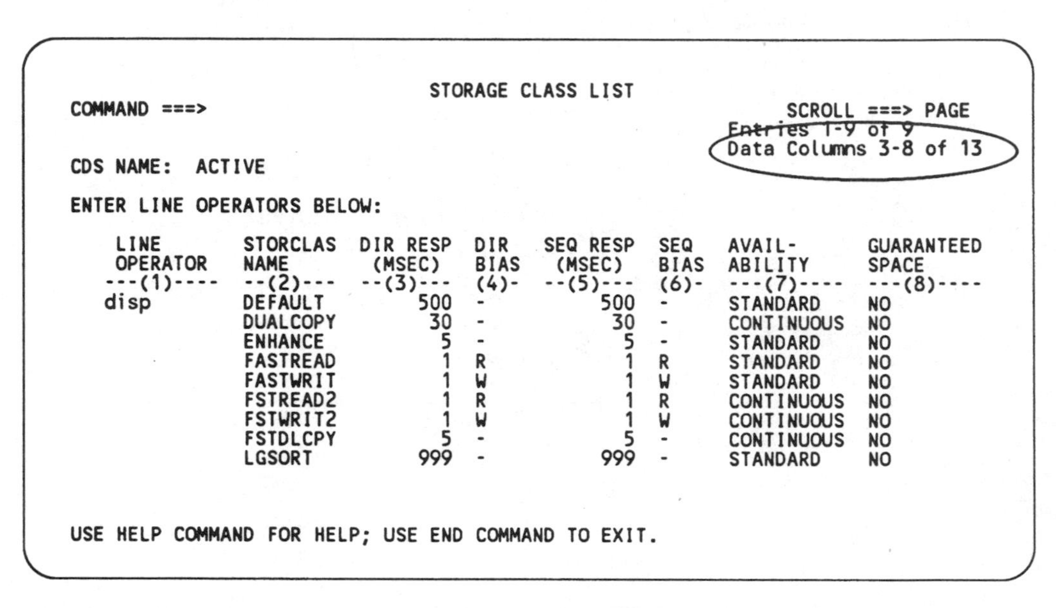

```
                                STORAGE CLASS LIST
COMMAND ===>                                              SCROLL ===> PAGE
                                                       Entries 1-9 of 9
                                                       Data Columns 3-8 of 13
CDS NAME:  ACTIVE

ENTER LINE OPERATORS BELOW:

  LINE      STORCLAS  DIR RESP  DIR   SEQ RESP  SEQ   AVAIL-       GUARANTEED
  OPERATOR  NAME       (MSEC)   BIAS   (MSEC)   BIAS  ABILITY      SPACE
  ---(1)--- --(2)---  --(3)---  (4)-  --(5)---  (6)-  ---(7)----   ---(8)----
  disp      DEFAULT       500   -         500   -   STANDARD     NO
            DUALCOPY       30   -          30   -   CONTINUOUS   NO
            ENHANCE         5   -           5   -   STANDARD     NO
            FASTREAD        1   R           1   R   STANDARD     NO
            FASTWRIT        1   W           1   W   STANDARD     NO
            FSTREAD2        1   R           1   R   CONTINUOUS   NO
            FSTWRIT2        1   W           1   W   CONTINUOUS   NO
            FSTDLCPY        5   -           5   -   CONTINUOUS   NO
            LGSORT        999   -         999   -   STANDARD     NO

USE HELP COMMAND FOR HELP; USE END COMMAND TO EXIT.
```

Figure 10.11 ISMF Storage Class List of Available STORCLASs (horizontal list)

```
                          STORAGE CLASS DISPLAY
COMMAND ===>

CDS NAME:            ACTIVE
STORAGE CLASS NAME:  DEFAULT

DESCRIPTION: DEFAULT STORAGE CLASS


PERFORMANCE OBJECTIVES
  DIRECT MILLISECOND RESPONSE:          500
  DIRECT BIAS:
  SEQUENTIAL MILLISECOND RESPONSE:      500
  SEQUENTIAL BIAS:
  INITIAL ACCESS RESPONSE SECONDS:

AVAILABILITY:                    STANDARD
GUARANTEED SPACE:                NO
GUARANTEED SYNCHRONOUS WRITE:    NO


USE HELP COMMAND FOR HELP; USE END COMMAND TO EXIT.
```

The attributes of a STORCLAS pertain mostly to performance and data availability, that is, how fast data must be delivered for direct and sequential access.

Figure 10.12 ISMF Storage Class Display of a Single STORCLAS (vertical list)

storage classes displayed on a list such as this. You cannot override any of the attributes associated with a storage class. By using the "disp" line command, the DEFAULT storage class can be displayed in vertical format. The screen produced in this way is shown in Figure 10.12.

10.14 ISMF MGMTCLAS Screens

Following the same procedure described earlier for data and storage classes, we can request ISMF to produce a list of all available management classes. This list is shown in Figure 10.13. Management attributes specify criteria used by the system to perform data set backup, migration, and expiration management.

Our experience indicates that the task of learning the meaning of attributes associated with each management class and the significance of each attribute for the system—and therefore your selection of appropriate management classes for new SMS-managed data sets—is one of the more confusing and difficult tasks involved in a conversion to SMS. Your installation's approach to the use of ACS routines determines the extent to which you will have to make decisions related to the use of management classes in your JCL.

A good example of the confusing nature of management class attributes is shown in the first three management class attributes, EXPIRE NON-USAGE, EXPIRE DATE/DAYS, and RET LIMIT, shown in data columns 3 to 5 of Figure 10.13. Although not readily apparent, these three attributes are

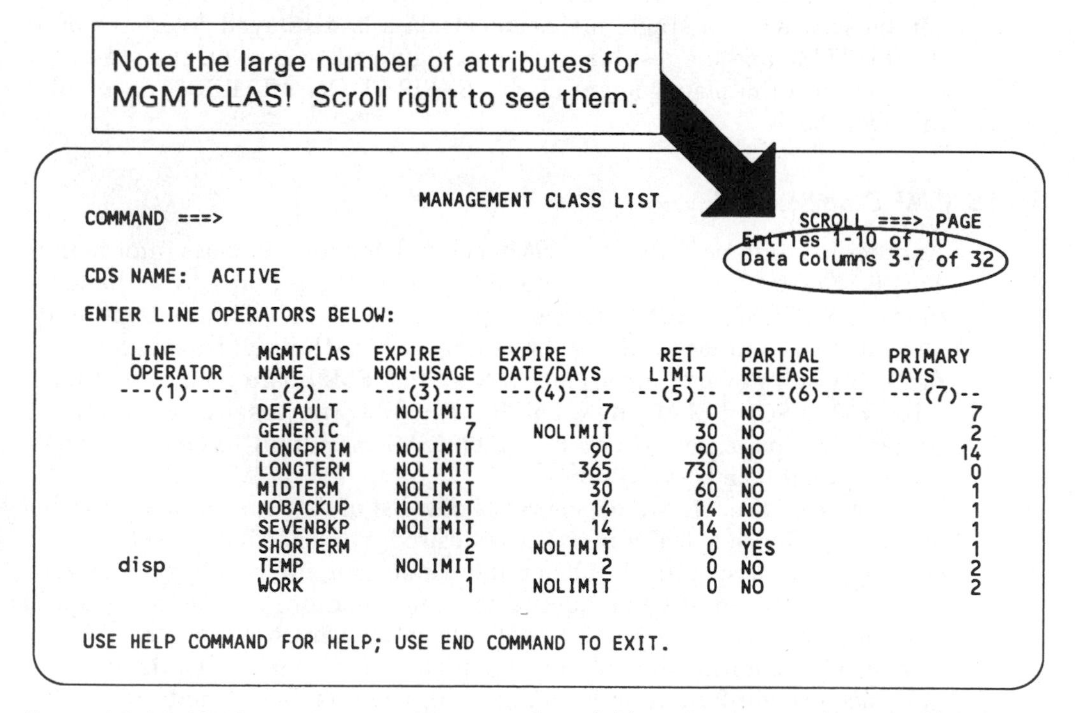

MANAGEMENT CLASS LIST

COMMAND ===> SCROLL ===> PAGE

Entries 1-10 of 10

Data Columns 3-7 of 32

CDS NAME: ACTIVE

ENTER LINE OPERATORS BELOW:

LINE OPERATOR ---(1)----	MGMTCLAS NAME --(2)---	EXPIRE NON-USAGE ---(3)---	EXPIRE DATE/DAYS ---(4)----	RET LIMIT --(5)--	PARTIAL RELEASE ----(6)----	PRIMARY DAYS ---(7)--
	DEFAULT	NOLIMIT	7	0	NO	7
	GENERIC	7	NOLIMIT	30	NO	2
	LONGPRIM	NOLIMIT	90	90	NO	14
	LONGTERM	NOLIMIT	365	730	NO	0
	MIDTERM	NOLIMIT	30	60	NO	1
	NOBACKUP	NOLIMIT	14	14	NO	1
	SEVENBKP	NOLIMIT	14	14	NO	1
	SHORTERM	2	NOLIMIT	0	YES	1
disp	TEMP	NOLIMIT	2	0	NO	2
	WORK	1	NOLIMIT	0	NO	2

USE HELP COMMAND FOR HELP; USE END COMMAND TO EXIT.

Figure 10.13 ISMF Management Class List of Available MGMTCLASs (horizontal list)

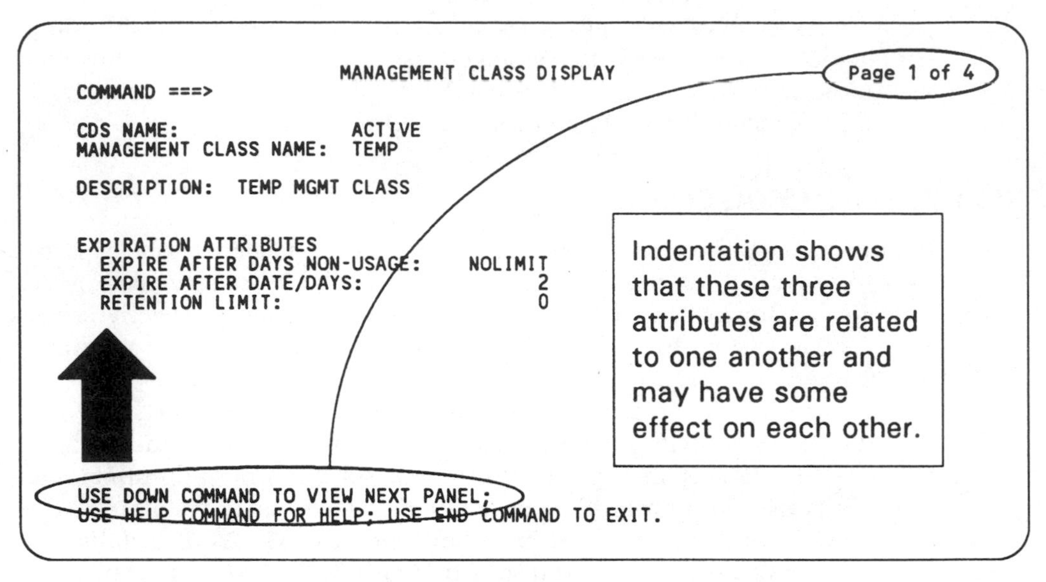

Figure 10.14 ISMF Management Class Display of a Single MGMTCLAS, First Screen (vertical list)

related to each other and together determine the expiration (deletion) criteria for each data set. That is, the way in which the system interprets the EXPIRE NON-USAGE value affects and is affected by the value coded for EXPIRE DATE/DAYS. That there is a relationship between these attributes can be seen when a single management class is displayed. We have done this for TEMP and the result is shown in Figure 10.14. As you can see by the indentations, the management class's EXPIRATION ATTRIBUTES involve three attributes.

10.15 ISMF Data Set Facility

Another function performed by ISMF is unrelated to SMS class information. This is the DATA SET facility, entered by selecting option 1 from the ISMF PRIMARY OPTION MENU screen (Figure 10.7). ISMF's Data Set option offers functions similar to ISPF's 3.4 option, but ISMF provides much greater flexibility and power. Once selected from the ISMF main menu, the first of four DATA SET SELECTION ENTRY PANELs appears. As Figure 10.15 shows, you then enter criteria by which ISMF will limit its search for data sets you want listed.

You can direct ISMF to generate a new list of data sets or bring up a list you previously saved. If a new list is desired, you can then direct ISMF to consult either a specific VTOC or the catalog for information about each data set to be listed. If you request catalog information, you can also request that the system search for additional data set information, not stored in the catalog, by consulting the volume on which each data set in the list is stored or by acquiring information from migrated data sets. Be warned: seeking information from each volume, and especially from migrated data sets, can be

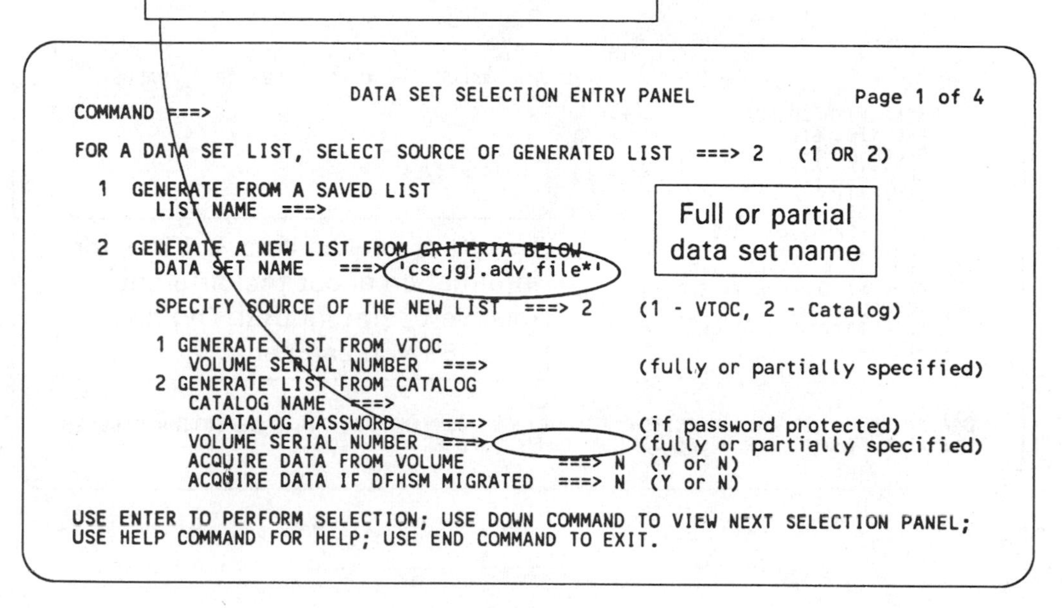

Enter MIGRAT here to generate information for migrated data sets.
DATA SET SELECTION ENTRY PANEL
Page 1 of 4
COMMAND ===>
FOR A DATA SET LIST, SELECT SOURCE OF GENERATED LIST ===> 2 (1 OR 2)
1 GENERATE FROM A SAVED LIST
LIST NAME ===>
2 GENERATE A NEW LIST FROM CRITERIA BELOW
DATA SET NAME ===> 'cscjgj.adv.file*'
Full or partial data set name
SPECIFY SOURCE OF THE NEW LIST ===> 2 (1 - VTOC, 2 - Catalog)
1 GENERATE LIST FROM VTOC
VOLUME SERIAL NUMBER ===> (fully or partially specified)
2 GENERATE LIST FROM CATALOG
CATALOG NAME ===>
CATALOG PASSWORD ===> (if password protected)
VOLUME SERIAL NUMBER ===> (fully or partially specified)
ACQUIRE DATA FROM VOLUME ===> N (Y or N)
ACQUIRE DATA IF DFHSM MIGRATED ===> N (Y or N)
USE ENTER TO PERFORM SELECTION; USE DOWN COMMAND TO VIEW NEXT SELECTION PANEL;
USE HELP COMMAND FOR HELP; USE END COMMAND TO EXIT.

Figure 10.15 ISMF Data Set List Function, Data Set Selection Entry Panel, First Screen

a very time consuming process, particularly if you try this for a large number of data sets!

Figure 10.15 shows that we want to produce a list of all data sets whose three-level names begin with "CSCJGJ.ADV.FILE" followed by any characters after "FILE", for example CSCJGJ.ADV.FILE3. To produce a list of all data sets whose high-level qualifier is CSCJGJ, you would enter "CSCJGJ.**" in the DATA SET NAME field.

To further limit the data set list, three additional panels are available on which search criteria can be entered. Paging forward one page with the PF8 key produces the screen shown in Figure 10.16. In our example we want to limit our search to data sets created on a specific CREATION DATE.

After limiting the search by date of creation, we again page forward with the PF8 key to the screen shown in Figure 10.17. Here we further restrict the search to SMS-managed data sets; we do not want the list to include non-SMS-managed (UNMANAGED) data sets. You can combine operators and values as you please. The on-line help facility explains the purpose of each field in Figures 10.16 and 10.17 and how to code them.

Having specified all the search criteria desired, we now press the *<Enter>* key to initiate the search. A fourth DATA SET SELECTION ENTRY PANEL is available, had we wished to use it. However, in our example we employed the first three panels to limit the data set list function to SMS-managed data sets, created on November 4, 1993, whose names conform to the specified criteria. Based on this, the system produces the list shown in Figure 10.18.

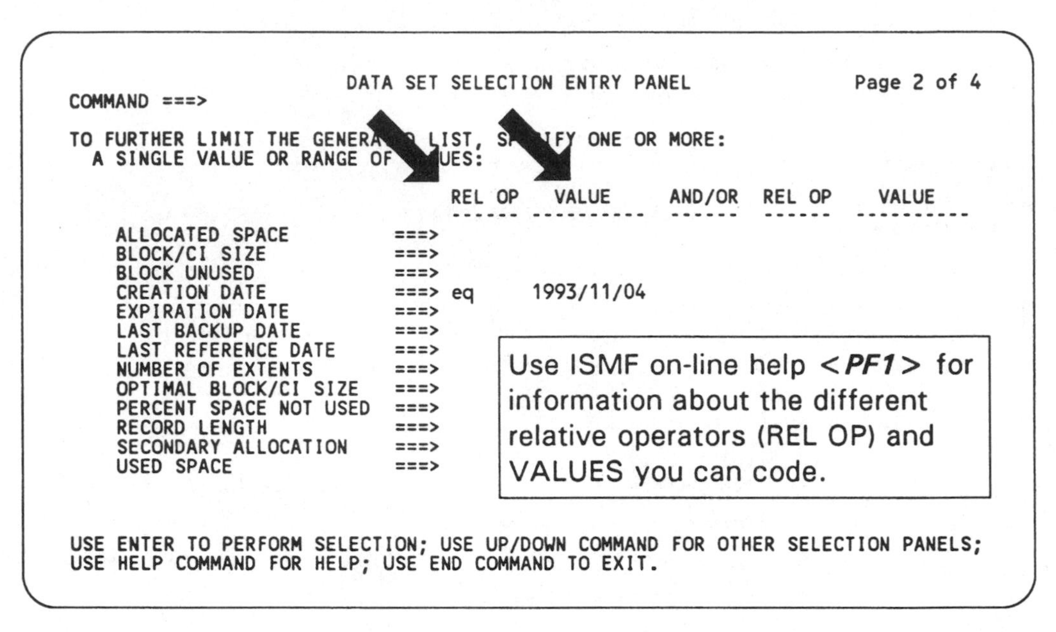

Figure 10.16 ISMF Data Set List Function, Data Set Selection Entry Panel, Second Screen

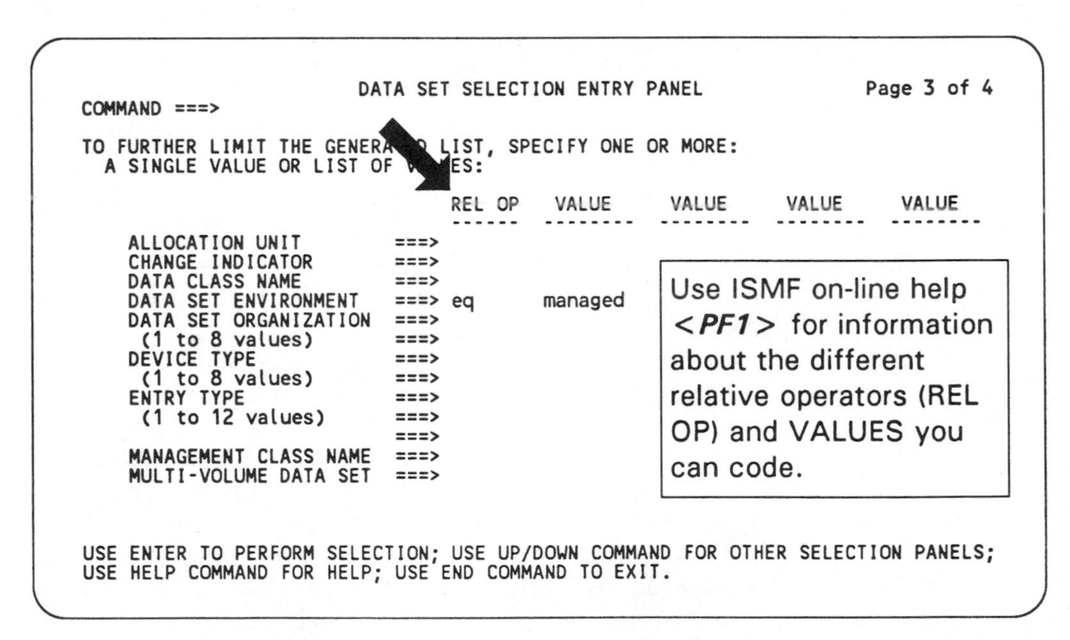

Figure 10.17 ISMF Data Set List Function, Data Set Selection Entry Panel, Third Screen

As with other ISMF lists, line and list commands can be performed against some or all of the data sets included in the list; for example, ALTER, COMPRESS, DELETE, and EDIT, can be entered for one or more data sets. The on-line help facility provides information about these and additional

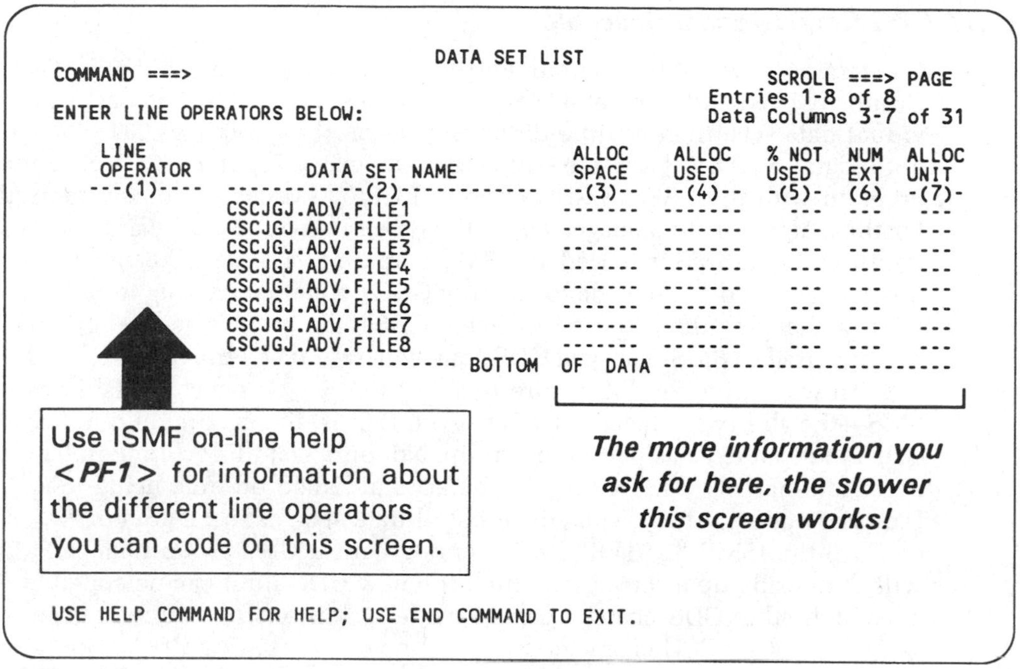

```
                                DATA SET LIST
COMMAND ===>                                                 SCROLL ===> PAGE
                                                        Entries 1-8 of 8
ENTER LINE OPERATORS BELOW:                             Data Columns 3-7 of 31

   LINE                                     ALLOC    ALLOC    % NOT   NUM   ALLOC
  OPERATOR          DATA SET NAME           SPACE    USED     USED    EXT   UNIT
  ---(1)----    ------------(2)------------ --(3)--  --(4)--  -(5)-   (6)   -(7)-
               CSCJGJ.ADV.FILE1             -------  -------   ---    ---    ---
               CSCJGJ.ADV.FILE2             -------  -------   ---    ---    ---
               CSCJGJ.ADV.FILE3             -------  -------   ---    ---    ---
               CSCJGJ.ADV.FILE4             -------  -------   ---    ---    ---
               CSCJGJ.ADV.FILE5             -------  -------   ---    ---    ---
               CSCJGJ.ADV.FILE6             -------  -------   ---    ---    ---
               CSCJGJ.ADV.FILE7             -------  -------   ---    ---    ---
               CSCJGJ.ADV.FILE8             -------  -------   ---    ---    ---
               ------------------- BOTTOM   OF  DATA -------------------------

USE HELP COMMAND FOR HELP; USE END COMMAND TO EXIT.
```

Use ISMF on-line help <PF1> for information about the different line operators you can code on this screen.

The more information you ask for here, the slower this screen works!

Figure 10.18 ISMF Data Set List Function, List of Selected Data Sets

commands available on this screen and others. Keep in mind that the amount of information displayed is determined by the GENERATE LIST criteria omitted or coded in Figure 10.15. The more information requested—for example, information from migrated data sets—the longer it takes to produce the list. Because there are *31 data columns,* much of the information available can only be seen by scrolling left and right.

10.16 ISMF On-Line Help

ISMF is a powerful tool that can effectively be used in an SMS environment. These pages have just scratched the surface of its capabilities. If you have access to it, begin exploring it and its help facility to learn much more about how SMS works now and how it will evolve in the future.

ISMF provides a highly informative on-line help facility. Entering "help" on the COMMAND line, or using the *<PF1>* key if it is so defined, brings up the help facility. We strongly encourage you to explore ISMF on-line help to enhance your knowledge of how MVS/ESA uses SMS class attributes and how SMS works. The help facility also provides information about list commands you can code on the COMMAND line and line commands that can be entered in the LINE OPERATOR field. List commands affect all classes included in the list while a line command only applies to the class displayed on the same line.

10.17 GDG Considerations Under SMS

Conversion to an SMS environment has some impact on Generation Data Groups (GDGs) and Generation Data Sets (GDSs). Since SMS manages individual data sets, there is little direct impact on the group (the GDG base is not a data set). GDG bases are still created by executing the IDCAMS utility program with the DEFINE GDG option; IEHPROGM can no longer be used for this. Also, due to management at the data set level, a GDG can contain a mixture of non-SMS-managed and SMS-managed data sets. This means that no changes need to be made to existing GDGs when converting to SMS. By simply changing the JCL used to create GDSs, the group's generations will be converted to SMS-managed GDSs one generation at a time.

However, one useful feature related to GDGs becomes available with SMS—the ability to change a GDG's level, that is, the maximum number of GDSs that can exist as part of the group. Not only can this be done in batch, by executing IDCAMS, it can also be accomplished on-line, using ISMF's Data Set option. After displaying a list of data sets, as in Figure 10.18, you can use the ISMF "ALTER" line operator with a GDG group name. ISMF will then bring up a screen on which the new GDG limit can be coded and on which other GDG changes can be made. Additionally, you may wish to assign the SCRATCH characteristic to all new and existing GDGs. Doing so ensures that GDSs that are no longer part of the group, and thus cannot be referenced by their relative generation numbers, are automatically deleted. Setting a GDG to SCRATCH can be done when it is created or, for existing GDGs, through IDCAMS or ISMF.

Although there is minimal SMS impact upon the generation data group, SMS implementation has greater impact on the data sets in the group. Remember that all SMS-managed data sets are cataloged at allocation time. Because of this, SMS interprets DISP=(NEW,KEEP,. . .) as DISP=(NEW,CATLG,. . .) for SMS-managed data sets. *But this change in DISP interpretation does not hold true for an SMS-managed GDS.*

If you code DISP=(NEW,KEEP,DELETE) for a GDS, MVS/ESA will keep and catalog the GDS at step termination, producing an output message of "RETAINED." But MVS/ESA does not make this GDS a full member of the group. In IBM's terminology, the new GDS is not "ROLLED IN" to the group as it should be. Thus, the GDS is retained and its named recorded in the catalog, but it cannot be accessed by its relative generation number as part of the GDG. However, by simply coding DISP=(NEW,CATLG,DELETE) when creating a new SMS-managed GDS, MVS/ESA will both catalog it at allocation and roll in the GDS at step termination, thus making it a full-fledged member of the GDG. ***IBM recommends that you always CATLG a new GDS, and not KEEP it, to avoid this problem.***

A more subtle problem exists related to allocating GDSs in an SMS environment. When creating an SMS-managed GDS, you no longer need to code a model data set control block (DSCB) as the first positional subparameter of your DCB parameter. DCB can be omitted and you can use DATACLAS or LIKE to obtain data set allocation attributes for a new SMS-managed GDS. You can also can take advantage of subparameter promotion and code LRECL and RECFM as stand-alone DD statement parameters, without DCB.

However, when a non-SMS-managed GDS is created, DCB subparameters cannot be promoted and used by themselves. If LRECL and RECFM are coded without DCB, DATACLAS, or LIKE, the data set allocation for a new non-SMS-managed data set fails and a "PATTERN DSCB NOT FOUND IN VTOC" message is produced in the output listing. This means you must code either DATACLAS, LIKE, or DCB=(model.name) when creating a non-SMS-managed GDS in an SMS environment. When this is done, LRECL and RECFM can then be coded as override values, if desired.

10.18 VSAM Changes with SMS

Prior to SMS, VSAM data sets could not be created through JCL DD statements, neither could VSAM data sets be deleted with the JCL DISP parameter. SMS allows you to create VSAM data sets in your JCL, and you can also intentionally and unintentionally delete VSAM data sets with JCL. Without SMS installed and activated, MVS/ESA interprets DISP=(OLD,DELETE) as DISP=(OLD,KEEP) when coded for an existing VSAM data set. But with SMS, DISP=(OLD,DELETE) is interpreted as just that for VSAM data sets! See Chapter 12 for an example of VSAM data set creation using JCL.

10.19 Converting to SMS: Comments, Questions, Recommendations

A decision to install and activate SMS usually initiates a major conversion effort on the part of the JCL programming community. Such a conversion extends beyond the limits of those who code JCL, affecting operators, production and quality control personnel, and users of TSO/ISPF, IDCAMS, and third-party packages. The extent to which your installation elects to make use of ACS routines can greatly impact the level of JCL changes and coding. In turn, your installation's data set naming conventions can influence the extent to which ACS routines can effectively be used with SMS.

Clear, consistent, and straightforward communication between the storage administrator, whose job it is to implement SMS, and the general programming community is highly desirable. To this end, Figure 10.19 lists some of the questions your may wish to address to those in your installation who are responsible for installing and converting to SMS.

Our experience shows that a great deal of the confusion associated with a conversion to SMS centers on two areas:

1. The meaning of the numerous MGMTCLAS attributes and thus the selection of appropriate management classes for new data sets. Other JCL changes, when compared to these, often appear to be simple mechanical adjustments. We've covered ISMF as a means of getting you started in this area.

- Is SMS installed and active on our system?
- Am I currently allowed to allocate SMS-managed data sets?
- Do our installation's data set naming conventions impact our use of ACS routines?
  —If so, what limitations exist related to automatic class selection?
- Do any installation-written ACS routines exist that automatically select STORCLAS, MGMTCLAS, or DATACLAS values when I allocate data sets?
  —If so, what classes will be assigned in this manner?
  —What are the conditions under which automatic class selection will occur? For example, do data sets whose names conform to certain patterns obtain automatic class selection while others do not?
- Am I allowed access to ISMF panels?
  —If so, how? That is, what ISPF option do I use to access ISMF?
  —If not, how do I obtain class information? That is, how do programmers and other users determine available STORCLAS, MGMTCLAS, and DATACLAS names, along with attribute values associated with each class?
- What classes, if any, are security-protected and thus limited in their use? For instance, am I prohibited from using certain STORCLASs?
- Is SMS configured on our system to support PDSE allocation?
- Do we have an installation-defined default symbolic device group name that allows me to omit UNIT when allocating non-SMS-managed data sets?
  —If so, what are the conditions under which I can omit UNIT for new non-SMS-managed data sets?

Figure 10.19 Checklist of Questions Related to SMS Implementation to Ask of Your Systems Programmers

2. Understanding how SPACE and the new SMS-supplied AVGREC parameter are interpreted by MVS/ESA and how to code them.

The next chapter is provided to help you get up to speed quickly and easily with AVGREC.

11

System-Determined Block Sizes and AVGREC

11.1 Why You Must Code SPACE
11.2 Comparing IBM Hard Disk Devices
11.3 Record Blocking
11.4 Traditional DD Statement Coding for New Data Sets
11.5 Traditional Space Requests by Data Block
11.6 New AVGREC Parameter Coding (MVS/ESA with DFSMS Only)
11.7 AVGREC Coding with Nongeneration Data Sets
11.8 AVGREC Coding with Non-SMS Generation Data Sets
11.9 How to Determine "Average" Record Length
11.10 Effect of AVGREC on Space Indication (TSO/ISPF)
11.11 Suggestions for Avoiding Problems with AVGREC
11.12 Do You Use AVGREC and SPACE with DFSMS?
11.13 Obtaining Additional Information About SPACE

11.1 Why You Must Code SPACE

Unlike the case with a UNIX, VAX VMS, or DOS, MVS doesn't give a data set disk space on an "open-ended" basis as needed. MVS requires you to plan your disk space usage and tell it, in advance, how much disk space a data set will use. You use the SPACE parameter, which applies only to disk data sets, to tell MVS how much disk space to allow for a data set you are creating. MVS/ESA Version 4 gives you powerful new ways to express a disk space specification, including AVGREC and DFSMS. I'll show you how to use these in this chapter.

11.2 Comparing IBM Hard Disk Devices

Different models of IBM mainframe hard disks have different track capacities, numbers of cylinders, and device capacity (Gb. means gigabytes, or billions of bytes; 1 Gb. equals 1,000 megabytes):

Disk Model	Bytes/ track	Tracks/ cylinder	Bytes/ cylinder	Total cylinders	Total bytes
3330-11	13,030	19	247,570	808	.200 Gb
3350	19,069	30	572,070	555	.317 Gb
3380-D	47,476	15	712,140	885	.630 Gb
3380-E	47,476	15	712,140	1,770	1.260 Gb
3380-K	47,476	15	712,140	2,655	1.890 Gb
3390-1	56,664	15	849,960	1,113	.946 Gb
3390-2	56,664	15	849,960	2,226	1.892 Gb
9340-1	46,456	15	696,840	1,440	1.003 Gb
9340-2	46,456	15	696,840	2,156	1.502 Gb

Disk devices in the MVS environment use a hard disk architecture known as "count, key, data" or "CKD." This is different from the sectored organization of mini- and microcomputers where tracks are divided into 512-byte sectors. CKD formatting creates tracks on the magnetic surface but does not carve up the tracks into sectors. As a result, the smallest unit of space on MVS hard disks is one whole track. As you can see from the preceding chart, the quantity of bytes that can be stored on a track varies from one model of hard disk to another. The models 3390 and 9340 disks are contemporary; the model 3380 is still in use but obsolescent. Disk track capacity is now approximately 50,000 bytes.

11.3 Record Blocking

We block records into groups for two reasons. Blocking records into groups eliminates many of the interrecord gaps that separate physical records on disk or tape, saving space, as Figure 11.1 indicates. A block of record combines several records into one physical record, just as a carton groups a dozen eggs. You go to the store and buy a carton of eggs at a time, so you can carry them home as one item. MVS/ESA can read a whole block of records in one action, instead of several input/output actions. You save time and energy carrying home a carton of eggs instead of making twelve trips, and MVS/ESA saves time and energy "carrying home" a block of records instead of several records individually.

How big should a block be to be most efficient? For tape data sets, this is a simple question to answer. You make the block size as large as possible, up to the MVS/ESA limit of 32,760 bytes, to squeeze out as many interrecord ("interblock") gaps as possible. But the single most burdensome thing connected with disk space is the determination of optimal block size for a given data set, and the amount of disk space required using this block size.

The number of blocks that fit on a disk track stays the same within a range of block sizes. This means that track capacity has a significant effect on the choice of physical record (block) size. As Figure 11.2 shows, deter-

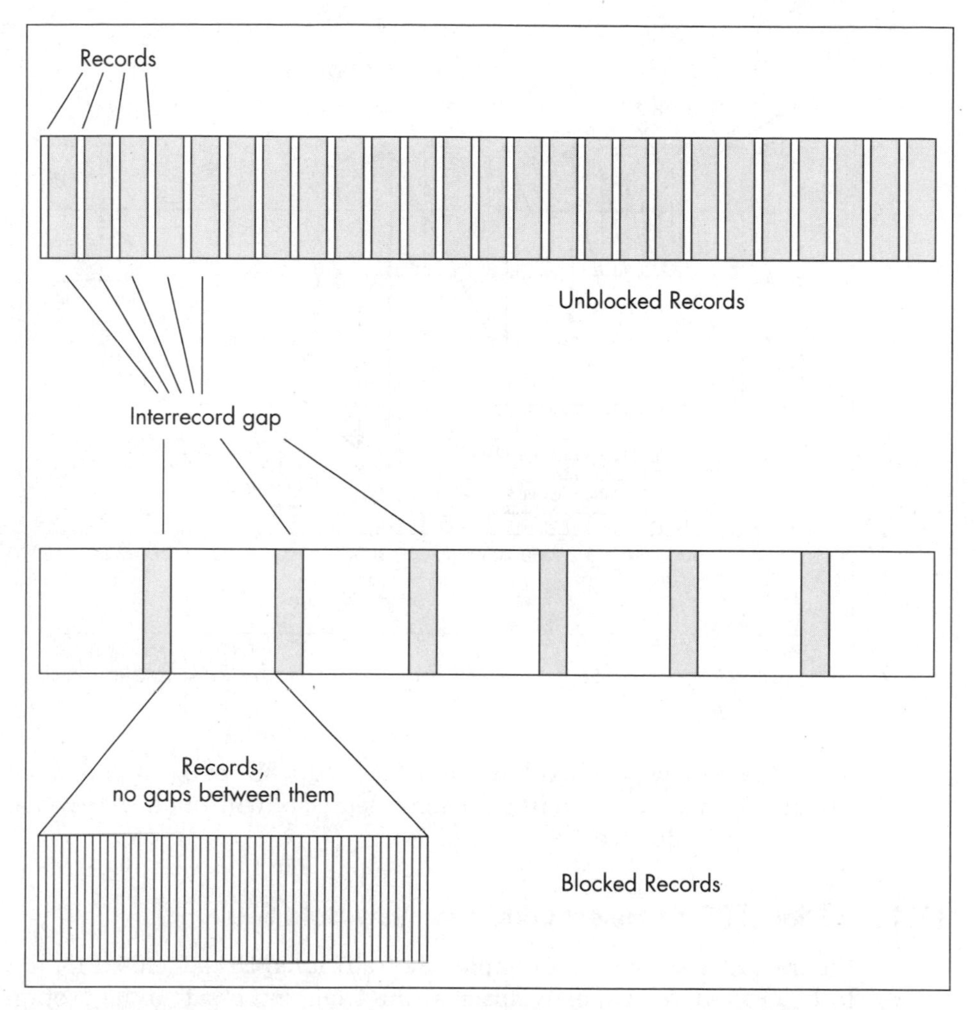

Figure 11.1 Blocking Eliminates Excessive Interrecord Gaps So It Saves Disk and Tape and Speeds Input/Output

mining an appropriate disk block size is a much more involved process than determining an adequate tape block size, because you cannot simply make disk block size larger to gain efficiency. As you move rightward on the horizontal scale, the block size increases linearly. But the efficiency (the percentage of the disk track actually used to store data) rises and falls. Generally speaking, we would prefer to remain within the "shark fins" representing block sizes that are 90 percent or more efficient. But the location of these shark fins varies from one disk device to another. A good "compromise" block size maximum of 6,233 coincides on most IBM disk models and IBM recommended this for a number of years as a target disk block size.

Under earlier versions of MVS it was your job to know the types of disk units your installation used and to do some arithmetic before coding SPACE. Under MVS/ESA Version 4 your job is much easier: you can let MVS determine the block size and simply talk about how many records you want to store.

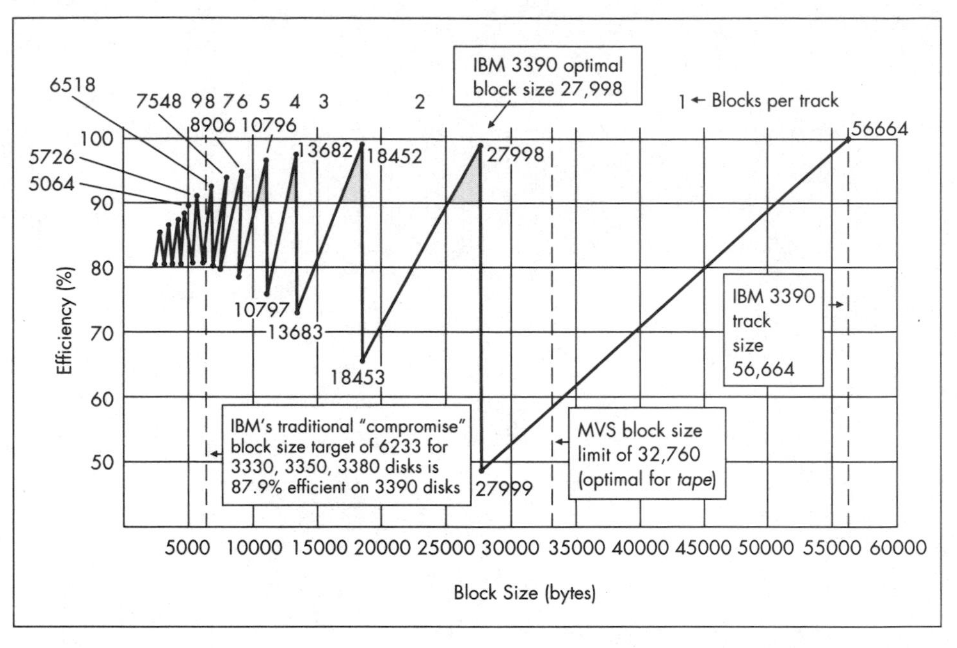

Figure 11.2 Track Utilization Efficiency Varies Nonlinearly with Block Size (Model 3390)

The best way to explore these new capabilties is to compare "traditional" DD statement coding for new data sets with modern DD statement coding, as I'll do next.

11.4 Traditional DD Statement Coding for New Data Sets

Figure 11.3 provides an example of a traditional DD statement for a data set to be created. You specify space at the time you create a data set, giving a figure for the primary space allocation. This is the amount of space you think the data set will require. You can specify this in terms of tracks, cylinder (an efficient collection of tracks), or data blocks. If you estimate too low for the primary space allocation and don't provide for secondary allocations, your job will fail when the data set is completely filled and you try to write more to it. You'll receive a system completion code of D37 as documented in Appendix E.

MVS/ESA ordinarily gives you your primary space allocation in one extent (that is, in one contiguous piece). But if available space on your mainframe disks is highly fragmented, it's possible that MVS will have to use multiple extents to meet your primary space allocation. MVS/ESA is allowed to use up to five extents to fulfill your primary space allocation. It can also use up to five extents for any secondary allocation.

When you create a disk data set, you can optionally give a value for secondary allocation. If you permit them, these "requested" secondary allocations can serve as a safety factor in case your estimate of the primary space allocation was too low. You will receive up to 15 secondary allocations in all. If the primary space allocation used more than one extent, you

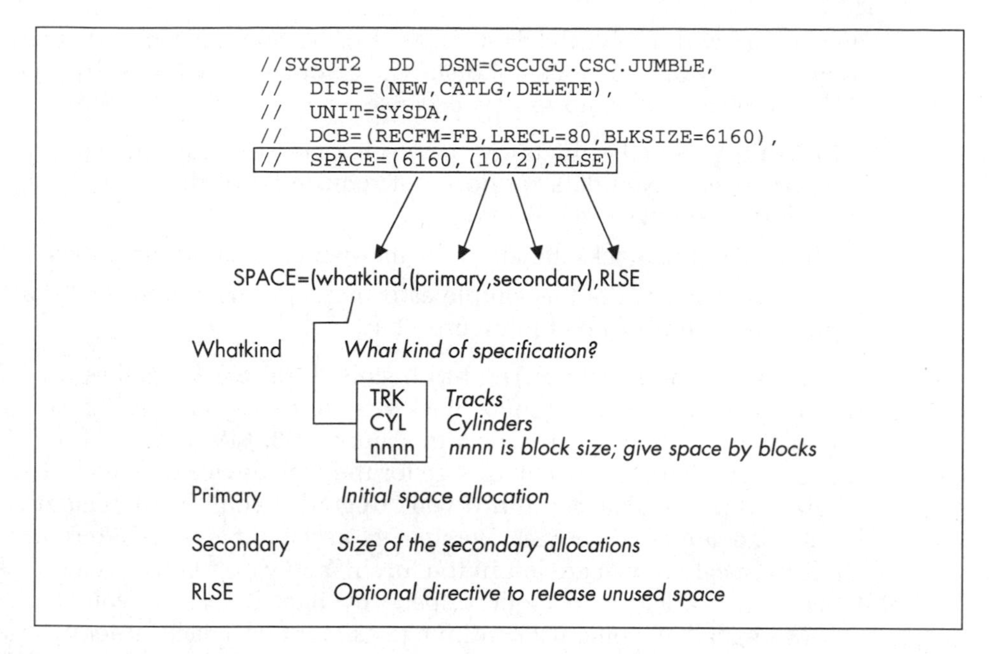
//SYSUT2 DD DSN=CSCJGJ.CSC.JUMBLE,
// DISP=(NEW,CATLG,DELETE),
// UNIT=SYSDA,
// DCB=(RECFM=FB,LRECL=80,BLKSIZE=6160),
// SPACE=(6160,(10,2),RLSE)
SPACE=(whatkind,(primary,secondary),RLSE
Whatkind
What kind of specification?
TRK
CYL
nnnn
Tracks
Cylinders
nnnn is block size; give space by blocks
Primary
Initial space allocation
Secondary
Size of the secondary allocations
RLSE
Optional directive to release unused space

Figure 11.3 Traditional DD Statement SPACE Coding

will receive fewer secondary allocations, since the maximum number of extents an ordinary data set can have is 16. (The limitation of 16 extents per data set per volume doesn't apply to VSAM data sets and the Partitioned Data Set Extended, which can exist with up to 123 extents.)

The ability to receive secondary allocations and their size are characteristics of the data set. Even though you code the SPACE parameter with your request for secondary allocation only when you create a data set, a data set allowed secondary allocations will receive them if it is later updated and expanded.

11.5 Traditional Space Requests by Data Block

Since tracks and cylinders vary in size between disk models, asking for disk space in these units only approximates the amount of storage needed for a certain quantity of records. Coding a space request by data block makes sense when you know how many records you want to store. To do this in a traditional DD statement, you code the block size at the "whatkind" field in the SPACE statement:

```
SPACE=(3840,200)
```

In this example, I had about 9,600 80-byte records to store. If I group $80 \times 48 = 3840$ of them together in each block, I need $9{,}600 / 48 = 200$ blocks to store them. But how much actual disk space (in tracks) will MVS/ESA give me?

When you specify disk space by blocks, MVS/ESA computes the number of tracks needed to provide sufficient space after it has chosen the disk device that will receive the data set. MVS/ESA contains tables that tell it the track capacity of each model of disk. The calculation will usually give you a little more space than necessary, because:

- MVS/ESA cannot split tracks between data sets, so you receive whole tracks, even if you data set does not require all of the room on the final track it receives.
- The size of the blocks dictates how many blocks can fit on a track.
- The calculation is not as simple as it may appear, due to the "shark fin" phenomenon illustrated in Figure 11.1.

Now, with or without DFSMS installed, MVS/ESA makes it unnecessary for you to worry about disk block size for new data sets. For example, if I omit the BLKSIZE specification in Figure 11.3, MVS/ESA will determine the most efficient (largest) block size for the disk device on which it chooses to place this new data set. But if you "upgrade" your DD statement to omit block size under MVS/ESA Version 4, and your system does *not* have DFSMS installed, you are left in the lurch! You won't know what block size to code in a SPACE to request space by data blocks. If you don't have DFSMS installed, you must continue to ask for disk space either by tracks or cylinders (BLKSIZE omitted), or continue to use traditional BLKSIZE coding and can request space in terms of blocks.

There are times when you won't know the block size of a data set to be written to disk, as in the case of sort work data sets. In these cases the program itself supplies the record length to MVS/ESA, not your DCB parameter. All you can do in such cases is to provide disk resources using TRK or CYL.

If you do know the record length or average record length, and you are using MVS/ESA with DSFSMS installed, you can omit block size *and* use the AVGREC parameter to simplify your work and your JCL, or you can use an appropriate locally defined DATACLAS and not code SPACE at all.

11.6 New AVGREC Parameter Coding (MVS/ESA with DFSMS Only)

Figure 11.4 shows you how the new AVGREC parameter works. Using AVGREC, you now have the capability to request disk space in terms of the quantity of *records* you wish to store. When you use AVGREC, MVS/ESA computes the quantity of disk tracks you need based on the length and quantity of the records that you indicate in the SPACE specification. But AVGREC is a little unusual for these reasons:

- It stands for "average record length" but the equals sign in it *does not* indicate anything about record length.
- AVGREC makes no sense coded alone; although it is a freestanding parameter of the DD statement, it must be coded with SPACE.
- The letter coded at the right side of the equals sign has a separate effect on SPACE than the word AVGREC at the left.

I drew the arrows in Figure 11.4 to make these points about how AVGREC works:

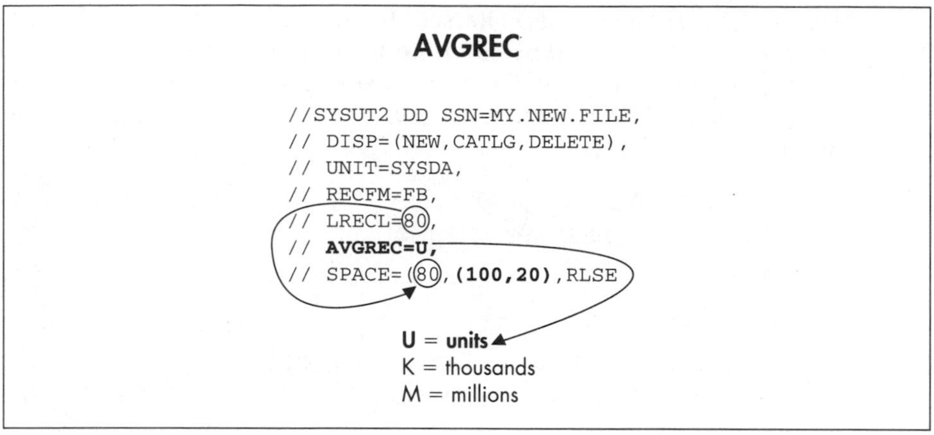

AVGREC

```
//SYSUT2 DD SSN=MY.NEW.FILE,
// DISP=(NEW,CATLG,DELETE),
// UNIT=SYSDA,
// RECFM=FB,
// LRECL=80,
// AVGREC=U,
// SPACE=(80,(100,20),RLSE)
```

U = units
K = thousands
M = millions

Figure 11.4 How AVGREC Changes the Way the SPACE Parameter Works

- The left arrow means that when AVGREC is present in a DD statement, the number at the SPACE parameter "whatkind" position is interpreted as a average record length, not block size.
- The right arrow means that the letter you code in AVGREC, which can be U, or K, or M, affects the meaning of the primary and secondary quantity numbers. U means "units," which is a multiplier of 1. K means "kilo," a multiplier of 1,000. M means "millions," a multiplier of 1,000,000.

Quite frankly, I think it would have been possible to design a clearer mechanism for JCL syntax to accomplish what AVGREC does. Let's examine some AVGREC coding variations and then some suggestions for its use.

11.7 AVGREC Coding with Nongeneration Data Sets

I have drawn some examples from the REG33UP7 job stream of Figure 8.2 in Chapter 8, to illustrate codings of SPACE with and without the use of AVGREC. First, let's look at the existing coding of the DD statements for two different data sets' output at STEP020 in this job stream. This DD statement requests space for a temporary data set, omitting BLKSIZE to let MVS/ESA compute the best block size for the data set:

```
//FINTRANS    DD DSN=&&FIN,     FINISHED TRANS
//   DISP=(NEW,PASS,DELETE),
//   UNIT=VIO,
//   RECFM=FB,
//   LRECL=92,
//   SPACE=(CYL,(1,1),RLSE)
```

Here, I have asked for a cylinder-sized chunk of space. MVS/ESA will find a cylinder of space for me, roughly about 50,000 × 15 = 750,000 bytes on modern disk drives. Suppose I knew that as an upper limit, 2,000 records would be written to this data set. The record length of 92 bytes × 2,000 indicates about 184,000 bytes would be needed for this data set. Clearly, my SPACE request, while not itself an excessive amount of space, represents overkill in this DD statement. I could do better by coding this DD statement with AVGREC:

```
//FINTRANS  DD DSN=&&FIN,            FINISHED TRANS
//   DISP=(NEW,PASS,DELETE),
//   UNIT=VIO,
//   RECFM=FB,
//   LRECL=92,                       ASK FOR SPACE FOR
//   AVGREC=U,                       2000 RECORDS TO START,
//   SPACE=(92,(2000,1000),RLSE)     1000 RECORDS SECONDARY
```

The revised DD statement asks for space by record length and record count in units. If I coded this as AVGREC=K, I could code the SPACE parameter as:

```
//FINTRANS  DD DSN=&&FIN,       FINISHED TRANS
//   DISP=(NEW,PASS,DELETE),
//   UNIT=VIO,
//   RECFM=FB,
//   LRECL=92,                  ASK FOR SPACE FOR
//   AVGREC=K,                  2K RECORDS TO START,
//   SPACE=(92,(2,1),RLSE)      1K RECORDS SECONDARY
```

Though this example deals with a temporary data set, the same coding applies to permanent nongeneration data sets.

11.8 AVGREC Coding with Non-SMS Generation Data Sets

DD statement coding for generation data sets (GDS) without DFSMS management relies on the use of a model data set control block (DSCB), which was (in the original scheme of MVS in the 1960s) intended to supply DCB information for every member of the generation data group. Coding in the DCB parameter can override the characteristics coded in the model DSCB, as in this traditional JCL from STEP020 of the REG33UP7 jobstream in Figure 8.2 of Chapter 8:

```
//NEWMAST  DD DSN=CSCJGJ.REG.STUACCTS(+1),
//   DISP=(NEW,CATLG,DELETE),
//   UNIT=SYSDA,
//   DCB=(CSCJGJ.CSC.MODEL,RECFM=FB,LRECL=177,BLKSIZE=22833),
//   SPACE=(CYL,(2,1),RLSE)
```

To allow MVS/ESA to determine the block size for a generation data set, you might be tempted to eliminate the BLKSIZE specification here. But that would cause a problem, because the BLKSIZE in the model data set label (the label for CSCJGJ.CSC.MODEL in this case) would then supply it. Instead, to have MVS/ESA compute the best block size, code BLKSIZE=0:

```
//NEWMAST   DD DSN=CSCJGJ.REG.STUACCTS(+1),
// DISP=(NEW,CATLG,DELETE),
// UNIT=SYSDA,
// DCB=(CSCJGJ.CSC.MODEL,RECFM=FB,LRECL=177,BLKSIZE=0),
// AVGREC=U,
// SPACE=(177,(15000,3000),RLSE)
```

This example asks for space to house 15,000 records, of 177 bytes length each, and secondary space in 3,000 record increments.

11.9 How to Determine "Average" Record Length

Average record length, coded at the beginning of a SPACE request when you use AVGREC, is simple for fixed-length record data sets, that is, RECFM=FB data sets. It is the record length. If you code a number here that is not actually record length, MVS/ESA will not complain. However, a grossly low number will probably not cause enough space to be allocated, since MVS/ESA uses this number to compute the quantity of disk tracks to allocate for the data set.

For variable-length records, determining the average record length accurately requires understanding the proportion of records of different lengths in the data set to be created. For illustration and practice purposes, I have listed here a few examples and the calculations required to determine an accurate average record length.

1. Records are of 100-byte and 200-byte sizes only; an equal number of 100- and 200-byte records exist in the data set. What is the average record length? If the data set contains about 100,000 records, how would you code AVGREC and SPACE?

   Answer: Half the records are 100 bytes long, and half are 200 bytes long:

   $.5 \times 100$ bytes + $.5 \times 200$ bytes =
   50 bytes + 100 bytes = 150 bytes average length

   Coding:
   ```
   AVGREC=U,
   SPACE=(150,100000,20000)
   ```

2. Records are of 100-byte, 80-byte, and 20-byte size; for every 100-byte record there are three 80-byte records and seven 20-byte records. What is the average record length? If the data set contains about 75,000 records, how would you code AVGREC and SPACE?

   Answer:

100-byte record	1
80-byte record	3
20-byte record	7
	11

(computed values rounded up)

$1/11 \times 100 + 3/11 \times 80 + 7/11 \times 20 =$

$10 \qquad 22 \qquad 13 = 45$

Coding:
```
AVGREC=U,
SPACE=(45,(75000,15000))
```

This example has ignored the four-byte record descriptor word (RDW) that MVS/ESA applies at the beginning of every variable-length record. The rounding up in the computation compensates for it.

3. Records contain a 27-byte root segment, and from 1 to 15 child segments of 18 bytes each; the maximum record length is therefore $4 + 27 + 15 \times 18 = 301$ bytes. (The four bytes at front is applied by MVS/ESA to variable length records.) No estimate is available as to the average number of child segments in the records. If 250,000 records exist to be written to the new data set, how would you code AVGREC and SPACE?

   Answer: Without knowing the distribution of 15-byte segments, you have two choices. You can look at space usage statistics for an existing data set of the same type and content, and compute an average record length based on the amount of space the data set occupies and the count of records it contains. Or, alternatively, you can simply code the maximum record length as the average record length and realize that part of your "safety" overallocation is now in the primary space allocation request rather than in the secondary space allocation request:

   Coding:
```
AVGREC=U,
SPACE=(301,(250000,50000))
```

11.10 Effect of AVGREC on Space Indication (TSO/ISPF)

You can use the TSO/ISPF 3.2 function to "tune in" to information about data sets stored in the system catalog and disk volume table of contents (VTOC). The way data set space information is presented to you depends on the way you allocated the data set.

When you allocate data sets using AVGREC, you can expect to see a change in the way TSO/ISPF reports space usage. Instead of seeing space reported in terms of tracks or cylinders, space will now be reported in terms of bytes allocated and bytes used. Space is, however, still allocated in units of tracks by MVS/ESA. Therefore, the smallest quantity of bytes that you will see allocated is a track of disk space, which is approximately 50,000 bytes depending on the specific type of disk devices used in your installation. Space is actually used in units of data blocks, not individual bytes. Since modern disk devices tracks are larger than the 32,760 block size limit of MVS/ESA, system-computed block sizes are determined based on two blocks per track, with block sizes of approximately 25,000 to 29,000 bytes. Expect to see small data sets allocated with AVGREC reported as having minimum "space used" indications in this range (see Figure 12.3).

11.11 Suggestions for Avoiding Problems with AVGREC

AVGREC represents a real improvement in JCL coding for systems where DFSMS is present, even if the data set being created is not DFSMS-managed. Here is some advice that will help you make implementation and use of it as smooth as possible.

1. To minimize the chance for misinterpretation by other people who might maintain the JCL, consistently code AVGREC close to SPACE, either on the line above SPACE, or on the same line:

   ```
   // AVGREC=U,                        2000 RECORDS TO START,
   // SPACE=(92,(2000,1000),RLSE)      1000 RECORDS SECONDARY
   ```

   or

   ```
   // AVGREC=U,SPACE=(92,(2000,1000),RLSE)
   ```

2. As a shop standard, consider *not* coding AVGREC with K or M. Both K and M obscure the real meaning of the numbers coded in SPACE and make it very easy to overlook the fact that a huge amount of space may be requested. I once suggested that participants in a corporate JCL class experiment with AVGREC coding, and before I could qualify this to say "but don't use M," a participant had tried it on a DD statement outputting a few 80-byte records. She immediately tied up the five largest chunks of space on an important disk pack (we deleted that data set fast)! If you stick to using U, the numbers coded in the JCL always represent what they literally say and you can minimize similar problems.
3. Always code secondary space with the intention of using it as a safety valve. One good rule of thumb is to make the secondary space allocation value one-fifth to one-half of the primary space allocation request, so that small increments of space will be provided to take care of any excess in record quantity. An alternative strategy is to limit the primary space allocation to that required for the smallest size data set likely to be written at the DD statement, and to make the secondary space allocation the size the maximum-sized data set would require. With both strategies your intention is to avoid space-related abends, while at the same time minimizing the number of extents a data set spans.
4. Unless you are allocating a data set for later use, such as a library, always code RLSE to release the tracks that the new data set does not use.

11.12 Do You Use AVGREC and SPACE with DFSMS?

DFSMS, the Storage Management Subsystem, assumes much of the responsibility for data set allocation decisions when it is activated. AVGREC and SPACE are two of several parameters that can be housed within a DATACLAS specification. If you code DATACLAS, you can omit from your DD statement the parameters coded in the specific data class in your installation. If you do code AVGREC and SPACE in the DD statement, along with

DATACLAS, your JCL *overrides* the AVGREC and SPACE housed in the DATACLAS.

11.13 Obtaining Additional Information About SPACE

This chapter has provided information about AVGREC, and was not intended to document all aspects of the SPACE parameter. If you need additional information about SPACE coding and operation, I suggest you examine *Practical MVS JCL Examples,* my introductory book on MVS/ESA JCL (ISBN 0-471-57316-7). That book was published by John Wiley & Sons, Inc., in 1993 and includes coverage of JCL starting with no assumption of prior JCL knowledge.

12

Miscellaneous MVS/ESA New Techniques

12.1 Creating SMS-Managed Data Sets Using TSO/ISPF 3.2

12.2 Partitioned Data Set Extended (PDSE)

12.3 LIKE and REFDD

12.4 Concatenation Improvements

12.5 Changing Generation Limit Using IDCAMS

12.6 Creating VSAM Data Sets with JCL Alone

You have no doubt heard introductory remarks or speeches that contained the phrase "and now, last but not least . . .". When a speaker uses such a phrase, he or she is usually trying to build or maintain momentum to close with a grand finale. In consciously arranging the content of this book, I use a variation of this phrase to begin this last chapter. I say, "and now, last by design, because they are least . . .". The features I have buried here in the last chapter are here because they deserve to be. You will probably find all of these features of much less use than the other MVS/ESA Version 4 and SMS features I have covered in the first 11 chapters! In trying to maximize this productivity of your time and attention, I have listed this potpourri of topics in the sequence I personally find them useful.

12.1 Creating SMS-Managed Data Sets Using TSO/ISPF 3.2

If your shop has installed and activated the Storage Management Subsystem as described in Chapter 10, your TSO/ISPF function 3.2, for data set allocation, has changed slightly, as shown in Figure 12.1. A new option, M, is now available to you. The traditional "a" allocate option still creates non-SMS-managed data sets. You can use the new "m" option to create a new SMS-managed data set, such as a TSO library, or an ordinary data set using DATACLAS. (Think of the letter "m" as standing for "managed" data sets, since the phrase "Enhanced Data Set Allocation" on the new 3.2 screen has neither an "m" in any of its words nor does it clearly suggest that enhanced allocation relates to SMS-managed data sets!) In the example shown in Figure 12.1 (prepared by Hal Breitenberg, to whom I give credit and thanks), the new option has been chosen to allocate an SMS-managed data set named CSCJGJ.ADV.FILE9.

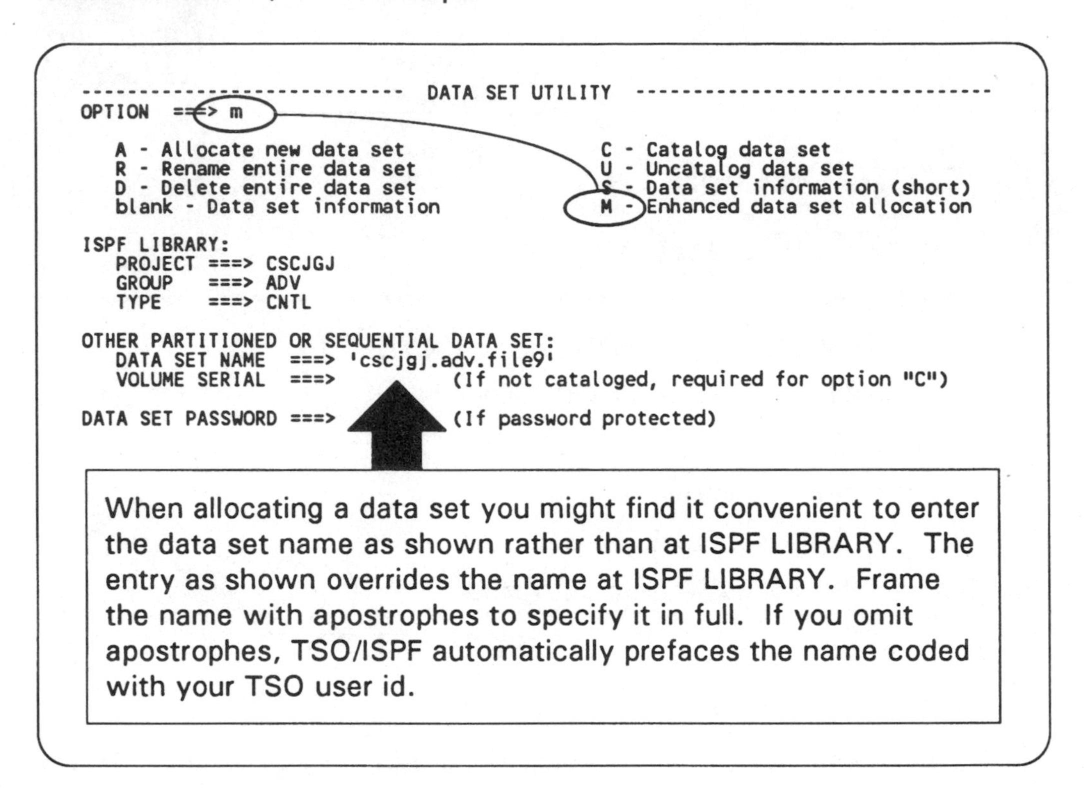

Figure 12.1 TSO/ISPF Option 3.2, Selecting Enhanced Data Set Allocation

After entering information on the first screen under option 3.2, you'll get the TSO/ISPF screen shown in Figure 12.2 when you initiate data set allocation. Here, this screen carries the default storage class (STORCLAS) DEFAULT, which happens to be a common DATACLAS name in this installation. We entered "shorterm" for the management class (MGMTCLAS) and "flatfile" for the data class (DATACLAS). With only this information specified, MVS/ESA creates an SMS-managed data set using attributes associated with the SMS classes indicated. For instance, data set allocation attributes, such as LRECL, RECFM, AVGREC, and SPACE information, are obtained by MVS/ESA from the FLATFILE data class.

To use SMS-supplied values on the enhanced allocation screen shown in Figure 12.2 to allocate a data set, you obviously have to know what the names and characteristics of your locally defined SMS constructs (classes) are. You get that information either by using ISMF, as described in Chapter 10, or from information distributed by your local storage administration group. The MGMTCLAS, STORCLAS, and DATACLAS names SHORTERM, DEFAULT, and FLATFILE shown in Figure 12.2 are not IBM-supplied names, but names defined locally.

If you leave the first three fields (MANAGEMENT CLASS, STORAGE CLASS, and VOLUME SERIAL) blank on the 3.2 allocation screen shown in Figure 12.2, the new data set will be assigned defaults or given none, de-

```
------------------------ ALLOCATE NEW DATA SET ----------------------------
COMMAND ===>

DATA SET NAME: CSCJGJ.ADV.FILE9

  MANAGEMENT CLASS       ===> shorterm    (Blank for default management class)
  STORAGE CLASS          ===> DEFAULT     (Blank for default storage class)
    VOLUME SERIAL        ===>             (Blank for authorized default volume)
  DATA CLASS             ===> flatfile    (Blank for default data class)
    SPACE UNITS          ===>             (BLKS, TRKS, CYLS, KB, or MB)
    PRIMARY QUANTITY     ===>             (In above units)
    SECONDARY QUANTITY   ===>             (In above units)
    DIRECTORY BLOCKS     ===>             (Zero for sequential data set) *
    RECORD FORMAT        ===>
    RECORD LENGTH        ===>
    BLOCK SIZE           ===>
    DATA SET NAME TYPE   ===>             (LIBRARY, PDS, or blank)        *
    EXPIRATION DATE      ===>             (YY/MM/DD, YYYY/MM/DD
                                           YY.DDD, YYYY.DDD in Julian form
                                           DDDD for retention period in days
                                           or blank)

  (* Specifying LIBRARY may override zero directory block)
```

DATA SET NAME TYPE appears only on the "m" enhanced allocation screen, not on the "ordinary" data set allocation screen ("a"). Putting LIBRARY in this field indicates that you want to allocate a partitioned data set extended (PDSE). Regardless of the type of data set you are allocating, you can leave the SPACE UNITS and other fields blank if you specify an appropriate STORAGE CLASS and DATA CLASS. If you make entries at SPACE UNITS and the other fields they override those characteristics of DATA CLASS.

Figure 12.2 TSO/ISPF Option 3.2, Supplying Information to Allocate an SMS-Managed Data Set

pending on locally defined settings. If you just specify DATA CLASS, you'll allocate an ordinary non-SMS-managed data set with the characteristics of the data class you indicated. If you want to use a data class but override any of the characteristics it includes, you enter the new values in the remaining fields. If you omit any SMS construct names on this new allocate screen, you may, depending on local settings, create a non-SMS-managed data set.

Notice that the fields shown in Figure 12.2 include one labeled DATA SET NAME TYPE. This field is new to the allocation process and appears only on the "enhanced" allocation. You can code LIBRARY here if you wish to allocate a partitioned data set extended (DSORG=PO-E), PDS if you want to allocate an ordinary partitioned data set (DSORG=PO), or you can leave this blank. If you leave this blank, but indicate a value other than zero for DIRECTORY BLOCKS, you still allocate an ordinary DSORG=PO partitioned data set. See the following section of this chapter for more information about the partitioned data set extended.

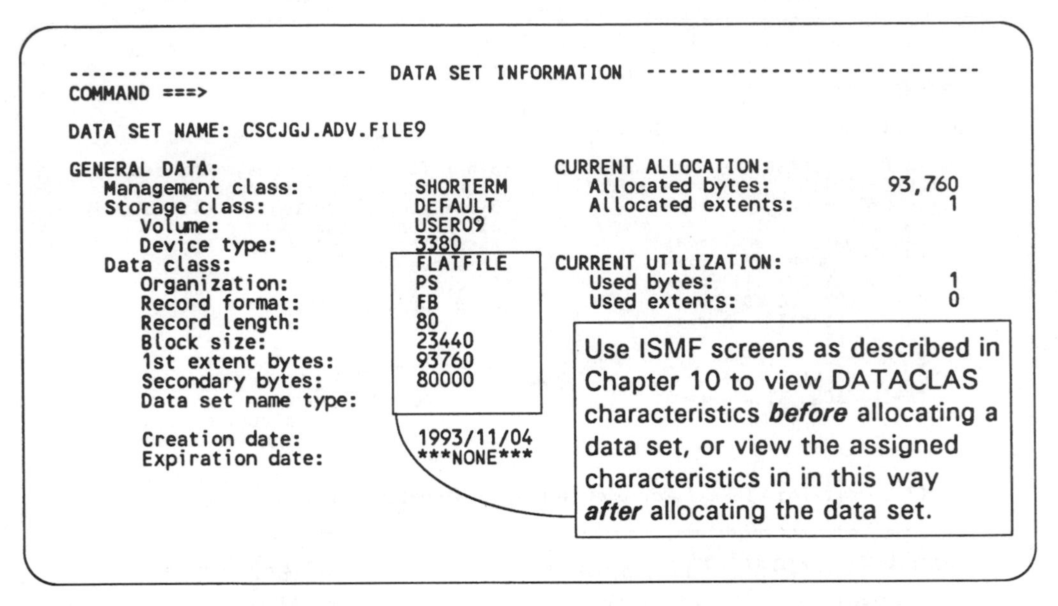

DATA SET INFORMATION
COMMAND ===>
DATA SET NAME: CSCJGJ.ADV.FILE9
GENERAL DATA:
Management class: SHORTERM
Storage class: DEFAULT
Volume: USER09
Device type: 3380
Data class: FLATFILE
Organization: PS
Record format: FB
Record length: 80
Block size: 23440
1st extent bytes: 93760
Secondary bytes: 80000
Data set name type:
Creation date: 1993/11/04
Expiration date: ***NONE***
CURRENT ALLOCATION:
Allocated bytes: 93,760
Allocated extents: 1
CURRENT UTILIZATION:
Used bytes: 1
Used extents: 0
Use ISMF screens as described in Chapter 10 to view DATACLAS characteristics before allocating a data set, or view the assigned characteristics in in this way after allocating the data set.

Figure 12.3 TSO/ISPF Option 3.2, Retrieval of Information About an SMS-Managed Data Set

Once you allocate a data set using the new 3.2 "enhanced" allocation function "m" you can press *<Enter>* at the screen shown in Figure 12.1, to view the actual characteristics of the data set you have allocated. Given how much of this information you might have taken on faith by using SMS construct names in the allocation process, you will find it interesting, and at least initially, reassuring, to view "as-built" this information! Figure 12.3 shows you the characteristics we obtained for our newly allocated CSCJGJ.ADV.FILE9 data set. Remember that MVS allocates disk space in full tracks, not portions of tracks. This accounts for any discrepancy between the number of bytes requested for allocations and the number of bytes actually allocated.

A "technical writing" flaw exists with the data set allocation screen shown in Figure 12.2, which carries a field labeled "SPACE UNITS." This terminology is only used in ISPF and represents the unit of measure for disk space to be allocated. You now have the option of allocating space by blocks, tracks, cylinders, kilobytes, or megabytes. However, you cannot code SPACE UNITS to allocate disk space based on a quantity of records, as you can in JCL with the AVGREC parameter! On the 3.2 screen shown in Figure 12.2, for example, a SPACE UNITS value of KB and a PRIMARY QUANTITY of 100 requests 100,000 bytes of disk space—regardless of the RECORD LENGTH (LRECL) coded.

In what seems to be an ever-accreting mass of similar-but-different specifications, SPACE UNITS might strike you as the same thing as a value named AVG VALUE that appears on ISMF screens. These two things are not actually the same, so if you have access to and use ISMF, keep that in mind as well.

12.2 Partitioned Data Set Extended (PDSE)

With MVS/ESA and SMS you can create two types of partitioned data sets: a partitioned data set ("slang" name PDS) and a partitioned data set extended ("slang" name PDSE). PDSEs, which must be SMS-managed, have certain advantages over PDSs:

- PDSEs never run out of directory blocks.
- They never need to be compressed (reorganized).
- They allow multiple jobs to concurrently create or use different members of the same PDSE using DISP=SHR.
- They are faster for MVS/ESA to access.
- Unlike PDSs, which can only acquire up to 16 extents, PDSEs, which make underlying use of VSAM files, can have up to 123 extents.

With early releases of MVS/ESA, you could not use a PDSE house machine language (a PDSE could not serve as a load module library). Newer releases of MVS/ESA promise to remove this restriction, which would make PDSEs useful for more than programmer and JCL libraries.

A partitioned data set is identified with the DSORG PO on TSO/ISPF 3.4 "data set list" and other screens. A partitioned data set extended is identified as DSORG=PO-E. But you do not specify DSORG as this value to create a PDSE using JCL. Instead, you use a a new keyword parameter, DSNTYPE, which you must code as DSNTYPE=LIBRARY. For example, the following DD statement creates a PDSE, with enough primary space to hold 50,000 80-byte records, and with secondary allocations large enough to hold 20,000 80-byte records. Since PDSEs must be SMS-managed, this example assumes that locally developed Automatic Class Selection (ACS) routines provide storage and management classes for the new data set.

```
//SYSUT2    DD  DSN=CSCJGJ.ADV.NEWPDSE,
//   DISP=(NEW,CATLG,DELETE),
//   RECFM=FB,
//   LRECL=80,
//   AVGREC=U,
//   SPACE=(80,(50000,20000,1)),
//   DSNTYPE=LIBRARY
```

Notice that we coded SPACE indicating the allocation of only one directory block. Since a PDSE has essentially unlimited directory block capacity, any nonzero quantity for directory blocks is sufficient, and the need to specify directory blocks when you use DSNTYPE=LIBRARY may be removed completely. If your installation has one or more data classes defined whose attributes fully or partially conform to those desired for this data set, you could simplify the DD statement by coding DATACLAS and omitting RECFM, LRECL, AVGREC, and SPACE.

A serious technical writing problem has been introduced with PDSE nomenclature. If you omit making an entry for DATA SET NAME TYPE on the TSO/ISPF enhanced allocation screen in Figure 12.2 (see section 12.1) or don't code DSNTYPE in JCL allocating a partitioned data set, you get a traditional DSORG=PO PDS. If you code DSNTYPE=PDS in JCL, or enter PDS at the DATA SET NAME TYPE on the TSO 3.2 enhanced allocation screen, you also create a traditional DSORG=PO PDS. To create a PDSE, you must code DSNTYPE=LIBRARY or enter LIBRARY at the DATA SET NAME TYPE field on the TSO 3.2 enhanced allocation screen. Yet the terms library, partitioned data set, and PDS have been used as synonyms for 30 years! The choice of the word "LIBRARY" as the required specification for a PDSE borders on the absurd, since it is guaranteed to cause unnecessary confusion. Frederick P. Brooks, the noted computer science author and scholar who wrote *The Mythical Man Month* and many other perceptive articles concerning software engineering, calls this type of unnecessary complication "accidental complexity."[1] I think the term is well chosen. The extra mental energy required to deal with these needlessly shifting sands of technobabble has nothing to do with the inherent complexity of the mainframe environment.

12.3 LIKE and REFDD

An MVS/ESA system with SMS can obtain data set characteristics such as RECFM, LRECL, BLKSIZE, and DSORG through a variety of means. To read existing sequential and partitioned data sets, MVS/ESA obtains this information from the data set label. But when creating new data sets, this information must be provided from other sources, such as the traditional DCB parameter and subparameters, or promoted parameters, as shown in Chapter 1. As an alternative to coding DCB or promoted parameters, you can use one of the three new parameters available with SMS: DATACLAS, LIKE, or REFDD. DATACLAS is described in Chapter 10, but LIKE and REFDD are independent of it, and I describe them here. You can use LIKE and REFDD with any data set, whether it is SMS-managed or not, but SMS must be present on your system.

Both LIKE and REFDD are similar to a traditional capability to copy DCB specifications from an existing data set label, and override some of them, a technique often used with the model data set label required to create a new generation of a non SMS-managed generation data set:

```
//   DCB=(CSCJGJ.CSC.MODLDSCB,RECFM=FB,LRECL=100,BLKSIZE=0),
```

You are not required to use LIKE or REFDD in place of DCB or promoted DCB parameters when you override DATACLAS characteristics, but doing so may make the data sets you create more consistent in their characteristics.

You can code LIKE in place of DCB=(dsname... to direct MVS/ESA to obtain allocation information for a new data set from the attributes of an existing, cataloged, disk data set, as shown in this example:

```
//*-------------------------------------------------------
//*   STEP 1
//*-------------------------------------------------------
//STEP010    EXEC   PGM=IEFBR14
//*
//NEWFILE1      DD   DSN=CSCJGJ.ADV.NEWFILE1,
//   DISP=(NEW,CATLG,DELETE),
//   STORCLAS=FASTWRIT,
//   MGMTCLAS=MIDTERM,
//   LIKE=CSCJGJ.ADV.OLDFILE
//*
//NEWFILE2      DD   DSN=CSCJGJ.ADV.NEWFILE2,
//   DISP=(NEW,CATLG,DELETE),
//   STORCLAS=FASTREAD,
//   MGMTCLAS=MIDTERM,
//   RECFM=FB,
//   LRECL=120,
//   AVGREC=U,
//   SPACE=(120,(20000,10000),RLSE),
//*-------------------------------------------------------
//*   NEXT STEP
//*-------------------------------------------------------
//STEP020    EXEC   PGM=IEFBR14
//NEWFILE3      DD   DSN=CSCJGJ.ADV.NEWFILE3,
//   DISP=(NEW,CATLG,DELETE),
//   STORCLAS=FASTREAD,
//   MGMTCLAS=MIDTERM,
//   REFDD=*.STEP010.NEWFILE2
```

LIKE copies LRECL, RECFM, SPACE, AVGREC, and DSNTYPE (if any) of the existing data set and uses these values when creating the new data set. If the existing data set is a VSAM data set, the system also obtains RECORG (instead of RECFM), KEYLEN, and KEYOFF. If the new data set is a tape data set, the system only obtains LRECL and RECFM from the existing data set. In no case is EXPDT or RETPD copied to the new data set. You will notice that STORCLAS and MGMTCLAS are coded in this example. This is because neither LIKE or REFDD copy SMS construct (class) information.

Be aware of a potential problem with LIKE. When you use LIKE, MVS/ESA determines the amount of space for the new data set taking into account only the first three extents' worth of space, not the full amount of space occupied by the referenced data set if it is spread over four or more extents. You could be surprised at the amount of space that you get (or don't get).

You can code REFDD=*.ddname in place of DCB=*.referback to direct MVS/ESA to obtain allocation information for a new data set from the coding on a previous DD statement in the same job, rather than from the label of an existing disk data set. When you code REFDD=*.ddname as in STEP020 in the preceding example, MVS/ESA acquires information similar to the information it gets when you code LIKE, but limited to the parameters ***actually present*** on the DD statement to which REFDD refers. Here too, only LRECL and RECFM are copied for tape data sets, and EXPDT and RETPD are never copied.

You have the option of overriding any of the allocation attribute values obtained through the use of LIKE and REFDD. You do this by coding parameters you want to override, such as SPACE and AVGREC, along with their values:

```
//NEWFILE1     DD  DSN=CSCJGJ.ADV.NEWFILE1,
//   DISP=(NEW,CATLG,DELETE),
//   STORCLAS=FASTWRIT,
//   MGMTCLAS=MIDTERM,
//   LIKE=CSCJGJ.ADV.OLDFILE,
//   AVGREC=U,
//   SPACE=(120,(20000,10000),RLSE),
```

Before using REFDD, you should check to make sure that it does not conflict with your installation's methods for recovering from job failures. Since REFDD is a referback, it may interfere with attempts to restart a job, unlike LIKE, which ties a step to the information provided in the data set label of a cataloged data set.

12.4 Concatenation Improvements

MVS/ESA Version 4 provides two improvements in data set concatenation when SMS is at least present on the system. When you code a DD statement such as this:

```
//*-----------------------------------------------------
//*  COPY A DATA SET
//*-----------------------------------------------------
//STEP010    EXEC  PGM=IEBGENER
//SYSPRINT     DD  SYSOUT=*
//SYSUT1       DD  DSN=CSCJGJ.ADV.FILE1,DISP=SHR
//             DD  DSN=CSCJGJ.ADV.FILE2,DISP=SHR
//             DD  DSN=CSCJGJ.ADV.FILE3,DISP=SHR
//SYSUT2...
```

you no longer have to worry about putting the file with the largest block size first. Older versions of MVS required this. It was necessary to relax this requirement to begin the process of divorcing programmers from the need to know physical block sizes. Without SMS, concatenated tape data sets must still be listed with the data set with the largest block size.

In addition, you can, with SMS present, intermix disk and tape devices in the list of concatenated data sets. Previously, concatenated data sets had to all be on the same type of device, either disk or tape. For fixed-length record data sets, the LRECL and RECFM of concatenated data sets must still be the same.

12.5 Changing Generation Limit Using IDCAMS

In previous versions of MVS, and without SMS installed, you could not readily change the number of generations of a generation data set. That is, if the generation data set base has been established specifying that seven generations be retained, you could not decide, later, that you needed 10 generations. Now, you can execute IDCAMS and have it process this control statement to change the limit:

```
ALTER  CSCJGJ.CSC.GDGBASE  LIMIT(10)
```

You input this command to IDCAMS at its //SYSIN DD statement. You code the name CSCJGJ.CSC.GDGBASE as the name of the GDS base that you want to change. If you make the limit lower than it had previously been defined, and excess generations exist as a result of the change, they are automatically eliminated.

12.6 Creating VSAM Data Sets with JCL Alone

VSAM was introduced as a replacement for ISAM in 1973. Since that time, creating a VSAM data set has required thinking about and deciding on its internal characteristics, which encompasses 60 or more settings. You express your choices for these specifications using control statements, as shown in Appendix B, and feed them to IDCAMS at its //SYSIN DD statement for execution. IDCAMS checks your specifications and if they are consistent, builds an entry, named the base cluster, for the data sets in a catalog. The base cluster retains information about the data set and controls its use.

Now, a full 20 years after VSAM was introduced, provision has finally been made to create a VSAM data set through JCL alone. Had this capability been provided earlier, the practice might have caught on. But even now, creating a VSAM data set through JCL does not have the flexibility of creating one with IDCAMS. This JCL creates a Key Sequenced Data Set if SMS is active:

```
//*---------------------------------------------------
//*  CREATE A VSAM KSDS
//*---------------------------------------------------
//STEP010    EXEC  PGM=IEBGENER
//SYSPRINT     DD  SYSOUT=*
//SYSUT1       DD  DSN=CSCJGJ.ADV.FILE4,DISP=SHR
//SYSUT2       DD  DSN=CSCJGJ.ADV.NEWKSDS,
//   DISP=(NEW,CATLG,DELETE),
//   UNIT=SYSDA,
//   RECORG=KS,
//   LRECL=90,
```

```
//   KEYLEN=5,
//   KEYOFF=0,
//   SPACE=(CYL,(5,5)),
//   VOL=SER=ACSCAC
//SYSIN         DD DUMMY
```

You can't specify IMBED, REPLICATE, CISIZE, FREESPACE, and SHARE-OPTIONS using JCL itself. But if these are contained in a DATACLAS, you can make them apply by specifying the DATACLAS in this DD statement. If you don't have them in a DATACLAS, they will assume defaults. But ERASE, KEYRANGES, MODEL, ORDERED, REUSE, SPANNED, SPEED, and RECATALOG can't be specified either in a DATACLAS or in JCL and will always assume default values for a VSAM data set created using JCL. If these latter definition options are of concern to the data set, you must still use ID-CAMS to create it.

VSAM data sets can be managed by SMS. A non-SMS-managed VSAM data set (but not an SMS-managed one) can be created without specifying a disk volume serial number. If you omit the volume serial number from the preceding example, MVS/ESA will pick out a disk to house the data set. This is something you still cannot do with IDCAMS! In addition, you can create a temporary VSAM data set using JCL, by coding the DISP parameter in the preceding example as

```
//   DISP=(NEW,PASS,DELETE),
```

IDCAMS cannot create temporary VSAM data sets. Both IDCAMS and JCL can, with SMS, delete VSAM data sets. If you code DISP=(OLD,DELETE) with a VSAM data set, the data set will be deleted. In the past, and still in MVS/ESA Version 4 without SMS active, the second DISP field always defaults to KEEP.

Notes

1. Frederick P. Brooks was a manager in charge of development of the original OS/360 in the 1960s. His *Mythical Man Month,* a classic book in the field of software engineering and project management, reveals much about the workplace environment in which OS and MVS was crafted. Brooks coined the term "accidental complexity" in an article entitled "No Silver Bullet: Essence and Accidents of Software Engineering," which appeared in the April 1987 issue of *Computer.*

The DFDSS Utility

A.1 The Data Facility Family
A.2 What Is DFDSS?
A.3 Accessing DFDSS Using JCL
A.4 Accessing DFDSS Using ISMF
A.5 DFDSS Logical and Physical Processing
A.6 How DFDSS Interacts with DFSMS
A.7 Printing Disk Data for Analysis
A.8 Filtering (Selecting) by Data Set Names with * and %
A.9 Filtering by Data Set Characteristics
A.10 COPY: Moving Data
A.11 COPY Support for SMS Data Sets
A.12 CONVERTV: Converting Disk Volumes to SMS-Managed
A.13 DUMP: Backing Up Data
A.14 COPYDUMP: Making Multiple Copies of Backup Data
A.15 RESTORE: Restoring Backup Data to Disk
A.16 COMPRESS and RELEASE: Managing Disk Space
A.17 DEFRAG: Defragmenting Disk Space
A.18 DFDSS Abbreviations and Acronyms
A.19 IBM Reference Materials Documenting DFDSS

A.1 The Data Facility Family

DFDSS is part of the Data Facility family of system software products, all of which deal with data management functions such as space allocation, space availability, and disk performance. DFSMS—the Storage Management Subsystem—simplifies the management and use of disk (and tape storage) by providing device independence. DFHSM—the Hierarchical Storage Management Subsystem—automates disk space management by creating backups and migrating data sets between disk and tape according to criteria established locally.

This appendix is intended to acclimate you to the wide range of data set housekeeping functions that can be accomplished using DFDSS. Since an appendix of this size cannot fully document all DFDSS command coding variations, additional readings in IBM reference manuals are suggested at its end.

This appendix was written in collaboration with Jim Turk, storage management consultant. Jim reviewed the manuscript for this appendix and prepared the content of the figures necessary to provide a concise highlight of DFDSS functionality.

A.2 What Is DFDSS?

IBM refers to DFDSS as the "primary data mover" of the Data Facility family. DFDSS helps you to copy or move data between like and unlike direct access (disk) storage devices, back up ("dump") and restore data, compress partitioned data sets, release unused disk space, and defragment disk volumes. DFDSS also converts data sets to and from the Storage Management Subsystem. DFDSS was designed for long-term use in the MVS/ESA environment and supports data set expiration dates beyond the year 1999. The actual name of the DFDSS program is ADRDSSU. In keeping with IBM's naming convention for informational and error messages, all messages from DFDSS begin with the letters "ADR," and the last four letters of the name stand for "data set services utility."

As a whole, DFDSS, DFSMS, and DFHSM make it easier for disk space management personnel to centralize and control the vast quantity of disk space installed in many mainframe installations. Because DFDSS is designed to support the activities of disk space managers and systems programmers as well as programmers, certain DFDSS commands and keywords can be protected against unauthorized use. If you are an applications programmer, your TSO user id or job names may not have sufficient privilege to use the complete range of DFDSS control statements, and you may not be able to use ISMF, the Interactive Storage Management Facility. In that case, regard this appendix as a "broadening" resource that can help you gain a perspective on powerful elements of the mainframe environment outside of your immediate purview.

DFDSS is a relatively new utility. Some specific coordination requirements exist for operating system and support software versions. For example, the Storage Management Subsystem (DFSMS) is not supported by DFDSS versions and releases prior to DFDSS Version 2 Release 4. Users of MVS/XA DFP Version 2 Release 2 or a later release must also install at least DFDSS Version 2 Release 2 or a later release for DFDSS to use it to process VSAM data sets.

A.3 Accessing DFDSS Using JCL

You can use job control language (JCL) statements to invoke DFDSS and to define the data sets that DFDSS accesses. As with all IBM utilities, control statements read by DFDSS at its //SYSIN DD statement control its execution, and it echoes back your control statements and writes a status report at SYSPRINT. The control statements specify one or more tasks that DFDSS is to perform. Figure A.1 shows you the general format of JCL used to invoke DFDSS.

A.4 Accessing DFDSS Using ISMF

Instead of using job control language, you can use the Interactive Storage Management Facility (ISMF), accessed from TSO, to form and submit the DFDSS COPY, DEFRAG, DUMP, RESTORE, COMPRESS, RELEASE, and CONVERTV commands, as shown in Figures A.2 through A.9. ISMF uses the information you supply on ISMF screens to build and submit job control language similar to the JCL you could write manually, shown in Figure A.10. As you can see in Figure A.8, you can either

```
EDIT ---- CSCJGJ.ADV.CNTL(A01) - 01.00 ---------------------- COLUMNS 001 072
COMMAND ===>                                                  SCROLL ===> PAGE
****** ***************************** TOP OF DATA ******************************
000100 //CSCJGJA   JOB 1,                    ACCOUNTING INFORMATION
000200 //  'BIN 7--JANOSSY',                 PROGRAMMER NAME AND DELIVERY BIN
000300 //  CLASS=A,                          INPUT QUEUE CLASS
000400 //  MSGLEVEL=(1,1),                   HOW MUCH MVS SYSTEM PRINT DESIRED
000500 //  MSGCLASS=X,                       PRINT DESTINATION X A L N OR O
000600 //  TIME=(5,0),                       ALLOW JOB TO RUN 5 MINUTES
000700 //* TYPRUN=SCAN,                      UNCOMMENT THIS LINE TO DO SCAN ONLY
000800 //  NOTIFY=CSCJGJ                     WHO TO TELL WHEN JOB IS DONE
000900 //*
001000 //*-----------------------------------------------------------------
001100 //* COPY AN ENTIRE DISK VOLUME
001200 //*-----------------------------------------------------------------
001300 //STEP010  EXEC  PGM=ADRDSSU,
001400 //  REGION=6M,
001500 //  PARM='UTILMSG=YES'
001600 //SYSPRINT   DD  SYSOUT=*
001700 //INDD1      DD  UNIT=3380,
001800 //  VOL=SER=VOL000,
001900 //  DISP=SHR
002000 //OUTDD1     DD  UNIT=3380,
002100 //  VOL=SER=VOL001,
002200 //  DISP=SHR
002300 //SYSIN      DD  *
002400     COPY       FULL                   -
002500                INDDNAME(INDD1)        -
002600                OUTDDNAME(OUTDD1)      -
002700                CPYV                   -
002800                ALLE                   -
002900                ALLDATA(*)
003000 //
```

UTILMSG = YES tells ADRDDSSU (the DFDSS utility) to print messages issued by other utilities it may call, such as ICKDSF. **CPYV** says "copy the input volume serial number to the output disk." **ALLE** copies all allocated space for each data set rather than just space actually used. **ALLDATA** forces empty data sets to be copied.

Figure A.1 General JCL Format and ddnames for DFDSS

```
                         ISMF PRIMARY OPTION MENU
ENTER SELECTION OR COMMAND ===> 2

SELECT ONE OF THE FOLLOWING:

 0  ISMF PROFILE               - Change ISMF user profile
 1  DATA SET                   - Perform Functions Against Data Sets
 2  VOLUME                     - Perform Functions Against Volumes
 3  MANAGEMENT CLASS           - Specify Data Set Backup and Migration Criteria
 4  DATA CLASS                 - Specify Data Set Allocation Parameters
 5  STORAGE CLASS              - Specify Data Set Performance and Availability
 6  STORAGE GROUP              - Specify Volume Names and Free Space Thresholds
 7  AUTOMATIC CLASS SELECTION  - Specify ACS Routines and Test Criteria
 8  CONTROL DATA SET           - Specify System Names and Default Criteria
 9  AGGREGATE GROUP            - Specify Data Set Recovery Parameters
10  LIBRARY MANAGEMENT         - Specify Library and Drive Configuration
 C  DATA COLLECTION            - Process Data Collection Function
 L  LIST                       - Perform Functions Against Saved ISMF Lists
 X  EXIT                       - Terminate ISMF

USE HELP COMMAND FOR HELP; USE END COMMAND TO EXIT.
```

Figure A.2 Accessing ISMF to Form DFDSS Control Statements

```
                        VOLUME LIST SELECTION MENU
ENTER SELECTION OR COMMAND ===> 1

SELECT ONE OF THE FOLLOWING:

 1  DASD                 - Generate a list of DASD volumes
 2  MOUNTABLE OPTICAL    - Generate a list of Mountable Optical volumes









USE HELP COMMAND FOR HELP; USE END COMMAND TO EXIT.
```

Figure A.3 Selecting Disk (DASD) Functions Within ISMF

```
                      VOLUME SELECTION ENTRY PANEL              Page 1 of 3
COMMAND ===>

SELECT SOURCE TO GENERATE VOLUME LIST ===> 2   (1 - Saved list, 2 - New list)

    1  GENERATE FROM A SAVED LIST
         LIST NAME ===>
    2  GENERATE A NEW LIST FROM CRITERIA BELOW
         SPECIFY SOURCE OF THE NEW LIST ===> 1  (1 - Physical, 2 - SMS)

         OPTIONALLY SPECIFY ONE OR MORE:
           TYPE OF VOLUME LIST     ===> 1        (1-Online,2-Not Online,3-Either)
           VOLUME SERIAL NUMBER    ===> VOL00*   (fully or partially specified)
           DEVICE TYPE             ===>          (fully or partially specified)
           DEVICE NUMBER           ===>          (fully specified)
             TO DEVICE NUMBER      ===>          (for range of devices)
           ACQUIRE PHYSICAL DATA   ===> Y        (Y or N)
           ACQUIRE SPACE DATA      ===> Y        (Y or N)
           STORAGE GROUP NAME      ===>          (fully or partially specified)
           CDS NAME  ===>
                                                 (fully specified or 'ACTIVE')

USE ENTER TO PERFORM SELECTION; USE DOWN COMMAND TO VIEW NEXT SELECTION PANEL;
USE HELP COMMAND FOR HELP; USE END COMMAND TO EXIT.
```

Figure A.4 Asking for a List of Disk Volumes that Meet Specific Criteria

```
                                VOLUME LIST
COMMAND ===>                                                SCROLL ===> PAGE
                                                         Entries 1-3 of 3
ENTER LINE OPERATORS BELOW:                              Data Columns 3-8 of 39

    LINE        VOLUME  FREE        %    ALLOC     FRAG   LARGEST   FREE
    OPERATOR    SERIAL  SPACE      FREE  SPACE     INDEX  EXTENT    EXTENTS
    ---(1)----  -(2)--  --(3)--    (4)-  --(5)--   -(6)-  --(7)--   --(8)--
    copy        VOL000  2749034     99     22466       0  2748259         2
                VOL001  1839311    100      8356       0  1838537         2
                VOL002  1254964     45   1516536       0  1254189         2
   ----------   ------  -----------  BOTTOM  OF  DATA  -----------  ------  ----









USE HELP COMMAND FOR HELP; USE END COMMAND TO EXIT.
```

Figure A.5 Selecting Volumes to Process from the List

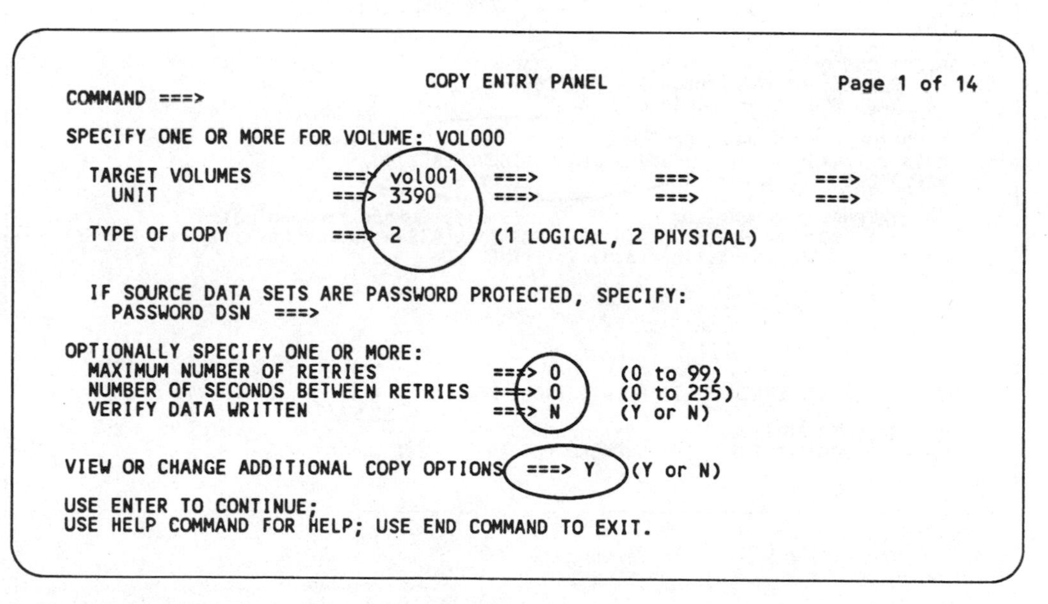

```
                              COPY ENTRY PANEL                    Page 1 of 14
COMMAND ===>

SPECIFY ONE OR MORE FOR VOLUME: VOL000

  TARGET VOLUMES        ===> vol001   ===>         ===>          ===>
    UNIT                ===> 3390     ===>         ===>          ===>

  TYPE OF COPY          ===> 2        (1 LOGICAL, 2 PHYSICAL)

  IF SOURCE DATA SETS ARE PASSWORD PROTECTED, SPECIFY:
    PASSWORD DSN   ===>

OPTIONALLY SPECIFY ONE OR MORE:
  MAXIMUM NUMBER OF RETRIES                ===> 0      (0 to 99)
  NUMBER OF SECONDS BETWEEN RETRIES        ===> 0      (0 to 255)
  VERIFY DATA WRITTEN                      ===> N      (Y or N)

VIEW OR CHANGE ADDITIONAL COPY OPTIONS ===> Y   (Y or N)

USE ENTER TO CONTINUE;
USE HELP COMMAND FOR HELP; USE END COMMAND TO EXIT.
```

Figure A.6 Specifying the Destination ("Target") for a Copy

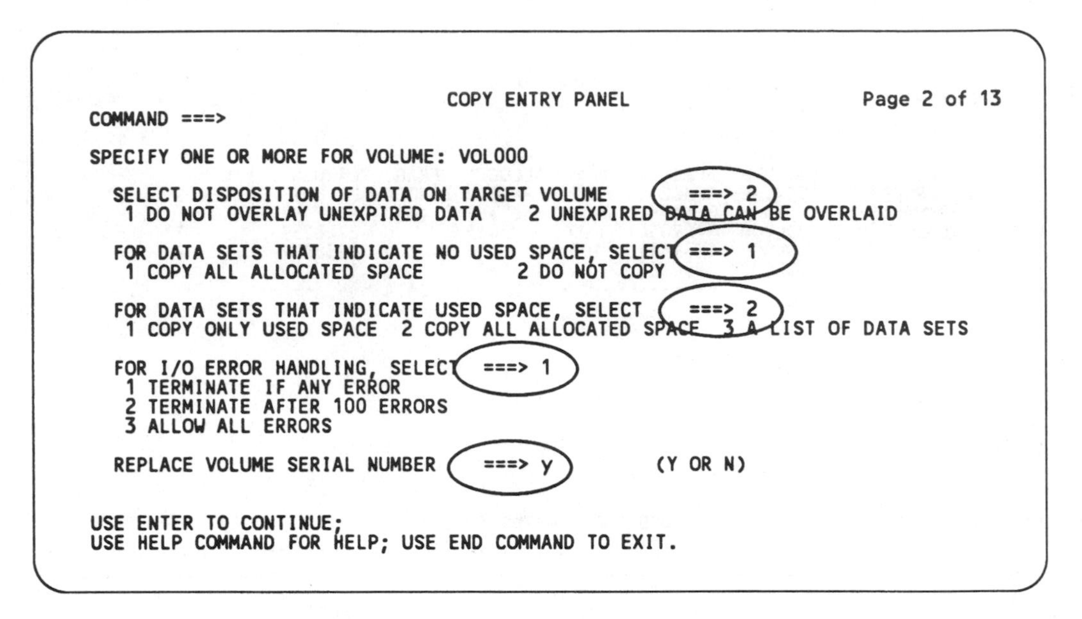

```
                                COPY ENTRY PANEL                      Page 2 of 13
COMMAND ===>

SPECIFY ONE OR MORE FOR VOLUME: VOL000

  SELECT DISPOSITION OF DATA ON TARGET VOLUME            ===> 2
   1 DO NOT OVERLAY UNEXPIRED DATA     2 UNEXPIRED DATA CAN BE OVERLAID

  FOR DATA SETS THAT INDICATE NO USED SPACE, SELECT ===> 1
   1 COPY ALL ALLOCATED SPACE          2 DO NOT COPY

  FOR DATA SETS THAT INDICATE USED SPACE, SELECT    ===> 2
   1 COPY ONLY USED SPACE  2 COPY ALL ALLOCATED SPACE  3 A LIST OF DATA SETS

  FOR I/O ERROR HANDLING, SELECT  ===> 1
   1 TERMINATE IF ANY ERROR
   2 TERMINATE AFTER 100 ERRORS
   3 ALLOW ALL ERRORS

  REPLACE VOLUME SERIAL NUMBER    ===> y           (Y OR N)

USE ENTER TO CONTINUE;
USE HELP COMMAND FOR HELP; USE END COMMAND TO EXIT.
```

Figure A.7 Entering Information About the Target Volumes for a Copy

```
                     COPY JOB SUBMISSION ENTRY PANEL
COMMAND ===>

SELECT ONE OF THE FOLLOWING ===> 2
  1  SUBMIT JOB FOR BACKGROUND PROCESSING
  2  SAVE GENERATED JOB IN A DATA SET

IF OPTION "2" IS SELECTED, SPECIFY:
 DATA SET NAME     ===> 'CSCJGJ.DFDSS.FIGURE9(A02JCL)'
 REPLACE CONTENTS ===> N               (Y or N)

JOB STATEMENT INFORMATION:              (verify before proceeding)
  ===> //CSCJGJA    JOB 1,'BIN 7--JANOSSY',CLASS=A,MSGLEVEL=(1,1),
  ===> //  MSGCLASS=X,TIME=(3,0),NOTIFY=CSCJGJ
  ===> //*
  ===> //*
  ===> //*
  ===> //*
  ===> //*

VIEW OR CHANGE EXECUTE STATEMENTS FROM PROFILE ===> Y       (Y or N)

USE ENTER TO CONTINUE;
USE HELP COMMAND FOR HELP; USE END COMMAND TO EXIT.
```

Figure A.8 Entering Job Submission Instructions to ISMF

have ISMF submit JCL generated this way or save it in a library and submit it yourself later.

For more information on using DFDSS with ISMF, see the ISMF on-line help screens built into ISMF itself, by pressing the *<PF1>* key within ISMF. The on-line help screens provide the most current information on the way ISMF handles your interactive requests for DFDSS services.

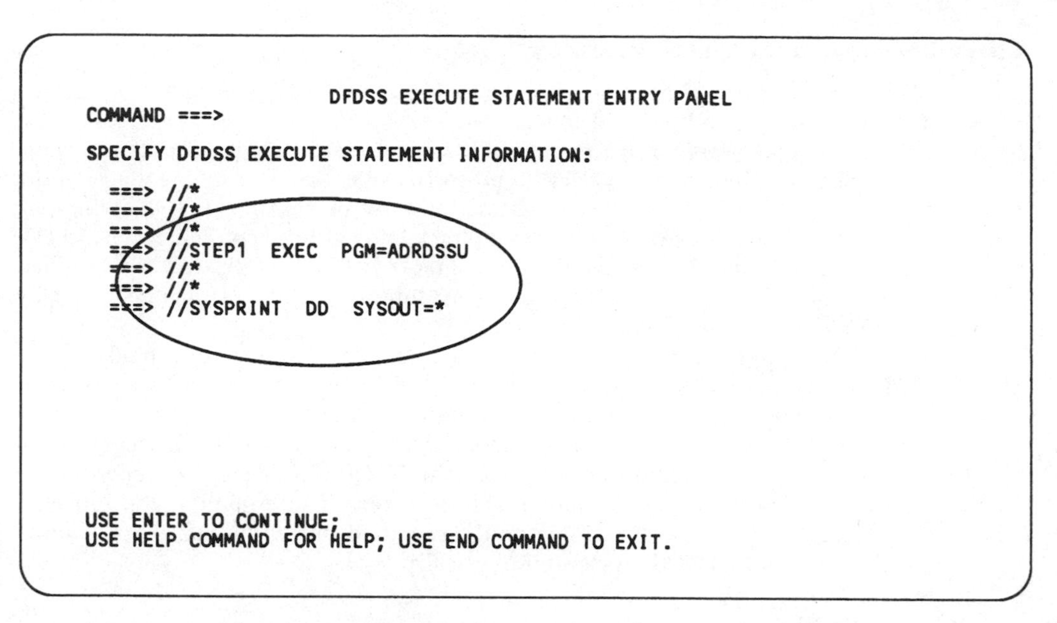

```
                        DFDSS EXECUTE STATEMENT ENTRY PANEL
COMMAND ===>

SPECIFY DFDSS EXECUTE STATEMENT INFORMATION:

  ===> //*
  ===> //*
  ===> //*
  ===> //STEP1   EXEC   PGM=ADRDSSU
  ===> //*
  ===> //*
  ===> //SYSPRINT   DD   SYSOUT=*

USE ENTER TO CONTINUE;
USE HELP COMMAND FOR HELP; USE END COMMAND TO EXIT.
```

Figure A.9 Entering Job Submission EXEC and DD Statements for DFDSS Submission

```
EDIT ---- CSCJGJ.DFDSS.FIGURE9(A02JCL)) - 01.00 -------------- COLUMNS 001 072
COMMAND ===>                                                   SCROLL ===> PAGE
****** ****************************** TOP OF DATA ******************************
000100 //CSCJGJA    JOB 1,'BIN 7--JANOSSY',CLASS=A,MSGLEVEL=(1,1),
000200 //  MSGCLASS=X,TIME=(3,0),NOTIFY=CSCJGJ
000300 //*
000400 //*
000500 //*
000600 //*
000700 //*
000800 //*
000900 //*
001000 //STEP1  EXEC  PGM=ADRDSSU
001100 //SYSPRINT  DD  SYSOUT=*
001200 //INVOL1     DD  VOL=SER=VOL000,UNIT=3390,DISP=SHR
001300 //OUTVOL1    DD  VOL=SER=VOL001,UNIT=3390,DISP=SHR
001400 //SYSIN      DD  *
001500        COPY  FULL -
001600              INDDNAME(INVOL1) -
001700              OUTDDNAME(OUTVOL1) -
001800              ALLDATA(*) -
001900              ALLEXCP -
002000              CANCELERROR -
002100              COPYVOLID -
002200              PURGE -
002300              WAIT(0,0)
002400 //
```

The ISMF screens help you build JCL to submit a run of the DFDSS utility. Ultimately the choices you make on ISMF screen lead to the formation of JCL such as this, which you can save and continue to tailor directly. If you prefer, you can code JCL like this yourself, without the aid of ISMF.

Figure A.10 JCL Constructed by ISMF from Information Gathered in Figures A.6, A.7, A.8, and A.9

A.5 DFDSS Logical and Physical Processing

DFDSS can perform either logical or physical processing. Each type of processing offers different capabilities and advantages.

When doing ***logical processing,*** DFDSS treats each data set and its associated information as a logical entity. DFDSS processes an entire data set before beginning the next one. DFDSS moves each data set as a set of data records, allowing data movement between devices with different track and cylinder configurations. DFDSS uses the catalog and the volume table of contents (VTOCs) of disk volumes to identify data sets for logical processing. If you dump (back up) a data set logically, DFDSS restores it logically.

During ***physical processing,*** DFDSS moves data in units of disk tracks. In this mode of processing the input and output disk device track sizes must be equal in other words, the processing must be done between "like" devices. Physical processing operates on whole disk volumes, ranges of tracks, or data sets. Physical processing relies only on volume information in the VTOC and VSAM volume data set (VVDS) for data set selection, not data block or record information, and processes only that part of a data set residing on the specified input volume. If you dump a data set physically, DFDSS restores it physically.

A.6 How DFDSS Interacts with DFSMS

Storage Management Subsystem (DFSMS) lets an installation define the way its mainframe allocates storage for each of potentially many categories of data. The categories of data sets are not specified by IBM; local study and decision must be made to group data sets into categories with similar requirements for space, disk availability, and performance. DFSMS provides a way for users of the mainframe to store and retrieve data without having to specify details about disk characteristics.

Automatic Class Selection is the DFSMS mechanism for assigning data sets to devices with various performance levels via DFSMS classes and storage groups, which IBM calls "constructs." When copying, restoring, and converting data, DFDSS invokes the Automatic Class Selection routines developed locally by your data storage management personnel.

A.7 Printing Disk Data for Analysis

You can use DFDSS to print disk-stored data to be able to analyze it in a "dump" format, which provides both hexadecimal and character forms of display. (This function is named "print" and not "dump" because DUMP is the name of another DFDSS function, which copies a data set for backup purposes.) You can print data to the sysout print spool or to a sequential data set as printlines for later printing or viewing. When you use DFDSS to print a data set, its contents are printed in the logical sequence of the data set on the volume, not in the physical sequence of disk cylinder number and disk head number sequence as the data might actually be stored. You can print:

- A non-VSAM data set specified by a full data set name
- VSAM data sets
- Ranges of disk tracks by number
- All or part of a disk volume table of contents (VTOC); you do not have to identify the VTOC location by disk track

```
EDIT ---- CSCJGJ.ADV.CNTL(A03A) - 01.00 --------------------- COLUMNS 001 072
COMMAND ===>                                                   SCROLL ===> PAGE
****** ****************************** TOP OF DATA ******************************
000100 //CSCJGJA   JOB 1,                 ACCOUNTING INFORMATION
000200 //   'BIN 7--JANOSSY',             PROGRAMMER NAME AND DELIVERY BIN
000300 //   CLASS=A,                      INPUT QUEUE CLASS
000400 //   MSGLEVEL=(1,1),               HOW MUCH MVS SYSTEM PRINT DESIRED
000500 //   MSGCLASS=X,                   PRINT DESTINATION X A L N OR O
000600 //   TIME=(0,30),                  SAFETY LIMIT: RUN TIME UP TO 30 SEC
000700 //*  TYPRUN=SCAN,                  UNCOMMENT THIS LINE TO DO SCAN ONLY
000800 //   NOTIFY=CSCJGJ                 WHO TO TELL WHEN JOB IS DONE
000900 //*
001000 //*  JCL TO PRINT A DATA SET IN DUMP FORMAT USING DFDSS
001100 //*  THIS JCL IS STORED AT CSCJGJ.ADV.CNTL(A03A)
001200 //*
001300 //*-----------------------------------------------------------------
001400 //*  PRINT A DATA SET
001500 //*-----------------------------------------------------------------
001600 //STEP010  EXEC  PGM=ADRDSSU,
001700 //   REGION=6M,
001800 //   PARM='UTILMSG=YES'
001900 //SYSPRINT   DD  SYSOUT=*
002000 //SYSIN      DD  *
002100      PRINT      DATASET(CSCJGJ.TEST.DATASET) -
002200                 INDYNAM(VOL000) -
002300                 SHARE
002400 //
```

INDYNAM tells DFDSS to dynamically build the **DCB** for the data set, making it unnecessary to code a **DD** statement for it.

Figure A.11 DFDSS Control Statements to Print a Data Set

For any type of printing, you can optionally print only the disk tracks on which read errors occur. If an error occurs while DFDSS is attempting to read a record, DFDSS attempts to print the contents of the record that is in error.

Figure A.11 shows you how to code DFDSS control statements to print the contents of a sequential data set, while Figure A.12 illustrates the print that results from such a job. Figure A.13 shows you how to print the contents of a disk volume table of contents (VTOC), and Figure A.14 illustrates the print that this produces. You could accomplish each of these things using older utilities such as IEBGENER, IDCAMS, IEHLIST, IEHATLAS, or (in some cases) by using TSO/ISPF. But DFDSS gives you new and powerful ways to select or "filter" data sets to be processed. Figure A.15 shows you how to print the contents of a specific disk track, something you cannot readily do without DFDSS. Figure A.16 illustrates how the contents of a track appear when printed.

```
PAGE 0001 DFDSS 5665-327  DATA FACILITY DATA SET SERVICES V2R5.0  93.323  14:38
   PRINT    DATASET(CSCJGJ.TEST.DATASET) -
            INDYNAM(VOL000) -
            SHARE
ADR101I        RI01 (01), TASKID 001 HAS BEEN ASSIGNED TO COMMAND 'PRINT '
ADR109I        RI01 (01), 93323 14:39:11 INITIAL SCAN OF USER CONTROL STATEMENTS COMPLETED.
ADR016I (001)-PRIME(01), RACF LOGGING OPTION IN EFFECT FOR THIS TASK
ADR006I (001)-SETUP(01), 93323 14:39:34 EXECUTION BEGINS

*** TRACK(CCHH)  0015000D          R0 DATA  0015000D02000000

   COUNT  0015000D01000384
 0000  E3C8C9E2 40C9E240 E3C8C540 C6C9D9E2  E340D3C9 D5C540D6 C640C140 E3C5E2E3  *THIS.IS.THE.FIRST.LINE.OF.A.TEST*
 0020  40C4C1E3 C1E2C5E3 40E6C8C9 C3C840E6  C1E240C3 D9C5C1E3 C5C440E3 D640C4C5  *.DATASET.WHICH.WAS.CREATED.TO.DE*
 0040  D4D6D5E2 E3D9C1E3 C540C4C6 C4E2E240  D7D9C9D5 E34B4040 4040E3C8 C9E240C9  *MONSTRATE.DFDSS.PRINT.....THIS.I*
 0060  E240E3C8 C540E2C5 C3D6D5C4 40D3C9D5  C540D6C6 40C140E3 C5E2E340 C4C1E3C1  *S.THE.SECOND.LINE.OF.A.TEST.DATA*
 0080  E2C5E340 E6C8C9C3 C840E6C1 E240C3D9  C5C1E3C5 C440E3D6 40C4C5D4 D6D5E2E3  *SET.WHICH.WAS.CREATED.TO.DEMONST*
 00A0  D9C1E3C5 40C4C6C4 E2E240D7 D9C9D5E3  4B404040 E3C8C9E2 40C9E240 E3C8C540  *RATE.DFDSS.PRINT....THIS.IS.THE.*
 00C0  E3C8C9D9 C440D3C9 D5C540D6 C640C140  E3C5E2E3 40C4C1E3 C1E2C5E3 40E6C8C9  *THIRD.LINE.OF.A.TEST.DATASET.WHI*
 00E0  C3C840E6 C1E240C3 D9C5C1E3 C5C440E3  D640C4C5 D4D6D5E2 E3D9C1E3 C540C4C6  *CH.WAS.CREATED.TO.DEMONSTRATE.DF*
 0100  C4E2E240 D7D9C9D5 E34B4040 4040E3C8  C9E240C9 E240E3C8 C540C6D6 E4D9E3C8  *DSS.PRINT.....THIS.IS.THE.FOURTH*
 0120  40D3C9D5 C540D6C6 40C140E3 C5E2E340  C4C1E3C1 E2C5E340 E6C8C9C3 C840E6C1  *.LINE.OF.A.TEST.DATASET.WHICH.WA*
 0140  E240C3D9 C5C1E3C5 C440E3D6 40C4C5D4  D6D5E2E3 D9C1E3C5 40C4C6C4 E2E240D7  *S.CREATED.TO.DEMONSTRATE.DFDSS.P*
 0160  D9C9D5E3 4B404040 E3C8C9E2 40C9E240  E3C8C540 C6C9C6E3 C840D3C9 D5C540D6  *RINT....THIS.IS.THE.FIFTH.LINE.O*
 0180  C640C140 E3C5E2E3 40C4C1E3 C1E2C5E3  40E6C8C9 C3C840E6 C1E240C3 D9C5C1E3  *F.A.TEST.DATASET.WHICH.WAS.CREAT*
 01A0  C5C440E3 D640C4C5 D4D6D5E2 E3D9C1E3  C540C4C6 C4E2E240 D7D9C9D5 E34B4040  *ED.TO.DEMONSTRATE.DFDSS.PRINT...*
 01C0  4040E3C8 C9E240C9 E240E3C8 C540E2C9  E7E3C840 D3C9D5C5 40D6C640 C140E3C5  *..THIS.IS.THE.SIXTH.LINE.OF.A.TE*
 01E0  E2E340C4 C1E3C1E2 C5E340E6 C8C9C3C8  40E6C1E2 40C3D9C5 C1E3C5C4 40E3D640  *ST.DATASET.WHICH.WAS.CREATED.TO.*
 0200  C4C5D4D6 D5E2E3D9 C1E3C540 C4C6C4E2  E240D7D9 C9D5E34B 40404040 E3C8C9E2  *DEMONSTRATE.DFDSS.PRINT.....THIS*
 0220  40C9E240 E3C8C540 E2C5E5C5 D5E3C840  D3C9D5C5 40D6C640 C140E3C5 E2E340C4  *.IS.THE.SEVENTH.LINE.OF.A.TEST.D*
 0240  C1E3C1E2 C5E340E6 C8C9C3C8 40E6C1E2  40C3D9C5 C1E3C5C4 40E3D640 C4C5D4D6  *ATASET.WHICH.WAS.CREATED.TO.DEMO*
 0260  D5E2E3D9 C1E3C540 C4C6C4E2 E240D7D9  C9D5E34B 4040E3C8 C9E240C9 E240E3C8  *NSTRATE.DFDSS.PRINT...THIS.IS.TH*
 0280  C540C5C9 C7C8E3C8 40D3C9D5 C540D6C6  40C140E3 C5E2E340 C4C1E3C1 E2C5E340  *E.EIGHTH.LINE.OF.A.TEST.DATASET.*
 02A0  E6C8C9C3 C840E6C1 E240C3D9 C5C1E3C5  C440E3D6 40C4C5D4 D6D5E2E3 D9C1E3C5  *WHICH.WAS.CREATED.TO.DEMONSTRATE*
 02C0  40C4C6C4 E2E240D7 D9C9D5E3 4B404040  E3C8C9E2 40C9E240 E3C8C540 D5C9D5E3  *.DFDSS.PRINT....THIS.IS.THE.NINT*
 02E0  C840D3C9 D5C540D6 C640C140 E3C5E2E3  40C4C1E3 C1E2C5E3 40E6C8C9 C3C840E6  *H.LINE.OF.A.TEST.DATASET.WHICH.W*
 0300  C1E240C3 D9C5C1E3 C5C440E3 D640C4C5  D4D6D5E2 E3D9C1E3 C540C4C6 C4E2E240  *AS.CREATED.TO.DEMONSTRATE.DFDSS.*
 0320  D7D9C9D5 E34B4040 4040E3C8 C9E240C9  E240E3C8 C540E3C5 D5E3C840 D3C9D5C5  *PRINT.....THIS.IS.THE.TENTH.LINE*
 0340  40D6C640 C140E3C5 E2E340C4 C1E3C1E2  C5E340E6 C8C9C3C8 40E6C1E2 40C3D9C5  *.OF.A.TEST.DATASET.WHICH.WAS.CRE*
 0360  C1E3C5C4 40E3D640 C4C5D4D6 D5E2E3D9  C1E3C540 C4C6C4E2 E240D7D9 C9D5E34B  *ATED.TO.DEMONSTRATE.DFDSS.PRINT.*
 0380  40404040                                                                      *....                            *

ADR013I (001)-CLTSK(01), 93323 14:39:49 TASK COMPLETED WITH RETURN CODE 0000
ADR012I        DSSU (01), 93323 14:39:50 DFDSS PROCESSING COMPLETE. HIGHEST RETURN CODE IS 0000
```

Figure A.12 Printed Contents of a Data Set

```
EDIT ---- CSCJGJ.ADV.CNTL(A04A) - 01.00 --------------------- COLUMNS 001 072
COMMAND ===>                                                  SCROLL ===> PAGE
****** ***************************** TOP OF DATA ******************************
000100 //CSCJGJA   JOB 1,                   ACCOUNTING INFORMATION
000200 //   'BIN 7--JANOSSY',               PROGRAMMER NAME AND DELIVERY BIN
000300 //   CLASS=A,                        INPUT QUEUE CLASS
000400 //   MSGLEVEL=(1,1),                 HOW MUCH MVS SYSTEM PRINT DESIRED
000500 //   MSGCLASS=X,                     PRINT DESTINATION X A L N OR O
000600 //   TIME=(1,0),                     SAFETY LIMIT: RUN TIME UP TO 1 MIN
000700 //* TYPRUN=SCAN,                     UNCOMMENT THIS LINE TO DO SCAN ONLY
000800 //   NOTIFY=CSCJGJ                   WHO TO TELL WHEN JOB IS DONE
000900 //*
001000 //* JCL TO PRINT A VTOC IN DUMP FORMAT USING DFDSS
001100 //* THIS JCL IS STORED AT CSCJGJ.ADV.CNTL(A04A)
001200 //*
001300 //*-----------------------------------------------------------------
001400 //* PRINT A DISK VTOC
001500 //*-----------------------------------------------------------------
001600 //STEP010  EXEC  PGM=ADRDSSU,
001700 //   REGION=6M,
001800 //   PARM='UTILMSG=YES'
001900 //SYSPRINT   DD  SYSOUT=*
002000 //SYSIN      DD  *
002100      PRINT    VTOC(1,1) -
002200               INDYNAM(NSW300)
002300 //
```

Figure A.13 DFDSS Control Statements to Print a VTOC

```
PAGE 0001 DFDSS 5665-327  DATA FACILITY DATA SET SERVICES V2R5.0  93.323   15:09
   PRINT    VTOC(1,1) -
            INDYNAM(NSW300)
ADR101I        RI01 (01), TASKID 001 HAS BEEN ASSIGNED TO COMMAND 'PRINT '
ADR109I        RI01 (01), 93323 15:10:11 INITIAL SCAN OF USER CONTROL STATEMENTS COMPLETED.
ADR016I (001)-PRIME(01), RACF LOGGING OPTION IN EFFECT FOR THIS TASK
ADR006I (001)-SETUP(01), 93323 15:10:16 EXECUTION BEGINS

*** TRACK(CCHH)  00030000         R0 DATA  0000000000000000

    COUNT  00030000012C0060
 0000  04040404 04040404 04040404 04040404  04040404 04040404 04040404 04040404  *................................*
 0020  04040404 04040404 04040404 F4000A00  0E3516E3 0D0B0000 000F8901 C0000D0C  *............4......T......i.{...*
 0040  000FBB60 00000020 0000352E 00000000  00000000 00000000 00000000 00000000  *...-............................*
 0060  00000000 00000000 00010000 03000000  0A000E00 00000000 00000000 00000000  *................................*
 0080  00000000 00000000 00000000                                                *............                    *

    COUNT  00030000022C0060
 0000  05050505 00000000 00000000 00000000  00000000 00000000 00000000 00000000  *................................*
 0020  00000000 00000000 00000000 F5000000  00000000 00000000 00000000 00000000  *............5...................*
 0040  00000000 00000000 00000000 00000000  00000000 00000000 00000000 00000000  *................................*
 0060  TO  007F    SAME AS ABOVE
 0080  00000000 00000000 00000000                                                *............                    *

   -
   -
   -

    COUNT  00030000352C0060
 0000  C9E2C7C7 D2F04BE2 D7C6D3D6 C7F14BD3  C9E2E340 40404040 40404040 40404040  *ISGGK0.SPFLOG1.LIST.............*
 0020  40404040 40404040 40404040 F1D5E2E6  F3F0F000 015D0143 00000001 0000C9C2  *............1NSW300..)........IB*
 0040  D4D6E2E5 E2F24040 4040405D 01438080  00814000 44000081 007D0000 00825000  *MOSVS2.....).....a.....a.'...b&.*
 0060  02330000 16880000 00010000 3C000300  3C000A00 00000000 00000000 00000000  *.....h..........................*
 0080  00000000 00000000 00000000                                                *............                    *

ADR013I (001)-CLTSK(01), 93323 15:10:32 TASK COMPLETED WITH RETURN CODE 0000
ADR012I        DSSU (01), 93323 15:10:32 DFDSS PROCESSING COMPLETE. HIGHEST RETURN CODE IS 0000
```

Figure A.14 Printed Contents of a VTOC

```
EDIT ---- CSCJGJ.ADV.CNTL(A05A) - 01.00 ---------------------- COLUMNS 001 072
COMMAND ===>                                                   SCROLL ===> PAGE
****** ******************************* TOP OF DATA ******************************
000100 //CSCJGJA   JOB 1,                  ACCOUNTING INFORMATION
000200 //   'BIN 7--JANOSSY',              PROGRAMMER NAME AND DELIVERY BIN
000300 //   CLASS=A,                       INPUT QUEUE CLASS
000400 //   MSGLEVEL=(1,1),                HOW MUCH MVS SYSTEM PRINT DESIRED
000500 //   MSGCLASS=X,                    PRINT DESTINATION X A L N OR O
000600 //   TIME=(3,0),                    SAFETY LIMIT: RUN TIME UP TO 3 MIN
000700 //*  TYPRUN=SCAN,                   UNCOMMENT THIS LINE TO DO SCAN ONLY
000800 //   NOTIFY=CSCJGJ                  WHO TO TELL WHEN JOB IS DONE
000900 //*
001000 //* JCL TO PRINT A PHYSICAL DISK TRACK USING DFDSS
001100 //* THIS JCL IS STORED AT CSCJGJ.ADV.CNTL(A05A)
001200 //*
001300 //*-----------------------------------------------------------------
001400 //* PRINT A TRACK
001500 //*-----------------------------------------------------------------
001600 //STEP010  EXEC  PGM=ADRDSSU,
001700 //   REGION=6M,
001800 //   PARM='UTILMSG=YES'
001900 //SYSPRINT   DD  SYSOUT=*
002000 //SYSIN      DD  *
002100     PRINT    TRACKS (55,1) -
002200              INDYNAM(NSW300)
002300 //
```

Figure A.15 DFDSS Control Statements to Print a Track

```
PAGE 0001 DFDSS 5665-327  DATA FACILITY DATA SET SERVICES V2R5.0  93.326  09:57

  PRINT    TRACKS (55,1) -
           INDYNAM(NSW300)

ADR101I        RI01 (01), TASKID 001 HAS BEEN ASSIGNED TO COMMAND 'PRINT '
ADR109I        RI01 (01), 93326 09:57:06 INITIAL SCAN OF USER CONTROL STATEMENTS COMPLETED.
ADR016I (001)-PRIME(01), RACF LOGGING OPTION IN EFFECT FOR THIS TASK
ADR006I (001)-SETUP(01), 93326 09:57:06 EXECUTION BEGINS

*** TRACK(CCHH)  00370001          R0 DATA  0037000102000000

    COUNT  0037000101001000
 0000  C3F5C4F5 F2F0F6F4 F0F0F4F0 F0F0F0F1  F0F0F2F4 F5F1F6F8 F7F6F7F9 F4F6F2F1  *C5D52064004000010024516876794621*
 0020  C4C4E240 C3F5C4F5 F2F0F6F4 F0F0F4F0  F0F0F0F2 F0F0F2F4 F5F1F6F8 F7F6F7F9  *DDS.C5D5206400400002002451687679*
 0040  F4F6F2F2 C4C4E240 C3F5C4F6 F3F0F8F9  F0F0F0F4 F0F0F0F1 F0F0F2F5 F5F6F1F1  *4622DDS.C5D630890004000100255611*
 0060  F7F6F8F3 F4F5F2F4 C4C4E240 C3F5C4F6  F3F0F8F9 F0F0F0F4 F0F0F0F2 F0F0F2F5  *76834524DDS.C5D63089000400020025*
 0080  F5F6F1F1 F7F6F8F3 F4F5F5F1 C4C4E240  C3F5C5F7 F5F5F2F2 F0F0F0F1 F0F0F0F1  *561176834551DDS.C5E7552200010001*
 00A0  F0F0F2F2 F4F4F2F0 F7F6F7F6 F8F8F7F2  C4C4E240 C3F5C5F7 F5F5F2F2 F0F0F0F1  *0022442076768872DDS.C5E755220001*
 00C0  F0F0F0F2 F0F0F2F2 F4F4F2F0 F7F6F7F6  F8F8F7F3 C4C4E240 C3F5C5F7 F9F6F3F9  *00020022442076768873DDS.C5E79639*
 00E0  F0F0F0F1 F0F0F0F1 F0F0F6F0 F4F0F5F3  F7F6F7F7 F4F9F5F0 C4C4E240 C3F5C5F7  *000100010060405376774950DDS.C5E7*
 0100  F9F6F3F9 F0F0F0F1 F0F0F0F2 F0F0F6F0  F4F0F5F3 F7F6F7F7 F4F9F5F7 C4C4E240  *9639000100020060405376774957DDS.*
 0120  C3F5C5F8 F0F6F0F1 F0F0F0F1 F0F0F0F1  F0F0F2F0 F3F5F4F2 F7F6F7F7 F6F4F5F0  *C5E80601000100010020354276776450*
 0140  C4C4E240 C3F5C5F8 F0F6F0F1 F0F0F0F1  F0F0F0F2 F0F0F2F0 F3F5F4F2 F7F6F7F7  *DDS.C5E8060100010002002035427677*
 0160  F6F4F6F5 C4C4E240 C3F5C5F8 F1F5F5F4  F0F0F0F1 F0F0F0F1 F0F0F2F8 F4F6F8F5  *6465DDS.C5E815540001000100284685*
 0180  F7F6F7F7 F7F8F9F6 C4C4E240 C3F5C5F8  F1F5F5F4 F0F0F0F1 F0F0F0F2 F0F0F2F8  *76777896DDS.C5E81554000100020028*
 01A0  F4F6F8F5 F7F6F7F7 F8F1F5F5 C4C4E240  C3F5C5F8 F4F2F3F0 F0F0F0F1 F0F0F0F1  *468576778155DDS.C5E8423000010001*
 01C0  F0F0F6F0 F7F4F5F5 F7F6F7F8 F1F9F5F8  C4C4E240 C3F5C5F8 F4F2F3F0 F0F0F0F1  *0060745576781958DDS.C5E842300001*
 01E0  F0F0F0F2 F0F0F6F0 F7F4F5F5 F7F6F7F8  F2F0F1F3 C4C4E240 C3F5C5F8 F7F7F9F2  *00020060745576782013DDS.C5E87792*
 0200  F0F0F0F2 F0F0F0F1 F0F0F6F0 F9F6F4F9  F7F6F8F1 F0F4F9F6 C4C4E240 C3F5C5F8  *000200010060964976810496DDS.C5E8*
 0220  F7F7F9F2 F0F0F0F2 F0F0F0F2 F0F0F6F0  F9F6F4F9 F7F6F8F1 F0F5F1F8 C4C4E240  *7792000200020060964976810518DDS.*
 0240  C3F5C5F9 F0F3F6F1 F0F0F0F1 F0F0F0F1  F0F0F1F3 F8F8F1F6 F7F6F7F9 F1F5F2F8  *C5E90361000100010013881676791528*
 0260  C4C4E240 C3F5C5F9 F0F3F6F1 F0F0F0F1  F0F0F0F2 F0F0F1F3 F8F8F1F6 F7F6F7F9  *DDS.C5E9036100010002001388167679*
 0280  F1F5F3F2 C4C4E240 C3F5C5F9 F0F4F0F9  F0F0F0F1 F0F0F0F1 F0F0F1F4 F8F9F2F3  *1532DDS.C5E904090001000100148923*
 02A0  F7F6F7F9 F1F6F0F0 C4C4E240 C3F5C5F9  F0F4F0F9 F0F0F0F1 F0F0F0F2 F0F0F1F4  *76791600DDS.C5E90409000100020014*
 02C0  F8F9F2F3 F7F6F7F9 F1F6F0F3 C4C4E240  C3F5C5F9 F0F7F5F3 F0F0F0F1 F0F0F0F1  *892376791603DDS.C5E9075300010001*
 02E0  F0F0F1F4 F8F9F2F3 F7F6F7F9 F2F5F1F4  C4C4E240 C3F5C5F9 F0F7F5F3 F0F0F0F1  *0014892376792514DDS.C5E907530001*
 0300  F0F0F0F2 F0F0F1F4 F8F9F2F3 F7F6F7F9  F2F5F2F7 C4C4E240 C3F5C5F9 F0F7F7F5  *00020014892376792527DDS.C5E90775*
 0320  F0F0F0F1 F0F0F0F1 F0F0F1F4 F8F9F2F3  F7F6F7F9 F2F2F0F5 C4C4E240 C3F5C5F9  *000100010014892376792205DDS.C5E9*
   -
   -
   -
```

Figure A.16 Printed Contents of a Track

A.8 Filtering (Selecting) by Data Set Names with * and %

You can select data sets for inclusion in or exclusion from DFDSS processing on the basis of their full data set names, or by partial names. IBM refers to selecting by partial names as "filtering." The % character acts as a place holder for DFDSS data set name filtering, and the * character acts as a wildcard. Figures A.17, A.18, A.19, A.20, and A.21 show you some examples of data set selection using data set name filtering.

```
EDIT ---- CSCJGJ.ADV.CNTL(A06A) - 01.00 --------------------- COLUMNS 001 072
COMMAND ===>                                                  SCROLL ===> PAGE
****** ****************************** TOP OF DATA ******************************
000100 //CSCJGJA   JOB 1,                        ACCOUNTING INFORMATION
000200 //  'BIN 7--JANOSSY',                     PROGRAMMER NAME AND DELIVERY BIN
000300 //  CLASS=A,                              INPUT QUEUE CLASS
000400 //  MSGLEVEL=(1,1),                       HOW MUCH MVS SYSTEM PRINT DESIRED
000500 //  MSGCLASS=X,                           PRINT DESTINATION X A L N OR O
000600 //  TIME=(3,0),                           SAFETY LIMIT: RUN TIME UP TO 3 MIN
000700 //* TYPRUN=SCAN,                          UNCOMMENT THIS LINE TO DO SCAN ONLY
000800 //  NOTIFY=CSCJGJ                         WHO TO TELL WHEN JOB IS DONE
000900 //*
001000 //* THIS JCL IS STORED AT CSCJGJ.ADV.CNTL(A06A)
001100 //*
001200 //*-----------------------------------------------------------------
001300 //* COPY DATA SETS THAT BEGIN WITH 'CSCJGJ' REGARDLESS OF THE
001400 //* NUMBER OF NODES OR THE VALUES OF THOSE NODES
001500 //*-----------------------------------------------------------------
001600 //STEP010  EXEC  PGM=ADRDSSU,
001700 //  REGION=4M,
001800 //  PARM='TYPRUN=NORUN'
001900 //SYSPRINT   DD   SYSOUT=*
002000 //SYSIN      DD   *
002100     COPY       DATASET( INCLUDE( CSCJGJ.** )  ) -
002200                OUTDYNAM(VOL000) -
002300                REBLOCK(**) -
002400                CANCELERROR -
002500                CATALOG -
002600                DELETE PURGE -
002700                TGTALLOC(TRK) -
002800                WAIT(2,2)
002900 //
```

The ** here at CSCJGJ is the wildcard that lets you specify that any number and value of remaining data set name parts is acceptable for selection. The comment "node" here refers to data set name parts. Examples of data set names selected for processing by this coding:

CSCJGJ.PRINT
CSCJGJ.CSC.LOADLIB
CSCJGJ.X
CSCJGJ.ADV.CNTL.NEWCOPY

*Figure A.17 Using the * as a Wildcard Filter*

```
EDIT ---- CSCJGJ.ADV.CNTL(A06B) - 01.00 --------------------- COLUMNS 001 072
COMMAND ===>                                                  SCROLL ===> PAGE
****** ***************************** TOP OF DATA ******************************
000100 //CSCJGJA   JOB 1,                    ACCOUNTING INFORMATION
000200 //   'BIN 7--JANOSSY',                PROGRAMMER NAME AND DELIVERY BIN
000300 //   CLASS=A,                         INPUT QUEUE CLASS
000400 //   MSGLEVEL=(1,1),                  HOW MUCH MVS SYSTEM PRINT DESIRED
000500 //   MSGCLASS=X,                      PRINT DESTINATION X A L N OR O
000600 //   TIME=(3,0),                      SAFETY LIMIT: RUN TIME UP TO 3 MIN
000700 //*  TYPRUN=SCAN,                     UNCOMMENT THIS LINE TO DO SCAN ONLY
000800 //   NOTIFY=CSCJGJ                    WHO TO TELL WHEN JOB IS DONE
000900 //*
001000 //* THIS JCL IS STORED AT CSCJGJ.ADV.CNTL(A06B)
001100 //*
001200 //*-----------------------------------------------------------------
001300 //* COPY ALL DATASETS THAT START WITH 'CSCJGJ.T.' OR CSCJGJ.P.'
001400 //* ANY ADDITIONAL NODES MAY HAVE ANY VALUES
001500 //*-----------------------------------------------------------------
001600 //STEP010  EXEC  PGM=ADRDSSU,
001700 //   REGION=4M,
001800 //   PARM='TYPRUN=NORUN'
001900 //SYSPRINT   DD   SYSOUT=*
002000 //SYSIN      DD    *
002100      COPY      DATASET(                  -
002200                  INCLUDE(                -
002300                          CSCJGJ.T.**     -
002400                          CSCJGJ.P.**     -
002500                          ))              -
002600                OUTDYNAM(VOL000)          -
002700                REBLOCK(**)               -
002800                CANCELERROR               -
002900                CATALOG                   -
003000                DELETE PURGE              -
003100                TGTALLOC(TRK)             -
003200                WAIT(2,2)
003300 //
```

The ** here at CSCJGJ is the wildcard that lets you specify that any number and value of remaining data set name parts is acceptable for selection. The comment "node" here refers to data set name parts.

*Figure A.18 Using the * as a Wildcard Filter and Concatenating Data Sets*

```
EDIT ---- CSCJGJ.ADV.CNTL(A06C) - 01.00 --------------------- COLUMNS 001 072
COMMAND ===>                                                  SCROLL ===> PAGE
****** ***************************** TOP OF DATA ******************************
000100 //CSCJGJA   JOB 1,                 ACCOUNTING INFORMATION
000200 //   'BIN 7--JANOSSY',             PROGRAMMER NAME AND DELIVERY BIN
000300 //   CLASS=A,                      INPUT QUEUE CLASS
000400 //   MSGLEVEL=(1,1),               HOW MUCH MVS SYSTEM PRINT DESIRED
000500 //   MSGCLASS=X,                   PRINT DESTINATION X A L N OR O
000600 //   TIME=(3,0),                   SAFETY LIMIT: RUN TIME UP TO 3 MIN
000700 //*  TYPRUN=SCAN,                  UNCOMMENT THIS LINE TO DO SCAN ONLY
000800 //   NOTIFY=CSCJGJ                 WHO TO TELL WHEN JOB IS DONE
000900 //*
001000 //* THIS JCL IS STORED AT CSCJGJ.ADV.CNTL(A06C)
001100 //*
001200 //*-------------------------------------------------------------------
001300 //* COPY ALL DATASETS THAT START WITH 'CSCJGJ', HAVE A SECOND NODE
001400 //* OF EXACTLY ONE CHARACTER, ANY REMAINING NODES CAN HAVE ANY VALUES
001500 //*-------------------------------------------------------------------
001600 //STEP010  EXEC  PGM=ADRDSSU,
001700 //   REGION=4M,
001800 //   PARM='TYPRUN=NORUN'
001900 //SYSPRINT   DD  SYSOUT=*
002000 //SYSIN      DD  *
002100      COPY     DATASET(                   -
002200                 INCLUDE(                 -
002300                        CSCJGJ.%.**       -
002400                        ))                -
002500               OUTDYNAM(VOL000)           -
002600               REBLOCK(**)                -
002700               CANCELERROR                -
002800               CATALOG                    -
002900               DELETE PURGE               -
003000               TGTALLOC(TRK)              -
003100               WAIT(2,2)
003200 //
```

The ** here at CSCJGJ is the wildcard that lets you specify that any number and value of remaining data set name parts is acceptable for selection. The % is like "?" under PC DOS and stands in for just one character. Examples of data set names selected for processing by this coding:

CSCJGJ.A.CNTL
CSCJGJ.K.COBOL.NEWCOPY
CSCJGJ.P.COBOL
CSCJGJ.X.OLD.TRANS.DATA.BACKUP
CSCJGJ.B.X

*Figure A.19 Using the % Placeholder and * Wildcard Together*

```
EDIT ---- CSCJGJ.ADV.CNTL(A06D) - 01.00 --------------------- COLUMNS 001 072
COMMAND ===>                                                  SCROLL ===> PAGE
****** ***************************** TOP OF DATA ******************************
000100 //CSCJGJA    JOB 1,                       ACCOUNTING INFORMATION
000200 //   'BIN 7--JANOSSY',                    PROGRAMMER NAME AND DELIVERY BIN
000300 //   CLASS=A,                             INPUT QUEUE CLASS
000400 //   MSGLEVEL=(1,1),                      HOW MUCH MVS SYSTEM PRINT DESIRED
000500 //   MSGCLASS=X,                          PRINT DESTINATION X A L N OR O
000600 //   TIME=(3,0),                          SAFETY LIMIT: RUN TIME UP TO 3 MIN
000700 //*  TYPRUN=SCAN,                         UNCOMMENT THIS LINE TO DO SCAN ONLY
000800 //   NOTIFY=CSCJGJ                        WHO TO TELL WHEN JOB IS DONE
000900 //*
001000 //* THIS JCL IS STORED AT CSCJGJ.ADV.CNTL(A06D)
001100 //*
001200 //*-------------------------------------------------------------------
001300 //* COPY DATASETS THAT START WITH 'CSCJGJ', HAVE A SECOND NODE OF
001400 //* ANY VALUE, AND HAVE A THIRD NODE THAT BEGINS WITH 'LIB' BUT HAS
001500 //* ONE ADDITIONAL POSITION OF ANY VALUE, SUCH AS LIB1, LIB2, LIBZ.
001600 //*-------------------------------------------------------------------
001700 //STEP010  EXEC  PGM=ADRDSSU,
001800 //   REGION=4M,
001900 //   PARM='TYPRUN=NORUN'
002000 //SYSPRINT   DD  SYSOUT=*
002100 //SYSIN      DD  *
002200      COPY     DATASET(                            -
002300                 INCLUDE(                          -
002400                          CSCJGJ.*.SOURCE.LIB%     -
002500                          ))                       -
002600               OUTDYNAM(VOL000)                    -
002700               REBLOCK(**)                         -
002800               CANCELERROR                         -
002900               CATALOG                             -
003000               DELETE PURGE                        -
003100               TGTALLOC(TRK)                       -
003200               WAIT(2,2)
003300 //
```

Here * is a wildcard for one data set name part (node) and % is a wildcard for one character.

Figure A.20 Using the % Placeholder at End of Data Set Name

```
EDIT ---- CSCJGJ.ADV.CNTL(A06E) - 01.00 ---------------------- COLUMNS 001 072
COMMAND ===>                                                   SCROLL ===> PAGE
****** ***************************** TOP OF DATA ******************************
000100 //CSCJGJA   JOB 1,                    ACCOUNTING INFORMATION
000200 //   'BIN 7--JANOSSY',                PROGRAMMER NAME AND DELIVERY BIN
000300 //   CLASS=A,                         INPUT QUEUE CLASS
000400 //   MSGLEVEL=(1,1),                  HOW MUCH MVS SYSTEM PRINT DESIRED
000500 //   MSGCLASS=X,                      PRINT DESTINATION X A L N OR O
000600 //   TIME=(3,0),                      SAFETY LIMIT: RUN TIME UP TO 3 MIN
000700 //*  TYPRUN=SCAN,                     UNCOMMENT THIS LINE TO DO SCAN ONLY
000800 //   NOTIFY=CSCJGJ                    WHO TO TELL WHEN JOB IS DONE
000900 //*
001000 //* THIS JCL IS STORED AT CSCJGJ.ADV.CNTL(A06E)
001100 //*
001200 //*-------------------------------------------------------------------
001300 //* COPY DATA SETS STARTING WITH ALL DATA SETS THAT BEGIN WITH
001400 //* 'CSCJGJ.' BUT EXCLUDE DATA SETS THAT HAVE THE CHARACTERS 'LOAD'
001500 //* ANYWHERE IN THE NAME.
001600 //*-------------------------------------------------------------------
001700 //STEP010  EXEC  PGM=ADRDSSU,
001800 //   REGION=4M,
001900 //   PARM='TYPRUN=NORUN'
002000 //SYSPRINT   DD  SYSOUT=*
002100 //SYSIN      DD  *
002200     COPY     DATASET(                  -
002300                INCLUDE(                -
002400                          CSCJGJ.**     -
002500                          )             -
002600                EXCLUDE(                -
002700                          **.*LOAD*.**  -
002800                          ))            -
002900              OUTDYNAM(VOL000)          -
003000              REBLOCK(**)               -
003100              CANCELERROR               -
003200              CATALOG                   -
003300              DELETE PURGE              -
003400              TGTALLOC(TRK)             -
003500              WAIT(2,2)
003600 //
```

Here the ** allows any number of data set name parts before or after the word LOAD, and any characters before or after LOAD within a name part. Data sets with "LOAD" anywhere within the name will be excluded from the copy rather than included. Here are some examples of data set names excluded by this coding:

CSCJGJ.LOAD
CSCJGJ.ADV.LOADLIB
ABCD.CSC.NEW.XYZLOAD1
HKJ2.ALOAD12.PROJECT.NEW
J7835.TEST.LOADER.BACKUP

*Figure A.21 Using the * Wildcard to Exclude Data Sets*

A.9 Filtering by Data Set Characteristics

In addition to filtering (selecting) on data set names, you can give DFDSS commands to select data sets for processing based on characteristics. You can filter on the following data set characteristics:

- Type of space allocation (cylinder, track, block, absolute track, or movable)
- Creation date (absolute or relative to the current date)
- Expiration date (absolute or relative to the current date)
- Last-referenced date (absolute or relative to the current date)
- Data set organization (sequential, partitioned, PDSE, BDAM, EXCP, ISAM, or VSAM)
- Data set size (number of allocated or used tracks)
- Number of extents
- Whether the data set is single-volume or multivolume
- Whether the data-set-changed flag is on or off
- DFSMS construct names (storage class, management class, and data class)
- Whether or not a data set is cataloged using the standard catalog search order

Figure A.22 shows you some examples of data set filtering by characteristics using the keywords FSIZE, which means filesize, and EXTNT, which means extents (allocations of noncontiguous disk space). This figure is especially interesting because it demonstrates a common technique used by disk storage management personnel to automate some of the tasks associated with their work. In Figure A.22, the disk volume serial numbers entering DFDSS at the data set member named CSCJGJ.BUILT.DASDLIST(VOLUMES1) were developed using a Statistical Analysis System (SAS) program, and appear as shown in Figure A.23. The SAS program (not shown) scanned a database that contains detailed information on all data set allocations and VTOC information for all disk devices on-line. Figure A.24 shows another form of data set filtering, this one excluding certain data sets based on the fact that they span multiple disk volumes and do not appear to have been accessed in the last three days.

Related to data set filtering is the ability to use the keyword INCAT to locate data sets by catalog in other than the default catalog search sequence for your system. Although JOBCAT and STEPCAT DD statements work for non-SMS data sets, you must use INCAT if you wish to indicate one or more specific catalogs using SMS-managed data sets. Figure A.25 shows you how to copy a data set using INCAT to specify the catalog in which its name is recorded.

```
EDIT ---- CSCJGJ.ADV.CNTL(A07A) - 01.00 --------------------- COLUMNS 001 072
COMMAND ===>                                                  SCROLL ===> PAGE
****** ***************************** TOP OF DATA ******************************
000100 //CSCJGJA   JOB 1,                ACCOUNTING INFORMATION
000200 //   'BIN 7--JANOSSY',            PROGRAMMER NAME AND DELIVERY BIN
000300 //   CLASS=A,                     INPUT QUEUE CLASS
000400 //   MSGLEVEL=(1,1),              HOW MUCH MVS SYSTEM PRINT DESIRED
000500 //   MSGCLASS=X,                  PRINT DESTINATION X A L N OR O
000600 //   TIME=(6,0),                  SAFETY LIMIT: RUN TIME UP TO 6 MIN
000700 //*  TYPRUN=SCAN,                 UNCOMMENT THIS LINE TO DO SCAN ONLY
000800 //   NOTIFY=CSCJGJ                WHO TO TELL WHEN JOB IS DONE
000900 //*
001000 //* THIS JCL IS STORED AT CSCJGJ.ADV.CNTL(A07A)
001100 //*
001200 //*-----------------------------------------------------------------
001300 //* THIS IS AN EXAMPLE OF A JOB USED TO COMPRESS PDS DATA SETS IN
001400 //* A LIST OF VOLUMES, WHERE THE LIST WAS CREATED BY A SAS
001500 //* PROGRAM.  THE SAS PROGRAM WAS USED TO ANALYZE DATA ABOUT A
001600 //* GROUP OF DISK VOLUMES AND CREATE A LIST OF VOLUMES THAT WERE
001700 //* IN NEED OF IMMEDIATE ATTENTION.  ONLY DATA SETS THAT ARE
001800 //* GREATER THAN 750 TRACKS AND HAVE GONE TO MORE THAN 9 EXTENTS
001900 //* WILL BE COMPRESSED.
002000 //*-----------------------------------------------------------------
002100 //STEP010  EXEC  PGM=ADRDSSU,
002200 //   REGION=6M,
002300 //   PARM='TYPRUN=NORUN'
002400 //SYSPRINT   DD SYSOUT=*
002500 //SYSIN      DD *
002600    COMPRESS
002700               DYNAM              -
002800 //            DD DSN=CSCJGJ.BUILT.DASDLIST(VOLUMES1),DISP=SHR
002900 //            DD *
003000               EXCLUDE(SYS1.**)   -
003100               BY(                -
003200                  (FSIZE,GT,750)  -
003300                  (EXTNT,GT,009)  -
003400                     )            -
003500 //
```

This example shows you concatenation of instream and file-stored control statements. CSCJGJ.BUILT.DASDLIST contains the list of volume serial numbers shown in Figure A.23, developed and stored by a program. DFDSS will "see" a set of control statements that includes that list of volume serial numbers. This concatenation may look strange. However, it is not specific to DFDSS, and works with any SYSIN input.

Figure A.22 Filtering Data Sets by Size and Extents

```
EDIT ---- CSCJGJ.BUILT.DASDLIST(VOLUMES1) - 01.00 ------------ COLUMNS 001 072
COMMAND ===>                                                   SCROLL ===> PAGE
****** ***************************** TOP OF DATA ******************************
000001 ((VL3005), -
000002  (VL5001), -
000003  (VL5002), -
000004  (VL5003), -
000005  (VL5004), -
000006  (VL5005), -
000007  (VL5006), -
000008  (VL5007), -
000009  (VL5008), -
000010  (VL5009), -
000011  (VL6008), -
000012  (VL6009), -
000013  (VL6010), -
000014  (VL6011), -
000015  (VL6012)) -
```

This file of volume serial numbers was developed by a SAS (Statistical Analysis System) program that analyzed a database of data set allocation and VTOC information. This file is concatenated with the other SYSIN control statements shown in Figure A.22 to accomplish a specific COMPRESS action using DFDSS.

Figure A.23 List of Volumes to Be Processed, Developed by a SAS Program

```
EDIT ---- CSCJGJ.ADV.CNTL(A07B) - 01.00 --------------------- COLUMNS 001 072
COMMAND ===>                                                   SCROLL ===> PAGE
****** ***************************** TOP OF DATA ******************************
000100 //CSCJGJA   JOB 1,                     ACCOUNTING INFORMATION
000200 //  'BIN 7--JANOSSY',                  PROGRAMMER NAME AND DELIVERY BIN
000300 //  CLASS=A,                           INPUT QUEUE CLASS
000400 //  MSGLEVEL=(1,1),                    HOW MUCH MVS SYSTEM PRINT DESIRED
000500 //  MSGCLASS=X,                        PRINT DESTINATION X A L N OR O
000600 //  TIME=(3,0),                        SAFETY LIMIT: RUN TIME UP TO 3 MIN
000700 //* TYPRUN=SCAN,                       UNCOMMENT THIS LINE TO DO SCAN ONLY
000800 //  NOTIFY=CSCJGJ                      WHO TO TELL WHEN JOB IS DONE
000900 //*
001000 //* THIS JCL IS STORED AT CSCJGJ.ADV.CNTL(A07B)
001100 //*
001200 //*-----------------------------------------------------------------
001300 //* COPY MULTIVOL DATA SETS UNREFERENCED MORE THAN 3 DAYS
001400 //*-----------------------------------------------------------------
001500 //STEP010  EXEC  PGM=ADRDSSU,
001600 //  REGION=6144K,
001700 //  PARM='TYPRUN=NORUN'
001800 //SYSPRINT   DD  SYSOUT=*
001900 //SYSIN      DD  *
002000     COPY       DS(INCLUDE(**)                                  -
002100                EXCLUDE(SYS1.**)                                -
002200                BY ((MULTI EQ YES) (REFDT LE *,-4)))            -
002300                LOGINDYNAM(VOL000)                              -
002400                OUTDYNAM(VOL001)                                -
002500                ALLDATA(*)                                      -
002600                ALLEXCP                                         -
002700                ALLMULTI                                        -
002800                CATALOG                                         -
002900                DELETE                                          -
003000                FORCE                                           -
003100                PURGE                                           -
003200                TGTA(SOURCE)
003300 //
```

"Today"

Figure A.24 Filtering Data Sets by Number of Disk Volumes Used and Days Elapsed Since Last Access

```
EDIT ---- CSCJGJ.ADV.CNTL(A08A) - 01.00 --------------------- COLUMNS 001 072
COMMAND ===>                                                  SCROLL ===> PAGE
****** ****************************** TOP OF DATA ******************************
000100 //CSCJGJA   JOB 1,                        ACCOUNTING INFORMATION
000200 //   'BIN 7--JANOSSY',                    PROGRAMMER NAME AND DELIVERY BIN
000300 //   CLASS=A,                             INPUT QUEUE CLASS
000400 //   MSGLEVEL=(1,1),                      HOW MUCH MVS SYSTEM PRINT DESIRED
000500 //   MSGCLASS=X,                          PRINT DESTINATION X A L N OR O
000600 //   TIME=(3,0),                          SAFETY LIMIT: RUN TIME UP TO 3 MIN
000700 //*  TYPRUN=SCAN,                         UNCOMMENT THIS LINE TO DO SCAN ONLY
000800 //   NOTIFY=CSCJGJ                        WHO TO TELL WHEN JOB IS DONE
000900 //*
001000 //* THIS JCL IS STORED AT CSCJGJ.ADV.CNTL(A08A)
001100 //*
001200 //*-------------------------------------------------------------------
001300 //* ALL DATASETS BEGINNING WITH 'CSCJGJ', LOOKING FIRST
001400 //* IN USERCAT1 CATALOG, THEN IN THE DEFAULT CATALOG IF NOT FOUND
001500 //*-------------------------------------------------------------------
001600 //STEP010  EXEC  PGM=ADRDSSU,
001700 //   REGION=4M,
001800 //   PARM='TYPRUN=NORUN'
001900 //SYSPRINT   DD  SYSOUT=*
002000 //SYSIN      DD  *
002100     COPY       DATASET(                   -
002200                  INCLUDE(                 -
002300                         CSCJGJ.**         -
002400                         ))                -
002500                INCAT(                     -
002600                   SYS1.ICFCAT.USERCAT1    -
002700                       )                   -
002800                OUTDYNAM(VOL000)           -
002900                REBLOCK(**)                -
003000                CANCELERROR                -
003100                CATALOG                    -
003200                DELETE PURGE               -
003300                TGTALLOC(TRK)              -
003400                WAIT(2,2)
003500 //
```

Figure A.25 Specifying a User Catalog Instead of Default Catalog

A.10 COPY: Moving Data

DFDSS provides a data set COPY command to move data sets. With COPY, you can move data sets or whole disk volumes from volumes not managed by Storage Management Subsystem to SMS-managed volumes, and vice versa. You can also convert any disk volume, without moving data, to and from the Storage Management Subsystem environment, as described in section A.11.

You can move data sets from one disk volume to another volume of like or unlike device type. Like devices have the same track capacity and number of tracks per cylinder (for example, IBM 3380 Standard and IBM 3380 Model D or E disk drives). Unlike disk devices have different track capacities or a different number of tracks per cylinder (such as model 3380 and 3390 disks).

When moving data to an unlike device, DFDSS offers a significant advantage when the receiving device has a larger track size than the sending device. DFDSS is designed to fill the track on the receiving device as completely as possible, instead of doing a simple track by track move. Each track on the receiving device is fully utilized, holding more records per track on the receiving disk drive than on the sending disk drive. Older utilities do not do this.

You can select data sets to be moved by searching catalogs and/or by searching a disk volume table of contents. Figure A.26 shows you how to copy a group of data sets having similar names for an application backup, limiting the selection of data sets to a specific user catalog with the ONLYINCAT option. Other options exist for the COPY command to:

- Delete data sets from the source volume after a successful copy, as shown in Figure A.27
- Copy or move multivolume data sets
- Retrieve readable data from a damaged volume
- Rename copied data sets
- Control data set placement on the target volume by copying to preallocated data sets. (In this way, you can place data sets on specific target volumes and even specific tracks.)
- Reblock partitioned and sequential data sets using the REBLOCK specification as shown in Figure A.28
- Copy an ordinary partitioned data set (PDS) to a partitioned data set extended, or vice versa, as shown in Figure A.29
- Copy data sets of undefined data set organization—in other words, machine language load modules—to an unlike device of larger track size, as shown in Figure A.30
- Process or exclude system (SYS1) data sets
- Move an entire VSAM sphere by invoking one COPY. You need not move each component individually. When you specify the base cluster name and SPHERE, DFDSS moves the entire sphere; that is, the base cluster and all associated alternate index components and paths. Figure A.31 shows you how to do this. (Once again, the lists of disk volume serial numbers to be accessed by DFDSS have been developed automatically by a SAS program, as discussed in section A.9, and are illustrated in Figure A.32.)

INDYNAM and OUTDYNAM on Figure A.31 tell DFDSS to build and open data control blocks for each disk volume listed. This allows you to externally specify lists of disk volumes as shown in this example.

```
EDIT ---- CSCJGJ.ADV.CNTL(A08B) - 01.00 --------------------- COLUMNS 001 072
COMMAND ===>                                                  SCROLL ===> PAGE
****** ***************************** TOP OF DATA ******************************
000100 //CSCJGJA   JOB 1,                     ACCOUNTING INFORMATION
000200 //   'BIN 7--JANOSSY',                 PROGRAMMER NAME AND DELIVERY BIN
000300 //   CLASS=A,                          INPUT QUEUE CLASS
000400 //   MSGLEVEL=(1,1),                   HOW MUCH MVS SYSTEM PRINT DESIRED
000500 //   MSGCLASS=X,                       PRINT DESTINATION X A L N OR O
000600 //   TIME=(3,0),                       SAFETY LIMIT: RUN TIME UP TO 3 MIN
000700 //*  TYPRUN=SCAN,                      UNCOMMENT THIS LINE TO DO SCAN ONLY
000800 //   NOTIFY=CSCJGJ                     WHO TO TELL WHEN JOB IS DONE
000900 //*
001000 //* THIS JCL IS STORED AT CSCJGJ.ADV.CNTL(A08B)
001100 //*
001200 //*-----------------------------------------------------------------
001300 //* COPY ONLY THE DATA SETS BEGINNING WITH "CSCJGJ"
001400 //* LISTED IN THE "INCAT" USER CATALOG.
001500 //*-----------------------------------------------------------------
001600 //STEP010  EXEC  PGM=ADRDSSU,
001700 //   REGION=4M,
001800 //   PARM='TYPRUN=NORUN'
001900 //SYSPRINT   DD  SYSOUT=*
002000 //SYSIN      DD  *
002100     COPY     DATASET(                     -
002200                INCLUDE(                   -
002300                        CSCJGJ.**          -
002400                        ))                 -
002500                INCAT(                     -
002600                 SYS1.ICFCAT.USERCAT1      -
002700                        )                  -
002800              ONLYINCAT                    -
002900              OUTDYNAM(VOL000)             -
003000              REBLOCK(**)                  -
003100              CANCELERROR                  -
003200              CATALOG                      -
003300              DELETE PURGE                 -
003400              TGTALLOC(TRK)                -
003500              WAIT(2,2)
003600 //
```

Figure A.26 Using ONLYINCAT to Limit Catalog Searching to the Specified User Catalog

```
EDIT ---- CSCJGJ.ADV.CNTL(A09A) - 01.00 --------------------- COLUMNS 001 072
COMMAND ===>                                                  SCROLL ===> PAGE
****** ***************************** TOP OF DATA ******************************
000100 //CSCJGJA   JOB 1,                       ACCOUNTING INFORMATION
000200 //   'BIN 7--JANOSSY',                   PROGRAMMER NAME AND DELIVERY BIN
000300 //   CLASS=A,                            INPUT QUEUE CLASS
000400 //   MSGLEVEL=(1,1),                     HOW MUCH MVS SYSTEM PRINT DESIRED
000500 //   MSGCLASS=X,                         PRINT DESTINATION X A L N OR O
000600 //   TIME=(3,0),                         SAFETY LIMIT: RUN TIME UP TO 3 MIN
000700 //*  TYPRUN=SCAN,                        UNCOMMENT THIS LINE TO DO SCAN ONLY
000800 //   NOTIFY=CSCJGJ                       WHO TO TELL WHEN JOB IS DONE
000900 //*
001000 //* THIS JCL IS STORED AT CSCJGJ.ADV.CNTL(A09A)
001100 //*
001200 //*-----------------------------------------------------------------
001300 //* COPY A GROUP OF SIMILARLY-NAMED DATA SETS
001400 //* ANY DATA SET WITH LAST PART 'TEST.SOURCE.LIB' WILL BE COPIED
001500 //*-----------------------------------------------------------------
001600 //STEP010  EXEC  PGM=ADRDSSU,
001700 //   REGION=4M,
001800 //   PARM='TYPRUN=NORUN'
001900 //SYSPRINT   DD  SYSOUT=*
002000 //SYSIN      DD  *
002100       COPY      DATASET(                  -
002200                    INCLUDE(               -
002300                       **.TEST.SOURCE.LIB  -
002400                              ))           -
002500                 OUTDYNAM(VOL000)          -
002600                 CANCELERROR               -
002700                 CATALOG                   -
002800                 DELETE PURGE              -
002900                 TGTALLOC(TRK)             -
003000                 WAIT(2,2)
003100 //
```

The **DELETE** here gets rid of the original data sets after the **COPY** has been accomplished, so this set of control statements really accomplishes a series of "moves" that consolidate the included group of data sets onto the disk volume specified at **OUTDYNAM**.

Figure A.27 Moving a Data Set by Copying It with Deletion of the Original Data Set After Copy

```
EDIT ---- CSCJGJ.ADV.CNTL(A11A) - 01.00 ---------------------- COLUMNS 001 072
COMMAND ===>                                                   SCROLL ===> PAGE
****** ***************************** TOP OF DATA ******************************
000100 //CSCJGJA   JOB 1,                       ACCOUNTING INFORMATION
000200 //   'BIN 7--JANOSSY',                   PROGRAMMER NAME AND DELIVERY BIN
000300 //   CLASS=A,                            INPUT QUEUE CLASS
000400 //   MSGLEVEL=(1,1),                     HOW MUCH MVS SYSTEM PRINT DESIRED
000500 //   MSGCLASS=X,                         PRINT DESTINATION X A L N OR O
000600 //   TIME=(3,0),                         SAFETY LIMIT: RUN TIME UP TO 3 MIN
000700 //* TYPRUN=SCAN,                         UNCOMMENT THIS LINE TO DO SCAN ONLY
000800 //   NOTIFY=CSCJGJ                       WHO TO TELL WHEN JOB IS DONE
000900 //*
001000 //* THIS JCL IS STORED AT CSCJGJ.ADV.CNTL(A11A)
001100 //*
001200 //*-------------------------------------------------------------------
001300 //* REBLOCK A DATA SET DURING COPY
001400 //*-------------------------------------------------------------------
001500 //STEP010  EXEC  PGM=ADRDSSU,
001600 //   REGION=4M,
001700 //   PARM='TYPRUN=NORUN'
001800 //SYSPRINT DD SYSOUT=*
001900 //SYSIN       DD  *
002000      COPY      DATASET(                  -
002100                  INCLUDE(                -
002200                     CSCJGJ.T.TEST.DATA   -
002300                        ))                -
002400                OUTDYNAM(VOL000)          -
002500                REBLOCK(**)               -
002600                CANCELERROR               -
002700                CATALOG                   -
002800                DELETE PURGE              -
002900                TGTALLOC(TRK)             -
003000                WAIT(2,2)
003100 //
```

You can have DFDSS reblock data sets during copy, so that they are stored with a block size most efficient for the target device.

Figure A.28 Reblocking a Data Set Using the REBLOCK Specification

```
EDIT ---- CSCJGJ.ADV.CNTL(A13A) - 01.00 ----------------------- COLUMNS 001 072
COMMAND ===>                                                    SCROLL ===> PAGE
****** ***************************** TOP OF DATA ******************************
000100 //CSCJGJA   JOB 1,                      ACCOUNTING INFORMATION
000200 //  'BIN 7--JANOSSY',                   PROGRAMMER NAME AND DELIVERY BIN
000300 //  CLASS=A,                            INPUT QUEUE CLASS
000400 //  MSGLEVEL=(1,1),                     HOW MUCH MVS SYSTEM PRINT DESIRED
000500 //  MSGCLASS=X,                         PRINT DESTINATION X A L N OR O
000600 //  TIME=(3,0),                         SAFETY LIMIT: RUN TIME UP TO 3 MIN
000700 //* TYPRUN=SCAN,                        UNCOMMENT THIS LINE TO DO SCAN ONLY
000800 //  NOTIFY=CSCJGJ                       WHO TO TELL WHEN JOB IS DONE
000900 //*
001000 //* THIS JCL IS STORED AT CSCJGJ.ADV.CNTL(A13A)
001100 //*
001200 //*-----------------------------------------------------------------
001300 //* COPY A PDS TO A PDSE
001400 //*-----------------------------------------------------------------
001500 //STEP010  EXEC  PGM=ADRDSSU,
001600 //  REGION=4M,
001700 //  PARM='TYPRUN=NORUN'
001800 //SYSPRINT   DD  SYSOUT=*
001900 //SYSIN      DD  *
002000      COPY      DATASET(                  -
002100                  INCLUDE(                -
002200                     CSCJGJ.LIB.SOURCE    -
002300                          ))              -
002400                STORCLAS(SCLSNAME)        -   /* PDSE MUST BE SMS */
002500                MGMTCLAS(MCLSNAME)        -   /* PDSE MUST BE SMS */
002600                REBLOCK(**)               -
002700                CANCELERROR               -
002800                CATALOG                   -
002900                DELETE PURGE              -
003000                TGTALLOC(TRK)             -
003100                CONVERT(PDSE(**))         - /* CONVERT DATA SET TO PDSE */
003200                WAIT(2,2)
003300 //
```

You can use DFDSS to copy an ordinary partitioned data set (commonly known as a PDS, with data set organization code PO) to a partitioned data set extended (PDSE, also known as a "library," with data set organization code PO-E). All PDSEs must be SMS-managed. The ** symbol is two wildcard characters, which is how you indicate "all data sets." This is analogous to PC-DOS *.* coding.

Figure A.29 Copying a Partitioned Data Set (PDS) to a Partitioned Data Set Extended

```
EDIT ---- CSCJGJ.ADV.CNTL(A14) - 01.00 ---------------------- COLUMNS 001 072
COMMAND ===>                                                 SCROLL ===> PAGE
****** ***************************** TOP OF DATA ******************************
000100 //CSCJGJA   JOB 1,                 ACCOUNTING INFORMATION
000200 //  'BIN 7--JANOSSY',              PROGRAMMER NAME AND DELIVERY BIN
000300 //  CLASS=A,                       INPUT QUEUE CLASS
000400 //  MSGLEVEL=(1,1),                HOW MUCH MVS SYSTEM PRINT DESIRED
000500 //  MSGCLASS=X,                    PRINT DESTINATION X A L N OR O
000600 //  TIME=(3,0),                    SAFETY LIMIT: RUN TIME UP TO 3 MIN
000700 //* TYPRUN=SCAN,                   UNCOMMENT THIS LINE TO DO SCAN ONLY
000800 //  NOTIFY=CSCJGJ                  WHO TO TELL WHEN JOB IS DONE
000900 //*
001000 //* THIS JCL IS STORED AT CSCJGJ.ADV.CNTL(A14A)
001100 //*
001200 //*-------------------------------------------------------------------
001300 //* THIS WILL COPY A LOAD LIBRARY AND DELETE THE ORIGINAL.
001400 //* NOTE THAT 'REBLOCK' IS NOT SPECIFIED.
001500 //*-------------------------------------------------------------------
001600 //STEP010  EXEC  PGM=ADRDSSU,
001700 //  REGION=4M,
001800 //  PARM='TYPRUN=NORUN'
001900 //SYSPRINT   DD  SYSOUT=*
002000 //SYSIN      DD  *
002100     COPY       DATASET(                    -
002200                  INCLUDE(                  -
002300                    USERID.TEST2.LOAD       -
002400                          ))                -
002500                STORCLAS(STANDARD)          -
002600                MGMTCLAS(WORK)              -
002700                ALLDATA(*)                  -
002800                CANCELERROR                 -
002900                CATALOG                     -
003000                DELETE PURGE                -
003100                TGTALLOC(TRK)               -
003200                WAIT(2,2)
003300 //
```

Load module library

Figure A.30 Copying a Load Module Library and Converting It to Be SMS-Managed

```
EDIT ---- CSCJGJ.ADV.CNTL(A10A) - 01.00 --------------------- COLUMNS 001 072
COMMAND ===>                                                  SCROLL ===> PAGE
****** ****************************** TOP OF DATA ******************************
000100 //CSCJGJA   JOB 1,                    ACCOUNTING INFORMATION
000200 //  'BIN 7--JANOSSY',                 PROGRAMMER NAME AND DELIVERY BIN
000300 //  CLASS=A,                          INPUT QUEUE CLASS
000400 //  MSGLEVEL=(1,1),                   HOW MUCH MVS SYSTEM PRINT DESIRED
000500 //  MSGCLASS=X,                       PRINT DESTINATION X A L N OR O
000600 //  TIME=(3,0),                       SAFETY LIMIT: RUN TIME UP TO 3 MIN
000700 //* TYPRUN=SCAN,                      UNCOMMENT THIS LINE TO DO SCAN ONLY
000800 //  NOTIFY=CSCJGJ                     WHO TO TELL WHEN JOB IS DONE
000900 //*
001000 //* THIS JCL IS STORED AT CSCJGJ.ADV.CNTL(A10A)
001100 //*
001200 //*-----------------------------------------------------------------
001300 //* COPY ALL VSAM DATA SETS AND ALL THEIR ASSOCIATED INDEXES AND
001400 //* ALTERNATE INDEXES FROM ONE SET OF VOLUMES TO ANOTHER SET
001500 //* OF VOLUMES, THE SETS OF VOLUMES ARE IDENTIFIED IN DATA SETS
001600 //*-----------------------------------------------------------------
001700 //STEP010  EXEC  PGM=ADRDSSU,
001800 //  REGION=6144K,
001900 //  PARM='TYPRUN=NORUN'
002000 //SYSPRINT   DD  SYSOUT=*
002100 //SYSIN      DD  *
002200      COPY      DATASET(               -
002300                EXCLUDE(SYS1.**)       -
002400                BY(                    -
002500                  (DSORG,EQ,VSAM)      -
002600                  ))                   -
002700                INDYNAM                -
002800 //             DD  DSN=CSCJGJ.BUILT.DASDLIST(VOLUMES2),DISP=SHR
002900 //             DD  *
003000                OUTDYNAM               -
003100 //             DD  DSN=CSCJGJ.BUILT.DASDLIST(VOLUMES3),DISP=SHR
003200 //             DD  *
003300                SPHERE
003400 //
```

This is another example of DFDSS control statements composed of the concatenation of file-stored lists of volume serial numbers and instream data. This job copies all VSAM data sets except those starting with SYS1 from one group of disks to another, selecting them simply by data set organization. SPHERE causes all indexes and alternate indexes to be copied along with the data component.

Figure A.31 Moving an Entire VSAM Sphere with One COPY Command

If the COPY command detects that you have not allocated enough space for a new sequential or partitioned data set being produced, it estimates the amount of additional space needed and extends the data set. The COPY then continues, using the additional space. The COPY command (and RESTORE command) has the capability to allocate multivolume VSAM data sets and can process VSAM linear data sets such as those that house DB2 databases. DFDSS preserves aliases when VSAM user catalogs are copied or dumped and restored; they do not have to be re-created. COPY gives you a choice in disk space allocation, allowing you to specify space by cylinders, blocks, or tracks, or to preserve the original space allocation type of the copied data set.

```
EDIT ---- CSCJGJ.BUILT.DASDLIST(VOLUMES2) - 01.00 ------------ COLUMNS 001 072
COMMAND ===>                                                   SCROLL ===> PAGE
****** ****************************** TOP OF DATA ******************************
000001  ((VL3005), -
000002    (VL5001), -
000003    (VL6001), -
000004    (VL6002), -
000005    (VL6003), -
000006    (VL6008), -
000007    (VL6009), -
000008    (VL6010), -
000009    (VL6011), -
000010    (VL6012)) -
```

This list of volumes containing VSAM data sets could have been composed manually or by a program. It is sandwiched between instream control statements with the coding shown in Figure A.31.

```
EDIT ---- CSCJGJ.BUILT.DASDLIST(VOLUMES3) - 01.00 ------------ COLUMNS 001 072
COMMAND ===>                                                   SCROLL ===> PAGE
****** ****************************** TOP OF DATA ******************************
000001    ((NV3005), -
000002      (NV5001), -
000003      (NV6002), -
000004      (NV6003), -
000005      (NV6005), -
000006      (NV6006), -
000007      (NV6008), -
000008      (NV6009), -
000009      (NV6010), -
000010      (NV6011), -
000011      (NV6012)) -
```

These are the target volumes to which the VSAM data sets will be copied. Since these records will be followed by additional instream control statements in Figure A.31, the last line ends with the continuation symbol, the hyphen.

Figure A.32 Lists of Disk Volume Serial Numbers to Be Accessed by DFDSS, as Developed by a SAS Program

A.11 COPY Support for SMS Data Sets

You can use the DFDSS COPY command to move data sets between SMS-managed volumes and non-SMS-managed volumes. COPY invokes Automatic Class Selection routines to determine the Storage Management Subsystem constructs of a new SMS-managed data set, such as STORCLAS and MGMTCLAS. You can, alternatively, specify the storage class name or the management class name for the new data set, or you can specify that Automatic Class Selection be bypassed. Figure A.33 shows you how you can use COPY to convert a group of data sets from non-SMS to SMS-managed status.

```
EDIT ---- CSCJGJ.ADV.CNTL(A15A) - 01.00 --------------------- COLUMNS 001 072
COMMAND ===>                                                  SCROLL ===> PAGE
****** ****************************** TOP OF DATA ******************************
000100 //CSCJGJA   JOB 1,                    ACCOUNTING INFORMATION
000200 //  'BIN 7--JANOSSY',                 PROGRAMMER NAME AND DELIVERY BIN
000300 //  CLASS=A,                          INPUT QUEUE CLASS
000400 //  MSGLEVEL=(1,1),                   HOW MUCH MVS SYSTEM PRINT DESIRED
000500 //  MSGCLASS=X,                       PRINT DESTINATION X A L N OR O
000600 //  TIME=(3,0),                       SAFETY LIMIT: RUN TIME UP TO 3 MIN
000700 //* TYPRUN=SCAN,                      UNCOMMENT THIS LINE TO DO SCAN ONLY
000800 //  NOTIFY=CSCJGJ                     WHO TO TELL WHEN JOB IS DONE
000900 //*
001000 //* THIS JCL IS STORED AT CSCJGJ.ADV.CNTL(A15A)
001100 //*
001200 //*-----------------------------------------------------------------
001300 //* CONVERT NON-SMS DATA SETS TO SMS-MANAGED WITH DATA MOVEMENT
001400 //*-----------------------------------------------------------------
001500 //STEP010  EXEC  PGM=ADRDSSU,
001600 //  REGION=4M,
001700 //  PARM='TYPRUN=NORUN'
001800 //SYSPRINT   DD  SYSOUT=*
001900 //SYSIN      DD  *
002000      COPY      DATASET(                    -
002100                  INCLUDE(                  -
002200                         CSCJGJ.T.**        -
002300                         CSCJGJ.P.**        -
002400                         CSCJGJ.LIB.**      -
002500                         CSCJGJ.JCL.PROCS   -
002600                         CSCJGJ.X%.**       -
002700                         ))                 -
002800                STORCLAS(SCLSNAME)          -
002900                MGMTCLAS(MCLSNAME)          -
003000                REBLOCK(**)                 -
003100                CANCELERROR                 -
003200                CATALOG                     -
003300                DELETE PURGE                -
003400                TGTALLOC(TRK)               -
003500                WAIT(2,2)
003600 //
```

Use of **STORCLAS** makes the new data set SMS-managed

Figure A.33 Using COPY to Convert Data Sets to SMS-Managed Data Set

A.12 CONVERTV: Converting Disk Volumes to SMS-Managed

DFDSS supports conversion of data sets to SMS without data movement. You can convert any disk volume, without moving data residing on it, to or from SMS-managed status. DFDSS facilitates this conversion by:

- Recognizing and preserving SMS constructs that identify the data set's data class, management class, and storage class. The construct names are either added to the data set when converted to SMS, or taken away from the data set if removed from SMS management.
- Filtering by SMS construct names. You can select data sets by construct names when processing data sets already managed by SMS.

DFDSS supports this conversion through the CONVERTV command, which processes whole disk volumes. Before attempting to convert a disk volume to SMS, you use a CONVERTV option named PREPARE to disable allocation of space on the volume by jobs running concurrently. Then you use the TEST option to verify that DFDSS can convert all data sets on that volume to SMS; you remove the data sets that TEST identifies as being unable to become SMS-managed. Finally, you use DFDSS to have CONVERT actually convert the volume to SMS-managed status. Figures A.34, A.35, and A.36 show you the sequence of runs by which you can use the CONVERTV specification.

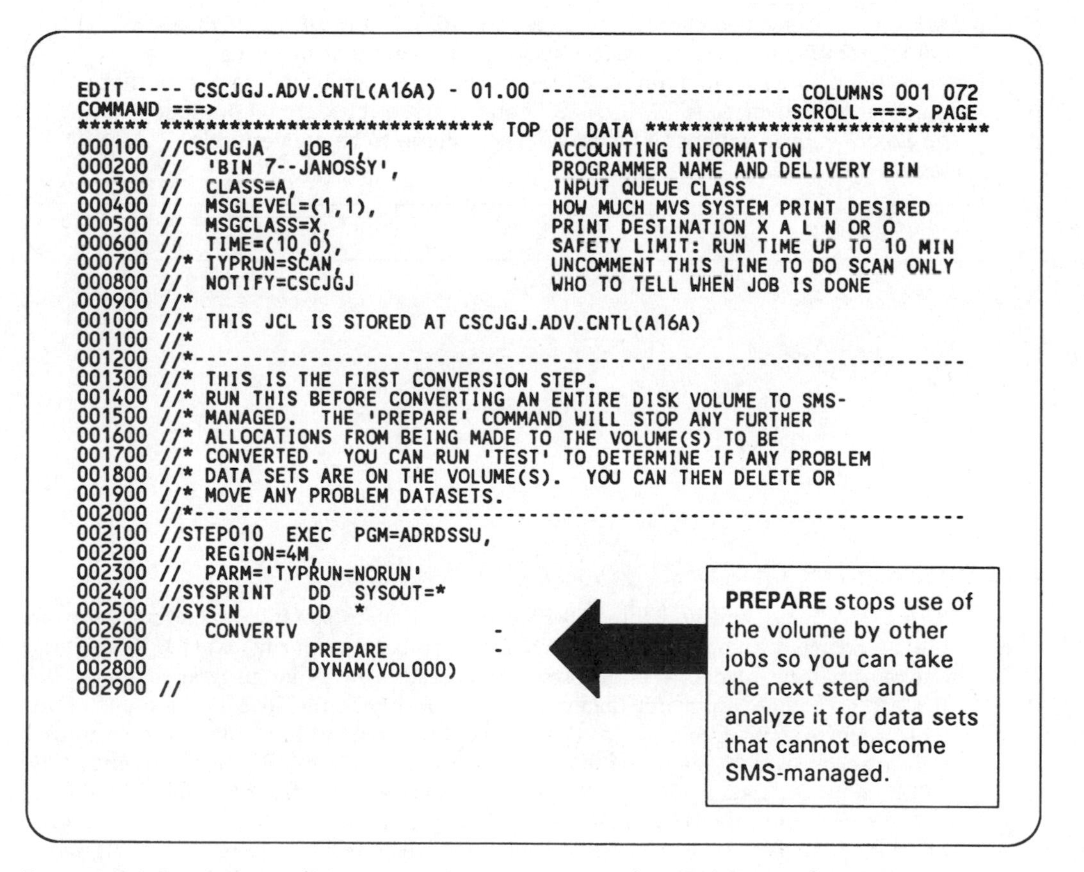

```
EDIT ---- CSCJGJ.ADV.CNTL(A16A) - 01.00 --------------------- COLUMNS 001 072
COMMAND ===>                                                  SCROLL ===> PAGE
****** ****************************** TOP OF DATA ******************************
000100 //CSCJGJA   JOB 1,                      ACCOUNTING INFORMATION
000200 //   'BIN 7--JANOSSY',                  PROGRAMMER NAME AND DELIVERY BIN
000300 //   CLASS=A,                           INPUT QUEUE CLASS
000400 //   MSGLEVEL=(1,1),                    HOW MUCH MVS SYSTEM PRINT DESIRED
000500 //   MSGCLASS=X,                        PRINT DESTINATION X A L N OR O
000600 //   TIME=(10,0),                       SAFETY LIMIT: RUN TIME UP TO 10 MIN
000700 //*  TYPRUN=SCAN,                       UNCOMMENT THIS LINE TO DO SCAN ONLY
000800 //   NOTIFY=CSCJGJ                      WHO TO TELL WHEN JOB IS DONE
000900 //*
001000 //* THIS JCL IS STORED AT CSCJGJ.ADV.CNTL(A16A)
001100 //*
001200 //*-------------------------------------------------------------------
001300 //* THIS IS THE FIRST CONVERSION STEP.
001400 //* RUN THIS BEFORE CONVERTING AN ENTIRE DISK VOLUME TO SMS-
001500 //* MANAGED.  THE 'PREPARE' COMMAND WILL STOP ANY FURTHER
001600 //* ALLOCATIONS FROM BEING MADE TO THE VOLUME(S) TO BE
001700 //* CONVERTED.  YOU CAN RUN 'TEST' TO DETERMINE IF ANY PROBLEM
001800 //* DATA SETS ARE ON THE VOLUME(S).  YOU CAN THEN DELETE OR
001900 //* MOVE ANY PROBLEM DATASETS.
002000 //*-------------------------------------------------------------------
002100 //STEP010  EXEC  PGM=ADRDSSU,
002200 //   REGION=4M,
002300 //   PARM='TYPRUN=NORUN'
002400 //SYSPRINT   DD  SYSOUT=*
002500 //SYSIN      DD  *
002600      CONVERTV                     -
002700               PREPARE             -
002800               DYNAM(VOL000)
002900 //
```

PREPARE stops use of the volume by other jobs so you can take the next step and analyze it for data sets that cannot become SMS-managed.

Figure A.34 First Step in Volume Conversion to SMS: Using the PREPARE Specification

```
EDIT ---- CSCJGJ.ADV.CNTL(A16B) - 01.00 ---------------------- COLUMNS 001 072
COMMAND ===>                                                  SCROLL ===> PAGE
****** ****************************** TOP OF DATA ******************************
000100 //CSCJGJA   JOB 1,                      ACCOUNTING INFORMATION
000200 //   'BIN 7--JANOSSY',                  PROGRAMMER NAME AND DELIVERY BIN
000300 //   CLASS=A,                           INPUT QUEUE CLASS
000400 //   MSGLEVEL=(1,1),                    HOW MUCH MVS SYSTEM PRINT DESIRED
000500 //   MSGCLASS=X,                        PRINT DESTINATION X A L N OR O
000600 //   TIME=(10,0),                       SAFETY LIMIT: RUN TIME UP TO 10 MIN
000700 //*  TYPRUN=SCAN,                       UNCOMMENT THIS LINE TO DO SCAN ONLY
000800 //   NOTIFY=CSCJGJ                      WHO TO TELL WHEN JOB IS DONE
000900 //*
001000 //* THIS JCL IS STORED AT CSCJGJ.ADV.CNTL(A16B)
001100 //*
001200 //*-----------------------------------------------------------------
001300 //* THIS IS THE SECOND CONVERSION STEP.  THIS IS RUN TO IDENTIFY
001400 //* ANY PROBLEM DATA SETS THAT EXIST ON THE VOLUME(S) TO BE
001500 //* CONVERTED TO SMS.
001600 //*-----------------------------------------------------------------
001700 //STEP010  EXEC  PGM=ADRDSSU,
001800 //   REGION=4M,
001900 //   PARM='TYPRUN=NORUN'
002000 //SYSPRINT   DD  SYSOUT=*
002100 //SYSIN      DD  *
002200       CONVERTV                    -
002300                 SMS               -
002400                 REDETERMINE       -
002500                 TEST              -
002600                 DYNAM(VOL000)
002700 //
```

TEST

SMS causes conversion actions to be taken. **REDETERMINE** tells DFDSS to again determine the class characteristics of data sets that might have been converted previously, in a run that later encountered "problem" data sets that could not be converted to SMS. **TEST** causes just a report to be produced, and no conversion actions to be done. The volume to be converted is identified at **DYNAM**.

Figure A.35 Second Step in Volume Conversion to SMS: Using the TEST Specification

A.13 DUMP: Backing Up Data

The COPY command and the DUMP command share some characteristics in that both can make a copy of disk-stored data for backup purposes. COPY creates a backed-up form of data that is directly accessible by other programs, much like IDCAM's REPRO command. Backup data created with the DUMP command, however, requires subsequent use of the RESTORE command to return the data to disk before access is possible by an application program. (In the PC environment under DOS, commands analogous to DUMP and RESTORE are BACKUP and RESTORE.)

You can use the DFDSS DUMP command to back up data on disk to tape or to another disk, and the RESTORE command to restore the backup if the original is lost, damaged, or inadvertently changed. Once you have used DFDSS DUMP to back

```
EDIT ---- CSCJGJ.ADV.CNTL(A16C) - 01.00 --------------------- COLUMNS 001 072
COMMAND ===>                                                  SCROLL ===> PAGE
****** ***************************** TOP OF DATA ******************************
000100 //CSCJGJA   JOB 1,                   ACCOUNTING INFORMATION
000200 //  'BIN 7--JANOSSY',                PROGRAMMER NAME AND DELIVERY BIN
000300 //  CLASS=A,                         INPUT QUEUE CLASS
000400 //  MSGLEVEL=(1,1),                  HOW MUCH MVS SYSTEM PRINT DESIRED
000500 //  MSGCLASS=X,                      PRINT DESTINATION X A L N OR O
000600 //  TIME=(10,0),                     SAFETY LIMIT: RUN TIME UP TO 10 MIN
000700 //* TYPRUN=SCAN,                     UNCOMMENT THIS LINE TO DO SCAN ONLY
000800 //  NOTIFY=CSCJGJ                    WHO TO TELL WHEN JOB IS DONE
000900 //*
001000 //* THIS JCL IS STORED AT CSCJGJ.ADV.CNTL(A16C)
001100 //*
001200 //*-----------------------------------------------------------------
001300 //* THIS IS THE LAST CONVERSION STEP.
001400 //* AFTER ALL PROBLEM DATA SETS HAVE BEEN REMOVED FROM THE
001500 //* VOLUME(S) YOU CAN RUN THE ACTUAL CONVERTV.
001600 //*-----------------------------------------------------------------
001700 //STEP010  EXEC  PGM=ADRDSSU,
001800 //  REGION=4M,
001900 //  PARM='TYPRUN=NORUN'
002000 //SYSPRINT   DD  SYSOUT=*
002100 //SYSIN      DD  *
002200    CONVERTV              -
002300              SMS         -
002400              DYNAM(VOL000)
002500 //
```

Neither **PREPARE** or **TEST** are specified

This run actually accomplishes the conversion-in-place to SMS-managed status. You should run this only after the **PREPARE** and **TEST** runs, and after removing any data sets from the volume that cannot be managed by SMS.

Figure A.36 Third Step in Volume Conversion to SMS: Using CONVERTV After Eliminating Problem Data Sets

up your data, you can also use DFDSS to make several copies of your backups. Backups can include specific tracks on a disk volume, or full disk volumes. DUMP and RESTORE can access disk or tape volumes.

Using DUMP, you can select data sets for backup by searching catalogs and by searching the volume table of contents (VTOC). You can back up data selectively by using filtering to choose only certain data sets. You can use other options of DUMP to:

- Back up either all the allocated space or only the used space in sequential or partitioned data sets
- Back up an entire VSAM "sphere" by invoking one dump; you need not separately back up the base cluster catalog entry, data component, index, and alternate index.

- Back up multivolume data sets
- Reset a field known as the data-set-changed flag of data sets successfully backed up. The next time you do a backup, you can specify that only data sets updated since the last reset (backup) are to be copied for backup.

In addition, other options of the DUMP command provide capabilities that affect the size, content, and handling of backup data:

- The COMPRESS command can save disk space by compressing backup data.
- The OPTIMIZE option can speed the data transfer rate by letting you specify a large number of disk tracks to be read at one time, as shown in Figure A.37.
- You can specify whether DFDSS continues or cancels a dump when a permanent read error occurs.
- You can retrieve readable data from a damaged disk volume.

```
EDIT ---- CSCJGJ.ADV.CNTL(A17A) - 01.00 --------------------- COLUMNS 001 072
COMMAND ===>                                                  SCROLL ===> PAGE
****** ***************************** TOP OF DATA ******************************
000100 //CSCJGJA   JOB 1,                      ACCOUNTING INFORMATION
000200 //  'BIN 7--JANOSSY',                   PROGRAMMER NAME AND DELIVERY BIN
000300 //  CLASS=A,                            INPUT QUEUE CLASS
000400 //  MSGLEVEL=(1,1),                     HOW MUCH MVS SYSTEM PRINT DESIRED
000500 //  MSGCLASS=X,                         PRINT DESTINATION X A L N OR O
000600 //  TIME=(10,0),                        SAFETY LIMIT: RUN TIME UP TO 3 MIN
000700 //* TYPRUN=SCAN,                        UNCOMMENT THIS LINE TO DO SCAN ONLY
000800 //  NOTIFY=CSCJGJ                       WHO TO TELL WHEN JOB IS DONE
000900 //*
001000 //* THIS JCL IS STORED AT CSCJGJ.ADV.CNTL(A17A)
001100 //*
001200 //*--------------------------------------------------------------------
001300 //* DO A LOGICAL DUMP OF ALL BUT SYS1 DATA SETS TO TAPE
001400 //* AND UNCATALOG THE DATA SETS
001500 //*--------------------------------------------------------------------
001600 //STEP010  EXEC  PGM=ADRDSSU,
001700 //  REGION=6144K,
001800 //  PARM='TYPRUN=NORUN'
001900 //VOL000      DD  UNIT=3380,
002000 //  VOL=SER=VOL000,
002100 //  DISP=SHR
002200 //TAPEOUT     DD  DSN=CSCJGJ.DUMP.VOL000,
002300 //  DISP=(NEW,CATLG,DELETE),
002400 //  UNIT=TAPE,
002500 //  VOL=(,,,10)
002600 //SYSPRINT    DD  SYSOUT=*
002700 //SYSIN       DD  *
002800      DUMP     DS(INCLUDE(**)                  -
002900                  EXCLUDE(SYS1.**))            -
003000               LOGINDDNAME(VOL000)             -
003100               OUTDDNAME(TAPEOUT)              -
003200               DELETE                          -
003300               PURGE                           -
003400               OPT(4)                          -
003500               COMPRESS                        -
003600               UNCAT
003700 //
```

OPT stands for **OPTIMIZE** and tells DFDSS how many tracks to read at a time according to this coding:

1 *means* 1 track
2 *means* 2 tracks
3 *means* 5 tracks
4 *means* 1 cylinder

COMPRESS causes data compression to save space, but requires additional **CPU** time to create and restore.

Figure A.37 Backing Up All Except SYS1 Data Sets on a Disk Volume with Optimized Reading

When processing a data set with the DUMP command, DFDSS preserves the construct names (storage class, management class, and data class) associated with SMS-managed data sets. As with COPY, you can filter data sets for processing based on storage class, management class, or data class name.

A.14 COPYDUMP: Making Multiple Copies of Backup Data

The COPYDUMP command lets you make from 1 to 255 copies of DFDSS-produced backup data, useful for either redundant archival of critical data or for distribution to other sites. You can copy a sequential data set that you backed up with the DUMP command to a tape or disk volume, as shown in Figure A.38. The sequential data set you are copying can reside on one or more tapes or on one or more disk volumes. If the backup data is produced from multiple disk volumes using a data set DUMP, you can selectively copy the data from one or more of the disk volumes.

```
EDIT ---- CSCJGJ.ADV.CNTL(A18A) - 01.00 --------------------- COLUMNS 001 072
COMMAND ===>                                                  SCROLL ===> PAGE
****** ****************************** TOP OF DATA ******************************
000100 //CSCJGJA   JOB 1,                    ACCOUNTING INFORMATION
000200 //  'BIN 7--JANOSSY',                 PROGRAMMER NAME AND DELIVERY BIN
000300 //  CLASS=A,                          INPUT QUEUE CLASS
000400 //  MSGLEVEL=(1,1),                   HOW MUCH MVS SYSTEM PRINT DESIRED
000500 //  MSGCLASS=X,                       PRINT DESTINATION X A L N OR O
000600 //  TIME=(3,0),                       SAFETY LIMIT: RUN TIME UP TO 3 MIN
000700 //* TYPRUN=SCAN,                      UNCOMMENT THIS LINE TO DO SCAN ONLY
000800 //  NOTIFY=CSCJGJ                     WHO TO TELL WHEN JOB IS DONE
000900 //*
001000 //* THIS JCL IS STORED AT CSCJGJ.ADV.CNTL(A18A)
001100 //*
001200 //*-----------------------------------------------------------------
001300 //* DO A LOGICAL DUMP CREATING THREE COPIES OF THE
001400 //* DATA SETS
001500 //*-----------------------------------------------------------------
001600 //STEP010  EXEC  PGM=ADRDSSU,
001700 //  REGION=6M,
001800 //  PARM='TYPRUN=NORUN'
001900 //ORIGINAL   DD  DSN=CSCJGJ.DUMP.VOL000,
002000 //  DISP=OLD
002100 //FIRSTCPY   DD  DSN=CSCJGJ.DUMP.VOL000.COPY1,
002200 //  DISP=(NEW,CATLG,DELETE),
002300 //  UNIT=TAPE,
002400 //  VOL=(,,,10)
002500 //SECNDCPY   DD  DSN=CSCJGJ.DUMP.VOL000.COPY2,
002600 //  DISP=(NEW,CATLG,DELETE),
002700 //  UNIT=TAPE,
002800 //  VOL=(,,,10)
002900 //THIRDCPY   DD  DSN=CSCJGJ.DUMP.VOL000.COPY3,
003000 //  DISP=(NEW,CATLG,DELETE),
003100 //  UNIT=TAPE,
003200 //  VOL=(,,,10)
003300 //SYSPRINT   DD  SYSOUT=*
003400 //SYSIN      DD  *
003500      COPYDUMP                          -
003600                INDD(ORIGINAL)          -
003700                OUTDD(FIRSTCPY,         -
003800                      SECNDCPY,         -
003900                      THIRDCPY)
004000 //
```

VOL=(,,,10) secures a quantity of scratch tape volumes beyond the normal MVS/ESA maximum of five. Here the coding acquires up to 20 (yes, 20) scratch tape volumes. For detailed information about scratch volume quantity, see section 15.12 of ***Practical MVS JCL Examples*** by James Janossy, published by John Wiley & Sons, Inc., in 1993.

Figure A.38 Using COPYDUMP to Create Multiple Copies of a Logical Dump

A.15 RESTORE: Restoring Backup Data to Disk

The RESTORE command is used only with backup data that was created with the DUMP command. You can use it to restore data to disk volumes from DFDSS-produced dumps, data set by data set, by ranges of tracks, or by whole volumes. You can restore data sets to SMS-managed volumes and non-SMS-managed volumes. RESTORE recognizes Automatic Class Selection routines to determine the Storage Management Subsystem constructs of the new data set. You can, alternatively, spec-

```
EDIT ---- CSCJGJ.ADV.CNTL(A19A) - 01.00 --------------------- COLUMNS 001 072
COMMAND ===>                                                  SCROLL ===> PAGE
****** ***************************** TOP OF DATA ******************************
000100 //CSCJGJA   JOB 1,                ACCOUNTING INFORMATION
000200 //   'BIN 7--JANOSSY',             PROGRAMMER NAME AND DELIVERY BIN
000300 //   CLASS=A,                      INPUT QUEUE CLASS
000400 //   MSGLEVEL=(1,1),               HOW MUCH MVS SYSTEM PRINT DESIRED
000500 //   MSGCLASS=X,                   PRINT DESTINATION X A L N OR O
000600 //   TIME=(3,0),                   SAFETY LIMIT: RUN TIME UP TO 3 MIN
000700 //*  TYPRUN=SCAN,                  UNCOMMENT THIS LINE TO DO SCAN ONLY
000800 //   NOTIFY=CSCJGJ                 WHO TO TELL WHEN JOB IS DONE
000900 //*
001000 //* THIS JCL IS STORED AT CSCJGJ.ADV.CNTL(A19A)
001100 //*
001200 //*-----------------------------------------------------------------
001300 //* RESTORE BACKED UP DATA FROM TAPE TO DASD
001400 //*-----------------------------------------------------------------
001500 //STEP010   EXEC  PGM=ADRDSSU,
001600 //   REGION=6M,
001700 //   PARM='TYPRUN=NORUN'
001800 //INTAPE      DD  DSN=CSCJGJ.P.WEEKLY.BKUP.VOL000(0),
001900 //   DISP=SHR
002000 //VOL000      DD  UNIT=3380,
002100 //   DISP=SHR,
002200 //   VOL=SER=VOL000
002300 //SYSPRINT    DD  SYSOUT=*
002400 //SYSIN       DD  *
002500     RESTORE   DS(INCLUDE(CSCJGJ.A2.SLBV.LOP21.MEDS,     -
002600                          CSCJGJ.A2.SLBV.LOP21.PREDATE,  -
002700                          CSCJGJ.A2.SLBV.LOP21.MESA,     -
002800                          CSCJGJ.A2.SLBV.LOP21.POP00,    -
002900                          CSCJGJ.A2.SLBV.LOP21.SSA,      -
003000                          CSCJGJ.T.RVSD.PRNTTP00,        -
003100                          CSCJGJ.T.RVSD.BBGUM,           -
003200                          CSCJGJ.LD.SLBV.IV.SMFTRPF,     -
003300                          CSCJGJ.LD.SLBV.IV.SMFTRPL,     -
003400                          CSCJGJ.LD.SLBV.IV.SMFBLOCN,    -
003500                          CSCJGJ.LD.SLBV.IV.WIGGLE))     -
003600               INDDNAME(INTAPE)                          -
003700               OUTDDNAME(VOL000)                         -
003800               REPLACE
003900 //
```

Coding a **DD** statement with the volume serial number as the ddname makes coding an **OUTDDNAME** specification easy.

Figure A.39 Using RESTORE to Return Backed-Up Data to Disk

ify STORCLAS and/or MGMTCLAS names for the new data set or you can specify that Automatic Class Selection be bypassed. Options are available with the RESTORE command to:

- Rename a data set during a restore
- Redefine the block size of sequential or partitioned data sets during the process of restoration
- Restore data sets having undefined format (machine language modules) to an unlike device of larger track capacity
- Restore an entire VSAM "sphere" by invoking one restore (you need not restore the base cluster, data, index, and alternate indexes separately)
- For MVS/XA Version 2 Release 3 or later, restore a user catalog without bringing down a continuously running application such as DB2 and or IMS
- Specify whether DFDSS should continue or cancel a restore when a permanent read error occurs

Figure A.39 illustrates the use of RESTORE and some of these features. DFDSS can do logical processing at a disk volume level. This lets disk space management and operations personnel restore data sets to an unlike device, and to incrementally back up disk volume data storage pools rather than always using a whole-volume backup method.

In addition to features of use to programmers, disk space managers, and computer operations personnel, DFDSS provides support for actions commonly performed by systems programmers. It includes a stand-alone restore program that can restore data to disk even if the computer system presently does not have a host operating system accessible on disk. Systems programmers can use DFDSS to restore the system residence (SYSRES) disk volume on which critical components of the operating system must reside.

A.16 COMPRESS and RELEASE: Managing Disk Space

DFDSS provides features to compress and release unused space in partitioned data sets, consolidate free space on disk volumes, and release unused space in partitioned and sequential data sets. These tasks are normally undertaken by disk space management personnel rather than individual programmers.

The DFDSS COMPRESS command provides a way to selectively compress multiple ordinary (non PDSE) partitioned data sets on specified disk volumes, as shown in Figure A.40. The compress does not reduce the space allocation of the partitioned data sets or release unused secondary extents, but does make space within the partitioned data sets available for the storage of new or changed members. The RELEASE command releases allocated but unused space from sequential and partitioned data sets on a specified disk volume. RELEASE options exist to:

- Release space only if the unused space is larger than the number of tracks you specify
- Retain a specified quantity of secondary space allocation, leaving space to add records to the data set after DFDSS releases secondary allocations beyond the specified amount

Systems programmers frequently deal with system data sets that carry names starting with SYS1. By using the DFDSS keyword PROCESS(SYS1) it is possible to release unused space in partitioned or sequential data sets with a high-level qualifier (data set name front part) of SYS1. It is also possible to move such data sets, and to specify the DELETE option with the DUMP command to dump, then delete them.

```
EDIT ---- CSCJGJ.ADV.CNTL(A20A) - 01.00 ---------------------- COLUMNS 001 072
COMMAND ===>                                                  SCROLL ===> PAGE
****** ***************************** TOP OF DATA ******************************
000100 //CSCJGJA   JOB 1,                    ACCOUNTING INFORMATION
000200 //  'BIN 7--JANOSSY',                 PROGRAMMER NAME AND DELIVERY BIN
000300 //  CLASS=A,                          INPUT QUEUE CLASS
000400 //  MSGLEVEL=(1,1),                   HOW MUCH MVS SYSTEM PRINT DESIRED
000500 //  MSGCLASS=X,                       PRINT DESTINATION X A L N OR O
000600 //  TIME=(3,0),                       SAFETY LIMIT: RUN TIME UP TO 3 MIN
000700 //* TYPRUN=SCAN,                      UNCOMMENT THIS LINE TO DO SCAN ONLY
000800 //  NOTIFY=CSCJGJ                     WHO TO TELL WHEN JOB IS DONE
000900 //*
001000 //* THIS JCL IS STORED AT CSCJGJ.ADV.CNTL(A20A)
001100 //*
001200 //*-------------------------------------------------------------------
001300 //* COMPRESS ALL BUT SYS1 DATA SETS ON TWO DISK VOLUMES.
001400 //* ONLY DATA SETS THAT ARE LARGER THAN 100 TRACKS AND HAVE
001500 //* ACCUMULATED MORE THAN 3 EXTENTS WILL BE COMPRESSED.
001600 //*-------------------------------------------------------------------
001700 //STEP010  EXEC  PGM=ADRDSSU,
001800 //  REGION=6M,
001900 //  PARM='TYPRUN=NORUN'
002000 //SYSPRINT   DD  SYSOUT=*
002100 //SYSIN      DD  *
002200      COMPRESS
002300                DYNAM                 -
002400                  ((VOL005),          -
002500                   (VOL012))          -
002600                EXCLUDE(SYS1.**)      -
002700                BY(                   -
002800                  (FSIZE,GT,100)      -
002900                  (EXTNT,GT,003)      -
003000                     )                -
003100 //
```

You can focus **COMPRESS** on data sets on specific volumes and with the coding at BY, which is here based on the number of tracks data sets are allocated and the number of extents they are fragmented into.

Figure A.40 Compressing Selected Partitioned Data Sets on Two Disk Volumes

A.17 DEFRAG: Defragmenting Disk Space

Access to a data set is most efficient when the tracks or cylinders it occupies are contiguous, that is, all together in one place. But the creation, extension, and deletion of data sets by the multiple jobs being run concurrently by MVS/ESA inevitably produces noncontiguous chunks of free space on disk volumes. This phenomenon is known as disk space "fragmentation" and results in degraded performance and an increase in space-related abends.

Disk space managers or computer operations personnel can use the DFDSS DEFRAG command to consolidate data sets into fewer physical locations (extents) and minimize data set fragmentation. DEFRAG also prints a report about free space and other volume statistics. Options of the DEFRAG command make it possible to:

- Identify free space and produce disk volume statistics without defragmenting a volume
- Specify that a volume be defragmented only if it is fragmented to a level greater than specified
- Use filtering to exclude selected data sets from defragmentation

Figure A.41 illustrates how a member of a disk space management group or a member of an operations group could use the DEFRAG command to defragment a disk volume. When protected data sets are relocated using the DEFRAG command, DFDSS automatically erases the data in the old location to ensure its security. Without this extra provision, it is conceivable that a job accessing the old data location on disk could acquire confidential information.

```
EDIT ---- CSCJGJ.ADV.CNTL(A21A) - 01.00 --------------------- COLUMNS 001 072
COMMAND ===>                                                  SCROLL ===> PAGE
****** ****************************** TOP OF DATA ******************************
000100 //CSCJGJA   JOB 1,                   ACCOUNTING INFORMATION
000200 //   'BIN 7--JANOSSY',               PROGRAMMER NAME AND DELIVERY BIN
000300 //   CLASS=A,                        INPUT QUEUE CLASS
000400 //   MSGLEVEL=(1,1),                 HOW MUCH MVS SYSTEM PRINT DESIRED
000500 //   MSGCLASS=X,                     PRINT DESTINATION X A L N OR O
000600 //   TIME=(10,0),                    SAFETY LIMIT: RUN TIME UP TO 3 MIN
000700 //*  TYPRUN=SCAN,                    UNCOMMENT THIS LINE TO DO SCAN ONLY
000800 //   NOTIFY=CSCJGJ                   WHO TO TELL WHEN JOB IS DONE
000900 //*
001000 //* THIS JCL IS STORED AT CSCJGJ.ADV.CNTL(A21A)
001100 //*
001200 //*-----------------------------------------------------------------
001300 //* DEFRAGMENT A DASD VOLUME
001400 //*-----------------------------------------------------------------
001500 //STEP010  EXEC  PGM=ADRDSSU,
001600 //   REGION=6M,
001700 //   PARM='TYPRUN=NORUN'
001800 //SYSPRINT   DD  SYSOUT=*
001900 //SYSUDUMP   DD  SYSOUT=*
002000 //SYSIN      DD  *
002100      DEFRAG                    -
002200                 DYNAM(VOL000)  -
002300                 DYNAL
002400 //
```

Defragment a disk volume

Figure A.41 Using DFDSS to Defragment a Disk Volume

A.18 DFDSS Abbreviations and Acronyms

Much of the IBM literature associated with DFDSS uses abbreviations and acronyms with which you may not be familiar. Some of these abbreviations are very old, dating from the 1960s; others are of recent vintage. The following list will help you deal with the nomenclature of DFDSS.

ABSTR Absolute track allocation by cylinder and track number

BDAM Basic direct access method, a primitive form of disk access support tied to track numbers on disk volumes

DAM Direct access method, a primitive form of disk access support tied to track numbers on disk volumes

DASD (pronounced "daz-dee") direct access storage device, IBM's term for disk

DAU Direct access unmovable, data set is tied to specific track locations on a given model of disk device and can't be relocated by the DEFRAG command

DSORG Data set organization, a specification of the DCB parameter in job control language; this also appears on TSO/ISPF screens describing the attributes of data sets, such as PO, PO-E, POU, PS, and PSU. Note that LIBRARY is the designation of a partitioned data set extended (PDSE) while, in a display of inconsistency, some TSO/ISPF screens refer to an ordinary partitioned data set as PDS rather than the actual DSORG code of PO.

EC Engineering change

ICKDSF Device Support Facility utility

IPL Initial program load, the "boot up" of the mainframe

ISMF Interactive Storage Management Facility, full screen interactive access to some DFDSS and DFHSM operations

ISPF Interactive System Productivity Facility, TSO full screen text editor and programmer's workbench

LDS VSAM linear data set, the underlying storage mechanism supporting the DB2 relational database

MDS Main device scheduling

MENTITY Model entity

MVOLSER Model volume serial number

PAM Partitioned access method supporting ordinary partitioned data sets

PDS Partitioned data set, synonym for a TSO/ISPF library; its actual DSORG code is PO, which stands for "partitioned organization"

PDSE Partitioned data set extended, a newer form of PDS for program and data libraries only, supported in the Storage Management Subsystem environment and referred to as of organization type LIBRARY or DSORG=PO-E

PO Partitioned organization, the DSORG code for partitioned data sets

PO-E The DSORG code for partitioned data set extended data sets

POU Partitioned organization unmovable, a PDS that can't be moved to different disk locations because its internal structure refers to specific track locations by number

PS Physical sequential, the DSORG of a simple sequential data set, the most primitive of data storage organizations

PSU Physical sequential unmovable, a sequential data set that can't be moved to different disk locations because its internal structure refers to specific track locations by number

QSAM Queued sequential access method

SAM Sequential access method, the manager of simple collections of records in sequential files

SMF System Management Facility, software that logs and captures information produced by MVS for analysis by disk space management and operations personnel

SP System Product, a descriptive term often associated with other software, such as "MVS/SP"

Sphere The complete set of VSAM data set components making up a data set, including the base cluster (the data set's characteristic information, recorded in the system catalog), the data component, index component, and all of the components of any alternate indexes

SYSRES System resident, meaning that the data set referred to is recorded on the high-speed hard disk that houses the operating system and other modules critical to mainframe operation

UIM User interaction module, a special form of program that receives control from system software at a documented "user exit" and can modify the standard operation of a system function

Undefined data set organization "Undefined" does not mean "unknown." It indicates a recording mode of "U" that is characteristic of machine language load modules, and tells MVS not to attempt record blocking or deblocking for the data set.

VVDS VSAM volume data set, housekeeping information recorded for VSAM's use on each disk volume

A.19 IBM Reference Materials Documenting DFDSS

This appendix is intended to familiarize you with the Data Facility Data Set Services (DFDSS) utility program, show you the format of its commands, and demonstrate several of its features. To apply this powerful utility to your own work, you will also need to consult documentation local to your installation, and you may wish to examine one or more of the following IBM publications.

Data Facility Data Set Services: User's Guide, SC26-4388
Shows how to copy, dump, and restore data sets and disk volumes and manage disk space using DFDSS.

Data Facility Data Set Services: Reference, SC26-4389
Provides complete illustrations of DFDSS utility command syntax.

Data Facility Data Set Services: Messages, SC26-4390
Provides complete documentation of all DFDSS warning and error messages.

MVS/ESA Interactive Storage Management Facility User's Guide, SC26-4508
Represents a guide to the use of ISMF to work with DFDSS and the Storage Management Subsystem (SMS).

MVS/DFP Version 3: General Information, GC26-4507
Provides a complete description of the Data Facility Storage Management Subsystem (SMS).

B

VSAM Key Sequenced Data Set (IDCAMS) Examples

B.1 VSAM Data Set Organizations

B.2 IDCAMS and Control Statements

B.3 Data to Load an Indexed File

B.4 Defining and Loading a Key Sequenced Data Set

B.5 Output from the Define and Load Run

B.6 Typical VSAM Backup/Update/Reload Job Streams

B.7 Alternate Key Access

B.8 Creating Data VSAM Sets Using JCL Alone (DFSMS Only)

B.9 Creating Temporary VSAM Data Sets (DFSMS Only)

Virtual Storage Access Method (VSAM) was introduced in 1973 as a replacement for IBM's Indexed Sequential Access Method (ISAM). VSAM is independent of the MVS/ESA operating system and exists on machines running DOS/VSE and VM. VSAM supports four forms of data set organization:

- *Sequential data sets,* known as Entry Sequenced Data Sets (ESDS)
- *Relative data sets,* known as Relative Record Data Sets (RRDS)
- *Indexed data sets,* known as Key Sequenced Data Sets (KSDS)
- *Linear space data sets,* analog of RECFM=U "undefined" format data sets

VSAM is typically used to support on-line operation if no database such as IMS, DB2, IDMS, Oracle, or other product is used.

B.1 VSAM Data Set Organizations

The internal organization of VSAM data sets is more complex than the sequential (PS) and partitioned (PO) data sets originally provided with OS. Records in a VSAM data set are stored in ***control intervals*** (roughly the equivalent of data blocks), which are themselves housed in larger physical groupings named ***control areas.*** Though VSAM could supplant these "ordinary" data set organizations, it hasn't been used for that purpose and we still use sequential and partitioned data sets. The most common use of VSAM is to support indexed files (Key Sequenced Data Sets) for batch or interactive processing. As with any indexed sequential access method, you can obtain records from a VSAM Key Sequenced Data Set sequentially in ascending order of the primary or an alternate key, or you can obtain them directly by key.

Entry Sequenced Data Sets, Relative Record Data Sets, and Key Sequenced Data Sets correspond to file organizations common across different types of IBM and non-IBM computer systems. But linear space data sets are unique to the IBM mainframe environment. What are they? As Mike Haupt, a noted author and technical consultant, describes in a capsule summary that bears repeating, VSAM itself is composed of two major logical parts. The "upper" part of VSAM is software that logically manages the ESDS, RRDS, and KSDS data set organizations. This part ultimately requires the services of a "lower" part, which provides a standard method to access disk space independent of differing disk device characteristics. Linear space data sets are what the lower part of VSAM provides.

Initially, upper VSAM was the only part directly accessible to programmers. Linear data set access now allows programmers and other IBM software to directly utilize lower VSAM services, just as does other IBM software. For example, DB2 databases are actually housed as linear space data sets.

B.2 IDCAMS and Control Statements

To create a VSAM data you must establish information about it in the system catalog. The traditional way to do this is to execute the IDCAMS utility, giving it control statements that describe up to 60 parameters that dictate the internal organization and placement of the data set on one or more disk volumes. It's possible, for example, to specify that the index for a data set reside on a different disk volume than the data, to speed access by reducing disk arm contention.

IDCAMS reads its control statement at //SYSIN. Control statements begin with a keyword such as DELETE or DEFINE, which identifies a function that IDCAMS is to perform. Each function has several specifications and can span multiple lines of coding. Unlike JCL, you continue an IDCAMS control statement with a hyphen, not a comma, just as with DFDSS.

These IDCAMS functions are accessed by control statements and are the most useful in creating and managing Key Sequenced Data Sets:

DELETE is analogous to IEFBR14 for eliminating all components of an existing VSAM data set.

DEFINE establishes the names and characteristics of a new VSAM data set.

SET LASTCC or SET MAXCC alter the COND CODE values left behind by IDCAMS (these values can be tested with IF control statements within the control statement input to IDCAMS).

REPRO copies data from one data set to another, and can be used to copy records from a sequential file to a VSAM data set to load it, or from a VSAM data set to a sequential backup.

BLDINDEX creates an alternate index for an existing key sequenced data set.

LISTCAT lists information about the data set, stored in the catalog, and makes it accessible for viewing.

PRINT allows printing the contents of a VSAM or nonVSAM data set in hexadecimal, character, or dump format.

I have provided the examples in this appendix to give you a complete model for defining, loading, and analyzing the contents of a key sequenced data set. The annotations on the figures are intended to explain the important points, and the places where you would have to make changes to use this model for other data sets.

B.3 Data to Load an Indexed File

Figure B.1 shows you the beginning of a file of 80-byte records that I wish to house in an indexed file. Each of these records documents a voyage that has been booked on a pleasure cruise ship. Figure B.2 documents the layout of these records, including the length and starting position of each field in the records. (I'd strongly suggest that you prepare a chart like this to document the location of primary and alternate key fields in any file to be loaded to VSAM.) You can see that the fields in the first record are:

```
             Ticket number: 49321
       Passenger last name: ABAMA
      Passenger first name: AL
     Sailing date (YYMMDD): 940507
         Number of berths: 001
                Deck code: B
              Sales agent: UWANNAGO TRAVEL AGENCY
Ticket purchase date (YYMMDD): 931105
```

These records are in order of the passenger name. To load them to an indexed file, the records will have to be sorted into ascending order of ticket number, the unique identifier that will be used as the primary key. (This example is further documented in *VS COBOL II Highlights and Techniques*, by James Janossy, published by John Wiley & Sons, Inc., 1992.)

```
BROWSE -- CSCJGJ.CSC.C204DATA(TICKETS) - 01.00 ----- LINE 00000000 COL 001 080
COMMAND ===>                                                    SCROLL ===> PAGE
*********************************** TOP OF DATA ***********************************
49321ABAMA          AL         940507001B UWANNAGO TRAVEL AGENCY 931105
31574AH             GEORGE     940216001S1WORLD TRAVEL, INC.     940103
35112CABOOSE        LUCE       940331001B2ULTIMATE TRAVEL AGENCY 940121
43261CANNON         LUCE       940415001C FOX VALLEY TRAVEL      931004
31259DAY            HOLLY      940216001B HOLIDAY TOURS, INC.    930803
49257FOOEY          O.         940507004B1JACK SPRAT TRAVEL      930803
31779HEAD           M. T.      940216002C KOOK'S TOURS           940113
35189HOE            IDA        940331002S JACK SPRAT TRAVEL      930603
43483INA            CAROL      940415002S FOX VALLEY TRAVEL      940118
31257IPPI           MRS.       940216001B2JACK SPRAT TRAVEL      930817
49892JOE            CURLY      940507001C UWANNAGO TRAVEL AGENCY 940402
49514LITTLE         CHIC N.    940507014B1WORLD TRAVEL, INC.     940213
31260MALLOW         MARSHA     940216001B HOLIDAY TOURS, INC.    930805
49891MOE            LARRY      940507005C2HOLIDAY TOURS, INC.    940320
31256NILLY          WILLIE     940216002S1ULTIMATE TRAVEL AGENCY 930718
43507RITA           MARGA      940415002S WORLD TRAVEL, INC.     940401
43103SHANDELEER     CRYSTAL    940415002S JACK SPRAT TRAVEL      930827
31310SHAW           ARKAN      940216007S1HOLIDAY TOURS, INC.    930911
31778SLEEPING       R. U.      940216001B1UWANNAGO TRAVEL, INC.  940107
43480TOUR           D.         940415003C1HOLIDAY TOURS, INC.    940117
49322TUCKY          KEN        940507002C ULTIMATE TRAVEL AGENCY 931105
31307WARE           DELLA      940216004B1WORLD TRAVEL, INC.     930909
43484ZONA           HARRY      940415002C1UNRAVEL TRAVEL, INC.   940222
31668ZOORI          MOE        940216004S1FOX VALLEY TRAVEL      940103
 -
 -
 -
```

Figure B.1 Records Documenting Passage Booked on a Pleasure Cruise Ship

		1	2 3	4			5 6	7	8
	----+	----0----+----	0----+----0----	+----0	---	-+	----0----+----0----+---	-0----	+----0
	49321	ABAMA	AL	940507	001	B	UWANNAGO TRAVEL AGENCY	931105	
	31574	AH	GEORGE	940216	001	S1	WORLD TRAVEL, INC.	940103	
	35112	CABOOSE	LUCE	940331	001	B2	ULTIMATE TRAVEL AGENCY	940121	
	43261	CANNON	LUCE	940415	001	C	FOX VALLEY TRAVEL	931004	
	31259	DAY	HOLLY	940216	001	B	HOLIDAY TOURS, INC.	930803	
	49257	FOOEY	O.	940507	004	B1	JACK SPRAT TRAVEL	930803	
	31779	HEAD	M. T.	940216	002	C	KOOK'S TOURS	940113	
	35189	HOE	IDA	940331	002	S	JACK SPRAT TRAVEL	930603	
	43483	INA	CAROL	940415	002	S	FOX VALLEY TRAVEL	940118	
	31257	IPPI	MRS.	940216	001	B2	JACK SPRAT TRAVEL	930817	
Field length	5	14	15	6	3	2	23	6	6
Start position	1	6	20	35	41	44	46	69	75
End position	5	19	34	40	43	45	68	74	80
Displacement	0	5	19	34	40	43	45	68	74
Field	TICK-NUM	LAST-NAME	FIRST-NAME	SAIL	QTY	DECK	SALES-AGENT	PURCH	

Figure B.2 Record Layout for Pleasure Cruise Passenger Records Showing Field Positions and Displacements

B.4 Defining and Loading a Key Sequenced Data Set

Figure B.3 shows you a two-step job stream that begins by sorting the ticket records into ascending sequence by the ticket number field, creating a temporary data set named &&TEMP1. In STEP020, I execute the IDCAMS utility to delete any existing copy of a data set named CSCJGJ.CSC.TICKKSDS, then define a data set of this name. Additional control statements copy the sorted ticket records to the newly defined data set, define and build an alternate index using the sales agent field as the alternate key, use LISTCAT to view the catalog information about the data set, and finally use PRINT to examine data set contents by primary key, alternate key, and the alternate index records themselves.

B.5 Output from the Define and Load Run

Figure B.4 shows you the full MVS/ESA system reporting for the define and load run, LISTCAT output that echoes back the data set characteristics stored in the catalog, and output of the print functions. I have edited the final PRINT output, showing the content of the alternate index records, so you can see how they are constructed to point to the primary keys of the records sharing a common (nonunique) alternate index value.

Figure B.3 Job Stream to Define and Load a VSAM Key Sequenced Data Set for the Pleasure Cruise Passenger Records (see facing page)

```
EDIT ---- CSCJGJ.ADV.CNTL(AB1KSDS) - 01.02 ------------------- COLUMNS 001 072
COMMAND ===>                                                   SCROLL ===> PAGE
****** ******************************* TOP OF DATA ******************************
000001 //CSCJGJA   JOB 1,                  ACCOUNTING INFORMATION
000002 //  'BIN 7--JANOSSY',                PROGRAMMER NAME AND DELIVERY BIN
000003 //  CLASS=A,                        INPUT QUEUE CLASS
000004 //  MSGLEVEL=(1,1),                 HOW MUCH MVS SYSTEM PRINT DESIRED
000005 //  MSGCLASS=X,                     PRINT DESTINATION X A L N OR O
000006 //  TIME=(0,6),                     SAFETY LIMIT: RUN TIME UP TO 6 SECS
000007 //  REGION=2M,                      ALLOW UP TO 2 MEGS VIRTUAL MEMORY
000008 //* TYPRUN=SCAN,                    UNCOMMENT THIS LINE TO DO SCAN ONLY
000009 //  NOTIFY=CSCJGJ                   WHO TO TELL WHEN JOB IS DONE
000010 //*
000011 //* DEMONSTRATE HOW TO DEFINE AND LOAD A KEY SEQUENCE DATA SET
000012 //* WITH AN ALTERNATE INDEX, AND TO DUMP INDEXES
000013 //* THIS JCL IS STORED AT CSCJGJ.ADV.CNTL(AB1KSDS)
000014 //*********************************************************************
000015 //*                                                                   *
000016 //*   SORT THE DATA TO BE LOADED IN TO KEY SEQUENCE                   *
000017 //*                                                                   *
000018 //*********************************************************************
000019 //STEP010  EXEC  PGM=SORT
000020 //SYSOUT     DD  SYSOUT=*
000021 //SORTIN     DD  DSN=CSCJGJ.CSC.C204DATA(TICKETS),
000022 //  DISP=SHR
000023 //SORTOUT    DD  DSN=&&TEMP1,
000024 //  DISP=(NEW,PASS,DELETE),
000025 //  UNIT=VIO,
000026 //  RECFM=FB,
000027 //  LRECL=80,
000028 //  SPACE=(CYL,1)
000029 //SORTWK01   DD  UNIT=VIO,SPACE=(CYL,1)
000030 //SORTWK02   DD  UNIT=VIO,SPACE=(CYL,1)
000031 //SORTWK03   DD  UNIT=VIO,SPACE=(CYL,1)
000032 //SYSIN      DD  *
000033    SORT FIELDS=(1,5,CH,A)
000034 //*
000035 //*********************************************************************
000036 //*                                                                   *
000037 //*   DEFINE AND LOAD THE CUSTOMER KSDS                               *
000038 //*                                                                   *
000039 //*********************************************************************
000040 //STEP020  EXEC  PGM=IDCAMS
000041 //SYSPRINT   DD  SYSOUT=*
000042 //MASTIN     DD  DSN=&&TEMP1,DISP=(OLD,DELETE)
000043 //*
000044 //WORKSRT1   DD  DSN=CSCJGJ.CSC.IDCUT1,
000045 //  UNIT=SYSDA,
000046 //  DISP=OLD,
000047 //  AMP='AMORG',
000048 //  VOL=SER=USER00
000049 //*
000050 //WORKSRT2   DD  DSN=CSCJGJ.CSC.IDCUT2,
000051 //  UNIT=SYSDA,
000052 //  DISP=OLD,
000053 //  AMP='AMORG',
000054 //  VOL=SER=USER00
000055 //*
000056 //SYSIN      DD  *
000057                                   /* HOUSEKEEPING DELETES  */
000058
000059     DELETE         CSCJGJ.CSC.TICKKSDS -
000060                    CLUSTER
000061
000062     DELETE         CSCJGJ.CSC.IDCUT1 -
000063                    CLUSTER
000064
000065     DELETE         CSCJGJ.CSC.IDCUT2 -
000066                    CLUSTER
000067
000068   SET LASTCC=0                    /* MAY NOT BE FOUND; GET */
000069   SET MAXCC=0                     /* RID OF COND CODE 8    */
```

Sort the records to be loaded to the indexed file into ascending order of primary key

These work files are used by the BLDINDEX function as it creates the alternate index

Delete the file before defining and loading only for first-time loading!

This job stream defines and loads an indexed file with the ticket records shown in Figure B.1. The following page shows the control statements used to define the characteristics of the file.

```
000071    /* - - - - - - - - - - - - - CREATE BASE CLUSTER - - - - -*/
000072
000073      DEFINE -
000074        CLUSTER     (    NAME(CSCJGJ.CSC.TICKKSDS) -
000075                         VOLUMES(USER01) -
000076                         RECORDSIZE(80 80) -
000077                         KEYS(5 0) -
000078                         TRACKS(1 1) -
000079                         SHAREOPTIONS(2 3) -
000080                         SPEED -
000081                         IMBED                                 ) -
000082                         -
000083        DATA        (    NAME(CSCJGJ.CSC.TICKKSDS.DATA) -
000084                         CONTROLINTERVALSIZE(4096) -
000085                         FREESPACE(6 1)                        ) -
000086                         -
000087        INDEX       (    NAME(CSCJGJ.CSC.TICKKSDS.INDEX)       )
000088
000089    /* - - - - - - - - - - - - - IF CREATE OKAY, LOAD IT - - -*/
000090
000091    IF LASTCC = 0 -
000092    THEN -
000093      REPRO          INFILE(MASTIN) -
000094                     OUTDATASET(CSCJGJ.CSC.TICKKSDS)
000095
000096    /* - - - - - - - - - - - - - DEFINE THE ALTERNATE INDEX - */
000097
000098       DEFINE -
000099         AIX        (    NAME(CSCJGJ.CSC.TICKKSDS.SALEAIX) -
000100                         RELATE(CSCJGJ.CSC.TICKKSDS) -
000101                         VOLUMES(USER02) -
000102                         RECORDSIZE(33 6600) -
000103                         KEYS(23 45) -
000104                         NONUNIQUEKEY -
000105                         TRACKS(1 1) -
000106                         SHAREOPTIONS(2 3) -
000107                         UNIQUE -
000108                         UPGRADE -
000109                         SPEED -
000110                         IMBED                                   ) -
000111                         -
000112         DATA       (    NAME(CSCJGJ.CSC.TICKKSDS.SALEAIX.DATA) -
000113                         CONTROLINTERVALSIZE(4096) -
000114                         FREESPACE(2 1)                          ) -
000115                         -
000116         INDEX      (    NAME(CSCJGJ.CSC.TICKKSDS.SALEAIX.INDEX) )
000117
000118       BLDINDEX      INDATASET(CSCJGJ.CSC.TICKKSDS) -
000119                     OUTDATASET(CSCJGJ.CSC.TICKKSDS.SALEAIX) -
000120                     WORKFILES(WORKSRT1 WORKSRT2) -
000121                     EXTERNALSORT
000122
000123       DEFINE -
000124         PATH       (    NAME(CSCJGJ.CSC.TICKKSDS.SALEAIX.PATH) -
000125                         PATHENTRY(CSCJGJ.CSC.TICKKSDS.SALEAIX) )
000126
000127     /* - - - - - - - - - - - - - LIST CATALOG TO SEE INFO  - -*/
000128
000129      LISTCAT -
000130        ENTRIES      ( CSCJGJ.CSC.TICKKSDS -
000131                       CSCJGJ.CSC.TICKKSDS.SALEAIX ) -
000132                     ALL
000133
000134     /* - - - - - - - - - - PRINT IT IN PRIMARY KEY SEQ  - -*/
000135
000136      PRINT          INDATASET(CSCJGJ.CSC.TICKKSDS) -
000137                     COUNT(50) -
000138                     CHARACTER
000139
000140     /* - - - - - - - - - - NOW PRINT IT IN ALT KEY SEQ  - -*/
000141
000142      PRINT          INDATASET(CSCJGJ.CSC.TICKKSDS.SALEAIX.PATH) -
000143                     COUNT(50) -
000144                     CHARACTER
000145
000146     /* - - - - - - - - - - THIS PRINTS THE AIX RECORDS  - -*/
000147
000148      PRINT          INDATASET(CSCJGJ.CSC.TICKKSDS.SALEAIX) -
000149                     COUNT(50) -
000150                     CHARACTER
000151 //
```

Define base cluster

Load the file

Define alternate index (key starts in displacement 45)

Show catalog info

Show contents

Figure B.3 (continued)

```
                  J E S 2  J O B  L O G  --  S Y S T E M  I B M 1  --  N O D E  N 1

17.09.53 JOB07869  IRR010I  USERID CSCJGJ   IS ASSIGNED TO THIS JOB.
17.09.54 JOB07869  ICH70001I CSCJGJ   LAST ACCESS AT 17:05:52 ON THURSDAY, MARCH 24, 1994
17.09.54 JOB07869  $HASP373 CSCJGJA  STARTED - INIT  1 - CLASS A - SYS IBM1
17.10.10 JOB07869  $HASP395 CSCJGJA  ENDED

------ JES2 JOB STATISTICS ------
  24 MAR 94 JOB EXECUTION DATE
        151 CARDS READ
        763 SYSOUT PRINT RECORDS
          0 SYSOUT PUNCH RECORDS
         41 SYSOUT SPOOL KBYTES
       0.27 MINUTES EXECUTION TIME

        1 //CSCJGJA   JOB 1,                     ACCOUNTING INFORMATION
          //  'BIN 7--JANOSSY',                  PROGRAMMER NAME AND DELIVERY BIN
          //  CLASS=A,                           INPUT QUEUE CLASS
          //  MSGLEVEL=(1,1),                    HOW MUCH MVS SYSTEM PRINT DESIRED
          //  MSGCLASS=X,                        PRINT DESTINATION X A L N OR O
          //  TIME=(0,6),                        SAFETY LIMIT: RUN TIME UP TO 6 SECS
          //  REGION=2M,                         ALLOW UP TO 2 MEGS VIRTUAL MEMORY
          //* TYPRUN=SCAN,                       UNCOMMENT THIS LINE TO DO SCAN ONLY
          //  NOTIFY=CSCJGJ                      WHO TO TELL WHEN JOB IS DONE
          //*
          //* DEMONSTRATE HOW TO DEFINE AND LOAD A KEY SEQUENCE DATA SET
          //* WITH AN ALTERNATE INDEX, AND TO DUMP INDEXES
          //* THIS JCL IS STORED AT CSCJGJ.ADV.CNTL(AB1KSDS)
          //*****************************************************************
          //*                                                               *
          //*   SORT THE DATA TO BE LOADED IN TO KEY SEQUENCE               *
          //*                                                               *
          //*****************************************************************
        2 //STEP010  EXEC  PGM=SORT
        3 //SYSOUT     DD  SYSOUT=*
        4 //SORTIN     DD  DSN=CSCJGJ.CSC.C204DATA(TICKETS),
          //  DISP=SHR
        5 //SORTOUT    DD  DSN=&&TEMP1,
          //  DISP=(NEW,PASS,DELETE),
          //  UNIT=VIO,
          //  RECFM=FB,
          //  LRECL=80,
          //  SPACE=(CYL,1)
```

This is the MVS/ESA system output that results from the submission of the AB1KSDS job stream in Figure B.3. I have included the complete output here, with annotations, to serve as a full example of VSAM Key Sequenced Data Set deletion, definition, loading, alternate index building, catalog information display, and data set content printing as accomplished with IDCAMS. At the very end of this listing you will find the third of three **PRINT** outputs, showing you the actual structure of the alternate index records as constructed by IDCAMS.

Figure B.4 MVS/ESA System Output for the Key Sequenced Data Set Define and Load Run

```
 6 //SORTWK01   DD  UNIT=VIO,SPACE=(CYL,1)
 7 //SORTWK02   DD  UNIT=VIO,SPACE=(CYL,1)
 8 //SORTWK03   DD  UNIT=VIO,SPACE=(CYL,1)
 9 //SYSIN      DD  *
   //*
   //*********************************************************************
   //*                                                                   *
   //*    DEFINE AND LOAD THE CUSTOMER KSDS                              *
   //*                                                                   *
   //*********************************************************************
10 //STEP020  EXEC  PGM=IDCAMS
11 //SYSPRINT   DD  SYSOUT=*
12 //MASTIN     DD  DSN=&&TEMP1,DISP=(OLD,DELETE)
   //*
13 //WORKSRT1   DD  DSN=CSCJGJ.CSC.IDCUT1,
   //   UNIT=SYSDA,
   //   DISP=OLD,
   //   AMP='AMORG',
   //   VOL=SER=USER00
   //*
14 //WORKSRT2   DD  DSN=CSCJGJ.CSC.IDCUT2,
   //   UNIT=SYSDA,
   //   DISP=OLD,
   //   AMP='AMORG',
   //   VOL=SER=USER00
   //*
15 //SYSIN      DD  *
```

The file at ddname **MASTIN** houses the sorted ticket records to be loaded to the Key Sequenced Data Set. **WORKSRT1** and **WORKSRT2** are sort work files used by the BLDINDEX function as it composes the alternate index. You may be able to eliminate explicit reference to these work files in your installation.

Figure B.4 (continued)

```
ICH70001I CSCJGJ   LAST ACCESS AT 17:05:52 ON THURSDAY, MARCH 24, 1994

IEF236I ALLOC. FOR CSCJGJA STEP010
IEF237I JES2 ALLOCATED TO SYSOUT
IEF237I 111  ALLOCATED TO SORTIN
IEF237I VIO  ALLOCATED TO SORTOUT
IEF237I VIO  ALLOCATED TO SORTWK01
IEF237I VIO  ALLOCATED TO SORTWK02
IEF237I VIO  ALLOCATED TO SORTWK03
IEF237I JES2 ALLOCATED TO SYSIN
IEF237I 116  ALLOCATED TO SORTDK01
IEF237I 115  ALLOCATED TO SORTDK02
IEF237I 117  ALLOCATED TO SORTDK03
IEF142I CSCJGJA STEP010 - STEP WAS EXECUTED - COND CODE 0000
IEF285I   CSCJGJ.CSCJGJA.JOB07869.D0000103.?           SYSOUT
IEF285I   CSCJGJ.CSC.C204DATA                          KEPT
IEF285I   VOL SER NOS= USER00.
IEF285I   SYS94083.T170954.RA000.CSCJGJA.TEMP1         PASSED
IEF285I   SYS94083.T170954.RA000.CSCJGJA.R0002792      DELETED
IEF285I   SYS94083.T170954.RA000.CSCJGJA.R0002793      DELETED
IEF285I   SYS94083.T170954.RA000.CSCJGJA.R0002794      DELETED
IEF285I   CSCJGJ.CSCJGJA.JOB07869.D0000101.?           SYSIN
IEF285I   SYS94083.T170954.RA000.CSCJGJA.S01           DELETED
IEF285I   VOL SER NOS= USER02.
IEF285I   SYS94083.T170955.RA000.CSCJGJA.S02           DELETED
IEF285I   VOL SER NOS= USER01.
IEF285I   SYS94083.T170955.RA000.CSCJGJA.S03           DELETED
IEF285I   VOL SER NOS= USER03.
IEF373I STEP /STEP010 / START 94083.1709
IEF374I STEP /STEP010 / STOP  94083.1709 CPU    0MIN 00.52SEC SRB    0MIN 00.01SEC VIRT  1040K SYS   228K EXT    4096K SYS    9084K

IEF236I ALLOC. FOR CSCJGJA STEP020
IEF237I JES2 ALLOCATED TO SYSPRINT
IEF237I VIO  ALLOCATED TO MASTIN
IEF237I 111  ALLOCATED TO WORKSRT1
IEF237I 111  ALLOCATED TO WORKSRT2
IEF237I JES2 ALLOCATED TO SYSIN
IEF237I 115  ALLOCATED TO SYS00001
IEF237I 116  ALLOCATED TO SYS00001
IEF285I   CSCJGJ.CSC.TICKKSDS                          KEPT
IEF285I   VOL SER NOS= USER01,USER02.
IEF237I 115  ALLOCATED TO SYS00002
IEF237I 115  ALLOCATED TO SYS00004
```

The sort left behind **COND CODE 0000** as an indication that it operated successfully

MVS/ESA shows the VSAM Key Sequenced Data Set on ***two*** volumes, because I placed its data component on disk volume serial number USER01 and the index component on disk volume USER02.

Figure B.4 (continued)

```
IEF285I   SYS94083.T171000.RA000.CSCJGJA.R0000002        KEPT
IEF285I   VOL SER NOS= USER01.
IEF285I   SYS94083.T171000.RA000.CSCJGJA.R0000004        KEPT
IEF285I   VOL SER NOS= USER01.
IEF237I 115  ALLOCATED TO SYS00006
IEF285I   CSCJGJ.CSC.TICKKSDS                            KEPT
IEF285I   VOL SER NOS= USER01.
IEF237I 116  ALLOCATED TO SYS00007
IEF237I 116  ALLOCATED TO SYS00009
IEF285I   SYS94083.T171002.RA000.CSCJGJA.R0000007        KEPT
IEF285I   VOL SER NOS= USER02.
IEF285I   SYS94083.T171002.RA000.CSCJGJA.R0000009        KEPT
IEF285I   VOL SER NOS= USER02.
IEF237I JES2 ALLOCATED TO SYSOUT
IEF237I 115  ALLOCATED TO SYS00011
IEF237I 116  ALLOCATED TO SYS00011
IEF237I 116  ALLOCATED TO SYS00012
IEF237I 117  ALLOCATED TO SORTWK01
IEF237I 117  ALLOCATED TO SORTWK02
IEF285I   SYS94083.T171004.RA000.CSCJGJA.R0000012        DELETED
IEF285I   VOL SER NOS= USER03.
IEF285I   SYS94083.T171005.RA000.CSCJGJA.R0000013        DELETED
IEF285I   VOL SER NOS= USER03.
IEF285I   CSCJGJ.CSC.TICKKSDS.SALEAIX                    KEPT
IEF285I   VOL SER NOS= USER02.
IEF285I   CSCJGJ.CSC.TICKKSDS                            KEPT
IEF285I   VOL SER NOS= USER01,USER02.
IEF237I 115  ALLOCATED TO SYS00015
IEF237I 116  ALLOCATED TO SYS00015
IEF285I   CSCJGJ.CSC.TICKKSDS                            KEPT
IEF285I   VOL SER NOS= USER01,USER02.
IEF237I 116  ALLOCATED TO SYS00016
IEF237I 115  ALLOCATED TO SYS00016
IEF285I   CSCJGJ.CSC.TICKKSDS.SALEAIX.PATH               KEPT
IEF285I   VOL SER NOS= USER02,USER01.
IEF237I 116  ALLOCATED TO SYS00017
IEF285I   CSCJGJ.CSC.TICKKSDS.SALEAIX                    KEPT
IEF285I   VOL SER NOS= USER02.
IEF142I CSCJGJA STEP020 - STEP WAS EXECUTED - COND CODE 0004
IEF285I   CSCJGJ.CSCJGJA.JOB07869.D0000104.?             SYSOUT
IEF285I   SYS94083.T170954.RA000.CSCJGJA.TEMP1           DELETED
IEF285I   CSCJGJ.CSC.IDCUT1                              KEPT
IEF285I   VOL SER NOS= USER00.
```

All of this MVS/ESA system reporting documents the allocation of devices to the many data sets accessed by IDCAMS as it follows my instructions to delete the existing CSCJGJ.CSC.TICKKSDS VSAM file (if it exists), define this data set catalog entry (cluster), populate its data component and build its index, and build its alternate index components. The listing of these allocation actions ends with the STEP WAS EXECUTED line, with **COND CODE 0004**.

IDCAMS accomplished all of the work I asked it to do, but left behind a "warning" indication with COND CODE 0004. You will see later in this system output the benign nature of this warning, and why in this case it poses no problem.

Figure B.4 (continued)

```
IEF285I   CSCJGJ.CSC.IDCUT2                                KEPT
IEF285I   VOL SER NOS= USER00.
IEF285I   CSCJGJ.CSCJGJA.JOB07869.D0000102.?               SYSIN
IEF285I   CSCJGJ.CSCJGJA.JOB07869.D0000105.?               SYSOUT
IEF373I STEP /STEP020 / START 94083.1709
IEF374I STEP /STEP020 / STOP  94083.1710 CPU    0MIN 03.13SEC SRB    0MIN 00.07SEC VIRT  1436K SYS   248K EXT    4120K SYS    9120K
IEF375I  JOB /CSCJGJA / START 94083.1709
IEF376I  JOB /CSCJGJA / STOP  94083.1710 CPU    0MIN 03.65SEC SRB    0MIN 00.08SEC

ICE143I 0 BLOCKSET     SORT  TECHNIQUE SELECTED
ICE000I 1 --- CONTROL STATEMENTS/MESSAGES ---- 5740-SM1 REL 11.1 ---- 17.09.54 MAR 24, 1994 --

          SORT FIELDS=(1,5,CH,A)

ICE088I 1 CSCJGJA .STEP010 .        , INPUT LRECL = 80, BLKSIZE = 3840, TYPE = F
ICE093I 0 MAIN STORAGE = (MAX,4194304,4194304), NMAX = 20800
ICE156I 0 MAIN STORAGE ABOVE 16MB = (4142928,4142928)
ICE128I 0 OPTIONS: SIZE=4194304,MAXLIM=1048576,MINLIM=450560,EQUALS=N,LIST=Y,ERET=RC16 ,MSGDDN=SYSOUT
ICE129I 0 OPTIONS: VIO=N,RESDNT=ALL ,SMF=NO    ,WRKSEC=Y,OUTSEC=Y,VERIFY=N,CHALT=N,DYNALOC=N            ,ABCODE=MSG
ICE130I 0 OPTIONS: RESALL=4096,RESINV=0,SVC=109 ,CHECK=Y,WRKREL=Y,OUTREL=Y,CKPT=N,STIMER=Y,COBEXIT=COB1
ICE131I 0 OPTIONS: TMAXLIM=4194304,ARESALL=0,ARESINV=0,OVERRGN=65536,EXCPVR=NONE ,CINV=Y,CFW=Y
ICE132I 0 OPTIONS: VLSHRT=N,ZDPRINT=N,IEXIT=N,TEXIT=N,LISTX=N,EFS=NONE    ,EXITCK=S,PARMDDN=DFSPARM ,FSZEST=N
ICE133I 0 OPTIONS: HIPRMAX=OPTIMAL
ICE084I 0 EXCP ACCESS METHOD USED FOR SORTOUT
ICE084I 0 EXCP ACCESS METHOD USED FOR SORTIN
ICE090I 0 OUTPUT LRECL = 80, BLKSIZE = 22880, TYPE = F  (SDB)
ICE080I 0 IN MAIN STORAGE SORT
ICE055I 0 INSERT 0, DELETE 0
ICE054I 0 RECORDS - IN: 50, OUT: 50
ICE134I 0 NUMBER OF BYTES SORTED: 4000
ICE165I 0 TOTAL WORK DATA SET TRACKS ALLOCATED: 45 , TRACKS USED: 0
ICE180I 0 HIPERSPACE STORAGE USED = 0K BYTES
ICE052I 0 END OF DFSORT
```

These messages from the sort utility are output at its //SYSOUT DD statement. Notice that it reports on the number of records it received ("in") and the number of records it output ("out").

Figure B.4 (continued)

```
IDCAMS  SYSTEM SERVICES                                  TIME: 17:09:57        03/24/94     PAGE    1
                                 /* HOUSEKEEPING DELETES  */

   DELETE       CSCJGJ.CSC.TICKKSDS -
                CLUSTER

IDC0550I ENTRY (R) CSCJGJ.CSC.TICKKSDS.SALEAIX.PATH DELETED
IDC0550I ENTRY (D) CSCJGJ.CSC.TICKKSDS.SALEAIX.DATA DELETED
IDC0550I ENTRY (I) CSCJGJ.CSC.TICKKSDS.SALEAIX.INDEX DELETED
IDC0550I ENTRY (G) CSCJGJ.CSC.TICKKSDS.SALEAIX DELETED
IDC0550I ENTRY (D) CSCJGJ.CSC.TICKKSDS.DATA DELETED
IDC0550I ENTRY (I) CSCJGJ.CSC.TICKKSDS.INDEX DELETED
IDC0550I ENTRY (C) CSCJGJ.CSC.TICKKSDS DELETED
IDC0001I FUNCTION COMPLETED, HIGHEST CONDITION CODE WAS 0

   DELETE       CSCJGJ.CSC.IDCUT1 -
                CLUSTER

IDC3012I ENTRY CSCJGJ.CSC.IDCUT1 NOT FOUND
IDC3009I ** VSAM CATALOG RETURN CODE IS 8 - REASON CODE IS IGG0CLA3-42
IDC0551I ** ENTRY CSCJGJ.CSC.IDCUT1 NOT DELETED
IDC0001I FUNCTION COMPLETED, HIGHEST CONDITION CODE WAS 8

   DELETE       CSCJGJ.CSC.IDCUT2 -
                CLUSTER

IDC3012I ENTRY CSCJGJ.CSC.IDCUT2 NOT FOUND
IDC3009I ** VSAM CATALOG RETURN CODE IS 8 - REASON CODE IS IGG0CLA3-42
IDC0551I ** ENTRY CSCJGJ.CSC.IDCUT2 NOT DELETED
IDC0001I FUNCTION COMPLETED, HIGHEST CONDITION CODE WAS 8

  SET LASTCC=0                   /* MAY NOT BE FOUND; GET */
  SET MAXCC=0                    /* RID OF COND CODE 8    */

  /* - - - - - - - - - - - - CREATE BASE CLUSTER - - - - -*/

   DEFINE -
     CLUSTER    (    NAME(CSCJGJ.CSC.TICKKSDS) -
                     VOLUMES(USER01) -
                     RECORDSIZE(80 80) -
                     KEYS(5 0) -
                     TRACKS(1 1) -
```

VSAM data set CSCJGJ.CSC.TICKKSDS already existed before this run, because I had run this job before. Here you see how IDCAMS reports the deletion of the components of the existing data set, starting with the alternate index path, then the alternate index, and finally the data, index, and base cluster itself. Every IDCAMS function such as **DELETE** returns a condition code value. The highest of these is reported as the COND CODE for the step at which IDCAMS is executed. The **DELETE**s for the sort work files, on the other hand, do not find these files present, and leave behind condition codes of 8. These condition codes could affect subsequent IDCAMS command processing unless I used **SET** to make the most recent (LASTCC) and highest (MAXCC) condition code values zero again.

Figure B.4 (continued)

```
                 SHAREOPTIONS(2 3) -
                 SPEED -
                 IMBED                              ) -
                 -
    DATA      (  NAME(CSCJGJ.CSC.TICKKSDS.DATA) -
                 CONTROLINTERVALSIZE(4096) -
                 FREESPACE(6 1)                     ) -
                 -
    INDEX     (  NAME(CSCJGJ.CSC.TICKKSDS.INDEX)    )

IDC0508I DATA ALLOCATION STATUS FOR VOLUME USER01 IS 0
IDC0509I INDEX ALLOCATION STATUS FOR VOLUME USER01 IS 0
IDC0001I FUNCTION COMPLETED, HIGHEST CONDITION CODE WAS 0

 /* - - - - - - - - - - - - - IF CREATE OKAY, LOAD IT - - -*/

 IF LASTCC = 0 -
 THEN -
   REPRO        INFILE(MASTIN) -
                OUTDATASET(CSCJGJ.CSC.TICKKSDS)

IDC0005I NUMBER OF RECORDS PROCESSED WAS 50
IDC0001I FUNCTION COMPLETED, HIGHEST CONDITION CODE WAS 0

 /* - - - - - - - - - - - - - DEFINE THE ALTERNATE INDEX - */

    DEFINE -
      AIX     (  NAME(CSCJGJ.CSC.TICKKSDS.SALEAIX) -
                 RELATE(CSCJGJ.CSC.TICKKSDS) -
                 VOLUMES(USER02) -
                 RECORDSIZE(33 6600) -
                 KEYS(23 45) -
                 NONUNIQUEKEY -
                 TRACKS(1 1) -
                 SHAREOPTIONS(2 3) -
                 UNIQUE -
                 UPGRADE -
                 SPEED -
                 IMBED                              ) -
                 -
    DATA      (  NAME(CSCJGJ.CSC.TICKKSDS.SALEAIX.DATA) -
                 CONTROLINTERVALSIZE(4096) -
                 FREESPACE(2 1)                     ) -
```

IDCAMS completed its base cluster **DEFINE** actions and reports here, with condition code 0, that all went well. The specifications I coded under CLUSTER, DATA, and INDEX have been recorded in the system catalog under the base cluster name. Next, you see that **REPRO** function worked and copied 50 records (the sorted ticket records that entered at ddname MASTIN) to the new VSAM Key Sequenced Data Set. Finally, you see the beginning of the echo of the **DEFINE** for the alternate index, which is in itself another Key Sequenced Data Set.

Figure B.4 (continued)

```
                 -
   INDEX      (   NAME(CSCJGJ.CSC.TICKKSDS.SALEAIX.INDEX) )

IDC0508I DATA ALLOCATION STATUS FOR VOLUME USER02 IS 0
IDC0509I INDEX ALLOCATION STATUS FOR VOLUME USER02 IS 0
IDC0001I FUNCTION COMPLETED, HIGHEST CONDITION CODE WAS 0

     BLDINDEX     INDATASET(CSCJGJ.CSC.TICKKSDS) -
                  OUTDATASET(CSCJGJ.CSC.TICKKSDS.SALEAIX) -
                  WORKFILES(WORKSRT1 WORKSRT2) -
                  EXTERNALSORT

IDC0652I CSCJGJ.CSC.TICKKSDS.SALEAIX SUCCESSFULLY BUILT
IDC0001I FUNCTION COMPLETED, HIGHEST CONDITION CODE WAS 0

     DEFINE -
       PATH       (   NAME(CSCJGJ.CSC.TICKKSDS.SALEAIX.PATH) -
                      PATHENTRY(CSCJGJ.CSC.TICKKSDS.SALEAIX) )

IDC0001I FUNCTION COMPLETED, HIGHEST CONDITION CODE WAS 0

  /* - - - - - - - - - - - - - LIST CATALOG TO SEE INFO - - -*/

    LISTCAT -
      ENTRIES     ( CSCJGJ.CSC.TICKKSDS -
                    CSCJGJ.CSC.TICKKSDS.SALEAIX ) -
                  ALL

CLUSTER ------- CSCJGJ.CSC.TICKKSDS
     IN-CAT --- SYS1.USERCAT
     HISTORY
       DATASET-OWNER-----(NULL)      CREATION--------1994.083
       RELEASE----------------2      EXPIRATION------0000.000
     PROTECTION-PSWD-----(NULL)      RACF----------------(YES)
     ASSOCIATIONS
       DATA-----CSCJGJ.CSC.TICKKSDS.DATA
       INDEX----CSCJGJ.CSC.TICKKSDS.INDEX
       AIX------CSCJGJ.CSC.TICKKSDS.SALEAIX

   DATA ------- CSCJGJ.CSC.TICKKSDS.DATA
     IN-CAT --- SYS1.USERCAT
     HISTORY
       DATASET-OWNER-----(NULL)      CREATION--------1994.083
```

IDCAMS has completed constructing the alternate index with **BLDINDEX**, and then **DEFINE**s the path, as specified. Now, I have used the **LISTCAT** function to print the catalog-stored information about the base cluster and alternate index. **LISTCAT** will confirm what MVS/ESA knows about the new data set, and the statistics in the base cluster will indicate (on the next page) how many records are in the data set, how many have been updated, and how many have been read (retrieved). **LISTCAT**, in fact, indicates more than you usually want to know, so various options and methods exist to trim down how much of this you actually receive and perhaps print.

Figure B.4 (continued)

```
    RELEASE----------------2      EXPIRATION------0000.000
  PROTECTION-PSWD-----(NULL)      RACF----------------(YES)
  ASSOCIATIONS
    CLUSTER--CSCJGJ.CSC.TICKKSDS
  ATTRIBUTES
    KEYLEN-----------------5      AVGLRECL--------------80      BUFSPACE------------8704      CISIZE--------------4096
    RKP--------------------0      MAXLRECL--------------80      EXCPEXIT----------(NULL)      CI/CA-----------------10
    SHROPTNS(2,3)      SPEED      UNIQUE           NOERASE      INDEXED         NOWRITECHK    IMBED          NOREPLICAT
    UNORDERED        NOREUSE      NONSPANNED
  STATISTICS
    REC-TOTAL-------------50      SPLITS-CI--------------0      EXCPS------------------5
    REC-DELETED------------0      SPLITS-CA--------------0      EXTENTS----------------1
    REC-INSERTED-----------0      FREESPACE-%CI----------6      SYSTEM-TIMESTAMP:
    REC-UPDATED------------0      FREESPACE-%CA----------1           X'A906610510F9D800'
    REC-RETRIEVED---------50      FREESPC-BYTES------32768
  ALLOCATION
    SPACE-TYPE---------TRACK      HI-ALLOC-RBA-------40960
    SPACE-PRI--------------2      HI-USED-RBA--------40960
    SPACE-SEC--------------2
  VOLUME
    VOLSER------------USER01      PHYREC-SIZE---------4096      HI-ALLOC-RBA-------40960      EXTENT-NUMBER----------1
    DEVTYPE------X'30102004'      PHYRECS/TRK-----------10      HI-USED-RBA--------40960      EXTENT-TYPE--------X'40'
    VOLFLAG------------PRIME      TRACKS/CA--------------2
    EXTENTS:
    LOW-CCHH-----X'002B000D'      LOW-RBA----------------0      TRACKS-----------------2
    HIGH-CCHH----X'002B000E'      HIGH-RBA-----------40959

INDEX ------ CSCJGJ.CSC.TICKKSDS.INDEX
  IN-CAT --- SYS1.USERCAT
  HISTORY
    DATASET-OWNER-----(NULL)      CREATION--------1994.083
    RELEASE----------------2      EXPIRATION------0000.000
  PROTECTION-PSWD-----(NULL)      RACF----------------(YES)
  ASSOCIATIONS
    CLUSTER--CSCJGJ.CSC.TICKKSDS
  ATTRIBUTES
    KEYLEN-----------------5      AVGLRECL---------------0      BUFSPACE---------------0      CISIZE---------------512
    RKP--------------------0      MAXLRECL-------------505      EXCPEXIT----------(NULL)      CI/CA-----------------41
    SHROPTNS(2,3)   RECOVERY      UNIQUE           NOERASE      NOWRITECHK           IMBED    NOREPLICAT      UNORDERED
    NOREUSE
  STATISTICS
    REC-TOTAL--------------1      SPLITS-CI--------------0      EXCPS------------------5      INDEX:
    REC-DELETED------------0      SPLITS-CA--------------0      EXTENTS----------------2      LEVELS-----------------1
```

These statistics are about the base cluster data component.

These statistics are about the primary index.

Figure B.4 (continued)

```
      REC-INSERTED-----------0    FREESPACE-%CI----------0     SYSTEM-TIMESTAMP:             ENTRIES/SECT-----------3
      REC-UPDATED------------0    FREESPACE-%CA----------0          X'A906610510F9D800'      SEQ-SET-RBA--------20992
      REC-RETRIEVED----------0    FREESPC-BYTES------20992                                   HI-LEVEL-RBA-------20992
   ALLOCATION
     SPACE-TYPE---------TRACK    HI-ALLOC-RBA-------21504
     SPACE-PRI--------------1    HI-USED-RBA--------21504
     SPACE-SEC--------------1
   VOLUME
     VOLSER------------USER01    PHYREC-SIZE----------512     HI-ALLOC-RBA-------20992      EXTENT-NUMBER----------1
     DEVTYPE------X'30102004'    PHYRECS/TRK-----------41     HI-USED-RBA------------0      EXTENT-TYPE--------X'00'
     VOLFLAG------------PRIME    TRACKS/CA--------------1
     EXTENTS:
     LOW-CCHH-----X'00190007'    LOW-RBA----------------0     TRACKS-----------------1
     HIGH-CCHH----X'00190007'    HIGH-RBA-----------20991
   VOLUME
     VOLSER------------USER01    PHYREC-SIZE----------512     HI-ALLOC-RBA-------21504      EXTENT-NUMBER----------1
     DEVTYPE------X'30102004'    PHYRECS/TRK-----------41     HI-USED-RBA--------21504      EXTENT-TYPE--------X'80'
     VOLFLAG------------PRIME    TRACKS/CA--------------2
     EXTENTS:
     LOW-CCHH-----X'002B000D'    LOW-RBA------------20992     TRACKS-----------------2
     HIGH-CCHH----X'002B000E'    HIGH-RBA-----------21503

AIX ----------- CSCJGJ.CSC.TICKKSDS.SALEAIX
   IN-CAT --- SYS1.USERCAT
   HISTORY
     DATASET-OWNER-----(NULL)     CREATION--------1994.083
     RELEASE----------------2     EXPIRATION------0000.000
     SMS MANAGED---------(NO)
   PROTECTION-PSWD-----(NULL)     RACF----------------(NO)
   ASSOCIATIONS
     DATA-----CSCJGJ.CSC.TICKKSDS.SALEAIX.DATA
     INDEX----CSCJGJ.CSC.TICKKSDS.SALEAIX.INDEX
     CLUSTER--CSCJGJ.CSC.TICKKSDS
     PATH-----CSCJGJ.CSC.TICKKSDS.SALEAIX.PATH
   ATTRIBUTES
     UPGRADE

   DATA ------- CSCJGJ.CSC.TICKKSDS.SALEAIX.DATA
     IN-CAT --- SYS1.USERCAT
     HISTORY
       DATASET-OWNER-----(NULL)     CREATION--------1994.083
       RELEASE----------------2     EXPIRATION------0000.000
     PROTECTION-PSWD-----(NULL)     RACF----------------(NO)
```

This information covers the alternate index, which is itself a Key Sequenced Data Set. Notice that IDCAMS and VSAM have already been updated to reflect the century in the date, so that problems surrounding the beginning of a new millennium in 2000 will be eliminated or at least minimized.

Figure B.4 (continued)

```
  ASSOCIATIONS
    AIX------CSCJGJ.CSC.TICKKSDS.SALEAIX
  ATTRIBUTES
    KEYLEN----------------23     AVGLRECL---------------33     BUFSPACE------------8704     CISIZE--------------4096
    RKP--------------------5     MAXLRECL------------6600     EXCPEXIT----------(NULL)     CI/CA-----------------10
    AXRKP-----------------45
    SHROPTNS(2,3)      SPEED     UNIQUE            NOERASE     INDEXED        NOWRITECHK     IMBED         NOREPLICAT
    UNORDERED        NOREUSE     SPANNED        NONUNIQKEY
  STATISTICS
    REC-TOTAL-------------10     SPLITS-CI--------------0     EXCPS-----------------2
    REC-DELETED------------0     SPLITS-CA--------------0     EXTENTS---------------1
    REC-INSERTED-----------0     FREESPACE-%CI----------2     SYSTEM-TIMESTAMP:
    REC-UPDATED------------0     FREESPACE-%CA----------1          X'A9066109490F4000'
    REC-RETRIEVED----------0     FREESPC-BYTES------36864
  ALLOCATION
    SPACE-TYPE---------TRACK     HI-ALLOC-RBA-------40960
    SPACE-PRI--------------2     HI-USED-RBA--------40960
    SPACE-SEC--------------2
  VOLUME
    VOLSER------------USER02     PHYREC-SIZE---------4096     HI-ALLOC-RBA-------40960     EXTENT-NUMBER----------1
    DEVTYPE------X'30102004'     PHYRECS/TRK-----------10     HI-USED-RBA--------40960     EXTENT-TYPE--------X'40'
    VOLFLAG------------PRIME     TRACKS/CA--------------2
    EXTENTS:
    LOW-CCHH-----X'00140007'     LOW-RBA----------------0     TRACKS----------------2
    HIGH-CCHH----X'00140008'     HIGH-RBA-----------40959

 INDEX ------ CSCJGJ.CSC.TICKKSDS.SALEAIX.INDEX
   IN-CAT --- SYS1.USERCAT
  HISTORY
    DATASET-OWNER-----(NULL)     CREATION--------1994.083
    RELEASE----------------2     EXPIRATION------0000.000
  PROTECTION-PSWD-----(NULL)     RACF----------------(NO)
  ASSOCIATIONS
    AIX------CSCJGJ.CSC.TICKKSDS.SALEAIX
  ATTRIBUTES
    KEYLEN----------------23     AVGLRECL---------------0     BUFSPACE---------------0     CISIZE---------------512
    RKP--------------------5     MAXLRECL-------------505     EXCPEXIT----------(NULL)     CI/CA-----------------41
    SHROPTNS(2,3)   RECOVERY     UNIQUE            NOERASE     NOWRITECHK           IMBED     NOREPLICAT     UNORDERED
    NOREUSE
  STATISTICS
    REC-TOTAL--------------1     SPLITS-CI--------------0     EXCPS-----------------4     INDEX:
    REC-DELETED------------0     SPLITS-CA--------------0     EXTENTS---------------2     LEVELS-----------------1
    REC-INSERTED-----------0     FREESPACE-%CI----------0     SYSTEM-TIMESTAMP:            ENTRIES/SECT-----------3
```

These statistics are about the alternate index. There are 10 unique values in the sales agent field, so 10 alternate index records were created.

Figure B.4 (continued)

```
      REC-UPDATED------------0      FREESPACE-%CA----------0           X'A9066109490F4000'     SEQ-SET-RBA--------20992
      REC-RETRIEVED----------0      FREESPC-BYTES------20992                                   HI-LEVEL-RBA-------20992
    ALLOCATION
      SPACE-TYPE---------TRACK      HI-ALLOC-RBA-------21504
      SPACE-PRI--------------1      HI-USED-RBA--------21504
      SPACE-SEC--------------1
    VOLUME
      VOLSER------------USER02      PHYREC-SIZE----------512      HI-ALLOC-RBA-------20992      EXTENT-NUMBER----------1
      DEVTYPE------X'30102004'      PHYRECS/TRK-----------41      HI-USED-RBA------------0      EXTENT-TYPE--------X'00'
      VOLFLAG------------PRIME      TRACKS/CA--------------1
      EXTENTS:
      LOW-CCHH-----X'0011000D'      LOW-RBA----------------0      TRACKS-----------------1
      HIGH-CCHH----X'0011000D'      HIGH-RBA-----------20991
    VOLUME
      VOLSER------------USER02      PHYREC-SIZE----------512      HI-ALLOC-RBA-------21504      EXTENT-NUMBER----------1
      DEVTYPE------X'30102004'      PHYRECS/TRK-----------41      HI-USED-RBA--------21504      EXTENT-TYPE--------X'80'
      VOLFLAG------------PRIME      TRACKS/CA--------------2
      EXTENTS:
      LOW-CCHH-----X'00140007'      LOW-RBA------------20992      TRACKS-----------------2
      HIGH-CCHH----X'00140008'      HIGH-RBA-----------21503

  PATH ------- CSCJGJ.CSC.TICKKSDS.SALEAIX.PATH
    IN-CAT --- SYS1.USERCAT
    HISTORY
      DATASET-OWNER-----(NULL)      CREATION--------1994.083
      RELEASE----------------2      EXPIRATION------0000.000
    PROTECTION-PSWD-----(NULL)      RACF----------------(NO)
    ASSOCIATIONS
      AIX------CSCJGJ.CSC.TICKKSDS.SALEAIX
      DATA-----CSCJGJ.CSC.TICKKSDS.SALEAIX.DATA
      INDEX----CSCJGJ.CSC.TICKKSDS.SALEAIX.INDEX
      DATA-----CSCJGJ.CSC.TICKKSDS.DATA
      INDEX----CSCJGJ.CSC.TICKKSDS.INDEX

    ATTRIBUTES
      UPDATE
        THE NUMBER OF ENTRIES PROCESSED WAS:
                  AIX -------------------1
                  ALIAS -----------------0
                  CLUSTER ---------------1
                  DATA ------------------2
                  GDG -------------------0
                  INDEX -----------------2
```

Finally, at the end of the complete **LISTCAT**, path information is listed, including the associations of the path, which are all of the various components involved in using the path for data set access. The summary print shown at the bottom of this page, which continues to the top of the next page, indicates how many different components of various type the **LISTCAT** accessed.

Figure B.4 (continued)

```
                 NONVSAM ---------------0
                 PAGESPACE -------------0
                 PATH ------------------1
                 SPACE -----------------0
                 USERCATALOG -----------0
                 TOTAL -----------------7
         THE NUMBER OF PROTECTED ENTRIES SUPPRESSED WAS 0
IDC0001I FUNCTION COMPLETED, HIGHEST CONDITION CODE WAS 0

  /* - - - - - - - - - -  PRINT IT IN PRIMARY KEY SEQ  - -*/

   PRINT          INDATASET(CSCJGJ.CSC.TICKKSDS) -
                  COUNT(50) -
                  CHARACTER

LISTING OF DATA SET -CSCJGJ.CSC.TICKKSDS

KEY OF RECORD - 31256
31256NILLY       WILLIE          940216002S1ULTIMATE TRAVEL AGENCY 930718

KEY OF RECORD - 31257
31257IPPI        MRS.            940216001B2JACK SPRAT TRAVEL      930817

KEY OF RECORD - 31258
31258MOOSE       MICKEY          940216004B2WORLD TRAVEL, INC.     930718

KEY OF RECORD - 31259
31259DAY         HOLLY           940216001B HOLIDAY TOURS, INC.    930803

KEY OF RECORD - 31260
31260MALLOW      MARSHA          940216001B HOLIDAY TOURS, INC.    930805

KEY OF RECORD - 31307
31307WARE        DELLA           940216004B1WORLD TRAVEL, INC.     930909

KEY OF RECORD - 31310
31310SHAW        ARKAN           940216007S1HOLIDAY TOURS, INC.    930911
 -
 -
 -

IDC0005I NUMBER OF RECORDS PROCESSED WAS 50
IDC0001I FUNCTION COMPLETED, HIGHEST CONDITION CODE WAS 0
```

The first **PRINT** I requested was by base cluster name. This will obtain the records in the data component in primary key sequence, regardless of how many records were added to the Key Sequenced Data Set in random access mode. (No such record additions were done in this job stream, but could have been done on-line.) All 50 records in the data set have been listed, but for publication purposes I edited some out.

Figure B.4 (continued)

```
/* - - - - - - - - - - - NOW PRINT IT IN ALT KEY SEQ - - -*/
  PRINT         INDATASET(CSCJGJ.CSC.TICKKSDS.SALEAIX.PATH) -
                COUNT(50) -
                CHARACTER

LISTING OF DATA SET -CSCJGJ.CSC.TICKKSDS.SALEAIX.PATH

KEY OF RECORD - FOX VALLEY TRAVEL
31375DUNNE          WILL B.        940216001B2FOX VALLEY TRAVEL         931015

KEY OF RECORD - FOX VALLEY TRAVEL
31668ZOORI          MOE            940216004S1FOX VALLEY TRAVEL         940103

KEY OF RECORD - FOX VALLEY TRAVEL
43261CANNON         LUCE           940415001C FOX VALLEY TRAVEL         931004

KEY OF RECORD - FOX VALLEY TRAVEL
43483INA            CAROL          940415002S FOX VALLEY TRAVEL         940118

KEY OF RECORD - FOX VALLEY TRAVEL
49662PIPER          PETER          940507005B FOX VALLEY TRAVEL         940301

KEY OF RECORD - HOLIDAY TOURS, INC.
31259DAY            HOLLY          940216001B HOLIDAY TOURS, INC.       930803

KEY OF RECORD - HOLIDAY TOURS, INC.
31260MALLOW         MARSHA         940216001B HOLIDAY TOURS, INC.       930805
 -
 -
 -

IDC0005I NUMBER OF RECORDS PROCESSED WAS 50
IDC0001I FUNCTION COMPLETED, HIGHEST CONDITION CODE WAS 0
```

The second **PRINT** I requested was by alternate index path name. This obtains the records in alternate key sequence. The system automatically reads the alternate index records in key sequence; the key of the alternate index records is a copy of the alternate key field value, in this case, the sales agent name. The alternate index records are used as "pointers" to obtain the data records themselves with random access behind the scenes. This form of access is inefficient and you should not consider it a substitute for sorting the data for high-volume access. It is useful, however, in specialized applications where part of an indexed file is "browsed" by alternate key.

Figure B.4 (continued)

```
/* - - - - - - - - - - -  THIS PRINTS THE AIX RECORDS  - -*/
 PRINT        INDATASET(CSCJGJ.CSC.TICKKSDS.SALEAIX) -
              COUNT(50) -
              CHARACTER

LISTING OF DATA SET -CSCJGJ.CSC.TICKKSDS.SALEAIX

KEY OF RECORD - FOX VALLEY TRAVEL
.....FOX VALLEY TRAVEL      31375 31668 43261 43483 49662

KEY OF RECORD - HOLIDAY TOURS, INC.
.....HOLIDAY TOURS, INC.    31259 31260 31310 31450 31780 35190 43480 49467 49891

KEY OF RECORD - JACK SPRAT TRAVEL
.....JACK SPRAT TRAVEL      31257 31573 35189 43103 43501 49257 49872

KEY OF RECORD - KOOK'S TOURS
.....KOOK'S TOURS           31777 31779 35114 49473 49738

KEY OF RECORD - PODUNK TRAVEL AGENCY
.....PODUNK TRAVEL AGENCY   35115

KEY OF RECORD - ULTIMATE TRAVEL AGENCY
.....ULTIMATE TRAVEL AGENCY 31256 31447 31800 35112 43102 49322 49469

KEY OF RECORD - UNRAVEL TRAVEL, INC.
.....UNRAVEL TRAVEL, INC.   35257 43378 43484 49258 49480

KEY OF RECORD - UWANNAGO TRAVEL AGENCY
.....UWANNAGO TRAVEL AGENCY 49261 49321 49892

KEY OF RECORD - UWANNAGO TRAVEL, INC.
.....UWANNAGO TRAVEL, INC.  31778

KEY OF RECORD - WORLD TRAVEL, INC.
.....WORLD TRAVEL, INC.     31258 31307 31574 43101 43377 43507 49514

IDC11462I REQUESTED RANGE END BEYOND END OF DATA SET.
IDC0005I NUMBER OF RECORDS PROCESSED WAS 10
IDC0001I FUNCTION COMPLETED, HIGHEST CONDITION CODE WAS 4

IDC0002I IDCAMS PROCESSING COMPLETE. MAXIMUM CONDITION CODE WAS 4
```

In this third **PRINT**, I have indicated the name of the alternate index itself. IDCAMS lists the contents of the alternate index records. VSAM is elegant in its simplicity of support for alternate indexes. An alternate index is simply a Key Sequenced Data Set in which each record carries a key that is an alternate key in another data set. The "data" part of each of these records is really the primary key of the one or more data component records that carries the alternate key value. For "nonunique" alternate keys (COBOL "with duplicates"), more than one primary key exists in the alternate index record for each alternate key value. I have edited this to put a space between primary key fields. In unedited **PRINT** output the primary keys fields are printed with no space between them.

Figure B.4 (continued)

B.6 Typical VSAM Backup/Update/Reload Job Streams

A VSAM data set supporting an application should be backed up periodically to preserve the data in case of disk or VSAM failure. Other processing can be combined with backup, such as sequential (batch) updating and subsequent restoration of the data set to disk. This combination offers speed, since sequential updating can proceed much more rapidly than direct-access update. As an added benefit, the restored VSAM data set is internally reorganized and is as efficient as possible for subsequent direct access processing.

In Figure B.5, you can see how IDCAMS can be arranged to copy a data set to tape, using the REPRO command. This command is coded almost identically to that in lines 93 and 94 of the AB1KSDS job stream in Figure B.3, except the VSAM data set is the "in" data set and the tape (or disk) copy is the "out" data set:

```
REPRO      INDATASET(CSCJGJ.CSC.TICKKSDS) -
           OUTDATASET(CSCJGJ.CSC.TICKKSDS.BACKUP)
```

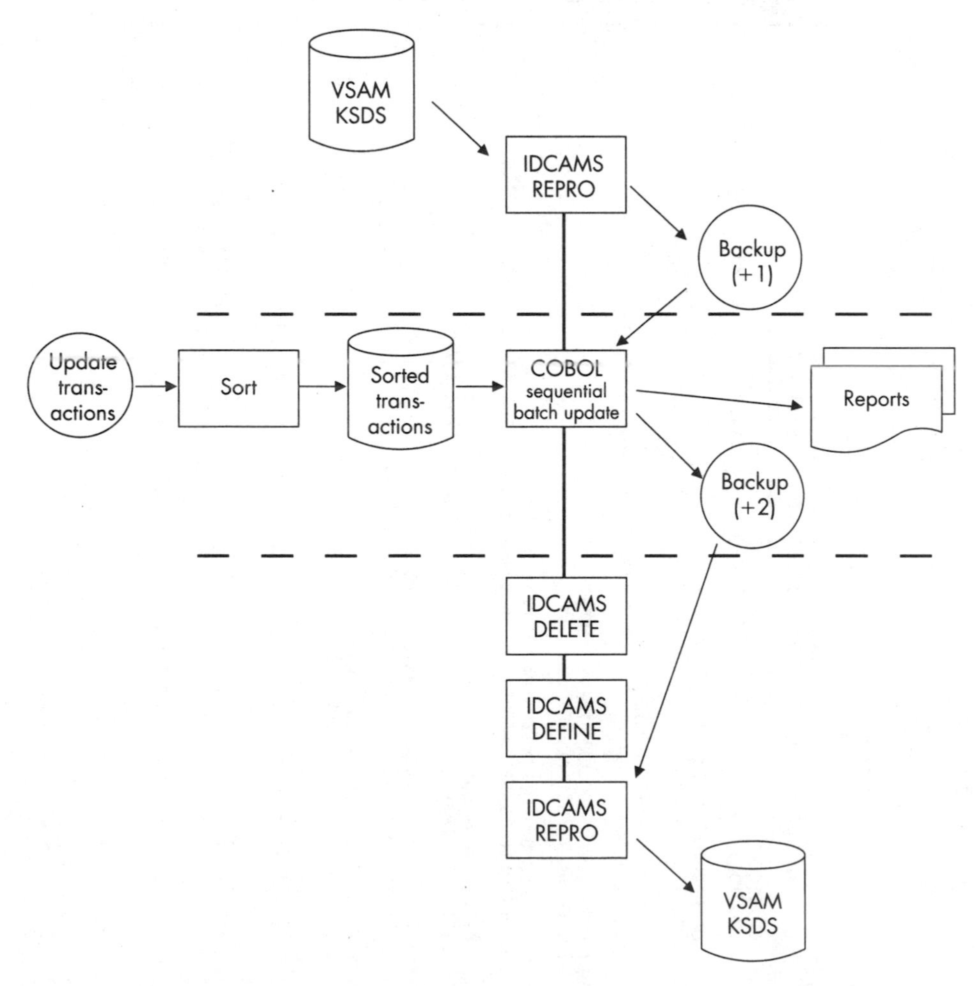

Figure B.5 Backup and Reload Job Stream Integrating Sequential Update with Data Set Reorganization

The second process shown in Figure B.5 is a sequential update. Raw update transactions intended to add, change, or delete records on the file are accumulated prior to the update, then sorted into ascending key sequence. An update program sequentially reads the sorted transaction and the backup file and "applies" the transactions to the backup, creating a new file and reporting. The third process is precisely the job stream of Figure B.3, in which the existing VSAM file is deleted, the file allocated again (perhaps differently, with more space or other parameters altered) and the newly created, updated sequential file loaded to the VSAM file.

B.7 Alternate Key Access

The CSCJGJ.CSC.TICKKSDS data set created in the AB1KSDS job stream provides for the creation of an alternate index, based on the alternate key of sales agent, a 23-byte field in positions 46 to 68 (displacement 45) of each record. You need to be aware of a special JCL requirement to access records in the Key Sequenced Data Set via the alternate key field.

Figure B.6 depicts the seven discrete components that exist for a Key Sequenced Data Set with an alternate index. The base cluster for the data set is its

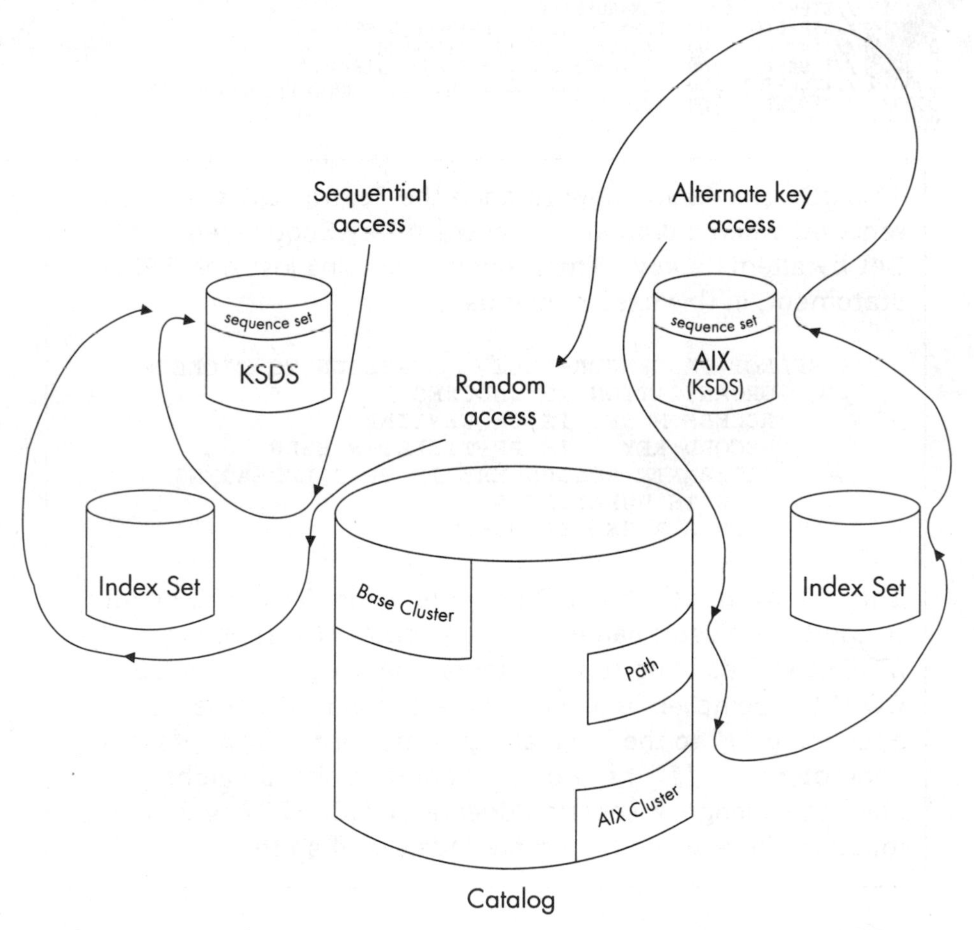

Figure B.6 Relationship of the Base Cluster and Alternate Index Components of a Key Sequenced Data Set

main catalog entry. No data is housed in the base cluster; it is information about data set characteristics, and the "statistics" made visible by LISTCAT. The index set, often separated into higher-level parts, and the lowest-level parts, called the sequence set, are a second component. The data component, where the data records

```
EDIT ---- CSCJGJ.ADV.CNTL(AB1JCL) - 01.00 ------------------- COLUMNS 001 072
COMMAND ===>                                                  SCROLL ===> PAGE
****** ****************************** TOP OF DATA ******************************
000001 //CSCJGJA   JOB 1,                 ACCOUNTING INFORMATION
000002 //  'BIN 7--JANOSSY',              PROGRAMMER NAME AND DELIVERY BIN
000003 //  CLASS=A,                       INPUT QUEUE CLASS
000004 //  MSGLEVEL=(1,1),                HOW MUCH MVS SYSTEM PRINT DESIRED
000005 //  MSGCLASS=X,                    PRINT DESTINATION X A L N OR O
000006 //  TIME=(0,6),                    SAFETY LIMIT: RUN TIME UP TO 6 SECS
000007 //  REGION=2M,                     ALLOW UP TO 2 MEGS VIRTUAL MEMORY
000008 //* TYPRUN=SCAN,                   UNCOMMENT THIS LINE TO DO SCAN ONLY
000009 //  NOTIFY=CSCJGJ                  WHO TO TELL WHEN JOB IS DONE
000010 //*
000011 //* DEMONSTRATE JCL TO EXECUTE A PROGRAM THAT ACCESSES A KSDS
000012 //* SEQUENTIALLY BY ALTERNATE KEY
000013 //* THIS JCL IS STORED AT CSCJGJ.ADV.CNTL(AB1JCL)
000014 //*-----------------------------------------------------------------
000015 //STEP101   EXEC  PGM=ALTEASY
000016 //STEPLIB     DD  DSN=CSCJGJ.ADV.LOADLIB,DISP=SHR
000017 //            DD  DSN=SYS1.COB2LIB,DISP=SHR
000018 //TICKETS     DD  DSN=CSCJGJ.CSC.TICKKSDS,DISP=SHR
000019 //TICKETS1    DD  DSN=CSCJGJ.CSC.TICKKSDS.SALEAIX.PATH,DISP=SHR
000020 //SYSOUT      DD  SYSOUT=*
000021 //
```

This JCL shows you how to code the "extra" DD statement required when a program accesses a Key Sequenced Data Set by alternate key. The program contains just one SELECT statement, in this case coded as:

```
SELECT PASSENGER-FILE     ASSIGN TO TICKETS
   ORGANIZATION IS INDEXED
   ACCESS MODE  IS SEQUENTIAL
   RECORD KEY   IS PR-TICKET-NUMBER
   ALTERNATE RECORD KEY IS PR-SALES-AGENT
      WITH DUPLICATES
   FILE STATUS  IS WS-STATUS.
```

The JCL must include a DD statement for //TICKETS pointing to the base cluster name, *and a second DD statement* for //TICKETS1 pointing to the alternate index path. The VS COBOL II compiler "makes up" the second DD name by appending "1" to the original DD name, or replacing its last character with "1" if the original name is already eight characters long. A second ddname of TICKETS2 would be made up for a second alternate index, and so forth.

Figure B.7 JCL to Access a Key Sequenced Data Set Via Its Alternate Index with the ALTEASY Program

for the data set are actually stored, is a third component. These three components are sufficient for a Key Sequenced Data Set that has no alternate index.

The alternate index for a Key Sequence Data Set is a Key Sequenced Data Set in itself. As such it has its own base cluster (the AIX cluster), its own index (the key to which is the alternate key value) that has higher-level and sequence set components, and its own data component, the alternate index data records. This accounts for six components.

The seventh and final component for a KSDS with one alternate index is the alternate index path, which is also an entry in the catalog. The path can contain security information and serves to link the alternate index to the data set that it indexes. Alternate index access proceeds along the arrow shown in Figure B.6. You can see that alternate index access requires a large amount of I/O activity and for this reason may proceed slowly if you attempt it for large quantities of data in a sequential mode.

Figure B.7 illustrates the special JCL coding necessary to access a VSAM data set by alternate key. In this example a VS COBOL II program named ALTEASY contains the SELECT statement shown in the figure, which demands a DD statement named //TICKETS in its execution JCL. But the VS COBOL II compiler generates a requirement for a second DD statement named //TICKETS1 to point to the alternate index path. If you forget this "extra" DD statement in your JCL, your job will fail. The ddname TICKETS is only seven characters long, so the "extra" ddname is TICKETS with "1" appended to it, TICKETS1. Had the ddname I coded with the SELECT statement been ABCDEFGH (eight characters) the extra ddname generated would have been ABCDEFG1, with the "1" replacing the last character. Figure B.8 shows you the actual source code of the ALTEASY program.

B.8 Creating Data VSAM Sets Using JCL Alone (DFSMS Only)

Under DFSMS you can create SMS-managed VSAM data sets using JCL alone. When you create a VSAM data set in this way, you can supply only the base cluster name. VSAM itself makes up the names of the data component and (for a Key Sequenced Data Set) the index component name by appendix .DATA or .INDEX to the base cluster name (or by replacing the word CLUSTER if you named the base cluster with this as the last part of its name.

To create a VSAM data set, MVS/ESA needs to obtain the RECORG parameter, and, for Key Sequenced Data Sets, KEYOFF and KEYLEN. These can be carried by DATACLAS. If DATACLAS does not carry these specifications or if you wish to override what DATACLAS carries, you can specify them in the DD statement. For example, this DD statement creates an SMS-managed Entry Sequenced VSAM data set:

```
//OUTDS  DSN=CSCJGJ.CSC.EMPMAST,
// DISP=(NEW,CATLG,DELETE),
// STORCLAS=STDVSAM,
// DATACLAS=VSAMD1,
// RECORG=ES
```

In this example the STORCLAS DFSMS parameter indicates UNIT and VOL information, while DATACLAS identifies the LRECL, SPACE, AVGREC, IMBED, REPLICATE, CISIZE, FREESPACE, SHAREOPTIONS, and volume count. RECORG is meaningful only if DFSMS is active, otherwise it is ignored. It is also ignored if the DD statement refers to an existing data set.

```
EDIT ---- CSCJGJ.ADV.COBOL(ALTEASY) - 01.00 ------------------ COLUMNS 007 078
COMMAND ===>                                                  SCROLL ===> PAGE
****** ***************************** TOP OF DATA ******************************
000100  ID DIVISION.
000200  program-id.  alteasy.
000300
000400 *  Copyright 1994 James Janossy    All rights reserved
000500 *  Internet  janossy@cs.depaul.edu
000600 *  DePaul University Department of Computer Science
000700 *  243 S. Wabash, Room 450, Chicago, IL 60604
000800 *-----------------------------------------------------------------
000900 *  This program reads a VSAM file sequentially by alternate
001000 *  key to demonstrate how START changes the key of reference
001100 *  and current record pointer (originated in RM/COBOL-85 and
001200 *  uploaded to the ES/9000 after testing).
001300
001400  ENVIRONMENT DIVISION.
001500  input-output section.
001600  file-control.
001700
001800 *--comment out the select statement that does not apply:
001900 *--select statement for RM/COBOL-85 on PC--------------------
002000 *
002100 *     select passenger-file      assign to 'tickksds.dat'
002200 *        organization            indexed
002300 *        access mode             sequential
002400 *        record key              pr-ticket-number
002500 *        alternate record key    pr-sales-agent  with duplicates
002600 *        file status             ws-status.
002700 *
002800 *--select statement for VS COBOL II & MVS/ESA----------------
002900 *
003000      select passenger-file      assign to tickets
003100         organization            indexed
003200         access mode             sequential
003300         record key              pr-ticket-number
003400         alternate record key    pr-sales-agent  with duplicates
003500         file status             ws-status.
003600
003700  DATA DIVISION.
003800  file section.
003900  fd  passenger-file
004000      record contains 80 characters.
004100  01  passenger-record.
004200      05 pr-ticket-number                pic x(5).
004300      05 pr-last-name                    pic x(14).
004400      05 pr-first-name                   pic x(15).
004500      05 pr-sailing-date                 pic x(6).
004600      05 pr-qty-people                   pic 9(3).
004700      05 pr-deck-code                    pic x(2).
004800      05 pr-sales-agent                  pic x(23).
004900      05 pr-purchase-date                pic x(6).
005000 *
005100  working-storage section.
005200  01  ws-status                          pic x(2).
005300  01  ws-records-read                    pic 9(5)   value 0.
005400 /
```

No **BLOCK CONTAINS** for VSAM file!

I developed this program to demonstrate how to use the START verb to change the key of reference and current record pointer to initiate sequential reading via alternate key. The program reads the VSAM Key Sequenced Data Set to which I have loaded the pleasure cruise ticket records shown in Figures B.1 and B.2. START shown at lines 9100 and 9200 involves the alternate key field, PR-SALES-AGENT. It positions the current record pointer to the first alternate index record that meets the requirement > = LOW-VALUES, which is the first record in the alternate index file. READ then obtains the first record according to the alternate index.

Figure B.8 Source Code of the ALTEASY Program

```
005500  PROCEDURE DIVISION.
005600 *---------------------------------------------------------------
005700 *  In RM/COBOL-85 you need declaratives (even in dummy form) to
005800 *  avoid abends even when non-zero File Status values are received
005900 *  such as '10' at end-of-file on sequential reading.  This code
006000 *  causes no harm on mainframe with VSAM.
006100 *---------------------------------------------------------------
006200  declaratives.
006300  0000-dummy    section.
006400      use after error procedure on passenger-file.
006500  0000-real-dummy.  exit.
006600  end declaratives.
006700 *
006800  0000-mainline-section   section.
006900  0000-mainline.
007000      perform 1000-boj.
007100      perform 2000-process
007200         until ws-status(1:1) = '1'.
007300      perform 3000-eoj.
007400      stop run.
007500 *
007600  1000-boj.
007700      display '*** start of program listalt'.
007800      open input passenger-file.
007900      if ws-status(1:1) = '0'
008000         or ws-status = '97'
008100            next sentence
008200       else
008300         display '*** Error opening indexed file, program ended'
008400         display '*** File status = ', ws-status
008500         stop run.
008600 *---------------------------------------------------------------
008700 *  This START uses the alternate key field to position the file
008800 *  access method to read sequentially on the alternate key:
008900 *---------------------------------------------------------------
009000      move low-values to pr-sales-agent.
009100      start passenger-file
009200         key >= pr-sales-agent.
009300      if ws-status(1:1) not = '0'
009400         display '*** Error on alt key start, program ended'
009500         display '*** File status = ', ws-status
009600         stop run.
009700      perform 2700-read.
009800
009900  2000-process.
010000      display  pr-ticket-number  ' '
010100               pr-last-name
010200               pr-first-name     ' '
010300               pr-sailing-date   ' '
010400               pr-qty-people     ' '
010500               pr-deck-code      ' '
010600               pr-sales-agent
010700               pr-purchase-date.
010800      perform 2700-read.
010900
011000  2700-read.
011100      read passenger-file.
011200 *---------------------------------------------------------------
011300 *  For sequential reading (RM/COBOL-85 and IBM VSAM KSDS too):
011400 *     File Status first-byte '0' means read was successful
011500 *     File Status first-byte '1' means end of file
011600 *     Any other file status value means access method failure
011700 *---------------------------------------------------------------
011800      if ws-status(1:1) = '0'
011900         add 1 to ws-records-read
012000       else
012100      if ws-status(1:1) = '1'
012200         next sentence
012300       else
012400         display '*** Error on read, program ended'
012500         display '*** File status = ', ws-status
012600         stop run.
012700 *
012800  3000-eoj.
012900      display '*** records read = ', ws-records-read.
013000      close passenger-file.
013100      if ws-status(1:1) not = '0'
013200         display '*** Error on file close, program ended'
013300         display '*** File status = ', ws-status
013400       else
013500      display '*** program ended normally'.
```

You have to check File Status after the OPEN. If you receive '0' in the first byte of File Status or '97' for the whole File Status value, the file opened properly.

START positions the current record pointer to the beginning of the alternate index. Subsequent READs follow the alternate index to read the data in the file.

Figure B.8 (continued)

A different RECORG code value exists for each organization of data set VSAM supports. RECORG code values and their meanings are:

ES Entry Sequenced Data Set

RR Relative Record Data Set

KS Key Sequenced Data Set

LS Linear Space Data Set

To create a Key Sequenced Data Set under DFSMS using JCL, you also code the KEYLEN and KEYOFF parameters. KEYLEN specifies the length of the key in bytes and KEYOFF specifies the starting position of the primary key field as an offset (position 1 is numbered 0):

```
//OUTDS    DSN=CSCJGJ.CSC.TICKKSDS,
//   DISP=(NEW,CATLG,DELETE),
//   STORCLAS=STDVSAM,
//   DATACLAS=VSAMD1,
//   RECORG=KS,
//   KEYLEN=5,
//   KEYOFF=0
```

Once again, if RECORG, KEYOFF, or KEYLEN are specified by DATACLAS, you can omit them from the DD statement. In this example, it's presumed that DATACLAS also contains a space allocation specification.

B.9 Creating Temporary VSAM Data Sets (DFSMS Only)

Under DFSMS you can create and pass temporary VSAM data sets, which are limited to one volume in size. For example, to create a temporary Key Sequenced Data Set to house the preceding file, you could code this:

```
//OUTDS    DSN=&&TICKKSDS,
//   DISP=(NEW,PASS),
//   LRECL=80,
//   SPACE=(80,(1000,300)),
//   AVGREC=U,
//   RECORG=KS,
//   KEYLEN=5
//   KEYOFF=0,
```

No STORCLAS was specified, so it is assumed that STORCLAS will be assigned by an installation-created Automatic Class Selection (ACS) routine. STORCLAS must be associated with this DD statement one way or another, since that's what makes the data set DFSMS-managed. If STORCLAS were to be specified to explicitly assign the storage class (unit and volume), this DD statement might appear as:

```
//OUTDS   DSN=&&TICKKSDS,
//   STORCLAS=STDVSAM,
//   DISP=(NEW,PASS),
//   LRECL=80,
//   AVGREC=U,
//   SPACE=(80,(100,30)),
//   RECORG=KS,
//   KEYLEN=5,
//   KEYOFF=0
```

C

Diagnosing File Status Errors in VS COBOL II

COBOL is by far the most common language used on mainframes. The present mainframe COBOL compilers are VS COBOL II and COBOL/370, both of which implement 1985 COBOL standards. This generation of software introduces changes in file handling that can cause you a large measure of frustration if you are not prepared for them. I have included this appendix because some of the file-handling changes affect MVS/ESA system reporting.

The most significant change in file handling in 1985 COBOL lies in support for "optional" files. Prior to the provision of support for optional files, you would receive a clear indication, with a DD STATEMENT MISSING from MVS, if you did not include a DD statement in your JCL matching the "ASSIGN TO" name in every SELECT statement in a COBOL program. You now will not receive such a message, as the figures in this appendix will show you. This makes coding errors in your program and JCL harder to detect!

Figure C.1 lists the JCL to execute a load module named COPYIT, which I created using VS COBOL II. This program is listed in Chapter 5 of my introductory MVS JCL book of *Practical MVS JCL Examples* (1993, John Wiley & Sons, Inc.). It's a simple read-and-write program that copies the records from a file to the printer and prints some minimal labeling information and a record count. The program contains only two SELECT statements, coded like this:

```
SELECT INPUT-FILE    ASSIGN TO  COPYIN.
SELECT OUTPUT-FILE   ASSIGN TO  COPYOUT.
```

Thus the program expects to be connected to a data set to be read at a DD statement carrying the ddname COPYIN, and the program expects to write records to a DD statement carrying the ddname COPYOUT.

For the run of the COPYIT program that produced the results shown in Figure C.2, I intentionally misspelled the ddname COPYIN in the execution JCL, making it XOPYIN instead. The result you see is a message from the VS COBOL II runtime environment, and mention of "status code" 35. "Status code" is actually the File Status value. File Status values are the same codes issued when VSAM files are accessed; they apply to sequential files as well. To diagnose this type of problem, you have to look up the meaning of File Status 35. You can look up such codes in this appendix.

In Figure C.3, you see the run results when I spell the ddname COPYIN correctly in the execution JCL, but I misspell COPYOUT as XOPYOUT. Now, no error at all is noted! The program ends execution with COND CODE 0000. This is potentially very dangerous. No listing of records emerges from COPYIT in this case; its record writing goes into the "bit bucket" of a system-created temporary file, which you will never see. If my execution JCL were coded to create a new file at the

```
EDIT ---- CSCJGJ.F92.CNTL(MYGO) - 01.07 ---------------------- COLUMNS 001 072
COMMAND ===>                                                    SCROLL ===> PAGE
****** ******************************** TOP OF DATA ********************************
000100 //CSCJGJA   JOB 1,                  ACCOUNTING INFORMATION
000200 //   'BIN 7--JANOSSY',              PROGRAMMER NAME AND DELIVERY BIN
000300 //   MSGLEVEL=(1,1),                HOW MUCH MVS SYSTEM PRINT DESIRED
000400 //   CLASS=A,                       INPUT CLASS
000500 //   MSGCLASS=X,                    PRINT DESTINATION X A L N OR O
000600 //*  TYPRUN=SCAN,                   UNCOMMENT IF WANT ONLY A JCL SCAN
000700 //   NOTIFY=CSCJGJ                  WHO TO TELL WHEN JOB IS DONE
000800 //*
000900 //*******************************************************************
001000 //* MYGO    RUN A LOAD MODULE                                       *
001200 //*******************************************************************
001300 //STEP010  EXEC  PGM=COPYIT
001400 //STEPLIB    DD  DSN=CSCJGJ.CSC.LOADLIB,DISP=SHR
001500 //           DD  DSN=SYS1.COB2LIB,DISP=SHR
001600 //COPYIN     DD  DSN=CSCJGJ.CSC.CNTL(WORKERS),DISP=SHR
001700 //COPYOUT    DD  SYSOUT=*
001800 //SYSOUT     DD  SYSOUT=*
001900 //
```

This JCL executes the load module for a simple VS COBOL II program named COPYIT, which is listed in Chapter 5 of the introductory book ***Practical MVS JCL Examples*** by James Janossy (John Wiley & Sons, Inc., 1993). COPYIT reads from a DD statement named COPYIN and writes to a DD statement named COPYOUT. The outputs from two runs of this JCL are shown in Figures C.2 and C.3. In Figure C.2 you see the result of a run with COPYIN spelled incorrectly as XOPYIN. In Figure C.3 you see the result of a run with COPYOUT spelled incorrectly as XOPYOUT. If you are experienced with MVS and older versions of COBOL, you may be surprised at both results!

Figure C.1 MVS/ESA JCL to Execute the Load Module for the COPYIT Program, Which Was Created Using VS COBOL II

ddname XOPYOUT, the data set would be allocated but would remain empty. The same effect would occur whether the misspelling exists in the SELECT statement in the program or in the JCL; any mismatch in SELECT name and ddname causes this problem. This problem can be very difficult to debug because you might at first suspect program logic and spend time tracing that.

You need to be especially careful in the "modern" environment about the correspondence between ddnames coded in SELECT statements within programs, and the corresponding names coded in your JCL. You can also take steps within programs to intercept some file opening problems by receiving the File Status value yourself and DISPLAYing it after each sequential file open, just as prudence dictates you do after opening and accessing VSAM files. Code the SELECT statement like this, and make the WS-INPUT-FILE-STATUS and WS-OUTPUT-FILE-STATUS fields each a PIC X(2) field.

```
 SDSF OUTPUT DISPLAY CSCJGJA  JOB08837  DSID     2 LINE 0       COLUMNS 02- 81
 COMMAND INPUT ===>                                             SCROLL ===> PAGE
*********************************** TOP OF DATA ***********************************
                     J E S 2  J O B  L O G  --  S Y S T E M  I B M 1  --  N

23.24.44 JOB08837  IRR010I  USERID CSCJGJ   IS ASSIGNED TO THIS JOB.
23.24.45 JOB08837  ICH70001I CSCJGJ   LAST ACCESS AT 23:23:25 ON SUNDAY, JANUARY
23.24.45 JOB08837  $HASP373 CSCJGJA  STARTED - INIT  1 - CLASS A - SYS IBM1
23.24.46 JOB08837  +IGZ035I There was an unsuccessful OPEN or CLOSE of file 'COP
                            program 'COPYIT' at relative location X'03E8'.  Neit
                            STATUS nor an ERROR declarative were specified.  The
                            status code was '35'.
23.24.46 JOB08837  IEA995I SYMPTOM DUMP OUTPUT
                     USER COMPLETION CODE=1035
                    TIME=23.24.45  SEQ=36076  CPU=0000  ASID=000F
                    PSW AT TIME OF ERROR  078D1000   8002C8CA  ILC 2  INTC 0D
                      ACTIVE LOAD MODULE=IGZCPCO   ADDRESS=0002C6A0  OFFSET=0000
                      DATA AT PSW  0002C8C4 - 00181610  0A0D47F0  C0E84820
                      GPR  0-3  80000000  8000040B  0000040B  000487FC
                      GPR  4-7  000470F0  80016C58  000489AA  000489A7
                      GPR  8-11 80006504  80016C58  000052E4  00031FC0
                      GPR 12-15 8002C7F2  000470A8  8002C84E  8001D838
                    END OF SYMPTOM DUMP
```

In this run of VS COBOL II program COPYIT I intentionally misspelled the ddname COPYIT as XOPYIT. The program attempts to open a data set at the ddname COPYIT, which does not exist in the JCL. *You do not receive a DD STATEMENT MISSING error message* as you might expect from prior experience with the older COBOL compiler, VS COBOL. Instead, you receive a user completion code and corresponding message from the COBOL runtime environment, starting with the letters "IGZ". The nature of the problem is now revealed to you in File Status code 35, which you can look up in Appendix C.

Figure C.2 Result from Executing COPYIT with JCL Using a DD Statement Labeled //XOPYIN Instead of //COPYIN

```
SELECT INPUT-FILE    ASSIGN TO  COPYIN
   FILE STATUS IS WS-INPUT-FILE-STATUS.

SELECT OUTPUT-FILE   ASSIGN TO  COPYOUT
   FILE STATUS IS WS-OUTPUT-FILE-STATUS.
```

Test each of these fields immediately after opening the respective file, and stop the run if you do not receive '00' after the open. This, however, works only for input files. For an output file such as COPYOUT, VS COBOL II automatically allocates the file as RECFM=U, LRECL=0, BLKSIZE=32760 and MVS/ESA makes it a temporary file. Tuck this tidbit away in your mind. It could save you hours of time trying to figure out why a report is not produced or a file is consistently created empty!

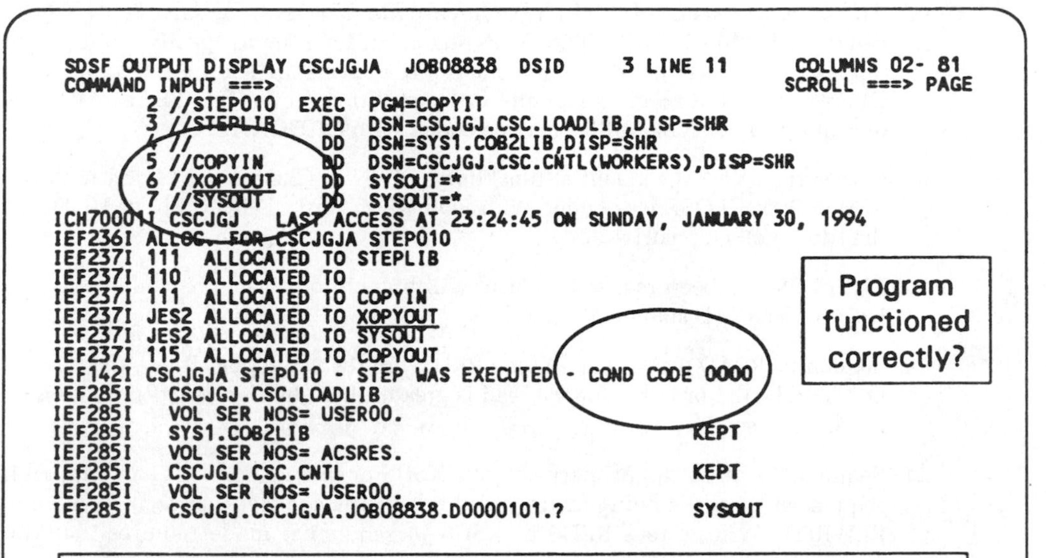

```
SDSF OUTPUT DISPLAY CSCJGJA  JOB08838  DSID     3 LINE 11      COLUMNS 02- 81
COMMAND INPUT ===>                                            SCROLL ===> PAGE
         2 //STEP010  EXEC  PGM=COPYIT
         3 //STEPLIB    DD  DSN=CSCJGJ.CSC.LOADLIB,DISP=SHR
         4 //           DD  DSN=SYS1.COB2LIB,DISP=SHR
         5 //COPYIN     DD  DSN=CSCJGJ.CSC.CNTL(WORKERS),DISP=SHR
         6 //XOPYOUT    DD  SYSOUT=*
         7 //SYSOUT     DD  SYSOUT=*
ICH70001I CSCJGJ    LAST ACCESS AT 23:24:45 ON SUNDAY, JANUARY 30, 1994
IEF236I ALLOC. FOR CSCJGJA STEP010
IEF237I 111  ALLOCATED TO STEPLIB
IEF237I 110  ALLOCATED TO
IEF237I 111  ALLOCATED TO COPYIN
IEF237I JES2 ALLOCATED TO XOPYOUT
IEF237I JES2 ALLOCATED TO SYSOUT
IEF237I 115  ALLOCATED TO COPYOUT
IEF142I CSCJGJA STEP010 - STEP WAS EXECUTED - COND CODE 0000
IEF285I   CSCJGJ.CSC.LOADLIB
IEF285I   VOL SER NOS= USER00.
IEF285I   SYS1.COB2LIB                                     KEPT
IEF285I   VOL SER NOS= ACSRES.
IEF285I   CSCJGJ.CSC.CNTL                                  KEPT
IEF285I   VOL SER NOS= USER00.
IEF285I   CSCJGJ.CSCJGJA.JOB08838.D0000101.?               SYSOUT
```


This JCL executes the load module for the COPYIT program, which was created using VS COBOL II. For this run I intentionally misspelled the ddname COPYOUT in the JCL as XOPYOUT. The program attempts to write records via the ddname COPYOUT, and as you can see by the COND CODE 0000, appears to work normally. *Why didn't it fail?* Because VS COBOL II supports "optional" files, which are files that don't have to exist! A DD statement named COPYOUT is actually missing here, but its absence is "absorbed" by the program, since it seems to be optional. This produces a very troublesome potential for error. If I were creating a new file at COPYOUT, the file would be created but be empty. The situation is even harder to detect if the misspelling occurred not in the JCL, but in the SELECT statement of the program. ***You must double-check the correspondence between your SELECT coding and your JCL to avoid this type of problem.***

Figure C.3 Result from Executing COPYIT with JCL Using a DD Statement Labeled //XOPYOUT Instead of //COPYOUT

File Status Reference

00 The action was successful.

02 READ was OK, next record on the file has the same alternate key; WRITE was OK, the alternate key duplicates an alternate key already on file. Applies only to indexed files (VSAM Key Sequenced Data Sets), when alternate keys exist.

04 READ executed successfully but the length of the record read was different than that defined for the file; the record may have been truncated.

05 An OPEN was successful for an "optional" file that does not exist. (OPTIONAL can be coded in the SELECT/ASSIGN statement for a file to specify that it might not exist and that no DD statement for it appears in JCL.) An optional file OPENed for input receives an end-of-file condition on the first READ. All types of sequential and VSAM files may be coded with OPTIONAL.

07 QSAM (non-VSAM sequential files) only; OPEN or CLOSE was coded with NO REWIND, or CLOSE was coded with FOR REMOVAL, FOR REEL, or UNIT but the file is not a tape drive.

10 End of file has been reached; control will branch to the actions coded after AT END in the READ statement.

14 Sequential READ was executed for a RRDS, but the value placed into the relative key field by the program for the read is greater than the limit of records defined for the data set.

21 Sequence error on the primary key of a KSDS or in a RRDS. This can happen if sequential access is being made and the key was changed between READ and REWRITE. Writing to a RRDS or KSDS in sequential mode requires that you write records in ascending sequence of the primary key. (This restriction and File Status value does not apply when you process these files in random access mode.)

22 Duplicate key for RRDS or KSDS file in random processing. This can happen for WRITE of a duplicate key for an RRDS READ, REWRITE with duplicate primary key (KSDS), or WRITE or REWRITE for a KSDS when the primary key is unique but an alternate key that is supposed to be unique is not. '22' makes no distinction between primary and alternate key errors!

23 "Desired record not found" in the RRDS or KSDS. This can happen if you do a READ with a nonexistent key, START with a relation condition that could not be satisfied, or START or random READ for an OPTIONAL file that is not present.

24 Out of space in a KSDS, or a WRITE to an RRDS with a key value greater than the limit of records defined for the file.

30 Data check or parity error on I/O device.

34 Out of space when WRITE was executed QSAM (non-VSAM sequential file) only.

35 OPEN with INPUT, I-O, or EXTEND specified as the SELECT/ASSIGN "access mode" but the file does not exist. The DD statement for the file may be missing from JCL. This file status is not issued if the file is defined as OPTIONAL in the SELECT statement (in that case READ actions against the file receive "end of file" or "record not found" indications).

37 The file being processed can't be accessed in the way that your OPEN implies. One of several reasons might exist for this. You may have specified OPEN OUTPUT or OPEN EXTEND but you can't use the WRITE verb with the file (are you trying a random WRITE on a tape?). Or you may have specified OPEN INPUT but you can't use the READ verb with the file (are you trying a random READ on a tape file?). Or you may have specified OPEN I-O but either the READ or WRITE verbs cannot be used with the file (are you trying this with a tape file?). Check your coding of the SELECT/ASSIGN statement. Have you specified ACCESS MODE IS RANDOM for a file that can't support this type of access?

38 You tried to OPEN a QSAM (non-VSAM sequential) file that was previously closed with the LOCK option.

39 OPEN failed because your file description and the catalog or label-stored characteristics of the file differ. You have coded the file organization, primary key position, alternate key position, record size, format, or block size incorrectly.

41 You tried to OPEN a file that was already open.

42 You tried to CLOSE a file that was already closed.

43 You are processing a file sequentially and did not execute a READ to obtain the record you are trying to REWRITE or DELETE. To rewrite or delete records with ACCESS MODE IS SEQUENTIAL you first have to read and obtain the record.

44 You are processing a QSAM (non-VSAM sequential) file and have either tried to REWRITE a record that is not the same size as the one you read, or you are trying to write or rewrite a variable length record that is shorter or longer than the FD states it should be.

46 You are either reading past the end-of-file (sequentially) or your prior random READ failed and, as a result, the current record pointer (CRP) is undefined for the READ/NEXT you are trying to do.

47 You are trying to READ from a file that is either not open or that you opened for OUTPUT or EXTEND.

48 You are trying to WRITE to a file that is either not open or that you opened for INPUT.

49 You are trying to do a DELETE or REWRITE, but you did not open the file for I-O.

90 Some form of program logic error has occurred.

91 The VSAM file you have tried to access is password protected under VSAM's own security scheme; you have not supplied the correct password to access it.

92 Some form of program logic error has occurred.

93 A required VSAM resource (memory or data set component) was not available.

94 The current record pointer was undefined when you attempted to do a sequential READ or READ/NEXT. You can only receive this under VS COBOL II Release 3 or 4 when you use the CMPR2 option to emulate the older releases of COBOL. Under "normal" Release 3 and 4 you get File Status value 46 for this condition.

95 Incomplete or invalid file information was available for the file. You formerly received this under some circumstances that now produce a File Status value of '39'.

96 You omitted the DD statement for the file in your JCL. Note that you can get this if you forget to code the extra DD statement matching the DDname "generated" by COBOL for the alternate index path when you have an alternate key. (For example, for DDname TICKETS with an alternate index the compiler "makes up" the DDname TICKETS1, and expect to have it pointed to the alternate index path in your JCL.)

97 OPEN was successful after the system itself initiated a VERIFY command to update the catalog about the file. This does not represent any error.

IBM Utility Program Return Code Reference

IBM utilities are programs supplied either as part of the MVS/ESA operating system or licensed separately by IBM. They are written in assembler language, PL/S (a system programming language internal to IBM) or C by IBM systems programmers. You execute utility programs the same as any other programs, that is, by using the EXEC statement. Documentation supplied by IBM in manuals tells you what ddnames each utility program expects in JCL.

Each utility program reads instructions you code to tell it what you want it to do. Your instructions take the form of 80-byte records called "control statements." Each utility reads its control statements at the ddname //SYSIN. Since many of these utilities were written by many different people almost 30 years ago, inconsistencies exist between them in the way they expect their control statements to be coded. For example, field positions within records are coded differently for DFSORT, IDCAMS, and IEBGENER, and IEBPTPCH.

All of the utilities communicate processing results to you via the return code, the four-digit number that you can test in subsequent job steps with the COND parameter. All utilities indicate successful processing with the return code 0000. Many utilities assign different meanings to other return code values. I have briefly described many of the utilities here and listed the COND CODEs issued by each for your convenience.

DFDSS (ADRDSSU)

Part of the Data Facility family of system software products. Copies or moves data between like and unlike information storage devices, backs up ("dumps") and restores data, defragments disk volumes, compresses partitioned data sets, releases unused disk space, and converts data sets to and from the Storage Management Subsystem.

0000 Successful execution

0004 Problem in a noncritical function; not usually fatal

0008 Error in requested function; some aspect bypassed

0012 Serious logical error; function abandoned

0016 Severe error; command processing terminated

DFSORT

General purpose sort/merge utility. Competing products such as CA-SORT and Syncsort issue similar condition codes.

0000 Successful execution

0004 (Not used)

0008 (Not used)

0012 (Not used)

0016 I/O error or out of sequence error; step terminated

0020 //SYSOUT ddname or message ddname missing

IDCAMS

Multipurpose Access Method Services utility to copy, print, dump, catalog, uncatalog, rename data sets, delete unexpired data sets and PDS members, define, alter and delete VSAM data sets, list catalog entries; create, alter, and delete generation data groups bases.

0000 Successful execution

0004 Problem in a non critical function; not usually fatal

0008 Error in requested function; some aspect bypassed

0012 Serious logical error; function abandoned

0016 Severe error; IDCAMS command processing terminated

IEBCOMPR

Compares data sets or whole partitioned data sets. One data set is indicated at //SYSUT1, and the other is indicated at //SYSUT2. The report produced at //SYSPRINT identifies records that differ but shows them only in hexadecimal.

0000 Successful completion

0004 (Not used)

0008 Unequal comparison; processing continues

0012 Grossly unequal comparison; step terminated

0016 User routine passed 0016 (rarely used)

IEBCOPY

Copies or merges partitioned data sets, or copies selected members. This utility is used for "compressing" (reorganizing) partitioned data sets. State the input PDS at //SYSUT1 and the output at //SYSUT2 and you can code DUMMY at //SYSIN. Not used for Partitioned Data Set Extended (PDSE) data sets.

0000 Successful completion

0004 Recoverable error; investigate

0008 Unrecoverable error; step terminated

IEBDG

Creates test data in patterns. The control statements you code at //SYSIN are tedious, but you may consider using this utility to create test data that contain packed decimal (COMP-3 or PACKED-DECIMAL) values.

0000 Successful completion

0004 User routine passed 0016 (rarely used)

0008 Error in control statements; processing continues

0012 Error during I/O; step terminated

0016 Unrecoverable error; step terminated

IEBEDIT

Manipulates JCL statements in batch mode.

0000 Successful completion

0004 Error; output may not be usable

0008 Unrecoverable I/O or control statement error

0012 (Not used)

0016 (Not used)

IEBGENER

Copies and optionally reformats records or inserts literal characters in fields

0000 Successful completion

0004 Warning error; probable successful completion

0008 User requested processing of data set labels only

0012 Unrecoverable error; step terminates

0016 User routine passed 0016 (rarely used)

IEBIMAGE

Creates and maintains forms control buffer (FCB) modules in SYS1.IMAGELIB control data set, electronically replacing physical carriage control tapes for printers; also creates or modifies printer character tables for certain laser printers, also housed in SYS1.IMAGELIB.

0000 Successful completion

0004 Operations performed; exceptions encountered

0008 Some operation not performed; investigate messages

0012 Severe exceptions encountered; possible termination

0016 Catastrophic exception; execution terminated

0020 //SYSPRINT data set could not be opened; terminated

0024 Control statements/parameters invalid; terminated

IEBISAM

Copies an ISAM data set (obsolete) to sequential data set or vice versa.

0000 Successful completion

0004 User routine passed 0004 or 0012

0008 Error terminated the operation

0012 User routine passed value not 00, 04, 08, or 12

0016 Error terminated the operation

IEBPTPCH

Produces formatted print from records; the control statements you code at //SYSIN can indicate two lines of titles up to 120 bytes each, and fields can be positioned in printlines in a sequence different from their positions within input.

0000 Successful completion

0004 Data set empty or PDS specified has no members

0008 PDS member specified does not exist

0012 Unrecoverable error or incorrect user routine return code

0016 User routine passed 0016 (rarely used)

IEBUPDTE

Used to modify records in sequential or partitioned data sets in batch mode. Programmers more commonly use TSO/ISPF for these functions now.

0000 Successful completion

0004 Incorrect syntax or use of control statement

0008 (Not used)

0012 Unrecoverable error; step terminated

0016 User routine passed 0016 (rarely used)

IEHATLAS

Recovers data from damaged disk volume; attempts to write on the defective track and reads back the data written. If a track is judged defective, this utility assigns an alternate track to replace it. Can produce a list of data on the defective track and can be used to place reconstructed data on the alternate track. The disk address of defective tracks is obtained from a dump or backup data. A more common recovery procedure is to entirely re-create a corrupted data set from a tape backup.

0000 Successful completion; alternate track assigned

0004 Device does not have software-assignable tracks

0008 All alternate tracks are in use

0012 Requested main memory not available

0016 I/O error in alternate track assignment

0020 Error other than data check or missing address marker

0024 Error in VTOC Format 4 DSCB record

0028 Alternate track information not reliable

0032 Error in count field of last record on track

0036 Errors in Home Address or in Record Zero

0040 Errors even after alternate track assignment

0044 (Not used)

0048 No error found and no alternate assigned

0052 I/O error; cannot reexecute the EXCP for it

0056 System does not support track overflow

0060 Track address indicated does not belong to data set

IEHDASDR

Initializes disk volumes, assigns alternate tracks for defective ones, dumps or restores disk contents (used by operations personnel).

0000 Successful completion

0004 Unusual condition but result satisfactory

0008 Operation did not complete successfully

0012 (Not used)

0016 Error invoking utility or opening input or //SYSPRINT

IEHINITT

Applies volume label and tape mark to a tape (used by operations personnel).

0000 Successful completion; //SYSPRINT present

0004 Successful completion; //SYSPRINT ddname not present

0008 Errors encountered and reported at //SYSPRINT

0012 Errors encountered and //SYSPRINT ddname not present

0016 Error in reading control statement or data set

IEHLIST

Lists partitioned data set members or disk VTOC (volume table of contents). Programmers routinely use TSO/ISPF to accomplish these tasks now.

0000 Successful completion

0004 (Not used)

0008 Error encountered, request ignored; processing continues

0012 Permanent I/O error encountered; step terminated

0016 Unrecoverable error reading data set; step terminated

IEHMOVE

Moves or copies data sets including OS catalogs (obsolete) but not ISAM or VSAM data sets. Can also rename or replace specified members of a partitioned data set. Most of these functions are now performed by IDCAMS.

0000 Successful completion

0004 Specified function not completed; processing continues

0008 Abnormal condition but recovery has been completed

0012 Unrecoverable error; step terminated

0016 Impossible to open //SYSIN or //SYSPRINT

IEHPROGM

Creates, modifies, and deletes OS passwords. Other functions formerly accomplished with IEHPROGM, such as creating generation data group indexes (bases), are now handled by IDCAMS.

0000 Successful completion

0004 Error in control statement name field or in PARM field of your EXEC statement

0008 Incorrect control statement or invalid request

0012 I/O error on disk VTOC, //SYSIN, or //SYSPRINT

0016 Unrecoverable error; step terminated

IEWL (also HEWL)

The standard MVS linkage editor, which combines object files produced by language compilers with service routines to create an executable load module. It accepts control statements at //SYSIN that identify ddnames pointing to libraries containing input object module or load module members. The resulting load module is written at //SYSLMOD as a member of a partitioned data set.

0000 Successful completion; processable load module created

0004 Warning messages listed but execution was successful

0008 Error message listed; load module execution may fail

0012 Severe errors in load module; execution impossible

0016 Operation terminated; incomplete load module produced

IGYCRCTL

The VS COBOL II compiler; this system software processes your COBOL source code statements to create a source code listing and an object file for link editing. VS COBOL supports 1985 ANSI COBOL standards. *Note:* The return codes listed here may be posted by the compiler as it processes your source code. As you execute your program, it may post a return code in the range of 1000–1999 to indicate a runtime error. Return codes in this range are built into your program load module automatically by the compiler. Runtime return codes are documented in IBM manuals for the VS COBOL II compiler.

0000 (I) Successful completion; informational messages only

0004 (W) Warning errors only; object module is not flawed

0008 (E) Error; object module flawed

0012 (S) Severe error in source code; object module flawed

0016 (U) Unrecoverable errors caused compiler to terminate

IKFCBL00

The VS COBOL compiler; this system software processes your COBOL source code statements to create a source code listing and an object file suitable for link editing. VS COBOL follows the 1974 ANSI COBOL standards. *Note:* The return codes listed here may be posted by the compiler as it processes your source code. As you execute your program, it may post a return code such as 0519 or 3505 to indicate a runtime error. Return codes such as 0519 and 3505 are built into your program automatically by this compiler. VS COBOL runtime return codes are documented for your convenience at the end of Appendix E in this book.

0000 Successful completion

0004 (W) Warning errors only; object module is not flawed

0008 (C) Caution; object module flawed

0012 (E) Serious error in source code; object module flawed

0016 (D) Disastrous problem in source code; object module flawed

0505 Compiler has failed and prematurely terminated due to gross source code syntax error; is unable to issue appropriate error messages

E

System Completion Code Reference

MVS tells you why a job failed using a three-position hexadecimal value known as the system completion code. When a program abends (ABnormally ENDs), the system completion code is printed in the job log as shown in Figure E.1. You can find the system completion code fastest by using the TSO/ISPF "find" command for the word "abend" as shown in Figure 7.5 on page 195.

When you find the word "abend" in the job log, and the system completion code following it, you sometimes have to look above in the system print to find the same code followed by a suffix, sometimes called a "reason code." The location of the system completion code and the suffix varies for different kinds of problems. This is admittedly not very user-friendly, in either location or content.

The range of 001 through FFF for the system completion code includes 4,095 possible values. But MVS uses only about 500 of these values. Some values are followed by a reason code, often abbreviated as "rc" in IBM manuals ("rc" is also referred to as "return code" in some IBM literature). IBM documents system completion codes in *MVS/370 Message Library: System Codes,* GC38-1008. I have listed the most commonly occurring system completion codes here for your convenience and have provided explanations of each in common language.

001 Record Length/Block Size Discrepancy

Your problem is in conflicting record or block size specifications in the program or JCL, damaged tape or disk media, a hardware error on a tape or disk drive, or incorrect logic attempting to read after end of data set has been reached.

001-0 A discrepancy exists between the record length and block size specified in the program or JCL and these values in the data set label. Examine and correct your JCL or program. A write was attempted for a data set opened for input, a read was attempted for a data set opened for output, data set concatenation was attempted for data sets of unlike blocking factor or other attributes, a read was attempted after end of file was reached, or for format U (undefined) type data sets the logical record length was not specified.

001-2 An error was detected in closing the data set

001-3 QSAM error could not be resolved by MVS

001-4 You probably forgot to code BLOCK CONTAINS 0 RECORDS in the FD for a file in a COBOL program. This phrase, when present, indicates that blocking for the file is specified in JCL. The blocking defaults to one record per block if the phrase is omitted, which almost always conflicts with the actual blocking of the data set if it is blocked. (In MVS technical terms, this reason code means that MVS was attempting to follow the dictates of the EROPT parameter of the DCB, which usually defaults to the code "ABE" for "abend the job upon error.")

```
EDIT ---- CSCJGJ.CSC.CNTL(A9ERROR) - 01.00 ------------------ COLUMNS 001 072
COMMAND ===> sub                                              SCROLL ===> PAGE
****** ***************************** TOP OF DATA ******************************
000100 //CSCJGJA   JOB  1,           ACCOUNTING INFORMATION
000200 //   'BIN 7--JANOSSY',        PROGRAMMER NAME AND DELIVERY BIN
000300 //   CLASS=A,                 INPUT QUEUE CLASS (WHICH INPUT QUEUE?)
000400 //   MSGCLASS=X,              PRINTING CLASS (WHICH OUTPUT QUEUE?)
000500 //   MSGLEVEL=(1,1),          HOW MUCH DETAIL DO YOU WANT IN MVS MESSAGES?
000600 //   NOTIFY=CSCJGJ            WHO SHOULD MVS TELL WHEN THE JOB FINISHES?
000700 //*
000800 //* THIS JCL IS STORED AT CSCJGJ.CSC.CNTL(A8ERROR)
000900 //*
001000 //STEP010  EXEC  PGM=XEBGENER
001100 //SYSUT1     DD  DSN=CSCJGJ.CSC.CNTL(WORKERS),      <=== INPUT
001200 //  DISP=SHR
001300 //SYSUT2     DD  SYSOUT=*                           <=== OUTPUT
001400 //SYSPRINT   DD  SYSOUT=*
001500 //SYSIN      DD  DUMMY
001600 //
****** **************************** BOTTOM OF DATA ****************************

JOB CSCJGJA(JOB04701) SUBMITTED
11.36.40 JOB04701 $HASP165 CSCJGJA  ENDED AT N1 - ABENDED CN(INTERNAL)
***
```

```
                    J E S 2   J O B   L O G  --  S Y S T E M   I B M 1  --  N O D

11.36.39 JOB04701  IRR010I  USERID CSCJGJ   IS ASSIGNED TO THIS JOB.
11.36.40 JOB04701  ICH70001I CSCJGJ   LAST ACCESS AT 11:29:40 ON TUESDAY, SEPTEMBER
11.36.40 JOB04701  $HASP373 CSCJGJA  STARTED - INIT  1 - CLASS A - SYS IBM1
11.36.40 JOB04701  CSV003I REQUESTED MODULE XEBGENER NOT FOUND
11.36.40 JOB04701  CSV028I ABEND806-04  JOBNAME=CSCJGJA   STEPNAME=STEP010
11.36.40 JOB04701  IEA995I SYMPTOM DUMP OUTPUT
                   SYSTEM COMPLETION CODE=806  REASON CODE=00000004
                    TIME=11.36.39  SEQ=01351  CPU=0000  ASID=000F
                    PSW AT TIME OF ERROR  070C1000   81031A30  ILC 2  INTC 0D
                      NO ACTIVE MODULE FOUND
                      DATA AT PSW  01031A2A - A6521810  0A0D186D  58E002FC
                      GPR  0-3  84806000  84806000  00000000  00FD6918
                      GPR  4-7  00000010  008F6EB8  008DD450  00FB8300
                      GPR  8-11 0103247C  008DD450  810314D2  01032480
                      GPR 12-15 008F6270  008DD450  810318CE  00000004
                    END OF SYMPTOM DUMP
11.36.40 JOB04701  IEF450I CSCJGJA STEP010 - ABEND=S806 U0000 REASON=00000004
11.36.40 JOB04701  $HASP395 CSCJGJA  ENDED

------ JES2 JOB STATISTICS ------
    22 SEP 92 JOB EXECUTION DATE
           15 CARDS READ
           70 SYSOUT PRINT RECORDS
            0 SYSOUT PUNCH RECORDS
            4 SYSOUT SPOOL KBYTES
         0.00 MINUTES EXECUTION TIME
                  -
                  -
                  -
```

System completion code

Figure E.1 TSO/ISPF Job Abend Message and Job Log Placement of the System Completion Code

001-5 You attempted I/O after the end of a file was reached

013 Conflicting DCB Parameters at Open

The actions you need to take to resolve a completion code of 013 depend on the specific reason code value received. Check the OPEN, FD, and SELECT/ASSIGN statements in the program, and your job control language spelling of data set names.

013-10 Dummy data set needs buffer space; specify BLKSIZE

013-14 The DD statement must specify a partitioned data set but currently does not

013-18 The member you specified was not found in the partitioned data set

013-1C I/O error searching partitioned data set directory

013-20 Block size is not a multiple of record length or is incorrect for variable length records. This occurs because of an inconsistency in the JCL DCB parameter between actual record length as specified in the program and BLKSIZE. It can develop if you mistakenly use the AFTER ADVANCING phrase in connection with records written to a data set rather than printed, and the ADV compiler PARM option is in effect.

013-34 Record length versus block size is inconsistent or a dummy data set needs buffer space

013-50 You tried to open a printer for other than output

013-60 Block size is not equal to record length for unblocked data set

013-64 DUMMY can only be used for sequential data sets

013-68 Block size cannot be greater than 32,760

013-A4 SYSIN or SYSOUT data sets must be sequential

013-A8 Invalid record format for SYSIN or SYSOUT data set

013-D0 Partitioned data set (PDS) cannot carry record format of FBS or FS

013-E4 The number of concatenated partitioned data sets (PDS) exceeds the limit of 16. (But the concatenation limit for sequential data sets or PDS members specified explicitly by name is 255.)

04E,04F DB2 Database Error

A connected user task or a task internal to the DB2 database has been terminated because the operating system has detected an internal DB2 error. Information may be displayed at the user's terminal and in a record written to SYS1.LOGREC, the system error log data set. Refer to *IBM DATABASE 2 Messages and Codes,* SC26-4113 for problem resolution suggestions.

0C1 Operation Exception

At the point of abend the machine is being directed to perform a machine language instruction that is not valid or that has not been implemented on the particular model of computer. A DD statement may be missing or the ddname spelled differently than in the program. Several things can cause an 0C1.

- //SYSOUT DD statement is missing from your JCL. Check to see if this ddname is present in your JCL for the step. DISPLAY, TRACE, and EXHIBIT in a VS COBOL program directs output to this ddname.
- The value after the AFTER ADVANCING phrase in a COBOL WRITE statement is outside the range of 0 to 99.
- A subscript value exceeds the bounds of the table with which it is associated, causing inappropriate access to a memory location.

- A data set was not open when an I/O was directed to it.
- Files have not been closed before a STOP RUN is executed.

0C2 Privileged Operation Exception

The program has attempted to invoke an operation available only to specially authorized programs. Several things can cause an 0C2.

- A DD statement is missing or incorrect.
- A data set was not open at the time I/O was directed to it.
- A subscript is uninitialized or carrying a value out of bounds for the table that it is associated with.

0C3 Execute Exception

An 0C3 results from seriously incorrect program logic that must be corrected. You may get this error in circumstances similar to those for 0C1 or 0C2.

0C4 Protection Exception

The program is attempting to access a memory address that is not within the memory area it is authorized to use. This can occur for several reasons.

- A SELECT/ASSIGN statement is missing.
- Your ASSIGN clause indicates an incorrect system name.
- You omitted the USING phrase after the procedure division heading in a CALLed program.
- A DD statement is incorrect or missing.
- A subscript or index is not initialized or has taken on a value outside the bounds of the table with which it is associated.
- You tried to access a field in the FD of a file that is not open.

0C5 Addressing Exception

The program is attempting to access a memory location that is outside the bounds of available real storage on the machine. Several things can cause this.

- A subscript of index out of bounds for the table with which it is associated.
- You left a subscript or index uninitialized (no VALUE clause or SET).
- You tried to close a data set a second time.
- You made an improper exit from a performed paragraph, which might occur when logic within the paragraph does a GO TO exit but the paragraph had not been performed THRU the exit.
- You supplied incorrect DD statement DCB values or forgot to code the DCB in your JCL.
- You tried to read or write to a data set before opening it.
- You tried to access a fields in FD of a COBOL program before an output file is opened, before reading the first record from an input file, or after execution of the AT END option for an input file.
- You coded a CALL using incorrect parameters.

0C6 Specification Exception

This exception indicates a problem with the alignment of a data field on a memory word boundary. Several things can cause an 0C6.

- You let a subscript take on a value outside the bounds of the table with which it is associated.
- You code an improper exit from a performed paragraph; this can occur when logic within the paragraph does a GO TO exit but the paragraph had not been performed THRU the exit.
- You use COMP fields for record storage, as opposed to use for internal program values only, and you position them without regard to forcing alignment on word boundaries.
- You make inconsistent usage of COMP linkage area fields between a calling program and a called program.
- You use a multiplier or divisor larger than 15 digits and a sign in a decimal arithmetic operation.
- You omit a DD statement or code it incorrectly.

0C7 Data Exception

An 0C7 indicates an attempt to perform an arithmetic operation on nonnumeric data. Logic is directing the machine to perform arithmetic processing with inappropriate data. This is the single most common cause for job failure on IBM mainframes. You can get 0C7s for many reasons.

- You forget to validate the contents of numeric fields (read from outside files) before trying to use them in arithmetic operations.
- You use a subscript or index value out of bounds.
- You forget to initialize a working storage field.
- You move nonnumeric data to a COBOL output picture such as $ZZ,ZZZ.99.

0C8 Overflow Exception, Fixed Point

A computed value is too large to be accommodated by the indicated receiving field. You can get this by dividing a value by a value that is too small (forcing a very large result), repeated computation involving the same fields within a loop, or multiplication of numbers that are too large.

0C9 Divide Exception, Fixed Point

A value that results from a division is too large to be accommodated by the indicated receiving field. This is usually caused by division by zero but can also be triggered by division by a value that is too small or repeated computation involving the same fields within a loop.

0CA Overflow Exception, Decimal

A computed value is too large to be accommodated by the indicated receiving field. This can be caused by division by a value that is too small, repeated computation involving the same fields within a loop, or multiplication of numbers that are too large.

0CB Divide Exception, Decimal

A value that results from a division is too large to be accommodated by the indicated receiving field. You can get this if you divide by zero, but it can also be triggered by division by a value that is too small or by repeated computation involving the same fields within a loop.

0CC Overflow Exception, Exponent

A value resulting from a floating point (COMP-1 or COMP-2) computation is too large to be accommodated by the receiving field. This can be caused by division by a value that is too small, repeated computation involving the same fields within a loop, or multiplication of numbers that are too large. Floating point numbers and arithmetic are designed for scientific processing and are not usually employed in business data processing. These formats store number values as a single-digit number followed by decimal values, multiplied by an exponent taken to be a power of 10.

0CD Underflow Exception, Exponent

The result of a floating point (COMP-1 or COMP-2) computation is so small that it cannot be represented. This may occur in multiplication by too small a number, division by too large a number, or a program loop involving repeated computation with the same quantities.

0CE Significance Exception

A computation involving floating point COMP-1 or COMP-2 data resulted in an absolute zero quantity, one possessing an all zero fraction. Floating point numbers and arithmetic are not widely used in business data processing; they are intended for scientific processing.

0CF Divide Exception, Floating Point

You tried to divide by a floating point COMP-1 or COMP-2 number that has a zero fraction.

106 Cannot Load and Run Program

A problem prevents MVS from running the program named on an EXEC statement. Try coding a larger REGION on the EXEC statement for the program. For reason code -0F investigate to see if the load module library (partitioned data set) has been damaged.

106-0B FETCH routine processing error

106-0C Not enough memory available for FETCH to do GETMAIN for the module or control blocks

106-0D Invalid record type in load module

106-0E Invalid address in load module

106-0F I/O error or load module partitioned data set is corrupted

122 Job Canceled with Dump

Check your program logic and its use of files. The program may have appeared to be in a loop, not outputting or producing a large amount of I/O. It may have demanded a data set that was not available.

137 I/O Error on Tape Data Set Labels

This usually results from flawed media, a malfunctioning device, or from an error that occurred in trailer label writing that escaped detection at the time it happened. Before re-creating a data set that cannot be processed, try different devices to access it. See the suggested use of IEBGENER under reason codes 1C and 20. Cleaning a tape may restore it to readability.

137-04	I/O error writing end-of-volume label or tape mark
137-08	I/O error while positioning tape for label processing
137-0C	I/O error reading trailer label
137-10	I/O error while positioning tape at end of data set
137-14	I/O error while reading header labels for data set opened INPUT or IN/OUT, or while reading trailer labels for data set being read backwards
137-18	I/O error positioning tape for first data record in data set
137-1C,-20	Invalid label during end-of-volume processing. Use IEBGENER to copy the data set in an attempt to salvage data. IEBGENER will successfully copy a tape data set with flawed labels and will merely post a return code of 0008. *Note:* In the case of 137-1C and 137-20 errors, some editions of the IBM manuals incorrectly suggest using IEBPTPCH to copy a tape that has I/O errors. This is a typographical error perpetuated in the manuals for several years; IEBGENER is the utility intended for this purpose.
137-24	The first data set on the second tape volume mounted as a scratch tape carries an expiration date that has not been reached. The operator was prompted for confirmation that the data set could be overwritten but responded negatively. Either do not request a specific series of volumes for output (let the system call for scratch tapes by omitting the VOL parameter) or specify a volume that is known to contain expired data sets.
137-28	System operator responded "no" for MVS request to write a VOL1 label record to the tape to be used for output; the tape contains unexpired data
137-2C	Tape being read contains an ASCII label format that is not processed by MVS
137-30	Tape label violation of standard for that type of label

213 Opening of a Disk Data Set Failed

A 213 is usually caused by an illogical DD statement, and MVS cannot process a data set it has been asked to access. Check your JCL for incorrect DSN and VOL=SER and check to see if the data set exists.

213-04	I/O error occurred reading data set label, the "format 1" data set control block (DSCB) in the disk VTOC. Alternatively, no such data set could be

found associated with the stated data set name. Check the spelling of the DSN in your JCL, and for the correct VOL=SER.

213-08 The data set is OS/MVS password protected but the password data set could not be located on the system residence volume. OS/MVS password protection is not the same as RACF, ACF2 or Top Secret security and is used only for system data sets. 213-0C I/O error occurred reading data set label, the "format 1" data set control block (DSCB) in the disk VTOC. Alternatively, no such item could be found associated with the stated data set name. Check the spelling of the DSN in your JCL, and for the correct VOL=SER.

213-18 I/O error occurred writing format-1 DSCB disk data set label in the VTOC. An I/O error creating a data set label in a disk VTOC is a serious matter and should be reported to the operations group.

213-20 The data set contains more than 16 extents and MVS cannot process. It is probably a DOS/VSE data set that must be re-created to be processable under MVS.

213-24 Data set has a type of split cylinder allocation not supported by MVS. It is likely a DOS/VSE data set that must be re-created.

213-28 The data set was assigned to a disk unit that already had 127 active users, the maximum number. Rerun the job; it may have no error.

213-2C The MVS system module that handles reason codes 04 and 0C experienced an internal problem. Advise the systems programmer.

214 Tape I/O Error

A hardware or tape media error exists or a tape mark is missing after the data. Have the tape cleaned and/or retry the operation on a different tape drive. If these actions fail, you must create the data set again.

214-04 Error reading a user label

214-08 Error positioning tape

222 Job Canceled without a Dump

Check your program logic and its use of files. The program may have appeared to be in a loop, not outputting anything or generating a large amount of I/O. It may have demanded a data set that was not available. The operator who canceled the job may have been required to provide a comment or reason; ask the operator if the reason is not apparent.

237 Invalid Block Count or Data Set Name

A 237 error stems from a failure in data set label verification processing. If the data set is not cataloged, you may have coded the incorrect VOL=SER. Check your JCL. If the VOL=SER is correct, have the tape cleaned and attempt to process it. If these steps do not resolve the problem, you have to re-create the data set.

237-04 Block count in the MVS (not JCL) data control block does not match the block count in trailer label. A block of data has probably been missed or skipped due to a hardware error.

237-08 Data set name on second or subsequent volumes of a tape data set is not correct. Verify that your JCL contains the correct data set name (and VOL=SER if the data set is not cataloged).

2FB JES3 Address Space Error

Contact the operations group to report this problem with Job Entry Subsystem 3 (JES3). You cannot correct this type of problem on your own.

2F3 System Failure Occurred During the Run

The computer system or MVS "crashed" while your job was running. Check to see if some of the data sets created by the job are on the system; if so, delete them and resubmit the job. Alternatively, modify the JCL to avoid trying to re-create the files already created, and resubmit the job.

313, 314, 317, 414, 417 I/O Error on Disk VTOC

This is a hardware problem. The data set being accessed very likely must be re-created because a defective volume or device may be involved. Notify the operations group, because a VTOC error affects large numbers of jobs.

322 Job Canceled: Exceeded Time Limit

The TIME parameter on the job statement or on an EXEC was too low. Check your program logic for loops. If your logic is correct, increase the TIME parameter.

413 Open Failed for a Tape Data Set

A system completion code of 413 usually means that you coded an illogical DD statement or that MVS cannot locate a specified tape data set.

413-04 No device available for data set, or device was allocated but is now not available. Specify another device in the UNIT parameter.

413-08 I/O error while a tape was being positioned

413-0C I/O error while reading tape label

413-10 I/O error while tape mark being written

413-18 Data set was to be opened for input, but you did not specify the volume serial number and the data set is not cataloged

413-1C Volume sequence number subparameter of VOL in the DD statement is higher than the number of volumes on which the data set resides

413-20 I/O error while reading disk VTOC

413-24 Tape density DEN coded in your DCB is not consistent with density capabilities of the device allocated

413-2C Mass storage system (MSS) operation error

413-30 MSS mounted incorrect volume

413-34 Multiple tape data set specified but no volume serial numbers were indicated

513 Open Failed for a Multiple Tape Data Set

This problem may occur if you try to open more than one data set on the same tape at the same time.

513-04 OPEN was attempted for a data set already open

513-08 Label format is invalid for the standard describing that type of label

513-0C Tape has a type of ASCII label not supported by MVS

522 Job Timed Out

The job had no activity for 30 minutes or more and was canceled by MVS. This type of cancellation is unusual and is often caused by program error or unavailable data sets. You can also receive a 522 cancellation during a TSO session if you don't press the <*Enter*> key or a PF key every few minutes.

613 Open Failed on a Tape Drive

The tape or drive may need cleaning. Tape cleaning may eliminate the error, but also try using a different drive, since this is usually a hardware problem.

613-04 I/O error while positioning tape on tape drive

613-08 I/O error during reading of tape label

613-0C Invalid tape label was read. The tape may be positioned improperly as a result of a prior step that did not complete successfully. Unload it with a disposition of (OLD,KEEP) and then cause it to be mounted again by attempting to access it.

613-10 I/O error while writing a tape label

613-14 I/O error writing tape mark after header labels

614 Closing Error on a Data Set

A defective disk or tape volume or device is involved. Notify the operations group so that media can be replaced or hardware maintenance initiated.

614-04 I/O error writing a disk end of file mark

614-08 Extent number in the MVS (not JCL) data control block indicates a value higher than the actual number of data set disk extents, and the location to write an end of file mark could not be determined.

614-0C The MVS CLOSE subsystem is not operating

614-10	Spooled or subsystem data set could not be closed; failing data control block could not be closed but others will continue to be processed.

637 Tape I/O Error or Improper Concatenation

The system is having a problem reading a tape. Defective tape or disk media or hardware is probably at fault. Have the tape and drive cleaned. You may have to re-create the data set on a different volume if several devices have trouble reading it.

637-04	I/O error reading tape label, writing tape mark, or in positioning a tape
637-08	I/O error occurred positioning tape after user trailer label processing
637-0C	You concatenated data sets with unlike characteristics; they must all be on tape or disk but not a mixture

637-10, -14, -18, 1C I/O Error Occurred Positioning a Tape

637-24,-2C	I/O error occurred rewinding a scratch tape
637-34	I/O error during end-of-volume processing while reading volume label
637-38	I/O error occurred positioning a tape without a label or with nonstandard labels
637-3C	I/O error occurred while positioning a concatenated tape
637-40	I/O error occurred positioning a tape
637-44	I/O error occurred checking sense byte to see if a write enable ring is on the tape
637-4C	I/O error occurred positioning a tape

706 Program Module Is Not Executable

The linkage editor marked the module "not executable," which means that it was recognized as incomplete or flawed. Check the diagnostic messages from the linkage editor when the program was compiled and linked. These messages are short and may be buried among the listing of module names that were used to form the final load module. Check also your JCL or proc used for link editing; it should test the return code of the link edit step and raise visible attention when a nonexecutable load module is created.

713 Open Failed: Data Set Is Not Expired

You tried to overwrite or "MOD onto" and extend an existing data set. This can happen if you code DISP=OLD to overwrite an existing data set or DISP=MOD to extend (append to) a data set. MVS seeks permission from the operator to do this when the LABEL parameter in the JCL that created the data set specifies an expiration date that is still in the future.

FORTRAN programs may require use of the VOL "IN" subparameter, because this language opens data sets for input and output processing depending on the way in which the data set is first accessed. Even reading a data set using FORTRAN ordinarily may require that MVS treat it as if output actions are to be taken. Coding

IN as the fourth subparameter allows a tape data set to be read without MVS presumption that you will also try to write to the data set:

```
LABEL=(,,,IN)
```

714 I/O Error Writing Trailer Label or Tape Mark

You have probably encountered defective hardware or tape, or the tape and/or tape drive need cleaning. Notify the operations group and rerun the job.

714-04 I/O error writing trailer label 1

714-08 I/O error writing trailer label 2

714-0C I/O error writing tape mark

717 I/O Error Closing a Tape Data Set

Probable defective media or media and/or tape drive needs cleaning. Notify the operations group and rerun the job with a different volume and tape drive.

717-04 I/O error writing tape mark following last data record

717-08 I/O error writing trailer label 1 or 2

717-10 I/O error reading trailer label 1

722 Outlim or JOBPARM Print Limit Exceeded

Your job tried to send more lines to SYSOUT than your OUTLIM or JES3 MAIN statement allows. If the job really should produce more print output, increase the limits and rerun it.

737 I/O Error at End of Disk Data Set

Several different kinds of input/output error can result in this system completion code. Use the individual reason codes to help resolve your problem; contact the operations group for assistance for VTOC problems.

737-04 I/O error while reading disk volume VTOC. Check your DSN and VOL=SER parameters of the DD statement for the ddname indicated in the error message.

737-08 I/O error when reading the disk volume label

737-0C I/O error when reading VTOC entries for a concatenated partitioned data set

737-10 I/O error writing a file mark on disk

737-14 I/O error while reading a VTOC entry in preparation for writing trailer labels

737-1C I/O error reading a format-3 DSCB in the VTOC; this entry documents the 4th through 16th of the disk extents for a data set.

737-24 Missing PDS member name was detected; your JCL indicated the member name in concatenation with other data sets. The error message indicates the number of the data set in the concatenated data set list in the DD statement. Check your JCL for an incorrectly spelled member name.

737-28 Functional or logical error in JES3 subsystem; contact systems programmer.

737-2C Error attempting to write file mark at end of disk data set. The number of disk extents that the data set includes, located in the DCBFDAD field of the data control block, is higher than the actual number of extents. Check your assembler logic dealing with the data control block.

737-34 Mass storage system (MSS) error on end-of-volume processing

737-38 Mass storage system (MSS) mounted an incorrect volume

737-3C The error routine that handles a "format-1 DSCB record not found" error has itself failed. The format-1 data set control block in the disk volume table of contents, or VTOC, is the data set label and it may have an I/O error or be missing. Contact the operations group.

804, 80A, 878 Program Needs More Memory

Check the REGION value on your JOB or EXEC statement. You may need to increase it because your program demands more memory than MVS is being allowed to let it use.

806 Program Load Module Cannot Be Found

Your JCL requested a program that could not be found and loaded. This may be a program named on an EXEC statement and housed in other than the default load library, but you left out a //STEPLIB DD (or //JOBLIB) statement that names the library. You can also get this problem when one program CALLs another and MVS can't locate the CALLed program. Check your EXEC statement or source code CALL for a misspelled program name. It is also possible that the load module was deleted or never created or that an I/O error occurred while MVS searched the directory of the load module library.

813 Open Failed; DSN in Label Does Not Match JCL

The DSN parameter and volume serial number are not consistent with what is contained in the tape data set label.

813-04 Check the spelling of the data set name in your JCL and the volume serial number you coded. If the tape is cataloged and you have not explicity coded the volume serial number, check to see if the data set may have been deleted but not uncataloged. You may have to use a dump utility to see the contents of the tape label to find out what data set name is present in it.

If you coded an explicit VOL=SER, the data set may originally have been written to the stated tape volume but has now expired, and the tape reused as scratch to receive another data set. Consult the tape management system (TMS) or check the JCL that created the data set for correct use of the LABEL=RETPD/EXPDT subparameter.

837 Error Occurred at the End of Volume

Check your logic to make sure your program is operating correctly. It may be outputting too much data as a result of a logic loop.

837-08 All space on specified volume was used and no additional volumes were specified. More space is needed to house the data being written. You need to specify more volume serial numbers explicitly or code the VOL parameter to indicate a larger volume count.

837-0C The tape volume indicated was mounted by MVS but another data set on the volume is currently in use. Rerun your job.

913 Security Problem

Several reason code values pinpoint the problem detected by the security system. To correct this problem you have to resolve your authorization to use the data set with your security coordinator.

922 Job Canceled Due to Machine or MVS Failure

Actual processing of the job had begun but an MVS abend was experienced, the console restart key was pressed, or some other machine problem occurred that forced this job and most likely all others to be canceled. There is almost certainly no error in the program; resubmit it.

A14 Error Releasing Disk Space at Data Set Closing

A defective disk or tape volume or device probably exists. Contact the operations group.

A22 Operator Forced Cancellation of the Job

No program logic may be in error. Check with the operator and find out why he/she canceled the job.

B14 Close Failed Trying to Write a PDS Member

Except for a reason code of -18, the partitioned data set probably requires reorganization before you can rerun the job. You may have to allocate more directory blocks for the PDS by copying it to a new PDS using IEBCOPY with an appropriate SPACE parameter on the DD statement for the new data set. For reason code -0C, the deletion of existing members of the PDS and its reorganization may also resolve the immediate problem.

B14-04 Duplicate member name

B14-0C The partitioned data set directory is full

B14-10 An I/O error occurred while writing the PDS directory

B14-14 A DCB inconsistency exists in the program or JCL and the PDS and directory

B14-18 Insufficient memory for the closing actions; increase REGION size for the step

B37 Disk Volume Is Out of Space

You received all the primary space you requested and as much of the secondary space as MVS could provide, but this was still not enough. A B37 usually means that you coded your SPACE parameter incorrectly or you have a logic loop involving a WRITE statement in your program. Check your program logic and SPACE coding for the data set.

B37-04 All space requested by the program on the disk volume has been used; MVS wants to mount another volume for the data set but cannot do so because the present disk is permanently mounted or is in use for other data sets of the failing job or other jobs.

B37-08 The data set must be re-created in a format that MVS can process; some DOS/VSE and MVS data sets are not compatible.

B37-0C The disk unit to which the data was assigned already has 127 jobs associated with it, which is the maximum that can be handled at one time. Rerun the job.

C13 Error on Concatenated PDS

Correct your JCL; you are violating one of the rules that apply to concatenated data sets.

C13-10 Output to a concatenated PDS is attempted. PDSs cannot be concatenated for output.

C13-18 An open for input has been attempted for concatenated PDSs, but one or more of the PDSs are not on disk. Concatenated PDSs must have like attributes, including being on disk, not tape.

C37 DOS/VSE Data Set Cannot Be Read by MVS

The next volume of the data set contained more than 16 extents or has a nonallowable form of split cylinder space allocation. Some DOS data sets are not compatible with MVS and must be re-created to be read by MVS.

CFB JES3 Initialization Problem

Contact the operations group; you cannot correct this problem on your own.

D37 Primary Space Exceeded, No Secondary

In writing a data set to a disk device, your JCL specified only a primary disk SPACE allocation and this was exceeded. Change your DD statement associated with the data set to specify more primary space or provide a secondary allocation of space. *Caution:* Make sure you delete the partially created data set resulting from this job before rerunning the job!

DFB JES3 System Support Module Problem

Contact the operations group; you cannot correct this problem on your own.

E37 Primary and Secondary Space Filled!

An E37 indicates a lack of appropriate disk resources to receive output. Check your program logic for a loop involving a statement involving output. You may have to change your JCL to specify larger primary or secondary allocations. Delete the partially created data set resulting from this job before rerunning it.

You can get an E37 under TSO when a TSO library needs to be reorganized. Keep a watch on your library status via TSO/ISPF function 3.2 and reorganize libraries ("compress" them) occasionally to avoid receiving an E37 during editing.

An E37-04 can also indicate that the disk volume table of contents (VTOC) is full. If no other explanation for the problem seems to apply contact the operations group, because a filled VTOC is a serious problem that will affect many other jobs.

E37-04 Not enough storage volumes were specified, a PDS was being written and filled the volume, a PDS being written used its maximum 16 extents, or the disk VTOC is full. A PDS can reside on only one disk volume; it cannot extend across volumes even if more than one volume is provided with the VOL or UNIT parameters.

E37-08 The next volume of a multivolume disk data set is not capable of receiving the data set because of a duplicate data set name or lack of space.

E37-0C Installation procedures prevent the extension of the data set.

VS COBOL User (Runtime) Return Codes

VS COBOL, IBM's 1974 COBOL compiler, is functionally obsolete, having been replaced by VS COBOL II. But if your shop is still running some older COBOL programs, you may find the following reference material of more than historical interest.

In certain circumstances, VS COBOL programs will post an unusual user return code. This happens because VS COBOL uses these return codes as an indication of certain execution-time errors. These code values were documented in Appendix K of the *IBM OS/VS COBOL Compiler and Library Programmer's Guide,* SC28-6483, which was not an especially easy technical manual to use. The following VS COBOL return codes are user return codes, not system completion codes. They appear as four-digit decimal numbers as if they had been moved by COBOL program logic to the RETURN-CODE register.

0187 Incorrect Verb Table

This error is caused by an internal problem in the compiler itself. IBM software support personnel must be notified to correct the compiler.

0203 Divide by Zero

You can avoid this error by using the ON SIZE ERROR option or by checking explicitly before dividing to make sure that the divisor is not zero or a small quantity less than one.

0295 Return Code Changed from − to +

Issued by a COBOL service routine, this provides information only.

0303 VSAM Time Stamp or Catalog Error

The last closure time stamp of a VSAM data set being processed appears to be out of synchronization with its catalog entry. This may be detected by checking File Status following the OPEN of the data set.

0304 VSAM Time Stamp/Index Error

A VSAM data set being processed is out of synchronization with its index. The time stamps on these do not match, indicating that one or the other has been updated independently as a result of prior system interruption or incorrect restoration of items to disk.

0400, 0505 VS COBOL Compiler Failure

Certain syntax errors can cause the VS COBOL compiler to fail. When this occurs, it posts a return code of 0400 or 0505 and quits. Since no abend occurs, you may think that your program actually ran and returned this code, but it was actually the compiler "giving up." Coding the word INDEX instead of INDEXED in defining a table to be searched can cause an 0505 user return code. You may also encounter it if you use the reserved word KEY as a data-name. Resolving an 0400 or 0505 error involves carefully inspecting your source code, since the compiler can't provide much help in locating your syntax violation.

0519 Error in Logic Flow

The next instruction to be executed is not identifiable. You probably branched out of a PERFORM and fell through the bottom of your program, or forgot to code a STOP RUN statement. Also check to make sure that called modules appropriately contain EXIT PROGRAM or GOBACK statements and that your use of the VS COBOL compiler PARM option DYN, needed for dynamically callable modules, is consistent.

1301 I/O Error But No DECLARATIVE Was Coded

Code declaratives in your program before the other statements in the procedure division, to intercept and handle I/O exceptions. Modern releases of VS COBOL and VS COBOL II do not require coding of declaratives.

3361 SYMDMP Option Error

Review your use of the VS COBOL SYMDMP debugging option; an error exists in control statement coding. Also, a COBOL library subroutine may lack sufficient workspace. Increase the REGION size parameter on the EXEC statement that invokes the program.

3440 Insufficient Memory for a Subroutine

Too little workspace is available for a COBOL library subroutine. Code REGION on the job step to specify a larger value.

3505 Flow of Control Error

This error can occur if you use a GO TO out of one SECTION of code into another and eventually "drop out the bottom" of the program. This error can also occur when an assembler (or PL/I) program CALLs a COBOL program. The assembler program needs to issue a call to library routine ILBOSTP0 before calliing a COBOL program but this has not been done. The assembler program must be corrected. This call initializes the COBOL environment so that the called program does not "think" it is the main program.

VS COBOL II User (Runtime) Return Codes

Programs compiled with VS COBOL II generate return codes in the range of 1000 through 1999 for conditions similar to those that caused VS COBOL to issue 0187, 0203, 0519, and so forth. For example, 1037 is the return code from VS COBOL II corresponding to the 0519 return code of VS COBOL. You don't need a printed reference to the meaning of these codes. VS COBOL II prints a plain-text description of each of its automatic return codes in your job log and system reporting.

Obtaining JCL and Programs for Local Use

You or your installation can acquire selected items of JCL from this text for local use. The programs, job streams, and SCANIT2 and SCANIT3 programs discussed in Chapter 7 are available in machine-readable form. Contact Norm Noerper, president of Caliber Data Training, Inc., for information concerning licensing and usage terms.

Caliber Data Training, Inc.
Suite 605
6160 N. Cicero Aveue
Chicago, Illinois 60646
Voice: (312) 794-1222
Fax: (312) 794-1225

I also offer on-site training in MVS/ESA JCL and related topics. I install items from this text such as SCANIT2 or SCANIT3 on your mainframe when I conduct such training. Contact Caliber Data Training for information, arrangements, and rates if you are interested in having the author at your facility to conduct training in MVS/ESA JCL, VS COBOL II, software reverse engineering techniques, software testing, or related subjects or reach me on Internet at janossy@cs.depaul.edu.

Index

A

Abend, 13, 27, 42–47, 53, 56, 60, 62, 68–69, 75, 77, 80–81, 188–89, 192–96, 229, 232, 238, 445
ABENDCC, 27, 81–82
Abnormal termination mode, 47–49, 53, 55, 65, 78
Absolute data set name, 244
ABSTR, 399
ACCESS MODE, 428
ACCESS MODE IS RANDOM, 436
ACCESS MODE IS SEQUENTIAL, 437
Accidental complexity, 354, 358
ACF2, 452
ACS routines, 309, 315–17, 321, 335, 353, 366, 389, 396, 430
ADRDSSU, 360, 438
AFTER ADVANCING (COBOL), 447
AGGR option, C/370, 292
AIX, 408, 415, 418, 425, 427
AIX cluster. *See* Cluster
ALLDATA, 361
ALLE, 361
Allocation. *See* Device allocation
ALTER, 332, 334, 357
Alternate index, 408, 412, 419, 422–23, 425, 428–29
Alternate index path, 426–27, 437
Alternate key, 425–26, 435
Alternate record key (COBOL), 426, 428
AMODE, 274, 276, 278, 286, 296–97
AND, 27, 28
argc, 262, 267, 280
argv[], 262, 267, 280
Array, 292
Ascii label, 451, 454
ASMCL, 262, 301, 307
ASMHCL, 263
Assemble and link, 262–63
Assembler, 1, 157–58, 248–50, 258–61, 305–306, 438
Automatic class selection routines. *See* ACS routines
Average record length computation, 345
AVG VALUE, 326–27, 35
AVGREC, 4, 6, 165, 168, 312–14, 318–19, 326–27, 336, 337, 342–48, 350, 352, 354–56, 427, 431

B

Backup, KSDS, 424
BAL (basic assembler language). *See* Assembler
Base cluster, 417. *See also* Cluster
BDAM, 399
BINARY, 291, 292
BLDINDEX, 403, 407–408, 410, 416
BLKSIZE, 7, 8, 9, 168, 312–13, 318–19, 342, 354, 447
BLOCK CONTAINS 0 RECORDS, 445
Block count, 452
Blocking, 338
Block size, 168
Breitenberg, Hal, 310, 349
Brooks, Frederick P., 354, 358
Bytes per disk cylinder, 338
Bytes per disk track, 338

C

C, 248–50, 262, 438
C/370, 248, 267–71, 273–75, 277, 279–87, 292–93, 297–98, 303–305
C/370 compile and link, 271, 299
C/370 environment 303, 305
C/utilities tool chest, 262
Caliber Data Training, Inc., 463
Call 293, 295–97, 457
Call, assembler to C/370, 304, 307
Call, C/370 to assembler, 299, 302
Call, C/370 to COBOL, 297
Call, COBOL to C/370, 287, 291
Catalog, 403, 425, 439
Catalog a GDS, 334
Cataloged procedure. *See* Proc
CCX4 procedure, 271, 293–94, 299, 307
CDS name, 325
Char, 292
Checklist, job stream restart, 208–209
CISIZE, 314, 358, 427
CKD (count, key, data), 338
Cluster, 408, 415, 425–27
CNTL, 129
COB2CLJ, 253, 257
COB2UCL, 253
COBOL, 248–49
COBOL/370, 42, 55, 59, 63, 253
COMP (COBOL), 291, 298, 449
COMP-1, COMP-2 (COBOL), 450
Compile, link, go (VS COBOL II), 29
Compiler failure, 461
Completion code, 12, 13, 43, 44, 50, 69, 78
Compound condition coding, 16

Compress, 332, 360, 379, 394, 397–98
Concatenation, 7, 91, 178–79, 230–31, 374, 459
Concatenation improvements, 356
COND, 11, 15, 16, 19, 28, 30, 47, 60–61, 65, 167
COND CODE, 12–14, 17, 20, 23, 30, 31, 33, 36, 43, 45–46, 48–50, 52, 55, 57, 65, 69–70, 72–73, 95, 106–11, 121, 167, 183–96, 192, 208, 234, 240, 278, 289, 290, 411–12, 414, 432
Cond codes, of utilities, 438–49, 438
Condition code. *See* COND CODE
Conditional expression. *See* Relational expression
Constructs. *See* DATACLAS; STORCLAS; MGMTCLAS
Control areas, 402
Control intervals, 402
CONVERT(PDSE), 386
CONVERTV 360, 390–93
COPIES, 181, 232, 242, 244
COPY 360, 363–64, 373–77, 380–82, 384–90, 392, 439
COPYDUMP, 395
CPYV, 361
Creation date, 331
CYL, 338, 341

D

DAM, 399
DASD, 399
DATACLAS 4, 5, 168, 313–20, 324, 326, 334–36, 347, 350, 354, 358, 378, 389, 390, 427, 430
Data class application screen, 324
Data class display, 327
Data class list screen, 326
Data component, 408, 411–12, 415, 417, 423
Data Facility Data Set Services. *See* DFDSS
Data set control block. *See* DSCB; Model data set label
Data set name type, 351, 354
Data set selection entry panel, 332
DAU, 399
DB2, 388, 402–03, 417
DCB 8, 163, 165, 312–13, 319–21, 335, 354, 445–46, 448, 453, 458
DCB=*.DDNAME, 355
DCB=(MODEL. . ., 335, 355
DCB elimination, 6, 7
DCB parameter promotion exceptions, 335
DDNAME, 140–41, 144, 146, 148
Deallocation, *See* Device deallocation
DECLARATIVES, 429
Defaults, 158–59, 163
DEFINE, 403, 408, 415, 416
DEFINE, GDG, 334
DEFRAG, 360, 398–99
DELETE, 332, 397, 403, 407, 414, 439
DELETE PURGE, 384, 387, 390
DEN, 453
Device allocation, 12, 13
Device deallocation, 12
DFDSS, 312, 315, 403, 438
DFHMAPS, 160
DFHSM, 310 315, 359
DFSMS. *See* SMS
DFSORT. *See* SORT
Directory, 458
Directory attributes, 327
Directory blocks, 351
Disk bytes per track, 338
Disk bytes per cylinder, 338
Disk track utilization efficiency, 340
DISP, 163, 165, 234, 237, 312–13, 320, 431
DISPLAY (COBOL), 209, 211, 447
Documentation, job stream recovery, 209–10, 224
DOS (PC), 337
DOS/VSE 452, 459
Double (C), 292
Doubleword (C), 292
Download 177, 182, 187, 228–29
DSCB, 442, 451, 452, 456, 457
DSN referback. *See* Referback, dsn
DSNTYPE, 85, 318–19, 355
DSNTYPE=LIBRARY, 353
DSNTYPE=PDS, 354
DSORG, 354, 388, 399
DSORG=PO, 351, 353–54, 386
DSORG=PO-E, 351, 353, 386
DUMMY, 447
DUMP (IDCAMS), 111–12, 360, 366, 392–94, 397, 439, 452
DYNAM, 392
Dynamic call, 293

E

EC, 399
EDCCLG, 270–71
EDCCOMP, 274, 277
EDCEPIL, assembler/C epilog, 303
EDCPRLG, assembler/C prolog, 303
ENDCNTL, 129

ENDIF
  apparent bug, 211, 213, 221
  basic example, 19–20
  elimination with ELSE, 110
  indentation, 82–83
End of volume, 458
Enhanced data set allocation, 349–50, 352
Enterprise system, 3
ENTRIES, 408, 416
Entry Sequenced Data Set. *See* ESDS
EQ, 27
ERASE, 358
EROPT, 445
ES, 430
ESDS, 402–03, 430
EVEN, 47, 50, 53, 58–61, 64–65
Execution deck, 211, 214, 223
EXHIBIT (COBOL), 447
EXPDT, 313–14, 318, 319, 355–56
Expiration attributes, 330
EXPIRE DATE/DAYS, 319, 329–30
EXPIRE NON-USAGE, 329–30
Extent, 340, 353, 355, 378, 452
EXTNT 378–79, 398

F

FALSE, 27, 80
File status, 50, 429, 433–34
File status reference, 435–37
Filtering with * and %, 373–78, 386, 390, 393
Find command (TSO/ISPF), 195
FORTRAN, 248, 455
FREESPACE, 314, 358, 427
FSIZE, 379, 398
Fullword (C), 292
Function (C), 298, 307

G

GDG base, 183, 439
GDG level, 334
GDS, 4, 127, 179–83, 186, 204–205, 210–11, 228–29, 234, 239, 245, 310, 312, 323, 334–35, 344, 357
GDS, mass access, 243
GE, 27
Generated ddname (VSAM, alternate index), 427, 437
Generation data set. *See* GDG; GDS
GT, 27

H

Hard disk, 337–38
Haupt, Mike, 403
HEWL, 443
Hexadecimal, 48, 445

I

ICKSDF, 361, 399
IDCAMS, 16, 17, 20, 23, 24, 30, 45, 52, 71, 88–89, 95, 105, 108, 110–12, 117, 121–22, 146, 148, 183, 334–35, 357, 367, 403, 406–407, 409, 412, 414, 416, 423, 438–39, 443
IEBCOMPR, 105–12, 121, 123, 146, 148, 439
IEBCOPY, 439, 458
IEBDG, 440
IEBEDIT, 440
IEBGENER, 7, 8, 16, 105, 111, 122–23, 134, 137, 141, 146, 169, 171, 242, 244, 356, 357, 367, 438, 440, 451
IEBIMAGE, 440
IEBISAM, 441
IEBPTPCH, 438, 441
IEBUPDTE, 441
IEFBR14, 7, 8, 16, 23, 24, 178–79, 181–82, 193, 232, 234, 320, 403
IEHATLAS, 367, 441
IEHDASDR, 442
IEHINITT, 442
IEHLIST, 367, 443
IEHMOVE, 443
IEHPROGM, 334, 443
IEWL, 443
IF/THEN/ELSE, 4, 6, 11, 15, 19, 20, 21, 23, 24, 27, 30, 31, 33, 34, 42, 50, 62, 65, 68, 116, 131, 150, 167, 178–79, 190, 234, 240
IGDZILLA, 310
IGYCRCTL, 444
ILBOABN0, 46, 50, 54, 58, 92
IMBED, 314, 358, 427
INCAT, 378, 381
INCLUDE, 87, 96, 98–103, 109, 124, 127–31, 203
INCLUDE group, 101, 127, 129
Index, 408, 412, 415
Index component, 411–12
Indexed data set, 402, 422
Indexed sequential access method. *See* ISAM
Index set, 425
INDYNAM, 367, 382, 388
Installation standards, and JCL templates, 169–71
Instream data, 5
Intentional user abend, 192

Interactive System Management Facility. *See* ISMF
Interactive System Productivity Facility. *See* ISPF
Interblock gap, 338
Interlanguage communication, 248, 258, 287
Internet, 463
Interrecord gap, 338
I/O error, 454–57
IPL, 399
ISAM, 5, 312, 357, 378, 402, 441, 443
ISMF, 309, 314, 319, 324, 326, 327–28, 330, 332–33 335–36, 350, 352–53, 360–62, 364–65, 400
ISMF on–line help, 333
ISPF, 310, 324, 400

J

JCL library, 127
JCL training, 463
JCLLIB, 37, 85–103, 105, 118, 124, 127–29, 142, 270, 277
Job, 15
Job failure, 173–74
Job stream, 15, 105–107, 113, 175–77
Job stream design, 207, 228
Job stream recovery instructions, 209–10
JOBCAT, 312, 378
JOBLIB, 42, 93, 98, 102, 127, 457
JOBPARM, 86

K

Kermit, 182
KEYLEN, 314, 318, 326, 355, 358, 427, 430–31
KEYOFF, 314, 318, 355, 358, 427, 430, 431
KEYRANGES, 358
Key Sequenced Data Set. *See* KSDS
KS, 430
KSDS, 174–76, 357, 402–403, 406, 409, 411, 418, 421, 423, 425–28, 430, 435–36

L

LABEL, 319
LABEL=(,,,, 456
LABEL=RETPD/EXPDT, 457
LASTCC. *See* SET LASTCC
LE, 27
Legacy system, 7
Library, 85, 127, 351, 354
LIKE 6, 275, 318–19, 334–35, 354–56
Linear Space Data Set. *See* LSDS
Link edit, 29
Linkage editor, 272, 278, 286, 443, 455
Linkage section, 253, 255, 258, 299
LIST, 439
LISTCAT, 403, 406, 408, 416, 420, 426
Load module, 34, 35, 42, 48, 89, 288
Load module library, 387
Logical processing, DFDSS 366
LOW-VALUES, 48, 428
LRECL, 7, 8, 9, 168, 311, 313, 314–15, 317–19, 321, 326, 335, 350, 354–57, 427, 431
LS, 430
LSDS, 400, 402–403, 430
LT, 27

M

Machine language, 1, 2, 287
MAIN, 86
Management class display, 330
Management class list screen, 329
MAXCC, 414. *See also* SET MAXCC
MDS, 400
MENTITY, 400
MGMTCLAS, 4, 5, 168, 313, 315–19, 321, 324, 329, 335, 336, 350, 355, 378, 389, 390, 397
MGMTCLAS screens, ISMF, 329
MIGRAT, 331
Migration levels (ML0, ML1, ML2), 316
Mix Software, Inc., 262
MOD, 234, 455
MODEL, 358
Model data set label. *See* Model DSCB
Model DSCB, 180–82, 312, 334, 344–45, 354
MSGCLASS, 222
Multi, 380
Multivolume data sets, 394
MVOLSER, 400
MVS, 2
MVS/ESA JCL training, 463
MVS/ESA Version 4, 4–5
MVS/XA, 2, 5, 297, 360, 397
Mythical Man Month, 354, 358

N

Narino, Bob, 248
NE, 27
Nested IF/THEN/ELSE, 82–83
Nested procs. *See* proc (procedure): nested
NG, 27
NL, 27
Noerper, Norm, 463
Nonunique alternate key, 423
Normal processing mode, 47, 52, 57
NOT, 27, 28, 69
NOT ABEND, 47, 71, 73

NOT CATLG 2, 225, 322
NOT RECATLG 2, 185

O

Object file, 263
OCCURS clause (COBOL), 292
ONLY, 47, 50, 53, 58, 60, 65–67
ONLYINCAT, 382–83
Operational documentation, 210
OPT, 394
OPTIMIZE, 394
Optional file, 432, 436
OR, 27, 28
ORDER, 96, 98, 124
ORDERED, 358
OS, 2
OS passwords, 443
OUTDYNAM, 382, 384, 388
OUTLIM, 456

P

Packed decimal and C, 292
PAM, 400
Parameter promotion, 7, 9
PARM, 90, 92, 117, 192, 248–52, 256, 258–59, 262, 264, 267, 287, 289, 290, 447
PARM for record selection, 255
PARM, runtime, 256
PARM validation, 255, 264
PARM.GO, 258
Partitioned data set. *See* PDS
Partitioned data set extended. *See* PDSE
PASS, 94
Path, 408, 416, 420, 425–26
"PATTERN DSCB NOT FOUND IN VTOC" message, 335
PDS, 319, 353, 386, 400, 439, 443, 447, 458, 460
PDS directory, 458
PDSE, 6, 85, 127, 319, 336, 341, 351, 353, 378, 400, 439
PEND, 87
PGM=* referback, 208
Physical Processing, DFDSS, 366
PL/I, 248
PL/S, 438
PO, 400
PO-E, 400
Poor JCL, 157
POU, 400
PowerC, 262
Pragma#, 287, 292, 298, 302, 305, 307, 390–91, 393
PREPARE, 391
Primary attributes, 327
Primary DASD, 316
Primary space, 459–60
Primary space allocation, 340
PRINT 366, 368–72, 403, 406, 408–409, 421–23, 439
Print rerun, 228, 241
Private proc library. *See* JCLLIB
Proc
  building using SET, 113–15
  examples, 209, 211–13
  IF/THEN/ELSE coding, 33–39
  levels of nesting, 152
  nested, 133–53
  procstepname, 31, 33, 37, 38, 39, 82, 136, 147, 151, 202, 223
  recursion, 152, 154–55
  statement, 87, 101–105, 107, 116–17, 167, 313
PROCESS(SYS1), 397
Production job streams, 42, 69, 173–245
PRT command, SDSF, 198–99, 201–202
PS, 400
PSU, 400

Q

QSAM, 400, 436–37, 445

R

RACF, 317, 319, 452
RAID (disks), 311
Random access, 425
RC, 13, 19, 26, 27, 29, 31, 45, 71, 73, 75, 232, 445
Reason code, 445
REBLOCK, 382, 385
RECATALOG, 358
RECFM, 7, 8, 168, 311, 313, 314, 318–19, 326, 335, 350, 354–57
RECFM=U, 401–402, 445
RECORG, 314, 318, 326, 355, 357, 427, 431
Recursion, proc. *See* proc (procedure): recursion
REDETERMINE, 392
REFDD, 6, 275, 318–19, 354–56
REFDD=*.ddname, 355–56
REFDT, 380
Referback, DSN, 8, 9, 147
Refurbished JCL, 159–72
REGION, 450, 457
Registers, 258–59, 301–302
Relational expression, 19, 21, 22, 32, 38, 39, 53, 68, 71, 74, 76, 150, 152
Relative Data Set, 402
Relative Record Data Set. *See* RRDS

RELEASE, 360, 397
Reload KSDS, 424
RENAME, 439
REPLICATE, 314, 358, 427
REPRO, 392, 403, 415, 424
Rerun, 225
Rerunnability, 227, 233, 240
RESTART, 174, 189–90, 202–207, 222–23, 227
RESTART checklist, 208–209
RESTORE, 360, 388, 392–93, 396–97
RET LIMIT, 319, 329
RETAINED message, 310, 320, 323, 334
RETPD, 313, 314, 318–19, 355–56
Return code, 13, 34, 445
Return codes (VS COBOL), 444
Return codes (VS COBOL II), 444
REUSE, 358
RLSE, 341, 347
RM/COBOL-85, 428
RMODE, 274, 286, 296–97
Robinson, Chris, 310
Robust user interface, 178
ROLLED IN message, 323, 334
RR, 430
RRDS, 402–03, 430, 436
Run, 27, 76–77, 80
Runtime return codes, 460

S

SAS, 380, 389
SAS/C, 248
SCANIT2 output analysis program, 184–85, 188, 190, 193–202, 205, 219, 222, 234–35, 237, 239, 240, 463
SCRATCH, 334
SDSF, 13, 194–202
Secondary attributes, 327
Secondary space, 459–60
Secondary space allocation, 340, 347
SELECT (COBOL), 426, 432–33, 436, 446, 448
SEP, 163, 165
Sequential, 428
Sequential access, 425
Sequential data set, 402
Sequential update program, 425
SET, 87, 96, 100–101, 104–105, 107, 113–14, 116–17, 125–26, 129–31, 242, 245, 262–63, 414
SET (1985 COBOL), 254
SET (COBOL), 448
SET LASTCC, 403, 407
SET MAXCC, 403, 407
SHAREOPTIONS, 314, 358, 427
Signed int (C), 292
SMS, 3, 4, 5, 7, 127, 129, 165, 168, 275, 309–313, 315–17, 319–22, 327, 329, 331, 334–37, 342, 344, 347, 350–52, 354–56, 358–60, 366, 378, 389, 391, 393, 396, 400, 427, 430
SMS constructs. *See* DATACLAS; STORCLAS; MGMTCLAS
Software portfolio, 159
Software reverse engineering training, 463
SORT, 45, 52, 141, 407, 409, 413, 438, 438
Source code, 248
SP, 400
SPACE, 6, 165, 311, 312, 314, 317, 318, 319, 320, 321, 336, 337, 341, 342, 343, 345, 346, 347, 348, 350, 353, 354, 355, 356, 427, 431, 458–59,
Space units, 352
SPANNED, 358
SPEED, 358
SPHERE, 382, 388, 393, 397, 400
Spool Display and Search Facility. *See* SDSF
Stacking, command, TSO/ISPF, 202
START (COBOL), 428–49, 436
Static call, 293
Statistics, LISTCAT, 417, 419
Step RESTART, 224. *See also* RESTART
STEPCAT, 312, 378
STEPLIB, 35, 42, 93, 127, 457
STOP RUN (COBOL), 448
Storage Management Subsystem. *See* SMS
STORCLAS, 4, 5, 168, 313, 315–20, 324, 328, 336, 350, 355, 378, 389–90, 397, 427, 430–31
STORCLAS screens, 328
Stored printlines, 231
Struct (C), 287, 292
Subprogram, C/370, 292
Subprogram, COBOL, 300
Substitution JCL, 115
SVC, 46
Symbolic device group name default, 336
Symbolic parameters
  and SET, 100, 113–17
  defaults, 125–26, 275
  for DSN, 212, 216, 218
  for generation numbers, 214, 218, 223, 241–44
  generalizing JCL with, 133
  installation in job stream, 130
  minimization in JCL streamlining, 167

Symbolic parameters *(continued)*
  nullification, 244
  substitutions, 120–21
SYS1.LINKLIB, 42, 127
SYS1.PROCLIB, 85, 87, 91–92, 98–99
SYSDA, 158, 167, 217
SYSOUT, 5, 167, 180, 209, 233, 242, 244, 456
SYSRES 397, 400
System/360, 1, 2
System abend, 48, 64, 66, 68, 74, 78
System catalog, 425. *See also* Catalog
System completion code, 14, 43, 44, 45, 48, 50, 59, 190, 235, 238, 340, 446
System completion code reference, 445–62, 445
System-determined block size, 4, 339, 342
System Display and Search Facility. *See* SDSF

T

31-bit address, 297
24-bit address, 297
Tape I/O error, 452
Tape label, 455
Templates, for JCL, 168–71
Temporary data set, 135, 186, 227, 312, 406, 409, 432, 434
Temporary VSAM data set, 358, 430
TEST, 391–93,
TIME, 453
TRACE (COBOL), 447
Trailer label, 456
Training, 171, 463
Trigraphs (C) 262, 267–69, 280–83, 298, 302, 307
TRUE, 27, 79, 81
TSO/ISPF, 249, 346, 349, 350, 367
Turk, Jim, 360
TYPRUN=SCAN, 128

U

UIM, 400
Uncatalog, 439
Uncataloged data sets, 224
Undefined record format. *See* RECFM=U
Unintentional user abend, 54
UNIT, 168, 311–12, 320–21, 336, 427, 453
Unix, 248, 337
Unix emulator, 262
UNMANAGED, 331
Update program, 425
Upload, 177, 228
User abend, 46, 54–56, 59, 62, 67, 74, 192
User abend code, 278
User completion code, 14, 43, 44, 45, 46, 63, 191, 193, 239
User condition code, 234
Utility program return codes, 438–44
UTILMSG=YES, 361, 371

V

VALUE (COBOL), 448
VAX, 337
VERIFY, 437
VIO, 90, 94–95, 158, 167, 217, 277, 312, 409
Virtual input/output. *See* VIO
Virtual storage, 2
Virtual storage access method. *See* VSAM
Virtual Storage Management System. *See* VSAM
VMS, 337
VOL, 312, 320–21, 427, 453
VOL=(,,,, 395
VOL1 label, 451
VOL=REF=* REFERBACK, 208
VOL=SER, 311, 451, 456–57
Volume count, 427
VSAM, 5, 50, 174, 181, 312–13, 326, 335, 341, 355, 357–58, 366, 378, 382, 388–89, 393, 397, 400–404, 412, 414, 418, 423–25, 427–28, 432–33, 435–37, 443, 461
VSAM allocation with JCL alone, 427
VS COBOL II
  compile and link, 253, 256, 294, 299
  compile, link, go, 257
  general reference, 14, 42, 54–55, 59–61, 63, 92, 176, 182 248, 250, 253–54, 287, 293, 297–98, 427, 432–37, 444
  MAP option, 292
  runtime return codes, 462
  training, 463
VS COBOL runtime return codes, 460
VTOC, 330, 366, 369–70, 378, 380, 393, 442–43, 451–53, 456–57
VVDS, 401

W

Wildcards * and %. *See* Filtering with * and %
WITH DUPLICATES (COBOL), 423, 426, 428
Work file, 263

X

XX replaces // in system reporting, 215